Current EC Legal Developments

Judicial Review of Anti-dumping and other
Safeguard Measures in the European Community

Many thanks for
all your help and
the 'odd' evening of
distraction.

Eugene.

Current EC Legal Developments

Judicial Review of Anti-dumping and other Safeguard Measures in the European Community

Eugene Creally, PhD

Butterworths
London, Dublin, Edinburgh, Brussels
1992

United Kingdom	Butterworth & Co (Publishers) Ltd, 88 Kingsway, LONDON WC2B 6AB 4 Hill Street, EDINBURGH EH2 3JZ
Australia	Butterworths Pty Ltd, SYDNEY, MELBOURNE, BRISBANE, ADELAIDE, PERTH, CANBERRA and HOBART
Belgium	Butterworth & Co. (Publishers) Ltd. 48 Rue de Namur/Namurstraat
Canada	Butterworths, TORONTO and VANCOUVER
Ireland	Butterworth (Ireland) Ltd, DUBLIN
Malaysia	Malayan Law Journal Sdn Bhd, KUALA LUMPUR
New Zealand	Butterworths of New Zealand Ltd, WELLINGTON and AUCKLAND
Puerto Rico	Equity de Puerto Rico Inc, HATO REY
Singapore	Malayan Law Journal Pte Ltd, SINGAPORE
USA	Butterworths Legal Publishers, ST PAUL, Minnesota, SEATTLE, Washington, BOSTON, Massachusetts, ORFORD, New Hampshire, AUSTIN, Texas and D & S Publishers, CLEARWATER, Florida

ISBN   0 406 01306 3
Printed in Great Britain by Ashford Colour Press Ltd, Gosport, Hampshire

Consultant Editor
DAVID VAUGHAN, Q.C.

Editors
HELEN BRITTON, B.A.
SANDRA DUTCZAK, LL.B.
CHARMIAN HARVEY, B.A.

Editorial Assistant
MARIA D'SOUZA

Produced by **Butterworths European Information Services**

PUBLISHER'S NOTE

With the momentum of change within the Community gathering pace it is hard to keep abreast of developments and obtain expert opinion and analysis together with original texts of legislation or cases as and when such events occur.

The *Current EC Legal Developments Series* is designed to provide the lawyer, consultant, researcher etc. with commentary and source materials of relevant practical interest on fundamental changes in Community law.

Each title in the series has a similar format presenting the full text of proposed or enacted legislation or judicial decisions under review and provides analysis and comment written by leading practitioners in the subject area under consideration.

The views expressed by the author are personal and are not intended to be applied to particular situations.

Any queries as to the nature or content of the *Current EC Legal Developments Series* or in respect of this title in the *Series* should be directed to the Managing Editor, Butterworths European Information Services, 88 Kingsway, London WC2B 6AB (071 405 6900).

Butterworth & Co (Publishers) Ltd.

To my father and to my mother's memory

ACKNOWLEDGMENT

The writer is indebted to Judge D.A.O. Edward, Dr. Robert C. Lane, Professor William Paterson, and Professor David O'Keeffe for their guidance and constructive criticisms in the compilation of this book. Margaret Ainslie is due a very special thanks for the enormous amount of time and effort spent in typing it and Una Doherty for her work on a close reading of it. A number of other persons provided assistance, notably Lesley Kelly, Marjorie Crozier, Sarah Barnetson, Gillian Caw and Iain Mackintosh.

CONTENTS

INTRODUCTION

Safeguard measures dating back to the beginning of the twentieth century have been used by the major trading nations of the Western world to combat unfair competition in the market place. This unfair competition normally, but not always, takes the form of price discrimination, ie subsidising low cost exports with profits from selling at high prices in the domestic market.

By far the greatest weapon in the European Community's arsenal of safeguard measures are the anti-dumping rules. Anti-dumping duties may be imposed if it can be established that dumping has caused injury to Community industry. Dumping occurs when a product is sold for export at a price lower than it is sold on the domestic market. Anti-dumping duties can be applied on a selective basis to those producers whose products cause injury to Community industry. It is one of the exceptions to the GATT (General Agreement on Tariffs and Trade) principle that safeguard measures must be applied on a non-discriminatory basis.

The Community's trading partners, in particular Japan, are now of the opinion that the Community is increasingly applying its anti-dumping legislation in a protectionist manner. Up to a few years ago Hong Kong was subject to only one anti-dumping proceeding which was subsequently discontinued. More recently, it has been the subject of an increasing number of investigations. Given the small size of its domestic market, Hong Kong, they contended, was not an example of dumping in the classical sense of subsidising low cost exports with high profits.

Another trend to emerge with the new anti-dumping policy is the greater number of "high tech" consumer products which inevitably are subjected to higher duties. Because such products involve greater amounts of money, investment and employment there is greater pressure on the Community authorities to take action where injury is established. It is due to the importance of the anti-dumping legislation that the chapters to follow hereon concentrate on the application and review of these rules. Reference will be made to the European Coal and Steel Community (ECSC) and European Atomic Energy Community (Euratom) Treaties only in passing. Therefore reference to the Treaty is intended to refer to the EEC Treaty (Treaty of Rome) and reference to the Community is intended to refer to the European Economic Community.

Apart from the anti-dumping legislation, the Community also has at its disposal anti-subsidy legislation to counteract the use by foreign governments of export and domestic subsidies. It can also impose quotas, designed to reduce the influx of low cost imports which have not been dumped but which nevertheless cause injury to Community industry. Legislation has been brought into force designed to combat "illicit commercial practices" which cause injury to both Community imports and exports.

The review of safeguard measures by the Court involves an analysis of the procedural and substantive rules relating primarily to an action for annulment of a Community act under article 173 since this is by far the most important right of action at the disposal of an affected party. Because the application of safeguard measures involves an evaluation of highly complex and technical findings, the writer also considers the extent to which the Court will review the exercise of powers which confer on the Community authorities a margin of discretion.

The law is stated, as much as is possible, as at 1 August 1992.

CHAPTER 1 : THE EXTERNAL COMPETENCE OF THE EUROPEAN COMMUNITY ON THE INTERNATIONAL PLANE AND THE POWERS OF THE COMMUNITY AUTHORITIES IN THE ADOPTION OF SAFEGUARD MEASURES

1.1   Introduction

In dealing with unfair trade practices by third countries in the European Community it is principally the Community authorities and not the Member States who regulate and adopt safeguard measures. This power flows from the fact that the Community has for the most part exclusive competence in dealing with matters affecting trade with third countries.

1.2   The external competence of the European Community

The scope and extent of the Community's capacity to act on the international plane is determined in accordance with the rules of international law, by the legal nature of the Community and by the powers assigned to it under the Treaties[1].

The further the Common Market comes to reciprocate a "domestic" market for goods originating within the Community the greater is the need for uniformity in the rules applying to the goods originating in third countries and imported into the Community. This is all the more crucial when one takes into account the increased economic interdependence of the major industrialised nations over the last two decades. Furthermore, the Community is increasingly dependent on the world economy both for the supply of raw materials and as an international market for its goods.

In the field of external relations, the EEC Treaty vests power in the Community in a limited number of areas, for example those articles[2] which deal with the Common Commercial Policy (hereinafter referred to as "the CCP").

---

1.   Ehlermann "Scope and extent of the capacity of the Community to act on the international plane", House of Lords Select Committee on European Affairs, Report 1985.
2.   Articles 110-116.

Apart from these express provisions, the European Court of Justice (hereinafter referred to as "the Court"), has developed a doctrine of implied powers[1]. In relation to the Community's Commercial Policy the Court stated in *Opinion 1/75*[2] that within the sphere of the CCP the Community is competent to conclude agreements with regard to a particular facet of that policy even if it has not yet established any Community rules which occupy the field internally.

1.2.1 The scope of the Community's powers within the CCP

The main Treaty provision with regard to the CCP is article 113. This confers on the Community the power to create and conduct a Common Commercial Policy based on uniform principles. It refers specifically to changes in tariff rates, the conclusion of tariff and trade agreements, the achievement of uniformity in measures of liberalisation, export policy and measures to protect trade such as those taken in the case of dumping or subsidies. Apart from these express powers the scope of Community powers in the area of the CCP depends on the definition of the term "Commercial Policy".

This was defined by the Court in *Opinion 1/75* when it held that its meaning may not be interpreted more narrowly for the sake of the Community than it is practised generally by the Member States[3]. It further stated that Commercial Policy is made up by the combination and interaction of internal and external measures without priority being taken by one over the other[4]. This echoed the dictum of the Court in the *Massey-Ferguson* case[5] where it had already emphasised the necessity of giving a broad construction to the articles of the Treaty relating to customs union and trade policy.

In *Opinion 1/78* the Court stated that the enumeration of article 113 was not exclusive[6]. It held that an interpretation restricting the CCP to the use of instruments intended to have effect only on the traditional aspects of external trade to the exclusion of more highly developed mechanisms would create a commercial policy destined to become nugatory in the course of time[7].

The EC Council was of the view that a measure, in order to be a measure of commercial policy, must have the object of altering the volume or the flow of

---

1.   Case 22/70 *EC Commission v EC Council* [1971] ECR 263.
2.   [1975] ECR 1355.
3.   Ibid at 1362.
4.   Ibid at 1363.
5.   Case 8/73 *Hauptzollamt Bremerhaven v Massey-Ferguson GmbH* [1973] ECR 897.
6.   [1978] ECR 2871 at 2913.
7.   Ibid.

trade[1]. Bourgeois[2] has argued that this definition, although it sounds convincing, had two main drawbacks. First, for the purposes of autonomous Community commercial measures, it produces results that are unsatisfactory when applied to measures that are inherent to the conduct of any Commercial Policy, eg customs formalities or marks of origin. Under the EC Council's interpretation these measures would be unlikely to fall within the ambit of article 113 as it would be difficult to show that they affected the volume or flow of trade. Second, the interpretation imported a subjective element which would allow reluctant Member States to argue that the measure was beyond the Community's powers or that it required unanimity. The EC Commission, on the other hand, argued that a measure of commercial policy must be assessed by reference to its specific characteristics as an instrument regulating international trade[3]. This definition is also unsatisfactory in that the term "instrument" is a very broad concept.

A better interpretation of the scope of the Community's Commercial Policy is a combination of both views[4], namely, all measures which regulate openly and specifically trade with third countries should always be considered as part of the Common Commercial Policy; they are *per se* measures of commercial policy unless the Treaty provides for an exception. Other measures should be considered as part of such policy by a sort of "rule of reason" viz. when their dominant purpose is to influence the volume or flow of trade.

The measures enumerated in articles 112 and 113 and measures ancillary to these, such as customs regulations and procedures for import and export licensing, would come within this formulation, as would measures such as taxes and measures having an effect equivalent to quantitative restrictions.

Bourgeois[5] provides some helpful guidelines in determining what constitutes "dominant purpose". They are as follows :

(a) the form of the agreement - the purpose, structure, instruments and effects;

(b) the framework within which it was concluded, for example if it takes place within an institutional organisation whose aim is to promote trade.

---

1. [1978] ECR 2871 at 2910.
2. "The Common Commercial Policy - Scope and Nature of the Powers" in (ed) Volker "Protectionism in the EEC", p4.
3. *Opinion 1/78* above at 2910-1.
4. See Ehlermann, Director-General for Commission Legal Service exposé at 10th Congress of International Federation for European Law held in Dublin, 24-26 June 1982.
5. Above.

The construction does, however, require further elucidation, but it goes some way in attempting to reconcile the differences in the views held by the EC Council and EC Commission. There is no doubt that the Community's safeguard measures used to counteract unfair trade practices are per se commercial policy measures and as such are within the scope of the Community's powers.

1.3   The nature of the powers within the CCP

The Court, since its judgment in the *ERTA* case[1], has consistently declared that the Community's external relations power is exclusive in nature. When such a power is exclusive the Member States may no longer unilaterally enter into international agreements or adopt autonomous measures in the field of external relations.

The principle in *ERTA*[2] was based on two grounds. First, the Community power excludes the possibility of concurrent or parallel powers on the part of the Member States since any steps taken outside the framework of the Community would be incompatible with the unity of the Common Market and the uniform application of Community law. Second, upon entry into force of a common internal rule it is the Community alone that is in a position to carry out contractual obligations towards third countries affecting the whole sphere of application of the Community legal system.

More specifically, in *Opinion 1/75*[3], which concerned an area of Commercial Policy, namely export credits, the Court concluded that the CCP was conceived in the context of the operation of a Common Market for the defence of the common interests of the Community. The Court stated that :

> "unilateral action on the part of the Member States would lead to disparities in the conditions for the grant of export credits, calculated to distort competition between undertakings of the various Member States in external markets ... It cannot therefore be accepted that in a field such as that governed by the understanding in question, which is covered by export policy and more generally by the common commercial policy, the Member States should exercise a power concurrent to that of the Community, in the Community sphere and in the international sphere."[4]

---

1.   Case 22/70 *EC Commission v EC Council* [1971] ECR 263.
2.   Ibid.
3.   [1975] ECR 1355 at 1363-4.
4.   Ibid at 1364.

At a later stage in its judgment the Court again unequivocally indicated that the Member States and the Community could not exercise powers concurrently in the sphere of commercial policy[1]. The Court reiterated the principle in *Donckerwolcke*[2] in which it indicated that at the end of the transitional period, responsibility in the field of Commercial Policy was transferred en bloc to the Community and unilateral action by the Member States was excluded across the whole field.

1.4 The basic powers of the Community authorities in the Member States and the adoption of safeguard measures

The EEC Treaty which established the European Economic Community (EEC), like the Treaty of Paris (hereinafter referred to as the ECSC Treaty) which established the European Coal and Steel Community (ECSC), created a Community with legal personality and four autonomous institutions. The European Atomic Energy Community (Euratom) was established by a separate Treaty at the same time as the EEC. It too had a separate legal personality and four autonomous institutions. The institutions included an Assembly (now known as the European Parliament[3]), a Council of Ministers, a Commission (equivalent to the High Authority under the ECSC Treaty but which had more limited autonomous powers) and a Court of Justice.

A single Court and Assembly were established for all three Communities by a Convention signed at the same time as the EEC and Euratom Treaties. On 1 July 1967, as a result of a Merger Treaty (Treaty of 8 April 1965 establishing a Single Council and Single Commission of the European Communities) a Single Council of Ministers was established. At the same time the ECSC High Authority and the EEC and Euratom Commissions were merged to form a single body known as the EC Commission.

Even though the three Communities have common institutions, they are legally distinct with the powers and functions of the institutions based on the terms of the Treaty under which they were established. This is of importance in relation to the EC Commission since it enjoys the more wide-reaching powers which are conferred on the High Authority under the ECSC Treaty.

---

1.   Ibid.
2.   Case 41/76 *Criel, née Donckerwolcke and Henri Schon v Procureur de la République* [1976] ECR 1921.
3.   Article 2, Single European Act.

1.4.1 The EC Commission

Under the safeguard measures discussed in the chapters to follow, the EC Commission has as its major role the task of determining whether there is sufficient evidence to initiate a proceeding and of investigating the facts to determine dumping and injury. In the United States, on the other hand, the task of determining whether foreign goods are dumped is entrusted to the International Trade Administration of the Department of Commerce whilst the determination of injury is carried out by the International Trade Commission.

This is quite a large undertaking for the EC Commission now that there are many more complex cases being brought to its attention. As the number of complaints increase rapidly the EC Commission is faced with an acute shortage of staff necessary to investigate unfair trading practices. This is particularly so in relation to anti-dumping cases. In 1986 only 26 officials were employed by the EC Commission to investigate complaints of dumping compared with 110 in the US for the same purpose[1]. To overcome this problem it was suggested that the EC Commission should consider employing private investigators to supplement its own staff[2]. In 1987 the number of case workers was increased to 33 and they were aided by 15 officials lent to the EC Commission by the Member States. There are currently 40 case workers assisted by 30 officials seconded from the Member States.

Under Regulation 2423/88[3], the EC Commission has the power, if certain conditions are fulfilled, to impose provisional anti-dumping and countervailing duties[4]. Such duties are valid only for six months, however, whereupon it is the responsibility of the EC Council to adopt definitive duties. Under Regulation 288/82[5] the EC Commission has the power to limit the period of validity of import documents or alter the rules for the product in question by providing that it may only be put into free circulation on production of an import authorisation[6]. This can be done either on the request of a Member State or on its own initiative. By virtue of article 1(b) of the New Commercial Policy Instrument - Regulation 2641/84[7] the EC Commission has the power to initiate, conduct and terminate formal international consultations or dispute settlement procedures.

---

1.   Financial Times, 8 October 1986.
2.   Ibid.
3.   Council Regulation (EEC) 2423/88 (OJ L209 2.8.88 p1). For an analysis of the regulation see Chapter 3 below.
4.   Article 11.
5.   Council Regulation (EEC) 288/82 (OJ L35 9.2.82 p1). For an analysis of the regulation see Chapter 3 below.
6.   Article 15.
7.   Council Regulation (EEC) 2641/84 (OJ L252 20.9.84 p1). For an analysis of the regulation see Chapter 3 below.

Under Regulation 2423/88 the EC Commission also has the power to terminate proceedings where there is no injury or where it is not in the interests of the Community to impose protective measures. This is the case, however, only where no objection is raised within the Advisory Committee, otherwise the matter must be submitted to the EC Council[1]. It can accept undertakings if it considers them appropriate instead of adopting anti-dumping or countervailing duties. Until very recently the EC Commission favoured settling most cases in this way. However, with the emergence of anti-dumping cases involving "high tech" consumer products from Japan and other Far East countries it has become less inclined to accept them owing mainly to the fact that large price increases are required in order to eliminate the injury caused by dumping. Although it does not specifically provide for it in Regulation 288/82, the EC Commission may accept a Voluntary Export Restraint agreement[2]. This is unlikely to occur very often since these agreements are for the most part offered on an industry to industry basis. To accept such an undertaking would mean that the appraisal of the injurious effects of imports on Community industry, as well as the choice of any protective measures, would be decided by someone other than the EC Commission.

1.4.2   The powers of the EC Commission under the ECSC Treaty

Under the ECSC Treaty, the High Authority was vested with the supreme powers of decision making. By virtue of the Merger Treaty, the High Authority and the Commissions which were established by the Treaties of Rome were merged into one single Commission. This does not mean that the EC Commission's powers are always the same. When acting under the ECSC Treaty it has all the decision-making powers which were vested in the High Authority.

This explains why the EC Commission, when acting under the ECSC anti-dumping rules, for example, has the power not only to order the definitive collection of provisional duties but also the power to impose definitive duties[3]. It is also competent to terminate proceedings when protective measures are thought to be unnecessary without seeking the permission of the Advisory Committee[4]. Even though it must consult the Advisory Committee throughout all the important stages of the procedure, it can adopt decisions quickly without having them vetoed as may be the case under the EEC Treaty.

---

1.   Article 9(1).
2.   See Chapter 3, Part 3.
3.   Article 12, Commission Decision 2424/88 (OJ L209 2.8.88 p18).
4.   Article 9(1), Commission Decision 2424/88. Cf Article 9(1) of Council Regulation (EEC) 2423/88 (OJ L209 2.8.88 p1).

1.4.3   The EC Council

Under the EEC Treaty the Council of Ministers is the institution endowed with supreme decision-making powers.

Under Regulation 2423/88 it is only the EC Council which is competent to impose definitive duties and to order the definitive collection of the provisional duties. Likewise it can adopt protective measures on a proposal from the EC Commission under Regulation 288/82 and Regulation 2641/84.

The fact that the EC Council adopts definitive duties has caused difficulties in the handling of cases before the Court mainly because it is the EC Commission which carries out the investigation. These difficulties have been made all the more acute by the number of highly complex cases that are coming before the Court[1]. In each of these cases it is the EC Council and not the EC Commission which is the defendant because the EC Council and not the EC Commission adopts the definitive duties. In most cases the EC Commission is only an intervener. Members of the EC Council Legal Service have intimated that they often find it difficult and unsatisfactory to represent the EC Council as defendant in anti-dumping cases with which the Commission officials are more familiar. At the moment the EC Commission Legal Service helps the EC Council draft its mémoire.

There are two possible means of avoiding duplication and also preventing the EC Council from being held responsible for errors made by the EC Commission. It is possible to introduce legislation enabling the definitive duties to be adopted by the EC Commission. The EC Commission has recently proposed such a change. This would have to be made subject to the proviso that the Member States be consulted. This solution has, however, its drawbacks, the major one being the political obstacles to the change. It is submitted, however, as Vermulst[2] suggests that the Member States now recognise that the application of anti-dumping laws is essentially a technical matter with limited room for political intervention. The alternative solution is an administrative one and it could take one of three forms. First, the EC Commission Legal Service could prepare the EC Council's mémoire. This tends to be the case, to a large extent, in the more complex cases now coming before the Court. Second, the two institutions could instruct counsel from one of the Member States. The problem with this alternative is that it is difficult to find suitable counsel. In anti-dumping cases especially, the questions which need most work are those on which the Community is in a weak legal position. Inevitably, the institutions will not wish to divulge the points they are most concerned about

---

1.   See Chapters 4, 5 and 6 below.
2.   "Anti-dumping Law and Practice in the United States and the European Community" (1987) at p311.

irrespective of whatever promises counsel makes regarding disclosure to private clients. Furthermore, anti-dumping actions will almost always give rise to issues of policy. It is difficult and often undesirable to make counsel aware of policy considerations. Third, in cases where there is no conflict of interest, there is no reason why the EC Commission's lawyer could not act as the EC Council's agent.

1.4.4   The Member States

The Member States have an important role to play in the administering of safeguard measures designed to counteract unfair trading practices. They, in the form of the Advisory Committee, are required to be consulted at each stage of the procedure. The Committee is made up of a representative from each of the Member States with a representative of the EC Commission as Chairman.

Under Regulation 2423/88, they also have the task of collecting the duties imposed by the Community institutions through their customs authorities.

Finally, under Regulation 288/82, the Member States have the power to adopt interim protective measures where there exists in their territory a situation authorising the adoption of protective measures; or where such measures are justified by a safeguard clause contained in a bilateral agreement between the Member State and a third party[1].

---

1.   Article 17(1)(a) and (b).

CHAPTER 2 : SAFEGUARD MEASURES : AN INTERNATIONAL PERSPECTIVE

2.1   Introduction

The General Agreement on Tariffs and Trade ("the GATT") came into existence in 1947[1]. It provides a framework of rules and standards for international trade. The GATT was based largely on the ill-fated International Trade Organisation Charter[2]. The contracting parties to the GATT aimed at :

> "raising the standard of living, ensuring full employment and a large and steadily growing volume of real income and effective demand, developing the full use of the resources of the world and expanding the production and exchange of goods"[3].

There were two means of contributing to these objectives. The GATT was concerned not only with the liberalising of trade policies by the reduction of tariffs but also with the elimination of discriminatory treatment and the anti-competitive effects of unfair trade practices such as dumping.

The GATT is based largely on three basic principles. First, there is the principle of non-discrimination. This means that goods of any contracting party are to be given no less favourable treatment than that given to any other contracting party. This principle - or most favoured nation clause as it is known in the GATT - is contained in article I[4]. The object of the clause is to ensure that all foreign goods are treated equally. As a corollary, article III attempts to impose the principle of non-discrimination between goods domestically produced and those which are imported with respect to internal taxation and other forms of governmental regulation. Such a provision is necessary, otherwise such measures would be substituted for tariff reductions.

---

1.   See generally, Jackson "World Trade and the Law of GATT" (1969); Dam "The GATT : Law and International Economic Organisation" (1970); GATT 4th supp. BISD (1956).
2.   Jackson, above, Chapter 2.
3.   Preamble of the GATT.
4.   There are a number of other mfn or non-discrimination clauses in the GATT, for example article III(7) (Internal mixing requirements); article IVb (Cinema films); article V(2), (5) and (6) (Transit of goods); article IX(1) (Marks of origin); article XIII(1) (Quantitative restrictions); article XVII(1) (State trading); article XVIII(20) (Measures to assist economic development); article XX(j) (Measures for goods in short supply).

The second principle is the prohibition on the use of quotas or other commercial measures as a means of protecting domestic industry[1]. Unlike tariffs, the impact of which an exporter can gauge, non-tariff restrictions such as quotas are arbitrary with the result that an exporter will be unable to assess how his product will be treated.

The third principle is that the GATT proceeds on the basis of consultation in resolving its trade disputes. The GATT outlines those situations when a contracting party can deviate from its obligations[2] and also the circumstances in which retaliatory action can be taken against unfair trading[3]. Furthermore, if a party considers that a benefit accruing to it under the GATT has been nullified or impaired as a result of another party's breach or adoption of other measures, the GATT dispute settlement procedure can be initiated under article XXIII[4].

In order to achieve reduction of tariffs and the elimination of discriminatory treatment, there have been a number of major rounds of multilateral trade negotiations[5]. Originally the objective of the negotiations was to bring about a substantial reduction in tariffs and the elimination of tariff preferences. From the outset it was agreed that the negotiations should be held on a "reciprocal and mutually advantageous basis"[6]. This idea of reciprocity, ie that one concession should be matched by another of similar value, was at the core of the international trade order. It worked well in relation to the reduction of tariffs. Great progress was made at the Kennedy Round on the reduction of tariffs with regard to industrial goods where the contracting parties applied a "linear" approach to cut tariffs[7]. This was in sharp contrast to the previous round of negotiations - the Dillon Round - where negotiations were conducted on a product by product basis[8]. The GATT is concerned not only with the reduction of tariffs but also with the elimination of other barriers to trade. As tariffs are reduced, the role of non-tariff barriers becomes more important. Kelly has defined a non-tariff barrier as any law, regulation, policy or practice of a government, other than an import duty that has a restrictive effect on trade[9].

---

1.   Article XI, GATT. See Jackson "World Trade and the Law of GATT" (1969).
2.   Article XIX (Safeguard Clause); articles XX and XXI (General Exceptions); article XXV (Waivers); article XXIV (Regionalism).
3.   Articles XI and XIII (Quantitative Restrictions); article XVI (Subsidies); article VI (Anti-dumping and Countervailing Duties).
4.   See generally Jackson, above, Chapter 8.
5.   Geneva 1947; Dillon Round 1960-1; Kennedy Round 1965-7; Tokyo Round concluded in 1979; Uruguay Round 1982.
6.   Article XXVIII bis para 1. Cf Part IV, GATT (added in 1964/5), provides that reciprocity will not be expected from less developed countries.
7.   GATT 13th supp. BISD 109 (1965).
8.   GATT 8th supp. BISD 119 (1960).
9.   "Non Tariff Barriers" in (ed) Balassa "Studies in Trade Liberalisation : Problems and prospects for industrial countries" (1967).

Most of the general clauses in the GATT deal with specific non-tariff barriers. As these barriers are reduced, those not controlled by the GATT become increasingly significant. Owing to their opacity, however, non-tariff barriers are much more difficult to value in terms of trade concessions and, as a result, it is much more difficult to achieve reciprocity.

The Tokyo Round of Multilateral Trade Negotiations concluded in 1979 was concerned with formulating new, fairer and more transparent rules on international trade relations in order to bring about the advantages in tariff reductions. Unlike the Kennedy Round, which was negotiated during an era of world economic expansion, unfavourable conditions - rising oil prices, world trade recession and rampant inflation - dominated the Tokyo Round Negotiations. In periods of expansion it is relatively easy to reduce barriers to trade since, generally speaking, imports do not give rise to a threat of loss of employment or closure of local industry. On the other hand, in times of recession, protectionist policies prevail and national frontiers are closed.

The result of the Tokyo Round was a number of Codes which improve and update the rules and procedures governing world trade in that they facilitate the abolition or reduction of a number of non-tariff barriers and improve surveillance. These Codes were seen as a way of reducing, if not eliminating, protectionism so as to facilitate more freedom in international trade[1].

In September 1982 the contracting parties agreed to launch a new Round of trade negotiations to be called the Uruguay Round. One of the objectives of the negotiations is to continue with the work of reducing tariffs and non-tariff barriers. These negotiations are special, however, in that they cover not only trade in goods but also trade in services. Trade in services has increased in importance owing to the development of communications and data processing technologies and the general trend towards deregulation in many service sectors and their trade. This has resulted in an increase in the proportion of services that can be traded across borders in recent years[2]. It was, therefore, considered important to negotiate a multilateral framework of principles and rules in order to increase transparency and to liberalise trade in services.

---

1. GATT 26th supp. BISD (1978-9).
2. See Focus : GATT Newsletter 57 (1988); GATT economists estimated that in 1988 trade in services amounted to some 600 US$ billion. (See Focus : GATT Newsletter 71 (1990)).

2.2   Dumping

2.2.1   Historical background

Prior to the GATT there was little international regulation of dumping[1]. The question first arose at an international level in 1920 at the World Economic Conference in The League of Nations. The general reaction to laws which would permit a country to impose anti-dumping duties was a fear that they would be used as a protectionist device by distorting competition and protecting domestic industry. Against this background, the power to impose anti-dumping duties where it could be shown that the dumping caused injury to the domestic producers of the like product was included in the new General Agreement on Tariffs and Trade[2]. However, the major drawback of the original anti-dumping provision was that it was subject to the grandfather clause contained in the Protocol of Provisional Application[3]. This meant that in relation to those provisions in Part II of the GATT (article VI was such a provision) the pre-existing legislation of the contracting parties was not superseded by the GATT. The result of this was that the requirements of article VI were disregarded, in particular by the United States whose legislation[4], which existed prior to the GATT, did not require injury to be proved.

Owing mainly to the insistence of the European Community, the question of dumping was considered at the Kennedy Round of Multilateral Trade Negotiations. The European Community was in favour of more specific and binding rules with regard to anti-dumping. The result was an Anti-dumping Code[5]. This Code, however, was only an extensive interpretation of article VI and binding only on those contracting parties which signed it.

At the Tokyo Round of Multilateral Trade Negotiations, the Anti-dumping Code concluded at the Kennedy Round was replaced by a new Code[6] which for the most part was incorporated into the legislation of those signatories to the Code, including the United States.

---

1.   At national level a number of countries had already in existence legislation which enabled them to impose anti-dumping duties. The first country to have such legislation was Canada in 1904 - an act to amend the Customs Tariff, 1897 SC 1904, c11, s19.
2.   Article VI, GATT. See Appendix 1.
3.   GATT, 1st supp. BISD 81 (1952).
4.   Tariff Act 1897 Chapter 11 30 Stat 205 as amended by the Tariff Acts 1922 and 1930.
5.   GATT 15th supp. BISD 24 (1968).
6.   GATT 26th supp. BISD 171 (1978-9).

2.2.2 Economic rationale

In his authoritative work *Dumping : a Problem in International Trade*[1], Jacob Viner defined dumping as price discrimination between national markets. This essentially means that the producers in one country sell their goods for whatever reason in the market of another producer at unusually low prices[2].

It is generally agreed that three preconditions are necessary for price discrimination between national markets to occur[3] :

(a) There have to be separate markets. This will usually be accompanied by the situation whereby the dumper's market will be insulated from the re-importation of the dumped goods. In order for this to occur certain barriers to trade will exist in order to distort the free flow of trade. They may take the form of high tariffs or transport costs, but more often they will be non-tariff barriers such as different technical standards[4].

(b) The dumper must exercise some form of control over the price in his domestic market. This, in essence, means that conditions of imperfect competition must exist. In other words, the producer of the dumped goods must have a relatively large share of the domestic market and must produce a product which can be differentiated from that which is sold by the other producers[5]. The dumper does not have to be a monopolist unless he is involved in predatory dumping, ie a foreign monopolist who sells his product in the importing country at a loss in order to eliminate his competitors in that market. Thereafter he will be able to sell at higher prices[6].

(c) There must exist in the importing country a greater elasticity of demand in order for the dumping to be profitable. This is more likely to be the case where demand in the domestic market for the product is inelastic[7]. In

---

1.   Reproduced in M Kellay, New York 1966; first published in 1923.
2.   See Fisher "The Anti-dumping Law of the US : A Legal and Economic Analysis" 5 Law and Policy in International Bus. (1973) 85 at 85-93; Bryan "Taxing Unfair International Trade Practices" pp31-43; De Jong "The Significance of Dumping in International Trade" 2 JWTL 162 at 168.
3.   Viner, above, pp94-101; Bryan, above, p33; Ehrenhaft "Protection against international price discrimination : US countervailing and anti-dumping duties" 58 Columbia Law Rev (1958) pp48-49.
4.   Bryan, above, pp31-1. This situation can be contrasted with one in which perfect competition prevails. Each firm sells a small amount of the total sold in any given market and each sells identical or homogeneous products.
5.   Barcelo "The Anti-dumping Law : Repeal or Revise it" (1979) NYB of International Legal Studies p65.
6.   De Jong, above, p168.
7.   An example of highly inelastic demand for a product was the case of *Electronic Typewriters* (Japan) OJ L335 22.12.84 p43. In the domestic market the demand for alphanumeric typewriters was small and inelastic. This enabled the Japanese manufacturers to maintain high prices.

such a case the price will be higher since a reduction in the price will have little effect on the level of sales.

In his analysis of dumping[1], Professor Viner broadly outlined three categories of dumping : sporadic dumping, short-term or intermittent dumping and continuous or long-term dumping.

Sporadic dumping usually takes the form of unloading excess stock on to foreign markets in order to protect the dumper's position in the domestic market. It may be that demand in the dumper's market is inelastic, in which case a reduction in the price will have little effect on sales. Viner saw this as not causing serious injury and at worst it deprived the consumer in the country of origin of the benefit of a bargain sale[2].

Short-term or intermittent dumping is aimed at gaining a foothold in the foreign market, or preventing the development of competition or eliminating competitors altogether[3]. This last situation is known as predatory dumping, and it occurs when a foreign producer sells abroad at a loss while maintaining monopoly profits in the domestic market. His temporary losses will in time be recouped by higher prices. Professor Viner saw this type of dumping as objectionable irrespective of whether or not predation was involved. He contended that, owing to its impermanence, it was liable to cause injury to the domestic producer in that its sudden cessation could render investment valueless or cut off a source of supply for materials. He argued that on the whole the injury to the domestic producers outweighed the short-term gain for the consumer[4].

Long-term or continuous dumping may occur as a result of the producer's determination to maintain the price structure in the domestic market or for reasons of maximising economies of scale. In both cases he will sell his product abroad at reduced prices in order to maintain high prices in his own home market[5]. Professor Viner noted that this was the only occasion in which dumping would benefit the foreign country in terms of efficiency and welfare[6].

---

1.   Viner "Dumping : a Problem in International Trade", reproduced in M Kellay, New York 1966.
2.   Ibid p101.
3.   Ibid pp26-27.
4.   Ibid pp132-140.
5.   Ibid pp28-30.
6.   Ibid p133; De Jong "The Significance of Dumping in International Trade" 2 JWTL 162 at 177.

2.2.3 The regulation of dumping in the GATT

Dumping is regulated primarily by article VI. However, as will be shown below, article VI suffered from a number of serious drawbacks.

First, it was subject to the grandfather clause which meant that it did not supersede the pre-existing legislation of the contracting parties[1]. Second, there were no multilateral procedural regulations to govern its application[2]. This meant in effect that by carrying out lengthy and time-consuming investigations the anti-dumping procedure could be used as a protectionist device. This was one of the main reasons why it was added to the list of non-tariff barriers to be discussed at the Kennedy Round. Finally, article VI suffered from a serious lack of definition of key concepts. Although the Expert Group on Anti-dumping and Countervailing Duties[3] went some way in clarifying the position, it was not really until the Anti-dumping Codes of the Kennedy Round[4] and the Tokyo Round[5] that a more specific set of standards was adopted with respect to the determination and investigation of dumping and injury.

In the following analysis of the GATT regulation of dumping, reference to the Anti-dumping Code is to the Code concluded at the Tokyo Round as it replaced that adopted at the Kennedy Round[6].

Dumping is defined in article VI(1) as the situation where the price of the product from one country to another is less than the comparable price in the ordinary course of trade for the like product when destined for consumption in the exporting country[7]. The term "like product" was not defined in article VI[8]. Because this is central to the question of dumping and injury, it was defined in article 2(2) of the Anti-dumping Code[9].

---

1.   See footnote 3, p16.
2.   See generally Curzon and Curzon "GATT" in (ed) Shonfield "International Economic Relations of the Western World" (1959-71).
3.   GATT 8th supp. BISD 146 (1960).
4.   Reproduced in GATT 15th supp. BISD 24 (1966-7).
5.   Reproduced in GATT 26th supp. BISD 171 (1978-9). See Appendix 2.
6.   Article 16(5), Anti-dumping Code (1979).
7.   This definition was maintained in article 2(1) of the Anti-dumping Code.
8.   The Expert Group defined "Like product" thus : "a product which is identical in physical characteristics subject however to such variations in presentation which are due to the need to adapt the product to special conditions in the market of the importing country" GATT 8th supp. BISD 146 at 149 (1960).
9.   In the Anti-dumping Code, "Like product" was defined as a product which is identical, ie alike in all respects to the product under consideration or, in the absence of such a product, another product which, although not alike in all respects, has characteristics closely resembling those of the product under consideration.

2.2.3.1 The determination of dumping

In order for dumping to exist the export price of the product must be less than its normal value. Article VI(1) provided that the export price was simply the price of the product exported from one country to another[1]. However, it did not deal with the situation where no export price existed or where the export price proved to be unreliable owing to association or compensatory arrangements. This was rectified by article 2(5) of the Anti-dumping Code. It provided that the export price may be constructed on the basis of the price :

(a) at which the imported products are first resold to an independent buyer; or

(b) if the products are not resold to an independent buyer or not resold in the condition imported, on such reasonable basis as the authorities may determine.

In both these cases allowances are permitted for costs incurred between importation and resale[2].

With regard to the normal value the preferred price was to be the domestic price, ie the comparable price in the ordinary course of trade for the like product when destined for consumption in the exporting country[3]. In the absence of the domestic price, article VI provided for two alternative methods of establishing normal value. It could be established by taking the highest comparable price for the like product for export to any third country in the ordinary course of trade[4]. Although it could be the highest price it had to be representative[5]. Alternatively, it could be established by taking the cost of production of the product in the country of origin and adding to it a reasonable amount for selling expenses and for profit[6].

In order to ensure a fair comparison between the normal value and the export price, article VI(1) provided that allowances should be made for differences in taxation, in conditions and terms of sale and for other differences affecting price comparability. Article 2(6) of the Anti-dumping Code added to this the requirement that the normal value and the export price should be compared at the same level of trade, ie the ex-factory level and in respect of sales made as near as

---

1. According to the Export Group on Anti-dumping and Countervailing Duties this was to be the price at which the product left the exporting country and not that at which it entered the importing country, GATT 8th supp. BISD 146 (1960).
2. Article 2(6), Anti-dumping Code.
3. Article VI(1)(a).
4. Article VI(1)(b)(i).
5. Article 2(4), Anti-dumping Code.
6. Article VI(1)(b)(ii).

possible in time. Once these allowances have been made the dumping margin could be determined.

2.2.3.2 Determination of injury

Dumping on its own, however, was not to be condemned unless its effect was such that material injury was caused to domestic industry in the importing country[1]. Unfortunately, article VI did not define injury[2] and it was not until the Anti-dumping Codes of the Kennedy Round and Tokyo Round that guidelines for the determination of injury were laid down.

Under article 3 of the Anti-dumping Code, a determination of dumping can only be made where the dumped imports are the cause of material injury to a domestic industry. This was a much less stringent test than that provided for in the Anti-dumping Code of the Kennedy Round, by which the authorities of the importing country had to show that dumping was demonstrably the principal cause of material injury[3].

According to article 3, the determination of injury must be based on positive evidence, involving an examination of the volume and prices of the dumped imports and the consequent impact on the domestic producers of the like product[4]. In other words, the dumped imports have to be the cause of injury and other factors such as the volume and prices of non-dumped imports which are causing injury are not to be attributed to the dumped imports[5]. As injury has to be caused to the producers of the like product in the importing country, it is important to know what constitutes domestic industry. Article 4 of Anti-dumping Code defines it as :

> "the domestic producers as a whole of the like products or to those of them whose collective output of the products constitutes a major proportion of the total domestic production of those products".

This general rule is subject to two exceptions. First, where the producer is related to the exporter or is himself the importer, then domestic industry may be interpreted as referring to the rest of the producers and second, the territory of a party may be

---

1.   Article VI(1); no precise definition or set of rules could be given in respect of the injury concept. With regard to a definition of industry, the Group of Experts agreed that a single firm within a large industry could generally not constitute an industry, GATT 8th supp. BISD 150 (1960).
2.   See article VI(1) and (6)(a).
3.   Article 3(a); Barcelo "The Anti-dumping Law : Repeal or Revise it" (1979) NYB of International Legal Studies, contends that article 3 of the Anti-dumping Code adopted at the Tokyo Round was a soft injury test.
4.   Article 3(2)-(3), Anti-dumping Code.
5.   Article 3(4), Anti-dumping Code.

divided into two or more competitive markets and the producers within each may be regarded as domestic industry[1].

2.2.3.3 Anti-dumping duties and undertakings

When it has been determined that the producers of the like product have been injured as a result of the effects of dumping, a contracting party can impose anti-dumping duties[2]. The amount of duty levied cannot exceed the margin of dumping in respect of such product[3] and the framers of the Code considered it desirable to impose a lesser duty if this would be adequate to remove injury[4]. Furthermore, the imposition of duties is not subject to the principle of non-discrimination. In other words, duties can be imposed selectively on the dumped goods while the same goods from other sources which were not dumped would be free of such duties[5]. Apart from the imposition of duties, the authorities in the importing country may accept price undertakings which revise the price or cease exports at dumped prices so as to eliminate the injurious effects of dumping[6]. The advantages of such undertakings are their flexibility and the fact that they bring about a more amicable solution.

2.2.3.4 Procedure

A major drawback of article VI was that it did not require the contracting parties to comply with any procedural requirements. This resulted in it being used as a protectionist device with investigations dragging on for many months. This situation was rectified by the Anti-dumping Code. It provided that anti-dumping investigations had to be concluded within one year after initiation[7] and furthermore that the investigation on dumping and injury had to be considered simultaneously[8]. The gathering of evidence and its verification is regulated by article 6 of the Anti-dumping Code. It provides that in cases where the offending exporter does not co-operate, the authorities in the importing country may proceed on the basis of facts available[9].

2.2.4 Evaluation

The Anti-dumping Code concluded at the Tokyo Round, like its predecessor, is binding only on those parties which signed it. Whereas most of the industrialised nations of the Western World signed it, the less developed countries did not. More

---

1.   Article 4(2), Anti-dumping Code.
2.   Article VI(6)(a).
3.   Article VI(2) : article 8(3), Anti-dumping Code.
4.   Article 8(1), Anti-dumping Code.
5.   This can be contrasted with article XIX of the GATT which permits the adoption of safeguard measures in cases of emergency. Such measures have to be applied on a non-discriminatory basis.
6.   Article 7(1), Anti-dumping Code.
7.   Article 5(5), Anti-dumping Code.
8.   Article 5(2), Anti-dumping Code.
9.   Article 6(8), Anti-dumping Code.

importantly, the United States bound itself by the injury criteria and it incorporated the Code into its domestic legal order[1].

The Code has also resulted in greater transparency with respect to the determination of dumping and injury. This process has continued through the work of the Anti-dumping Committee and in particular with regard to its recommendations on greater transparency in anti-dumping proceedings and on-the-spot investigations, to name but two[2].

As a result of the recent GATT Panel's report in the dispute between the European Community and Japan concerning the importation of anti-dumping duties by the Community on "screwdriver assembly" products[3], the delegates at the Uruguay Round are at present debating the question of introducing provisions into the Anti-dumping Code to counteract the circumvention of duties by such methods[4].

2.3   Subsidies and countervailing duties

2.3.1   Historical background

The GATT rules on subsidies are much stricter than those regulating dumping. Whereas dumping is prohibited by the GATT only when it causes injury, some subsidies are prohibited altogether, notably export subsidies on non-primary goods, while others are to be restricted in their application.

The main GATT provision on subsidies is article XVI[5]. It distinguishes between export subsidies and subsidies in general, the former being subdivided into export subsidies on primary goods and those on non-primary goods[6].

The term "subsidy" is not defined in the GATT nor in the Code on Subsidies and Countervailing Duties, though it is generally accepted that it involves a net loss to government[7]. In 1961 the GATT Panel of Experts agreed that a definition was neither feasible nor necessary. Further, they pointed out that to formulate a

---

1.   Trade Agreements Act 1979, s2(b)(3), 19 USC s2503(b)(3).
2.   GATT 30th supp. BISD (1982-83).
3.   See Chapter 3, below.
4.   See Focus : GATT Newsletter 70 (1990).
5.   See Appendix 1.
6.   Article XVI(3) and (4).
7.   Pestieau "Revising GATT approach to Subsidies : A Canadian View" p95 in (ed) Warnecke "International Trade and Industrial Policies" (1978).

definition might give rise to a situation where measures are included which were never intended to come within the meaning of article XVI[1].

Originally, the country granting the subsidy had to notify the GATT bodies of the nature, extent and effects of the subsidy[2]. Not surprisingly, this provision was ignored, largely because it meant confessing to a practice that was trade distorting. The reason for such a weak provision was twofold. First, subsidies were regarded as a less serious obstacle to trade than, for instance, tariffs or quotas. Second, as we live in a buyers' market rather than a sellers' market, most countries tend to use subsidies as a means of increasing their exports[3]. This is due largely to the fact that the economies of the various contracting parties are at different stages of development and many have industries which are not internationally competitive[4].

In 1955 new rules on subsidies were added in order to strengthen article XVI. These new rules banned export subsidies on non-primary goods altogether and limited the application and effect of export subsidies on primary goods[5].

The new Code on Subsidies and Countervailing Duties[6] recognises that subsidies are used by governments to promote important objectives of social and economic policy[7]. However, at the same time it provides that the signatories should seek to avoid the use of any subsidy which causes :

(a)   injury to domestic industry of another signatory;

(b)   nullification or impairment of the benefits accruing directly or indirectly to another signatory;

(c)   serious prejudice to another signatory[8].

---

1.   GATT 10th supp. BISD at 208 (1962).
2   Article XVI(1).
3.   See generally Kock "International Trade Policy and the GATT 1947-67".
4.   Warnecke "Government Intervention and Open Global Trading System" p15 in (ed) Warnecke "International Trade and Industrial Policies" (1978).
5.   Article XVI(3) and (4).
6.   See Appendix 3.
7.   Article 8(1), Subsidies Code.
8.   Article 8(3), Subsidies Code.

2.3.2   Export subsidies and domestic subsidies

Article XVI deals almost entirely with export subsidies. This is due to the fact that domestic subsidies were seen as less harmful than export subsidies since they were used primarily to further social and economic goals.

2.3.2.1 Export subsidies

Barcelo defines an export subsidy as a subsidy conditioned on the export of a product or on export performance[1]. The primary aim of the exporting country in granting a subsidy is not to further socio-economic goals but is rather an attempt to increase their share of the market in the importing country[2]. The GATT further distinguishes between export subsidies on non-primary goods and those on primary goods[3].

Article XVI(4) prohibits contracting parties from granting subsidies on non-primary goods which result in the sale of such products for export at a lower price than the comparable price charged for the like product in the domestic market. The 1960 Working Group had the task of giving effect to article XVI(4). The result was an illustrative list of those subsidies they considered were not compatible with article XVI(4)[4]. This prohibition and illustrative list is reproduced in article 9 of the Subsidies Code. It is, however, subject to one qualification in that the developing countries can grant such subsidies provided they do not cause serious prejudice to the trade or production of another signatory[5].

Article XVI(3) provides that the contracting parties should seek to avoid the use of subsidies on the export of primary products. Primary products are defined as :

> "any product of farm, forest, or fishery, or any mineral, in its natural form or which has undergone such processing as is customarily required to prepare it for marketing in substantial volume in international trade."[6]

Article XVI(1) then provides an exception to article XVI(3) in that a contracting party can grant an export subsidy on a primary product but only if this is applied in a manner which does not result in that party having more than an equitable share of world trade in that product. What is meant by the term "more than an equitable

---

1.   Barcelo "Subsidies, Countervailing Duties and Anti-dumping Duties after Tokyo Round" 13 Cornell L J 257 at 261.
2.   Ibid at 261-2.
3.   At the Uruguay Round of Multilateral Trade Negotiations the United States proposed that this distinction should be ended.
4.   GATT 9th supp. BISD 187 (1961).
5.   Article 14 (3)-(6), Subsidies Code.
6.   Notes to article XVI section B para (2).

share of world trade" is uncertain. Phegan argues that since the term "equitable" connotes fairness what may seem fair to one producer may not be fair to another[1]. Unfortunately, the Subsidies Code has failed to resolve the difficulties posed by the term. Article 10(1) reproduces article XVI(3) and article 10(2) attempts to define what is meant by the term "more than an equitable share of world trade". It states that the term shall include :

> "any case in which the effect of an export subsidy granted by a signatory is to displace exports of another signatory bearing in mind development in world markets."

2.3.2.2 Domestic subsidies

Barcelo regards these as being primarily production subsidies which are granted irrespective of output destination[2]. Such subsidies are granted largely for social and economic reasons though they may have the effect of indirectly increasing a country's exports. They are often used as a tool in a country's industrial policy in order to prevent or promote structural change. Such subsidisation can be justified from an economic point of view in that it eliminates distortions that are not self-correcting such as those brought about by the problems associated with infant industries and foreign government interference[3]. As a tool of industrial policy, subsidies have become more apparent today. This is due largely to the worldwide recession which has resulted in high inflation coupled with stagnation. There is therefore a need for temporary measures to protect jobs and prevent the collapse of industry. However, as the number of firms in trouble continually grows, these temporary measures inevitably become more permanent.

We, today, are also witnessing an industrial revolution in the Far East countries. These newly industrialised countries such as Taiwan, Korea, etc, along with Japan, produce large quantities of high-tech goods, the majority of which are exported at very low prices. In such cases subsidies are used to counteract fierce competition and protect infant industries.

Domestic subsidies can, however, have adverse effects. They can, and often do, amount to protectionism which runs contrary to the liberal trade order as laid down by the GATT. Second, they may have the effect of increasing the number of imports into the country complaining of low priced imports. Third, as a corollary of the above, such subsidies may bring about a reduction in the number of exports of other countries to third country markets[4].

---

1.   "GATT Article XVI. 3 : Export subsidies and equitable shares" 16 JWTL 251.
2.   Barcelo, above.
3.   See generally Curzon Price "Industrial Policies in the EEC" (1981).
4.   Barcelo, above.

The Subsidies Code refers to domestic subsidies as subsidies other than export subsidies. On the whole the GATT takes a more tolerant view of these subsidies. Prior to the Tokyo Round no separate provision dealing with such subsidies existed. Now, article 11 of that Code recognises that domestic subsidies could be used as important instruments for the promotion of social and economic policy objectives[1] and therefore as such are not prohibited. However, it was also noted that such subsidies may have adverse effects on trade[2]. In such a case they may be subject to countervailing duties if they cause injury to the domestic industry of the like product in the importing country[3]. On the other hand, where such subsidies are being maintained in such a manner as to cause injury or serious prejudice or nullification or impairment of benefits accruing to other signatories, they may be subject to whatever countermeasures are deemed appropriate by the Committee on Subsidies and Countervailing Measures[4].

2.4 The procedures for counteracting the adverse effects of subsidies

The new Subsidies Code provides two different procedures for counteracting the adverse effects of subsidies whether they be export or domestic subsidies.

2.4.1 Countervailing duties

The effect of a subsidy is similar to that of dumping. It results in the importation of unfairly low priced products on to the domestic market. The difference between the two lies in the fact that whereas dumping is practised by the individual firm, subsidies are granted by foreign governments or out of public funds.

Article VI(3) provides that a countervailing duty may be imposed to offset a bounty or subsidy which has been granted directly or indirectly on the manufacture, production or export of a product. Where the subsidy causes or threatens to cause injury to the domestic producers of the like product the GATT permits the

---

1. The objectives noted in article 11 are as follows:
    (a) the elimination of industrial, economic and social disadvantages of specific regions;
    (b) to facilitate the restructuring, under socially acceptable conditions, of certain sectors especially where this has become necessary by reason of changes in trade and economic policies including international agreements resulting in lower barriers to trade;
    (c) generally to sustain employment and to encourage retraining and change in employment;
    (d) to encourage research and development programmes, especially in the field of high technology industries;
    (e) the implementation of economic programmes and policies to promote the economic and social development of developing countries;
    (f) redeployment of industry in order to avoid congestion and environmental problems.
2. Article 11, Subsidies Code.
3. Article VI, GATT : Part I Subsidies Code.
4. Article 13, Subsidies Code.

contracting parties to impose countervailing duties[1]. In such a situation it is of no relevance whether the subsidy in question is prohibited under the GATT[2] or the Subsidies Code[3].

Article VI, however, was not uniformly applied by all the contracting parties. More importantly, the United States did not require that injury be determined before it could impose countervailing duties. It relied on the grandfather clause which provided that pre-existing legislation was not superseded by the GATT, in order to avoid some of the requirements of article VI[4].

Now, by virtue of article 1 of the Subsidies Code, the signatories to the Code must take the necessary steps to ensure that the imposition of countervailing duties is in accordance with article VI. Part I of the Subsidies Code deals at length with the procedures involved in determining whether or not a subsidy has caused injury to the domestic producer of the like product in the importing country. The procedures relating to anti-subsidy actions are similar to those which apply to anti-dumping actions and therefore they do not need to be considered here.

2.4.2   Dispute settlement procedure

Article 13 of the Subsidies Code provides that signatories may, after authorisation has been given, adopt such countermeasures as they consider appropriate including withdrawal of concessions or obligations, in order to counteract export subsidies that are inconsistent with the Code or any subsidy which may cause injury or serious prejudice or nullification or impairment of benefits accruing to a signatory.

However, such measures cannot be adopted unilaterally. They may only be authorised by all the contracting parties[5] or by the Committee on Subsidies and Countervailing Measures[6]. Furthermore, authorisation will be granted only after the necessary consultation, conciliation and dispute settlement procedures have been complied with[7].

---

1. Article VI(6), GATT : article 6, Subsidies Code.
2. Article XVI(4). See also Report of GATT Experts, GATT, 8th supp. BISD 146 (1960).
3. Article 9(1), Subsidies Code.
4. See footnote 3, p16.
5. Article XXV(1) GATT.
6. Article 15, Subsidies Code.
7. Articles 12, 13, 17 and 18, Subsidies Code.

2.4.3 Evaluation

It was hoped that the new Code would strengthen the multilateral regulation of subsidies and go some way in helping to achieve the primary aim of the Tokyo Round Negotiations - a greater expansion and liberalisation of world trade. Some success was achieved with a need to prove injury before countervailing duties could be imposed but at the same time it did not bring about a greater control over subsidisation policies *per se*. Owing to their variety and ambiguity a large proportion of subsidies tend to remain outside the ambit of the GATT multilateral regulation. Instead of it becoming more difficult to distort international trade, it has become easier by the device of domestic subsidies[1]. The problems and difficulties raised by the Code on Subsidies and Countervailing Duties are very much on the agenda at the Uruguay Round of Multilateral Trade Negotiations[2].

The United States in particular has called for greater transparency in countervailing duty proceedings and the establishment of clearer guidelines for the administration of multilateral rules on subsidies. It has also proposed updating the Code by including provisions designed to prevent circumvention of countervailing duties[3].

2.5 Safeguard measures

2.5.1 Historical background

By virtue of article XIX of the GATT[4], a contracting party can take emergency action on imports where :

> "if, as a result of unforeseen developments and of the effect of the obligations incurred by a contracting party under this Agreement, including tariff concessions, any product is being imported into the territory of that contracting party in such increased quantities and under such conditions as to cause or threaten serious injury to domestic producers in that territory of like or directly competitive products, the contracting party shall be free, in respect of such product, and to the extent and for such time as may be necessary to prevent or remedy such injury, to suspend the obligation in whole or in part or to withdraw or modify the concession."

---

1.   Curzon Price "Industrial Policies in the EEC" (1981).
2.   Bulletin of the European Communities No 9 (1986) 16/19 pp13-21.
3.   See Focus : GATT Newsletter 70 (1990).
4.   See Appendix 1.

The situation envisaged by article XIX is that in which serious injury is caused by a large influx of imports of a particular product at prices lower than those on the domestic market but which are not at dumped or subsidised prices[1].

As a result of a number of serious drawbacks inherent in article XIX, the contracting parties tend to resort to other means of relief permitted by the GATT[2]. The main drawbacks are as follows :

  (a) The injury criterion under article XIX is much more stringent than that under article VI (article VI refers to material injury rather than serious injury). This can be explained by the fact that they have not been imported at dumped or subsidised prices.

  (b) Article XIX is subject to the rule of non-discrimination in that safeguard measures must not be applied in a discriminatory or selective manner. This in effect means that protective action must be taken against all contracting parties even though the problem imports come only from a few.

  (c) Resort to article XIX tends to be expensive in that the country wishing to rely on the escape clause will have to offer equivalent compensation to any contracting party having a substantial interest at stake[3].

2.5.2 Voluntary Export Restraint Agreements (VERs)

As a result of these drawbacks in article XIX, Voluntary Export Restraint agreements (VERs) have become more prolific. As a non-tariff barrier they are much more difficult to control and are not subject to multilateral surveillance.

The concept has been defined by Metzger as follows :

"Action of restraint by the exporting country taken because of its concern that unilateral quotas would otherwise be imposed against it by an importing country which might well produce more adverse trade effects than those

---

1.   This corresponds to what the special Working Party in 1960 described as "market disruption". They concluded that this concept had a number of elements :
         (i)   sharp and substantial increase (or potential increase) of imports of particular products from particular sources;
         (ii)   offered at prices substantially lower that those on the domestic market;
         (iii) serious damage or threat of it to domestic producers;
         (iv)   difference in price is not due to either subsidies or dumping.
2.   Merciai "Safeguard Measures in GATT", 15 JWTL 41 at 45-6.
3.   Article XIX(3).

voluntarily agreed to by the exporting country through a more flexible medium."[1]

VERs are based on either :

(a)   formal bilateral voluntary restraint agreement between exporting and importing country; or

(b)   unilateral action on the part of an exporting country[2].

As a means of counteracting injury from a large influx of imports of a particular product they are more flexible than action taken under article XIX, which normally takes the form of quotas. As far as VERs are concerned it is the exporting country which for the most part maintains control over them. Their duration and severity are open to periodic review through the negotiation process. Quotas on the other hand are applied by the importing country on the basis of an independent and non-negotiable decision.

The flexibility of VERs is enhanced by the fact that they can be applied on a discriminatory basis and, unlike action under article XIX, they do not involve payment of compensation.

2.5.3   The need for selective safeguards

Because of the proliferation of VERs and the fact that the Contracting Parties tend not to resort to article XIX some countries, and notably the Community, advocated at the Tokyo Round of Multilateral Trade Negotiations a Code on Safeguard Measures. Behind this call for a new Code was the hope that safeguard measures could be adopted on a selective basis.

Certain advantages would be gained from having selective safeguard measures. First, it would limit the action taken to the problem imports, with the result that this would be less disruptive to trade. Second, it would avoid the need to pay compensation which is required in the case of official action under article XIX. Thus, it has the advantage over VERs in that they would be subject to multilateral surveillance.

---

1.   "Injury and market disruption from imports" in Williams Commission Papers 1 at 167, 168-73 (1971).
2.   See generally McGovern "International Trade Regulation" (1982).

On the other hand, strong legal, economic and political arguments can be put forward against the introduction of selective safeguards[1]. The adoption of safeguard measures on a discriminatory basis is against the spirit and aims of the GATT which is based for the most part on the principle of non-discrimination. To allow such measures would, in the words of Curzon-Price[2], "open the floodgates of discrimination in all kinds of circumstances". There must be a commitment to the non-discriminatory application of such measures in order to expose and control protectionist interventions. In the absence of non-discrimination, small and weaker countries would suffer from the abuse of power by the larger and more powerful ones. A discriminatory system also has the effect of penalising the most disruptive producers, ie the most efficient, the result of which is a reduction in world income. Lastly, from the political viewpoint, the GATT would lose. It would find itself virtually unable to handle the disputes and trade wars that would inevitably arise under a discriminatory system.

Since the Tokyo Round, there has been little progress with regard to selective safeguard measures. At the GATT Ministerial Meeting in 1982 there was a call for more predictability and clarity of safeguard measures in order to bring about a greater security for both importing and exporting countries. In doing so the results of trade liberalisation to date would be preserved and it would avoid the proliferation of restrictive measures[3].

At the Uruguay Round of Multilateral Trade Negotiations the question of safeguard measures has arisen. In remaining true to the spirit and aim of the GATT, one of the objectives specified in the Ministerial Declaration was an agreement on safeguards based on the principles of the GATT including the fact that they should apply to everyone.

The European Community has again raised the question of selective safeguards[4]. It has proposed a selective safeguard regime applicable in special circumstances[5]. Its proposal would allow interim precautionary action against one or more suppliers whose products have been found to be causing serious injury to domestic producers as a result of the large influx of imports.

Following consultations, action to restrict these imports would have to be proportional to the injury suffered and would be removed after a maximum of eight

---

1.   Curzon Price "Industrial Policies in the EEC" (1981) pp5-10.
2.   Ibid at p8.
3.   See full text of the GATT Ministerial Declaration reproduced in 17 JWTL 67.
4.   See generally FOCUS : GATT Newsletter 69 (1990).
5.   Ibid.

months or at the end of a full injury investigation. Where serious injury is definitively established, the importing country would be able, following consultations, to adopt selective safeguard measures for a period which should be the subject of negotiations at the Uruguay Round. Those countries affected either by the interim or definitive measures would be free to withdraw equivalent concessions to the importing country. During the period in which the measures are in force, imports of the product from other countries can be monitored. If they are found to be causing injury to domestic producers, the countries covered by the measures could request that they be extended to these suppliers.

This proposal has not received broad support. The majority of the less developed countries are of the opinion that such a regime would benefit only the more powerful trading nations. The idea of the affected exporters being able to request the extension of safeguard measures to other exporters is seen as an attempt to shift the political burden from importer to exporter.

It appears, therefore, that while the question of selective safeguards will continue to be discussed, it is unlikely that agreement will be reached, at least not in the foreseeable future.

2.5.4   Evaluation

Because of the shortcomings of article XIX, an increasing number of cases are determined on the basis of the Anti-dumping Rules. In essence, the Anti-dumping Rules are used as a surrogate escape clause because they are less rigid than emergency action under article XIX.

In order to make safeguard measures more effective, they have to be much more predictable and precise. This could be achieved by shortening the duration of the measures and by allowing imports to increase at a reasonable rate while at the same time bringing about the adjustment of the domestic industry in question[1]. Also, VERs and similar arrangements have to be monitored in order to prevent the movement away from trade liberalisation to protectionism[2].

Apart from the issue of selective safeguards, the Negotiating Group on Safeguards are at present discussing a draft text of a new code[3].

---

1.   Bulletin of the European Communities No 9 (1986) Vol 19 pp13-21 at 19.
2.   Executive Branch GATT Studies No 8, GATT Provisions on Relief from Injurious Imports, 124-9.
3.   See generally FOCUS : GATT Newsletter 63 (1989).

2.6   Illicit commercial practices

2.6.1   Historical background

Inevitably there are other forms of unfair trade practices not caught by the anti-dumping, anti-subsidy or safeguard measure provisions. The majority of these take the form of non-tariff barriers, such as discriminatory treatment of imported goods vis-à-vis domestic goods and infringement of intellectual property rights, to name but two.

In 1964 the EC Commission had discussed the idea of "common principles and a Community procedure concerning abnormal trade practices of Third Countries[1]" with the EC Council. The idea received little attention and it was temporarily dropped. It was not until 1980 that the matter was again discussed by the Welsh Committee, the Committee for External Economic Relations in the European Parliament. In its report, the Committee recommended that new legislation should be considered by the Community authorities to cover those areas of unfair trading practices not covered by the existing legislation[2].

In 1983, the EC Commission submitted a proposal to the EC Council for a new regulation designed to strengthen the Common Commercial Policy. The result was the adoption of Regulation 2641/84. Regulation 2641/84[3] is aimed primarily at illicit commercial practices not covered by the existing trade policy instruments in the Community[4]. The regulation was designed to produce the same effects as Section 301 of the US Trade Act 1974[5]. Unlike Section 301, however, it does not aim at opening up third markets but seeks to protect European trade interests in such markets against illicit commercial practices. In effect it is a means of permitting the Community to use its existing rights with regard to the commercial practices of third countries.

The regulation in part allows the Community authorities, if certain conditions are satisfied, to take unilateral action[6]. Prior to this, unilateral action could be taken

---

1.   EEC Bulletin 1964, supp. 1.
2.   European Parliament, Doc. 1 422/811.
3.   See Chapter 3 Part 4 below.
4.   Article 13, Council Regulation (EEC) 2641/84 (OJ L252 20.9.84 p1).
5.   19 USC 241. The Regulation was not modelled on section 301 as the Community institutions saw it as a substantial derogation from the spirit of the GATT.
6.   By virtue of article 10(2) of Council Regulation (EEC) 2641/84 (OJ L252 20.9.84 p1), countermeasures can only be taken if they are compatible with the Community's international obligations and procedures. This means that where there is provision for consultation and dispute settlement, this must be exhausted before retaliatory action can be taken. However, where an applicant cites a breach of a rule outside the GATT then the Community may take unilateral action if injury has been caused to Community industry as a result of the illicit commercial practices see : *Unauthorised Reproduction of Sound Recordings* (Indonesia) OJ C136 21.5.87 p3.

only in the case of dumping and subsidisation. In all other cases unfairness had first to be established by the GATT membership before a complainant could retaliate[1].

Regulation 2641/84 provides the Community authorities with procedures allowing them to :

(a) respond to illicit commercial practices causing injury;

(b) ensure full exercise of the Community's rights with regard to the commercial practices of third countries[2].

The regulation is aimed at strengthening the Community's hand in the GATT dispute settlement procedure under article XXIII. It is important to first consider the type of practices which are to be regarded as illicit.

2.6.2 Illicit commercial practices

The term illicit commercial practice is defined in Regulation 2641/84 as :

"any international trade practices attributable to third countries which are incompatible with international law or with the generally accepted rules"[3].

The regulation further provides that the Community authorities can respond to such practices where they affect either Community imports or exports. The definition focuses on trade practices "attributable to third countries". This would therefore seem to suggest that it covers trade practices only of governments and not of private companies[4].

It is not yet clear what activities of third countries are caught by Regulation 2641/84. A number of complaints have however been brought to the attention of the Community authorities[5]. Four of these have concerned practices in

---

1. MCE Bronckers "Private response to foreign unfair trade practices" NWJ Int. Law & Bus. (No 3 Winter 1985) 651 at 718.
2. Article 1.
3. Article 2(1).
4. See Steenbergen "The New Commercial Policy Instrument" (1985) CMLRev 421 at 425 where he contends that one cannot rule out the possibility that the new instrument can be used where unfair trade practices of private companies are directly or to a substantial degree caused or promoted by government intervention in third countries, for example, in the fields of government contracts, price regulations, rules on advertisements, technical standards, etc.
5. *Aramid Fibres* (US) OJ C25 5.2.86 p2; *Sound Recordings* (Indonesia) OJ C136 21.5.87 p3; *Soya Meal* (Argentina) unpublished decision 22nd December 1986; Commission Decision rejecting complaint lodged by Smith Kline & French Laboratories Ltd against Jordan OJ L30 1.2.89 p67; *Port charge or fee used for the creation of Harbour Management Fund* (Japan) OJ C40 16.2.91 p18; *Piracy of Community Sound Recordings* (Thailand) OJ C189 20.7.91 p26.

third countries which have affected Community exports and have been held to constitute illicit commercial practices[1].

Aramid Fibres[2] concerned the exclusion from the United States market of the unlicensed importation of certain aramid fibres manufactured by Akzo NV or its affiliated companies outside the United States under Section 337 of the US Tariff Act 1930. The complainant, Enka, Akzo's fibre subsidiary, contended that this was a breach of article III(4) of the GATT and the exclusion of the unlicensed importation of aramid fibres was not necessary under article XX(d) of the GATT. Article III(4) sets out the obligation to treat imported products no less favourably than like products of national origin in respect of all laws, regulations and requirements affecting their internal sale, purchase, transportation, distribution or use. Enka claimed that, by not being able to challenge the standing of DuPont in the United States aramid fibre industry, it was deprived of establishing that DuPont's position was achieved as a result of an infringement of Enka's patent.

The complaint, as the EC Commission noted, raised important questions of interpretation which had considerable economic implications. It referred the matter to the GATT under article XXIII[3]. In November 1989, the GATT Council adopted a panel report finding Section 337 of the United States Tariff Act 1930 to be inconsistent with article III(4)[4]. The importance of this finding lies in the fact that it was not the substantive elements of the law that were contrary to the GATT rules but rather the procedures for enforcing it in the national courts[5].

In *Unauthorised Reproduction of Sound Recordings*[6] the complainant, the association of members of the International Federation of Phonogram and Videogram Producers (IFPI), alleged that Indonesia was in breach of both international law and of generally accepted rules. The breach of international law was article 10 of the Paris Convention for the Protection of Intellectual Property of which Indonesia was a signatory.

The complaint also referred to a breach of "generally accepted rules". How does a rule become generally accepted? Professor Sohn provides us with several ways in which a rule can become generally accepted[7]. This may occur when a rule is

---

1. See *Aramid Fibres, Sound Recordings, Port charge or fee used for creation of Harbour Management Fund* and *Piracy of Community Sound Recordings* above.
2. OJ C25 5.2.86 p2.
3. OJ L117 5.5.87 p18.
4. 36th supp. BISD (1990).
5. Ibid.
6. OJ C136 21.5.87 p3.
7. "Generally Accepted International Rules" 61 Washington L. Rev (1986) 1073 at 1073-4.

supported by the constant practice of states who consider that the practice is obligatory[1]. It is not clear how generally accepted the practice of states must be, but "universality" is not required[2]. Sohn identified two factors which had to be taken into account : first, there had to be express acceptance of the rule by a reasonable number of states representing different political, economic and ideological views and, second, acquiescence by other states[3].

In *Unauthorised Reproduction of Sound Recordings*, the complainant relied on the Berne Convention for the Protection of Literary and Artistic Works and the Paris text of Universal Copyright Convention. Indonesia was not a signatory to either Convention but it was argued that in view of the large number and importance of the countries adhering to those Conventions they constituted generally accepted rules[4]. As a result of an undertaking by the Indonesian authorities, the EC Commission suspended[5] and more recently terminated the proceedings without further examination of the complaint[6].

Port charge or fee for the creation of the Harbour Management Fund[7] concerned the imposition of a charge or fee on all cargoes moving through Japanese ports. The charge applied to all shipping companies which carried cargoes to, from or within Japan. The complainants, the European Community Shipowners' Association (ECSA) maintained that the charge constituted an illicit commercial practice in that it conferred no commercial benefit to the Community shipping companies and further it was discriminatory owing to the fact that a different fee was charged depending on whether it was an international or domestic cargo. As a result of an undertaking from the Japanese government to discontinue the fund, the EC Commission has suspended proceedings without further investigation into the complaint[8].

Piracy of Community Sound Recordings[9] concerned allegations that Thailand was in breach of the Berne Convention for the Protection of Literary and Artistic Works (as revised) and in particular article 4(1) by failing to protect European sound recordings against unauthorised reproduction.

1.   Ibid at 1073.
2.   Brownlie "Principles of Public International Law" 7, (3rd ed) (1979).
3.   "Generally Accepted International Rules" 61 Washington L. Rev (1986) at 1074.
4.   OJ C136 21.5.87 p3.
5.   OJ L335 25.11.87 p22.
6.   OJ L123 17.5.88 p50.
7.   OJ C40 11.2.91 p18.
8.   OJ L74 20.3.92 p47.
9.   OJ C189 20.7.91 p26.

On the other hand, the EC Commission has in two cases rejected complaints on the basis that the alleged act of unfair competition was not incompatible with international law or generally accepted rules. In *Soya Meal*[1], FEDIOL, the Community association of oil-seed crushers and oil processors, alleged that Argentina's system of differential export taxes for soya goods and export restrictions were incompatible with the GATT and in particular with articles III and XI thereof. In an unpublished decision the EC Commission refused to initiate proceedings on the basis that the measures complained of were not contrary to the GATT.

FEDIOL appealed to the Court against this decision[2]. They argued that article III was not designed simply to remove any discrimination whereby imported products were adversely affected by a system of domestic charges but also to prevent the protection of domestic products by a differential export tax system as existed in the present case, from harming production in another country to which those products were imported. The Court rejected this argument. It held that article III could not be applied to a case such as the one in issue which related to a system of differential charges on exports levied solely on categories of domestic products. The applicant also argued that the fixing of artificial reference prices as a basis for calculating the differential charges on soya products intended for exportation constituted a measure having an effect equivalent to a quantitative restriction and was therefore contrary to article XI. The Court rejected this argument on the ground that article XI applied only to quantitative restrictions and could not be interpreted as covering measures having an effect equivalent to quantitative restrictions. It also rejected the applicants' subsidiary arguments based on articles XX and XXIII.

The EC Commission also rejected a complaint lodged by Smith Kline & French Laboratories Limited against Jordan[3]. In that case the complainant alleged that an amendment to Jordan's intellectual property law amounted to "an act of unfair competition" in terms of article 10 bis (1) of the Paris Convention for the Protection of Industrial Property. In refusing to initiate proceedings, the EC Commission held that the term "act of unfair competition" could not include the legislative acts of a signatory state.

As these complaints were brought by "natural or legal persons", this may be an indication of how the new instrument will develop. Along with the courts in many other contracting states the Court has, however, until recently denied the direct

---

1. Unpublished Decision dated 22nd December 1986.
2. Case 70/87 EEC *Seed Crushers' and Oil Processors' Federation (Fediol) v EC Commission* [1989] ECR 1781.
3. OJ L30 1.2.89 p67.

effect of the GATT provisions[1]. The Court has in the *Third Fediol*[2] case held that for the purpose of the new Commercial Policy instrument natural or legal persons can rely directly on the provisions of the GATT. The Court relied on the fact that the GATT forms part of the Rules of Public International law, and by virtue of article 2(1) of Regulation 2641/84 the applicants were entitled to apply to the Court to review the legality of the EC Commission decision applying those provisions.

2.6.3   Dispute settlement under article XXIII of the GATT

Protective measures under the new regulation may be adopted only insofar as they are compatible with the Community's international obligations and procedures[3]. This in essence means that the procedures providing for consultation and dispute settlement at international level must be exhausted before the Community authorities can adopt any protective measures. Only where there is no provision for such procedures can retaliatory action be taken unilaterally. It should also be noted that the procedure laid down in article 1(b) of Regulation 2641/84 (ie ensuring the full exercise of the Community's rights with regard to the commercial practices of third countries) relates specifically to the implementation of the relevant dispute settlement procedures under international law.

2.6.3.1   Article XXIII[4]

A party which believes that a benefit accruing to it has been nullified or impaired by another contracting party's breach or other measure may seek consultations with the aid of other interested parties and the GATT secretariat[5].

What is meant by the term "nullification or impairment" in article XXIII? As the term has never been defined it is necessary to look at the decided cases to date for guidance. It is arguable that the term implies that some sort of injury must have occurred to the trade expectations of a contracting party before it can invoke article XXIII[6].

---

1.   See Petersmann "Application of GATT by the Court of Justice of the European Communities" 20 CMLRev (1983) 397-437; Chapter 6, below.
2.   Case 70/87 *EEC Seed Crushers' and Oil Processors' Federation (Fediol) v EC Commission* [1989] ECR 17681; see also Brand "Private Parties and GATT Dispute Resolution: Implications of Panel Report on Section 337 of US Tariff Act of 1930" 24 JWTL (vol 3) 5.
3.   Article 10(2), Council Regulation (EEC) 2641/84 (OJ L252 20.9.84 p1).
4.   See Appendix 1.
5.   Article XXIII(1).
6.   This became clear in one of the earliest cases : see *Chile v Australia* GATT 2nd supp. BISD 188 (1952) : see also *DISC* case 23rd supp. BISD 98 (1977) : Jackson "The jurisprudence of international trade : the *DISC* case in GATT" 72 AJIL (1978) 747 at 755; Klabbers and Vrengdenhil "Dispute settlement in GATT : *DISC* and its successor" (1986) 1 LIEI 115 at 118.

Owing to the lack of definition, however, there has developed the principle of prima facie nullification or impairment[1]. This principle presumes nullification or impairment in at least three situations :

(a) when a quantitative restriction has been imposed on a product;

(b) when a domestic production subsidy is introduced on a product which has previously been the subject of a tariff concession resulting from tariff negotiations;

(c) when a state has been held by a GATT panel to have violated its GATT obligations.

By presuming nullification or impairment the burden of proof is shifted on to the defendant state which as a result has to prove its innocence[2]. If a contracting party fails to reach a satisfactory solution through consultations, it can by virtue of article XXIII(2) request the setting up of a working party or a panel to investigate the dispute[3]. If the recommendations of the panel are not implemented then the contracting party can ask the GATT plenary body to authorise the suspension of the GATT obligations or application of concessions[4].

Some of the Codes negotiated at the Tokyo Round of Multilateral Trade Negotiations have their own dispute settlement procedures[5]. For the most part these correspond to the general system under article XXIII. The Code on Subsidies and Countervailing Duties, however, contains more stringent time limits and it also allows the Committee administering the Code to authorise the injured parties to take a number of wide-ranging counter measures.

2.6.3.2 Evaluation

Most of the leading commentators on the GATT have criticised the dispute settlement procedure under article XXIII[6]. The major criticism is that the system is

---

1.   Klabbers and Vrengdenhil, above, at 119.
2.   Ibid.
3.   The main difference between a working party and a panel is that the former consists of national representatives whereas the latter normally consists of GATT experts.
4.   Article XXIII(2); see also *Netherlands v US* GATT 1st supp. BISD 32 (1953) : GATT 7th supp. BISD 23 (1959) - the only case in which the provision was invoked.
5.   Code on Technical Barriers to Trade; Code on Government Procurement; Code on Customs Valuation and Code on Subsidies and Countervailing Duties. See generally GATT 26th supp. BISD (1978-9).
6.   See Jackson "The Jurisprudence of International Trade: the *DISC* case in GATT" 72 AJIL (1978) at 747; Bronckers "Selective Safeguard Measures in Multilateral Trade Relations" (1985); Hofbauer and Schott "Trading for growth : the next Round of Trade Negotiations" 11 Inst. Int'l Econ. 79 (1985) : Richard Sutherland Whitt "The Politics of Procedure : An examination of the

subject to many delays. Furthermore, it is often the case that diplomatic or other political pressures ensure compliance with the panel's recommendations. These extra-legal means are inappropriate to an adjudicatory procedure which, if it is to succeed, needs to develop trust and confidence[1]. Inevitably, diplomatic and political pressure works well in the case of the more powerful contracting parties but less so in the case of the less developed countries.

The panel procedure is also criticised. It is argued that it is often difficult to find an impartial panel where members are not allied to one of the parties to the dispute. Owing to the fact that consensus is required at each stage of the process this also results in endless delays.

Whatever the solution to the problems facing the GATT dispute settlement process and the panel procedure, one has to be very aware of the restrictive political environment in which it operates. Reform of the rules is one of the objectives of the Uruguay Round of Multilateral Trade Negotiations. According to the Ministerial Declaration of Punta del Este, the aim of the negotiations in this area was to improve the rules and procedures of the dispute settlement process, with the object of ensuring compliance with the adopted recommendations[2]. In this respect the special negotiating group have produced a new decision of the contracting parties styled "Improvements to the GATT Dispute Settlement Rules and Procedures". The result is a more adjudicatory approach to dispute settlement in the GATT and a movement away from the institutionalised negotiating forum it was designed to be[3].

Because the GATT Dispute Settlement Procedure lacks both the political will to ensure effectiveness and also consensus on the interpretation of certain GATT Rules[4], the new regulation can be seen as strengthening the Community's hand within the system. As Steenbergen points out, much will depend on the attitude of the EC Commission, the EC Council (especially the Member States who insisted on the insertion of article 10(2)) and, in the last instance, on the Court if not on the contracting parties[5].

GATT Dispute Settlement Panel and article XXI, Defense in the context of the US embargo of Nicaragua" (1987) Law, Policy & Int'l Bus. 603.

1. See Jackson, ibid at 780.
2. See Focus : GATT Newsletter 47 (June 1987).
3. GATT, 36th supp. BISD 1990; see also Eric Canal-Forques and Rudolf Ostrihansky "New Developments in the GATT Dispute Settlement Procedures" 24 JWTL 5 (vol. 2). They noted a shift in emphasis from consultations to panel proceedings, strict determination of time limits, inclusion of arbitration provisions, to name but a few.
4. See Richard Sutherland Whitt, above, at p628.
5. Steenbergen "The New Commercial Policy Instrument" (1985) CMLRev at 430.

CHAPTER 3 : SAFEGUARD MEASURES IN THE EUROPEAN COMMUNITY

3.1   Introduction

In order to consider the extent to which the findings of the Community authorities are reviewed by the Court, it is important to be familiar with the manner in which safeguard measures are applied in the Community. The substantive and procedural rules of the main Community safeguard measures are as follows :

Part 1 -   Anti-dumping Measures under Regulation 2423/88[1].

Part 2 -   Countervailing Measures under Regulation 2423/88[2].

Part 3 -   Common Rules for Imports under Regulation 288/82 (as amended)[3].

Part 4 -   Response to Illicit Commercial Practices under Regulation 2641/84 - the New Commercial Policy Instrument[4].

Reference is made in passing to the United States anti-dumping rules by way of comparison.

PART 1 : ANTI-DUMPING MEASURES UNDER REGUALTION 2423/88

3.2   General

Dumping occurs when a supplier sells his product at different prices in different countries[5]. Such a practice is regarded as a form of unfair and undesirable competition. As a result, the majority of industrialised nations in the western world have adopted legislation which permits them to impose anti-dumping measures against such practices. A number of commentators have, however, questioned the economic rationale of such measures[6].

---

1.   See Appendix 4.
2.   See ibid.
3.   See Appendix 5.
4.   See Appendix 6.
5.   Dale "Anti-dumping in Liberal Trade Order" 1980, p1.
6.   See generally Dale, above; Barcelo "The Anti-dumping Law : Repeal it or Revise it", 2 [1979] 1 Michigan Yearbook of International Legal Studies 53; Davey "An analysis of European

In the European Community, it is the institutions of the Community which have the power to take action against dumped products from third countries. This power stems from article 113 of the EEC Treaty, which provides for a Common Commercial Policy after the end of the transitional period based on uniform principles including measures to protect trade such as those to be taken in the case of dumping or subsidies[1]. This competence is exclusive with the exception of new Member States, which can adopt national measures against dumped goods during the transitional period[2].

The anti-dumping rules are laid down in Regulation 2423/88[3]. They do not, however, apply to the field of coal and steel. The relevant instrument here is Commission Decision 2424/88[4]. This section will deal primarily with the rules as laid down by Regulation 2423/88[5].

Dumping must cause injury[6] to Community industry before anti-dumping duties may be imposed. Regulation 2423/88 also provides that the imposition of such duties must be in the interests of the Community[7].

3.3   Dumping

Article 2(2) of Regulation 2423/88 states that "a product shall be considered to have been dumped if its export price to the Community is less than the normal

---

Communities legislation and practice relating to anti-dumping and countervailing duties" in (ed) B. Hawk "Anti Trust and Trade Policy in International Trade" (1983).

1.   Prior to the end of the transitional period (1969) the Member States were competent to apply their own anti-dumping legislation. From 1962 onwards there was an obligation to consult at Community level. By virtue of article 91 of the Treaty, the Member States could adopt measures against intra-Community dumping. This, however, was no longer applicable at the end of the third stage of the transitional period.

2.   Eg article 380 of the Act of Accession of Spain and Portugal. Note : the EC Commission can also take action against dumping within the Common Market - see article 91(1) of the EEC Treaty.

3.   OJ L209 2.8.88 p1. The first regulation adopted was in 1968 (Regulation 459/68 - OJ L93 16.4.68 p1); for a commentary see Beseler "EEC Protection against dumping and subsidies from Third States" [1968] CMLRev 327. It was substantially revised in 1979 (Regulation 3017/79 - OJ L339 31.12.79 p1) as a result of the new Anti-dumping Code which was adopted at the Tokyo Round of Multilateral Trade Negotiations (reproduced in OJ L71 22.3.79 p90) and the opinion of Advocate General Warner in Case 113/77 *NTN Toyo Bearing Co Ltd v EC Council* [1979] ECR 1185 at 1212; Regulation 2176/84 (OJ L201 30.7.84 p1) was adopted in 1984 and amended by Regulation 1761/87 (OJ L167 26.6.87 p9) permitting the Community authorities to impose anti-dumping duties on components of products which were already subject to duties.

4.   OJ L209 2.8.88 p18.

5.   For the most part, the anti-dumping rules involving EEC products and ECSC products are the same. Where they differ, specific reference to the differences will be made.

6.   Article 2(1), Council Regulation (EEC) 2423/88.

7.   Articles 11(1), 12(1).

value of the like product". In order to determine whether dumping has taken place, the following must be considered :

— the normal value of the product[1].
— the export price of the product[2].
— the comparison of the normal value and the export price properly adjusted[3].

3.3.1 The like product

Dumping can take place only if the product sold abroad is a like product to that exported to the Community and if it causes injury to the Community producers of the like product. In the United States, the product sold abroad merely requires to be "such or similar merchandise to that exported to the United States"[4]. Arguably, this term violates the GATT but, as Vermulst points out, the authorities, in carrying out their investigation into injury and dumping, restrict the scope of the products to be compared[5].

"Like product" is defined in the regulation as :

"a product which is identical, ie alike in all respects, to the product under consideration, or, in the absence of such a product, another product which has characteristics closely resembling those of the product under consideration[6]."

The Community authorities have recently held that the requirement that a product be similar to an imported product should not be interpreted narrowly and that only differences in quality or basic use are grounds for considering that a product is not similar to another[7]. The position under Regulation 2423/88 can be compared to the regime under Regulation 288/82 (safeguard measures) where the term "like product" applies to both producers of like and also directly competing products[8].

---

1. Article 2(3)-(7), Council Regulation (EEC) 2423/88. This concept is known in the United States as the foreign market value.
2. Article 2(8), Council Regulation (EEC) 2423/88.
3. Article 2(9)-(10), Council Regulation (EEC) 2423/88.
4. Section 771(16) of Tariff Act 1980, 19 USC section 1677(16).
5. "Anti-dumping law and Practice in the United States and the European Community" (1987) pp340-3.
6. Article 2(12). This was taken directly from article 2(2) of the GATT Anti-dumping Code.
7. See *Small Screen Colour Televisions* (Korea) OJ L314 28.10.89 p1. The EC Commission excluded higher range small screen colour televisions which included features such as flat square screens, teletext modules and digital chassis. It noted that these more innovative and enhanced technical characteristics were not found in the Korean export models. See also *Synthetic Fibres of Polyester* (USA, Mexico, Taiwan, Romania, Turkey, Yugoslavia) OJ L348 17.12.88 p49.
8. Article 15(1), Council Regulation (EEC) 288/82.

In ascertaining whether the exported product and that sold on the domestic market are like products within the meaning of article 2(12), the EC Commission for the most part relies on their physical characteristics and the degree of interchangeability of the products in question. For example, the EC Commission held that nickel produced in the Community had a purity the same as that originating in the USSR and that each product was almost interchangeable in application with one another[1].

The degree of interchangeability has not, however, been defined. It is essential, therefore, to look at the decisions to date. In one case the EC Commission noted that the products under consideration all had the same chemical component, magnesium oxide. Although the content varied, it lay within a range between 71-90%. While this and other factors may be relevant for certain specific uses, all products were used for the same purposes[2]. In another case, however, the EC Commission was satisfied on the basis of available data that sodium carbonate in light and dense forms were not randomly interchangeable by end users. They were therefore held not to be like products[3]. Where a large variety of models are concerned, the EC Commission has to decide whether they form one single category of products or whether they fall into different categories separated by clearly defined dividing lines. Such a situation arose in *Dot Matrix Printers*[4]. In order to determine this, the EC Commission considered the following criteria :

(a) the physical and technical characteristics of the printers;

(b) their application and use;

(c) particularities of the printer market and the consumers' perceptions of these products; and

(d) other factors, inter alia, production, equipment, and personnel.

It concluded that the printers formed one single category of products.

---

1. *Unwrought Nickel* (USSR) OJ L286 19.10 83 p29. See also *Bisphenol* (USA) OJ L23 26.1.83 p9, where the EC Commission noted that the few differences between the specifications for the US and the Community were minimal. In *Glass textile fibres (Rovings)* (GDR, Czechoslovakia) OJ L354 16.12.83 p15, the EC Commission concluded that, as regards the physical characteristics, the products closely resembled one another and that in a large number of cases they could be used for the same application. In *Radio Broadcast Receivers* (South Korea) OJ L34 11.2.92 p8, the EC Commission noted that car radios produced in the Community were manufactured using the same basic technology which was comparable to that used to produce the equipment sold in South Korea. They also possessed common basic physical and technical characteristics which enabled them to be broadly interchangeable.

2. *Natural Magnesite (caustic burned)* (China) OJ L371 30.12.82 p21.

3. *Sodium Carbonate* (Bulgaria) OJ L283 6.10.82 p9.

4. Commission Regulation (EEC) 1418/88 OJ L130 26.5.88 p12 imposing a provisional anti-dumping duty on imports of serial-impact dot-matrix printers originating in Japan. See also *Daisy Wheel Printers* (Japan) OJ L177 8.7.88 p1; *Compact Disc Players* (Japan, South Korea) OJ L205 18.7.89 p5.

In a number of cases, the EC Commission has held that the products in question were not "like products". It held that transparent drawn glass and transparent float glass obtained by the float method were not like products[1]. It took into account the fact that the process of manufacturing drawn glass led to optical defects which were evident when regarded at an angle. Also the float process made it possible to obtain larger rectangles which were essential for certain uses. Finally, only float glass could be used for certain purposes. Similarly, in *Freezers* it concluded that chest freezers and upright freezers were not like products[2].

On the other hand, the EC Commission has held that even where the products sold in the domestic market and those for export are not in exactly the same form, the product sold on the domestic market is a like product because it has characteristics that closely resemble that exported to the Community[3].

3.3.2   Normal value

3.3.2.1 The domestic market price

The preferred basis for the determination of normal value is the domestic market price, ie the price actually paid or payable in the exporting country or the country of origin. A similar preference exists in the United States. This price is known as the foreign market price.

Normal value is defined in the regulation as :

> "the comparable price actually paid or payable in the ordinary course of trade for the like product intended for consumption in the exporting country or country of origin."[4]

---

1.   See *Glass* (Turkey, Yugoslavia, Romania, Bulgaria, Hungary, Czechoslovakia) OJ L51 28.2.86 p73 (Note : for the purpose of an investigation under Council Regulation (EEC) 288/82 the two types of glass were regarded as directly competing products OJ L128 14.5.86 p7); see also *Outboard Motors* (Japan) OJ L152 10.6.83 p18, EC Commission excluded Outboard Motors (above) 85 h.p. since Community industry did not produce the models in question and because there was no evidence that the establishment in the EC of such production was being envisaged; *Small Screen Colour Televisions* (Korea) OJ L314 28.10 89 p1.

2.   OJ L259 11.10 86 p14.

3.   See *Sensitised Paper for Colour Photographs* (Japan) OJ L124 11.5.84 p45. Two of the exporters sold the product for export in large width rolls but for the domestic market these were cut into smaller widths. Exporter suggested that normal value should be based on the export prices to non-EC countries or on their constructed value. The EC Commission, however, considered that the product sold on the domestic market was a like product since it had characteristics which closely resembled the product exported to the EC; see also *Aluminium Foil* (Austria) OJ L339 1.12.82 p58, 1982. The EC Commission held that the product sold to the Community was not in exactly the same form as that sold on the domestic market. It therefore based normal value on the cost of production of the like product in Austria.

4.   Article 2(3)(a).

Article 2(3)(a) of Regulation 2423/88 provides that this price shall be net of all discounts and rebates directly linked to the sales under consideration provided that the exporter claims and supplies sufficient evidence that any such reduction from the gross price has actually been granted. In *Compact Disc Players*[1] one of the exporters claimed that normal value established for sales on the domestic market should take account of the purchase value of compact discs which were given in the form of rebates on the price paid for the product under consideration. They argued that these were directly related to the sales under consideration. The EC Commission noted that the compact discs were purchased by the exporter several years before the investigation period. They were not provided with any indication of their cost nor an estimate of the effect of these goods on the market value of the compact disc players. In these circumstances, the EC Commission estimated this effect to be the cost of similar compact discs purchased during the investigation period by the exporter. This cost was deducted from the domestic selling price.

On the other hand, in *Small Screen Colour Televisions*[2], it refused to deduct a rebate which it held was not directly related to the sales under consideration. Two of the Korean producers operated a form of rebate to their customers, ie retailers. This was paid when the products under consideration were resold by their customers to final customers on instalment terms. The EC Commission held that this was an event posterior to and independent of the producer's sale to their customers.

Article 2(3)(a) also permits the EC Commission to take into account deferred discounts, provided they are directly related to the sales under consideration and evidence is produced to show that these discounts were based on consistent practice in prior periods or on an undertaking to comply with the conditions required to qualify for the deferred discount.

In three main situations, the domestic market price will not be used, namely, when there are no sales of the like product on the domestic market; when there are no sales of the like product in the ordinary course of trade; and when such sales do not provide a proper comparison, ie insufficient sales[3].

---

1. OJ L13 17.1.90 p21; see also *Synthetic Fibres of Polyester* (Mexico, Romania, Taiwan, Turkey, USA, Yugoslavia) OJ L348 17.12.88 p49.
2. OJ L314 28.10. 89 p1; See also *Audio Tapes in Cassettes* (Japan, Hong Kong, Republic of Korea) OJ L313 13.11 90 p5.
3. Article 2(3)(b), Council Regulation (EEC) 2423/88.

3.3.2.1.1 No sales of the like product on the domestic market

The domestic market price will be disregarded when there are no sales of the like product on the domestic market. Such a situation will normally arise if, for example, the exporter only manufactures the product in question for export[1], or where there are no sales on the domestic market of the models comparable to those exported to the Community[2].

A new article 2(3)(c) was introduced by Regulation 2423/88 to deal with the increase in the number of original equipment manufacturers (hereinafter referred to as OEMs), ie importers who sell in the Community under their own brand names, products which they neither sell nor produce in the country of origin but which are purchased from other producers of the product who export the product in question to the Community. This article provides that in such cases, the normal value shall be established on the basis of prices or costs of other sellers or producers in the country of origin either by reference to their domestic market price or the constructed value[3]. Where normal value is constructed, the EC Commission will normally apply a reduced profit rate based on that realised by the exporter/producer on his domestic brand sales, or if he has no sales, on the basis of the profit realised by those exporters/producers who do[4].

3.3.2.1.2 No sales in the ordinary course of trade

The domestic market price will also be disregarded when there are no sales in the ordinary course of trade. This concept is not defined in the regulation. It does, however, signify the fact that the EC Commission will disregard the domestic price when it does not reflect normal trading conditions[5]. In other words, the domestic prices used to determine the normal value must be arms length prices[6].

The regulation expressly refers to the fact that sales made at a loss[7] and sales between parties who are associated or who have a compensatory arrangement are not made in the ordinary course of trade[8]. Sales are made at a loss when they are

---

1.   See for example *Ballbearings* (Thailand) OJ L113 30.4 86 p61; *Stainless Steel House Cooking Ware* (South Korea) OJ L74 19.3.86 p83; *Chemical Fertiliser* (USA) OJ L15 19.1.83 p1.
2.   See *Electronic Scales* (Japan) OJ L80 24.3.84 p9.
3.   See *Small Screen Colour Televisions* (Republic of Korea) OJ L314 28.10.89 p1; *Glutamic Acid and its Salts* (Indonesia, Republic of Korea, Taiwan, Thailand) OJ L56 3.3.90 p23.
4.   See *Linear Tungsten Halogen Lamps* (Japan) OJ L188 20.7.90 p10; *Audio Tapes in Cassettes* (Japan, Hong Kong, Republic of Korea) OJ L119 14.5.90 p35.
5.   See Van Bael and Bellis "EEC Anti-dumping and other Trade Protection Laws" (1985) at p33.
6.   Article 2(4), Council Regulation (EEC) 2423/88.
7.   Ibid.
8.   Article 2(7).

made at a price less than the cost of production[1]. Such sales may be considered as not having been made in the ordinary course of trade if they :

(a) have been made in substantial quantities during the investigation period as defined in article 7(1)(c) and;

(b) are not at prices which permit recovery, in the normal course of trade and within the period referred to in paragraph (a), of all costs reasonably allocated[2].

The changes made to article 2(4)(a) and (b) confirm that the EC Commission must confine its examination to the investigation period.

Transactions between parties which appear to be associated or to have a compensatory arrangement with each other may be considered as not being in the ordinary course of trade[3]. This means that the EC Commission can disregard prices charged in transactions between associated companies unless the prices and costs involved are comparable to those involved in transactions between parties which have no such link[4].

The term "associated" is not defined in the regulation. It has, however, been the subject of controversy in relation to sales companies which form part of the corporate structure. In *Electronic Typewriters*, it was held that the sales from the manufacturing company to its sales company were in reality transactions between associated companies. In arriving at such a conclusion, the EC Council took into account that they both formed part of the corporate structure in which the sales company had a function similar to a sales department. It also noted that although they were legally separate entities, this did not alter the existence of a single economic entity, and what was relevant was not the legal structure but the fact that the principal function of these sales companies was to sell or facilitate the sale of

---

1.   "Cost of production" is defined in article 2(3)(b)(ii) of Council Regulation (EEC) 2423/88 as : "... all costs, in the ordinary course of trade, both fixed and variable, in the country of origin, of materials and manufacture plus a reasonable amount for selling, administrative and other general expenses..."

2.   Article 2(4)(a) and (b), Council Regulation (EEC) 2423/88. See for example *Dot Matrix Printers* (Japan) OJ L317 24.11.88 p33; *Video Cassette Tapes* (South Korea, Hong Kong) OJ L174 22.6.89 p1; *DRAMS* (Japan) OJ L20 25.1.90 p5; *Salmon* (Norway) OJ L69 16.3.91 p32; *Ferro-Silicon* (Brazil) OJ L111 3.5.91 p1; *Polyester Yarns* (Man-Made Staple Fibres) (India, Taiwan, Indonesia, Republic of Korea, China, Turkey) OJ L276 3.10 91 p7.

3.   Article 2(7), Council Regulation (EEC) 2423/88.

4.   *Electronic Typewriters* (Japan) OJ L163 22.6.85 p1; *Compact Disc Players* (South Korea, Japan) OJ L205 18.7 89 p5.

the corporate product[1]. This approach has since been followed by the EC Commission[2].

Even if an association does exist, article 2(7) does not rule out the possibility of allowing the EC Commission to use the sales in question if the prices are comparable to those at which the like product is sold to unrelated parties[3].

Article 2(7) also allows the EC Commission to treat as associated, parties who have a compensatory arrangement[4]. The term, however, is not defined in the regulation. It could, for example, be an arrangement between an exporter and an importer which involved the sale of a product at an artificially high price (in order to avoid dumping) with the loss compensated by his receiving other goods at artificially low prices[5].

3.3.2.1.3 Sales not permitting a proper comparison, ie insufficient sales

Finally, the domestic market price will be disregarded when the quantity of sales involved is so residual or so negligible that they cannot be considered as reliably reflecting prices in the ordinary course of trade[6]. The EC Commission has now set a threshold below which sales on the domestic market should be disregarded. It held that given the commercial importance of the Community as an import market, sales on the domestic market should be used if they exceed 5% of the volume of exports to the Community[7]. The EC Commission has recently held that even if sales on the

---

1. Ibid, see also *Electronic Typewriters* (Japan) OJ L335 22.12 84 p13. The EC Commission considered that an exporter had a controlling interest in a Japanese sales company because "all other shareholders have individually only minor shareholdings" and because "the main reason for the sales company's existence is to sell the exporter's product in Japan".
2. See for example *Electronic Scales* (Japan) OJ L275 16.10.85 p5; *Photocopiers* (Japan) OJ L239 26.8.86 p5; *Synthetic Fibres of Polyester* (GDR, Romania, Turkey, Yugoslavia) OJ L103 15.4.87 p38; *UREA* (GDR, USSR, Czechoslovakia, Yugoslavia, Kuwait, Saudi Arabia, Libya, Trinidad and Tobago) OJ L121 9.5.87 p11; *Daisy Wheel Printers* (Japan) OJ L177 8.7.88 p1; *Compact Disc Players* (South Korea, Japan) OJ L205 18.7.89 p5.
3. *Sensitised Paper for Colour Photographs* (Japan) OJ L124 11.5.84 p45.
4. See *Polypropylene Film* (Japan) OJ L172 18.6.82 p44. The EC Commission excluded sales because of the existence of a special processing arrangement; *Polyester Yarn* (USA) OJ L50 23.2.83 p14 - textural arrangement; *Phenol* (USA) OJ L195 18.7.81 p22 - Conversion operation.
5. See Cuanne and Stanbrook "Dumping and Subsidies" (1983) p34/5; Briët "Anti-dumping in de EEG - De Kinderschoenen ontgroeid?" SEW (1982) 145 at 150 note 30 - he suggests that it could include buy back arrangements, swap deals and conversion operations.
6. The EC Commission simply stated that domestic sales did not permit a proper comparison because "minimal quantities were involved" - *Potato Granules* (Canada) OJ L116 28.4.81 p11; "quantities involved were insufficient" - *Ferrochromium* (South Africa, Surinam, Turkey, Zimbabwe) OJ L161 15.6.83 p15; "small quantities were involved" - *Unwrought Aluminium* (Norway, USSR, Yugoslavia, Surinam) OJ L57 28.2.84 p19; "virtually no sales" - *Ballbearings* (miniature) (Singapore, Japan) OJ L79 23.3.84 p8.
7. *Electronic Typewriters* (Japan) OJ L335 22.12.84 p43; see also *Photocopiers* (Japan) OJ L239 26.8.86 p5; *Dot Matrix Printers* (Japan) OJ L130 26.5.88 p12; *Video Cassette Tapes* (Hong Kong, South Korea) OJ L174 22.6.89 p1; *Compact Disc Players* (Japan, South Korea) OJ L205 18.7.89 p5; *Ferro Silicon* (Iceland, Norway, Sweden, Venezuela, Yugoslavia) OJ L38 10.2.90 p1; *Ballbearings* (Thailand) OJ L152 16.6.90 p24; *Small Screen Colour TV Receivers* (Hong Kong, China) OJ L14 19.1.91 p31.

domestic market are low in absolute terms, so long as they exceed the threshold amount, such sales will be used to determine normal value[1]. In the United States, the competent authorities will use sales on the domestic market where such sales exceed 5% of the total sold in the United States, and failing that, the exporter's sales to countries other than the United States if they meet the 5% threshold. In order to prevent foreign producers establishing a "fictitious" foreign market price, the United States' Anti-dumping Rules now permit the competent authorities to consider contrasting movements in the prices of different forms of a product as evidence of a fictitious market price if such price movements appear to reduce the amount by which the foreign market value exceeds the US price[2].

3.3.2.2 The alternative methods of determining normal value

In those cases where the EC Commission cannot use the domestic market price, it has the power to base the normal value of the product in question in one of the following ways :

    3.3.2.2.1   The comparable price of the like product when exported to any third country, ie export price to a third country[3].

    3.3.2.2.2   The constructed value[4].

There are two further methods by which normal value can be determined where the sales are made at a loss in the country of origin[5] :

    3.3.2.2.3   The remaining sales on the domestic market made at a price which is not less than the cost of production.

    3.3.2.2.4   Adjusting the sub-production cost price in order to eliminate the loss and provide for a reasonable profit.

Finally, with regard to state trading countries, normal value is determined by a different set of rules[6].

---

1.   *Compact Disc Players* (Japan, South Korea) OJ L205 18.7.89 p5. The EC Council concurred with the EC Commission OJ L13 17.1.90 p21.
2.   Section 1316, Omnibus Trade and Competitiveness Act 1988.
3.   Article 2(3)(b)(i), Council Regulation (EEC) 2423/88.
4.   Article 2(3)(b)(ii), Council Regulation (EEC) 2423/88.
5.   Article 2(4), Council Regulation (EEC) 2423/88.
6.   Article 2(5), Council Regulation (EEC) 2423/88.

3.3.2.2.1 The export price to a third country

Normal value may be determined by the comparable price of the like product when exported to any third country[1]. This may be the highest such export price, but it should also be a representative one[2]. This method has been used by the EC Commission infrequently[3], as more often than not, export sales to another country will also be at dumped prices[4].

3.3.2.2.2 The constructed value

The constructed value is the method most often used by the EC Commission when the domestic market price cannot be used. It is calculated by adding the cost of production plus a reasonable margin for profit[5]. The cost of production is to be computed on the basis of all costs in the ordinary course of trade, both fixed and variable, in the country of origin, of materials and manufacture plus a reasonable amount for selling, administrative and other general expenses[6].

Article 2(3)(b)(ii) of Regulation 2423/88 permits the EC Commission to calculate selling, general and administrative expenses (hereinafter referred to as "SGAs") by reference to the expenses incurred by the producer or exporter on the profitable sales of the like product on the domestic market. In *Compact Disc Players*, the EC Commission calculated SGAs on the basis of the weighted average of SGAs incurred by the exporters who had insufficient sales for some models by reference to sales of their other profitable models[7].

If such data is unavailable or unreliable or is not suitable for use, SGAs will be calculated by reference to the expenses incurred by other producers or exporters in the country of origin or export on their profitable sales of the like product[8]. In *Compact Disc Players*, the EC Commission calculated the SGAs for those exporters who had no sales, insufficient sales or who made sales at a loss on the domestic

---

1.   Article 2(3)(b)(i), Council Regulation (EEC) 2423/88.
2.   Ibid.
3.   See *Saccahrin and its Salts* (Korea) OJ L331 9.12.80 p25, where normal value was calculated on the basis of exports to the United States and Australia.
4.   See *Ballbearings* (miniature) (Japan, Singapore) OJ L79 23.3.84 p8. The Minebea Group requested that normal value be constructed on the basis of the prices at which its products exported from Singapore are first resold to an independent buyer on the Japanese market. The EC Commission held that with regard to these exports it could not be ruled out that dumping was being practised by Minebea on the Japanese market. See also *UREA* (Libya, USSR, GDR, Yugoslavia, Czechoslovakia, Saudi Arabia, Kuwait, Trinidad and Tobago) OJ L317 7.11 87 p1; *Ferro Silicon* (Iceland, Norway, Sweden, Venezuela, Yugoslavia) OJ L38 10.2.90 p1.
5.   Article 2(3)(b)(ii), Council Regulation (EEC) 2423/88.
6.   Ibid. For a detailed analysis of the factors involved in the calculation of cost of production see Van Bael and Bellis "EEC Anti-dumping and other Trade Protection Laws" (1985) pp37-40.
7.   OJ L205 18.7.89 p5; see also : *Linear Tungsten Halogen Lamps* (Japan) OJ L188 20.7.90 p10; *Silicon Metal* (Brazil) OJ L96 10.4.92 p17.
8.   Article 2(3)(b)(ii).

market, by reference to the weighted average of SGAs realised by all the other producers on the domestic sales of profitable models of compact disc players[1].

Article 2(3)(b)(ii) concludes by stating that, if neither of the above two methods can be applied, the expenses incurred shall be calculated by reference to the sales made by the exporter or other producers or exporters in the same business sector in the country of origin or export or on any other reasonable basis. In *Daisy Wheel Printers*, the EC Commission noted that the exporters in question had no or insufficient profitable sales of the product under consideration on the domestic market. It therefore calculated the SGAs for one exporter on its profitable sales of dot matrix printers and for the other, on its profitable sales of line printers. The EC Commission concluded these to be the most appropriate products in the same business sector[2].

This concept of SGAs has given rise to controversy in the context of whether the selling expenses of sales companies should be included in the determination of the constructed value. In *Electronic Typewriters*,[3] these sales companies were held in essence to be sales departments of the manufacturing company. The EC Commission held that such expenses should be included because :

— where normal value is based on domestic selling prices, these prices if they are in the ordinary course of trade cover all SG&A incurred by the sales organisation;

— where normal value is based on constructed value under the structure of Regulation 2176/84, this surrogate method should yield the same result as above. Article 2(3)(b)(ii) therefore expressly provides that SG&A expenses be included[4].

---

1. OJ L205 18.7.89 p5; see also : *Linear Tungsten Halogen Lamps* (Japan) OJ L188 20.7.90 p10; *Silicon Metal* (Brazil) OJ L96 10.4.92 p7.
2. OJ L177 8.7.88 p1; see also *Container Corner Fittings of Worked Cast Steel* (Austria) OJ L165 19.6.92 p37 : the same business sector was deemed to be the foundry division.
3. OJ L335 22.12.84 p43.
4. Ibid. See also *Electronic Scales* (Japan) OJ L275 16.10.85 p5 where the EC Commission held that : "this method [constructed value] is designed to lead to normal value as would be established if sales on the domestic market had taken place. Since sales prices have necessarily to reflect *SG & As* by the seller, the amount of such expenses is equal to that usually reflected in sales prices in the ordinary course of trade of a product of the same general class or kind has to be included in the constructed value"; *Ballbearings* (Thailand) OJ L113 30.4.86 p61; *Photocopiers* (Japan) OJ L239 26.8.86 p5; *Dot Matrix Printers* (Japan) OJ L130 26.5.88 p12.

This means, and rightly so, that the constructed value is a constructed normal value. It should, therefore, yield as far as possible the same result as if there had been sufficient sales on the domestic market and if article 2(3)(a) had applied[1].

With regard to selling expenses, it should be emphasised that these do not refer to expenses related to export sales as some authors have suggested[2]. Such a contention confuses a constructed export price with a constructed normal value. It is true that normal value and export price should be on an equal footing for the purposes of article 2(9) of Regulation 2423/88[3]. Article 2(9), however, refers to the adjustments which have to be made in order to make the normal value and the export price comparable. It has nothing to do with the constructed normal value.

To the cost of production, a reasonable margin of profit has to be added. Article 2(3)(b)(ii) states that the margin of profit is to be determined, on the basis of "the profitable sales of like products on the domestic market". This new wording, as opposed to that under Regulation 2176/84, namely "the profit normally realised on the sales of products of the same general category on the domestic market of the country of origin" reflects the recent EC Commission practice of using profit margins from profitable sales[4].

Where an exporter has no domestic sales or insufficient domestic sales, or where these are made at a loss, article 2(3)(b)(ii) permits the EC Commission to calculate the margin of profit by reference to the profit realised by other exporters in the country of origin on profitable sales of the like product. In *Electronic Typewriters*, the EC Commission, in considering the profit margins of those exporters who had insufficient sales on the domestic market, thought it reasonable to include a margin of 32.39%, which corresponded to the lowest profit margin of the three exporters who had sufficient domestic sales[5]. In the absence of profitable sales of other producers of the like product on the domestic market, the Community authorities are permitted by article 2(3)(b)(ii) to determine a profit margin by reference to any other reasonable basis. In *Ballbearings*, the EC Commission considered it appropriate to use the profit realised on certain NMB Thai bearings exported from Thailand but re-imported into Thailand by an independent company which incorporated them into disc drives[6].

---

1. See Joined Cases 260/85 and 106/86 *TEC Co Ltd v EC Council* [1988] ECR 5855. The Court condoned the practice of the Community authorities.
2. Cf Van Bael and Bellis "EEC Anti-dumping and other Trade Protection Laws" (1985) at p40.
3. Ibid.
4. *Photocopiers* (Japan) OJ L54 24.2.87 p12; OJ L239 26.8.86 p5; *Radio Broadcast Receivers* (South Korea) OJ L34 11.2.92 p8.
5. OJ L163 22.6.85 p1; see also *Dot Matrix Printers* (Japan) OJ L317 24.11.88 p33; *Radio Broadcast Receivers* (South Korea) OJ L34 11.2.92 p8.
6. OJ L152 16.6.90 p24.

Article 2(3)(b)(ii) does not specify a single percentage rate of profit, unlike the American regulations, which state that profits shall not be less than 8% of direct costs and general overheads[1].

Exporters have argued that the present practice of the Community authorities in determining profit margin results in high dumping margins and does not reflect the true position[2]. The practice, now codified in article 2(3)(b)(ii), allows them to use artificially high profit margins in constructing normal value given that unprofitable unit sales do not have to be included.

The EC Commission has on occasions constructed the normal value on the "basis of facts available"[3]. It has used, for example, the highest weighted average domestic price[4]; information supplied by the complainant[5]; and the cost of manufacture of equivalent exported models of another producer on the domestic market plus selling general and administrative costs and a reasonable profit[6].

3.3.2.2.3 Remaining sales on the domestic market, if they have been made at a price not less than the cost of production

When some sales on the domestic market have been made at a loss, the EC Commission can, if it wishes, determine normal value by using the remaining sales if they have been made at a price not less than the cost of production[7]. For instance, in *Potato Granules*[8], the EC Commission concluded that since one-third of the sales on the domestic market were not made at a loss, these could be used as a reliable basis for determining normal value. The EC Commission in *Photocopiers*[9] established normal value on the basis of remaining, ie profitable sales only, even though according to some exporters, by restricting the calculation to these sales and thereby eliminating certain sales at a loss, an artificially high profit margin was established.

---

1.   CFR s353 (6)(a)(2) 1983.
2.   See Joined Cases 277 and 300/85 *Canon Inc v EC Council* [1988] ECR 5731. The Court held, however, that the authorities were not in error when they established normal profit on the basis of data relating to other electronic typewriter models.
3.   Article 7(7)(b), Council Regulation (EEC) 2423/88.
4.   *Vinyl Acetate Monomer* (Canada, USA) OJ L53 1.3.90 p1.
5.   *Photo Albums* (South Korea, Hong Kong) OJ L138 31.5.90 p48.
6.   *Small Screen Colour TV Receivers* (China, Hong Kong) OJ L14 19.1.91 p31.
7.   Article 2(4), Council Regulation (EEC) 2423/88.
8.   OJ L116 28.4.81 p11.
9.   OJ L54 24.2.87 p12.

3.3.2.2.4 Adjusting the sub-production cost price in order to eliminate loss and allow for a margin of profit

Alternatively, when sales are made at a loss, the EC Commission can calculate normal value by adjusting the sub-production cost price in order to eliminate loss and allow for a margin of profit. It is basically a simplified form of the constructed value and is quite often used by the EC Commission to determine normal value[1]. For example in *Outboard Motors*[2], the prices of the product on the domestic market by one company were lower than the costs ordinarily incurred in its production. Normal value was therefore determined by adjusting the sub-production cost prices in order to eliminate losses and allow for a reasonable margin of profit.

3.3.2.2.5 State trading countries

In the case of state trading countries (or non-market economies)[3], the domestic market prices are not used. Instead, the regulation lays down special rules for the determination of the normal value[4]. It states that :

"... normal value shall be determined in an appropriate and not unreasonable manner on the basis of one of the following criteria :

(a) the price at which the like product of a market economy third country is actually sold :

    (i) for consumption on the domestic market of that country; or

    (ii) to other countries, including the Community; or

(b) the constructed value of the like product in a market economy third country;

(c) if neither price nor constructed value as established under (a) or (b) provides an adequate basis, the price actually paid or payable in the

---

1.   See Van Bael and Bellis "EEC Anti-dumping and other Trade Protection Laws" (1985) p42 at footnote 78.

2.   OJ L152 10.6.83 p18. See also *Textured Polyester Fabrics* (USA) OJ L133 20.5.81 p17; *Perchlorethylene* (Czechoslovakia, Romania, Spain, USA) OJ L371 30.12.82 p47; *Electronic Scales* (Japan) OJ L80 24.3.84 p9; *Artificial Corundum* (Czechoslovakia, China, Spain, Yugoslavia) OJ L255 25.9.84 p9; *Hydraulic Excavators* (Japan) OJ L68 8.3.85 p13.

3.   This concept is not defined in article 2(5). It basically refers, however, to those state trading countries outlined in Council Regulations (EEC) 1765/82 and 1766/82. (They are : Bulgaria, Romania, Poland, GDR, USSR, Hungary, Czechoslovakia, Vietnam, North Korea, Mongolia, People's Republic of China). The use of the words "in particular" in article 2(5) suggests, however, that other countries could be classified as non-market economies. It should be noted that, as a result of the changes in Eastern Europe, the German Democratic Republic formally became part of the Federal Republic of Germany to form a unified Germany in the EEC. See *Barium Chloride* (GDR, China) OJ L60 7.3.91 p1. The EC Commission having noted the above held that the anti-dumping proceeding concerning imports of Barium Chloride originating in the GDR no longer had any legal basis.

4.   Article 2(5).

Community for the like product, duly adjusted, if necessary, to include a reasonable profit margin[1]."

In determining normal value, the first step is to select the analogue country, ie the comparable free market economy. In doing this the EC Commission is guided by article 2(5), which states that normal value has to be determined in an appropriate and not unreasonable manner[2]. In most cases, the EC Commission will proceed by considering the proposal put forward by the complainants. In a number of cases this was not objected to by the other parties involved[3]. It will, however, consider the alternatives suggested by the importer or exporter in question. For example in *Barium Chloride*, the main importer of the product from China suggested the German Democratic Republic. This was rejected, however, since the prices were not representative, ie they were made at a loss and fell outside the reference period[4]. Generally speaking, if the case involves a market and a non-market economy, the EC Commission will invariably use the prices on the free market economy[5].

In determining the analogue country, the EC Commission will normally look to see if the product in question has undergone a similar production process and whether it is subject to the same degree of technology and technical standards[6]. On a number of

---

1. Ibid. Note : the US anti-dumping laws allow for ten ways in which normal value or foreign market value may be determined : see s773(c) of the Tariff Act 1930, 19 USC s1677b(c).
2. Under the United States Anti-dumping Rules, this is to be determined using the "factors of production" approach, ie constructing value by taking the volume of inputs in the imported product and finding their value in market economy. Section 1316, Omnibus Trade and Competitiveness Act 1988.
3. See *Photographic Enlargers* (Poland, USSR, Czechoslovakia) OJ L212 21.7.82 p32 (Japan was used); *Trichloroethylene* (GDR, Poland, Romania, Spain USA, Czechoslovakia) OJ L223 31.7.82 p76 (prices on American domestic market were used); *Kraftliner* (USSR) OJ L64 10.3.83 p25 (American domestic prices were used); *Sanitary Fixtures* (Czechoslovakia, Hungary) OJ L325 22.11.83 p18 (Austria was used); *Paint, Distemper, Varnish and Similar Brushes* (China) OJ L46 14.2.87 p45 (Sri Lanka was used); *Potassium Permanganate* (Czechoslovakia) OJ L42 16.2.90 p1 (USA was used).
4. OJ L110 27.4.83 p11. See also *Natural Magnesite* (China) OJ L371 30.12.82 p21 (the importer suggested Austria, no evidence was produced to show that this would be more suitable); *Unwrought Nickel* (USSR) OJ L159 17.6.83 p43 (the exporter and one dealer suggested the London Metal Exchange quotations. The EC Commission rejected this on basis that it doubted whether the quotations covered production costs in market economy countries) : *Non-alloyed Unwrought Aluminium* (USSR) OJ L57 28.2.84 p19 (London Metal Exchange was again suggested as an alternative, again rejected).
5. See *Codeine* (Hungary) OJ L16 20.1.83 p30. The Hungarian exporter suggested that normal value should be based on the export price in Germany and not the domestic price in Yugoslavia. The EC Commission held, however, that the additional administrative burden which would be imposed on it by carrying out investigations in a further market economy country would be unjustified, unless it could be demonstrated that it would be manifestly more appropriate and reasonable to use another third country's normal value rather than use the prices or costs in Yugoslavia.
6. See for example *Oxalic Acid* (China, Czechoslovakia) OJ L19 27.1.82 p26; *Standardised Multiphase Electric Motors* (Bulgaria, Czechosolovakia, GDR, USSR, Poland, Romania) OJ L85 31.3.82 p9; *Refrigerators* (Yugoslavia, USSR, GDR, Poland, Romania, Hungary, Czechoslovakia) OJ L184 29.6.82 p23; *Sodium Carbonate* (GDR, Bulgaria, Poland, Romania, USSR) OJ L160 18.6.83 p18; *UREA* (GDR, Czechoslovakia, USSR) OJ L121 9.5.87 p11; *Gas Fuelled, Non Refillable Pocket Lighters* (Japan, Republic of Korea, China, Thailand) OJ L133 28.5.91 p20.

occasions, it has also taken into account the fact that production has been carried out on a substantial scale[1] and that there has been strong internal competition. This latter factor usually guarantees that price levels are in a reasonable proportion to costs[2]. In the United States, on the other hand, the authorities will also take into consideration other factors including, inter alia, the level of development of the country, population and division of labour. Vermulst, in criticising the Community authorities' determination of the analogue country, has argued that this concept should be known as "analogue industry", given the reliance on a sector rather than country approach[3].

Usually, the EC Commission uses the domestic price prevailing on the analogue market in order to determine the normal value[4]. When this is unreliable the EC Commission has used either the constructed value[5] or the export prices of the analogue country[6].

As a last resort, the EC Commission can establish normal value by the price actually paid or payable in the Community for the like product duly adjusted, if

1.   See for example *Sodium Carbonate* (USSR) OJ L297 24.11.79 p12; *Lithium Hydroxide* (USA, USSR) OJ L23 30.1.80 p19; *Standardised Multiphase Electric Motors* (Bulgaria, Czechoslovakia, GDR, USSR, Romania, Poland) OJ L85 31.3.82 p9; *Natural Magnesite* (China) OJ L371 30.12.82 p21; *Hexamethylenetetramine* (GDR, Czechoslovakia, Romania) OJ L40 12.2.83 p24; *Glass Textile Fibre (Rovings)* (Japan, GDR, Czechoslovakia) OJ L160 18.6.83 p18; *Methenamine* (Hexamethylenetetramine) (Hungary, Poland, Bulgaria, Romania, Yugoslavia, Czechoslovakia) OJ L104 24.4.90 p14.

2.   See for example *Hexamethylenetetramine* (GDR, USSR, Czechoslovakia, Romania) OJ L40 12.2.83 p24; *Glass Textile Fibre (Rovings)* Japan, GDR, Czechoslovakia) OJ L160 18.6.83 p18; *Methenamine* (Hexamethylenetramine) (Hungary, Poland, Bulgaria, Romania, Yugoslavia, Czechoslovakia) OJ L104 24.4.90 p14. Note : the existence of price controls also ensures that price levels are in reasonable proportion to costs; *Sodium Carbonate* (USSR) OJ L297 24.11.79 p12.

3.   Vermulst "Anti-dumping law and Practice in the United States and the European Community" "The New Amendments to the EC'sop437.

4.   *Sodium Carbonate* (USSR) OJ L297 24.11.79 p12; *Lithium Hydroxide* (USA, USSR) OJ L23 30.1.80 p19; *Cylinder Vacuum Cleaners* (Poland, GDR, Czechoslovakia) OJ L172 18.6.82 p47; *Kraftliner* (USSR, Sweden, USA, Austria, Canada, Finland, Portugal) OJ L64 10.3.83 p25; *Methenamine* (Hexamethylenetetramine) (Poland, Hungary, Bulgaria, Romania, Yugoslavia, Czechoslovakia) OJ L104 24.4.90 p14.

5.   *Angles, Shapes and Sections of Iron and Steel* (Romania) OJ L56 29.1.80 p34; *Hardboard* (Czechoslovakia, Spain, Hungary, Poland, Bulgaria, Sweden, Norway, Finland, USSR Romania) OJ L181 25.6.82 p19; *Paracetamol* (INN) (China) OJ L236 11.8.82 p23; *Unwrought Nickel* (USSR) OJ L159 17.6.83 p43; *Asbestos-Cement Corrugated Sheets* (GDR, Czechoslovakia) OJ L259 28.9.84 p48; *Woven Polyolefin Sacks* (China) OJ L187 19.7.90 p36; *Small Screen Colour TV Receivers* (Hong Kong, China) OJ L14 19.1.91 p31.

6.   *Mechanical Alarm Clocks* (GDR, USSR) OJ L158 25.6.80 p5 (exports to EEC) : *Saccharin and its Salts* (China, Japan and USA) OJ L331 9.12.80 p41 (exports to third countries) : *Ballbearings* (Japan, Romania, USSR, Poland) OJ L152 11.6.81 p44 (exports to EEC); *Photographic Enlargers* (Poland, USSR, Czechoslovakia) OJ L212 21.7.82 p32 (exports to EEC); *Sanitary Fixtures* (Czechoslovakia, Hungary) OJ L325 22.11.83 p18 (export prices to third countries); *Mechanical Wrist Watches* (USSR) OJ L213 4.8.87 p5 (exports to third countries and the EEC).

necessary, to include a reasonable margin of profit[1]. The EC Commission did so in *Oxalic Acid*[2], having rejected every other possibility. It rejected the following :

—   South Korea : the South Korean exporters refused to co-operate.

—   Domestic prices charged in China : China was one of the countries under investigation. Article 2(5) did not cover such a possibility.

—   Taiwan : it was rejected on the ground that the prices charged on the Taiwanese market were artificially high.

—   Japan : as the manufacturing processes and raw materials were different, Japan was rejected.

—   Prices of exports to the United States from Brazil : the EC Commission considered that it was highly likely that such products were dumped. It therefore rejected this possibility.

—   Domestic prices charged in Brazil : the Brazilian exporter refused to co-operate.

—   India : the Indian producer also refused to co-operate.

3.3.2.2.6 Imports made via a third country

Article 2(6) of Regulation 2423/88 provides that where a product is not imported directly from the country of origin but is exported to the Community from an intermediate country, the normal value shall be the comparable price actually paid or payable for the like product on the domestic market of either the country of export or the country of origin. The latter basis might be appropriate, inter alia, where the product is merely transhipped through the country of export, where such products are not produced in the country of export or where no comparable price for it exists in the country of export. In *Potassium Permanganate*, imports were not made direct to the Community from the USSR, but via Austria. The EC Commission considered that the product was not produced in Austria and was merely transhipped through this country. In such circumstances, the country of origin was appropriate for the purposes of calculating normal value[3]. On the other hand, in *Aspartame*, the Japanese product was imported to the Community via the United States. The EC Commission's investigation revealed that the product was not

---

1.   Article 2(5)(c), Council Regulation (EEC) 2423/88.

.2   OJ L343 13.12.88 p34; see also *Silicon Metal* (China) OJ L80 27.3.90 p9, the producers in the suggested market economy countries refused to co-operate; *Video Cassette Tapes* (China) OJ L106 26.4.91 p15, as above; *Pure Silk Typewriter Ribbon Fabrics* (China) OJ L174 7.7.90 p27, the Community producer and the Chinese exporter were the only producers of the product in question.

3.   OJ L145 8.6.90 p9.

merely transhipped through the United States but was actually sold to and imported by the US producer/exporter before exportation to the Community. Furthermore, there was substantial production in the United States and there was a comparable price for the product. In such circumstances, the EC Commission concluded that the conditions under which the country of origin might be considered appropriate were not fulfilled. Normal value was based on the comparable price paid for the like product on the US domestic market[1].

3.3.3   Export price

Dumping is determined by comparing normal value with the export price of the like product. In the United States, the export price is known as the United States price (USP). Article 2(8)(a) of Regulation 2423/88 states that :

"The export price shall be the price actually paid or payable for the product sold for export to the Community net of all taxes, discounts and rebates actually granted and directly related to the sales under consideration. Deferred discounts shall also be taken into consideration if they are actually granted and directly related to the sales under consideration."

This price, however, may not always be reliable where, for example, there is no export price, or where there is an association or compensatory arrangement between the exporter and the importer or a third party[2]. In such a case, the EC Commission can construct the export price on the basis of "the price at which the imported product is first resold to an independent buyer, or if the product is not resold to an independent buyer, or not resold in the condition imported, on any reasonable basis"[3]. In the United States, this concept is known as the exporters' sales price (ESP).

The normal method for constructing the export price is on the basis of the price at which the product is first resold to an independent buyer. In constructing this, the regulation states that allowance shall be made for all costs incurred between importation and resale including all duties and taxes and for a reasonable profit margin[4]. The regulation provides in article 2(8)(b) that these costs shall include

---

1.   OJ L134 29.5.91 p1.
2.   Article 2(8)(b), Council Regulation 2423/88. See footnote 5, p51.
3.   Article 2(8)(b), Council Regulation 2423/88. The latter method, ie on any reasonable basis, has never been used by the EC Commission. In *Textured Polyester Fabrics* (USA) OJ L133 20.5.81 p17, an adjustment was made to the processing costs where the products were not resold in the state in which they had been imported.
4.   Article 2(8)(b) of Council Regulation (EEC) 2423/88 provides that :
      "the allowances shall include, in particular the following :
            (i)   usual transport, insurance, handling, loading and ancillary costs;
            (ii)   customs duties, any anti-dumping duties and other taxes payable in the importing country by reason of the importation on the sale of the goods;

those normally borne by an importer but paid by any party either in or outside the Community which appears to be associated or to have a compensatory arrangement with the importer or exporter. This provision permits the Community authorities to deduct not only the costs of the related sales subsidiary, but also the export costs borne by the parent company, for example where the parent company has paid the advertising costs of its subsidiary in the Community. One commentator has criticised this provision on the basis that it permits the Community authorities to construct the export price in such a way that it results in a higher dumping margin[1].

The EC Commission will not use the profit margin of the related importer since this is in essence a transfer price between associated companies. Rather, it will look to an independent importer and the profit margin it would have made if it had been in the position of the related importer[2]. Such a profit margin has so far ranged from 2 to 12.7%[3].

In calculating the export price, the EC Commission will normally include all exports to the Community, even those which enter the Community for inward processing and which will subsequently be re-exported[4]. Finally, the EC Commission has, on a number of occasions, constructed the export price on the "basis of the facts available" where it lacked full and reliable information on the real export prices[5]. In the majority of cases it used the Community's import statistics[6].

      (iii)   a reasonable margin for overheads and profit and/or any commission usually paid or agreed."

For an analysis of the institutions' practice with regard to allowances see Van Bael and Bellis "EEC Anti-dumping and Other Trade Protection Laws""The New Amendments to the EC'so at pp52-54.

1.   See Norall "The New Amendments to the EC's Basic Anti-dumping Regulation" 29 CMLRev 83 at 89.

2.   See EC Commission intervention in the *Electronic Typewriter* cases : Case 250/85 *Brother v EC Council* [1988] ECR 5683; Joined Cases 260/85 and 106/86 *TEC & Co Ltd v EC Council* [1988] ECR 5855; Joined Cases 273/85 and 107/86 *Silver Seiko Ltd v EC Council* [1988] ECR 5927; Joined Cases 277 and 300/85 *Canon Inc v EC Council* [1988] ECR 5731; Case 301/85 *Sharp v EC Council* [1988] ECR 5813.

3.   For example, *Chemical Fertiliser* (USA) OJ L39 12.2.81 p4 (3%); *Textured Polyester Fabrics* (USA) OJ L133 20.5.81 p17 (5%); *Ballbearings* (Japan, USSR, Poland, Romania) OJ L152 11.6.81 p44 (6%); *Phenol* (USA) OJ L12 18.1.82 p1 (5%); *Polypropylene* (Japan) OJ L152 10.6.83 p18 (5%); *Dicumyl Peroxide* (Japan) OJ L203 27.7.83 p13 (5%); *Caravans for Camping* (Yugoslavia) OJ L240 30.8.83 p12 (5%); *Ballbearings* (Japan, Singapore) OJ L79 23.3.84 p8 (6%); *Electronic Scales* (Japan) OJ L80 24.3.84 p9 (8%); *Sensitised Paper for Colour Photographs* (Japan) OJ L124 11.5.84 p45 (5%); *Artificial Corundum* (Czechoslovakia, China, Spain, Yugoslavia) OJ L255 25.9.84 p9 (5%); *Electronic Typewriters* (Japan) OJ L335 22.12.84 p43; *Ballbearings* (Japan) OJ L340 28.12.84 p37 (6%); *Ballbearings* (Thailand) OJ L113 23.4.85 p61 (6%). *Housed Bearing Units* (Japan) OJ L35 6.2.87 p32 (6%); *Urea and Ammonium Nitrate* (USA) OJ L208 30.7.87 p1 (2%); *Vinyl Acetate Monomer* (USA) OJ L213 4.8.87 p32 (5%); *Video Cassette Recorders* (South Korea, Japan) OJ L57 28.2.89 p55 (12.7%); *Small Screen Colour TV Receivers* (China, Hong Kong) OJ L14 19.1.91 p31 (10%).

4.   *Acrylonitrile* (USA) OJ L101 20.4.83 p29; *Propan-I-OL* (USA) OJ L106 19.4.84 p55.

5.   Article 7(7)(b), Council Regulation (EEC) 2423/88.

6.   *Trichloroethylene* (GDR, Poland, Romania) OJ L223 31.7.82 p76; *Perchlorethylene* (Czechoslovakia, Romania) OJ L371 30.12.82 p47; *Silicon Metal* (China) OJ L80 27.3.90 p9; *Potassium Permanganate* (USSR) OJ L145 8.6.90 p9; *Artificial Corundum* (USSR, China, Hungary, Poland, Brazil, Yugoslavia, Czechoslovakia) OJ L275 2.10.91 p27.

3.3.4 The comparison between normal value and the export price

Once the normal value and the export price have been determined, the regulation stipulates that :

> "For the purposes of ensuring a fair comparison, due allowance in the form of adjustments shall be made in each case, on its merits, for the differences affecting price comparability, ie for differences in :
>
> (i) physical characteristics;
>
> (ii) import charges and indirect taxes;
>
> (iii) selling expenses resulting from sales made :
>
> — at different levels of trade, or
>
> — in different quantities, or
>
> — under different conditions and terms of sale[1]."

The regulation further provides that the comparison shall be made as nearly as possible at the same time[2]. As in the United States, the objective is to compare normal value with the export price of the like product at the *ex factory* level, ie the price at which the product leaves the factory. The adjustments will be granted if an interested party can show that they are justified[3], which more often than not constitutes an insurmountable hurdle.

The adjustments listed in article 2(9)(a) which are required to be made in order to take account of the differences affecting price comparability shall be made in accordance with the rules laid down in article 2(10)(a) to (e). In *Freezers*[4], it was argued that the list of factors in article 2(9) of Regulation 2176/84 was not exhaustive and that article 2(10) of the said regulation merely laid down guidelines for determining these allowances. The EC Commission rejected this, concluding that the list of factors enumerated was exhaustive. The new wording of articles 2(9) and (10) of Regulation 2423/88 put beyond doubt the fact that the only adjustments allowed to effect a fair comparison are those listed in article 2(10). On a number of occasions, the EC Commission has made adjustments even though these were not requested by the parties involved[5]. There is nothing in the wording of the revised articles to suggest, that should the need arise again, the EC Commission may not make such adjustments.

---

1. Article 2(9)(a). The US Anti-dumping Rules permit similar adjustments if these can be established and in addition allow adjustment for packing and delivery costs. For a discussion of how these allowances have been applied in the United States, see : Vermulst "Anti-dumping Law and Practice in the United States and the European Community" (1987) pp 369 - 384.
2. Ibid.
3. Article 2(9)(b), Council Regulation (EEC) 2423/88.
4. OJ L259 11.9.86 p14.
5. *Upright Pianos* (USSR, GDR, Poland, Czechoslovakia) OJ L101 16.4.82 p30; *Photographic Enlargers* (Czechoslovakia, Poland, USSR) OJ L212 21.7.82 p32.

Article 2(10) specifies the rules to be considered in establishing whether an adjustment will be granted. It is an area in which the EC Commission has considerable discretion, with the result that it has a powerful influence on what the level of the dumping margin will be.

The new articles 2(9) and (10) were introduced in order to codify the existing practice of the Community authorities in the granting of adjustments in effecting a fair comparison between the normal value and export price as established under their separate rules.

When constructing the export price, the EC Commission will normally deduct all costs of a related sales subsidiary in the Community from its prices to independent buyers. Many exporters whose sales were made through an associated sales company have argued that an identical approach should be adopted when constructing the normal value[1]. The EC Commission has consistently argued that this confused two distinct issues namely, the establishment of normal value and the export price with the adjustments allowed for differences affecting price comparability when comparing these prices.

For the purpose of constructing the export price, Regulation 2423/88 permits the deduction of all costs incurred between importation and resale, thereby arriving at an export price which is not influenced by the relationship between the exporter and its associated importer. Normal value is established by using the comparable price in the ordinary course of trade or on a constructed basis where no such price is available. As regards the subsequent comparison between normal value and export price as determined above, other rules apply which lead to price adjustments for all allowable expenses. The same criteria apply whether the factors to be taken into consideration are in respect of sales on the domestic market or those destined for export. Many commentators[2] have argued that such a practice invariably leads to a finding of dumping.

The position in the United States is different. Where an exporter sells his products through a related sales company, the competent authorities, in adjusting the foreign market value, will deduct not only that exporter's direct selling expenses in his domestic market but also all indirect selling expenses to an amount not exceeding

---

1.   See *Electronic Typewriters* (Japan) OJ L163 22.6.85 p1; *Photocopiers* (Japan) OJ L239 26.8.86 p5; *Compact Disc Players* (Japan, South Korea) OJ L205 18.7.89 p5.
2.   See Norall "The New Amendments to the EC's Basic Anti-dumping Regulation" at p97; Bell "Anti-dumping Practice in the EEC : the Japanese Dimension" LIEI (1987) 21; Kuzmik "A Community Export Price Offset" [1988] 2 CMLRev 317; Vermulst "Anti-dumping Law and Practice in the United States and the European Community" (1987) p497-9.

the indirect selling expenses allocated to his sales in the United States. This latter adjustment is known as the Exporter's Sales Price offset (ESP offset)[1]. In so doing, the authorities will reduce the dumping margin and redress the imbalance which resulted from the deduction of all costs on the export side. Vermulst observes, however, that this is merely a compromise owing to the fact that the limit on the amount of indirect selling expenses which may be deducted does not result in a fair comparison[2].

The EC Commission's practice has, however, been endorsed by the Court, in particular in the *Mini Ballbearing*[3] and *Electronic Typewriter*[4] cases. The Court has held that :

> "there are three sets of distinct rules, each of which must be complied with separately for the respective purposes of determining the normal value, establishing the export price and making the comparison between the two[5]."

3.3.4.1 Differences in physical characteristics

The regulation provides that where there are differences in the physical characteristics of the product, normal value "shall be adjusted by an amount corresponding to a reasonable estimate of the value of the difference in the physical characteristics of the product concerned"[6]. In *Photocopiers* some exporters supplied photocopiers without reprographic drums. Where a comparable machine was sold for export along with a reprographic drum, an adjustment to normal value was allowed in order to take account of this difference. For some exporters the prices of drums on the domestic market were not separately available and in such cases the adjustment was calculated on the basis of the constructed value of the drums. This was determined by adding the cost of production as defined in article 2(3)(b)(ii) plus a reasonable margin of profit[7]. In the majority of cases, adjustments under this heading have involved the price of an exported product being compared with a similar rather than an identical product[8].

---

1.   This adjustment has no statutory base. It is merely an administrative practice. For a discussion of how it is applied in practice, see Vermulst, above, pp377-380.
2.   Vermulst, above, p498.
3.   Case 240/84 *NTN Toyo Bearing Co Ltd v EC Council* [1987] ECR 1809; Case 255/84 *Nachi Fujikoshi Corpn v EC Council* [1987] ECR 1861; Case 256/84 *Koyo Seiko Co Ltd v EC Council* [1987] ECR 1899; Case 258/84 *Nippon Seiko KK v EC Council* [1987] ECR 1923; Case 260/84 *Minebea Co Ltd v EC Council* [1987] ECR 1975.
4.   See footnote 2, p62.
5.   Joined Cases 260/85 and 106/86 *TEC & Co Ltd v EC Council* above at 5920 para 31 of judgment.
6.   Article 2(10)(a).
7.   *Photocopiers* (Japan) OJ L239 26.8.86 p5.
8.   Note that in article 2(12) of Council Regulation (EEC) 2423/88 the definition of 'like product' includes products which have characteristics which closely resemble those of the product under consideration. See also section 3.3.1 above.

The EC Commission has granted adjustments for differences in physical specifications[1] and in the quality of the product in question[2]. It has in the past relied on its own judgment in determining the amount of the adjustment, although on one occasion it consulted an outside expert[3]. Article 2(10)(a) now provides that the amount of the adjustment shall be calculated on the basis of relevant data for the investigation period or the data for the last available financial year.

3.3.4.2 Differences in import charges and indirect taxes

Article 2(10)(b) states that normal value shall be reduced by an amount corresponding to any import charges or indirect taxes as defined in the notes to the Annex, borne by the like product and by materials physically incorporated therein, when destined for consumption in the country of origin or export and not collected or refunded in respect of the product exported to the Community. Such an adjustment was allowed in *Video Cassette Recorders* in respect of import charges included in video cassette recorders destined for consumption on the Korean market. The EC Commission did not have sufficient information to prove the exact amount of the import charges on parts physically incorporated into the domestically sold models. In these circumstances, it estimated the adjustment on the basis of the value of the raw materials directly imported into Korea by the companies in question using an average import tax rate of 20%[4]. This approach was confirmed by the EC Council[5].

---

1. See *Upright Pianos* (USSR) OJ L101 16.4.82 p30, (adjustments were allowed for differences in quality of action, the type of sound board used and the raw material of the cabinet); *Refrigerators* (Yugloslavia, USSR, Hungary, Poland, Romania, GDR, Czechoslovakia) OJ L184 29.6.82 p23 (adjustments were allowed for differences in volume freezing capacity and type of defrosting system); *Photographic Enlargers* (Poland, USSR, Czechoslovakia) OJ L212 21.7.82 p32 (10% adjustment for differences in physical characteristics); *Ceramic Tiles* (Spain) OJ L168 28.6.84 p35 (adjustments were allowed for differences in size, colour and pattern); *Ferroboron Alloy* (Japan) OJ L73 20.3.90 p6 (adjustments were allowed for differences in boron content of the product); *Small Screen Colour TV Receivers* (China, Hong Kong) OJ L195 18.7.91 p1 (adjustment was allowed for lack of cable tuner); *Dihydrostreptomycin* (DHS) (Japan, China) OJ L187 13.7.91 p23 (adjustment of 9% allowed). No adjustment for differences in physical specifications was allowed in the following : *Refrigerators* (Hungary, Poland) OJ L184 29.6.82 p23; *Glycine* (Japan) OJ L107 18.4.85 p8.
2. *Studded Welded-Link Chain* (Spain, Sweden) OJ L231 2.9.80 p10 (differences in steel qualities); *Upright Pianos* (USSR) OJ L101 16.4.82 p30 (adjustment was allowed to take account of inferior conditions in which the pianos were delivered); *Photographic Enlargers* (Czechoslovakia, Poland, USSR) OJ L212 21.7.82 p32 (adjustment of 5% allowed for differences in quality with Japanese product (10% for Poland)); *Copper Sulphate* (USSR, Czechoslovakia) OJ L151 9.6.83 p24 (adjustment was allowed for the lower quality of the product); *Sanitary Fixtures* (Czechoslovakia, Hungary) OJ L325 22.11.83 p18 (allowance was made for inferior glazing and polishing of the imported product); *Artificial Corundum* (Spain, China, Yugoslavia, Czechoslovakia) OJ L255 25.9.84 p9 (allowances were made for any transformation of the product after its importation from the point of view of quality). Adjustments were rejected in the following cases because of the lack of proof : *Hardboard* (Hungary, Czechoslovakia, Poland, Spain, Bulgaria, Norway, Sweden, Finland, USSR, Romania) OJ L181 25.6.82 p19; *Barium Chloride* (GDR, China) OJ L110 27.4.83 p10; *Video Cassette Tapes* (China) OJ L106 26.4.91 p15 (Adjustment of 20% was allowed).
3. *Mechanical Clocks* (GDR, USSR) OJ L344 19.12.80 p34.
4. OJ L57 28.1.89 p55; see also : *Polyester Yarn* (Mexico, South Korea, Taiwan, Turkey) OJ L151 17.6.88 p39; *Cotton Yarn* (India, Turkey, Brazil, Egypt, Thailand) OJ L271 27.9.91 p17.
5. OJ L240 31.8.88 p5.

3.3.4.3 Differences in selling expenses

3.3.4.3.1 Sales made at different levels of trade

The EC Commission has granted adjustments for differences in the level of trade only in a small number of cases[1]. The new text of article 2(10) retains the possibility of such an adjustment but gives no guidance on how it should apply.

3.3.4.3.2 Sales made in different quantities

The old regulation - Regulation 2176/84 - set out at length the adjustment allowed for differences in quantities. Unlike the present regulation, it did not limit the claim to adjustments for differences in *selling expenses* resulting from sales made in different quantities[2].

3.3.4.3.3 Sales made under different conditions and terms of sale

The regulation provides that the normal value shall be reduced by the directly related costs incurred for conveying the product under consideration from the premises of the exporter to the independent buyer[3]. This wording gives effect to previous practice in that it excludes the possibility of deducting transport costs incurred by the manufacturer to its warehouse or related sales company. In the same way, the export price shall be reduced by any directly related costs incurred by the exporter for conveying the product from its premises in the exporting country to its destination in the Community[4]. In both cases these costs include transport[5], insurance, handling, loading and ancillary costs.

The regulation provides that both the normal value and export price shall be reduced by the respective directly related costs of the packing for the product concerned[6] and they shall be reduced by the cost of any credit granted for the sales under consideration[7]. The amount of the reduction for the cost of any credit given shall be calculated by reference to the normal commercial credit rate applicable in the country of origin or export in respect of the currency expressed on the invoice[8].

---

1.   *Vinyl Acetate Monomer* (USA) OJ L311 21.11.80 p13; *Electronic Scales* (Japan) OJ L80 24.3.84 p9; *Copper Sulphate* (Poland, Spain, Hungary, Bulgaria) OJ L275 18.10.84 p12.
2.   Emphasis added.
3.   Article 2(10)(c)(i).
4.   Ibid.
5.   See *Synthetic Fibres of Polyester* (USA, Mexico, Taiwan, Romania, Turkey, Yugoslavia) OJ L348 17.12.88 p49.
6.   Article 2(10)(c)(ii).
7.   Article 2(10)(c)(iii).
8.   See *Synthetic Fibres of Polyester* (USA, Romania, Mexico, Taiwan, Turkey, Yugoslavia) OJ L348 17.12.88 p49; *Video Cassette Recorders* (South Korea, Japan) OJ L57 28.2.89 p55; *Small Screen Colour TV Receivers* (China, Hong Kong) OJ L14 19.1.91 p31 (adjustment rejected).

The regulation provides that both the normal value and export price shall be reduced by an amount corresponding to the direct costs of providing warranties, guarantees, technical assistance and services[1]. In *Mica*, the exporter claimed an adjustment corresponding to the direct costs incurred for cutting the product into slices. This was rejected by the EC Commission on the grounds that article 2(10)(c)(iv) only covers after-sales services, whereas the services allegedly being rendered related to pre-sales services[2].

Where commissions have been paid in respect of the sales under consideration, both the normal value and the export price shall be reduced by the corresponding amount paid[3]. Article 2(10)(c)(v) also provides that the salaries paid to salesmen shall be deducted. The term "salesmen" is defined as "personnel wholly engaged in direct selling activities". In *Audio Tapes in Cassettes*[4], the EC Commission rejected a claim for the deduction of sales staff expenses by way of adjustment to the normal value. These expenses included car and telephone expenses. The EC Commission observed that such expenses did not form part of salaries but were selling, general and administrative expenses.

Regulation 2176/84 provided that as a general rule no allowance or adjustment could be made for overheads, research and development and advertising costs[5]. This is due mainly to the fact that there are huge difficulties involved in allocating overhead costs satisfactorily[6]. The position regarding these costs was explained in *Electronic Typewriters* :

> "... Under Regulation (EEC) 2176/84 allowances can only be granted for differences in the factors mentioned in article 2(9). One of these factors is "conditions and terms of sale". This is a relatively narrow technical term referring to the obligations inherent in a sales contract which may be laid down in the contract itself or in the general conditions of sale issued by the seller. What is decisive is whether the costs are strictly necessary to fulfil the terms of the sales under consideration. Where this first criterion is met it must

---

1.   Article 2(10)(c)(iv).
2.   OJ L284 3.10.89 p45.
3.   Article 2(10)(c)(v), Council Regulation (EEC) 2423/88. See *Synthetic Fibres of Polyester* (USA, Romania, Mexico, Taiwan, Turkey, Yugoslavia) OJ L348 17.12.88 p49.
4.   OJ L313 13.11.90 p5.
5.   This meant that allowances may only have been granted for overheads and general expenses where it could be shown that they had a "direct relationship to domestic or export sales under consideration". For example, one could have a situation where the overhead is related directly to the individual sale, for instance, in relation to the sale of a particular car. The person buying it wants to leave the country for six months and therefore wants the car stored. He pays for this. It can therefore be said that such an overhead is directly related to the sale in question and will be granted.
6.   The question of overheads was discussed at great length in the GATT during the Tokyo Round of Trade Negotiations. Because of the difficulties involved, no rule was incorporated into the new GATT Code.

be shown in addition that these costs bear a direct functional relationship to the sales under consideration, ie that they are incurred because a particular sale is made. In general, overheads and general expenses, wherever they occur, do not have such a direct functional relationship and are therefore not allowable ....[1]"

Under the wording of the new regulation, no mention is made of these costs, thereby confirming the fact that they are not deductible.

3.3.4.4 Amount of adjustment

The regulation provides that the amount of the adjustment shall be calculated on the basis of the relevant data for the investigation period or the data for the last available financial year[2].

3.3.4.5 Insignificant adjustments

A new provision has been introduced by Regulation 2423/88[3], whereby claims for individual adjustments having an ad valorem effect of less than 0.5% of the price or value of the affected transactions shall be considered insignificant.

3.3.5 The reference period

In considering whether or not a product has been dumped, the EC Commission compares the normal value and the export price over a given period of time. This is known as the reference period. This is important when considering the dumping margin, because prior to the changes in Regulation 2176/84, the EC Commission had complete discretion to choose whatever reference period it liked[4]. The problem with this was that if dumping occurred for only a short time and if the reference period happened to be during that time, then the resultant dumping margin may

---

1.   OJ L163 22.6.85 p1.
2.   Article 2(10)(d).
3.   Article 2(11)(e).
4.   See for example *Lithium Hydroxide* (USA, USSR) OJ L274 31.10.79 p26 (January-April 1979 : four months); *Mounted Piezo-Electric Quartz Crystal Units* (USA, Japan, Republic of Korea) OJ L162 27.6.80 p62 (1.1.79 - 31.1.80 : 13 months); *Chemical Fertiliser* (USA) OJ L39 12.2.81 p5 (1.1.80 - 30.9.80 : nine months); *Hermetic Compressors* (Spain) OJ L113 25.4.81 p53 (1.7.80 - 31.12.80 : six months) : *Fluid Cracking Catalysts* (USA) OJ L11 16.1.82 p25 (1.1.80 - 30.4.81 : 16 months); *Hardboard* (USSR, Romania, Hungary, Bulgaria, Poland, Spain, Sweden, Finland, Norway, Czechoslovakia) OJ L181 25.6.82 p19 (1.1.80 - 30.6.80 : six months).

have been higher than would otherwise have been the case. The regulation now provides that the reference period shall :

"cover a period of not less than six months immediately prior to the initiation of the proceeding[1]."

More recently, in a number of complex cases, the investigation has exceeded the normal time for its completion[2]. In the United States, the reference period normally covers a period consisting of 150 days prior to and 30 days after, the first day of the month during which the complaint was received in an acceptable form. There is provision also for the reference period to be extended upon the request of the complainant, or if the Department of Commerce concludes that those concerned by the investigation are co-operating and the case is extraordinarily complicated[3].

3.3.6   The dumping margin

Once the normal value and the export price of the like product have been calculated and the proper adjustments made to make them comparable, the dumping margin is determined. This is defined as "the amount by which the normal value exceeds the export price"[4]. The regulation further provides that where dumping margins vary, weighted averages may be established[5].

The new article 2(13) of Regulation 2423/88 confirms the Community authorities' existing practice when prices vary[6]. It provides that normal value shall normally be established on a weighted average basis. For the weighted average method, all the domestic prices are averaged, the average being weighted by the volume of the

---

1.   Article 7(1)(c).
2.   See for example : *Glutamic Acid and its Salts* (Indonesia, Taiwan, Thailand, Republic of Korea) OJ L56 3.3.90 p23; *Small Screen Colour TV Receivers* (Republic of Korea) OJ L107 27.4.90 p56; *Ballbearings* (Japan, Singapore) OJ L256 20.9.90 p1; *Espadrilles* (China) OJ L365 28.12.90 p28; *Small Screen Colour TV Receivers* (Hong Kong, China) OJ L14 19.1.91 p31; *EPROMs* (Japan) OJ L65 12.3.91 p1.
3.   Section 733(c) of the Tariff Act 1930, 19 USC s167b(c). A case may be extraordinarily complicated by reason of :
   - the number and complexity of the transactions to be investigated or adjustments to be made;
   - the novelty of the issues presented;
   - the number of firms whose activities must be investigated;
   - the necessity of additional time to make a preliminary determination.
4.   Article 2(14)(a), Council Regulation (EEC) 2423/88.
5.   Article 2(14)(b).
6.   See *Ballbearings (Miniature)* (Japan, Singapore) OJ L193 21.7.84 p1. The EC Commission held that a comparison of normal value with a weighted average export price comprising dumped and non-dumped sales would be in contradiction with the EC Council's amendment of the Community's anti-dumping legislation. Therefore it has been a consistent practice of the EC Commission not to use weighted average export prices for the determination of the dumping margin except in cases where for administrative reasons it was not considered feasible to employ the transaction-by-transaction method or where the averaging of the export prices would have had no effect on the overall outcome of the proceedings.

goods sold at each price. With regard to the export price, the regulation provides that these prices shall normally be compared with the normal value on a transaction-by-transaction basis[1] except where the use of weighted averages would not materially affect the results of the investigation[2]. By the transaction-by-transaction method, normal value is compared with the export price for each sale to the Community. All transactions below normal value are considered, but sales above normal value (say 10%) are not allowed to offset sales below normal value by the same volume (say 10%). Export prices above normal value are treated as if they were made at normal value. The Trade and Tariff Act 1984 in the United States permits the authorities if they wish to establish a weighted average export price[3]. Lastly, article 2(13) provides for the use of sampling, ie the use of the most frequently occurring or representative prices may be applied to establish normal value and export prices in cases in which a significant volume of transactions is involved[4].

It is the practice of the Community authorities to treat non-co-operating producers differently from those who co-operate. Non-co-operation justifies the use of the "best available information" in accordance with article 7(7)(b) of Regulation 2423/88. Normally, the EC Commission will apply the highest dumping margin found for co-operating firms to those companies which did not co-operate[5]. Its reasoning is two-fold. First, it limits the opportunity for the non-co-operating producer to circumvent the duty. Second, the application of a lower margin to a non-co-operating producer would constitute a bonus for non-co-operation.

More recently, the EC Commission has adopted a tougher stance with non-co-operating producers and, in particular, where this non-co-operation represents the majority of exports to the Community. In *Thermal Paper*[6], the EC Commission observed that the investigation had been characterised by the non-co-operation of a significant proportion of the Japanese companies concerned. Furthermore, it had serious doubts as to whether the results of the dumping investigation for the four producers who co-operated were really representative for the rest of the producers. In these circumstances, it took the view that it would not be appropriate to apply the highest dumping margin found for the co-operating producers to those which did not co-operate. It concluded that the data contained in the complaint provided the most reliable and reasonable basis for establishing the dumping margin.

1.　　See for example *Sodium Carbonate* (USA) OJ L317 13.11.82 p5; *Electronic Typewriters* (Japan) OJ L335 22.12.84 p43.
2.　　*Ballbearings II* (Japan, Poland, Romania, USSR) OJ L152 11.6.81 p44.
3.　　Vermulst "Anti-dumping Law and Practice in the United States and the European Community" (1987) p385.
4.　　See for example *Salmon* (Norway) OJ L69 16.3.91 p32.
5.　　See for example *Ballbearings* (Japan, Singapore) OJ L256 27.4.90 p1; *Aspartame* (Japan, USA) OJ L330 29.11.90 p16; *EPROMs* (Japan) OJ L65 12.3.91 p1.
6.　　OJ L270 26.9.91 p15.

It is therefore in the interests of a producer/exporter to co-operate. Failure to do so will inevitably result in him being placed at a competitive disadvantage vis-a-vis his fellow producers.

Where the dumping margin is 1% or less, the EC Commission will consider this minimal, and therefore not such as would cause injury to the Community producers[1].

3.4   Injury

There must be injury to Community industry in order for anti-dumping duties to be imposed. The criteria for the determination of injury are laid out in article 4 of Regulation 2423/88. It provides that :

"A determination of injury shall be made only if the dumped or subsidised imports are, through the effects of dumping or subsidisation, causing injury ie causing or threatening to cause material injury to an established Community industry or materially retarding the establishment of such an industry."[2]

This involves three main stages, each of which will be considered individually. They are as follows :

3.4.1   What constitutes Community industry?

3.4.2   What is meant by the terms "material injury", "material retardation", and "threatening to cause material injury"?

3.4.3   Is there a "causal link" between the dumped imports and the injury to Community industry?

Before considering these criteria, two points should be made. First, it should be noted that the effect of the dumped imports has to be assessed in relation to the Community production of the like product[3]. Secondly, in the majority of cases where

---

1.   See *Polyester Yarn* (USA) OJ L358 31.12.80 p91 (for non-textured yarn a dumping margin of 0.2% was considered de minimis); for textured yarn a dumping margin of 0.5% and 1.1% were considered de minimis; *Non-alloyed Unwrought Aluminium* (Egypt) OJ L161 15.6.83 p13 (a dumping margin of 0.3% was considered de minimis); *Sensitised Paper for Colour Photographs* (Japan) OJ L124 11.5.84 p45 (a dumping margin of 0.54% was considered de minimis); *Ceramic Tiles* (Spain) OJ L168 28.6.84 p35 (a dumping margin of less than 0.5% was considered de minimis); *Denim* (Turkey, Indonesia, Hong Kong, Macao) OJ L222 17.8.90 p50 (dumping margin was less than 1%); *Polyester Yarns* (Mexico) OJ L275 2.10.91 p21 (dumping margin of 0.53% was considered de minimis); *Polyester Yarns* (Taiwan, Indonesia, India, China, Turkey) OJ L276 3.10.91 p7 (dumping margins of 0.43% and 0.26% were considered de minimis).
2.   Article 4(1).
3.   Article 4(4), Council Regulation (EEC) 2423/88. See also section 3.3.1 above.

dumping has been found to exist, a determination of injury has been made. However, in a small number of cases, even though there has been dumping, this has resulted in a no injury determination[1].

3.4.1 What constitutes Community industry?

Community industry is defined in the regulation as :

> "the Community producers as a whole of the like product or to those of them whose collective output constitutes a major proportion of the total Community production of those products."[2]

What constitutes "a major proportion of total Community production" has not been defined in the regulation or in decided cases[3]. For instance, in one case the EC Commission still held that the rest of the Community producers represented a major part of the Community production of the product in question even though the main Community producer did not support the complaint and where the German producer considered that it was not injured[4]. Furthermore, in some cases the EC Commission has held that a producer in one Member State may satisfy the requirements of article 4(5), if its output constitutes a major proportion of the total Community production[5]. On the other hand, the failure of a large proportion of

---

1.   The cases in which no injury determinations have been made are as follows :
  - (i)   when dumping is considered de minimis : see above (footnote 1, p72);
  - (ii)   when the Community producers show no interest in the investigation : see *Peaches* (Greece) OJ L110 29.4.80 p35; *Hammers* (China) OJ L29 4.2.86 p36; *Stainless Steel House Cooking Ware* (South Korea) OJ L74 19.3.86 p33; *High Carbon Ferro Chromium* (Albania, USSR) OJ L90 11.4.91 p38;
  - (iii)   low level of market penetration so that material injury is not being caused : see *Mechanical Wrist Watches* (USSR) OJ L11 16.1.82 p14; *Methenamine* (Hexamethylenetetramine) OJ L104 24.4.90 p14; *Portland Cement* (Yugoslavia) OJ L16 22.1.91 p34; *Audio Tapes in Cassettes* (Japan, Hong Kong, Republic of Korea) OJ L119 14.5.90 p35; *Thin Polyester Film* (Republic of Korea) OJ L151 15.6.91 p89; *Dihydrostreptomycin* (Japan, China) OJ L187 13.7.91 p23; *Polyester Yarns* (man-made staple fibres) (Republic of Korea, Taiwan, Indonesia, India, China, Turkey) OJ L187 13.7.91 p23;
  - (iv)   the prior existence of other safeguard measures : see *Mechanical Wrist Watches* (USSR) OJ L11 16.1.82 p14 (existence of quantitative restrictions) : *Seamless Tubes of Non-alloy Steel* (Spain) OJ L196 30.7.80 p34 (existence of countervailing duties);
  - (v)   decrease in consumption and increase in the volume of imports from other countries : see *Glass Textile Fibres (Rovings)* (GDR, Japan, Czechoslovakia) OJ L160 18.6.83 p18; *NPK Fertilisers* (Hungary, Poland, Romania, Yugoslavia) OJ L188 20.7.90 p63;
  - (vi)   the complainant, who accounted for 90% of Community industry, was the main importer of the dumped imports. Furthermore, he was able to increase his market share : see *Ice Skates* (Czechoslovakia, Hungary, Romania, Yugoslavia) OJ L52 12.2.85 p48.
2.   Article 4(5).
3.   Dr Beseler, then Head of the Commercial Defence Division DG-1 at the CEFIC Anti-dumping Seminar held in Brussels on 2-3 April 1981, suggested that a share of production of 25 % or more would be regarded as acceptable.
4.   See *Cylinder Vacuum Cleaners* (Czechoslovakia, Poland, GDR) OJ L172 18.6.82 p47.
5.   See *Edible and Pharmaceutical Gelatine* (Sweden) OJ C219 27.8.80 p2; *Louvre Doors* (Malaysia, Singapore) OJ C286 5.11.80 p4; *Mechanical Wrist Watches and Movements* (USSR) OJ C181 19.7.80 p3 - in all three cases, the Member State involved was the United Kingdom;

Community producers to reply to the EC Commission's questionnaire may mean that the combined production of the remaining producers who did reply will not constitute a major proportion of the total Community production[1]. In such circumstances, the Community authorities would not have the information available to establish whether injury is being caused to the Community.

Two major exceptions are provided for in article 4(5) to this basic rule : related parties and regional industry.

3.4.1.1   Related parties

The regulation provides that "when producers are related to the exporters or importers or are themselves importers of the allegedly dumped product the term 'Community industry' may be interpreted as referring to the rest of the producers"[2]. This provision has been used on a few occasions to exclude Community producers from the examination of injury suffered by the complainant industry[3].

The decision to exclude a Community producer must be made by the Community authorities on a case by case basis on reasonable and equitable grounds and taking into consideration all aspects involved[4]. It may be reasonable for a Community producer to import the dumped goods and still be included in the assessment of injury in certain cases[5]. This has now been recognised by the Court[6]. First, a Community producer of certain models of the product in question may import some models which have been dumped and include them as part of its overall range at prices corresponding to its own prices. In this case, the producer is not causing injury to itself or anyone else. For example, in *Dot Matrix Printers*, one of the grounds considered by the EC Commission for not excluding three Europrint members who imported dumped printers from Japan, was that it was necessary for printer manufacturers to offer a full range of printers in order to defend their position on the market. Potential clients are more likely to buy equipment from a supplier who offers a full range of products[7]. Second, a Community producer may import dumped

---

Portland Cement (Yugoslavia) OJ L16 22.1.91 p34 - the Member State involved was Italy; *Welded Wire Mesh* (Yugoslavia) OJ L123 18.5.91 p54 - the Member State involved was Greece, *Asbestos Cement Pipes* (Turkey) OJ L209 31.7.91 p37 - the Member State involved was Italy.

1. *Certain Cotton Terry Towelling Articles* (Turkey) OJ L17 23.1.91 p22.
2. Article 4(5).
3. See for example *Textured Polyester Yarn* (USA) OJ L133 20.5.81 p17; *Electronic Scales* (Japan) OJ L80 24.3.84 p9; *Skates* (Czechoslovakia) OJ L52 22.2.85 p48; *Video Cassette Recorders* (South Korea, Japan) OJ L240 31.8.88 p5; *DRAMS* (Japan) OJ L20 25.1.90 p5; *Ballbearings* (Japan, Singapore) OJ L256 27.4.90 p1; *EPROMs* (Japan) OJ L65 12.3.91 p1; *Large Electrolytic Aluminium Capacitors* (Japan) OJ L152 4.6.92 p22.
4. *Large Electrolytic Aluminium Capacitors* (Japan) OJ L152 4.6.92 p22.
5. Private conversation with Commission officials, November 1985.
6. See Joined Cases 133 and 150/87 *Nashua Corpn v EC Commission and EC Council* [1990] ECR 719; Case C-156/87 *Gestetner Holdings Plc v EC Commission and EC Council* [1990] I ECR 781.
7. OJ L130 26.5.88 p12; OJ L317 24.11.88 p33. See also : *Photo Albums* (South Korea, Hong Kong) OJ L138 31.5.90 p48; *Radio Broadcast Receivers* (South Korea) OJ L34 11.2.92 p8.

products in order to avoid or minimise injury to itself or as part of its overall policy to maximise its competitiveness while at the same time not taking advantage of the dumped imports to make windfall profits[1]. Lastly, a Community producer may import dumped products as a means of self protection while an anti-dumping investigation is ongoing[2]. It should be stressed that these situations will arise only where the Community producer is an importer and is not related to the exporter[3].

3.4.1.2 Regional industry
In exceptional circumstances, the producers within a region of the Community may be treated as constituting Community industry if the producers within such a market sell all or almost all of their production of the product in question in that market, and if the demand in that market is not to any substantial degree supplied by producers of the product in question located elsewhere in the Community[4].

This concept of regional industry was considered by the EC Commission in *Portland Cement*[5]. It held that as the producers in Ireland, the United Kingdom and Denmark sold almost all their production in their domestic markets (95%, 99% and 93% respectively) and that the demand in each of these markets was not supplied to any substantial degree by producers of the product in question located elsewhere in the Community, they therefore constituted isolated markets within the meaning of article 4(5)(a) and (b). In *Synthetic Fibres of Polyester*, the Italian market was most affected by the dumped imports. The EC Commission considered article 4(5)(a) and (b) with a view to possible measures on a regional basis. It concluded, however, given the size of the Italian market (30% in 1985), the share held by other Community producers and the volume of sales made by Italian producers outside their home market, that the Italian market could not be considered an isolated market within the meaning of article 4(5)(a) and (b)[6].

Finally, where the Community production of the like product has no separate identity, the effect of the dumped imports "shall be assessed in relation to the production of the narrowest group or range of production which includes the like product for which the necessary information can be found"[7]. This provision has the

---

1. See *Large Electrolytic Aluminium Capacitors* (Japan) OJ L152 4.6.92 p22.
2. See *Photo Albums* (South Korea, Hong Kong) OJ L138 31.5.90 p48.
3. See *Electronic Scales* (Japan) OJ L80 24.3.84 p9; *Photocopiers* (Japan) OJ L239 26.8.86 p5; *Dot Matrix Printers* (Japan) OJ L130 26.5.88 p12.
4. Article 4(5)(a) and (b), Council Regulation (EEC) 2423/88.
5. OJ L202/43 1986; see also *Portland Cement* (Yugoslavia) OJ L16 22.1.91 p34 (Italian market); *Welded Wire Mesh* (Yugoslavia) OJ L123 18.5.91 p54; *Asbestos Cement Pipes* (Turkey) OJ L209 31.7.91 p37.
6. OJ L103 15.4.87 p38.
7. Article 4(4), Council Regulation (EEC) 2423/88.

effect of widening the scope of Community industry, but to date it has never been used by the EC Commission[1].

3.4.2 What is meant by the terms "material injury" "material retardation" and "threatening to cause material injury"?

3.4.2.1 Material injury

The term "material injury" is not defined in the regulation. Article 4(2) provides, however, that :

"An examination of injury shall involve the following factors, no one or several of which can necessarily give decisive guidance :

(a) volume of dumped or subsidised imports, in particular whether there has been a significant increase, either in absolute terms or relative to production or consumption in the Community;

(b) the prices of dumped or subsidised imports, in particular whether there has been a significant price undercutting as compared with the price of a like product in the Community;

(c) the consequent impact on the industry concerned as indicated by actual or potential trends in the relevant economic factors such as :

— production,
— utilisation of capacity,
— stocks,
— sales,
— market share,
— prices (ie depression of prices or prevention of price increases which otherwise would have occurred),
— profits,
— return on investment,
— cash flow,
— employment."

In establishing whether the dumped imports have caused material injury to Community industry, the EC Commission may, where more than one country is under investigation, decide whether to cumulate overall imports originating in all these

---

1.   *Standardised Multiphase Motors* (Bulgaria, Czechoslovakia, GDR, Hungary, USSR, Poland, Romania) OJ L53 27.1.80 p15; *Louvre Doors* (Malaysia, Singapore) OJ L135 22.5.81 p33.

countries[1]. In coming to its decision, the EC Commission will take into account the comparability of the imported products in terms of their physical characteristics, the volumes imported, price levels and the degree of competition with similar Community products[2].

In *Polyester Yarn*[3], the EC Commission, having considered these factors, held that between 1986-87 the volume of imports from all the countries had increased. In these circumstances, there should be cumulation. On the other hand, in *Synthetic Fibres of Polyester*[4], the United States contended that their products should be viewed in isolation from those of the other countries under investigation. It argued that the volume of exports was small, their market share had fallen and the quality of the product exported differed from the exports of other countries. The EC Commission held that all imports except those of the American producers should be cumulated.

3.4.2.1.1 The volume of dumped imports

Under this heading the EC Commission normally examines the increase in the volume of the dumped imports in the Community and also the market share they attain. Unlike the investigation to determine whether or not dumping has taken place, which usually covers a period of less than a year[5], the EC Commission views the effect of the volume of dumped imports over the preceding few years[6]. Generally speaking, this is the reason for the small number of decided cases which refer to the increase in the volume of dumped imports[7]. Normally they refer to the increase in the total volume of imports.

---

1. A similar power exists under the United States rules, see 19 USC s1677 (7)(c)(iv) as amended by s1330 Omnibus Trade and Competitiveness Act 1988.
2. *Synthetic Fibres of Polyester* (Mexico, Romania, Turkey, Taiwan, USA, Yugoslavia) OJ L151 17.6.88 p47; *Glutamic Acid and its Salts* (Taiwan, Thailand, Indonesia, Republic of Korea) OJ L56 3.3.90 p23.
3. OJ L151 17.6.88 p39. See also *Glutamic Acid and its Salts*, above; *Methenamine* (Hexamethylenetetramine) (Poland, Hungary, Bulgaria, Romania, Yugoslavia, Czechoslovakia) OJ L104 24.4.90 p14; *Photo Albums* (South Korea, Hong Kong) OJ L138 31.5.90 p48; *Audio Cassettes in Tapes* (Japan, Hong Kong, Republic of Korea) OJ L313 13.11.90 p5; *Small Screen Colour TV Receivers* (China, Hong Kong) OJ L14 19.1.91 p31; *Artificial Corundum* (USSR, Poland, China, Hungary, Brazil, Yugoslavia, Czechoslovakia) OJ L275 2.10.91 p27.
4. OJ L151 17.6.88 p47; see also *Tungsten Carbide* (China, Republic of Korea) OJ L83 30.3.90 p36; *Audio Tapes in Cassettes* (Japan, Hong Kong, Republic of Korea) OJ L119 14.5.90 p35 (imports from Hong Kong not cumulated); *Dihydrostreptomycin* (Japan, China) OJ L187 13.7.91 p23 (no cumulation); *Cotton Yarn* (Brazil, Egypt, Turkey, India, Thailand) OJ L271 27.9.91 p17 (imports from India not cumulated).
5. See article 7(1)(c).
6. Eg *Electronic Scales* (Japan) OJ L275 16.10.85 p5 (imports rose from 4167 units in 1980 to 8315 units in 1982, 11, 605 units in 1983 and 10, 222 units in first half of 1984); *Paint, Distemper, Varnish and Similar Brushes* (China) OJ L79 22.3.89 p24. (In 1980 imports amounted to 10 million pieces, in 1986 to 33 million pieces, in 1987 to 46 million pieces and in 1988 to 31 million pieces - equivalent to 62 million pieces per annum); *Thermal Paper* (Japan) OJ L270 26.9.91 p15 (imports rose from 1725 tonnes in 1987 to 23,750 tonnes in the first six months of 1990, an increase of 1276%).
7. Eg *Paraxylene* (USA, Puerto Rico, Virgin Islands) OJ L158 16.6.81 p7, approximately 80% of the total imports were made at dumped prices. Increase in the volume of dumped imports, eg *Mechanical Wrist Watches* (USSR) OJ L11 16.1.82 p14.

For the most part, the EC Commission considers the increase in the volume of dumped imports and the market share they attain in relation to the Community as a whole, though on a few occasions it considered these in relation to specific Member States[1]. In the majority of cases, the increase in the volume of dumped imports is represented by an increase in absolute volume[2].

3.4.2.1.2 The prices of the dumped imports

A finding of price undercutting has been made in virtually all cases. It is an essential prerequisite to a finding of injury and the imposition of an anti-dumping duty, since no duty can be imposed if the export price is at existing price levels in the Community[3].

A finding of price undercutting as high as 68% has been made by the EC Commission[4]. In some cases the EC Commission found that undercutting persisted even though the Community producers reduced their prices in order to meet the competition and preserve their market share[5]. In determining whether or not price undercutting is taking place, the EC Commission will compare the exporters' and Community producers' weighted average selling prices, free of all rebates and taxes and calculated on the basis of sales to the first unrelated customer[6]. Where the product in question is comprised of a range of models, the EC Commission will select those models which are comparable with Community models and which are sold in sufficient quantities[7]. In some cases the EC Commission has employed outside experts to carry out the analysis of price undercutting. In *Photocopiers*, the EC Commission, in order to facilitate a more comprehensive analysis of price undercutting, entered into a contract with a German Market Research agency, Info-Markt, to undertake a technical study of model comparisons on the German market. It concluded that undercutting took the form not just of lower prices but also of more highly featured machines being sold at prices at or even below those of the Community producers[8].

---

1.   Market share attained eg *Chromium Sulphate* (Yugoslavia) OJ L205 3.8.85 p12 (Italy most affected).

2.   Eg *Polystyrene* (Spain) OJ L97 4.4.85 p30 average annual rate of increase in imports of around 100% over 1980-84 period.

3.   See the Opinion of Advocate General VerLoren van Themaat in Joined Cases 239/82 and 275/82 *Allied Corporation and Ors v EC Commission* [1984] ECR 1005 at 1037.

4.   *Audio Cassettes in Tapes* (Japan, Hong Kong, Republic of Korea) OJ L313 13.11.90 p5.

5.   *Polyester Yarn* (USA) OJ L231 2.9.80 p5.

6.   See for example *Ballbearings* (Thailand) OJ L152 16.6.90 p24, *Thermal Paper* (Japan) OJ L270 26.9.91 p15.

7.   Eg : *Small Screen Colour TV Receivers* (Hong Kong, China) OJ L14 19.1.91 p31 (selected only 10 and 14 inch models as they accounted for more than 50% of sales of comparable models of the Community producers in the markets concerned).

8.   OJ L54 24.2.87 p12. See also *Dot Matrix Printers* (Japan) OJ L317 24.11.88 p33. The analysis of price-undercutting was based on an Ernst & Whinney Conseil Study.

3.4.2.1.3 Consequent impact on Community industry

Under this heading the Community authorities consider the effects of the dumped imports on the overall performance of the Community producers of the like product. The factors listed in article 4(2)(c) are merely a guide and are by no means exhaustive[1]. Further, the Community authorities do not have to consider all the factors in article 4(2)(c) but only those which provide a sufficient basis for forming a judgment[2].

An analysis of the impact of dumped imports on Community industry generally begins with a reference to their effect on the Community production of the like product. In most cases, the fall in production will be quite evident, though in one case the EC Commission held that a fall in production of 2% had an impact on Community industry[3]. In some cases it has referred to the fact that the effect on production was so severe that it ceased either temporarily or completely[4]. Closely interrelated with the fall in production is the resultant under-utilisation of capacity[5] and the accumulation of unsold stocks[6].

In addition to these, the EC Commission normally considers how the dumped imports have affected the share of the market held by the Community producers. In the majority of cases they have had quite a marked effect[7]. However, in a number of other cases a small decrease has been held by the EC Commission to have had an impact on Community industry[8]. A corollary to the reduction in the market share is a fall in sales[9]. On a number of occasions, the EC Commission has noted that the detrimental effect caused by a fall in sales would have been greater but for

---

1.   *Paraxylene* (Puerto Rico, USA, Virgin Islands) OJ L158 16.6.81 p7, referred to orders lost by Community producers; *Orthoxylene* (Pureto Rico, USA) OJ L141 27.5.81 p7, referred to cancellation of contracts; *Electronic Typewriters* (Japan) OJ L335 22.12.84 p43, referred to the fact that research and development investment was threatened.
2.   Joined Cases 277 and 300/85 *Canon Inc v EC Council* [1988] ECR 5731 at 5808 para 56 of judgment.
3.   *Paraformaldehyde* (Spain) OJ L282 26.10.84 p58.
4.   *Ferro-Chromium* (Sweden, South Africa) OJ L165 22.6.78 p20 (production was ceased temporarily) : *Copper Sulphate* (Poland, Bulgaria, Hungary, Spain) OJ L275 18.10.84 p12 (fall of 40%); *Glutamic Acid and its Salts* (Thailand, Taiwan, Indonesia, Republic of Korea) OJ L56 3.3.90 p23 (temporary closure of one Community producer and also a fall in production at the works of the other producers).
5.   Eg *UREA* (Austria, Hungary, Malaysia, Romania, USA, Venezuela) OJ L235 25.8.88 p5; *EPROMs* (Japan) OJ L65 12.3.91 p1.
6.   Eg *Copper Sulphate* (Yugoslavia) OJ L308 4.11.82 p7; *Chromium Sulphate* (Yugoslavia) OJ L205 3.8.85 p12; *Glass* (Bulgaria, Romania, Turkey, Yugoslavia, Hungary, Czechoslovakia) OJ L51 28.2.86 p73; *Potassium Permanganate* (China) OJ L138 3.6.88 p1; *EPROMs* (Japan) OJ L65 12.3.91 p1.
7.   Eg *Glass* (Czechoslovakia, Turkey, Romania, Yugoslavia, Hungary, Bulgaria) OJ L51 28.2.86 p73 (decrease of 41.9%); *Linear Tungsten Halogen Lamps* (Japan) OJ L188 20.7.90 p10 (market share fell from 57-29%).
8.   Eg *Glycine* (Japan) OJ L107 18.4.85 p8 (decrease of 2.3%).
9.   Eg *Glass* (Czechoslovakia, Turkey, Romania, Yugoslavia, Hungary, Bulgaria) OJ L51 28.2.86 p73 (fall of 70%). At the other end of the spectrum : *Non-alloyed Unwrought Aluminium* (USSR, Norway, Yugoslavia, Surinam) OJ L57 28.2.84 p19 (only a fall of 4%).

the fact that the producer increased his sales outside the Community. This meant a reduction in profits because products were sold at lower prices[1].

One of the most important factors is the depression of prices[2] or the prevention of price increases which otherwise would have occurred. Frequently, the EC Commission refers to the fact that prices have failed to develop in line with production costs, resulting in these costs not being covered[3]. The overall picture is usually one of a fall in profits with an associated fall in employment.

In *Electronic Typewriters*, the EC Commission noted that apart from the fall in profits, profitability had reached a level where there was little or no investment in research and development facilities, vital for the future of the industry[4]. This was also a factor referred to by the EC Commission in *Photocopiers*. It noted that not only would there be insufficient resources devoted to research and development, but Community producers would either have to postpone or abandon the launching of new models[5].

As regards the effect on employment, this normally takes the form of a reduction in working hours[6], the absence of new orders[7] or plant closures[8].

3.4.2.2 Material retardation
Article 4(1) of Regulation 2423/88 also provides that a determination of injury may be made where the dumped imports are materially retarding the establishment of Community industry[9]. This term is not defined in the regulation and, up until very recently, it had not been resorted to by the Community authorities.

---

1. Eg *Chromium Sulphate* (Yugoslavia) OJ L205 3.8.85 p12.
2. See *Video Cassette Recorders* (Japan) OJ L240 31.8.88 p5. The sharp and accelerating price depression for video cassette recorders coincided with the appearance of the exporters in question on the Community market. The European producers were forced to follow in order to maintain a foothold in the market; see also *Glutamic Acid and its Salts* (Thailand, Taiwan, Indonesia, Republic of Korea) OJ L56 3.3.90 p23; *Ferro Silicon* (Brazil) OJ L111 3.5.91 p1; *Cotton Yarn* (Brazil, Egypt, Turkey, India, Thailand) OJ L271 27.9.91 p17.
3. Eg *Vinyl Acetate Monomer* (Canada) OJ L57 28.2.84 p17.
4. OJ L335 22.12.84 p43.
5. OJ L239 26.8.86 p5.
6. *Louvre Doors* (Taiwan) OJ L158 16.6.81 p5.
7. *Herbicide* (Romania) OJ L44 21.2.79 p8.
8. *Roller Chains for Cycles* (China, USSR) OJ L217 14.8.85 p7; *Glutamic Acid and its Salts* (Thailand, Taiwan, Indonesia, Republic of Korea) OJ L56 3.3.90 p23.
9. Until recently, the US authorities were permitted only to examine the negative effects of dumped imports on established industry (19 USC, s 1677 (7)). By virtue of s1328 of the Omnibus Trade and Competitiveness Act 1988 they may consider the effects of the dumped imports on the establishment of new industry.

In *DRAMs*[1], however, the EC Commission, in determining whether injury had been caused to the complainant industry, had to consider whether the complainant industry was established. If this was not the case then it had to consider whether it had been materially retarded. As far as it was concerned, the decisive factor in determining establishment was the existence of commercial production. The EC Commission noted that Community industry had all the necessary production facilities, equipment, technical know-how and that it had produced DRAMs though not on a commercial basis.

On the assumption that the complainant industry was not yet an established industry, the EC Commission noted the following :

— The three complainant companies had made detailed plans on investment, production, costs, marketing and strict timing schedules with a view to commercial DRAM production in the Community. It noted that funds were available to implement these plans. All three companies had acquired the most advanced technical know-how necessary for DRAM production, very costly new facilities were built and state of the art machinery acquired and installed. Prior to the investigation period, several hundred million Ecus had been spent. In these circumstances, these three companies had made a serious commitment to start commercial production of DRAMs. This was confirmed by the fact that two of the companies successfully produced one mega bit DRAMs.

— Due to low prices, two of the companies delayed the start of mass production. The third company temporarily abandoned its DRAM project.

— All three companies suffered heavy financial losses as a result of the delay or abandonment of mass production. There was no return or a smaller return on investment and two of the companies had to lay off staff.

Taking into account all these factors, the EC Commission held that Community industry had been materially retarded.

---

1.   OJ L20 25.1.90 p5.

3.4.2.3 Threatening to cause material injury

Article 4(1) further provides that a determination of injury may be made where the dumped imports are threatening to cause material injury. Article 4(3) Regulation 2423/88 states that a determination of threat of injury may only be made where a situation is likely to develop into actual injury. It then provides that account may be taken of the rate of increase in the dumped imports[1]; the export capacity already in existence in the country of origin or that which will be operational in the foreseeable future[2]; and the likelihood that such exports will be exported to the Community[3]. In the United States, the competent authorities are also entitled to take into account as part of their test of threat of material injury, dumping by the same party of the same class or kind of merchandise in other GATT member markets[4].

In the case of *Small Screen Colour Televisions*[5], the EC Commission considered that there was a threat of increased injury to Community industry from Korean exports in the future, in view of the availability of a large production capacity. This, it noted, was out of proportion to the size of the domestic market - the capacity of twenty-five million tubes per year corresponded to one-third of the world's consumption. In addition, the Korean companies had been installed in the United States for some time, with the result that it was no longer capable of absorbing the huge volumes involved, leading them to turn for expansion to the Community.

On the other hand, in *Photocopiers*, the EC Commission, guided by the factors in article 4(3), decided there was no threat of injury from the imports of a certain model of copier from the end of the reference period. It concluded that there was little evidence that such copiers made in Japan had increased their share of the market rapidly since the end of the reference period. Furthermore, there was no evidence regarding the export capacity of the exporter for the copier in question[6].

---

1. Eg *Methylamine, Dimethylamine, Trimethylamine* (GDR, Romania) OJ L238 15.8.82 p35; *Vinyl Acetate Monomer* (Canada) OJ L57 28.2.84 p17: *Binder and Baler Twine* (Brazil) OJ L34 5.2.87 p55.
2. Eg *Barium Chloride* (China, GDR) OJ L228 20.8.83 p28; *Electronic Typewriters* (Japan) OJ L335 22.12.84 p43; *Herbicide* (Romania) OJ L26 30.1.88 p107; *Small Screen Colour Televisions* (Republic of Korea) OJ L314 28.10.89 p1; *Ferro Silicon* (Brazil) OJ L111 3.5.91 p1.
3. Eg *Methylamine, Dimethylamine, Trimethylamine* (GDR, Romania) OJ L238 13.8.82 p35; *Barium Chloride* (GDR) OJ L228 20.8.83 p28; *Vinyl Acetate Monomer* (Canada) OJ L58 29.2.84 p17; *Electronic Typewriters* (Japan) OJ L335 22.12.84 p43; *Synthetic Fibres of Polyester* (GDR, Romania, Turkey, Yugoslavia) OJ L103 15.4.87 p38; *Small Screen Colour Televisions* (Republic of Korea) OJ L314 28.10.89 p1; *Ferro Silicon* (Brazil) OJ L111 3.5.91 p1.
4. Section 1329, Omnibus Trade and Competitiveness Act 1988.
5. OJ L314 28.10.89 p1.
6. OJ L54 24.2.87 p12; see also *Synthetic Fibres of Polyester* (GDR, Romania, Turkey, Yugoslavia) OJ L103 15.4.87 p38; *Mica* (Japan) OJ L284 3.10.89 p45; *Dense Sodium Carbonate* (USA) OJ L283 16.10.90 p38.

3.4.3   Is there a "causal link" between the dumped imports and the injury to Community industry?

Article 4(1) states that :

"A determination of injury shall be made only if the dumped or subsidised imports are, through the effects of dumping or subsidisation, causing injury ..."

This causality test, taken from the Anti-dumping Code concluded at the Tokyo Round of Multilateral Trade Negotiations in 1979, is much more lenient than its predecessor in article 4(1) of Regulation 459/68[1]. It stated that a determination of injury could only be made if the dumped imports were the principal cause of such injury[2].

The Community authorities have recently held that article 4(1) should not be interpreted narrowly. In *Dot Matrix Printers*[3], the EC Commission had concluded that dumped imports had caused injury to Community industry. The exporters argued, however, that the EC Commission had failed to show specific injurious effects of the dumped imports on each of the complainant producers. The EC Council contended that such an approach would in most cases be impossible and would render Regulation 2423/88 unworkable. It referred to the decision of the Court of Justice in *Technointorg v EC Commission and EC Council*[4] where it was held that :

"It should also be borne in mind that where, as in this case, the dumped products come from different countries, it is in principle necessary to assess the combined effects of such imports. It is consistent with the objectives of Regulation 2176/84 that Community authorities should be able to examine the effect on Community industry of all such imports and consequently take appropriate action against all exporters, even if the volume of each individual exporter's exports is relatively small."[5]

Article 4(1) also stipulates that :

"Injuries caused by other factors, such as volume and prices of imports which are not dumped or subsidised, or contraction in demand, which, individually or in combination, also adversely affect the Community industry must not be attributed to the dumped or subsidised imports."

---

1.   OJ L93 16.4.68 p1. See footnote 5, p43 above.
2.   This was taken directly from article 3(c) of the Anti-dumping Code concluded at the Kennedy Round of Multilateral Trade Negotiations in 1967; reproduced in GATT 1968, GATT 15th supp. BISD 1966-7 at p14.
3.   OJ L317 24.11.88 p33.
4 .   Joined Cases 294/86 and 77/87 [1988] ECR 6077.
5.   Ibid at 6116 para 41 of judgment.

These, however, are only guidelines with the result that the list is not exhaustive[1]. For example, the EC Commission has referred to other factors in the decided cases to date : exchange rate fluctuations[2], miscalculations regarding investment[3], decrease in exports from the Community[4], substitution by other products[5], competition among Community producers[6] and environmental problems[7] to name a few. On the other hand, in *Large Electrolytic Aluminium Capacitors*[8], some of the Japanese exporters sought to argue that the Community producers had been inflicting injury on themselves by importing the dumped product from Japan. The EC Commission took the view that this was not self-inflicted injury so that this did not constitute "other factors" within the meaning of article 4(1).

By far the most important factors considered are the volume and prices of other non-dumped imports. In one case, the EC Commission concluded that the fall in imports from other sources benefited the dumped imports more than Community production[9]. In another case, the EC Commission rejected the exporter's argument that injury was caused by imports from other countries. It noted that, with the exception of the German Democratic Republic, these imports declined in line with the fall in demand[10].

The EC Commission has also referred to the changes in the pattern of consumption as an important factor in considering causality[11]. In *Paraformaldehyde*, the EC Commission found that whilst consumption in the Community had dropped, the market share of the imported products increased. It concluded that the decline in consumption affected the Community producers more than the imported products[12]. The EC Commission noted in *Photocopiers* that whereas the market share held by other exporters remained around 1%, that held by the Community producers fell from 19% to 15%, whilst consumption increased by 100%[13].

---

1.   Article 3(4) of the GATT Anti-dumping Code refers to the following : changes in the pattern of consumption, trade restrictive practices of and competition between foreign and domestic producers, developments in the technology and the export performance and productivity of the domestic industry.

2.   Eg *Upright Pianos* (USSR) OJ L101 16.4.82 p30.

3.   Eg *Dicumyl Peroxide* (Japan) OJ L203 27.7.83 p13; *Photocopiers* (Japan) OJ L239 26.8.86 p5.

4.   Eg. *Cycle Chains* (Taiwan) OJ L312 13.11.76 p41.

5.   Eg *Mechanical Wrist Watches* (USSR) OJ L11 16.1.82 p4; *Hardboard* (Switzerland, Yugoslavia, Argentina) OJ L157 12.6.86 p61.

6.   Eg *Textured Polyester Fabrics* (USA) OJ L133 20.5.81 p17; *Freezers* (USSR, GDR, Yugoslavia) OJ L259 11.9.86 p14.

7.   *Asbestos Cement Pipes* (Turkey) OJ L209 31.7.91 p37.

8.   OJ L152 4.6.92 p22.

9.   See *Electronic Scales* (Japan) OJ L80 24.3.84 p9.

10.   See *Shovels* (Brazil) OJ L231 29.8.84 p29.

11.   See *Electronic Typewriters* (Japan) OJ L335 22.12.84 p43; *Glass Mirrors* (South Africa) OJ L36 8.2.85 p10.

12.   OJ L282 26.10.84 p58.

13.   OJ L239 26.8.86 p5; see also *Denim* (Turkey, Indonesia, Hong Kong, Macao) OJ L222 17.8.90 p50.

3.5   Community interests

Even though it has been established that dumping exists and, as a result, injury has occurred, a further condition has to be satisfied before duties can be imposed. The Community authorities must show that it is in the interests of the Community to impose such duties[1]. This concept is peculiar to the Community. Neither article VI of the GATT nor the Anti-dumping Code refer to the need to take into account the interests of others who may be affected by the imposition of duties such as consumers and processors.

From the decided cases to date, the Community authorities tend to give more weight to the interests of the complainant industry than that of the processors or consumers. For example, in *Electronic Typewriters*, the Community authorities held that it was in the Community's overriding interest to maintain the stability of the industry. They contended that in the long term it was in the consumers' interest to have a viable Community industry which would compete with and offer an alternative to imports[2]. On the other hand, in *Photo Albums*, the Community authorities took the view that consumer interest took precedence over the interests of the Community industry. It limited protective measures to two categories of photo albums. With respect to the other category, it noted that the Community industry would be unable to meet demand[3].

In a number of cases, the consumers have argued that it would be in the interests of the Community for imports to continue, since this would give them another source of supply and would increase the competition among the suppliers[4]. The EC Commission normally rejects this argument, stating that if the Community producers were to disappear from the market, this would mean a dependence on an external source of supply, something which is not in the interests of the Community[5].

Since the effect of an anti-dumping duty is to raise the price of the product, users and processors have argued in a number of cases that their competitiveness will decrease[6]. In *Sensitised Paper*, it was argued that the increase in price could not be passed on either by the photo-finishing laboratories or the dealers to the consumers

---

1.   Articles 11(1), 12(1), Council Regulation (EEC) 2423/88.
2.   OJ L163 22.6.85 p1.
3.   OJ L138 31.5.90 p48.
4.   Eg *Sodium Carbonate* (USA) OJ L317 13.11.82 p5; *Kraftliner* (USSR, USA, Sweden, Austria, Finland, Canada, Portugal) OJ L64 10.3.83 p25; *Sodium Carbonate* (USA) OJ L206 2.8.84 p15.
5.   Eg *Natural Magnesite* (China) OJ L371 30.12.82 p21.
6.   Eg *Methylamine, Dimethylamine, Trimethylamine* (GDR, Romania) OJ L238 13.8.82 p35; *PVC Resin Compounds* (Czechoslovakia, GDR, Romania, Hungary) OJ L274 24.9.82 p15; *Orthoxylene* (Puerto Rico, USA) OJ L101 20.4.83 pOJ L101 20.4.83 p4.

thereby resulting in losses for them. The EC Commission rejected this, contending that since only one quarter of the total cost of colour print was attributable to the cost of sensitised paper, a moderate increase in the price of this product would have a minor impact on the cost for the consumer[1]. Furthermore, as the EC Commission pointed out in *Dot Matrix Printers*, the price advantages which buyers previously enjoyed originated from unfair business practices[2].

In *UREA*[3], the importers argued that it was not in the Community interest to take protective measures against Malaysia. They argued that this was in conflict with the Community's general policy of increasing commercial co-operation with ASEAN countries. The EC Commission noted that, although it was in the interests of the Community to maintain good relations with ASEAN countries, the maintenance of free trading systems implied that sales did not take place at dumped prices. The Community would be acting in a discriminatory manner if it took protective measures against exporters in some countries which sold at dumped prices in the Community, but not against exporters in other countries which were engaged in the same practices. Furthermore, neither international law nor Community law prevents the imposition of anti-dumping duties where it has been established that injury has been caused despite the existence of regional quantitative limits[4].

In some cases, the Community authorities have decided that it is in the Community interest to adopt protective measures without fully eliminating injury. For example, in *Glycine* it was held that in view of the competitive situation and structure in the Community market characterised by the presence essentially of one Community producer and two non-Community firms, it was considered in the interests of the Community to take protective measures without fully eliminating the injury[5]. The concept was also used in *Unwrought Nickel* to limit the amount of duty imposed[6]. There was a genuine fear in this case that the goods from the Soviet

---

1.   OJ L124 11.5.84 p45; see also *Potassium Permanganate* (Czechoslovakia) OJ L42 16.2.90 p1; *Ballbearings* (Japan, Singapore) OJ L256 27.4.90 p1 *Small Screen Colour TV Receivers* (China, Hong Kong) OJ L14 19.1.91 p31; *Ferro Silicon* (Brazil) OJ L111 3.5.91 p1.

2.   OJ L130 26.5.88 p12; OJ L317 24.11.88 p33; see also *Daisy Wheel Printers* (Japan) OJ L177 8.7.88 p1.

3.   OJ L235 25.8.88 p5.

4.   *Woven Polyolefin Sacks* (China) OJ L187 19.7.90 p36; *Espadrilles* (China) OJ L365 28.12.90 p25.

5.   OJ L218 15.8.85 p11.

6.   OJ L159 17.6.83 p43. See also Van Bael and Bellis "International Trade Law and Practice of the European Community - EEC Anti-dumping and Other Trade Protection Laws" (1985) at p89 who contend that "it may be questioned whether the Community interest criterion is at all relevant for the determination of the level of duty. It would seem to result form the wording of articles 11(1) and 12(1) of the Regulation that "Community interests" come into play only to determine whether "intervention" is called for but that once a decision to intervene has been made, the level of the duty must be fixed exclusively on the basis of the dumping and injury findings". Cf Opinion of Advocate General VerLoren van Themaat in Joined Cases 239 and 275/82 *Allied Corporation v EC Council and EC Commission* [1985] ECR 1005 where he developed a theory that the amount of the duties should not exceed the level required by the Community interest.

Union would be displaced from the market thereby opening the way for other low priced products from other third countries[1].

Finally, on a number of occasions the Community authorities have not adopted any protective measures since they considered this was in the best interests of the Community[2].

3.6   Protective measures

The protective measures that can be taken under Regulation 2423/88 are :

    3.6.1   Anti-dumping duties

    3.6.2   Undertakings.

3.6.1   Anti-dumping duties

Such duties can either be provisional[3] or definitive[4]. They apply in general to future imports of the product, with the result that if the duty collected exceeds the dumping margin, then the only remedy available to the exporter is to apply for a refund[5].

Article 13 of Regulation 2423/88 lays down a number of general points in relation to anti-dumping duties. First, the duties are to be imposed by regulation[6]. Second, the rate of duty will normally conform to the margin of dumping. However, article 13(3) gives the Community authorities the discretion to impose a lesser duty if the lesser amount would be sufficient to eliminate injury[7]. No such rule exists in the United States' Anti-dumping Rules where an anti-dumping duty must always equal the margin of dumping thereby resulting inevitably in over protection. The duty may take the form of an ad valorem duty, ie a percentage of the import price[8],

---

1.   Ibid.
2.   *Furfural* (Dominican Republic, China, Spain) OJ L189 11.7.81 p57; *Codeine* (Czechoslovakia, Hungary, Poland, Yugoslavia) OJ L16 20.1.83 p30; *Acrylonitrile* (USA) OJ L101 20.4.83 p29; *Non-alloyed Unwrought Aluminium* (USSR, Norway, Yugoslavia, Surinam) OJ L57 28.2.84 p19; *Tube and Pipe Fittings* (Japan, Taiwan, Brazil, Yugoslavia) OJ L313 8.11.86 p20.
3.   Article 11, Regulation 2423/88.
4.   Article 12, Regulation 2423/88.
5.   Article 16, Regulation 2423/88.
6.   In the case of provisional duties this is a Commission regulation, and for definitive duties, a Council regulation. A regulation is defined in article 189 of the EEC Treaty in this way : "[a regulation] shall have general application. It shall be binding in its entirety and directly applicable in all Member States".
7.   See *Photocopiers* (Japan) OJ L54 24.2.87 p12; *Oxalic Acid* (South Korea, Taiwan) OJ L72 18.3.88 p15.
8.   Eg *Glass Mirrors* (South Africa) OJ L36 8.2.85 p10 (rate of duty was 17.5%); *Clogs* (Sweden) OJ L32 7.2.86 p1 (rate of duty was 7%); *Copper Sulphate* (Yugoslavia) OJ L113 30.4.86 p4 (rate of duty was 27%); *Paint, Distemper, Varnish and Similar Brushes* (China) OJ L272 4.10.88 p16

or a variable duty, ie the difference between a floor price and the import price[1], or it could be a specific duty, ie a fixed amount[2]. The Court has held that the Community authorities have a wide discretion in deciding the appropriate type of duty in each case to afford the most effective defence against dumped imports[3]. Third, Regulation 2423/88 provides that anti-dumping duties shall be neither imposed nor increased with retroactive effect[4]. There are two exceptions to this general rule, however. Anti-dumping duties may be imposed on products which were entered for consumption not more than 90 days prior to the imposition of provisional duties where :

— there is a history of dumping which caused injury or where the importer was, or should have been, aware that the exporter practises dumping and that such dumping would cause injury, and

— the injury is caused by sporadic dumping, ie massive dumped imports of a product in a relatively short period, to such an extent that, in order to preclude it recurring, it appears necessary to impose an anti-dumping duty retroactively on those imports, or

— an undertaking has been violated[5].

In three cases, the EC Commission has had to consider whether, pursuant to article 13(4)(b) of Regulation 2423/88, the imposition of anti-dumping duties with retroactive effect was warranted[6]. In *Mercury*, the EC Council confirmed the EC Commission's finding that this was a case of sporadic dumping, but it did not consider it necessary to impose an anti-dumping duty with retroactive effect on these imports. It took into account that imports from the USSR during the ninety days preceding the importation of the provisional duty were negligible[7]. Fourth, the duty must be imposed on a non-discriminatory basis where the product is imported into the Community from more than one country[8]. Finally, the regulation stipulates that no product shall be subject to both anti-dumping and countervailing duties for the purpose of dealing with the same situation arising from dumping or

---

(rate of duty was 69%); *Pure Silk Typewriter Ribbons* (China) OJ L174 7.7.90 p27. Rate of duty was 24.6%.

1.   Eg *Copper Sulphate* (Czechoslovakia, USSR) OJ L274 7.10.83 p1; *Vinyl Acetate Monomer* (Canada) OJ L198 28.7.90 p57; *Espadrilles* (China) OJ L365 28.12.90 p25.

2.   Eg *Sodium Carbonate* (USA) OJ L317 13.11.82 p5; *Silicon Metal* (China) OJ L198 28.7.90 p57.

3.   Case 189/88 *Cartorobica SpA v Ministero delle Finanze dello Stato* [1990] ECR 1269 at paras 24 and 25 of judgment.

4.   Article 13(4). Note the position with regard to article 13(11), Council Regulation (EEC) 2423/88. See section 3.8 below.

5.   See article 13(4)(b)(i) and (iii), Council Regulation (EEC) 2423/88.

6.   *UREA* (Czechoslovakia, GDR, Kuwait, Libya, USSR, Saudi Arabia, Trinidad and Tobago, Yugoslavia) OJ C34 12.2.87 p3; *Mercury* (USSR) OJ C67 22.3.86 p3; *Video Cassette Tapes* (South Korea, Hong Kong) OJ L174 22.6.89 p1. Note the Department of Commerce in the United States has applied duties retroactively in 17 cases (see Vermulst "Anti-dumping Law and Practice in the United States and the European Community" (1987) at p97).

7.   OJ L346 10.12.87 p27.

8.   Article 13(5), Council Regulation (EEC) 2423/88

the granting of a subsidy[1]. This provision was considered by the Community authorities in *Ballbearings*. They were required to determine whether an anti-dumping duty could be imposed in addition to a countervailing duty without double counting. In order to do so, they were required to examine the impact of the countervailable subsidies on normal value and export price. They concluded that the elimination of the subsidies in question by a countervailing duty had no effect on the dumping margin. In these circumstances, it was appropriate to impose an anti-dumping duty in addition to the countervailing duty[2].

3.6.2 Undertakings

The injurious effects of dumping may also be eliminated with the acceptance by the EC Commission of a price undertaking, in which case the investigation is brought to an end without the imposition of anti-dumping duties[3].

The decision whether or not to accept the undertaking is that of the EC Commission subject, when appropriate, to the powers of the EC Council and review by the Court. In *Minebea v EC Council*[4] the EC Commission suggested that the Court should be slow to interfere with the decision of whether an undertaking should be accepted on the grounds that this has been made on purely pragmatic, practical and administrative grounds and in the light of the EC Commission's manpower and workload, and not on grounds of principle. The Court held that there was no provision in Regulation 2176/84 which compelled the institutions to accept an undertaking offered. It was clear from article 10 of that regulation that it was for the institutions in the exercise of their discretionary power to determine whether such undertakings were acceptable[5].

Neither the GATT Anti-dumping Code nor the regulation itself specify what conditions have to be fulfilled for the undertaking to be acceptable. Some idea of the necessary conditions may be obtained by considering the reasons given for rejecting price undertakings. In a number of cases, the undertaking was found unacceptable because, in view of its special features, its implementation could not have been adequately monitored[6]. The EC Commission has also rejected undertakings on the ground that the price increase was not sufficient to eliminate

---

1. Article 13(9), Council Regulation (EEC) 2423/88; see *Seamless Steel Tubes* (Spain) OJ L165 23.6.81 p27.
2. OJ L152 16.6.90 p24 ; OJ L281 12.10.90 p1.
3. Article 10(1), Council Regulation (EEC) 2423/88.
4. Case 260/84 [1987] ECR 2049.
5. Ibid at 2011, para 48 of judgment. See also Joined Cases 133 and 150/87 *Nashua Corpn v EC Commission and EC Council* [1990] ECR 719.
6. Eg *Sodium Carbonate* (USA) OJ L206 2.8.84 p15; *Small Screen Colour TV Receivers* (China, Hong Kong) OJ L14 19.1.91 p31; *Cotton Yarns* (Brazil, Thailand, Egypt, India, Turkey) OJ OJ L82 27.3.92 p1.

the injury[1]. In one case, it rejected the undertaking because of the non-existence in the country of origin of a similar procedure[2]. Where there has been a breach of a previous undertaking, a new undertaking will usually be rejected[3].

Undertakings have the advantage that the investigation is terminated in a friendly manner. For the exporter, it means that the price increase will accrue to him and not to the Community, which would be the case if duties were imposed. Undertakings, furthermore, are highly flexible and they save on administrative cost and time. On the other hand, they do have certain drawbacks. First and foremost, they are very often difficult to draft so as to prevent their circumvention. Second, in a small number of cases they have proved to be difficult to monitor and supervise, eg the ballbearing industry[4]. Third, as a corollary of the above, undertakings require compliance, which is not the case for anti-dumping duties. Lastly, there are no sanctions for breach of the undertaking except that duties may be imposed retroactively in terms of article 13(4)(b).

Between 1980 and 1983, 50% of all anti-dumping proceedings were terminated by undertakings. However, this policy has been reversed, as the Community authorities strive to bring about more transparency to anti-dumping proceedings. This change is reflected in the Community authorities' attitude towards the acceptance of undertakings in relation to potential exporters. In *Sodium Carbonate*, the EC Council concluded that, in general, undertakings from potential exporters should not be accepted on the following grounds :

(a) it is difficult to determine an appropriate export price for a company that has not exported to the Community;

(b) it is difficult or impossible to determine the volume of any possible future exports and the impact they would have on the Community;

(c) an anti-dumping investigation should, in the interests of all parties, be conducted expeditiously[5].

---

1.   Eg *Electronic Scales* (Japan) OJ L275 16.10.85 p5.
2.   Eg *Vinyl Acetate Monomer* (Canada) OJ L170 29.6.84 p70.
3.   Eg *Hardboard* (Czechoslovakia, Poland, Sweden) OJ L361 24.12.83 p6.
4.   See *Ballbearings* (Miniature) (Japan, Singapore) OJ L193 21.7.84 p1.
5.   OJ L311 29.11.84 p26; see also *Electronic Typewriters* OJ L335 22.12.84 p43; *Hydraulic Excavators* (Japan) OJ L63 2.3.85 p13.

Finally, the regulation provides that where an undertaking has been withdrawn[1] or where it has been violated[2], the EC Commission can, if it considers it to be in the interests of the Community, apply provisional anti-dumping duties on the basis of facts established before the acceptance of the undertaking[3].

3.7   The dumping of components

If a component is sold in the ordinary course of trade to independent buyers in both the exporting country and the importing country, an anti-dumping duty may be imposed on it if the conditions for doing so are fulfilled. In this way, the component is treated in the same manner as any other product that has been dumped.

Over the past few years, it has been the practice of exporters, in particular the Japanese who face anti-dumping duties imposed on products that have been dumped, to circumvent those duties by setting up so-called "screwdriver" assembly plants in the Community. These plants produce the same product but rely heavily on cheap imported components. The existing anti-dumping rules would not permit an anti-dumping duty to be imposed on such a component, since no finding of dumping has been or could be made, merely because a finding of dumping has been made in respect of the complete product. For this reason, the EC Council adopted Regulation 1761/87[4] which provided the Community authorities with the means, if certain conditions were fulfilled, of imposing duties on such components. In the United States, Section 1321 of the Omnibus Trade and Competitiveness Act 1988 gives the competent authorities the power to prevent circumvention of duties by permitting them to extend duties to include later developed versions of that product, products that are altered in minor respects from the product originally investigated, parts of the product that are imported from the country under investigation and assembled or finished in the United States and products assembled in third countries from parts or components from the country originally under investigation.

Regulation 1761/87 was incorporated into article 13(10) of Regulation 2423/88. It provides that definitive anti-dumping duties may be imposed by way of derogation from the second sentence of paragraph (4)(a) which states that anti-dumping duties shall *neither be imposed nor increased with retroactive effect*[5].

---

1.   See for example *Sodium Carbonate* (Bulgaria) OJ L246 29.8.81 p14; *Fibre Building Board.* (Czechoslovakia) OJ L241 31.8.83 p9.
2.   See for example *Hardboard* (USSR) OJ L61 2.3.84 p21; *Copper Sulphate* (Yugoslavia) OJ L296 8.11.85 p26.
3.   Article 10(6), Regulation 2423/88. See also *Paint, Distemper, Varnish and Similar Brushes* (China) OJ L272 4.10.88 p16.
4.   OJ L167 26.6.87 p9.
5.   Emphasis added.

Such duties are only to be imposed on products that are introduced into the commerce of the Community after having been assembled or produced in the Community where three criteria are fulfilled[1]. First, the assembly or production has to be carried out by a party which is related or associated to any of the manufacturers whose exports of the like product are subject to a definitive anti-dumping duty. In *Electronic Scales* the EC Commission found that TEC (UK) Ltd was a subsidiary of TEC (Japan) and that TEC-Keylard had substantial capital links and close economic and commercial links with TEC (Japan)[2]. In *Electronic Typewriters*, Silver Reed International (Europe) Ltd contended that it should not be included in the investigation because the assembly was not carried out by Silver Reed but by Astec Europe Ltd. The EC Commission held, however, that they were in essence those of Silver Reed. It noted that Astec Europe Ltd simply assembled the parts of typewriters which were delivered to its premises by Silver Reed. Furthermore, these assembled typewriters were exclusively sold on the Community market by the Silver Reed Group which bore all the costs between importation of the parts and the sale of the finished product[3]. Second, the assembly or production operation has to be started or substantially increased after the opening of the anti-dumping investigation[4]. Third, the value of the parts or materials used in the assembly or production operation and originating in the country of exportation of the product subject to the anti-dumping duty must exceed the value of all other parts or materials used by at least 50%. This is usually determined on the basis of the company's purchase prices of the parts or materials when delivered to the factories in the Community, ie on an into-factory duty paid basis[5]. However, in *Electronic Typewriters*, some companies' purchase prices were not used since they did not adequately reflect their true value. In these cases, the sales prices were adjusted in order to ensure that they reflected the companies' purchase prices of those parts manufactured by third parties on the totality of the companies' own production costs plus the sales, general and administrative expenses incurred by them and shown in their public accounts[6]. In *Dot Matrix Printers*[7], the value supplied to the EC Commission for some parts corresponded to the parent company's purchase price on the Japanese market, adjusted to include costs of transport and customs duties paid. The EC Commission rejected this method of determining the value of the products on the ground that it did not reflect a reasonable profit and did not include selling expenses for the selling company. It considered that such

1.   Article 13(10)(a), Council Regulation (EEC) 2176/84. Proceedings have been initiated in six cases. *Electronic Typewriters* (Japan) OJ C235 1.9.87 p2; *Electronic Scales* (Japan) OJ C235 1.9.87 p2; *Hydraulic Excavators* (Japan) OJ C285 23.10.87 p4; *Plain Paper Photocopiers* (Japan) OJ C44 17.2.88 p3; *Ballbearings* (Japan) OJ C150 8.6.88 p4; *Dot Matrix Printers* (Japan) OJ L291 10.10.89 p52.
2.   OJ L101 20.4.88 p1.
3.   OJ L101 20.4.88 p4.
4.   *Electronic Typewriters* (Japan) OJ L101 20.4.88 p4; *Electronic Scales* (Japan) OJ L101 20.4.88 p1; *Plain Paper Photocopiers* (Japan) OJ L284 19.10.88 p60; *Dot Matrix Printers* (Japan) OJ L291 10.10.89 p52.
5.   *Electronic Scales* (Japan) OJ L101 20.4.88 p1; *Dot Matrix Printers* (Japan) OJ L291 10.10.89 p52.
6.   OJ L101 20.4.88 p4, (Canon, Kyshu Matsushita, Sharp).
7.   OJ L291 10.10.89 p52.

prices appeared to be influenced by a relationship between the seller (the parent company) and the buyer (the subsidiary company).

In determining the value of the parts, some exporters have argued that certain sub-assembled items of significant value used for some models were of Community origin and therefore should not be included. In *Electronic Scales* the product was assembled in the Community by an independent Community producer from parts imported from Japan and from parts manufactured by this producer itself. The EC Commission held that this constituted a substantial process or operation as required by article 5 of Regulation 802/68 and was therefore of Community origin[1].

In *Electronic Typewriters,* Canon contended that the product was assembled in the Community entirely from parts imported from Japan by a subsidiary company of a Japanese producer which normally manufactured them in Japan and supplied Canon's mother company there. On the other hand, Sharp Corporation sold all the individual parts to an unrelated Community company which carried out the sub-assembly and subsequently sold to Sharp. In both cases, the EC Commission held that the assembly was of a basic and unsubstantial nature compared with the manufacture of the components which was performed in Japan. The parts were therefore not of Community origin[2].

In a recent case[3], the Court stated the tests which require to be fulfilled in order to satisfy article 5 of Regulation 802/68. It held that the assembly in Taiwan of electronic typewriters from Japanese components would be the last substantial process and would thereby confer Taiwanese origin, if technically and in the light of the definition of the goods, the assembly represented the decisive production stage. If that test was inconclusive then it could be supplemented by a test of applicable value. The Court went on to hold that even if it passed those tests - under article 5 of Regulation 802/68 - the assembly could still be disregarded if it was transferred solely in order to circumvent anti-dumping duties on typewriters from Japan.

The EC Commission noted in two cases[4] that for some companies the weighted average value of the Japanese parts produced by them for all models did not exceed 50%. In such cases, anti-dumping duties could not be extended to such parts.

---

1.   OJ L101 20.4.88 p1.
2.   OJ L101 20.4.88 p4 para 11.
3.   Case 26/88 *Brother International GmbH v Hauptzollamt Giessen* [1989] ECR 4253.
4.   Ibid, *Photocopiers* (Japan) OJ L34/28 1990.

The regulation states that each case is to be decided on its merits and that account should be taken of the circumstances of each case. In doing so, it provides a number of factors that can be taken into consideration, namely : the variable costs incurred in the assembly or production operation, research and development carried out and the technology applied within the Community[1].

3.7.1   Source of the parts

The EC Commission noted in *Electronic Typewriters* that, with the exception of Brother, the nature of the parts sourced in the Community was relatively simple and that they were of a low value. Those parts of a higher technological value were imported from Japan. It concluded that there were few attempts substantially to change the sourcing pattern[2].

3.7.2   Research and development

In *Electronic Scales*, TEC (UK) Ltd claimed that its technical manager visited TEC Japan's factory for two months in order to receive training. It also claimed that its decision to set up a Research and Development Centre should be taken into consideration. The EC Commission held that these did not constitute research and development[3]. Likewise in *Electronic Typewriters*, the EC Commission was not convinced that the activities of Sharp's "Creative Center Europe" or its "Engineering Research Office" related to *Electronic Typewriters*[4].

3.7.3   Effects on employment

In both *Electronic Scales* and *Electronic Typewriters*, the EC Commission found that only a limited number of jobs had been created. It noted that the companies investigated carried out simple assembly operations of a very basic nature, whereas the Community producers normally had an integrated in-depth production which required more personnel. The net result of these assembly operations was that there had been a fall in sales by Community producers leading inevitably to a loss of employment in the Community[5].

---

1.   Article 13(10)(a), Council Regulation (EEC) 2423/88.
2.   OJ L101 20.4.88 p4; see also *Plain Paper Photocopiers* (Japan) OJ L284 3.10.89 p60.
3.   OJ L101 20.4.88 p1.
4.   OJ L101 20.4.88 p4.
5.   OJ L101 20.4.88 p1; OJ L101 20.4.88 p4; see also *Plain Paper Photocopiers* (Japan) OJ L284 3.10.89 p60.

3.7.4 Protective measures

When components are found to have been dumped, protective measures can take one of two forms :

>   3.7.4.1   Application of an anti-dumping duty;

>   3.7.4.2   Acceptance of an undertaking.

3.7.4.1 Application of an anti-dumping duty

The regulation provides that the rate of duty shall be that applicable to the manufacturer in the country of origin of the like product subject to an anti-dumping duty to which the party in the Community carrying out the assembly or production is related or associated[1]. In both *Electronic Scales* and *Electronic Typewriters*, the EC Commission held that the rate of duty was to be calculated in a manner to ensure that it corresponded to the percentage rate of duty applicable to the exporters in question, on a CIF value of the parts from Japan as established for the investigation period[2]. In *Dot Matrix Printers*, a flat rate duty on two companies was imposed[3].

3.7.4.2 Acceptance of an undertaking

The provisions of Regulation 2423/88 relating to undertakings apply also to the dumping of components[4]. In *Electronic Typewriters*, the EC Commission accepted an undertaking from Kyushu Matsushita (UK) which removed the conditions justifying the extension of anti-dumping duties to typewriters assembled in the Community[5].

3.7.5 Protective measures unnecessary

Where the value of the Japanese parts for the product in question is less than 60%, the EC Commission has concluded that the adoption of protective measures are unnecessary and has consequently terminated proceedings[6].

---

1.   Article 13(10)(c).
2.   OJ L101 20.4.88 p1; OJ L101 20.4.88 p4.
3.   OJ L291 10.10.89 p52.
4.   Article 13(10)(d).
5.   OJ L128 21.5.88 p39. See also *Plain Paper Photocopiers* (Japan) OJ L284 3.10.89 p60; OJ L355 23.12.88 p66; OJ L340 23.11.89 p25; *Dot Matrix Printers* (Japan) OJ L291 10.10.89 p52; OJ L 340 23.11.89 p25.
6.   *Hydraulic Excavators* (Japan) OJ L101 20.4.88 p24 - Komatsu (UK) Ltd; *Electronic Typewriters* (Japan) OJ L101 20.4.88 p26 - Brother; *Electronic Scales* (Japan) OJ L101 20.4.88 p28 - TEC Keylard; cf *Plain Paper Photocopiers* (Japan) OJ L126 9.5.89 p83 the weighted average value of parts and materials of Japanese origin incorporated in all models assembled or produced by Sharp Manufacturing (UK) Limited was more than 60%.

3.7.6   Application of anti-dumping laws to components : some problems

This provision was shrouded in controversy even before it was adopted and it is likely that this will continue[1]. It is possible to pinpoint three main problem areas :

3.7.6.1   The legality of the new law in relation to the GATT and the Anti-dumping Code

3.7.6.2   Administration of the new law

3.7.6.3   Effect on foreign investment.

3.7.6.1   The legality of the new law in relation to the GATT and the Anti-dumping Code

Neither the provisions of article VI nor the articles of the Anti-dumping Code suggest in any way that an anti-dumping duty can be imposed on components as such[2]. Furthermore, article VI and the Code constitute exceptions to the rules of the GATT. For this reason, they should be interpreted narrowly. It would be contrary to such an interpretation to hold that they allow duties to be imposed on components which are not necessarily sold elsewhere and which, if sold separately, had not been dumped merely because there had been dumping of the completed product of which the components form a part[3].

In introducing an anti-dumping law which produces such a result, the Community authorities have increased the protectionist and anti-competitive effect of the anti-dumping rules. The European Community has long argued that its approach differed from the United States in respect of article VI and the GATT Code in that it remained within the parameters of the GATT whereas the United States felt able to ignore such constraints. The position now, however, is that the Community seems to be shifting away from respecting the spirit of the GATT. It appears concerned more with maximising the benefits that accrue from interpreting the rules to its own advantage[4].

The Japanese, at whom this new law was chiefly aimed, filed a complaint with the GATT. In October 1988 they requested the GATT Council to establish a panel to examine their complaint. They argued that the anti-dumping measures adopted by the Community authorities on the basis of this provision were contrary to the GATT in that they had been applied without the requirements in article VI having been fulfilled and further, they were aimed at obliging firms to use parts originating in

---

1.   Following a GATT panel report concluding that the provision was contrary to the GATT and the GATT anti-dumping code, the EC Commission decided to avoid invoking the provision, at least until the question of selective safeguard measures has been decided at the Uruguay Round of Trade Negotiations.
2.   See Chapter 2 above.
3.   Private conversation with Commission officials.
4.   Financial Times, 22 June 1987.

the Community. The Community authorities, on the other hand, contended that this new law was fully justified by article XX(d) which permitted a party to adopt measures necessary to secure compliance with laws or regulations which were not inconsistent with the GATT rules[1].

The Panel, in its report in March 1990[2], concluded that article 13(10) of Regulation 2423/88 was contrary to article III. It provided further that article XX(d) could not be invoked by the Community authorities to justify this law. The Panel recommended that the Community bring its application of article 13(10) Regulation 2423/88 into conformity with its obligations under the GATT. The Community has advised that it will not oppose the adoption of the report, but that the implementation of its recommendations will have to wait until the results of the Uruguay Round are clear with respect to the circumvention of anti-dumping duties[3]. In the meantime, however, the EC Commission took the decision to stop initiating parts cases under article 13(10) and instead to initiate them under the normal anti-dumping rules.

Recently, the EC Commission initiated its first case under the normal rules against parts of products already the subject of anti-dumping measures[4]. In so doing it has shown that it will not hesitate to take action against exporters who circumvent anti-dumping duties. There may well be problems with the determination of dumping, injury and customs classification. The results of the EC Commission's investigation are awaited with interest.

3.7.6.2 Administration of the law relating to components

The administration of this law was also not free from problems. Even before it came into force, the average time taken for an investigation over the past few years, from the moment of initiation until the imposition of duties, doubled from four and a half months to almost nine. Two main reasons could explain this. First, the nature of the products involved in the complaint had changed from simple products in small markets, such as fertilisers, to technologically complicated items, such as electronic typewriters, photocopiers, semi-conductors, etc. In economic and monetary terms these are very important. Second, until recently only twenty-six officials were employed by the EC Commission to investigate complaints of dumping made by European manufacturers, compared with one hundred and ten in the United States for the same purpose. This new provision was in effect creating another and even more complex type of investigation, which meant more work for the already over-stretched officials and longer delays.

---

1.   Focus, GATT Newsletter 58 (1988).
2.   GATT BISD 36th supp. 1990.
3.   Focus : GATT Newsletters 70 and 71 (1990).
4.   *Parts for Pocket Lighters* (Japan) OJ C202 1.8.91 p4.

3.7.6.3   Effect on foreign investment

This new provision affected Japan more than any other third country owing to its many related or associated firms in the Community manufacturing products comprised mainly of Japanese components. The Japanese at the time declared that the new provision would slow down investment in the European Community. Some Japanese producers contended that the reason imported components were used was due to the fact that European components were not always reliable[1]. Upon the adoption of the new provision, Commissioner De Clercq, then Commissioner for External Relations, declared that the provision would only discourage assembly plants with small added value and very limited, if any, transfer of technology.

3.8   Power to increase anti-dumping duties

Regulation 2423/88 introduced another new provision which permits the Community authorities to impose an additional duty where an exporter bears the existing duty in whole or in part instead of increasing its prices[2]. In theory, it was possible under the old regulation to deal with such a situation by initiating a review under article 14. In practice, however, due to the EC Commission's limited resources, the procedure was never invoked. The new procedure was introduced in order to provide the authorities with a less onerous procedure. It can also be viewed as a means of discouraging exporters from bearing the duties, and instead raising their prices.

Like article 13(10) referred to above, this provision is also shrouded in controversy, given that its legality is also questionable in the light of the GATT and the GATT Anti-dumping Code. First, the provision does not require a full investigation to be carried out. It is drafted in such terms that the EC Commission does not intend to look at the exporter's position, merely that of the importer, thereby ignoring normal value. Second, failure to increase prices will be regarded as evidence that the exporter has borne the duties, even though it may be the case that a decrease in the costs of production in the exporting country is the reason for the lack of price increase. It will be interesting to see if the Japanese raise the matter in the GATT as they did with article 13(10).

The article viewed as a whole appears to be aimed primarily at related importers. For example, it provides that :

"Insofar as the results of the investigation show that the absence of a price increase by an amount corresponding to the anti-dumping duty is not due to a

---

1.   Financial Times, 24 June 1987.
2.   Article 13(11)(a).

reduction in the costs and/or profits of the importer for the product concerned then the absence of such price increase shall be considered as an indicator that the anti-dumping duty has been borne by the exporter."[1]

Such a provision, as Norall points out[2], makes no sense in the case of an unrelated importer. He notes, however, that it seems the provision does apply in the case of a related importer but there is no clear indication of what proof is necessary.

The regulation provides that there has to be a complaint from an interested party before the procedure can be set in motion[3]. The EC Commission has initiated three investigations under this provision to date[4] and issued one decision. In *Silicon Metal*[5], the EC Commission had received a complaint from the Liaison Committee of Ferroalloy Industries in the Community on behalf of all Community producers of silicon metal, alleging that all or part of the definitive anti-dumping duty imposed on imports of silicon metal from China had been borne by the exporters.

The EC Commission, having considered that the complaint contained sufficient evidence of dumping, initiated an investigation under article 13(11). None of the exporters and only three of the importers concerned, accounting for a small fraction of the total imports, co-operated.

The EC Commission compared the prices found in the original reference period with those found in the period immediately after the imposition of the provisional duty up to the publication of the notice of initiation of the investigation under article 13(11).

Given the extent of the non-co-operation, the EC Commission based its findings on the facts available under article 7(7)(b) of Regulation 2423/88. It considered it appropriate to make an assessment of the import price (prior to payment of customs duties and anti-dumping duty) on the basis of customs statistics. It concluded that this price fell considerably following the imposition of the provisional duty, thereby indicating that the exporters had borne either completely or partially the

---

1.   Article 13(11)(c).
2.   Norall "The New Amendments to the EC's Basic Anti-dumping Regulation" 26 CMLRev pp83-101.
3.   Article 13(11)(b).
4.   *Woven Polyolefin Bags* (China) OJ C157 15.6.91 p5; *Compact Disc Players* (Japan, Republic of Korea) OJ C174 5.7.91 p15. (Note : this has been turned into a full scale review OJ C334 28.12.91 p8); *Silicon Metal* (China) OJ C273 18.10.91 p20.
5.   OJ L170 25.6.92 p1.

anti-dumping duty. The amount of the absorption of the duty expressed as a percentage of the anti-dumping duty was 178%.

If the EC Commission finds that the anti-dumping duty has been borne in whole or in part by an exporter, then the duty can be imposed in accordance with articles 11 and 12[1]. This implies that the duty can be increased at either the provisional or definitive stage. In *Silicon Metal* [2], the EC Council, having concluded that the definitive duty had been borne in full by the exporter, imposed an additional duty for the same amount namely, 198 Ecu per tonne.

The imposition of an additional duty is not automatic where the Community authorities make a finding that an exporter has borne the duty. On the contrary, it has to be in the interests of the Community[3]. In *Silicon Metal*, the EC Council observed that it was in the Community's interest to restore the effect of the definitive duty, given that the absorption of the duty by the exporter prevents the removal of the injury suffered by Community industry[4].

The regulation also provides that the duties may be applied retroactively[5]. It appears to be the case that the idea of retroactivity in this context is the same as that which applies in respect of article 13(10). If this is so, then retroactive application can be justified in circumstances other than those specified in article 13(4). In theory, this would mean that additional duties could be applied from the moment that the exporter bore the duty. It is unlikely, however, that this would extend back beyond the adoption date of the new regulation.

Finally, owing to the problems associated with proof and the fact that the EC Commission's resources are limited, it is unlikely that the EC Commission will extend the new provision to article 13(10)[6].

3.9   Procedure

3.9.1   Initiation

The initiation of an anti-dumping investigation is preceded by the lodging of a written complaint. According to the regulation a complaint may be made by "any

---

1.   Article 13(11)(b).
2.   Above.
3.   Article 13(11)(b).
4.   Above.
5.   Article 13(11)(b).
6.   See Norall "The New Amendments to the EC's Basic Anti-dumping Regulation" 26 CMLRev at pp98-100.

natural or legal person, or any association not having legal personality, acting on behalf of a Community industry which considers itself injured or threatened by dumped or subsidised imports"[1]. In the United States, on the other hand, an investigation may be initiated by the Department of Commerce on its own initiative[2] or at the request of the affected domestic industry[3]. They are usually brought by European manufacturers' associations, for example "The European Council of Chemical Manufacturers' Federation (CEFIC)"[4], but it can be brought by an individual company so long as it states that it is acting on behalf of a Community industry[5]. A complaint may be lodged in the United States by a number of interested parties namely, a manufacturer, producer or wholesaler of the like product; a certified or recognised union or group of workers representative of an industry engaged in the manufacture, production, or wholesale of the like product; a trade or business association, a majority of whose members manufacture, produce or wholesale the like product; and finally, an association, the majority of whose members are the interested parties referred to above[6].

A complaint may be withdrawn[7]. In such a case, the proceedings may be terminated unless such action would not be in the interests of the Community[8]. This has occurred on five occasions. In *Paracetemol*, the main Community producer withdrew its support but the EC Commission decided to continue the investigation[9]. However, in *Television Image and Sound Recorders or Reproducers*, the complaint was withdrawn after the Japanese offered a unilateral restraint agreement, whereupon the EC Commission decided that it was not in the Community's interest to continue[10]. In *Portland Cement*, the EC Commission continued with its investigation even though a Greek manufacturer, representing approximately 11% of the total Community production, withdrew its support from the complaint, on the ground that the allegation of dumped imports was not likely to cause it injury[11]. The complainants in *NPK Fertilisers* withdrew their complaint on two grounds, namely, as regards the companies located in Hungary, Poland and Romania, in view of new developments in these markets, and as regards the companies located in Yugoslavia, in view of the need for a non-discriminatory approach[12]. In *Audio*

---

1.   Article 5(1).
2.   Section 732(a)(1), Tariff Act 1930 (as amended), 19 USC s1673(a)(1) (1985).
3.   Section 732(b)-(d), Tariff Act 1930 (as amended), 19 USC s1673a(b) - (d) (1985).
4.   Eg *Styrene Monomer* (USA) OJ L42 14.2.81 p14.
5.   Eg *Copper Sulphate* (Yugoslavia) OJ L308 4.11.82 p17; *Welded Wire Mesh* (Yugoslavia) OJ L123 18.5.91 p54.
6.   See footnote 3 above.
7.   Article 5(4), Council Regulation (EEC) 2423/88. See *Cellular Mobile Radio Telephones* (Canada, Hong Kong, Japan) OJ L362 30.12.88 p59.
8.   Ibid.
9.   OJ L236 11.8.82 p23.
10.   OJ L86 31.3.83 p23.
11.   OJ L202 25.7.86 p43.
12.   OJ L188 20.7.90 p63.

Tapes on Reels, the complainants withdrew their complaint owing to the adoption of a definitive duty on audio tapes in cassettes[1].

The regulation stipulates that "the complaint shall contain sufficient evidence of the existence of dumping and the injury resulting therefrom"[2]. The usual practice, however, is for the EC Commission to send the complainants a questionnaire which specifies the information required. The regulation does not provide a time limit by which the EC Commission must determine whether the complaint contains sufficient information to justify the initiation of an investigation. On the other hand, under the American system, a "sufficiency determination" must be issued by the Department of Commerce within 20 working days after the date on which the complaint is lodged[3]. If both the authorities in the Community and the United States prefer not to provide any information regarding the complaint prior to the formal initiation, the deadline provided for in the American system avoids or limits the possibility of leaks[4]. If the EC Commission decides that there is sufficient evidence to justify initiating a proceeding, after consultation with the Advisory Committee, it announces this in the Official Journal of the European Communities[5].

3.9.2 Investigation

All interested parties are invited by way of a questionnaire to supply information to the EC Commission within a specified time, usually 30 days (which may be extended by seven days)[6].

Basically, the EC Commission is seeking to determine whether there are sufficient domestic sales in the country of origin to allow it to calculate the normal value using the domestic prices and so enable it to establish whether dumping is taking place. Once the information is received it can be verified, if necessary, by carrying out investigations in the countries involved. This can only be done, however, with the consent of the firms involved and if the governments in those countries raise no objections[7].

1.　　　OJ L28 4.2.92 p25.
2.　　　Article 5(2).
3.　　　19 CFR s353.37 (a).
4.　　　See Vermulst "Anti-dumping Law and Practice in the United States and the European Community" (1987) at p314.
5.　　　Article 7(1)(a), Council Regulation (EEC) 2423/88.
6.　　　See Van Bael and Bellis "EEC Anti-dumping and other Trade Protection Laws" (1985), p110 at footnote 4.
7.　　　Article 7(2)(b), Council Regulation (EEC) 2423/88.

Unlike the field of competition law, an anti-dumping investigation does not give rise to any question of extraterritoriality[1]. Extraterritoriality refers simply to the application of laws outside the territory of the state which enacted them. Controversy arises, however, where this concept is used in another sense. This is where a state extends its jurisdiction, on the basis of an effect on its own territory, to conduct outside the limits of that state (ie the "effects doctrine").

International law permits a state to legislate as it wishes on virtually any matter whatsoever so long as that state respects the sovereignty of other states in the execution of its laws. What is objected to with respect to the "effects doctrine" is that it occurs wholly outside the territory of the state where its effects are felt.

The problems associated with extraterritoriality do not arise in anti-dumping investigations for a number of reasons. First, the investigating country does not claim a right to investigate any matter whatsoever on the territory of another state. The investigation is carried out on the basis of co-operation. The Community authorities can, however, proceed on the basis of the facts available[2] where the country alleged to have dumped refuses to co-operate. It is further provided that where any interested party or third party has supplied the EC Commission with false or misleading information, it may disregard any such information and disallow any claim to which this refers. It is, however, in the interests of those concerned to co-operate since the EC Commission will very often rely on the complainants' allegations[3]. A similar rule exists in the United States anti-dumping legislation[4]. As *Vermulst*[5] points out, the rule is not limited to information received during the verification, but allows the relevant authority to use the best evidence available in ascertaining the existence of dumping whenever a party or any other person refuses or is unable to produce information requested timeously and in a form required, or otherwise significantly impedes an investigation[6]. Second, both article VI and the GATT Anti-dumping Code permit States to impose duties. Finally, the authorities carrying out the investigation are concerned with the prices at which the goods are sold in the importing country[7].

---

1. See generally Lowe "Extraterritorial Jurisdiction"; an annotated collection of legal materials (1983).
2. Article 7(7)(b), Council Regulation (EEC) 2423/88.
3. Eg *Chromium Sulphate* (Yugoslavia) OJ L205 3.8.85 p12 (the EC Commission used prices quoted in the complaint to determine normal value); *Paratungstate* (China, Korea) OJ L83 30.3.90 p117. (The export price was determined on the basis of a reply to the questionnaire received from one importer and information gathered during inspections at the premises of the two Community importers which imported Ammonium Paratungstate from China during the investigation.)
4. 19 CFR 207.8; 19 CFR 353.52(b).
5. Vermulst "Anti-dumping Law and Practice in the United States and the Europen Community" (1987).
6. Ibid, pp63-64.
7. See Temple Lang "European Community Anti-dumping and Competition Laws : their actual and potential application to EFTA countries" (unpublished).

During the investigation, the interested parties have certain rights. These are access to information "relevant to the defence of their interests and which is not confidential within the meaning of article 8"[1], and a right to be heard[2]. The EC Commission has recently announced that on the request of an interested party, a "hearing officer" will be appointed at the commencement of an investigation. His responsibility will be to hear complaints from interested parties and ensure the proper conduct of the investigation. Such appointments will no doubt increase the transparency of anti-dumping investigations. Their operation in practice will be awaited with interest.

3.9.3   Access to information and confidentiality

Interested parties have the right to inspect, on a written request, any information made available to the EC Commission which is relevant to the defence of their interests and which is not confidential. The Court has held that failure to comply with this procedural requirement will lead to the regulation in question being annulled. In *Timex v EC Council and EC Commission* the Court held that :

> "all non-confidential information, whether supplied by a Community undertaking or an undertaking in a non-member country which has been used by the EC Commission during its investigation and which has had a decisive influence on its decision regarding the anti-dumping duty must be made available to the complainant requesting it."[3]

Furthermore, the regulation provides that the exporters and importers of the product in question may request to be informed of the essential facts and considerations on the basis of which the definitive duties are to be imposed, or the collection of amounts secured by way of provisional duties[4].

All information submitted to the EC Commission is subject to the confidentiality rules. Such information can be used only for the purpose for which it was requested[5]. This rule is important for two reasons. First, it means that the information submitted for an anti-dumping action cannot be passed on to other Directorates-General, eg D.G. IV (Directorate-General for Competition). Second, it is important in securing the co-operation of an analogue country, which is necessary in order to determine the normal value of a product originating in a state trading country. There is no provision for the disclosure of confidential information, unlike the system in the United States, which permits such information to be disclosed to the

---

1.   Article 7(4)(a), Council Regulation (EEC) 2423/88.
2.   Article 7(5) and (6), Council Regulation (EEC) 2423/88.
3.   Case 264/82 [1985] ECR 849 at para 25 of judgment.
4.   Article 7(4)(b).
5.   Article 8(1), Council Regulation (EEC) 2423/88.

lawyer or any other representative of a party to the proceeding under an administrative protective order[1]. Advocate General Darmon in the *Al Jubail* case[2] has advocated that the time is ripe for the Community authorities to adopt a similar system, thereby increasing the transparency of anti-dumping determination and ensuring that all parties to the investigation are in a position to adequately defend their interests.

The regulation defines information as confidential "if its disclosure is likely to have a significantly adverse effect upon the supplier or the source of such information"[3]. For example, in *Thiophen*, the EC Commission held that the information which it received, if published, even in summarised form, would have a significantly adverse effect upon these firms[4].

The regulation allows the EC Commission to disregard the information submitted as confidential where the request for confidentiality is not warranted and the supplier is unwilling either to make it public or to authorise its disclosure in generalised or summary form, or the request for confidentiality is warranted but the supplier is unwilling to submit a non-confidential summary, provided that the information is susceptible of such a summary[5].

Furthermore, the confidentiality rules do not prevent the disclosure of general information by the Community authorities, in particular, the reasons on which decisions taken are based or the evidence relied on by the Community authorities which are necessary to explain those reasons in court proceedings[6]. Such disclosure must take into account the legitimate interests of the parties so as to ensure that their business secrets are not divulged.

3.9.4 The right to be heard

The regulation provides for two types of hearing[7]. First, there is an oral hearing which takes place between one of the parties and Commission representatives[8]. The EC Commission will hear an interested party if it has made a written request

---

1. Section 777, Trade Agreements Act 1979; 19 USC s1677f. As amended by s1332 of the Omnibus Trade and Competitiveness Act 1988.
2. Case 49/88 *Al-Jubail Fertiliser Co (SAMAD) and Saudi Arabian Fertiliser Co v EC Council* [1991] 3 CMLR 377.
3. Article 8(3).
4. OJ L295 21.10.82 p35; see also *Diesel Engines* (Finland, Sweden) OJ L76 22.3.90 p28.
5. Article 8(4). See also *Thiophen* (United States) OJ L295 21.10.82 p35.
6. Order of the Court in Case 236/81 *Celanese Chemical Inc v EC Council and EC Commission* [1982] ECR 1183.
7. The EC Commission has in the past used another type of meeting - A "Disclosure Conference" - this depends on the acquiescence of the parties. Source : private conversation with Commission officials. See *Ballbearings* (Japan) OJ L167 27.6.85 p3.
8. Article 7(5), Council Regulation (EEC) 2423/88.

and can show that it is likely to be affected by the results of the proceeding and that there are particular reasons why it should be heard orally[1]. These meetings tend to be informal with no official record being kept of the proceedings. Some Commission officials would, however, favour a more formal approach to these meetings similar to the system under United States law, where official records are kept. Such records would be of great value should the outcome of the anti-dumping proceedings lead to court action[2]. Second, there is a confrontation meeting which takes place between the complainants and those accused of dumping, with a Commission official presiding[3]. Confrontation meetings are not as common as oral hearings[4]. The regulation states that there is no obligation on any party to attend. This is usually what happens when the EC Commission arranges such a meeting[5], since the issues raised are those at the centre of the dispute and no doubt involve confidential information.

3.9.5 Termination of proceedings

An anti-dumping investigation can be terminated in one of three ways :

3.9.5.1 Termination of proceedings where protective measures are unnecessary;

3.9.5.2 The acceptance of an undertaking;

3.9.5.3 The imposition of anti-dumping duties.

3.9.5.1 Termination of proceedings where protective measures are unnecessary

If, after consultation, it becomes apparent that protective measures are unnecessary, and where the Advisory Committee does not object, the proceedings shall be terminated[6]. This usually occurs where there is no evidence of dumping (or where it is minimal) or where there is no injury to Community industry[7]. If the Advisory Committee objects, the EC Commission can submit a proposal to the EC Council that the proceedings be terminated. The proceedings will stand terminated, if the EC Council acting by qualified majority has not decided otherwise[8].

---

1.   Ibid.
2.   Private conversation with Commission officials.
3.   Article 7(6), Council Regulation (EEC) 2423/88.
4.   Confrontation meeting was arranged and took place in the following cases : *Mechancial Wrist Watches* (USSR) OJ L11 16.1.82 p4. *Decabromodiphenylether* (USA) OJ L319 16.11.82 p16.
5.   See *Barium Chloride* (China) OJ L110 27.4.83 p11; *Outboard Motors* (Japan) OJ L152 10.6.83 p18; *Ferro-chromium* (South Africa) OJ L161 15.6.83 p15; *Nickel* (USSR) OJ L159 17.6.83 p43; *Caravans for Camping* (Yugoslavia) OJ L240 30.8.83 p12; *Sensitised Paper for Colour Photographs* (Japan) OJ L124 11.5.84 p45; *Glycine* (Japan) OJ L207 5.8.85 p85; *Hardboard* (Argentina, Switzerland, Yugoslavia) OJ L157 12.6.86 p61; *Ferro Silicon* (Brazil, USSR) OJ L219 8.8.87p24; *Herbicide* (Romania) OJ L26 30.1.88 p107; *Oxalic Acid* (China, Czechoslovakia) OJ L343 13.12.88 p34.
6.   Article 9(1), Council Regulation (EEC) 2423/88.
7.   See footnote 1, p72 and footnote 1, p73.
8.   Article 9(1), Council Regulation (EEC) 2423/88; see for example *Portland Cement* (GDR, Poland, Yugoslavia) OJ L202 25.7.86 p43; *Artificial Corundum* (USSR, Hungary, Poland, Czechoslovakia, China, Brazil, Yugoslavia) OJ L275 2.10.91 p27.

3.9.5.2 The acceptance of an undertaking

The EC Commission may terminate proceedings if, after consultation, it finds the offering of an undertaking acceptable[1]. Such undertakings are offered by the exporters or producers of the product in question. As such, they are considered on an individual basis. This can be contrasted with the system in the United States which provides for the termination of an investigation on the basis of a public restraint agreement concluded between the United States government and the governments of the country in which the goods are produced. Vermulst argues that whilst such agreements can be objected to on ideological grounds, they have certain practical advantages including, inter alia, less expense in dealing with one party rather than a number of exporters or producers; greater bargaining power on the part of foreign governments; and control of the agreement by the foreign governments[2]. An undertaking may not be offered later than the end of the period during which representations may be made under article 7(4)(c)(iii). The EC Commission may continue the investigation, even if it accepts the undertaking either after consultation or where it is requested to do so by exporters representing a significant percentage of the trade involved[3]. In such a situation, if a no injury determination is made the undertaking lapses[4].

3.9.5.3 The imposition of anti-dumping duties

The Community authorities may impose protective measures which take the form of :

    3.9.5.3.1 Provisional duties;

    3.9.5.3.2 Definitive duties.

3.9.5.3.1 Provisional duties

If, after the preliminary examination, the EC Commission determines that, as a result of dumping, injury has been caused to Community industry, and where it is in the interests of the Community, it may impose a provisional anti-dumping duty[5]. It may do this either by acting on a request of a Member State[6] or alternatively on its own initiative[7]. Owing to the fact that a definitive determination will be made shortly thereafter, at most three months, the EC Commission will normally have verified most of the information before it at the provisional stage. This can be contrasted with the United States, where owing to the fact that the determination of injury and dumping is carried out by the different authorities, the Department of

---

1.   Article 10(1), Council Regulation (EEC) 2423/88.
2.   Vermulst "Anti-dumping Law and Practice in the United States and the European Communities" (1987) pp81-82.
3.   Article 10(4), Council Regulation (EEC) 2423/88.
4.   Ibid.
5.   Article 11(1), Council Regulation (EEC) 2423/88.
6.   Article 11(2)-(3) Council Regulation (EEC) 2423/88.
7.   Article 11(1), Council Regulation (EEC) 2423/88.

Commerce need only be satisfied that it has a reasonable basis to believe or suspect dumping[1].

Even though the EC Commission decides not to impose a duty, this does not rule out the possibility of imposing one at a later date[2]. Provisional duties are valid for four months[3] but they can be extended for a further two months[4] by submitting a proposal to the EC Council not later than one month before the expiry of the period of validity of the provisional duty[5]. This also applies in the case of a proposal for definitive action.

When a duty has been imposed, the product in question cannot enter the Community unless a security for the amount of the duty has been posted[6]. On the expiry of the period of validity, the security shall be released only to the extent that the EC Council has not decided to collect it definitively[7].

3.9.5.3.2   Definitive duties

When it is finally established that the injury has resulted from dumping, and where it is in the Community's interest, a definitive duty may be imposed[8]. Such duties are imposed by the EC Council on a producer-by-producer basis, and it also decides the proportion of the provisional duty that is to be definitively collected. As the duty is imposed on a country-wide basis, in order to avoid circumvention, the EC Council will impose a residual duty for non-co-operating producers or those producers who have not been investigated. This will normally be equivalent to the highest margin found for co-operating producers. In the United States, however, the authorities distinguish between non-co-operating producers and non-investigated producers. The former will be subject to a duty equivalent to the highest dumping margin found, whereas the latter will be subject to a duty equivalent to the weighted average of the margins found for the co-operating producers. As a result, the effect on new market entrants is less draconian. The EC Council usually collects the amount secured by way of provisional duties or those secured by way of provisional duties to a maximum of the duty definitively imposed[9].

1.　　　　Section 733(b) of the Tariff Act 1930, 19 USC s1673b(b).
2.　　　　Article 11(4), Council Regulation (EEC) 2423/88.
3.　　　　Article 11(5), Council Regulation (EEC) 2423/88.
4.　　　　Ibid.
5.　　　　Article 11(6), Council Regulation (EEC) 2423/88.
6.　　　　Article 11(1), Council Regulation (EEC) 2423/88.
7.　　　　Article 11(7), Council Regulation (EEC) 2423/88.
8.　　　　Article 12(1), Council Regulation (EEC) 2423/88.
9.　　　　Eg *Electronic Typewriters* (Japan) OJ L163 22.6.85 p1; *Ballbearings* (Miniature) (Japan, Singapore) OJ L193 21.7.84 p1; *Video Cassette Tapes* (Hong Kong, South Korea) OJ L174 22.6.89 p1.

The EC Commission has proposed to the EC Council the establishment of a new procedure for the imposition of duties. It has suggested that it be given the power to impose not only provisional but also definitive duties. Such a power would be exercised in conjunction with the Anti-dumping Committee. In other words, the EC Commission would send its proposal to impose a definitive duty to the Committee rather than the EC Council. If the Committee does not object, then the EC Commission would impose the definitive duty. If it objects, then a procedure similar to the termination of proceedings, namely a referral to the EC Council for a decision within a prescribed time limit, should apply. In the event that the EC Council does not make a decision, the EC Commission could impose a definitive duty. Such an amendment would be welcomed given that it is the EC Commission who carries out the investigation both at the provisional and definitive stage.

3.10   The review procedure

Regulation 2423/88 provides that the regulation imposing the definitive duties and the decisions to accept undertakings are subject to review[1]. Such a review may be initiated :

(a)   at the request of a Member State;

(b)   on the initiative of the EC Commission; or

(c)   where an interested party so requests and submits evidence of changed circumstances sufficient to justify the need for such a review, provided that at least a year has elapsed since the conclusion of the investigation[2].

With regard to this last category, it would appear that the concept of "changed circumstances" includes an increase in the prices of an exporter who previously dumped, as the aim of article 14 is to bring about an increase in prices, thereby eliminating dumping. Moreover, the lodging of successful refund applications may serve as evidence that the dumping margin has been eliminated or at least lowered[3]. In such circumstances, it would be difficult for the EC Commission in exercising its discretion to reject a review application.

---

1.   Article 14(1).
2.   Ibid.
3.   See for example *Compact Disc Players* (Japan) OJ C173 4.7.91 p3.

In the majority of cases, it is the complainant industry which requests a review[1], as self-initiated reviews by the EC Commission or at the request of the Member States tend to be infrequent. This can be compared with the United States, where the Commerce Department reviews anti-dumping duties once a year[2] in addition to reviews on request owing to "changed circumstances"[3]. Where, after consultation, it becomes apparent that a review is warranted, the investigation shall be reopened in accordance with article 7 where the circumstances so require. The reopening of an investigation does not, however, affect the operation of the measures in question[4]. If, as a result of the review investigation, the measures are to be repealed, annulled or amended, this is the task of the Community institution which was responsible for their introduction[5].

3.11   The "Sunset" procedure

Article 15 of Regulation 2423/88 provides that anti-dumping duties and undertakings lapse after five years from the date on which they entered into force or were last modified or confirmed[6]. As Vermulst[7] notes, this provision ensures that anti-dumping duties or undertakings do not remain in force long beyond the needs of the complaining industry.

It is also stipulated, however, that if an interested party shows that such an expiry would lead again to injury or a threat thereof, the EC Commission shall carry out a review of the measure[8]. In such a situation, the measure shall remain in force pending the outcome of the review[9]. The regulation further provides that, where the initiation of the review has not been published within six months after the end of the relevant five year period, the measure shall lapse at the end of that six month period[10]. Furthermore, the new text of article 15 states that, where anti-dumping duties and undertakings lapse, the EC Commission shall publish a notice to that effect in the Official Journal stating the date of expiry of the measure[11].

---

1.   Eg *Lithium Hydroxide* (USA, USSR) OJ C181 19.7.80 p4; *Sodium Carbonate* (Bulgaria) OJ C220 1.9.81 p2; *Kraftliner* (USA, Austria, Canada, Finland, Portugal) OJ C217 21.8.82 p2; *Herbicide* (Romania) OJ C142 29.5.87 p4. But see for example *Saccharin and its Salts* (China, South Korea, USA) OJ C119 4.5.83 p3 (The American exporter requested a review of its undertaking); *Compact Disc Players* (Japan) OJ C173 4.7.91 p3 (Japanese exporters requested a review).
2.   Section 751(a) of the Tariff Act 1930, 19 USC s1675(a).
3.   Section 751(b) of the Tariff Act 1930, 19 USC s1675(b).
4.   Article 14(2), Council Regulation (EEC) 2423/88.
5.   Article 14(3), Council Regulation (EEC) 2423/88.
6.   This concept was introduced in 1984 under Council Regulation (EEC) 2176/84.
7.   Vermulst "Anti-dumping Law and Practice in the United States and the European Communities" (1987) p331.
8.   Article 15(3). See for example *Paracetamol* (China) OJ C236 2.9.87 p2.
9.   Ibid.
10.   Ibid.
11.   Article 15(6).

The EC Commission has stated[1] that it will on its own initiative review the position of individual exporters (but not all the exporters of the product under consideration) who, because they had been subject to an earlier review, are not eligible for one under the "Sunset provisions".

3.12 Refunds

A definitive duty remains in force for a period of five years[2] unless, as a result of a review, it is amended[3]. However, during this period, a refund can be obtained, if an importer can show that the duty exceeds the actual dumping margin, ie the amount by which the price of the consignment in question is less than the normal value as calculated for the purposes of obtaining the definitive duty[4]. The refund is merely a corrective factor designed to enable the rate of duty fixed by the regulation imposing definitive duties to be adjusted in a particular case. It presupposes that the duty is lawfully collected[5]. Furthermore, article 16 does not permit the validity of the regulation to be challenged or a review of the general findings made during the previous investigations to be requested[6].

Prior to the new text in article 16 of Regulation 2423/88, the EC Commission published a set of guidelines for importers[7] in order to create a greater transparency in deciding whether or not refunds were to be granted. The new text of article 16 codifies the existing practice outlined in the guidelines referred to above and, in particular, the practice of deducting anti-dumping duties as a cost on the export side where the exports sales are made through a sales subsidiary[8]. This practice has recently been condoned by the Court[9].

The regulation provides that all refund calculations shall be made in accordance with the provisions of articles 2 or 3 and shall be based, as far as possible, on the same method applied in the original investigation, in particular, with regard to any application of averaging or sampling techniques[10].

---

1.   Statement to the Working Party on Commercial Questions of the Council of Ministers of 14 June 1988.
2.   See footnote 6, p110.
3.   See section 3.10 above.
4.   Article 16(1), Council Regulation (EEC) 2423/88.
5.   Opinion of Advocate General Darmon in Case 312/84 *Continentale Produkten Gesellschaft v EC Commission* [1987] ECR 841 at 860.
6.   Case 312/84 ibid, at para 12 of judgment.
7.   OJ C266 22.10.86 p2 "Commission notice concerning the reimbursement of anti-dumping duties".
8.   See for example *Vinyl Acetate Monomer* (USA) OJ L240 3.9.90 pp19,21 and 23.
9.   Case C-188/88 *NMB Deutschland et al v EC Commission* (1992) Transcript 10 March 1992.
10.   Article 16(1).

The importer has to submit an application to the EC Commission via the Member State in which the products were released for free circulation. This must be done within three months of the date on which the amount of the definitive duty was determined or the date on which the decision was made to definitively collect the provisional duties[1]. This application has to be forwarded to the EC Commission which then informs the other Member States and produces an opinion on the matter[2]. If the Member States do not object within one month, the EC Commission may act in accordance with the opinion[3]. In all other cases, it shall, after consultation, decide whether and to what extent the application should be granted[4]. If it is granted, the excess amount shall be reimbursed. To date the EC Commission has only published a small number of decisions on the question of refunds[5].

3.13 Special rules and measures

Regulation 2423/88 does not preclude the application of any special rules laid down in agreements concluded between the Community and third countries[6], nor the application of special measures, provided that such action does not run counter to obligations under the GATT[7].

3.14 The differences between the EEC and ECSC anti-dumping rules

The Treaty establishing the European Coal and Steel Community, as its name suggests, covers coal and steel products[8]. Anti-dumping investigations concerning these two products are governed by Commission Decision 2424/88[9] and the rules relating to the substance and procedure of such investigations are by and large the same as those under Regulation 2423/88.

---

1. Article 16(2), Council Regulation (EEC) 2423/88; see *Vinyl Acetate Monomer* (US) OJ L240 3.9.90 pp19, 21 and 23.
2. Ibid.
3. Ibid.
4. Ibid.
5. See *Cotton Yarns* (Turkey) OJ L11 12.1.85 p34; *Glass Textile Fibres* (Czechoslovakia, Japan) OJ L63 2.3.85 p29; *Acrylic Fibres* (USA) OJ L125 11.5.85 p32; *Ballbearings* (Singapore) OJ L148 15.6.88 p26; *Light Sodium Carbonate* (Bulgaria) OJ L60 9.3.90 p14; *Vinyl Acetate Monomer* (USA) OJ L240 3.9.90 pp19, 21 and 23; *Dense Sodium Carbonate* (USA) OJ L47 20.2.91 p9; *Compact Disc Players* (Japan) OJ L104 24.4.91 p44; OJ L143 7.6.91 pp51 and 54, and OJ L151 15.6.91 p86.
6. Article 17(1).
7. Article 17(3); see also *Nuts of Iron or Steel* (Taiwan) OJ C53 28.2.92 p4. These special measures took the form of a special duty of 15%.
8. The Treaty of Paris - the Treaty establishing the European Coal and Steel Community - was signed in 1951. It should be noted that steel products which are the result of manufacturing basic steel products, such as tubes and pipes, are subject to the anti-dumping rules governed by Council Regulation (EEC) 2423/88.
9. OJ L209 2.8.88 p18.

There are, however, two major differences. First, Decision 2424/88 allows the EC Commission to determine normal value by using basic prices. Second, because of the institutional framework under the ECSC Treaty, the EC Commission's powers are much broader than those under the EEC Treaty.

3.14.1 The basic price system

Apart from the methods described earlier for determining normal value[1], Decision 2424/88 allows for the determination of normal value on the basis of "basic prices". It states that :

> "where several suppliers from one or more countries are involved and it is deemed appropriate to establish a basic price system the normal value may be derived from the basic price; however, normal value shall be determined in accordance with the preceding provisions of this article where it becomes apparent that such a method of determination would produce a significantly different result."[2]

Originally, a list of basic prices was compiled by reference to the lowest normal costs in the supplying country or countries where normal conditions of competition prevail[3]. This list is regularly revised by the EC Commission[4]. Generally speaking, in anti-dumping proceedings under Decision 2424/88, basic prices are used by the EC Commission to determine normal value.

3.14.2 The powers of the EC Commission

The institutional framework under the ECSC Treaty is different from that under the EEC Treaty[5]. Under the ECSC Treaty, the EC Commission has the power to take action which, under the EEC Treaty, is within the exclusive competence of the EC Council. The reason for this is that the EC Commission, when it deals with matters involving coal and steel, does so with the decision-making powers that were vested in the High Authority under the ECSC Treaty[6].

---

1. See the methods for determining normal value under Council Regulation (EEC) 2423/88, section 3.3.2 above.
2. Article 6(2)(b), Commission Decision (EEC) 2424/88.
3. See recommendation (ECSC) 3004/77 OJ L352 31.12.77 p13. Article 14 of the ECSC Treaty defines recommendation thus : "[Recommendations]" shall be binding as to the aims to be pursued but shall leave the choice of the appropriate methods for achieving these aims to those to whom the recommendations are addressed".
4. Eg OJ L321 17.11.82 p1.
5. See Chapter 1 above which sets out the institutional framework under both Treaties.
6. As a result of the 1965 Merger Treaty, since 1967 the three Communities (EEC, ECSC, Euratom) have been represented by the one Commission.

With regard to anti-dumping proceedings, the EC Commission has the power not only to impose provisional duties, but also definitive duties[1], and to order the definitive collection of provisional duties[2]. Even though the EC Commission has to consult the Advisory Committee in all instances, it can take decisions without the Committee being able to veto them.

3.14.3   Other minor differences

First, with regard to the question of judicial review[3], appeals can only be made to the Court by Community producers[4] and not by exporters[5]. Secondly, representatives of Directorate General III, which supervises the Community's steel industry, are actively involved in ECSC anti-dumping actions.

PART 2 : COUNTERVAILING MEASURES UNDER REGULATION 2423/88

3.15   Introduction

Countervailing duties provide a defence to the introduction of unfairly low priced imports which take the form of subsidies granted to an exporter by its government. Regulation 2423/88[6] provides that the Community authorities can impose countervailing duties on subsidised imports whose release for free circulation cause injury. This regulation governs anti-subsidy actions for all products except those covered by the ECSC Treaty[7].

The rules with respect to the substance and procedure in anti-subsidy actions are for the most part the same as those for anti-dumping actions. The one major exception, however, is that the Community authorities are not required to determine the normal value and the export price. It is only necessary to establish that there is a subsidy which is causing injury and to determine the amount of that subsidy.

Unlike anti-dumping actions, which are a common occurrence, there have been only a small number of anti-subsidy cases[8]. Various reasons for this state of affairs have been cited by writers who specialise in the field. For example, subsidies are granted

---

1.   Article 12(1), Commission Decision (EEC) 2424/88.
2.   Article 12(1)(a), Commission Decision (EEC) 2424/88.
3.   See Chapters 4, 5 and 6 below.
4.   See Articles 33 and 80 ECSC Treaty.
5.   See Joined Cases 239 and 275/82 *Allied Corpn and Ors v EC Commission* [1984] ECR 1005.
6.   OJ L209 2.8.88 p1.
7.   Commission Decision (EEC) 2424/88 (OJ L209 2.8.88 p18) governs those goods covered by the ECSC Treaty.
8.   See Davey "An analysis of European Communities legislation and practice relating to anti-dumping and countervailing duties" in (ed) B Hawk "Anti Trust and Trade Policy in International Trade" at pp114-115.

by governments, whereas dumping is practised by individual undertakings, with the result that this involves accusing foreign governments of unfair trading practices. Furthermore, anti-subsidy actions are usually initiated at the same time as anti-dumping actions. Normally, this results in the imposition of anti-dumping rather than countervailing duties[1].

Since the rules relating to anti-subsidy actions are virtually the same as those in the anti-dumping actions, only the major differences between the two will be considered here[2].

3.16   The existence of a subsidy

Article 3(1) states that :

"A countervailing duty may be imposed for the purpose of offsetting any subsidy bestowed, directly or indirectly, in the country of origin or export, upon the manufacture, production, export or transport of any product whose release for free circulation in the Community causes injury."

Unfortunately, the regulation does not define what is meant by a subsidy. Rather, it lists a number of export subsidies in an annex to the regulation but stresses that subsidies bestowed on exports include but are not limited to the practices listed[3].

In the majority of cases decided thus far, the subsidies held to be subject to duties have been mainly export subsidies. The EC Commission in *Soya Meal* identified two factors that are crucial in determining whether a subsidy is subject to duties. There has to be government intervention, in other words some charge on the public account, and there has to be a benefit to the recipient with a resultant cost to the exchequer[4].

---

1.   See article 13(9) of Council Regulation (EEC) 2423/88 which states that : "no product shall be subject to both anti-dumping and countervailing duties for the purpose of dealing with one and the same situation arising from dumping or from the granting of any subsidy"; but see *Ballbearings* (Thailand) OJ L152 16.6.90 p24; OJ L281 12.10.90 p1 where countervailing duties were in existence and the EC Commission considered it appropriate to impose anti-dumping duties in addition.

2.   For an analysis of the rules relating to the substance and procedure see the preceding section on the anti-dumping rules.

3.   Article 3(2).

4.   OJ L106 18.4.85 p19; see generally Cuanne and Stanbrook "Dumping and subsidies. The law and procedures governing the imposition of anti-dumping and countervailing duties in the Europen Community" 1983 at pp51-54. In the *Second Fediol Case* (Case 188/85 [1988] ECR 4193) the Court held that article 3 of Council Regulation (EEC) 2176/84 presupposed the grant of an economic advantage through a charge on the public account.

Some of the export subsidies held by the EC Commission to give rise to countervailing duties are as follows :

1. *Credit premiums*, eg in a number of cases the EC Commission held that the excessive remission of tax on industrial products (IPI), where the tax credit which was granted exceeded the amount of tax actually collected at the production stage, constituted an export subsidy[1].

2. *Access to working capital* at lower rates of interest than those obtained on the commercial market[2], or the availability of government loans to obtain working capital[3], were held to be export subsidies.

3. *Concessionary financing for exports.* This occurred where the Banks who offered the finance facility obtained the re-financing at rates lower than the rate of increase in the value of variable treasury bonds[4].

4. *Export credits.* All export rediscount credit programmes and post shipment credit programmes were held to be export subsidies. It was observed that the interest rates applicable were between 36-37%, whereas the interest rates on bonds issued by the government of the exporting country were between 44-58%, thereby constituting a cost to the government[5].

5. *Low interest credits for investment purposes.* An export subsidy was held to exist where it was noted that the interest rates on such credits varied between 33-45% as compared to the interest rates on bonds issued by the government of the exporting country which varied between 44-58%, thereby constituting a cost to the government[6].

6. *Exemption from income tax.* Where the government exempted from income tax, profits made by the soya bean crushers from forward exchange (hedging) transactions on foreign markets, this was held to constitute an export subsidy[7].

7. *Corporate tax exemption.* This was held to constitute an export subsidy where certificates of promotion conditional on all production being exported were issued to companies exempting them from payment of corporate income tax for the eight years following on start up of

1.   *Stainless Steel Bars* (Brazil) OJ L139 5.6.80 p30; *Sheets and Plates of Iron and Steel* (Brazil) OJ L45 17.2.83 p11 (ECSC); *Binder and Baler Twine* (Mexico, Brazil) OJ L34 5.2.87 p55.
2.   Ibid.
3.   *Soya Meal* (Brazil) OJ L106 18.4.85 p19.
4.   Ibid. See also *Binder and Baler Twine* (Mexico, Brazil) OJ L34 5.2.87 p55.
5.   *Polyester Yarns and Fibres* (Turkey) OJ L137 31.5.91 p8.
6.   *Polyester Yarns and Fibres* (Turkey) OJ L137 31.5.91 p8.
7.   Ibid. See also *Binder and Baler Twine* (Mexico, Brazil) OJ L34 5.2.87 p55.

operation[1]. Likewise, an export subsidy was held to exist where companies were exempted from corporate taxation on up to 20% of their export earnings (25% if the exporter did not produce the goods)[2].

8.   *Tax rebate.* This was held to constitute an export subsidy where the exporters received a tax rebate on the export of the finished product designed to offset indirect taxes levied on the finished product and on all prior transactions of the raw material involved in its production[3].

9.   *Customs duty and indirect tax exemption on imports of machinery and essential materials*[4]. This was held to constitute an export subsidy, given that the exemption was contingent on export performance.

10.   *Rebates on electricity rates for exporters*[5].

11.   *Resource utilisation support fund.* This fund was designed to support the utilisation of domestic resources in the products for export. Between 2-4% of the volume of net foreign exchange income corresponding to the exports realised was paid as a premium[6].

The regulation is not limited solely to export subsidies. It does not rule out the possibility of a domestic subsidy giving rise to the imposition of duties[7]. In *Soya Meal*, the EC Commission stipulated that two factors had to be present before such a subsidy could give rise to duties. First, it has to distort competition. Therefore, as long as the impact of such interventions is "general" they do not distort competition. Second, the advantages must be conferred selectively, ie with the aim of helping specific firms[8].

Measures which are regarded as being in the public interest, eg improving the infrastructure, health, education, etc, do not have a distorting effect on competition. Any attempt to call a measure of general nature a subsidy would be absurd, because by ignoring the fact that policies of all modern states imply to

---

1.   *Ballbearings* (Thailand) OJ L152 16.6.90 p59.
2.   *Polyester Yarns* (Turkey) OJ L137 31.5.91 p8.
3.   *Tube and pipe fittings* (Spain) OJ L322 19.11.83 p13; see also *Polyester Fibres & Yarns* (Turkey) OJ L137 31.5.91 p8.
4.   *Ballbearings* (Thailand) OJ L152 16.6.90 p59.
5.   *Ballbearings* (Thailand) OJ L152 16.6.90 p59.
6.   *Polyester Fibres and Yarns* (Turkey) OJ L137 31.5.91 p8.
7.   Article 3(1). See also article 11(3) of the GATT Code on Subsidies and Countervailing Duties (Reproduced in OJ L71 17.3.80 p72).
8.   See OJ L106 18.4.85 p19; see generally Cuanne and Stanbrook "Dumping and subsidies. The law and procedures governing the imposition of anti-dumping and countervailing duties in the European Community" (1983) at pp51-4.

varying degrees some financial intervention of government, it would make large sections of social and economic policy subject to countervailing duties[1].

In *Sheets & Plates of Iron or Steel*, it held that an investment programme which granted duty-free treatment and exemption from tax on imported machinery warranted a countervailing duty[2]. In *Polyester Fibres & Yarns*[3], the EC Commission noted that a number of subsidies constituted domestic or production subsidies and were countervailable. They were as follows :

— *Resource utilisation support programme.* The government provided a cash premium based on the level of the company's own resources used for investment purposes;

— *Incentive premium.* The government granted a cash grant based on the percentage of the value of purchases of locally produced machinery and equipment used.

— *Investment incentive allowance.* The government permitted a tax deduction based on the percentage of total fixed investment.

— *Customs duty exemption.* A complete exemption was granted on the imports of machinery and equipment. By virtue of not having to pay such duties the cost of production was lower.

— *Low interest credit during first three months of production.*

On the other hand, in *Soya Meal*, the EC Commission held that the provision of a flat rate finance for the preparation and storage of soya beans constituted a domestic subsidy, but not such as to give rise to the imposition of a duty, since the loans were generally available[4].

Article 3(4) governs the valuation of the subsidy in question. First, the regulation provides that the exemption of a product from indirect taxes does not constitute a subsidy[5]. Second, the amount of the subsidy is to be determined per unit of the

---

1.   Ibid.
2.   OJ L45 14.2.83 p11 (ECSC).
3.   OJ L137 31.5.91 p8.
4.   OJ L106 18.4.85 p19.
5.   Article 3(3); see also *Tube and Pipe Fittings* (Spain) OJ L103 19.4.86 p4.

subsidised product exported to the Community[1], but the regulation allows for the following deductions to be made, if they are justified :

(a)   application fees or other costs incurred in order to qualify for the subsidy[2].

(b)   export taxes, duties or other charges intended to offset the subsidy[3].

The burden of proving these rests on the party making the claim[4].

Where the subsidy is not granted by reference to quantities manufactured, produced, exported or transported, the amount shall be determined by allocating the value of the subsidy over the appropriate level of production and over a suitable period of time[5]. However, where the subsidy is based upon the acquisition or future acquisition of fixed assets, the value of the subsidy shall be calculated by spreading the subsidy across a period which reflects the normal depreciation of such assets in the industry concerned[6].

Finally, with respect to state trading countries, the amount of the subsidy is to be determined in an "appropriate and not unreasonable manner". This is to be established using the same methods used to determine dumping from state trading countries[7].

As in the case of dumping, where the authorities refuse to supply the EC Commission with the relevant information, the EC Commission will proceed on the basis of the facts available[8].

3.17   Community interests

Where the Community authorities conclude that, as a result of subsidisation, Community industry has been injured, they may impose a countervailing duty, but

---

1.   Article 3(4)(a), Council Regulation (EEC) 2423/88.
2.   Article 3(4)(b)(i).
3.   Article 3(4)(b)(ii).
4.   Article 3(4)(b), Council Regulation (EEC) 2423/88.
5.   Article 3(4)(c), Council Regulation (EEC) 2423/88; see *Ballbearings* (Thailand) OJ L152 16.6.90 p59.
6.   Ibid. Where the assets are non-depreciating, the subsidy shall be valued as an interest-free loan - see *Sheets and Plates of Iron or Steel* (Brazil) OJ L205 29.7.83 p29.
7.   Article 3(4)(d), Council Regulation (EEC) 2423/88. See also section 3.3.2.2.5 above.
8.   Article 7(7)(b), Council Regulation (EEC) 2423/88. See also *Seamless Tubes* (Spain) OJ L196 30.7.80 p34 (here information supplied by one of the complainants was used).

only where it is in the interests of the Community to do so[1]. In *Soya Meal*[2], it held that it was no longer in the interests of the Community to require the collection of a countervailing duty, since the Brazilian Government had stopped granting concessionary financing for exports of soya meal. It held that the position with regard to subsidies can, in this respect, be distinguished from that faced in dumping, where it is essential that account is only taken of the facts and elements which have occurred during the period covered by the investigation. It referred to the fact that a subsidy is granted not by an exporter but by a government, and its introduction or removal normally follows considerations which are different from those which an exporter would take into account. It concluded that the risk of having a subsidy which has been removed in the course of an investigation and subsequently re-introduced is not the same as the subsequent re-appearance of dumping which had stopped during the investigation. This difference, it noted, is reflected in the relevant international rules which distinguish in this respect between anti-dumping and countervailing action.

3.18   Protective measures

The Community authorities can either impose a countervailing duty (provisional[3] or definitive[4]) or they can accept an undertaking from the exporter in question[5].

3.18.1   The imposition of a countervailing duty

For the most part, the rules are the same as those applying to anti-dumping actions[6], therefore only the differences will be considered. First, the regulation provides that the duty should be less if such lesser duty would be adequate to remove the injury[7]. In *Soya Meal*, the EC Commission held that where the benefit to the recipient of the subsidy is less than the cost to the exchequer, a countervailing duty could only reflect the lesser amount[8]. Second, with regard to the question of retroactivity, like anti-dumping duties, a countervailing duty shall be neither imposed nor increased with retroactive effect[9].

---

1.   Articles 11(1), 12(1), Council Regulation (EEC) 2423/88.
2.   OJ L106 18.4.85 p19.
3.   Article 11(1), Council Regulation (EEC) 2423/88.
4.   Article 12(1), Council Regulation (EEC) 2423/88.
5.   Article 10, Council Regulation (EEC) 2423/88.
6.   See generally section 3.6 of Anti-dumping Rules above.
7.   Article 13(3).
8.   OJ L106 18.4.85 p19.
9.   Article 13(4)(a), Council Regulation (EEC) 2423/88. Article 13(4)(b) specifies a number of situations where a countervailing duty may be imposed retroactively. They are as follows :
       (i)   in critical circumstances that injury which is difficult to repair is caused by massive imports in a relatively short period of a product benefiting from export subsidies paid or bestowed inconsistently with the provisions of the GATT and of the Agreement on Interpretation and Application of articles VI, XVI and XXIII of the GATT, and
       (ii)   that it is necessary, in order to preclude the recurrence of such injury, to assess countervailing duties retroactively on these imports;
     (iii) that an undertaking has been violated.

3.18.2 The acceptance of an undertaking

With respect to the acceptance of an undertaking, the rules are similar to those in anti-dumping actions[1]. The regulation states that the EC Commission may accept an undertaking in an anti-subsidy action where :

(i)   the subsidy is eliminated or limited, or where other measures concerning its injurious effects are taken by the government of the country of origin or export[2]; or

(ii)   prices are revised or exports ceased to the extent that the EC Commission is satisfied that the amount of the subsidy or the injurious effects thereof, are eliminated. In the case of subsidisation the consent of the country of origin or export shall be obtained[3].

Thus far there have only been three cases in which the EC Commission has accepted an undertaking[4].

PART 3 : COMMON RULES FOR IMPORTS UNDER REGULATION 288/82

3.19   Introduction

In situations where the importation of goods is not objectionable either because it does not result from dumping or subsidisation, the Community authorities are permitted to adopt protective measures, if the goods in question are imported in such greatly increased quantities and on such terms or conditions as to cause injury or the threat thereof, to the Community producers of the like or directly competing goods[5].

Imports into the European Community from third countries, except for goods from state trading countries[6], China[7] and Cuba[8] are governed by Regulation 288/82[9] (as

---

1.   See generally section 3.6 of the Anti-dumping Rules above.
2.   Article 10(2)(a).
3.   Article 10(2)(b), Council Regulation (EEC) 2423/88.
4.   *Women's Shoes* (Brazil) OJ L327 14.11.81 p39; *Ballbearings* (Thailand) OJ L152 16.6.90 p59; *Polyester Fibres and Yarns* (Turkey) OJ L272 28.9.91 p92; in *Tubes and Pipe Fittings* (Spain) OJ L322 19.11.83 p13, the EC Commission rejected the undertakings offered.
5.   Article 15(1), Council Regulation (EEC) 288/82; see also the Preamble to the Regulation.
6.   Council Regulation (EEC) 1765/82 (OJ L195 5.7.82 p1). Amended by Act of Spanish and Portuguese Accession and by Council Regulation (EEC) 1243/86 (OJ L113 30.4.86 p1) and Council Regulation (EEC) 848/92 (OJ L89 4.4.92 p1) : the name "USSR" or "Soviet Union" is to be replaced by the names of each of the countries which emerge from the break-up of the Union.
7.   Council Regulation (EEC) 1766/82 (OJ L195 5.7.82 p21). Amended by Act of Spanish and Portuguese Accession and by Commission Regulation (EEC) 35/83 (OJ L5 7.1.83 p12), Commission Regulation (EEC) 101/84 (OJ L14 17.1.84 p7), Commission Regulation (EEC) 268/85 (OJ L28 1.2.85 p39) and Council Regulation (EEC) 1243/86 (OJ L113 30.4.86 p1).
8.   Article 1(1), Council Regulation (EEC) 288/82.

amended by Regulation 842/92[1]). This section of the chapter will deal largely with the adoption of protective measures under Title V of Regulation 288/82. In order to complete the picture with regard to the common rules for imports, it is important to note the following :

(a)   Common rules for imports from state trading countries;

(b)   Imports from state trading countries not liberalised at Community level; and

(c)   Surveillance measures under Title IV Regulation 288/82.

(a)   Common rules for imports from state trading countries

Regulation 1765/82 governs imports from state trading countries[2] and Regulation 1766/82 governs imports from China[3]. Both regulations provide a common liberalisation list for those goods not subject to quantitative restrictions[4]. A product may be added to the list by the EC Council and in certain cases by the EC Commission. The EC Commission may add a product to the list where, by virtue of the revocation of a quantitative restriction by a Member State, a product has become liberalised in the Community. The Member State can, however, request that the matter be sent to the EC Council[5].

(b)   Imports from state trading countries not liberalised at Community level

Regulation 3420/83 (as amended) governs the products from state trading countries which are not liberalised at Community level, ie those products which are still subject to quantitative restrictions at national level[6]. Even though this is a matter within the exclusive competence of the Community, the Member States are, by virtue of specific authorisation from the EC Commission, permitted to maintain national measures with respect to goods that are economically or politically sensitive[7].

---

9.   OJ L35 9.2.82 p1. Successive Regulations have been in effect since 1969. Council Regulation (EEC) 288/82 concerns goods covered by the EEC Treaty. As regards goods covered by the ECSC Treaty the relevant legislation is Recommendation 77/328 ECSC.

1.   OJ L89 4.4.92 p1. The name "USSR" or "Soviet Union" is to be replaced by the names of each of the countries which emerge from the break-up of the Union.

2.   Footnote 6, p121.

3.   Footnote 7, p121.

4.   Article 1 and Annex of Council Regulations (EEC) 1765/82 and 1766/82.

5.   Article 2(2), Council Regulations (EEC) 1765/82 and 1766/82.

6.   OJ L346 8.12.83 p6; amended by Council Regulations 848/92 (OJ L89 4.4.92 p1). The name "USSR" or "Soviet Union" is to be replaced by the names of each of the countries which emerge from the break up of the Union.

7.   See Case 41/76 *Donckerwolcke v Procureur de la République* [1976] ECR 1921 at 1937.

(c)   Surveillance measures under Title IV of Regulation 288/82

The Community authorities do not have to impose protective measures. Instead, they can if they wish adopt surveillance measures[1]. The primary aim of such action is to gather information on import trends, in that this may prove to be useful in deciding whether protective measures should be adopted.

In the majority of cases, it is the EC Commission which adopts surveillance measures[2], but the EC Council can do so when the imposition of such measures is taken simultaneously with the liberalisation of the importation of the product in question[3]. Surveillance may be at Community level[4] or at national level[5] and, unlike the adoption of protective measures, it can be taken at any time regardless of the Community investigation procedure under Title III[6]. In both cases, however, the products in question can only be put into free circulation on the production of an import document[7].

3.20   Safeguard measures

Regulation 288/82 lays down the basic principle that importation of goods from third countries into the Community shall be free and therefore not subject to any quantitative restrictions without prejudice to :

—   measures which may be taken under Title V (adoption of protective measures);

—   measures maintained under Title IV (surveillance);

—   quantitative restrictions for products listed in Annex 1 and maintained in the Member States indicated opposite these products in that Annex[8].

3.21   The substantive rules

Title V of Regulation 288/82 provides for the adoption of protective measures where a product is imported in such greatly increased quantities and/or on such terms or conditions as to cause, or threaten to cause, substantial injury to Community

---

1.   Article 10, Council Regulation (EEC) 288/82.
2.   Article 15(2), Council Regulation (EEC) 288/82.
3.   Ibid.
4.   Article 10, Council Regulation (EEC) 288/82.
5.   Article 12(2), Council Regulation (EEC) 288/82.
6.   Article 7(4), Council Regulation (EEC) 288/82.
7.   Article 11(1) and 13, Council Regulation (EEC) 288/82.
8.   Article 1(2).

producers of like or directly competing products[1]. Before protective measures are adopted, the Community authorities carry out an investigation with respect to the imported product that is allegedly causing injury to Community industry[2].

3.21.1   Like or directly competing products

In determining whether injury has been caused to Community industry, Regulation 2423/88 governing anti-dumping and countervailing duties refers only to the Community producers of the like product[3]. Regulation 288/82, on the other hand, refers to producers not only of the like product but also those of directly competing products.

Since the term is not defined in the regulation, it is therefore necessary to consider the decided cases to date. This question confronted the EC Commission in *Quartz Watches*[4], when it had to decide whether imported digital watches and Community mechanical and analogue quartz watches, were directly competing products. The EC Commission defined directly competing products as :

> "products which can essentially be substituted one for the other, that is to say, which are suitable for the same purposes and therefore are basically interchangeable."

It concluded that because of their high degree of interchangeability for the user, the watches in question were directly competing products. In coming to this conclusion, it took into account the fact that as regards general aspect, all watches look similar, all the watches in question possessed an essential function - that of giving the time, and that once a consumer bought a digital watch, he would not be concerned with buying another watch.

In *Glass*[5], the EC Commission, having decided that drawn and float glass were not like products, had to determine whether they were directly competing products. It held that they could be substituted for one another and were therefore directly competing products. In arriving at this conclusion, the EC Commission noted that they used the same raw material and their chemical composition was virtually the same; they were the same shape and except for special uses were precut in standard sizes and thicknesses; finally, when looked at straight on, they were substantially the same and were both used for the same purposes.

---

1.   Article 15(1) and 16(1)(a).
2.   Title III, Council Regulation (EEC) 288/82.
3.   See section 3.3.1 Anti-dumping Rules, above.
4.   OJ L106 19.4.84 p31.
5.   OJ C128 27.5.86 p7.

3.21.2 The determination of injury

The regulation expressly stipulates that the injury resulting from the imports in question must be "substantial" in order to permit the imposition of protective measures[1]. Because such imports are not objectionable, in the sense that they are neither dumped nor subsidised, the use of the word "substantial" suggests that a higher degree of injury is required than the material injury requirement under Regulation 2423/88[2].

Regulation 288/82 uses the same criteria used in anti-dumping and anti-subsidy rules for determining injury. They are as follows :

3.21.2.1 The volume of imports, in particular, where there has been a significant increase, either in absolute terms or relative to production or consumption in the Community[3].

3.21.2.2 The prices of the imports, in particular where there has been a significant price undercutting as compared with the price of a like product in the Community[4].

3.21.2.3 The consequent impact on the Community producers of similar or directly competitive products as indicated by actual or potential trends in the relevant economic factors, such as :

— production
— utilisation of capacity
— stocks
— sales
— market share
— prices (ie depression of prices or prevention of price increases which otherwise would have occurred)
— profits
— return on investment
— cash flow
— employment[5].

3.21.2.1 The volume of imports

As in the case of dumping and subsidisation, the EC Commission examines the increase in the volume of the imports and their consequent effect on the market

---

1. Article 15(1).
2. See section 3.4.2.1 Anti-dumping Rules above.
3. Article 9(1)(a).
4. Article 9(1)(b).
5. Article 9(1)(c).

share they attain in the Community. In some cases, the EC Commission will not only look at the Community as a whole, but will also take into account the Member States most affected[1]. In the decided cases to date, it has tended to rely on a period of three to five years in order to determine the effect of the imports in question on Community industry. The increase in volume is normally represented in absolute terms, though sometimes the EC Commission will also refer to the rate of import growth[2].

3.21.2.2 The price of imports

The wording of articles 15(1) and 16(1)(a) tends to suggest that a finding of injury could be made with reference to an increase in the volume of imports alone[3]. However, the EC Commission normally considers the other criteria laid down in article 9(1) when making a determination of injury, and in all cases it usually makes a finding of price undercutting. In the decided cases to date, it has found varying degrees of price undercutting, and in one case it noted that the price differences ranged from 12.1% to 77.4%[4].

3.21.2.3 Impact on Community industry

Article 9(1)(c) outlines a number of economic factors which may be considered in determining whether or not such imports have had an adverse impact on Community industry. In most cases, the EC Commission has usually found that over a three to four year period, a decline in production has resulted from an increase in the imports of the product in question[5]. A corollary of this, though not often referred to by the EC Commission in its decided cases, is a decline in the utilisation of capacity. However, the EC Commission noted in *Glass* that this resulted in the closing down of the largest and most modern furnace in the Community[6]. A fall in sales, with the resultant increase in stocks has been noted, in some cases, by the EC Commission. In one case, the increase in stocks had to be financed and buildings had to be erected for storage, therefore leading to an increase in costs[7].

---

1. Eg *Quartz Watches* (Hong Kong, Japan, Macao, South Korea, Taiwan) OJ L106 19.4.84 p31 (looked at the effect of imports on the French and German market); *Glass* (Spain, Turkey, Yugoslavia) OJ C128 27.5.86 p7 (looked at the Greek market which was most affected); *Slide Fasteners* (Taiwan) OJ L353 16.12.87 p11 (looked at Spanish and Italian market).
2. See *Stoneware* (South Korea, Taiwan) OJ L369 29.12.82 p27 - the EC Commission held that the increase in the volume of imports represented an average annual rate of import growth of 44.7% for the period 1977-81 and 31.2% for the period 1977-82.
3. See Van Bael and Bellis "International Trade Law and Practice of the European Community - EEC Anti-dumping and other Trade Protection Laws" (1985) at pp176-177 for a discussion of the wording of the two sections, which they see as being contrary to article XIX of the GATT.
4. *Quartz Watches* (Hong Kong, Macao, Japan, South Korea, Taiwan) OJ L106 19.4.84 p31.
5. In *Quartz Watches* (Hong Kong, Macao, Japan, South Korea, Taiwan) OJ L106 19.4.84 p31 - German watch production fell by 46.6%.
6. OJ C128 27.5.86 p7.
7. Ibid.

Two other factors that have a cumulative effect on each other are prices and market shares. The EC Commission has noted that price depression usually results in a fall in market share[1]. A fall in profits is not often expressly referred to by the EC Commission, but in *Glass* it concluded that the overall effect of the imports in question had resulted in an erosion of profitability and financial losses[2].

Finally, a decline in employment has been mentioned in all decided cases to date. In one case, the EC Commission noted that employment had fallen by 91%[3]. Apart from a reduction in the workforce, the EC Commission has also referred to the fact that in one case, the number of manufacturers fell from 82 to 65[4].

3.21.3 Threat of injury

As in anti-dumping and anti-subsidy actions, this can only be made where the situation is likely to develop into actual injury[5]. In order to determine whether or not there is a threat of injury, the EC Commission may take account of the following :

(a)   the rate of increase of exports into the Community; and

(b)   the export capacity in the country of origin or export, already in existence or which will be operational in the foreseeable future, and the likelihood that the resulting exports will be to the Community[6].

3.21.4   Causality

The regulation expressly provides that there has to be a causal link between the import of the goods in question and the injury caused to Community industry[7]. Unlike Regulation 2423/88, it does not expressly state that injury caused by other factors, such as contraction in demand or competition, should be excluded[8]. The EC Commission has discussed the question of causality in *Quartz Watches*[9] and also in *Glass*[10].

---

1.   *Quartz Watches* (Hong Kong, Macao, Japan, South Korea, Taiwan) OJ L106 19.4.84 p31. The EC Commission noted that the market share had dropped below 10% in 1983.
2.   OJ C128 27.5.86 p7.
3.   *Stoneware* (South Korea, Taiwan) OJ L369 29.12.82 p27.
4.   *Quartz Watches* (Hong Kong, Macao, Japan, South Korea, Taiwan) OJ L106 19.4.84 p31; see also *Beach Slippers* (China) OJ L340 28.12.84 p30 where the number of producers dropped from 24 firms and 14 craftsmen in 1979 to 16 firms and 10 craftsmen in 1983.
5.   Article 9(2), Council Regulation (EEC) 288/82. The threat of injury was found to exist in *Beach Slippers* OJ L340 28.12.84 p30. Protective measures were therefore extended.
6.   Article 9(2), Council Regulation (EEC) 288/82.
7.   Article 15(1).
8.   Article 4(1), Council Regulation (EEC) 2423/88.
9.   OJ L106 19.4.84 p31.
10.   OJ C128 27.5.86 p7.

In *Quartz Watches*[1], the EC Commission noted that the imports of mechanical watches had never been in such quantities as to contribute significantly to the creation of substantial injury. Furthermore, it rejected the claim that the cause of economic difficulties was the drop in demand for mechanical watches in favour of quartz watches for reasons of consumer taste, and the fact that the digital watch had created its own market. The EC Commission contended that consumer preference would be reflected uniformly throughout the Community. Therefore, it held that the increase in demand for quartz watches was due to the low level of prices. Second, since the Community market was stable, any influx of imports on such a marked scale as that of the digital quartz watches would have led to a reduction in the outlets for domestic production. It concluded, therefore, that the imports of digital quartz watches, taken in isolation, caused substantial injury to the Community producers. On the other hand, the imports of analogue quartz watches contributed only to a minor degree in causing injury due to the lack of significant price undercutting.

In *Glass* [2], the EC Commission considered whether the imports of wired and figure glass on the one hand, and the imports of drawn and float glass on the other, caused substantial injury to Community industry. With regard to the former, it concluded that the imports in question were not in themselves the cause of any serious injury to Greek industry, owing to the fact that its problems had occurred before the increase in penetration of the imports in 1984. On the other hand, the EC Commission held that the imports of drawn and float glass contributed, to some extent, to the worsening of the difficulties facing Greek industry. At the same time, however, it noted that imports from the rest of the Community and from non-Community countries not covered by the investigation also increased and these were at prices lower than the countries under investigation. It referred to the fact that there had been a contraction in demand for drawn glass and a corresponding increase for float glass. The Greek industry, it concluded, did not have the necessary technology for producing float glass and, to add to its difficulties, the industry had recently invested in a drawn glass production line.

3.21.5   No injury determination

To date there has been only one instance in which the EC Commission has made a no injury determination. In *Stoneware*[3], it concluded that cheap imports into the Community of articles of common pottery could not, taken in isolation, be considered as constituting substantial injury. In coming to this conclusion, the EC Commission referred to the fact that imports of common pottery increased only slightly while the share of the Community market they held had remained stable.

---

1.   OJ L106 19.4.84 p31.
2.   OJ C128 27.5.86 p7.
3.   OJ L369 29.12.82 p27.

3.21.6 Community interests

Even though it has been established that substantial injury has been caused by the imports in question, protective measures will only be taken if it is in the interests of the Community to do so[1]. Since this term is not defined in the regulation, it is necessary to look at the findings of the EC Commission in the decided cases to date. The EC Commission has, in *Quartz Watches*[2], discussed this term at length. It considered the effect of the imports in question on the Community industry in France and Germany. In the case of France, it concluded that it was in the interest of the Community to adopt protective measures. On reaching this conclusion it noted that the French industry was largely concerned with the production of assembled watches. Secondly, the social consequences for the French were much higher, since watchmaking in the Franche-Comté area was the main source of employment. On the other hand, the EC Commission held that in relation to Germany, protective measures were not necessary for the moment. This was due to the fact that the restructuring of the German industry was geared mainly to large scale watchmaking.

3.21.7 Protective measures which may be adopted under Title V

Under Title V of Regulation 288/82, protective measures may be taken both by the EC Commission and the EC Council[3]. Also, if certain conditions are satisfied, the Member States may adopt interim protective measures[4].

To date, only quotas have been imposed by the Community authorities under Title V, though in *Stoneware*[5] and in *Footwear*[6] the EC Commission replaced the quota with an export restraint agreement. In order to gain an indication of how these quotas operate in practice, reference has to be made to the decided cases[7]. First, the EC Commission has the discretion either to make it an overall quota, applicable to all third countries, or, within this, to make an allocation of quantities among the main supplier countries[8]. As the EC Commission pointed out in *Quartz Watches*[9], account had to be taken not only of direct imports but also of those in free circulation. It must be noted, however, that Regulation 288/82 does not apply to goods already in free circulation. In order to restrict such imports, the Member State in question has to seek authorisation from the EC Commission under

---

1.   Articles 15(1) and 16(1), Council Regulation (EEC) 288/82.
2.   OJ L106 19.4.84 p31.
3.   Articles 15(1)(a) and (b) and article 16(1).
4.   Article 17, Council Regulation (EEC) 288/82.
5.   OJ L369 29.12.82 p27.
6.   OJ L54 1.3.88 p59.
7.   The Regulation lays down a few guidelines with reference to quotas. See article 15(2).
8.   *Quartz Watches* (Hong Kong, Japan, Macao, South Korea, Taiwan) OJ L106 19.4.84 p31; *Slide Fasteners* (Taiwan) OJ L353 16.12.87 p11; *Footwear* (South Korea, Taiwan) OJ L54 1.3.88 p59.
9.   OJ L106 19.4.84 p31.

article 115 of the EEC Treaty. Second, the quota may be set in volume terms[1] or in both volume and value terms[2]. Third, the duration of the quota should only be for as long as the injury remains[3]. The date on which these measures are to expire should be fixed immediately and the level of protection should be progressively reduced, by means of an annual increase of the quotas in question[4]. Last, and most importantly, the protective measures taken, whether they be quotas or some other measure, must be compatible with the Community's international obligations[5]. This means that they must apply to all third countries covered by Regulation 288/82 which import the product in question[6].

Unlike Regulation 2423/88, which expressly provides that the EC Commission may accept undertakings[7], Regulation 288/82 contains no similar provision. In *Stoneware*[8], however, the South Korean government offered an export restraint agreement[9], with the result that the EC Commission decided to replace the protective measures with a system of automatic authorisation for the imports in question. It indicated that it would not be prepared to accept an export restraint agreement on an industry-to-industry basis, arguing that it considered such action as tantamount to a deviation from the procedure conducted under Regulation 288/82. In support of its argument, it contended that the appraisal of the injurious effects of the imports on the Community industry, as well as the choice of any defensive measures, were matters which may be undertaken only by the Community authorities[10].

---

1. *Quartz Watches* (Hong Kong, Japan, Macao, South Korea, Taiwan) OJ L106 19.4.84 p31; *Footwear* (South Korea, Taiwan) OJ L54 1.3.88 p59.
2. *Stoneware* (South Korea, Taiwan) OJ L369 29.12.82 p27.
3. *Quartz Watches* (Hong Kong, Japan, Macao, South Korea, Taiwan) OJ L106 19.4.84 p31; *Footwear* (South Korea, Taiwan) OJ L54 1.3.88 p59 (limited period of two and a half years).
4. Ibid.
5. *Stoneware* (South Korea, Taiwan) OJ L369 29.12.82 p27.
6. The EC Commission has been prepared to apply the safeguard measures on a mfn basis in line with the GATT rules (ie on a non-discriminatory basis.) This has been so even though it was in favour of a code on safeguard measures during the Tokyo Round of Multilateral Trade Negotiations which would permit the imposition of such measures on a discriminatory or selective basis. It has again raised the question of selective safeguard measures during the present round of trade negotiations. (See section of GATT Safeguard Measures in chapter 2, above); The only exception to this general rule, are those countries with which the EEC has concluded a Free Trade Agreement. This is permitted under article XXIV (5)(b) GATT.
7. Article 10.
8. OJ L269 18.9.82 p27; see also *Footwear* (Taiwan, South Korea) OJ L54 1.3.88 p59.
9. On export restraint agreements see section on GATT Safeguard Measures in chapter 2 above.
10. *Footwear* (Taiwan, South Korea) OJ L54 1.3.88 p59; the EC Commission favours a state-to-state approach to export restraint agreements.

3.22   Procedure

The rules relating to procedure are laid down in Titles II and III of Regulation 288/82. This is divided roughly into the following four stages :

3.22.1   Information and consultation;

3.22.2   Investigation;

3.22.3   Adoption of protective measures;

3.22.4   Review procedure.

3.22.1   Information and consultation

Unlike the regime under Regulation 2423/88, where it is the Community industry which makes the complaint[1], under Regulation 288/82 it is the Member State which informs the EC Commission should trends in imports appear to call for surveillance or protective measures[2].

Consultation takes place in an Advisory Committee, which is comprised of representatives of each Member State presided over by a Commission official[3]. Consultation may be held either at the request of the Member State or on the initiative of the EC Commission. It should take place within eight working days following the receipt of information provided by the Member State, and in any event before the adoption of any measure whether it be one of surveillance or protection[4].

It is provided that consultation should cover : terms and conditions of importation; import trends and the various aspects of the economic and commercial situation as regards the product in question; and the measures, if any, to be taken[5].

3.22.2   Investigation

Where, after consultation, there is sufficient evidence to justify an investigation, the EC Commission announces the opening of the investigation in the Official Journal[6]. Some information may be confidential. The applicable rules are in article 8 and they are the same as those for anti-dumping and anti-subsidy proceedings[7]. Where information is generally not forthcoming, the EC Commission

---

1.   See footnote 1 p101 above.
2.   Article 3. See *Stoneware* (South Korea, Taiwan) OJ L369 29.12.82 p27.
3.   Article 5(1), Council Regulation (EEC) 288/82.
4.   Article 4, Council Regulation (EEC) 288/82.
5.   Article 5(3), Council Regulation (EEC) 288/82.
6.   Article 6(1)(a), Council Regulation (EEC) 288/82.
7.   See section 3.9.3 Anti-dumping Rules above.

has the right to proceed on the basis of the facts available[1]. To date, it has not had to revert to this provision. The interested parties have a right to be heard, if they can show that they are likely to be affected by the outcome of the investigation and that there are special reasons for them to be heard orally[2].

At the end of the investigation, the EC Commission submits a report of its findings to the Advisory Committee[3]. If the EC Commission considers that no Community surveillance or protective measures are necessary, it publishes a notice of termination along with its reasons in the Official Journal, after consulting with the Advisory Committee[4]. Only on one occasion has the EC Commission held this to be the case. In *Glass*, the EC Commission held that, because of anti-dumping measures and protective measures under article 108(3) of the EEC Treaty already in force, the Greek glass industry enjoyed a degree of protection which was likely to obviate the effect of imports from non-EEC countries[5].

3.22.3 Protective measures

The regulation provides for the adoption of protective measures by the EC Commission and the EC Council and for the adoption of interim protective measures by the Member States. Where intervention is requested of the EC Commission by a Member State, then it has to take a decision within five working days of receipt of such a request[6]. Such a decision has to be communicated to the EC Council and the Member State, whereupon any Member State may, within one month, refer such a decision to the EC Council[7]. The EC Council then has the power to amend, confirm or revoke the decision of the EC Commission[8]. If it has not given a decision within three months, the measure taken by the EC Commission is deemed to be revoked[9]. By virtue of article 16, the EC Council may adopt appropriate measures. Such a decision is final, subject only to judicial review. Before a Member State adopts interim protective measures, it has to inform the EC Commission and the other Member States of the reasons for and the details of the proposed measures. After the Advisory Committee has been consulted, the Member State may adopt these measures[10]. Where the matter is urgent, consultation shall take place within five working days after the information has been given to the EC Commission. At the end of the period, the Member State may adopt the measures. During that period, it may make imports of the product subject to the production of

1.   Article 6(5), Council Regulation (EEC) 288/82.
2.   Article 6(4), Council Regulation (EEC) 288/82.
3.   Article 7(1), Council Regulation (EEC) 288/82.
4.   Article 7(2), Council Regulation (EEC) 288/82.
5.   OJ C128 27.5.86 p7.
6.   Article 15(4), Council Regulation (EEC) 288/82.
7.   Article 15(5), Council Regulation (EEC) 288/82.
8.   Article 15(6), Council Regulation (EEC) 288/82.
9.   Ibid.
10.   Article 17(2)(a), Council Regulation (EEC) 288/82.

an import authorisation which is to be granted at the end of the period[1]. The EC Commission has to be notified of the measures immediately following their adoption and such measures will operate until the adoption of a decision by the EC Commission[2].

3.22.4 Review procedure

Article 18(1) allows for consultations with the Advisory Committee either at the request of a Member State or on the initiative of the EC Commission while any surveillance or protective measure is in operation in order to examine the effects of the measure and to ascertain whether its application is still necessary.

PART 4 : RESPONSE TO ILLICIT COMMERCIAL PRACTICES UNDER REGULATION 2641/84 - THE NEW COMMERCIAL POLICY INSTRUMENT

3.23   Introduction

In 1984, the EC Council adopted Regulation 2641/84 "on the strengthening of the Common Commercial Policy with regard, in particular, to the protection against illicit commercial practices"[3]. This was justified by the need to defend vigorously the legitimate interests of the Community in the appropriate bodies, in particular the GATT, and to make sure that the Community, in managing trade policy, acts with as much speed and efficiency as its trading partners[4].

The regulation, therefore, provides the Community authorities with procedures enabling it :

(a)   to respond to any illicit commercial practices with a view to removing the injury resulting therefrom; and

(b)   to ensure full exercise of the Community's rights with regard to the commercial practices of third countries[5].

Because the rules relating to these procedures are different, they will be discussed separately.

---

1.   Article 17(2)(b), Council Regulation (EEC) 288/82.
2.   Article 17(3), Council Regulation (EEC) 288/82.
3.   OJ L252 20.9.84 p1. For a detailed analysis of the new instrument see Bourgeois and Laurent "Le nouvel instrument de politique commerciale" : un pas en avant vers l'élimination des obstacles aux échanges internationaux" 1985 RTDE 41; Steenbergen "The New Commercial Policy Instrument" 1985 CMLRev 421; Van Bael & Bellis "International Trade Law and Practice of the European Community - EEC Anti-dumping and other Trade Protection Laws" (1985) p197 et seq.
4.   See Preamble to Council Regulation (EEC) 2641/84.
5.   Article 1.

3.24 ILLICIT COMMERCIAL PRACTICES

3.24.1 What constitutes an illicit commercial practice?

The regulation defines an illicit commercial practice as :

> "any international trade practices attributable to third countries which are incompatible with international law or with the generally accepted rules."[1]

Except for the few cases to date[2], it is not clear what constitutes an illicit commercial practice. In the explanatory memorandum which accompanied the draft regulation, the EC Commission gave the following examples :

— restrictions on exports of raw materials contrary to the GATT;

— import restrictions and other charges that are incompatible with the GATT[3].

Some commentators have indicated that illicit commercial practices are those trade practices which violate the rules laid down by international trade agreements such as the GATT or the GATT Codes[4] and also those laid down by the bilateral and multilateral agreements to which the Community or the Member States are a party[5]. An indication of the type of commercial practice that is to be

---

1. Article 2(1).
2. Notice of initiation of an examination procedure concerning illicit commercial practices within the meaning of Council Regulation (EEC) 2641/84 consisting of the exclusion from the United States market of the unlicensed importation of certain aramid fibres manufactured by AKZO'NV or its affiliated companies outside the United States, OJ C25 5.2.86 p2; Notice of initiation of an "illicit commercial practice" procedure concerning the unauthorised reproduction of sound recordings in Indonesia, OJ C136 21.5.87 p3; *Soya Meal* (Argentina) unpublished Decision dated 22 December 1986; Commission Decision rejecting the complaint lodged by Smith Kline & French Laboratories Ltd against Jordan OJ L30 1.2.89 p67; Notice of initiation of an examination procedure concerning illicit commercial practice within the meaning of Regulation (EEC) 2641/84 consisting of the imposition in Japan of a port charge or fee used for the creation of the Harbour Management Fund OJ C40 16.2.91 p18; Notice of initiation of an examination procedure concerning illicit commercial practice within the meaning of Regulation (EEC) 2641/84, consisting of piracy of Community sound recordings in Thailand OJ C189 20.7.91 p26.
3. Com (83) 87 final p2 note 1.
4. Such violations under the GATT or the GATT Codes include :
   - export restrictions applied in an illicit manner.
   - export subsidies prohibited by the GATT which cause injury to the Community exporters on a third country market.
   - non respect for the rules relating to customs valuation of imported merchandise.
   - violation of Code on Technical Barriers to Trade.
   - systematic eviction of Community enterprises from the markets of States, contracting parties to the Government Procurement Code.
   - violation of the Code on Import Licensing.
   Source : Bourgeois and Laurent "Le nouvel instrument de politique commerciale : un pas en avant vers l'élimination des obstacles aux échanges internationaux" 1985 RTDE 41 p51.
5. See generally Bourgeois and Laurent, above, pp50-54; Van Beal and Bellis "International Trade Law and Practice of the European Community - EEC Anti-dumping and other Trade Protection Laws" (1985) p202; Bourgeois "EC Rules against 'Illicit Trade Practices' Policy

regarded as illicit is demonstrated by the four complaints to date which have given rise to the initiation of an examination under Regulation 2641/84. In *Aramid Fibres*[1], the illicit commercial practice complained of was the finding by the United States International Trade Commission that Enka BV (the sole producer in the Community of aramid fibre) had violated section 337 of the United States Tariff Act 1930, by the unauthorised importation and sale of aramid fibres manufactured abroad by a process that, if practised in the United States, would infringe United States Patent Law. Enka BV claimed that this constituted a denial of national treatment in respect of the application of United States patent law which affected their sale in the United States, ie breach of article III(4) of the GATT. Furthermore, such an exclusion order could not be exempted under article XX(d) of the GATT. After investigating the matter, the EC Commission agreed with Enka BV's complaint that the procedure under section 337 was less favourable to them than that exercised by the American courts in respect of American goods, with the result that there was a denial of national treatment contrary to article III[2]. In November 1989, the GATT Council adopted a panel report finding Section 337 of the United States Tariff Act to be inconsistent with article III(4)[3].

Second, a complaint was submitted by the International Federation of Phonogram and Videogram Producers (IFPI), on behalf of the Community producers in the sound recording industry that, by failing to provide Community industry with effective protection against unauthorised reproduction of sound recordings, Indonesia was in breach of both international law and of generally accepted rules. The breach of international law to which it referred was article 10 bis and 10 ter of the Paris Convention for the Protection of Intellectual Property, to which Indonesia was a signatory. The unauthorised reproduction of phonograms in Indonesia, they argued, was an "act of unfair competition" since it enabled competitors to profit at no cost from major investments made by other firms. Second, Indonesia provided no effective protection or appropriate legal remedies to counter such unfair competition. The breach of generally accepted international rules related to the Rules of the Berne Convention for the Protection of Literary and Artistic Works and the Paris text of the Universal Copyright Convention, to which Indonesia was not a signatory. They contended that these must be regarded as generally accepted international rules, in view of the large number and importance of countries adhering to them. More specifically, it was argued that Indonesian copyright law failed to respect the national treatment rules laid down in these conventions[4].

Cosmetics or International Law Enforcement?" (ed) B Hawk in "North American and Common Market Antitrust and Trade Law" (1988).

1. OJ C25 5.2.86 p2.
2. OJ L117 5.5.87 p18.
3. 36 supp. BISD (1990).
4. Ibid.

Third, a complaint was submitted by the European Community Shipowners' Association (ECSA) concerning the imposition of a port charge or fee on all cargoes moving through Japanese ports[1]. The charge applied to all shipping companies which carried cargoes to, from, or within Japan.

It was maintained that the revenue derived from the charge was to be used for the creation of a so-called "Harbour Management Fund" for the purpose of ensuring a regular supply of dock labour and of updating and modernising a Japanese import distribution system. It was further alleged that the fund was authorised and guided by the Japanese government.

The complainants argued that the charge or fee constituted an illicit commercial practice in that first, shipping lines were forced to contribute towards a fund which would bring no commercial benefit to the Community shipping companies and secondly, the charge or fee was discriminatory owing to the fact that it was imposed at two levels, ie one for all shipping companies which carried international export or import cargoes to and from Japan and another (approximately 75% lower than the former) for Japanese domestic carriers which operated in their coastal cabotage trades.

The complainants maintained that the discriminatory nature of the fund was confirmed by the accounts for the period October 1989 to September 1990 which showed that over 96% of the money collected was contributed by shipping lines in international trade with Japanese coastal operators only contributing 3.6%. Following a consultation with the Member States, the EC Commission considered that there was sufficient evidence to justify the initiation of an examination.

Fourth, a complaint was lodged by the International Federation of the Phonographic Industry (IFPI) concerning the piracy of sound recordings, ie the unauthorised duplication of Community sound recordings, in Thailand[2].

The complainants alleged that Thailand was in breach of the Berne Convention for the Protection of Literary and Artistic Works (as revised). It was argued that Thailand, pursuant to its obligations under the above-mentioned international law and in particular article 4(1), should have accorded producers of sound recordings from the EC Member States national treatment and the minimum level of copyright protection. It was noted that Thailand had adopted a Copyright Act in 1978,

---

1.   OJ C40 16.2.91 p18.
2.   OJ C189 20.7.91 p26.

which appeared to comply with the Thai commitments concerning the protection of foreign sound recordings. It was argued, however, that this Act was not effectively implemented, as piracy of foreign sound recordings on a massive scale was still taking place.

Furthermore, the complainant alleged that Thailand's failure to protect European sound recordings against piracy has the effect of denying the producers fair and equitable market opportunities in Thailand, while Thai sound recording manufacturers did not encounter the same problems.

In two other cases, the EC Commission refused to initiate proceedings on the ground that the measures complained of were not contrary to international law or generally accepted rules[1]. In *Soya Meal*, it held that the allegations of differential export taxes for soya products and export restrictions were not contrary to articles III and XI of the GATT. They did not, therefore, constitute an illicit commercial practice. The EC Commission's decision has been upheld by the Court in the *Third Fediol*[2] case. In the complaint lodged by Smith Kline & French Laboratories Ltd against Jordan, the allegation that an amendment to Jordan's intellectual property laws was contrary to the Paris Convention for the protection of intellectual property rights was rejected by the EC Commission, on the basis that legislative acts of a signatory state could not amount to "an act of unfair competition" as laid down in article 10 bis(1) of the Convention.

This new regulation, unlike the other Trade Protection Laws, is aimed at illicit commercial practices that affect not only imports into the Community, but Community exports to third countries[3]. This, however, is subject to two qualifications. First, the scope of the regulation is limited to illicit commercial practices which are "attributable" to third countries. This, in essence, means unfair practices by foreign governments and not those carried out by private undertakings[4]. Second, it does not apply to cases covered by the other existing rules in the field of trade regulation[5].

1.　　*Soya Meal* (Argentina) unpublished Commission Decision dated 22 December 1986; Commission Decision rejecting the complaint of Smith Kline and French Laboratories Ltd against Jordan OJ L30 1.2.89 p67.
2.　　Case 70/87 [1989] ECR 1781.
3.　　Article 2(4) Council Regulation (EEC) 2641/84.
4.　　Cf the Economic and Social Committee contended that the practices do not refer solely to the practices of governments but also those of other public authorities - OJ C211 8.8.83 p24.
5.　　Article 13, Council Regulation (EEC) 2641/84.

3.24.2 Injury

Before action can be taken by the Community authorities, the illicit commercial practice has to cause injury to Community industry[1]. "Injury" is defined in the regulation as :

"any material injury caused or threatened to Community industry."[2]

3.24.2.1 What is meant by the term "Community industry"

This is defined[3] in the regulation to mean all Community producers of products identical or similar to the product which is the subject of illicit practices or of products competing directly with that product[4], or which are consumers or processors of the product which is the subject of illicit practices, or all those producers whose combined output constitutes a major proportion of total Community production of the products in question.

In *Aramid Fibres*, the complaint was lodged on behalf of the AKZO Group by ENKA BV, the sole producer of aramid fibre in the Community[5]; in *Sound Recordings*, by the International Federation of Phonogram and Videogram Producers (IFPI) on behalf of the European producers said to represent virtually the whole Community sound recording industry[6] and in *Port Charge of Fee used for the Creation of the Harbour Management Fund*, by the European Community Shipowners' Association (ECSA) which represented approximately 90% of all Community shipping lines trading to and from Japan[7]. It is arguable that the Association, which appeared to represent Community providers of services, did not have such a right, unless it was in fact representing Community producers of goods. In *Piracy of Community Sound Recordings* the complaint was lodged by the International Federation of the Phonographic Industry (IEPI) representing virtually all producers of sound recordings in the Community[8]. As stated above, producers, processors and consumers of the product in question have the right to lodge a complaint. The fact that consumers and processors are covered by the term "Community industry" goes further than Regulation 2423/88 and Regulation 288/82.

There are, however, two exceptions to this basic principle. First, when the producers are related to the exporters or the importers or are themselves importers

---

1.   Article 1(a), Council Regulation (EEC) 2641/84.
2.   Article 2(3).
3.   Article 2(4).
4.   This is similar to Council Regulation (EEC) 288/82 where consideration is taken not only of producers of the like product but also those of directly competing products.
5.   OJ C25 5.2.86 p2.
6.   OJ C136 21.5.87 p3.
7.   OJ C40 16.2.91 p18.
8.   OJ C189 20.7.91 p26.

of the product alleged to be the subject of an illicit practice, the term "Community industry" may be interpreted as referring to the rest of the producers[1]. Second, a particular region of the Community may be regarded as a Community industry if their collective output constitutes a major proportion of the output of the product in question in the Member State or States where the region is located. However, they must show that the effect of the illicit practice where it concerns imports is concentrated in that Member State or States. Further, where the illicit practice concerns Community exports to a third country, a significant proportion of the output of those producers is exported to the third country concerned[2].

3.24.2.2 What is meant by the term "material injury"?

The term itself is not defined in the regulation, but article 8(1) provides a list of criteria similar to those found in Regulation 2423/88 and 288/82 which are to be used in determining whether or not injury has been caused. They are as follows :

(i) the volume of Community imports or exports concerned, notably where there has been a significant increase or decrease, either in absolute terms or relative to production or consumption on the market in question[3];

(ii) the prices of Community producers' competitors, in particular in order to determine whether there has been, either in the Community or in third country markets, significant undercutting of the prices of Community producers[4];

(iii) the consequent impact on Community industry as defined in article 2(4) and as indicated by trends in certain economic factors, such as :

— production
— utilisation of capacity
— stocks
— sales
— market share
— prices (that is, depression of prices or prevention of price increases which would normally have occurred)
— profits
— return on capital
— investment
— employment

---

1. Article 2(4)(a), Council Regulation (EEC) 2641/84.
2. Article 2(4)(b), Council Regulation (EEC) 2641/84.
3. Unlike Council Regulation (EEC) 2423/88, reference here is made not only to the increase in the volume of the imports or exports but also to their decrease.
4. Unlike Council Regulation (EEC) 2423/88, reference here is made to the prices of the Community producers' competitors.

How these provisions will operate in practice is unclear in the absence of decided cases. Unfortunately, the complaint in *Aramid Fibres* was concerned with the threat of injury rather than material injury[1]. However, in *Sound Recordings*, the complainant contended that the unauthorised reproduction of phonograms was causing serious injury to Community producers, in that it was restricting market access to the Indonesian and, more importantly, to the Middle Eastern countries with the result that there would be a significant loss of sales[2]. In *Port Charge or Fee used for the Creation of the Harbour Management Fund*, the complainants contended that the Community shipping lines had only paid the charge because failure to do so would have created considerable problems regarding the availability of dock labour to load and unload cargoes. Such a situation would have seriously disrupted and restricted their normal commercial operations. Furthermore, the charge paid would result in increased costs. The amount paid by the shipowners was approximately 10% of the overall fee charged by Japan Harbour Transport Association for the period from October 1989 to March 1990. The European companies had estimated that the total costs borne by them, estimated at 4.5 million US dollars per year, could not be fully passed on to the shippers[3].

In *Piracy of Sound Recordings* it was estimated that the percentage of the Thai market for international repertoire music, controlled by pirated sound recordings extended to more than 90% of the units sold in Thailand from 1985 to 1990. It was argued that the unauthorised duplication of sound recordings injured the Community producers in two respects : first, their sales of legitimate phonograms in Thailand were significantly reduced and, secondly, Thai pirated recordings were exported in large quantities to third countries, thereby restricting the Community producers' access and sales to third countries. They estimated that the losses sustained by the community producers during the past ten years amounted to 200 million Ecu (retail values)[4].

3.24.2.3 Threat of injury

Where a threat of injury is alleged, it has to be clearly foreseeable that a particular situation is likely to develop into actual injury[5]. In order to determine this, the EC Commission may take into account inter alia[6] factors such as :

(a)   the rate of increase of the exports to the market where the competition with the Community products is taking place;

---

1.   OJ L117 5.5.87 p18.
2.   OJ C136 21.5.87 p7.
3.   OJ C40 16.2.91 p18.
4.   OJ C189 20.7.91 p26.
5.   Article 8(2), Council Regulation (EEC) 2641/84.
6.   Ibid.

(b)   the export capacity in the country of origin or export already in existence, or which will be operational in the foreseeable future, and the likelihood that the exports resulting from that capacity will be to the market referred to in point (a).

In *Aramid Fibres*, the EC Commission considered whether there was a threat of injury as alleged by the complainant. It examined whether or not any future injury was clearly foreseeable, and concluded that the arguments of loss of direct sales to the United States and the Community in the period up to 1990 and beyond were convincing[1].

3.24.2.4 Community interests

As in the case with the other trade protection laws, the interests of the Community play a major part in determining whether protective measures are to be adopted[2] or whether the procedure is to be terminated[3]. In *Aramid Fibres*, the EC Commission noted that in the light of the results of the investigation, it appeared that an important question of the application of the GATT was at issue which had serious economic implications. It concluded, therefore, that it was in the Community interest to initiate international consultation and dispute settlement procedures, with a view to achieving the alignment of United States legislation with its international obligations[4]. In *Port Charge or Fee used for the Creation of the Harbour Management Fund*, the EC Commission concluded that it was in the interests of the Community to suspend the examination procedure following formal assurances given by the Japanese government that the Harbour Management Fund would be discontinued[5].

In *Piracy of Sound Recordings*, the complainants argued that it was in the Community interest to initiate an examination, given that the failure of Thailand to grant effective protection affected the rights of Community authors and artists to participate economically in the exploitation of their works and performances[6].

---

1.   OJ L117 5.5.87 p18. In the complaint ENKA BV contended that prior to the exclusion order exports were to be some 1,000 tonnes by 1990. OJ C25 5.2.86 p2.
2.   Article 10(1) where it states that "where it is found as a result of the examination procedure that action is necessary in the interests of the Community ...".
3.   Article 9(1) where it states that "when it is found as a result of the examination procedure that the interests of the Community do not require any action to be taken".
4.   OJ L117 5.5.87 p18.
5.   OJ L74 20.3.92 p47.
6.   OJ C189 20.7.91 p26.

3.25   Full exercise of the Community's rights

The regulation defines "Community rights" as

> "those international trade rights of which it may avail itself either under international law or under generally accepted rules."[1]

The major difference with regard to this procedure as compared with that in article 1(a) as outlined above is that action may be taken without injury to Community industry being proved. As the EC Commission explained in its memorandum which accompanied the draft regulation, the practices covered by this procedure would be those involving recourse to the GATT dispute settlement procedures, notably articles XXII and XXIII and those provisions of the GATT Codes that specifically lay down rules governing dispute settlement, eg Title II of the Subsidies Code[2].

3.26   Protective measures

3.26.1   Acceptance of an undertaking

The EC Council may accept an undertaking offered by a third country or by the country concerned, if this is considered satisfactory[3]. In *Reproduction of Sound Recordings*[4], Indonesia undertook, pending its eventual accession or adherence to the relevant international conventions, to provide for sound recordings by nationals of the Community Member States the same protection on their territory as for sound recordings by Indonesian nationals. The EC Commission concluded that it was in the interests of the Community to accept the undertaking and terminate the procedure without taking protective measures pursuant to article 10(3). If the measures proposed are considered satisfactory, the procedure will be terminated[5]. It is the EC Commission which is entrusted with the task of supervising the application of these measures[6]. If they are rescinded, suspended or improperly implemented, or where the EC Commission has grounds for believing that this is the case, the Member States shall be informed and protective measures may be adopted in accordance with article 11, where these are necessary and justified[7].

---

1.   Article 2(2).
2.   See Chapter 2, section 2.4.2 above.
3.   Article 9(2)(a), Council Regulation (EEC) 2641/84.
4.   OJ L123 17.5.88 p51.
5.   Article 9(2)(a) Council Regulation (EEC) 2641/84.
6.   Article 9(2)(b), Council Regulation (EEC) 2641/84.
7.   Article 9(2)(c), Council Regulation (EEC) 2641/84.

3.26.2 Adoption of commercial policy measures

The adoption of commercial policy measures is subject to the prior discharge of an international procedure for consultation or for the settlement of disputes where the Community's international obligations so require[1]. Once this has been completed and account has been taken of the results, commercial policy measures may then be imposed[2]. The regulation provides that "any" commercial policy measure may be taken[3] but stresses that such measures must be compatible with existing international obligations and procedures[4]. It then expressly refers to the following :

(a)   the suspension or withdrawal of any concession resulting from commercial policy agreements;

(b)   the raising of existing customs duties or the introduction of any other charge on imports;

(c)   the introduction of quantitative restrictions or any other measure modifying import or export conditions or otherwise affecting trade with the third country concerned[5].

3.27   Procedure

For the most part, the procedural rules are the same for both regimes under article 1 - where there are differences these shall be noted. The procedure to be followed can be divided into three main stages :

3.27.1   The complaint or referral;
3.27.2   The examination;
3.27.3   The adoption of measures.

3.27.1   The complaint or referral

The regulation provides that :

"Any natural or legal person, or any association not having legal personality, acting on behalf of a Community industry which considers that it has suffered injury as a result of illicit commercial practices may lodge a written complaint."[6]

---

1.   Article 10(2), Council Regulation (EEC) 2641/84.
2.   Ibid.
3.   Article 10(3) : The adoption of commercial policy measures applies equally to both procedures in article 1.
4.   Ibid.
5.   Ibid.
6.   Article 3(1).

This provision, however, does not apply in relation to the procedure for ensuring the full exercise of the Community's rights. The complaint must contain sufficient evidence of the existence of an illicit commercial practice and the injury resulting therefrom[1]. The complaint may be withdrawn, in which case the procedure may be terminated unless such termination would not be in the interests of the Community[2]. If it becomes apparent after consultation (in the Advisory Committee[3]) that there is insufficient evidence to justify initiating an investigation, the complainant is informed[4]. In the complaint lodged by Smith Kline & French Laboratories Ltd against Jordan, the EC Commission rejected the complaint on the basis that it did not contain sufficient evidence in law of the existence of an illicit commercial practice as required by article 3(2) of Regulation 2641/84[5]. The complainant had argued that new legislation in Jordan amending its patent laws, infringed articles 10bis and 10ter of the Paris Convention for the Protection of Industrial Property by depriving it of the protection previously afforded. The EC Commission concluded that "acts of unfair competition" within the meaning of article 10bis could only cover acts carried out by competitors and therefore could not include acts of a signatory state, eg the adoption of a new law[6].

As far as a referral by a Member State is concerned, it may ask the EC Commission to initiate the procedures referred to in article 1[7]. The EC Commission will have to be supplied with the necessary evidence to support the requests, and in the case of illicit commercial practices, proof of these and the resultant injury must be given[8]. If, after consultation, it is decided that an investigation should be initiated, the Member State shall be informed[9].

3.27.2   The examination

Where, after consultation, it is apparent that there is sufficient evidence to justify the start of an investigation and where this is in the interests of the Community, the EC Commission shall announce this in the Official Journal[10]. It then notifies the representatives of the country or countries involved[11].

---

1.   Article 3(2), Council Regulation (EEC) 2641/84.
2.   Article 3(4), Council Regulation (EEC) 2641/84.
3.   Article 5, Council Regulation (EEC) 2641/84.
4.   Article 3(5), Council Regulation (EEC) 2641/84.
5.   OJ L30 1.2.89 p67.
6.   Ibid.
7.   Article 4(1), Council Regulation (EEC) 2641/84. This provision applies to both article 1(a) and 1(b).
8.   Article 4(2), Council Regulation (EEC) 2641/84.
9.   Article 4(4), Council Regulation (EEC) 2641/84.
10.   Article 6(1)(a), Council Regulation (EEC) 2641/84.
11.   Article 6(1)(b), Council Regulation (EEC) 2641/84.

The regulation gives the EC Commission the power to ingather all the information necessary and to check this with the importers, traders, agents, producers, trade associations and organisations, provided that the undertakings or organisations give their consent[1]. The EC Commission can also carry out investigations in the territory of the countries concerned provided that their governments have been officially notified and raise no objection within a reasonable period[2]. Where such information is not supplied, the EC Commission may proceed on the basis of the facts available[3]. The EC Commission shall be assisted in its investigation by officials of the Member State in whose territory the checks are carried out, provided that the Member State so requests[4]. Finally, the Member States, when requested, shall supply the EC Commission with all the information necessary for the examination[5].

All interested parties may inspect the information available to the EC Commission[6]. This information is limited to all internal documents for the use of the EC Commission and the administrations, provided that it is relevant to the protection of their interests, not confidential within the meaning of article 7 and is used by the EC Commission in its examination procedure[7]. With regard to the rules relating to confidentiality, these are similar to those applied in anti-dumping proceedings[8]. Finally, the interested parties concerned may ask to be informed of the principal facts and considerations resulting from the examination procedure[9].

The interested parties concerned have a right to be heard by the EC Commission provided that the request is made in writing within the prescribed period laid down in the Official Journal and that they are a party primarily concerned with the result of the procedure[10]. The regulation also provides for a confrontation meeting. However, no party is under any obligation to attend and failure to do so will not be prejudicial to that party's case[11].

When it has concluded its examination, the EC Commission reports to the Advisory Committee. The report should normally be presented within five months (this can be extended to seven) of the announcement of the initiation of the procedure[12].

---

1.   Article 6(2)(a).
2.   Article 6(2)(b), Council Regulation (EEC) 2641/84.
3.   Article 6(7), Council Regulation (EEC) 2641/84.
4.   Article 6(2)(c), Council Regulation (EEC) 2641/84.
5.   Article 6(3), Council Regulation (EEC) 2641/84.
6.   Article 6(4)(a), Council Regulation (EEC) 2641/84.
7.   Ibid.
8.   Article 7, Council Regulation (EEC) 2641/84. See section 3.9.3 under the Anti-dumping Rules above.
9.   Article 6(4)(b), Council Regulation (EEC) 2641/84.
10.   Article 6(5), Council Regulation (EEC) 2641/84.
11.   Article 6(6).
12.   Article 6(9), Council Regulation (EEC) 2641/84.

The procedure can be terminated, without the adoption of protective measures, in one of two ways. When it is found, as a result of the examination, that it is in the interests of the Community that no action need be taken, the procedure shall be terminated in accordance with article 12[1]. By virtue of article 12, it is the EC Commission which takes the decision, subject to a referral by the Member States to the EC Council. In such a situation, if the EC Council has not given a ruling within thirty days, the EC Commission's decision stands. However, where the third country concerned has taken measures that are satisfactory, the procedure is terminated in accordance with article 11[2]. In this case, it is the EC Council on a proposal from the EC Commission that takes the decision.

3.27.3   The adoption of measures

Where the Community has to fulfil the requirement of following formal international consultation or dispute settlement procedures in response to an illicit commercial practice within the meaning of article 1(a), any decisions relating to the initiation, conduct or termination of such procedure shall be taken in accordance with article 12[3]. In *Aramid Fibres*, the EC Commission initiated the procedure for consultation and dispute settlement referred to in article XXIII of the GATT[4].

The EC Council has the power to take decisions in accordance with the procedure in article 11 where after the conclusion of formal international consultation or dispute settlement in response to an illicit commercial practice, measures of commercial policy are to be adopted[5] or where the full exercise of the Community's right within the meaning of article 1(b) is to be ensured[6].

---

1.   Article 9(1), Council Regulation (EEC) 2641/84.
2.   Article 9(2)(a), Council Regulation (EEC) 2641/84; see *Reproduction of Sound Recordings* (Indonesia) OJ L123 17.5.88 p51; *Port Charge or Fee used for the Creation of Harbour Management Fund* (Japan) OJ L74 20.3.92 p47.
3.   Article 11(2)(a), Council Regulation (EEC) 2641/84.
4.   OJ L117 5.5.87 p18.
5.   Article 11(2)(b), Council Regulation (EEC) 2641/84.
6.   Article 11(3), Council Regulation (EEC) 2641/84.

CHAPTER 4 : PROCEDURAL ASPECTS OF JUDICIAL REVIEW

PART 1 : "LOCUS STANDI" - GENERAL

4.1   Introduction

In the legal systems of the Member States limits are laid down with regard to the powers exercised by the Executive. In the Community legal order the Executive institutions are the EC Commission and to some extent the EC Council, though the latter's function is primarily legislative.

The control of the Executive by the European Parliament is weaker than that by the Parliaments in the Member States. The Court is entrusted with the task of supervising the activities of the Executive. It is only proper that the acts of the EC Council and EC Commission are subject to review by the Court. In this way, the rule of law is seen to be applied in that not only do the Community authorities enforce the law but they are also bound by it.

The Community authorities have considerable powers in the field of external relations and no more so than in relation to the measures designed to counteract unfair trade practices by Third Countries. In these circumstances it is necessary to ensure that there are "appropriate and corresponding judicial safeguards"[1].

The question of "locus standi" or the right of an interested party to challenge an act of the institutions imposing safeguard measures before the Court will vary according to whether it is a direct or an indirect action. The former, for example an action for annulment, is where the interested party can bring his case directly before the Court. The object is to have the act declared void. The latter, for example an article 177 reference, is where an action is brought via the national court to the European Court of Justice for a ruling on the validity of a Community act. The effect of the ruling is to have the act declared invalid in the particular case. The distinction between the effect of the two actions is slowly being eroded away. This will be considered in more detail below.

---

1.   Bebr "Development of judicial control of the European Communities" p19.

The first part of the Chapter deals generally with the jurisprudence of the Court with respect to locus standi in relation to both direct and indirect actions. The second part deals more specifically with the jurisprudence of the Court with respect to safeguard measures. Emphasis will be placed on article 173 of the EEC Treaty since by far the greatest number of actions involving safeguard measures have been raised under article 173 and in particular judicial review of anti-dumping measures.

The system of judicial remedies in the European Community, and in particular articles 173 and 184 on the one hand and article 177 on the other, according to the Court, forms a complete system designed to permit it to review the legality of measures adopted by the institutions[1]. As a result, natural and legal persons are protected against the application to them of general measures which they cannot contest directly before the Court by reason of the criteria set down in article 173, 2nd para which will be considered below. Where the Community authorities are responsible for the implementation of such measures, natural or legal persons may bring a direct action against such measures which are addressed to them or which are of direct and individual concern to them and, in support of such an action, plead the illegality of the general measure on which they are based. If implementation is a matter for the national authorities, such parties may plead the invalidity of general measures before the national courts and the latter may or must in some situations request the Court for a preliminary ruling[2]. Each of these actions will be considered in detail below together with an analysis of article 175 (action for failure to act) and article 215, 2nd para (action for damages).

4.2   Action for annulment - article 173 of the EEC Treaty

This is the procedure whereby a direct challenge may be made against a Community measure which, it is claimed, is illegal. The object of the procedure is to secure the annulment of the measure.

4.2.1   What measures can be reviewed by the Court ?
Article 173, 1st para, states that :

> "The Court of Justice shall review the legality of acts of the Council and the Commission other than recommendations or opinions."

---

1.   Case 294/83 *Parti Ecologiste "Les Verts" v European Parliament* [1986] ECR 1357 at 1365.
2.   Ibid.

The Court has interpreted this provision liberally. In *IBM v EC Commission* the Court stated that :

> "Any measure the legal effects of which are binding on, and capable of affecting the interest of, the applicant by bringing about a distinct change in his legal position is an act or decision which may be the subject of an action under article 173 for a declaration that it is void"[1].

More recently, in *Gestetner Holdings plc v EC Council and EC Commission* the Court held that the rejection by the EC Commission of a proposed undertaking was not a measure having binding legal effects of such a kind as to affect the interests of the applicant. Such a rejection was an intermediate measure whose purpose was to prepare for the final decision[2].

The Court has held that the form in which such acts are cast is immaterial in determining whether they are open to challenge under article 173[3]. For example, in *Cement Convention* it held that a "communication" issued by the EC Commission under article 15 of Regulation 17 did not constitute a decision[4]. On the other hand in the *IBM* Case[5] it did not accept that a statement of objections which, under Regulation 17, the EC Commission is required to issue to a firm whose marketing practices are under investigation constituted a decision. The Court has not restricted its interpretation to mean those binding acts in article 189[6]. In its *ERTA* judgment it held that :

> "Article 173 treats as acts open to review by the Court *all* measures adopted by the institutions which are *intended to have legal force.*[7]"

4.2.2 The capacity to bring an action

4.2.2.1 Privileged applicants

By virtue of article 173, 1st para the EC Council, EC Commission or the Member States may contest the legality of a Community act so long as the action is taken

---

1. Case 60/81 *IBM v EC Commission* [1981] ECR 2639 at 2651.
2. Case 156/87 *Gestetner Holdings plc v EC Council and EC Commission* [1990] ECR 781; see also Joined Cases 133 and 150/87 *Nashua Corpn v EC Council and EC Commission* [1990] ECR 719.
3. Case 60/81 *IBM v EC Commission* [1981] ECR 2639.
4. Case 8-11/66 *Cimenteries CBR Cementsbedrijven NV v EC Commission* [1967] ECR 75.
5. Case 60/81 *IBM v EC Commission* [1981] ECR 2639.
6. The binding acts enumerated in Article 189 are Regulations, directives and decisions. Recommendations and opinions have no binding force.
7. Case 22/70 *EC Commission v EC Council* [1971] ECR 263 at 276. Emphasis added. See also Case 230/81 *Luxembourg v European Parliament* [1983] ECR 255.

within the prescribed time limits provided for in the Treaty[1]. In an action for annulment by a Member State or by a Community institution there is no need to distinguish among the various binding acts. It is perfectly possible for a privileged plaintiff to challenge the legality of a regulation under article 173, 1st para. In certain narrow circumstances which are not of concern in this paper, an action may also be raised by the European Parliament[2].

4.2.2.2 Non-privileged applicants

Article 173, 2nd para states that :

"Any natural or legal person may, under the same conditions, institute proceedings against a decision addressed to that person or against a decision which, although in the form of a regulation or a decision addressed to another person, is of direct and individual concern to the former."

The first thing one notices about article 173, 2nd para is that, on its face, the only act a natural or legal person can challenge is a decision.

A natural or legal person has little problem where a decision is addressed to them[3]. A common example is where a natural or legal person has been held to have infringed the Community's competition law. In such a case, the EC Commission will usually issue a decision to that effect addressed to the individual concerned[4].

In the second situation enumerated in article 173, 2nd para, a natural or legal person has to show that the decision, although addressed to someone else, is of direct and individual concern to him. In the last situation a natural or legal person has to show three things :

(i)   that the act in question, although in the form of a regulation is in essence a "decision";

(ii)   that it is of individual concern to him;

(iii) that it is of direct concern to him.

---

1.   Case 166/78 *Italy v EC Commission* [1979] ECR 2575; the right of action conferred upon Member States to seek the annulment of a Community act is unconditional.
2.   Case 70/88 *European Parliament v EC Council* (Chernobyl) [1990] ECR 2041.
3.   See for example Case 789/79 *Calpak and Ors v EC Commission* [1980] ECR 1949.
4.   Eg Cases 56 and 58/64 *Consten and Grundig v EC Commission* [1966] ECR 299; Case 17/74 *Transocean Marine Paint v EC Commission* [1974] ECR 1063.

The concepts "direct" and "individual" concern have been interpreted narrowly so that it is difficult for a natural or legal person to challenge a Community regulation. The reasons for the Court's restrictive interpretation of these concepts will be considered later.

4.2.2.2.1 What is a "decision"?

The annulment of a regulation can only be contested by a natural or legal person where it is in essence a decision, irrespective of its form. In *Alcan v EC Commission* the Court held quite generally with regard to article 173, 2nd para that :

> "The aim of this provision is to ensure the legal protection of individuals in all cases in which they are directly and individually concerned by a Community measure - in whatever form it appears - which is not addressed to them.[1]"

It reiterated this view in *Hans-Otto Wagner GmbH and Ors v EC Commission* with specific reference to regulations when it stated that the purpose of article 173, 2nd para is :

> "to prevent the Community institutions from being able to bar proceedings instituted by an individual against a decision of direct and individual concern to him by simply choosing the form of a regulation.[2]"

In cases where a natural or legal person seeks to have a regulation annulled, that natural or legal person not only has to show that the measure is of direct and individual concern to him but also that by its nature it is a decision. The literal reading of article 173, 2nd para points to the fact that this condition is important.

The case law of the Court has at times, however, not helped in reinforcing this point. There have developed two separate lines of case law. There are certain judgments of the Court, notably *CAM v EC Commission*[3] and *Société pour l'Exportation des Sucres v EC Commission* [4], which are authority for the view that a natural or legal person will have locus standi irrespective of the fact that the measure is a regulation in form and substance if he satisfies the conditions of direct and individual concern.

---

1. Case 69/69 *Alcan Aluminium Raeren SA v EC Commission* [1970] ECR 385 at 393.
2. Case 162/78 *Hans-Otto Wagner GmbH and Ors v EC Commission* [1979] ECR 3467 at 3487.
3. Case 100/74 *Société C.A.M. SA v EC Commission* [1975] ECR 1393.
4. Case 88/76 *Société pour l'exportation des sucres SA v EC Commission* [1977] ECR 709.

These decisions must, however, be put into the context of the earlier and later judgments which stress the importance of establishing that the regulation is in essence a decision. In these cases, the Court takes the view that if the act at issue is in the nature of a regulation then it is immaterial that the measure is of direct and individual concern to the individual[1]. In *Compagnie Française Commerciale et Financière SA v EC Commission* the Court held that the regulation's legislative nature was not detracted from by the fact that the persons that it affected might be more or less ascertainable, ie individually concerned[2]. The test for determining whether the regulation in question is in essence a decision is analogous but not always the same as that for determining whether a measure is of individual concern to a particular person[3].

The starting point is to decide whether the measure in question is a regulation or a decision. In so doing, the Court will invariably revert to the definitions laid down in article 189[4]. The Court was faced with such a situation in *Confédération nationale des producteurs de fruits et légumes v EC Council*[5]. It referred to article 189 and then stated that the criterion for the distinction must be sought in the "general application" or otherwise of the measure in question[6]. In other words, where the applicant is affected as a member of a general class, then the measure will be regarded as a regulation. If, however, he is affected as an individual, the measure will be regarded as a decision. The Court reiterated the point in *Koninklijke Scholten Honig NV v EC Council and EC Commission*[7] when it stated that if the measure is applicable to objectively determined situations and involves legal consequences for categories of persons viewed in a general and abstract manner, then it is a regulation. If, on the other hand, it is applicable to a limited number of persons defined or identifiable it will be a decision.

A number of authors[8] observed that this distinction is difficult to apply where, although the number of persons is small, they are designated as a general class, even though their identity is fixed and ascertainable at the time when the measure is adopted. It is submitted that no difficulty arises if it can be established that the regulation in question produces legal effects for a closed category of persons. As

---

1. See Case 64/69 *La Compagnie Française Commerciale et Financière SA v EC Commission* [1970] ECR 221; Case 162/78 *Hans Otto Wagner GmbH and Ors v EC Commission* [1979] ECR 3467.
2. Ibid.
3. See Opinion of Advocate General Warner in Case 100/74 *Cam v EC Commission* above at 1411.
4. A Regulation is defined thus : "[A Regulation] shall have general application. It shall be binding in its entirety and directly applicable in all Member States". A decision is defined thus: "[A decision] shall be binding in its entirety upon those to whom it is addressed".
5. Cases 16 and 17/62 *Confédération nationale des producteurs de fruits et légumes and Fédération nationale des producteurs de raisins de table v EC Council* [1962] ECR 471 at 478.
6. Ibid at 478.
7. Case 101/76 *Koninklijke Scholten Honig NV v EC Council and EC Commission* [1977] ECR 797 at 808.
8. See for example Vaughan "Law of European Communities" (Butterworths, London) p200; Hartley "The Foundation of EEC law", pp357 et seq.

Advocate General Van Gerven observed in *Weddel v EC Commission*[1] the decisive factor is not whether many persons are affected or only a few or the fact that "it is possible to determine the number or identity of the persons to whom it applies at any given time"[2] but it is the fact that, at the time at which the contested regulation was adopted, it affected the legal situation of a closed category of persons[3]. Both the Advocate General and the Court[4] noted that in the present case the category of applicants affected by the regulation was closed. No more persons could be added at the time the regulation was adopted[5].

4.2.2.2.2 Individual concern

The test of individual concern was first formulated in *Plaumann & Co v EC Commission*[6]. Plaumann was an importer of clementines. The Court held that :

> "the applicant is affected by the disputed decision as an importer of clementines, that is to say, *by reason of a commercial activity which may at any time be practised by any person* and is not therefore such as to distinguish the applicant in relation to the contested decision as in the case of the addressee."[7]

In order to be individually concerned the Court stressed that the decision must affect them "by reason of certain attributes which are peculiar to them or by reason of circumstances in which they are differentiated from all other persons and by virtue of these factors distinguishes them individually just as in the case of the person addressed"[8]. Advocate General Roemer noted that "concern" does not arise from the individuality of particular persons but from the membership of the abstractly defined group of all those who wished to import clementines during the period in question. This group he considered was not ascertainable when the decision was issued since it was constantly changing even though this in practice was only to a limited degree[9].

The Court also noted in *Plaumann* that it was appropriate to consider the question of individual concern first because if the applicant did not satisfy this criterion

---

1. Case 354/87 *Weddel & Co BV v EC Commission* [1990] I ECR 3847.
2. See Case 26/86 *Deutz v EC Commission* [1987] ECR 941 at para 8 of judgment.
3. Case 354/87 *Weddel & Co BV v EC Commission* above at pp3871-2; see also Case 244/88 *Usines Coopératives de déshydration du Vexin v EC Commission* [1989] ECR 3811 at para 10 of judgment.
4. Ibid, p3886 at paras 20-23 of judgment.
5. Ibid, p3872.
6. Case 25/62 *Plaumann & Co v EC Commission* [1963] ECR 95.
7. Ibid at 107. Emphasis added.
8. Ibid.
9. Ibid, at 116.

then it became unnecessary to consider the question of direct concern[1]. The Court, it is submitted, was concerned with the "economy of judicial reasoning". There is nothing, however, to prevent it considering direct concern first if it so chooses.

From the case law of the Court, "individual concern" will be satisfied when the applicant can show that he belongs to a group of interested persons who can be identified and ascertained at the time when the decision was made. In such a case, as the Court has held, the applicant would be in position "similar to the persons to whom the decision was addressed"[2]. At this point there is really no distinction between the notion of individual concern and the criteria necessary to establish that the measure in question is a decision as opposed to a regulation.

4.2.2.2.3 Direct concern

On the question of direct concern, the Court has adopted the attitude that a measure will be of "direct concern" to a natural or legal person only if it affects that person's legal position without need for any further implementing action. As Advocate General Roemer stated in *Plaumann & Co v EC Commission* :

> "Only when the Member State avails itself of the authorisation, which is left to its discretion, are legal effects created for the individual. The decision of the Member State is therefore an essential link inserted in the chain of various legal measures between the decision of the Commission and the concrete legal effect falling on the individual."[3]

The Court did not rule on the question of direct concern, because it was of the opinion that if an applicant was not individually concerned there was no need to consider whether direct concern was satisfied[4].

In the *Toepfer* case, the Court considered the question of direct concern first. It held that the applicant was directly concerned by the measure in question. The measure provided that the EC Commission's decision "shall" come into force immediately. The Court held that the decision therefore to amend or abolish protective measures was directly applicable and concerned the interested parties subject to it as directly as the measures it replaced[5].

---

1.   Case 25/62 *Plaumann & Co v EC Commission* [1963] ECR 95 at 107.
2.   Cases 106 and 107/63 *Toepfer v EC Commission* [1965] ECR 405.
3.   Case 25/62 *Plaumann & Co v EC Commission* [1963] ECR 95 at 115.
4.   See footnote 1 above.
5.   Cases 106 and 107/63 *Toepfer v EC Commission* [1965] ECR 405 at 411.

In many ways, the Court's ruling was similar to Advocate General Gand's finding in the *Getreide-Import* case when he held that :

> "Where the intervention of a Member State is a purely technical implementation, the Community decision is of *direct* concern to the individual."[1]

On the whole, because regulations are by their nature directly applicable, there will be little difficulty in showing that the natural or legal person caught by their provisions is directly concerned. Only in cases where the regulations require or allow the authorities in the Member States to adopt implementing measures may the link between the authority adopting the measure and the individual affected by it be broken[2].

4.2.3   Why is article 173, 2nd para, interpreted so restrictively?

Smit and Herzog[3] in their Commentary on the EEC Treaty are of the opinion that the restrictive interpretation of article 173, 2nd para is to be regretted. They contend that the rule of law would have been better served if each citizen were given the opportunity to take an action directly before the Court where their legal rights had been prejudiced by a Community measure. Why then has the Court interpreted article 173, 2nd para against individuals?[4]

Advocate General Lagrange considered this question in *Confédération Nationale des Producteurs de Fruits et Légumes v EC Council*[5]. He noted that there existed two indirect remedies for individuals to challenge a Community regulation, namely a plea of illegality under article 184 and a ruling on validity under article 177, 1st para, point (b). More importantly, he emphasised the quasi-legislative character which regulations normally assume and the fact that extremely grave consequences would follow from even a partial annulment of the regulations. Rasmussen[6] rejects this argument on the basis that the Court has annulled regulations where their validity has been called into question under article 177, 1st para, point (b) as well

---

1.   Case 38/64 *Getreide-Import Gesellschaft mbH v EC Commission* [1965] ECR 203 at 211.

2.   See Case 123/77 *UNICME v EC Council* [1978] ECR 845 where the Court ruled that even though the persons affected by the Council measure could be determined more or less precisely the measure was not of "direct concern" to them as long as no application for an import permit had been denied by the national authorities. See also Case 11/82 *Piraiki Patraiki v EC Commission* [1985] ECR 207.

3.   Volume 5 at p379.

4.   See generally Rasmussen "Why is Article 173 interpreted against Private Plaintiffs" 5 ELRev (1980) 112; J Dinnage "Locus Standi and Article 173" ELRev (1979) 15.

5.   Cases 16 and 17/62 *Confédération nationale des producteurs de fruits et légumes and Fédération nationale des producteurs de raisins de table v EC Council*[1962] ECR 471 at 486.

6.   Ramussen, above, at p120.

as under article 173, 2nd para[1]. He points to the fact that the Court will take into account the instability that may occur as a result of the annulment when dealing with the merits of the case.

Stein and Vining[2] advance the argument that political considerations are buttressed by the inherent aversion of administrators to judicial control. Rasmussen[3] rejects this argument, since he believes there is little evidence that it has any bearing on the Court's rationale. There is also the argument by some[4] that the Court's attitude to article 173, 2nd para is aimed at trying to maintain a balance between allowing individuals an opportunity to seek annulment of acts of the EC Council and EC Commission, and a fear of opening itself up to a flood of such actions.

Finally, and possibly the most convincing reason for the Court's restrictive interpretation of article 173, 2nd para, is the "appellate court" argument put forward by Rasmussen[5]. He contends that not only the Court's interpretation of article 173 but also of articles 175 and 215(2), is evidence of the Court's policy to establish itself as an appellate court. This argument has gained weight with the establishment of the Court of First Instance[6].

4.2.4   The position under the ECSC Treaty

In order to understand the reasoning for the Court's restrictive interpretation of article 173 it is important to note the main differences under the ECSC Treaty.

Article 33, the provision which covers an action for annulment, differs from article 173 in several respects. First and foremost, only undertakings engaged in the production of coal and steel may sue. Second, an undertaking may challenge a decision or a recommendation[7]. It must show, however, that either the decision or

---

1.   See for example Case 114/76 *Bele-Mühle Josepf Bergmann v Grows-Farm GmbH* [1977] ECR 1211; *Japanese Ballbearing Cases*, Cases 113/77 *NTN Toyo Bearing Co Ltd and Ors v EC Council and EC Commission*; Case 118/77 *Import Standard Office (ISO) v EC Council*; Case 119/77 *Nippon Seiko KK and Ors v EC Council*; Case 120/77 *Koyo Seiko Co Ltd and Ors v EC Council and EC Commission* and Case 121/77 *Nachi Fujikoshi Corporation and Ors v EC Council* [1979] ECR 1185 et seq.

2.   "Citizen Access to Judicial Review of Administrative Action in Transnational and Federal Context" in (ed) Jacobs "European Law and the Individual" 116 at 123.

3.   Ramussen "Why is Article 173 interpreted against Private Plaintiffs" 5 ELRev (1990) 112 at p121.

4.   See for example Stein and Vining, above, at p123; Brown and Jacobs "The Court of Justice of the European Communities" p97.

5.   Ramussen, above, p124.

6.   Council Decision (ECSC, EEC, Euratom) 88/591 (OJ L319 25.11.88 p1); amended text in OJ C215 21.8.89 p1.

7.   Decisions are defined in article 14 thus : "[Decisions] shall be binding in their entirety". Recommendations are defined in article 14 thus : "[Recommendations] shall be binding as to the aims to be pursued but shall leave the choice of the appropriate methods for achieving these aims to those to whom the recommendations are addressed".

recommendation "is individual in character" or, if it is general in character, that it involves a misuse of powers affecting that undertaking. Finally, there is no need to show direct concern. This invariably stems from the fact that it is the High Authority and not the Member States that has the power to adopt legally binding measures. In these circumstances, the High Authority's relationship with coal and steel undertakings is assumed to be direct.

Because article 33 is limited to a small number of undertakings, the Court has interpreted the provision in a very liberal manner. For example, where an undertaking challenges a decision addressed to someone else, it does not have to show that the decision concerns them individually or directly. In the *Second Limburg Coalmines Case* the Court stated that :

> "... to enable an undertaking to institute proceedings against a decision concerning it which is individual in character, it is not necessary that it should be the only, or almost the only, party concerned by the decision."[1]

4.2.5   Is there a time limit?

Article 173, 3rd para states that there is a period of two months within which an interested party can bring proceedings to have a measure annulled. This period is calculated from the date of publication of the measure or from its notification or in the absence of both, from the date when it first came to the knowledge of the applicant[2].

4.3   Action for failure to act - article 175 of the EEC Treaty

This action provides a remedy when the EC Council or EC Commission fail to act where they are obliged to do so under the Treaties. The Court has indicated that it regards an action for annulment and an action for failure to act as "one and the same procedure"[3] though the latter should not be used simply for purposes of evading the conditions for the former[4].

---

1.   Case 30/59 *De Gezamenlijke Steenkolenmijnen in Limburg v High Authority* [1961] ECR 1 at 17.
2.   Under the ECSC Treaty the time limit is only one month. For the method of computing time limits see Case 152/85 *Misset v EC Council* [1987] ECR 223.
3.   Case 15/70 *Chevalley v EC Commission* [1970] ECR 975 at 979.
4.   Joined Cases 10 and 18/68 *"Eridania" v EC Commission* [1969] ECR 459 at 483.

4.3.1   Capacity to bring an action

4.3.1.1 Privileged applicants

The Member States and the other institutions of the Community can bring an action against the EC Council or EC Commission where they have failed to act, in infringement of the Treaty[1].

4.3.1.2 Non-privileged applicants

Article 175, 3rd para provides that :

> "Any natural or legal person may ... complain to the Court of Justice that an institution of the Community has failed to address to that person any act other than a recommendation or an opinion."

The term "act" should be given the same meaning as that under article 173 and as a result is not limited solely to those binding acts enumerated in article 189[2]. Article 175, 3rd para should be interpreted to allow any natural or legal person to raise any action against the EC Commission or EC Council for failure to perform any act that would have been of direct and individual concern to him. Only this interpretation would, as the Court pointed out in *Chevalley*, permit articles 173 and 175 to be viewed as one and the same procedure[3].

4.3.2   Preconditions of an action

An action under article 175 involves two separate stages. First, the institution must be called upon to act as required by Community law[4]. There is no time limit within which this must take place though it should be within a reasonable time of the institution having shown its intention not to act[5]. Within two months of being called upon to act, the institution concerned must define its position. Second, if at the end of the two months, the institution has not defined its position, article 175, 2nd para states that the applicant may bring proceedings within a further period of two months.

The grounds of review must be the same as those enumerated in article 173 if the two articles are to be of a mutually complementary nature. The effect of a successful article 175 action is that the institution whose failure to act has been declared

---

1.　　　Article 175(1).
2.　　　Case 15/70 *Chevalley v EC Commission* [1970] ECR 975.
3.　　　Case 15/70 *Chevalley v EC Commission* [1970] ECR 975. See also the Opinion of Advocate General Dutheillet de Lamothe in Case 15/71 *Mackprang v EC Commission* [1971] ECR 797.
4.　　　Article 175(2).
5.　　　Case 59/70 *Netherlands v EC Commission* [1971] ECR 639.

contrary to the Treaty must take the necessary measures to comply with the Court's judgment[1]. There has been to date only one successful action[2].

4.3.3 Proceedings under the ECSC Treaty

Under article 35 of ECSC Treaty, the procedure is similar in most respects in that the object and the effect of the judgment are the same. There are, however, a number of minor differences.

First, the only possible defendant is the EC Commission, while the only applicants entitled to bring an action are the EC Council, the Member States and undertakings or associations[3]; second, undertakings or associations may only challenge decisions which are individual in character[4]; third, the only acts which the institution can be required to take are recommendations or decisions[5]; fourth, a request for action under the ECSC Treaty can only be satisfied by a binding act, and this may be subject to an action for annulment under article 33 ECSC; fifth, the time limits are different in that proceedings have to be initiated within one month of a failure to take any decision or make any recommendation[6]; and lastly, proceedings are initiated against the implied decision of a refusal which is in essence an annulment of that decision[7].

4.4 Plea of illegality : article 184 of the EEC Treaty

Article 184 is designed to overcome the limitations of an action for annulment under article 173, namely the restrictions on locus standi.

The plea of illegality permits a natural or legal person who cannot challenge a true regulation, ie a general legislative act, to do so indirectly when it is applied to him by a subsequent individual act in order that the underlying "general measure" is

---

1. Article 176(1).
2. Case 13/83 *European Parliament v EC Council* [1985] ECR 1513; there have also been two successful actions under the ECSC Treaty.
3. Article 35(1).
4. Action for failure to act must have the same characteristics as an action for annulment. Joined Cases 7 and 9/54 *Groupement des Industries Sidérurgiques Luxembourgeoises v High Authority* [1954-56] ECR 175 at 191-2.
5. Article 35(1).
6. Article 35(3).
7. Ibid.

declared inapplicable to him. The term "general measure" is used even though article 184 specifically refers to a regulation. The reason for this is that the Court in *Simmenthal* held that :

> "The field of application of [article 184] must therefore include acts of the institutions which, although they are not in the form of a regulation, nevertheless produce similar effects and on those grounds may not be challenged under article 173 by natural or legal persons other than the Community institutions and Member States."[1]

The plea cannot be brought independently but must arise in another action, hence its description by one commentator - "it forms a shield not a sword"[2]. Because it is an ancillary action, the plea will fail if the other action is unsuccessful. Furthermore, a plea of illegality is applicable only in the context of proceedings brought before the Court under some other provision of the Treaty[3].

The grounds upon which the plea may be raised are the same as those laid down in article 173. The effect of a successful plea is that the general act in question will be declared inapplicable to the party challenging it and the individual act, deprived of its legal basis, annulled. Unlike an action for annulment, the act would not be declared void, though in practical terms the institution responsible for it will replace it in order to avoid a multiplicity of actions.

4.5 Action for damages - article 215, 2nd para of the EEC Treaty

Article 215, 2nd para states that :

> "The Community shall, in accordance with the general principles common to the laws of the Member States, make good any damage caused by its institutions or by its servants in the performance of their duties."

---

1. Case 92/78 *Simmenthal SpA v EC Commission* [1979] ECR 777 at 800.
2. Paisley "Guide to EEC Law in Northern Ireland" (1986).
3. Cases 31 and 33/62 *Milchwerke Heinz Wöhrmann and Sohn KG and Alfons Lütticke GmbH v EC Commission* [1962] ECR 501 at 507.

The action for damages is a distinct and separate form of legal recourse from Articles 173 and 175[1]. In *Lütticke v EC Commission* the Court held that :

> "The action for damages provided for by article 178 and the second paragraph of article 215 was established by the Treaty as an independent form of action with a particular purpose to fulfil within the system of actions and subject to conditions for its use, conceived with a view to its specific purpose."[2]

As Vaughan[3] stresses, the Court in developing its case law has proceeded cautiously in order to avoid extending the non-contractual liability of the institutions. The result has been that a number of limitations have been placed on the liability of the Community. This is especially so in relation to liability for legislative measures. Undoubtedly, this restrictiveness does have consequences in the field of external relations, where safeguard measures adopted to counteract unfair trade practices invariably take the form of regulations.

The aim of an action for damages is not to bring about the annulment of an act or measure but to establish subjective rights to financial compensation for actual loss sustained. The Court held in *Atkien-Zuckerfabrik Schöppenstedt v EC Council* that a claim for damages :

> "differs from an application for annulment in that its end is not the abolition of a particular measure, but compensation for damages caused by an institution in the performance of its duties."[4]

While an action for damages can and often does result from the illegality of Community behaviour or the lack of it, it can in fact occur without that precondition. The law relating to an action for damages does not require the prior formal declaration of annulment of a Community act or the declaration of failure to act as a prerequisite for the admissibility of a damages action[5].

Even though a claim for damages and an action for annulment are conceptually different this does not mean that they need be the subject of separate proceedings.

---

1. Originally the Court treated an action for damages under Article 215(2) as a subsidiary form of action in that it had to be coupled with an action for annulment under Article 173 or an action under Article 175 for failure to act. If these failed so also did the action for damages; see generally Case 25/62 *Plaumann v EC Commission* [1963] ECR 95.
2. Case 4/69 *Lütticke v EC Commission* [1971] ECR 325 at 336.
3. Vaughan "Law of the European Communities" (Butterworths, London).
4. Case 5/71 *Atkien-Zuckerfabrik Schöppenstedt v EC Council* [1971] ECR 975 at 983. See also Case 43/72 *Merkur v EC Commission* [1973] ECR 1055 at 1069.
5. Conditions for the admissibility of an action for damages are autonomous of any annulment procedure. See generally Case 43/72 *Merkur v EC Commission* above.

For instance, it is possible to make them both the subject of the same proceedings. In such a case the admissibility and the merits of each will be judged separately according to their own different rules.

Article 215, 2nd para does not define the conditions or limits to Community liability. It refers simply to the "non-contractual liability" of the Community which has to be determined "in accordance with the general principles common to the laws of the Member States".

Four basic conditions have to be established in order to establish liability. They are as follows :

    4.5.1   The conduct of the institutions must be illegal.

    4.5.2   There must be a causal connection between the alleged injury and the conduct with which the institutions are charged.

    4.5.3   There must be injury.

    4.5.4   The conduct of the institutions must be culpable, ie the act or omission must constitute an official fault or a misconduct on the part of its author.

4.5.1 Illegality of the conduct of the institutions

The non-contractual liability of the Community arises from the existence of a wrongful act or omission on the part of the Community institutions or its servants in the performance of their duties. There are basically two main activities associated with the performance of their duties, namely, in their capacity as law makers and in carrying out their administrative duties.

Under the first category, the Court will be required to consider the illegality of the Community measure itself, whereas the second category is concerned mainly with the question of administrative fault.

One of the most important questions to be answered definitively by the Court is whether illegality of a Community measure is a pre-condition for liability. Generally speaking, the non-contractual liability of the Community requires that the measure or omission be illegal. In most cases a failure to establish illegality under article 173 would be sufficient evidence that there had not been a breach of official duty and would lead to the action being dismissed. For example, in *Kampffmeyer v EC Commission* the Court held that :

"the Commission applied article 22(2) of Regulation 19 [safeguard measures] in circumstances which did not justify protective measures ... As it was aware of the existence of applications for licences, it caused damage to the interests of importers who had acted in reliance on the information provided in accordance with Community Rules. The Commission's conduct constituted a wrongful act or omission capable of giving rise to liability on the part of the Community."[1]

More recently there have been indications that the Court might under exceptional circumstances rule that Community liability arises irrespective of illegality. Applicants have sought to rely on the German legal concept of *Sonderopfer* (special sacrifice) and the equivalent French concept of *égalité devant les charges publiques* (equality of all citizens in sharing public burdens) in order to found a claim for compensation in respect of lawful Community acts. Where a lawful act is involved, the applicant would have to show the following :

(a)   the damage is particular to one or several persons;

(b)   the loss is abnormally severe; and

(c)   the source of damage must be shown not to have been made in the interest of public order[2].

As is the case under article 173, 2nd para, the Court in applying article 215, 2nd para, considers whether the applicant was affected in a special and individual way. It would contravene the logic of the system for the direct challenge by individuals of the legality of Community measures if an individual were allowed an unqualified right to challenge normative measures under the guise of seeking compensation for alleged damage resulting from them. As the Court held in *Koninklijke Scholten Honig NV v EC Commission and EC Council* :

"even though an action for damages under article 178 and 215(2) constitutes an independent action, it must nevertheless be assessed having regard to the whole of the system of legal protection of individuals set up by the Treaty. If an individual takes the view that he is injured by a Community legislative measure which he regards as illegal he has the opportunity, when the implementation of the measure is entrusted to national authorities, to contest

---

1.   Case 5, 7, 13-24/66 *Kampffmeyer v EC Commission* [1967] ECR 245 at 262.
2.   See Opinion of Advocate General Verloren van Themaat in Case 26/81 *Oleifici Mediterranei SA v EEC* [1982] ECR 3057 at 3089-90 and Opinion of Advocate General Slynn in Case 59/83 *SA Biovilac NV v EEC* [1984] ECR 4057 at 4082 et seq.

the validity of the measure at the time of its implementation, before a national court in an action against the national authority. Such a court may, or even must, in pursuance of article 177, refer to the Court of Justice a question on the validity of the Community measure in question. The existence of such an action is by itself of such a nature as to ensure the efficient protection of the individuals concerned."[1]

However, where legislative action involving measures of economic policy are concerned, illegality on its own is not sufficient to give rise to liability even though it may give rise to annulment in the context of article 173 or invalidity in the context of article 177. Two further criteria have to be fulfilled. There must be a breach of a superior rule of law for the protection of the individual[2] and the institution in question must have "manifestly and gravely disregarded the limits on the exercise of its powers[3].

Community liability is limited by insisting that there has to be a breach of a superior rule for the protection of the individual because in the view of the EC Commission, if this were not the case :

"the institutions would be submerged in a spate of actions entailing considerable interference with their proper working"[4].

The Court has equated the idea of breach of a superior rule for the protection of the individual with breach of general principles common to the laws of the Member States. For example, in the *CNTA* case, the general principle concerned was legitimate expectation. It held :

"the Commission has violated a superior rule of law, thus rendering the Community liable, by failing to include in Regulation 189/72 transitional measures for the protection of the confidence which a trader might legitimately have had in the Community rules"[5].

---

1. Case 143/77 *Koninklijke Scholten Honig NV v EC Commission and EC Council* [1979] ECR 3583 at 3626.
2. Eg Case 5/71 *Atkien-Zuckerfabrik Schöppenstedt v EC Council* [1971] ECR 975 at p984.
3. Joined Cases 83 and 94/76 and 4, 15, 40/77 *Bayerische HNL v EC Council and EC Commission* [1978] ECR 1209 at 1224-5.
4. Seventh General Report of EC Commission (1973) point 596.
5. Case 74/74 *Compoir national téchnique agricole (CNTA) v EC Commission* [1975] ECR 533 at 550; in Case 5/71 *Atkien-Zuckerfabrik Schöppenstedt v EC Council* [1971] ECR 975, it was the principle of non-discrimination.

In *Ireks-Arkady* the Court ruled that there was a breach of the principle of equality in that the provisions of the regulation provided for quellmehl and pre-glutinised starch to receive different treatment in respect of production refunds[1]. Advocate General Capotorti in the *Bayerische HNL* case identified three elements which he considered would be sufficient to make unlawfulness serious to qualify as a breach of a superior rule of law. First, the level of importance of the infringed rule; second, the degree of blame to be attached to the author of the measure; and third, the extent of the loss suffered[2].

In determining whether the institutions have manifestly and gravely disregarded the limits on the exercise of their powers, the Court takes into account the extent to which the harm is concentrated on a small number of victims and the degree of that harm[3].

4.5.2 Causal connection

The applicant must show that injury was caused by an act or omission on the part of the Community institutions. In other words, injury must result from conduct of Community institutions and it must result from that conduct directly, immediately and exclusively[4]. In *Kampffmeyer* [5] the act that had been committed by the German Government and expressly approved by the EC Commission was held by the Court to constitute the causal link between the act of approval and the damage suffered.

4.5.3 There must be injury

There must exist an actual and certain damage which is both appreciable and definitive. The damage must have crystalised by the time the claim for compensation is made, since an action under article 215, 2nd para which concerns only future or potential loss will generally be dismissed as premature[6]. An applicant will generally have to show that he has been affected in a special and individual manner.

The burden of proof rests with the party bringing the action. The applicant must provide satisfactory evidence as to the existence and precise amount of damage to

---

1.   Case 238/78 *Ireks-Arkady GmbH v EC Commission* [1979] ECR 2955 at 2973.
2.   Joined Cases 83 and 94/76 and 4, 15, 40/77 *Bayerische HNL v EC Council and EC Commission* [1978] ECR 1209 at 1232.
3.   Case 238/78 *Ireks-Arkady GmbH v EC Commission* [1979] ECR 2955; and Joined Cases 83 and 94/76, and 4, 15, 40/77 *Bayerische HNL v EC Council and EC Commission* above.
4.   See Smit and Herzog "The Law of the European Economic Community : A Commentary on the EEC Treaty" Volume 6 p95.
5.   Case 5, 7, 13-24/66 *Kampffmeyer v EC Commission* [1967] ECR 245.
6.   See for example, Joined Cases 9 and 25/64 *Third Feram Case* [1965] ECR 311 at 320.

enable the Court to determine the appropriate compensation. The damage must be certain and specific. It must be quantifiable in that it is capable of being expressed as a specified sum of money.

In deciding on quantum, the Court will allow for direct loss and other additional expenses necessarily and reasonably incurred as a direct consequence of the Community act, for example indemnity payments for failure to honour contracts. As regards loss of profits, the Court is not quite as generous owing to the speculative nature of assessing them[1].

4.5.4   Culpability of the institution's conduct

Culpability is taken to mean that the illegal act or omission must constitute an official fault or misconduct on the part of its author. For example, such conduct may consist of the enactment of an improper Community measure. In this case, liability may arise if it can be shown that the institutions were negligent. Other types of conduct may include grave misjudgment of market relations, or inexcusable forecasting errors[2].

4.5.5   Time limit

An action must be brought within five years from the occurrence of the event.

4.6   A preliminary ruling on the validity of acts of the institutions - article 177, 1st para, point (b) of the EEC Treaty

The Court has the duty to ensure the uniform interpretation and application of Community law in the courts of the Member States. For this purpose, the EEC Treaty confers on all courts the power - article 177, 2nd para - and on some the duty - article 177, 3rd para - to refer questions of Community law to the Court for its ruling. By virtue of article 177, 1st para, point (b), the Court has jurisdiction to give a preliminary ruling concerning the validity of acts of the institutions of the Community.

4.6.1   The acts whose validity may be the subject of a preliminary ruling

Article 177 is broadly drafted and makes no reference to article 189 which enumerates Community acts which are binding and those which are non-binding. As a result, it may be assumed that any act originating with the Community

---

1.   See Case 5, 7, 13-24/66 *Kampffmeyer v EC Commission* [1967] ECR 245; Case 74/74 *CNTA v EC Commission* [1975] ECR 533.
2.   See for example, Joined Cases 116 and 124/77 *G.R. Amylum NV and Tunnel Refineries Ltd v EC Council and EC Commission* (Isoglucose cases) [1979] ECR 3497.

institutions and forming part of the Community legal order comes within the ambit of article 177[1].

Just because an action for the annulment of a regulation is held inadmissible by the Court does not mean that the applicant can no longer challenge the validity of that regulation. In *Koninklijke Scholten Honig NV v EC Commission and EC Council*, the applicant's action for annulment was held to be inadmissible but they were able to have the regulation declared invalid under article 177, 1st para, point (b)[2].

4.6.2 The questions to be referred

The formulation of the question(s) referred is a matter for the national court alone to decide. The role of the European Court is to rule on its validity, not to apply Community law to the facts of the case facing the national court.

4.6.3 The courts which may make a reference

Article 177, 2nd para grants a discretion to courts or tribunals of the Member States to refer a question as laid down in article 177, 1st para to the Court on condition that a decision on the question is necessary for the court or tribunal to give judgment. Article 177, 2nd para attributes the right to request a preliminary ruling to any court or tribunal of the Member States. In *BRT v SABAM*, the Court held that this right cannot be fettered by regulation of the Communities and that the preliminary ruling procedure will continue so long as "the request of the national court has neither been withdrawn nor become devoid of object"[3]. In this latter respect, the Court in the *Second Rheinmuühlen* case held that "in the case of a court against whose decisions there is a judicial remedy under national law, article 177 does not preclude a decision of such a court referring a question to this Court for a preliminary ruling from remaining subject to the remedies normally available under national law"[4].

The Court was not prepared to follow Advocate General Warner's opinion. He took the view that the discretion to refer may not be fettered by any rule or provision of national law[5]. The Court's view has been criticised[6] on the basis that it was

---

1. Case 322/88 *Grimaldi v Fonds des Maladies Professionnelles Bruxelles* [1989] ECR 4407 at para 8 of judgment.
2. Case 143/77 *Koninklijke Scholten Honig NV v EC Council and EC Commission* [1979] ECR 3583.
3. Case 127/73 *Belgische Radio en Televisie and Société Belge des Auteurs, Compositeurs et Editeurs v SV SABAM and NV Fonior* [1974] ECR 51 at 63.
4. Case 146/73 *Rheinmuhlen-Dusseldorf v Einfuhr- und Vorrastsstelle für Getreide und Futtermittel* [1974] ECR 139 at para 3 of judgment.
5. Case 146/73 *Rheinmuhlen-Dusseldorf v Einfuhr- und Vorrastsstelle für Getreide und Futtermittel* [1974] ECR 139 at para 3 of judgment.
6. See O'Keefe "Appeals against an order to refer under Article 177 of the EEC Treaty" [1983] ELRev 87-104.

contrary to its normal practice of interpretation and furthermore such an interpretation could lead to undesirable consequences for the uniform application and interpretation of Community law.

4.6.3.1 What constitutes a court or tribunal?

This is answered by reference to Community law. The concept of judicial function is difficult to define, but normally a body is regarded as being judicial if it has power to give binding determinations of legal rights and obligations of individuals. One commentator has argued that three criteria have to be fulfilled before a body can be considered a court or tribunal. They are as follows :

(a)   the requirement to solve a dispute between the parties;

(b)   the existence of various institutional factors;

(c)   the involvement of public authorities[1].

4.6.3.2 Necessity

A decision on the question raised before the Court must be "necessary" to enable the national court to give judgment. It is not the reference to the Court which must be necessary but a decision on the question. Furthermore, the Treaty makes it clear that this is a question for the national court to decide.

When is a decision necessary in order to give judgment? Bebr has noted that this should be understood in the sense of a question being relevant for pending litigation rather than as one being indispensable[2].

4.6.4   The courts which must make a reference

Article 177, 3rd para states that :

> "Where any such question [in sense of article 177, 1st para] is raised in a case pending before a court or tribunal of a Member State, against whose decisions there is no judicial remedy under national law, that court or tribunal shall bring the matter before the Court of Justice."

---

1.   W. Alexander and E. Grabandt "National Courts entitled to ask Preliminary Rulings under Article 177 of the EEC Treaty : The case law of the Court of Justice" 19 CMLRev 413-420.
2.   Bebr "Development of judicial control of the European Communities".

What constitutes a court or tribunal against whose decisions there is no judicial remedy?

In an attempt to answer this question, two distinct theories have developed. The first theory, the so-called "abstract theory", is that the only courts within the scope of the provision are those whose decisions are never subject to appeal. Arguments in favour of this theory include considerations of national legal policy from the viewpoint of the costs involved and the prevention of long drawn out proceedings. The second theory, the so-called "concrete" theory, is that the courts or tribunals within the scope of the provision are those against whose decisions there is no judicial remedy. If the courts against whose decision there is no judicial remedy were identical with the highest courts of the Member States, an abstract theory presumes that the notion of judicial remedy would be irrelevant. The abstract theory also assumes that only cases brought before the highest courts are of the greatest importance for the interpretation and validity of Community law[1].

Article 177, 3rd para does not reiterate the qualification that a decision on the question must be necessary. Does this mean that the courts within the scope of article 177, 3rd para are always compelled to ask for a preliminary ruling even if they do not consider a ruling to be necessary? In *CILFIT v Ministero della Sanità* the Court held that it :

> "follows from the relationship between the second and third paragraphs of article 177 that the courts or tribunals referred to in the third paragraph have the same discretion as any other national court or tribunal to ascertain whether a decision on a question of Community law is necessary to enable them to give judgment"[2].

4.6.5 The effect of a ruling as to the validity of the measure under article 177, 1st para, point (b)

At strict law, the effect of a ruling of invalidity (under article 177, 1st para, point (b)) is that it is binding only on the court which requested the ruling. This is similar to the effect of a plea of illegality under article 184. Technically, the measure remains in force but because of its invalidity it cannot be applied in the instant case.

---

1.   Hartley "The Foundation of EEC Law" at p261 et seq.
2.   Case 283/81 *CILFIT v Ministero della Sanità* [1982] ECR 3415 at 3429 para 10 of judgment.

There is, however, judicial authority from the Court which now infers that a ruling under article 177, 1st para, point (b) may have general effect. In *International Chemical Corporation v Amministrazione delle Finanze dello Stato* the Court held that :

> "... Although a judgment of the Court given under article 177 of the Treaty declaring an act of an institution, in particular a Council or Commission regulation, to be void is directly addressed only to the national court which brought the matter before the Court, it is sufficient reason for any other national court to regard that act as void for the purposes of a judgment which it has to give"[1].

The general effect of an article 177, 1st para, point (b) ruling may also stem from the subsequent behaviour of the Community institutions. The institution responsible for the measure may repeal it and replace it with a valid measure. In *Providence Agricole de la Champagne v ONIC* the Court held that :

> "Although the Treaty does not expressly lay down the consequences which flow from a declaration of invalidity within the framework of a reference to the Court for a preliminary ruling, articles 174 and 176 contain clear rules as to the effects of the annulment of a regulation within the framework of a direct action. Thus article 176 provides that the institution whose act has been declared void shall be required to take the necessary measures to comply with the judgment of the Court of Justice. In its judgments of 19 October 1977 in Joined Cases 117/76 and 16/77 (*Ruckdeschel and Hansa-Lagerheus Ströh* (Quellmehl) [1977] ECR 1753) and in Joined Cases 124/76 and 20/77 (*Moulins et Huileries de Pont-à-Mousson* and *Providence Agricole de la Champagne* (Maize Groats and meal) [1977] ECR 1975) the Court has already referred to that rule within the context of a reference to it for a preliminary ruling"[2].

PART 2 : "LOCUS STANDI" - SAFEGUARD MEASURES

4.7   Action for annulment : article 173

4.7.1   Introduction

Generally speaking, protective measures adopted by the Community authorities are in the form of a regulation. To date, where such measures have been challenged, proceedings have been raised under article 173. For this reason, the analysis of judicial review of safeguard measures will concentrate largely on article 173.

---

1.   Case 66/80 *International Chemical Corporation v Amministrazione delle Finanze dello Stato* [1981] ECR 1191 at 1216 para 18(a) of judgment.
2.   Case 4/79 *Providence Agricole de la Champagne v ONIC* [1980] ECR 2823 at 2853 para 44.

Unlike Community acts relating to the implementation of competition rules, which are now subject to the jurisdiction of the Court of First Instance[1], Community acts imposing protective measures and in particular anti-dumping and countervailing duties are solely subject to the jurisdiction of the Court.

By virtue of article 3(3) of the decision establishing the Court of First Instance[2], it was envisaged that the competence to exercise jurisdiction in such matters subject to a right of appeal to the Court on a point of law would be reviewed. The EC Commission has recently issued its opinion on the draft EC Council decision, prepared by the Court of Justice, amending the decision establishing the Court of First Instance with a view to extending that Court's jurisdiction[3].

In essence, the Court has proposed that the jurisdiction of the Court of First Instance be extended to all direct actions brought by individuals. The EC Commission is in principle in favour of the proposed changes on the ground that the transfer of jurisdiction in direct actions would allow the Court to concentrate on its primary role of interpreting Community law for the national courts. It is not in favour of extending the jurisdiction of the Court of First Instance where state aids or the review of safeguard measures, in particular the review of anti-dumping measures, are concerned[4].

It takes the view that the addition of a second tier to the judicial system would render the decision-making process even more cumbersome than it is at present given the existing two stage administrative procedure. Inevitably there would be a real danger that certainty as to the law for all interested parties and the effectiveness of the Community's trade law policy might be prejudiced[5].

In this respect, the EC Commission has observed that its fears regarding the transfer of jurisdiction in these matters would be alleviated if the EC Council were to adopt its proposal to reduce the administrative proceedings to one stage only with the power to adopt both provisional and definitive anti-dumping duties being delegated to the EC Commission[6].

---

1.   Council Decision (ECSC, EEC, Euratom) 88/591 (OJ L319 25.11.88 p1); amended text in OJ C215 21.8.89 p1.
2.   Ibid.
3.   Bulletin of European Communities No 3 1992 at 114-115.
4.   Ibid at p115.
5.   Ibid.
6.   Clifford Chance 'EC Trade Law Quarterly' April-June 1992.

The attitude of the Court to the admissibility of actions where safeguard measures are concerned varies according to the parties who seek to have the measures annulled. In these circumstances, the analysis will proceed on the basis of considering separately the position of those interested parties which are most likely to challenge safeguard measures. As stated above, where a natural or legal person wishes to challenge the legality of a regulation under article 173, 2nd para they will have to show three things : that the regulation in question is in essence a decision, that it concerns them directly and that it concerns them individually.

From what has been stated above, the Court's attitude to the interpretation of article 173, 2nd para is very restrictive. The Court will only in very exceptional circumstances annul a Community regulation where it is an individual who challenges the legality of that regulation. The Court adopts a much more liberal approach to the admissibility of an action under article 173, 2nd para where safeguard measures are concerned, otherwise virtually all those parties most affected by the regulation in question would have little prospect of challenging the legality of the regulation. As a general rule of thumb, the Court, in determining whether an interested party has locus standi, will consider whether :

— it has been named specifically in the measure challenged; or

— it is concerned by the findings relating to the existence of dumping complained of; or

— its procedural guarantees under the basic regulation have been infringed.

4.7.2 Exporters/producers

4.7.2.1 Regulation 2423/88
(a) Anti-dumping duties
Anti-dumping regulations are peculiar in that they apply to all products of a certain type from a particular country but which are based on the findings of the prices charged by a small number of exporters. In these circumstances, a regulation imposing anti-dumping duties does not fall neatly into the definition of a regulation or a decision for that matter, in terms of article 189.

This peculiarity may have been the reason why Advocate General Warner in the *Japanese Ballbearing* cases[1] was of the opinion that the regulation imposing the

---

1.   Case 113/77 *NTN Toyo Bearing Co Ltd and Ors v EC Council* [1979] ECR 1185, Advocate General Warner's opinion at 1212.

anti-dumping duties was a "hybrid instrument". He referred to this "hybrid instrument" as a kind that the Court has not had to consider before and may seldom have to consider. In other words, for everyone except the four named exporters in the regulation, it was a measure of general application. However, as far as each of the exporters were concerned, it constituted a decision of direct and individual concern[1].

The Court did not follow the Advocate General's approach, nor did it adopt his idea of a "hybrid instrument". It held that the regulation imposing definitive duties was of direct and individual concern not only to the named exporters, but also to those importers specifically named in the operative part of the regulation which were subsidiaries of the exporters. As there was no need to make a distinction between the producers/exporters on the one hand and the importers on the other, all the applicants had locus standi[2]. The reason put forward by the Court for not making the distinction was that the EC Commission in its investigations applied the special provisions concerning export prices where the exporters and importers were associated[3].

A much broader approach to the question of whether exporters had locus standi to challenge regulations imposing anti-dumping duties was adopted by the Court in the *First Allied* case[4]. The Court held that the question of locus standi must be resolved in the light of the system established by the basic regulation (now Regulation 2423/88) and more particularly, of the nature of the anti-dumping measures provided for by that regulation, regard being had to the provisions of the second paragraph of article 173[5].

It then stated that although regulations imposing anti-dumping duties, and for that matter countervailing duties, are legislative in character since they apply to all the traders concerned, taken as a whole, the provisions may nonetheless be of direct and individual concern to those exporters charged with dumping. Anti-dumping duties can only be imposed on the basis of the findings resulting from investigations concerning the production prices and export prices of undertakings which have been individually identified[6]. In these circumstances the Court held that the measures imposing anti-dumping duties are liable to be of direct and individual concern to those producers and exporters who are able to establish that

---

1.   Ibid at 1246.
2.   Ibid at 1204-5.
3.   Ibid at 1204, para 9 of judgment.
4.   Joined Cases 239 and 275/82 *Allied Corporation and Ors v EC Commission* [1984] ECR 1005.
5.   Ibid at 1029, para 10 of judgment.
6.   Joined Cases 239 and 275/82 *Allied Corporation and Ors v EC Commission* [1984] ECR 1005 at 1030, para 11 of judgment.

they were identified in the measures adopted by the Community institutions or that they were concerned by the preliminary investigations[1].

In concluding that the exporters had locus standi the Court referred to the fact that the EC Commission had during the oral procedure noted that, on balance, it was in favour of the admissibility of direct actions brought by undertakings from non-Member States[2].

The decision in the *First Allied* case should not be seen as amounting to a licence for all exporters to raise an action under article 173, 2nd para. In *Sermes SA v EC Commission*[3], the Court in summarising its case law held that it was "generally" true that exporters and producers would be directly and individually concerned on the basis that they were able to establish that they were identified in the measure adopted or that they had been concerned by the preliminary investigations.

Identification in the measure in question or involvement in the investigations will be regarded as prima facie evidence that the exporter or producer in question has locus standi. Advocate General Mischo in *Nashua Corporation v EC Commission and EC Council*[4] considered that the determining factor is that the exporter or producer must have been charged with dumping on the basis of information about their business activities. Identification or involvement afforded a strong presumption but not proof that this was indeed the case[5]. The Court did not go as far as the Advocate General. It concluded that the crucial factor was whether the economic agent in question was concerned by the findings relating to the existence of dumping complained of. The Court, on the basis of the principles enunciated in the *First Allied* case, held that this was generally true in relation to exporters and producers[6].

Temple Lang was of the opinion that the refusal of an offer of an undertaking would be a decision addressed to the undertaking in question, with the result that it would

---

1.   Joined Cases 239 and 275/82 *Allied Corporation and Ors v EC Commission* [1984] ECR 1005 at 1030, para 12 of judgment.
2.   Ibid at 1029, para 9 of judgment.
3.   Case 279/86 [1987] ECR 3109 at para 15 of Order. See also Case 301/86 R *Frimodt Pedersen A/S v EC Commission* [1987] ECR 3123 at para 15 of Order; Case 205/87 *Nuova Ceam SrL v EC Commission* [1987] ECR 4428 at para 15 of Order.
4.   Joined Cases 133 and 150/87 *Nashua Corporation v EC Commission and EC Council* [1990] ECR 719 at 742.
5.   Joined Cases 133 and 150/87 *Nashua Corporation v EC Commission and EC Council* [1990] ECR 719 at 748.
6.   Ibid at 772.

have locus standi under article 173, 2nd para[1]. The Court, however, has taken a different view. In a number of the *Plain Paper Photocopier* cases it held that such a rejection was an intermediate measure whose purpose was to prepare for the final decision and was not, therefore, a measure which may be challenged before the Court. It is only at the stage of the imposition of definitive duties that traders can, by challenging the regulation imposing the duties, raise an irregularity associated with the rejection of their proposed undertaking[2].

(b) Countervailing duties

For the most part, the rules governing the imposition of countervailing duties are similar to those relating to anti-dumping duties. They are both governed by the same basic regulation, namely Regulation 2423/88.

In anti-dumping cases it is the export or production prices of individually identified undertakings that are considered. On the other hand, in anti-subsidy cases it is the activities of governmental or public bodies which are crucial. Frequently, in anti-subsidy cases, countervailing duties will be imposed without a finding being made about the exporters, for example, where a subsidy is given simply as a payment of so much per tonne exported. In such a situation, there would be no investigation into the activities of the exporters in question[3]. The exporters would therefore have no locus standi.

The Court has held that in considering the distinction between a regulation and a decision this "may be based only on the nature of the measure itself and the legal effects which it produces and not on the procedures for its adoption"[4]. As a consequence of this principle most exporters would have difficulty in challenging anti-subsidy regulations.

Notwithstanding this principle, the Court has held in *Fediol* that an interested party may derive locus standi from the procedural rights laid down in the basic

---

1.   "Judicial Review of Trade Safeguard Measures in the European Community" in 1985 (ed) B. Hawk 'Antitrust and Trade Policy in the United States and the European Community' Fordham University School of Law, at p644.
2.   See Joined Cases 133 and 150/87 *Nashua Corporation v EC Commission and EC Council* above, paras 9 and 10 of judgment; Case 156/87 *Gestetner Holdings plc v EC Commission and EC Council* [1990] ECR 781 at paras 8 and 9 of judgment.
3.   Only when the granting of a subsidy requires an investigation to be carried out will the exporter be able to show that they are directly and individually concerned.
4.   Case 307/81 *Alusuisse Italia SpA v EC Council and EC Commission* [1982] ECR 3463 at 3473, para 13 of judgment. See also Case 279/86 *Sermes SA v EC Commission*, [1987] ECR 3109; Case 301/86 R *Frimodt Pedersen A/S v EC Commission*, [1987] ECR 3123 and Case 205/86 *Nuova Ceam Srl v EC Commission*, [1987] ECR 4427. These cases all related to anti-dumping duties and whether independent importers had locus standi. The decisions are nonetheless applicable to all safeguard measures.

regulation, where those rights have been disregarded or infringed during the investigation[1]. This is likely only to arise where an exporter or producer is involved in an EC Commission investigation. In such a situation, one would expect that if a duty is imposed it will be on the basis of findings made about that exporter.

4.7.2.2 Regulation 288/82

Protective measures under Regulation 288/82 are imposed if the EC Commission concludes that serious injury is being caused to Community industry and that it is in the interests of that industry that protective measures are adopted. These measures usually take the form of quotas which may be applied to imports from all countries, or in some situations, to specific countries. Generally speaking, the imposition of such measures will rarely be based on the findings of individually identified exporters.

An exporter may have a right to challenge measures adopted under Regulation 288/82 where its procedural rights laid down by the basic regulation have been infringed or disregarded during the investigation. Article 6 of Regulation 288/82 states that the announcement of the opening of an investigation must specify a period within which interested parties make their views known in writing. By virtue of article 6(2), the EC Commission is empowered to collect all information it deems necessary and to endeavour to check this information with importers, traders, agents, producers, trade associations and organisations. More importantly, however, Article 6(4) allows the EC Commission to hear interested natural or legal persons. Such parties, where they have applied in writing, must be heard.

Temple Lang[2] has argued that the Court's judgment in the *Piraiki-Patraiki* case[3] has given exporters more scope to challenge quantitative restrictions adopted under Regulation 288/82. In this case, which is discussed below, the Court held that where the performance of identifiable contracts was made impossible by the imposition of quantitative restrictions and where the exporters had entered into these contracts, they would have locus standi[4].

---

1.   Case 191/82 *EEC Seed Crushers' and Oil Processors' Federation (Fediol) v EC Commission* [1983] ECR 2913 at 2935.
2.   Temple Lang "Judicial Review of Trade Safeguard Measures in the European Community" in 1985 (ed) B. Hawk 'Anti-trust and Trade Policy in the United States and the European Community' Fordham University School of Law, p650.
3.   Case 11/82 *Piraki Patraili v EC Commission* [1985] ECR 207.
4.   Ibid at 246.

4.7.2.3 Regulation 2641/84

Regulation 2641/84 is aimed at curtailing the illicit trade practices of third countries and not individual firms, and for this reason is more akin to anti-subsidy cases.

The regulation is based largely on Regulation 2423/88. As discussed above, the types of measures that are likely to be imposed under Regulation 2641/84, namely quantitative restrictions, suspension of tariff concessions, the raising of tariffs, etc, would be general and legislative in nature. In these circumstances, exporters would encounter the same difficulties facing exporters in anti-subsidy cases. In order to be able to challenge the acts imposing protective measures, exporters would have to show that they are concerned by the findings relating to the existence of dumping complained of or that their procedural rights as guaranteed by the basic regulation have been infringed or disregarded.

Regulation 2641/84 is unique in that it permits the adoption of protective measures to counteract illicit trade practices in a third country which affect Community exports. Many exporters may be affected because such protective measures will have the consequence of limiting imports from that country. Such exporters will not have locus standi as they are not involved in the investigation leading to the adoption of such measures, nor are they individually identified in the measure in question.

Temple Lang[1] identifies one possible situation in which exporters would have locus standi. This is where a non-Member State encourages certain undertakings to become parties to a restrictive trade practice or a misuse of monopoly power.

4.7.3   Complainants

4.7.3.1 Regulation 2423/88

The position of complainants in the context of trade measures first arose in the *Fediol* case[2]. Fediol was a trade association. It had lodged a complaint pursuant to Regulation 3017/79 requesting the initiation of anti-subsidy proceedings against the importation of soya bean oil cake from Brazil. The EC Commission informed Fediol by letter that it did not intend to initiate proceedings. As a result Fediol brought an action under article 173, 2nd para of the EEC Treaty seeking a declaration that the decision contained in the letter was void.

---

1.   Temple Lang, above, at 649.
2.   Case 191/82 *EEC Seed Crushers' and Oil Processors' Federation (Fediol) v EC Commission* [1983] ECR 2913.

The Court began as it did in the *First Allied* case, by stating that the question of admissibility must be assessed in the light of the whole scheme of investigation and protection created by the basic regulation[1]. The Court proceeded to analyse the provisions of the basic regulation which related to anti-subsidy cases. It then in some detail concluded that complainants could bring proceedings before the Court alleging that the EC Commission had disregarded specific rights granted to them under the basic regulation. It held that :

"It appears from a comparison of the provisions governing the successive procedural stages described above that the regulation recognises the existence of a legitimate interest on the part of Community producers in the adoption of anti-subsidy measures and that it defines certain specific rights in their favour, namely the right to submit to the Commission all evidence which they consider appropriate, the right to see all information obtained by the Commission subject to certain exceptions, the right to be heard at their request and to have the opportunity of meeting the other parties concerned in the same proceeding and finally the right to be informed if the Commission decides not to pursue a complaint. In the case of the proceedings being terminated on the completion of the stage of preliminary investigation provided for in article 5 that information must comprise at least a statement of the Commission's basic conclusions and a summary of the reasons therefore as is required by article 9 in the event of the termination of formal investigations."[2]

It noted that whilst the EC Commission had a duty to establish objectively the facts concerning the existence of subsidisation practices and of the injury caused as a result to Community industry, it had nevertheless a very wide discretion in deciding what measures were necessary taking into account the interests of the Community. It was in the light of these considerations that it was necessary to consider whether complainants have a right to bring an action. It held that :

"It seems clear, first, in that respect - and the point is not disputed by the Commission - that complainants must be acknowledged to have a right to bring an action where it is alleged that the Community authorities have disregarded rights which have been recognised specifically in the regulation, namely the right to lodge a complaint, the right, which is inherent in the aforementioned right, to have that complaint considered by the Commission with proper care and according to the procedure provided for, the right to receive information within the limits set by the regulation and finally, if the Commission decides not to proceed with the complaint, the right to receive

---

1.   Ibid at 2932, para 15 of judgment.
2.   Case 191/82 *EEC Seed Crushers' and Oil Processors' Federation (Fedio) v EC Commission* [1983] ECR 2913 at 2934, para 25 of judgment.

information comprising at the least the explanations guaranteed by article 9(2) of the regulation.

Furthermore it must be acknowledged that, in the spirit of the principles which lie behind articles 164 and 173 of the Treaty, complainants have the right to avail themselves, with regard both to the assessment of the facts and to the adoption of protective measures provided for by the regulation of a review by the Court appropriate to the nature of the powers reserved to the Community institutions on the subject.

It follows that complainants may not be refused the right to put before the Court any matters which would facilitate a review as to whether the Commission has observed the procedural guarantees granted to complainants by Regulation 3017/79 and whether or not it has committed manifest errors in its assessment of the facts, has omitted to take into consideration any essential matters of such a nature as to give rise to a belief in the existence of subsidisation or has based the reasons for its decision on considerations amounting to a misuse of powers. In that respect, the Court is required to exercise its normal powers of review over a discretion granted to a public authority, even though it has no jurisdiction to intervene in the exercise of the discretion reserved to the Community authorities by the aforementioned regulation."[1]

The Court concluded by stating that the basic regulation acknowledged that undertakings and associations of undertakings injured by subsidisation practices on the part of non-Member countries have a legitimate interest in the initiation of protective action by the Community. In these circumstances they have a right of action within the framework of the legal status which the regulation confers on them[2].

The question of locus standi of complainants came before the Court again in *Timex Corporation v EC Council and EC Commission*[3] shortly after its decision in *Fediol*. This was an anti-dumping case. Timex, who, as it happened, was the leading manufacturer of mechanical wrist watches and watch movements in the Community had lodged a complaint with the EC Commission. The result of the subsequent investigation was a finding that dumping had taken place and that this dumping had caused injury to Community industry. An anti-dumping duty was therefore imposed on watches originating in the Soviet Union. Timex challenged this duty on the grounds that it was insufficient in respect of watches and furthermore, no duty

1. Case 191/82 *EEC Seed Crushers' and Oil Processors' Federation (Fedio) v EC Commission* [1983] ECR 2913 at 2935-6, paras 28-30 of judgment.
2. Ibid at 2936, para 31 of judgment.
3. Case 264/82 *Timex Corpn v EC Coucil and EC Commision* [1985] ECR 849.

had been imposed on the movements of such watches. They argued that this breached the procedural and substantive rules laid down by the basic regulation.

Advocate General Darmon, in his opinion for the Court, reiterated the principles enunciated in *Fediol*. He stated that :

> "Complainants may apply to the Court for a review of the procedural guarantees laid down by that regulation [Regulation 3017/79] and of the substantive question whether any manifest errors of assessment and misuse of power have been committed. This is a principle derived from the scheme of Regulation 3017/79 and from the general principles of the Treaty. As such, it applies to all measures adopted by the institutions in anti-dumping and anti-subsidy proceedings, and in particular to the regulations imposing duties."[1]

The Advocate General then proceeded to consider whether the regulation was in essence a decision and if so, whether Timex was directly and individually concerned. He concluded by stating that as the Community's production was practically Timex alone and the procedure was determined exclusively on the basis of the effect on Timex, it was directly and individually concerned. The Court agreed with him. On the question of standing it held that :

> "It should be pointed out first of all that the complaint under article 5 of Regulation 3017/79 which led to the adoption of Regulation 1882/82 was lodged by the British Clock and Watch Manufacturers' Association Limited on behalf of manufacturers of mechanical watches in France and the United Kingdom, including Timex. According to the documents before the Court, that association took action because a complaint which Timex had itself lodged in April 1979 had been rejected by the Commission on the ground that it came from only one Community manufacturer.

> The complaint which led to the opening of the investigation procedure therefore owes its origin to the complaints originally made by Timex. Moreover, it is clear from the preamble to Commission Regulation 84/82 and the preamble to Council Regulation 1882/82 that Timex's views were heard during that procedure.

> It must also be remembered that Timex is the leading manufacturer of mechanical watches and watch movements in the Community and the only remaining manufacturer of those products in the United Kingdom. Furthermore, as is also clear from the preambles to Regulations Nos. 84/82 and 1882/82, the

---

1.   Case 264/82 *Timex Corpn v EC Coucil and EC Commision* [1985] ECR 849 at 853.

conduct of the investigation procedure was largely determined by Timex's observations and the anti-dumping duty was fixed in the light of the effect of the dumping on Timex. More specifically, the preamble to Regulation 1882/82 makes it clear that the definitive anti-dumping duty was made equal to the dumping margin which was found to exist "taking into account the extent of the injury caused to Timex by the dumped imports". The contested regulation is therefore based on the applicant's own situation.

It follows that the contested regulation constitutes a decision which is of direct and individual concern to Timex within the meaning of the second paragraph of article 173 of the EEC Treaty."[1]

As in the *Fediol* case, the Court based its judgment insofar as complainants are concerned on their procedural rights as laid down in the parent regulation. This will be the situation whether or not injury findings have been made about them. These decisions run contrary to the Court's judgment in *Alusuisse* where it held that locus standi to challenge is based on the legal nature of the regulation imposing the duty and the legal effects it produces[2].

The effect of the Court's rulings is that the number of interested parties who may claim locus standi to challenge Community acts imposing safeguard measures has been extended to cover those parties whose procedural rights as provided for in the parent regulation have been infringed.

4.7.3.2 Regulation 288/82

Unlike Regulation 2423/88, it is only the Member States who have the right to complain under Regulation 288/82. For this reason complainants are less likely, if at all, to have locus standi to challenge protective measures. In certain limited circumstances they may, however, have locus standi if their procedural rights under the basic regulation have been infringed or disregarded. Like any other interested party, an individual producer by reason of article 6(4) of Regulation 288/82 has a right to be heard. Individual producers may have locus standi if they can show that the protective measures adopted are inadequate to them in relation to the findings of "substantial injury" or threat thereof.

---

1. Case 264/82 *Timex Corpn v EC Coucil and EC Commision* [1985] ECR 849 at 865-6, paras 13-16 of judgment.
2. Case 307/81 *Alusuisse Italia SpA v EC Council and EC Commission* [1982] ECR 3463.

4.7.3.3 Regulation 2641/84

Regulation 2641/84 endows complainants with much greater procedural rights due to the fact that the regulation, as far as procedure is concerned, is based on the anti-dumping rules. By virtue of article 3, private individuals are given a right to complain and a right to be informed if the complaint does not provide sufficient evidence to justify initiating an investigation. Furthermore, article 6 gives complainants a right to make submissions and to inspect non-confidential information in the possession of the EC Commission. They also have a right to be heard and to oppose parties having adverse interests. In the light of the Court's judgments in *Fediol* and *Timex*, complainants would have locus standi to challenge measures adopted under the basic regulation if they could show that these procedural rights had been disregarded or infringed.

4.7.4   Independent and associated importers

4.7.4.1 Regulation 2423/88
(a)   Anti-dumping duties
Generally speaking, importers are not referred to in regulations imposing anti-dumping duties. In the normal case, dumping will be determined on the basis of the export prices of non-Community producers. In certain situations, however, the importers are subsidiaries of the exporters and as such the sales between them are not at arms length. In these circumstances, the Community institutions may determine dumping by reference to the prices charged to independent importers. Where the export price is determined by reference to resale prices, associated importers as such will have had findings made about them[1]. In such circumstances they will be identified and would therefore have locus standi[2].

In *Canon Inc v EC Council*[3] the Court indicated that regulations imposing anti-dumping duties may also be of direct and individual concern to importers by virtue of other provisions than those concerning a finding of dumping. Such a situation arose in *Neotype Techmashexport v EC Commission and EC Council*[4]. There, the applicants were associated with Energomachexport and exporter of the products at issue. The intervener, GIMELEC (Association of Electrical Equipment and Industrial Electronic Industries) maintained that the action brought by Neotype against the definitive regulation as to the existence of dumping did not concern the applicant

1.   Article 2(8)(b), Council Regulation (EEC) 2423/88.
2.   See Case 118/77 *ISO v EC Council* [1979] ECR 1277; Joined Cases 239 and 275/82 *Allied Corporation and Ors v EC Commission* [1984] ECR 1005; Case 2179/86 *Sermes v EC Commission* [1987] ECR 3109; Case 301/86 *Frimodt Pedersen A/S v EC Commission* [1987] ECR 3123.
3.   Joined Cases 277/85 and 300/85 *Canon Inc v EC Council* [1988] ECR 5731.
4.   Joined Cases 305/86 and 160/87 *Neotype Techmashexport GmbH v EC Commission and EC Council* [1990] ECR I 2945; see also Joined Cases 304/86 and 185/87 *Enital SpA v EC Council and EC Commission* [1990] ECR 2939; Joined Cases 320/86 and 188/87 *Stanko France v EC Commission and EC Council* [1990] ECR 3103; Case 157/87 *Electroimplex and Ors v EC Council* [1990] ECR 3021.

directly since the export price was established on the basis of the prices paid and not by reference to the resale prices charged by Neotype.

The Court rejected GIMELEC's argument. It referred to its established case law relating to the locus standi of associated importers and held that the considerations underlying that case law were applicable not only in connection with a finding of dumping by reference to the importer's resale prices, but also in connection with the calculation of the anti-dumping duty itself[1]. As far as Neotype was concerned the Court noted :

"As is apparent from article 1(4)(a) of the definitive regulation for associated importers the net unit price, free-at-Community-frontier, in accordance with which the amount of anti-dumping duty to be paid is determined, is the customs value as determined in accordance with article 6 of Council Regulation (EEC) 1224/80 of 28 May 1980 on the valuation of goods for customs purposes (Official Journal 1980 L134, p. 1). Under that provision the customs value is based essentially on the price at which the imported products are sold by the importer in question to persons not connected with the vendor. Associated importers are therefore in a position to influence, by means of the resale prices charged for the products in question to independent buyers, the amount of the duty payable.

In those circumstances Neotype, which is associated with the exporter of the products in question, Energomashexport, and to which the method of calculation mentioned above was applied in accordance with article 1(4)(b) of the definitive regulation, is directly and individually concerned by that regulation."[2]

However, now that exporters have locus standi to challenge regulations imposing anti-dumping duties before the Court as a result of the decision in the *First Allied* case, there is less importance and less need to show that associated importers have locus standi. The position of independent importers is less straightforward. This was first discussed at great length by the Court in the *Alusuisse* case[3]. Alusuisse was an importer of orthoxylene. It did not manufacture the product itself nor did it belong to a group of undertakings which included a manufacturer. It was basically an independent importer. Alusuisse brought proceedings under article 173, 2nd para of the EEC Treaty seeking a declaration that the EC Council and EC Commission regulations were void.

---

1.   Joined Cases 305/86 and 160/87 *Neotype Techmashexport GmbH v EC Commission and EC Council* [1990] ECR I 2945 at 2999, para 20 of judgment.
2.   Ibid p2999 paras 20 and 21 of judgment.
3.   Case 307/81 *Alusuisse Italia SpA v EC Council and EC Commission* [1982] ECR 3463.

Advocate General Rozès distinguished the position of Alusuisse from the importers in the *Japanese Ballbearing* cases. She held that unlike the importers in the *Japanese Ballbearing* cases, Alusuisse was not specifically referred to in the regulation[1]. Alusuisse had argued that owing to the special nature of the procedure leading to the adoption of anti-dumping regulations, they could not be regarded as measures of general application[2]. The Advocate General, referring to the previous decisions of the Court, was of the opinion that such a line of argument could not be upheld. In her view, the argument wrongly assimilated the position preparatory to the adoption of the regulation to the adoption itself. In other words it confused the nature of the investigation with the nature of the measure[3]. She further noted that the distinction in the Court's case law between a regulation and a decision was founded on the nature and effects of the measure and not on the manner of its adoption[4].

The Court emphasised the fact that the regulations at issue had as their object the imposition of anti-dumping duty on all imports of orthoxylene originating in the United States and Puerto Rico. In these circumstances, such measures as regards independent importers who, in contrast to exporters, were not expressly named in the regulations, were measures having general application within the meaning of the second paragraph of article 189 of the Treaty because they applied to objectively determined situations and entailed legal effects for categories of persons regarded generally and in the abstract[5].

The Court agreed with Advocate General Rozès in holding that the distinction between a regulation and a decision could be based only on the nature of the measure itself and the legal effects which it produces and not on the procedures for its adoption[6]. In doing so it rejected Alusuisse's argument that the particular features of the procedure leading to the adoption of the anti-dumping regulations, in particular the participation of the various interested parties in the successive stages of that procedure, led to the conclusion that the measures in question constituted individual administrative acts which could be contested under article 173, 2nd para[7].

The Court confirmed the position of independent importers in the *First Allied* case. It noted that Demufert, one of the applicants, was an importer established in one of the Member States and was not referred to in any of the measures which were

---

1.   Case 307/81 *Alusuisse Italia SpA v EC Council and EC Commission* [1982] ECR 3463 at 3475-6.
2.   Ibid at 3477.
3.   Case 307/81 *Alusuisse Italia SpA v EC Council and EC Commission* [1982] ECR 3463 at 3477.
4.   Ibid.
5.   Ibid at 3472, para 9 of judgment.
6.   Ibid at 3473, para 13 of judgment.
7.   Ibid at 3473, para 12 of judgment.

contested in the applications before the Court[1]. It contrasted its position with the importers in the *Japanese Ballbearing* cases and it noted that in the former, the existence of dumping was established by reference to the export prices of the American producers and not by reference to the retail prices charged by European importers. In such circumstances, the findings relating to the existence of dumping were not of direct concern to Demufert whereas they were of direct concern to the producers and exporters[2]. The Court stressed, however, that insofar as the importer was compelled to pay anti-dumping duties it was open for it to bring an action in the national court to challenge the validity of the regulation[3].

The position of independent importers was again considered by the Court in relation to a sole importer and two exclusive importers[4] none of which had an association or a compensatory arrangement with the exporter of the product at issue.

In *Sermes SA v EC Commission*[5], the applicant, a sole importer into France of electric motors exported from the German Democratic Republic, sought a declaration under article 173, 2nd para that the Commission regulation imposing a provisional anti-dumping duty on electric motors was void.

The EC Commission argued that Sermes had no locus standi to challenge the regulation in issue since it was not of direct and individual concern to it but was of general application. Furthermore, the nature of the measure was not affected by the fact that Sermes was concerned by the anti-dumping investigation or was identified in the contested measure. Sermes' position was not specifically taken into account because the dumping was substantiated by reference to the export price, not to the resale price which Sermes was charged.

Sermes, on the other hand, argued that the regulation was of direct and individual concern to it. First, it was concerned by the preliminary investigations conducted by the EC Commission inasmuch as it took part in all stages of the anti-dumping proceedings. Secondly, it was the sole importer of electric motors from the German Democratic Republic and as such was unique in France. Thirdly, it was also identified in the preamble of the regulation and was therefore treated differently

---

1. Joined Cases 239 and 275/82 *Allied Corporation and Ors v EC Commission* [1984] ECR 1005 at 1031, para 15 of judgment.
2. Joined Cases 239 and 275/82 *Allied Corporation and Ors v EC Commission* [1984] ECR 1005 at 1031, para 15 of judgment.
3. Ibid.
4. Case 279/86 *Sermes SA v EC Commission* [1987] ECR 3109; Case 301/86 *R Frimodt Pedersen A/S v EC Commission* [1987] ECR 3123; Case 205/87 *Nuova Ceam Srl v EC Commission* [1987] ECR 4428.
5. Case 279/86 *Sermes SA v EC Commission* [1987] ECR 3109 .

from importers who were not included in it. Furthermore, by reason of article 7 of Regulation 2176/84, importers were put on the same footing as exporters being treated as "an interested party likely to be affected by the result of the proceeding".

The Court held that Sermes did not have the locus standi to challenge the EC Commission regulation in issue as it was a measure of general application and not a decision to which Sermes was directly and individually concerned within the meaning of article 173, 2nd para.

It noted that regulations imposing an anti-dumping duty were in fact legislative, as regards their nature and scope, inasmuch as they applied to all traders concerned taken as a whole. Notwithstanding this the Court held that :

> "... certain provisions of such regulations may nevertheless be of direct and individual concern to those producers and exporters who are charged, on the basis of information derived from their business activities, with practising dumping. That is generally true of producers and exporters who are able to establish that they were identified in the measures adopted by the Commission or the Council or were concerned by the preliminary investigations (see the judgments of 21 February 1984 *Allied Corporation v EC Commission*, cited above, and 23 May 1985 in Case 53/83 *Allied Corporation v EC Council* [1985] ECR 1621).

> It is also true of those importers who are directly concerned by findings of dumping inasmuch as export prices have been determined by reference to those importers' resale prices and not to the export prices charged by the producers or exporters in question (see the judgments of 29 March 1979 in Case 118/79 *ISO v EC Council* [1979] ECR 1277 and 21 February 1984 *Allied Corporation v EC Commission*, cited above). Under article 2(8)(b) of Regulation 2176/84 export prices may be constructed in that way inter alia where there is an association between exporter and importer."[1]

The Court concluded that Sermes belonged to neither category of trader. It also observed that Sermes had conceded that it was not associated with the exporter of the product at issue. The Court further noted that the dumping was substantiated not by reference to Sermes' resale prices but by reference to the prices actually paid or payable, on exportation[2].

---

1.   Case 279/86 *Sermes SA v EC Commission* [1987] ECR 3109 at 3114, paras 15-16 of Order.
2.   Ibid p3114 at para 17 of Order; see also Case 301/86 R *Frimodt Pedersen A/S v EC Commission* [1987] ECR 3123 and Case 205/87 *Nuova Ceam Srl v EC Commission* [1987] ECR 4428 at para 16 of Order.

The Court rejected Sermes' assertion that as sole importer in France of electric motors from the German Democratic Republic it was directly and individually concerned by the regulation at issue. It held :

"The contested regulation concerns the applicant not by reason of certain attributes which are peculiar to it or by reason of circumstances in which it is differentiated from all other persons but merely by virtue of its objective capacity as an importer of the goods in question in the same manner as any other trader who is, or might be in the future, in the same situation (see the judgment of 14 July 1983 in Case 231/82 *Spijker v EC Commission* [1983] ECR 2559)."[1]

The Court also rejected Sermes' argument that, given that it had participated in the successive stages of the investigation, its application was admissible. The Court noted that the distinction between a regulation and the legal effects which it produces can only be based on the nature of the measure itself and the legal effects which it produces and not on the procedures for its adoption.

Extramet Industrie SA v EC Council[2] is the latest decision of the Court concerning the locus standi of independent importers. It is the first occasion that the Court has been prepared to hold that an independent importer had the right to challenge a Council regulation imposing a definitive anti-dumping duty. The case was decided on its special facts and is not to be regarded as a precedent giving independent importers an unlicensed right to challenge such measures. It is unfortunate that the Court did not follow the Advocate General's line of reasoning, as discussed below, where he held that there was no logical distinction between the position of a related importer on the one hand and an independent importer on the other.

Extramet sought the annulment of the Council regulation imposing a definitive duty on imports of calcium metal originating in the USSR and China. The complaint had been lodged by Péchiney, the sole producer of the product in the Community. Apart from being the most important importer of calcium metal, Extramet was the main end user of the product, processing it into granules of pure calcium. Only after Péchiney refused to supply it with calcium metal did Extramet commence importing from the USSR and China. Furthermore, it had lodged a complaint with the competent French authorities that Péchiney's refusal to supply it with calcium metal constituted an abuse of a dominant position within the meaning of article 86 of the EEC Treaty.

---

1.   Case 279/86 *Sermes SA v EC Commission* [1987] ECR 3109 at 3114, para 18 of Order.
2.   Case C-358/89 *Extramet Industrie SA v EC Council* (1991) Transcript 16 May.

The EC Council maintained that Extramet had no standing to challenge the regulation in question owing to the fact that as an independent importer, its sales prices had not been taken into consideration when establishing export price.

The Court observed that according to its consistent case law, it had recognised that on the one hand, a foreign exporter or producer who was identified in the act in question or was concerned by the preliminary investigations and on the other, an importer whose resale prices had been used as a basis for establishing the export price had locus standi[1]. Such recognition the Court held, however, did not prevent other undertakings from being individually concerned where those undertakings have certain qualities or attributes which are particular to them and which distinguish them from all other persons[2].

The Court held that Extramet had locus standi to challenge the regulation in question. In particular, it observed that it had established a number of factors which distinguished it from all other persons, namely :

— it was the most important importer of calcium metal;

— it was an end user of the product;

— its economic activities depended largely on the imports of calcium metal with the result that it was seriously affected by the imposition of the duties taking into account the small and limited number of producers concerned and given the fact that it was also experiencing difficulties in receiving supplies from the only producer in the Community, Péchiney who also was its principal competitor[3].

The Court did not take into account that Extramet was identified albeit implicitly in the regulation and also that it participated in the preliminary investigations. Advocate General Jacobs, on the other hand, in noting these factors considered that there was no logical basis for distinguishing between producers, exporters,

---

1.   Case C-358/89 *Extramet Industrie SA v EC Council* (1991) Transcript 16 May, at para 15 of judgment.
2.   Ibid at para 16 of judgment.
3.   Ibid at para 17 of judgment.

complainants and importers insofar as the question of locus standi was concerned. In his view, similar criteria should be applied to undertakings in each of these categories in determining this question. More importantly, he observed that :

> "There is a particularly strong case for acknowledging the admissibility of an action brought by an undertaking whose participation in the proceedings before the Commission can be regarded as having affected their outcome."[1]

Vermulst[2] has noted that in his opinion there is no good reason why the Advocate General's reasoning should not be followed so as to allow independent importers the right to challenge Commission and Council regulations imposing anti-dumping duties. He has suggested one modification, namely that the test should simply be whether or not the independent importer participated in the preliminary investigations. Such a test would avoid the anomalous situation of, on the one hand, regarding an independent importer whose information is verified and used, as having locus standi whilst on the other hand rejecting an action brought by an independent importer who provided information which was not used.

Arguably, the Court's decision in *Extramet* arose from the special situation in which Extramet found itself. It is regrettable that the Court did not adopt the Advocate General's reasoning.

In a number of other situations it may be possible to argue that an independent importer has locus standi to challenge a regulation imposing a definitive anti-dumping duty. First, it may be part of an identifiable and ascertainable group where it has given a bond or a guarantee for payment of provisional duties. It may, therefore, have locus standi to challenge the regulation imposing the definitive duties if the regulation also orders the definitive collection of provisional duties. Secondly, as a result of the Court's ruling in *Piraiki-Patraiki*[3], an independent importer may have locus standi to challenge a measure imposing anti-dumping duties if it can establish that it had entered into a contract to buy goods which would be subject to a duty and that it would be responsible for the payment of that duty rather than the exporter.

On the other hand, an importer will not have locus standi to challenge a regulation imposing a provisional duty where the EC Council has subsequently imposed a

---

1.   Opinion dated 21 March 1991 at para 66.
2.   [1992] CML Rev No 29 p387.
3.   Case 11/82 *Piraiki Patraiki v EC Commission* [1985] ECR207.

definitive duty and ordered the definitive collection of the provisional duties. As the Court held in *Neotype Techmashexport v EC Council and EC Commission*[1] :

> "... it should be stated that, as the amounts secured as provisional anti-dumping duties were collected, in accordance with article 2(1) of the definitive regulation, at the rate of duty definitively imposed, Neotype may place no reliance on any legal effect arising out of the provisional regulation (see the judgments in Case 56/85 *Brother v EC Commission* [1988] ECR 5655 paragraph 6; and in Joined Cases 294/86 and 77/87 *Technointorg v EC Commission and EC Council* [1988] ECR 6077, paragraph 12)."[2]

It also noted that an importer could plead the illegality of the definitive regulation, insofar as that regulation ordered the definitive collection of the provisional duties, in support of a claim for compensation for any damage caused by the provisional regulation. To that extent the definitive regulation replaced the provisional regulation and the legality of the provisional regulation therefore had no bearing on any damages claim[3].

Likewise, an independent importer and for that matter an associated importer will not have locus standi to challenge a EC Commission decision accepting price undertakings[4]. Such decisions can only be of direct and individual concern to that trader who is a party to the undertaking given.

(b)   Countervailing duties

It is only in very exceptional circumstances that importers, whether associated or independent, will have locus standi in anti-subsidy cases given that the Community authorities will rarely, if at all, look at the prices charged by importers to their customers in the Community. The most likely situation in which an importer will have locus standi is where the regulation orders the definitive collection of the provisional duties or where the importer has entered into a contract before the protective measures were adopted, ie the situation in the *Piraiki-Patraiki* case.

---

1.   Joined Cases 305/86 and 160/87 *Neotype Techmashexport GmbH v EC Commission and EC Council* [1990] I ECR 2945.
2.   Joined Cases 305/86 and 160/87 *Neotype Techmashexport GmbH v EC Commission and EC Council* [1990] ECR I 2945 at 2997, para 13 of judgment.
3.   Ibid p2997 at para 14 of judgment.
4.   Case 295/86 *SA Garelly v EC Commission* [1987] ECR 3117 at 3122 para 14 of judgment.

4.7.4.2 Regulation 288/82

Importers, whether associated or independent, are unlikely to have locus standi to challenge measures imposing protective measures under Regulation 288/82 as they are less likely to be affected by quantitative restrictions or to be the subject of specific findings. Where an importer, however, can prove that it fulfils the criteria laid down in *Piraiki-Patraiki* case[1], it may then have locus standi. Importers on the whole, unlike exporters, are less likely to be affected by quantitative restrictions or to be the subject of specific findings.

Piraiki-Patraiki concerned an application by a number of Greek undertakings that a EC Commission decision authorising France to impose quotas on imports of cotton yarns from Greece was void. The EC Commission argued that the decision was addressed to the French Republic and the Hellenic Republic and although the applicants were touched by the effects of the protective measures authorised, the decision in question was not of direct or individual concern to them[2]. The applicants argued, however, that their situation could be distinguished from that of any other exporter to France of cotton yarn of Greek origin inasmuch as they had entered into a series of contracts of sales with French customers, to be performed during the period of application of the decision and covering quantities of cotton yarn in excess of the quotas authorised by the EC Commission. According to the applicants the EC Commission was in a position and even under the obligation to identify the traders who, like the applicants, were individually concerned[3].

The Court then held :

> "It must be concluded that the Commission was in a position to obtain sufficiently exact information on the contracts already entered into which were to be performed during the period of application of the decision at issue. It follows that the undertakings which were party to contracts meeting that description must be considered as individually concerned for the purpose of the admissibility of this action, as members of a limited class of traders identified or identifiable by the Commission and by reason of those contracts particularly affected by the decision at issue."[4]

Therefore, in circumstances where an importer has entered into a contract before the imposition of protective measures under Regulation 288/82 it may have locus standi to challenge those measures.

---

1. Case 11/82 *Piraiki Patraiki v EC Commission* [1985] ECR 207.
2. Ibid at 241, para 3 of judgment.
3. Ibid at 242-3, paras 12-15 of judgment.
4. Ibid at 246, para 31 of judgment.

4.7.4.3 Regulation 2641/84

An importer under Regulation 2641/84 is in a similar position to an importer under an anti-subsidy action. For this reason it is unlikely that he would have locus standi except in exceptional cases.

4.7.5 Original Equipment Manufacturers (OEMs)

Original Equipment Manufacturers (hereinafter referred to as OEMs) may be defined as importers who sell in the Community, under their own brand names, products which they neither sell nor produce in the country of origin but which are purchased from exporters of the products to the Community.

The admissibility of an article 173 action by OEMs has arisen recently in some of the *Photocopiers*[1] cases. In *Nashua Corporation v EC Commission and EC Council*[2], the applicant was defined as "the supplier of Nashua brand photocopiers which it sells in the Community and numerous other countries". It was not disputed and was certain that Nashua bought most of its photocopiers from Ricoh Co Limited of Japan which manufactured Nashua brand machines at its production facilities in Japan.

The EC Council, relying on the decision of the Court in *Sermes SA v EC Council*[3] which reiterated those categories of economic agent who had locus standi to challenge Community measures imposing anti-dumping duties, considered that the application was inadmissible[4]. It argued that the applicant was neither a producer/exporter nor an associated importer and therefore not individually concerned. The EC Council was of the view that Nashua, if it was to be categorised, would be regarded as an independent importer, ie an importer not associated to an

---

1. See Joined Cases 133/87 and 150/87 *Nashua Corporation v EC Commission and EC Council* [1990] ECR 719; and Case 156/87 *Gestetner Holdings plc v EC Commission and EC Council* [1990] ECR 781.
2. Joined Cases 133 and 150/87, above, at 20-21.
3. Case 279/86 *Sermes SA v EC Council* [1987] ECR 3109.
4. The Court summarised the case law as follows : "However, the Court has held that certain provisions of such regulations may nevertheless be of direct and individual concern to those *producers* and *exporters* who are charged, on the basis of information derived from their business activities, with practising dumping. That is 'generally' true of producers and exporters who are able to establish that they were identified in the measures adopted by the EC Commission or the EC Council or were concerned by the preliminary investigations (see the judgments of 21 February 1984, *Allied Corporation v EC Commission* [1984] ECR 1005 and of 23 May 1985 in Case 53/85, *Allied Corporation v EC Council* [1985] ECR 1621). It is also true of those *importers* who are directly concerned by findings of dumping inasmuch as export prices have been determined by reference to those importers' resale prices and not to the export prices charged by the producers or exporters in question (see the judgments of 29 March 1979 in case 118/77, *ISO v EC Council* [1979] ECR 1277, and of 21 Feburary 1984, *Allied Corporation v EC Commission*, [1984] ECR 1005). Under article 2(8)(b) of Council Regulation (EEC) 2176/84 export prices may be constructed in that way inter alia where there is an association between exporter and importer" (paras 15 and 16).

exporter or producer. Such economic agents have been held by the Court not to be individually concerned by an anti-dumping regulation[1].

In reaching this conclusion, the EC Council argued that Nashua had not been singled out by the contested regulation. This view was based on two grounds. First, the export price was established on the basis of sales to Nashua by Ricoh who was a producer and exporter and not on Nashua's resale price. Second, the construction of normal value for sales to OEMs was based not on information from Nashua but from Ricoh.

In his Opinion[2], Advocate General Mischo agreed that the EC Council's application of the principles in the *Sermes* case was correct. He disagreed, however, with their conclusion, holding that Nashua was directly and individually concerned by the contested regulation. He was of the opinion that the determining factor in deciding whether the applicant had locus standi was not its status, ie whether it was an exporter/producer or associated importer, but the manner in which its actual situation was taken into account[3].

He noted that the anti-dumping duty imposed on Nashua photocopiers did not apply indiscriminately to all OEMs. Rather, Nashua was not only affected by the regulation on account of its status as an OEM but more importantly in its capacity as an OEM selling products manufactured by Ricoh. (Ricoh being one of the exporters whose products were dumped and which were subject to a definitive duty). As a result, Nashua's products were also subject to the same anti-dumping duty as Ricoh. In such circumstances, it was correct to hold that Nashua was affected by those findings and by the imposition of duties in the same was as Ricoh[4].

On the assumption that Ricoh was individually concerned by the contested regulation it would be illogical not to treat Nashua as being in the same position in respect of products sold under its own brand name. It would have been wrong to treat

---

1.   Case 307/81 *Alusuisse Italia Spa v EC Council and EC Commission* [1982] ECR 3463.
2.   Joined Cases 133 and 150/87 *Nashua Corporation v EC Commission and EC Council* [1990] ECR 719 at 742.
3.   Ibid at 748.
4.   Ibid at 749.

Nashua as if it were Ricoh, as the photocopiers imported by Nashua had a distinctive "logo" which characterised them to Nashua products. Advocate General Mischo was of the opinion that :

> "Once a product imported under a given brand name is subject, on entry into the Community, to special customs arrangements, the act which established those arrangements is of direct and individual concern to the business whose product bears the distinctive brand name (or which is the holder or owner of that brand name), even if it is not considered to be an exporter for the purpose of the anti-dumping legislation."[1]

The brand name was a distinctive badge, he argued, which identified the owner and placed him in a situation which distinguished him from any other person.

He noted further that the application of the contested regulation, in particular, to Gestetner was a perfect example of the argument that the brand name distinguishes the product and its owner - in particular an OEM - from any other person. The customs authorities would naturally impose on Gestetner products entering the Member States a general duty of 20%, since its name was not included in the list of exporters in the contested regulation which were subject to different duties. At the hearing, however, the EC Council confirmed that Gestetner photocopiers which were manufactured by Mita, should only be subject to a duty of 12.6%. There was nothing in the regulation to this effect, with the result that the customs officials would had to have had the position clarified by the national authorities or the EC Commission in order to obtain confirmation of that fact. Customs officials in the Member States subsequently received an explanatory memorandum setting out the position. It was, therefore, the case that during customs clearance, Gestetner brand products were distinguished from all other products. It could not be denied that they were directly and more importantly individually concerned in the same way as Mita[2].

Further, Nashua had in its submissions contended that the EC Council had failed to treat it as an exporter of its own products. Rather, the EC Council had treated it as an importer of the products which, although bearing Nashua's brand name, were in actual fact Ricoh products. The Advocate General took the view that if the EC Council were allowed to determine the admissibility of such claims by OEMs by how it perceived the functions and role of a particular OEM, then such a decision

---

1.   Joined Cases 133 and 150/87 *Nashua Corporation v EC Commission and EC Council* [1990] ECR 719 at 750.

2.   Joined Cases 133 and 150/87 *Nashua Corporation v EC Commission and EC Council* [1990] ECR 719 at 750, para 45; see also Case C-156/87 *Gestetner Holdings plc v EC Commission and EC Council* [1990] I ECR 781.

would be removed from direct review by the Court. He held that, reiterating the decision of the Court in the *Mini Ballbearing* cases, the exercise of discretion by the Community authorities was still subject to review by the Court in determining whether procedural rules had been complied with, whether facts on which a decision was based were accurately stated and whether there had been a manifest error of appraisal or misuse of powers[1].

The Advocate General also relied on a further ground for holding that Nashua was directly and individually concerned by the contested regulation. As stated above, the refusal to accept an undertaking and the subsequent imposition of definitive duties amounted to a decision of direct and individual concern to the applicant in question. Such circumstances, the Advocate General contended, existed in the present case, thereby conferring on Nashua locus standi[2].

The Court concurred with the Advocate General that Nashua had locus standi. In reaching this conclusion the Court's reasoning differed from that of the Advocate General. It restated the principles enunciated by the Court in the *First Allied* case and considered that it was necessary to establish whether Nashua was concerned by the findings relating to the existence of dumping complained of[3]. It noted that it was by reference to the particular features of Ricoh's sales to OEMs as compared with its costs in sales of the product under its own brand name that the EC Council in constructing the normal value used a profit margin of 5%. This was lower than the average profit margin which was estimated at 14.6%. Proceeding on the basis of the normal value thus constructed for sales by Ricoh to OEMs, the Community authorities arrived at a dumping margin lower than that determined for the sales of the products bearing Ricoh's own brand name. For these reasons, the Court concluded that Nashua was concerned by the findings relating to the existence of dumping complained of and the provisions of the regulation regarding Ricoh's dumping practices were therefore of direct concern to it[4].

In conclusion, the category of persons which have locus standi to challenge Community measures imposing anti-dumping duties has been extended to include OEMs. This, however, does not amount to a licence for all OEMs to challenge such measures. Locus standi will only be conferred on those OEMs who can show that they are concerned by a finding relating to the dumping complained of.

---

1.   Joined Cases 133 and 150/87 *Nashua Corporation v EC Commission and EC Council* [1990] ECR 719 at 751. See for example, Case 240/84 *NTN Toyo Bearing Co Ltd v EC Council* [1987] ECR 1809.
2.   Joined Cases 133 and 150/87 *Nashua Corporation v EC Commission and EC Council* [1990] ECR 719 at 751.
3.   Ibid at 772-773, paras 14-16 of judgment.
4.   Ibid at 773, paras 17-20 of judgment.

4.7.6   Trade associations

In *Confédération Nationale des Producteurs de Fruits et Légumes v EC Council*[1] the Court held that an Association in its capacity as the representative of a category of businessmen was not individually concerned by a measure such as a regulation which affected the general interests of that category.

The position of trade associations with reference to safeguard measures is likely only to arise in relation to anti-dumping and countervailing measures and to illicit commercial practices. The major reason for this is that Trade Associations are specifically mentioned in Regulation 2423/88 and Regulation 2641/84 as having a right to lodge a complaint .

The position of a trade association was considered by the Court in *Fediol*. The EC Commission observed that on a strict interpretation of article 173, 2nd para, a trade association had no right to institute proceedings or to appear in Court. However, taking account of the powers of a procedural nature given by the parent regulation to Associations lacking legal personality, it would be illogical to refuse such an Association the right to bring an action. It was therefore appropriate to give a broad interpretation of the concept of "legal person" within the meaning of article 173, 2nd para of the EEC Treaty[2].

Advocate General Rozès noted with regard to trade associations that it was not formal legal personality that mattered, but whether the association in question was recognised by the law and given certain powers to fulfil the duties given to it. In this respect she noted that the Anti-dumping regulation endowed associations with procedural powers. She proceeded to hold that associations :

> "while not possessing legal personality, operate in the context of one economic sector of the Community; it must therefore be concluded that such associations do have the capacity to institute proceedings in order to protect such procedural interests."[3]

The Court agreed with the Advocate General. It held that Associations have "a right of action within the framework of the legal status which the regulation confers on them"[4].

---

1.   Cases 16 and 17/62 *Confédération nationale des producteurs de fruits et légumes and Fédération nationale des producteurs de raisins de table v EC Council* [1962] ECR 471.

2.   Case 191/82 *EEC Seed Crushers' and Oil Producers' Federation (FEDIOL) v EC Commission* [1983] ECR 2913 at 2918.

3.   Ibid at 2940.

4.   Ibid at 2936, para 31 of judgment.

Under Regulation 288/82, the interests of trade associations could only be protected by means of intervention before the Court. This will only come about when the trade association can show to the satisfaction of the Court that it has an interest in the result of the case. The right of intervention is discussed below in relation to the position of users and processors.

4.7.7 Users, processors and consumers

The interests of users, processors and consumers who are neither importers nor complainants will normally be protected in the event of an action for annulment being brought by an exporter, by intervention in proceedings before the Court.

Article 37 of the Court's statute provides that :

> "Member States and institutions of the Community may intervene in cases before the Court.
>
> The same right shall be open to any other person establishing an interest in the result of any case submitted to the Court, save in cases between Member States, between institutions of the Community or between Member States and institutions of the Community.
>
> Submissions made in an application to intervene shall be limited to supporting the submissions of one of the parties."[1]

The right of an organisation such as the European Office of Consumer Unions to intervene depends upon that organisation being able to establish that it constitutes "any other person" and has an interest in the result of proceedings before the Court. The case law of the Court to date tends to suggest that these questions are treated quite liberally. For example, in *Chris International Foods* the Court was prepared to allow several non-Member States, namely Granada, Dominica, St. Lucia and St.Vincent to intervene[2]. It also allowed the Banana Growers Association to intervene. It is difficult to glean from the Court's reasoning why an intervention is justified but it is safe to say, that it will usually be permitted where the intervener can show that it has an economic interest in the result of the case.

---

1. Protocol on Statute of Court of Justice of the EEC, art 37. See also Rules of the Single Court of the Three Communities (OJ L350 28.12.74 p1); as Temple Lang states "submissions should be seen more as conclusions rather than arguments"("Judicial Review of Trade Safeguard Measures in the European Community"). See also Rule 93 Rules of Procedure of the Court.
2. Joined Cases 91 and 200/82 *Chris International Foods Ltd v EC Commission* [1983] ECR 417.

It is unlikely that processors, users, consumers, etc will have locus standi to challenge a regulation imposing an anti-dumping duty. It may be, however, that during the course of an anti-dumping investigation such persons may be adversely affected by a decision of the Community authorities which may give rise to an action under article 173.

Recently, the Court has had to consider the admissibility of an action by the Bureau Européen des Unions de Consommateurs (BEUC) (The European Office of Consumer Unions)[1]. BEUC were not challenging a regulation imposing an anti-dumping duty but a decision contained in a letter dated 15 March 1989 refusing to permit them to inspect the EC Commission's non-confidential file and information made available by all the parties in an anti-dumping investigation concerning the imports of audio cassettes and audio cassette tapes from Japan, the Republic of Korea and Hong Kong. The question the Court had to decide was whether the letter could be regarded as an act which could be the subject of an action under article 173.

The EC Commission contended that BEUC's application was inadmissible as the letter of 15 March 1989 did not constitute a decision as it merely informed BEUC of its legal position under article 7(4)(a) of Regulation 2423/88 and did not alter its position in any way. In its view the letter did not produce any legal effect and was merely an opinion.

BEUC, on the other hand, argued that the EC Commission had a discretion concerning access to the non-confidential file and its refusal to allow BEUC the opportunity to inspect it constituted a decision and not merely an explanation of the legal position.

The Court agreed with BEUC and held that :

> "inasmuch as the letter refuses the BEUC access to the non-confidential file, it constitutes not merely a communication but a decision which adversely affects the interests of BEUC. The EC Commission's letter must therefore be regarded as an act adversely affecting the BEUC which may be the subject of an action under article 173 EEC."[2]

---

1.   Case C-170/89 *Bureau européen des unions de consommateurs (BEUC) v EC Commission* [1992] 1 CMLR 820.
2.   Ibid at 848, para 11 of judgment.

4.7.8   Non-Member States

As stated above, Member States of the Community have by virtue of article 173, 1st para locus standi to challenge any binding legal act whatever its form. The right of a non-Member State to challenge safeguard measures may in some situations be of the utmost importance and in particular in relation to illicit commercial practices and anti-subsidy actions. Non-Member States are specifically referred to in article 7(1) of Regulation 2423/88 and article 6(1) of Regulation 2641/84.

Circumstances may arise where an exporter cannot challenge an act imposing safeguard measures and for this reason it may be important that non-Member States should have the right to intervene on their behalf. As stated above, the Court considered the question of the right of non-Member States to intervene in the *Chris International Foods* case[1]. In that case, the Court held that non-Member States had a right to intervene. The non-Member States put forward three reasons why they considered they had sufficient interest for intervention[2]. They contended that they were entitled to preferential treatment for their bananas in part of the Community market; they were dependent on bananas for their export earnings and if the application by Chris International Foods succeeded the rights of non-Member States concerned under the Fourth Protocol of the Lomé II Convention would be seriously affected. The Court held in the light of these arguments that Granada, Dominica, St. Lucia and St. Vincent had shown sufficient interest in the outcome of the case before it[3].

Apart from having a right to intervene, a more important question is whether it is possible for a non-Member State to be directly and individually concerned by an act imposing safeguard measures[4]. It may be that a non-Member State which is operating a subsidy or illicit commercial practice is directly and individually concerned by a Community measure designed to counteract such practices. It is perfectly feasible for non-Member States to put forward the arguments detailed in the *Chris International Foods* case in order to show that they have locus standi under article 173.

It is unlikely that a non-Member State would have standing under Regulation 288/82 on the ground that it is not a material factor where the product originates. What is important is that the product is being imported into the Community in substantial quantities which are causing serious injury to Community producers and that it is in the interest of the Community to take action. Only in a situation where

---

1.   Case 91/82 *Chris International Foods Ltd v EC Commission* [1983] ECR 417.
2.   Ibid at 418-9.
3.   Ibid at 419.
4.   In some cases involving state trading countries the trader is the state - Raznoimport Cases, eg,
       Case 120/83R *Raznoimport v EC Commission* [1983] ECR 2573.

it specifically relates to a product from the non-Member State in question and only when other factors are in existence could the non-Member State have locus standi.

4.7.9 Refusal to accept an undertaking

As discussed earlier, the EC Commission has the power under Regulation 2423/88 to accept an undertaking. Its reasons for doing so will be practical and non-legal. Likewise, it will have similar reasons for refusing to accept an undertaking. The Court in a number of the *Photocopier* cases[1] has discussed the question of whether the rejection of an undertaking constituted a measure having binding legal effects so that it could be challenged before the Court. The EC Council in its observations argued that a decision by the EC Commission to refuse an undertaking was merely a stage in the process leading to a further decision and therefore could not be challenged in a separate action. Advocate General Mischo was of the opinion that such a refusal of itself could be regarded as an act liable to affect an applicant's interests. However, such a consequence, he observed, was merely a potential one until the EC Council takes its final decision[2].

The Court agreed with the Advocate General. It held that the refusal by the EC Commission of a proposed undertaking could not be considered as a measure having binding legal effects of such a kind as to affect the interests of the applicant as the EC Commission may revoke its decision or the EC Council may decide not to impose a duty. Such a rejection is an intermediate measure and is not one capable of being challenged[3]. It was clear, held the Court, that as a result of the decisions in the *Mini Ballbearing* cases[4] it was by challenging the regulation introducing definitive duties that traders could raise an irregularity associated with the rejection of their proposed undertakings[5].

Locus standi to challenge a decision rejecting an exporter's exemption from a duty or the refusal to accept an undertaking will only be conferred on an exporter if that exporter initiates proceedings to challenge the regulation imposing the definitive duties.

---

1. See Joined Cases 133 and 150/87 *Nashua Corporation v EC Commission and EC Council* [1990] ECR 719; Case C-156/87 *Gestetner Holdings plc v EC Commission and EC Council* [1990] I ECR 781.
2. See Advocate General's Opinion in Joined Cases 133 and 150/87 *Nashua Corporation v EC Commission and EC Council* [1990] ECR 719 at 745.
3. Joined Cases 133 and 150/87 *Nashua Corporation v EC Commission and EC Council* above at paras 9-10 of judgment; Case 156/87 *Gestetner Holdings plc v EC Commission and EC Council* [1990] ECR 781, at paras 8-9 of judgment.
4. Cases 240/84 *NTN Toyo Bearing Co Ltd v EC Council* [1987] ECR 1809, an 255/84 *Nachi Fujikoshi Corporation v EC Council* [1987] ECR 1899, below.
5. Joined Cases 133 and 150/87 *Nashua Corporation v EC Commission and EC Council* above at para 10 of judgment and Case C-156/87 *Gestetner Holdings plc v EC Commission and EC Council* above, at para 8 of judgment.

4.8   Action for failure to act : article 175

When the EC Commission or EC Council fail to act where they are obliged to do so under the Treaties then an interested party, provided they have sufficient locus standi can raise an action under article 175. In actual fact a complainant is the only interested party that would have a right to raise an action under article 175 and only where the institution in question has a duty to adopt an act addressed to the complainant. A complainant will require to establish that it has locus standi to raise an action under article 175 by satisfying the Court that it would be directly and individually concerned by the institutions' failure to perform the act in question or where the institutions have infringed or disregarded their procedural rights under the basic regulation in question.

4.8.1   Regulation 2423/88

A complainant could raise an action under article 175, where the EC Commission fails despite the request in the complaint to communicate to the complainant the decision not to initiate anti-dumping or anti-subsidy proceedings. In this respect it should be observed that the applicants in *Fediol*[1] maintained that they would have raised an action under article 175 if such a decision had not been communicated to them. There is no doubt that by either issuing a decision refusing to initiate proceedings or a decision to initiate them, the complainants' legal rights are affected in a fundamental way, and in particular, in exercising its procedural rights under article 7 of Regulation 2423/88 during the investigation. The Court concluded in *Fediol* that the complainants had a legitimate interest in having safeguard measures adopted and as a result they had to be granted the right to challenge a decision of the EC Commission to initiate or refuse to initiate an investigation[2].

A complainant could also raise an action under article 175 where a decision has been taken by the EC Commission to terminate the proceeding and it has failed to communicate this to the complainant. This decision constitutes an act other than a recommendation or opinion which has to be addressed to all parties known to be concerned, including complainants.

To conclude, it is submitted that it is possible in two cases for a complainant to raise an action under article 175. It can force the EC Commission to address to it the decision not to open formal anti-dumping or anti-subsidy investigations and second

---

1.   Case 191/82 *EEC Seed Crushers' and Oil Processors' Federation (Fediol) v EC Commission* [1983] ECR 2913 at 2923.
2.   Ibid.

it can demand the EC Commission to notify it of the termination of anti-dumping and anti-subsidy proceedings.

4.8.2   Regulation 288/82

Natural or legal persons as such do not enjoy judicial protection under Regulation 288/82. As such they will normally not derive any right from article 175.

4.8.3   Regulation 2641/84

Owing to the similarity of the procedural provisions of Regulation 2641/84 with the Anti-dumping Rules similar conclusions can be reached with regard to a complainant's standing to challenge under article 175.

4.9   Plea of illegality : article 184

As stated above, article 184 is a shield and not a sword in that it is an ancillary action to other proceedings - normally an action for annulment under article 173. In order that the plea can be considered, a party will have to show that it has the locus standi to challenge the act imposing the safeguard measures.

Article 184 is aimed at the basic regulation upon which the act imposing safeguard measures is based. It should be emphasised that a plea of illegality is the only means by which an applicant can challenge these measures as they are true regulations. They are measures of general application and immune from challenge under article 173 by natural or legal persons. The effect of a successful application under article 184 is to have the regulation in question, or a provision of it, declared inapplicable in the particular case. The net practical result is that the Community institutions would be forced into amending the legislation.

In *Bureau Européen des Unions de Consommateurs v EC Commission*[1] the applicants sought inter alia a declaration pursuant to article 184 that article 7(4)(a) of Regulation 2423/88 was inapplicable insofar as it prohibited BEUC from inspecting the non-confidential file and the information made available by all parties to the anti-dumping investigation in question.

The Court rejected this submission. It noted that from the wording of article 7(4)(a) it was apparent that the EC Council chose to grant the right of access to the non-confidential file to those most directly concerned by the alleged dumping namely

---

1.   Case C-170/89 *Bureau européen des unions de consommateurs (BEUC) v EC Commission* [1992] 1 CMLR 820.

complainants, importers and exporters known to be concerned. Such a right was not granted to consumers against whom no complaint was made. Users and processors would be in a similar position. By making this choice the EC Council had not infringed the right to a fair hearing or principle of sound administration. Nor was this altered by the fact that the Community authorities were required to take into account amongst others the interests of consumers in determining the interests of the Community[1].

It was for the Community legislature, the Court observed, to consider whether the basic anti-dumping regulation should allow an association like BEUC to consult the non-confidential file, but there was nothing in the wording of article 7(4)(a) to prevent the EC Commission from allowing persons who have a legitimate interest to inspect the non-confidential file[2].

In *NMB v EC Commission*[3], the applicants challenged a number of EC Commission decisions which rejected in part their request for a refund of anti-dumping duties levied in 1985 and 1986 on the imports of ballbearings originating in Singapore.
The EC Commission objected to the admissibility of the applicants' submission that in the event of the Court not accepting that anti-dumping duties paid as a cost could be deducted in calculating the constructed export price where the importers are associated to the exporters, the basic regulation was unlawful under article 184. It maintained that the provisions of the regulation which the applicants sought to attack were not specified; that there was no claim relating to them in the application; and lastly that article 184 allows a claim to be made that the regulation was inapplicable but not that it was invalid.

The Court rejected the EC Commission's arguments holding that :

"... since the dispute concerns the deduction of anti-dumping duties made in the three contested decisions pursuant to article 2(8)(b) of the basic regulation, it is clear that the applicants contest the legality of that provision insofar as it is applied to the refund of anti-dumping duties and not the legality of the basic regulation as a whole. In addition, a submission that a regulation is unlawful put forward in support of an action brought against individual decisions constitutes a plea in law raised in connection with the application. It follows that such a plea need not appear in the form of the Order sought in the application but need merely be mentioned in the body thereof. It is clear from the application that it seeks the annulment not of the basic regulation or of

---

1.   Case 170/89 *Bureau européen des unions de consommateurs (BEUC) v EC Commission* [1992] 1 CMLR 820 at 851, para 28 of judgment.
2.   Ibid p851 at paras 29 and 30 of judgment.
3.   Case C-188/88 *NMB V EC Commission* (1992) Transcript 10 March.

certain provisions thereof but of the three contested decisions, on the ground that they are based on an illegal provision of that regulation which should be declared inapplicable under article 184 of the EEC Treaty."[1]

The Court was not required to consider the legality of article 2(8)(b) having decided that the EC Commission was entitled to do what it had done. Advocate General Tesauro upheld the applicant's submissions but on the basis that the EC Commission had wrongly interpreted the legislation.

4.10   Preliminary ruling on validity : article 177, 1st para, point (b)

It is possible to challenge the validity of safeguard measures indirectly in the national courts under article 177, 1st para, point (b) of the EEC Treaty. In the usual situation, an importer who will normally pay the duties may decide to raise proceedings in the national courts following the collection of them by the customs authorities[2]. Such a duty is normally paid by the importer residing within the Community.

The effect of a ruling on the validity of a measure by the Court under article 177, 1st para, point (b) is to have a measure declared inapplicable in the particular case. However, as a result of the case law of the Court and in particular its ruling in the *ICC* case discussed above[3], the effect of a ruling under article 177, 1st para, point (b) has the same practical result as the annulment of a measure under article 173.

References under article 177 are aimed primarily at ensuring that Community law is applied in a uniform manner throughout the Member States. Where a Member State decides the case without referring a question to the Court, the decision will inevitably be less predictable than if a reference had been made. This is due mainly to the fact that the national court will be less familiar with Community law than the Court. The finding by the national court is binding only in that Member State and not in any other. The Court has also recently held that only it can declare a Community measure invalid[4].

---

1. Ibid at para 25 of judgment.
2. There have been five preliminary references to the Court concerning the validity of anti-dumping measures. They are as follows : Case 239/84 *Gerlach and Co BV Internationale Expedite v Minister for Economic Affairs* [1985] ECR 3507; Case 248/87 *Continentale Produkten Gesellschaft Ehrhardt-Renken v Hauptzollamt München West* [1989] ECR 1151; Case 189/88 *Cartorobica SpA v Ministero delle Finanze dello Stato* [1990] ECR 1269; Case 323/88 *Sermes SA v Directeur des Services des Douanes de Strasbourg* [1990] ECR 3027; Case 16/90 *D Nölle t/a Eugen Nölle v Hauptzollamt Bremen Freihafen* (1991) Transcript 22 October.
3. See footnote 1, p170.
4. Case 314/85 *Firma Foto-Frost v Hauptzollamt Lübeck-Ost* [1988] ECR 4199.

A ruling under article 177, 1st para, point (b) is less satisfactory than bringing a direct action under article 173[1]. In the first place and most importantly, the proceedings are raised against the customs authorities and not against the proper defendants, the EC Council and the EC Commission, thereby creating difficulties with respect to the discovery of documents. Secondly, not all national courts are under an obligation to make an article 177 reference. Those that are, namely courts from which there is no judicial remedy, do not have to make a reference if the national court considers that a ruling on the validity of the measure is not necessary in order to decide the case. Thirdly, proceedings in the national court will undoubtedly take a substantial amount of time and expense to follow through. Fourthly, as Advocate General Van Gerven observed in *Sermes SA v Directeur des Services des Douanes de Strasbourg*[2], the preliminary reference procedure can give rise to a number of problems from a procedural point of view[3].

First, the question referred to the Court in that case was in very general terms. It was as follows :

> "Is Council Regulation (EEC) 864/87 ... valid in the light of Community law, in particular the basic regulation, Council Regulation 2176/84, and the fundamental principles of Community law?"

The Advocate General noted that the Court had held in *Continentale Produkten Gesellschaft Erhardt-Renken v Hauptzollamt München-West*[4] that when a question in such general terms is referred to it, the Court examines whether the grounds of the decision making the reference can supply any clarification. Where those grounds disclose the submissions by the applicant in the main proceedings before the national court, the Court endeavours to give a reply to the question referred for a preliminary ruling after examining those submissions[5]. He noted that in the present case, the decision making the reference referred to the applicant's submissions only in very general terms, and in particular did not specify the provisions of the basic regulation which were said to be infringed[6].

Secondly, Sermes had previously brought an action for annulment of the EC Commission regulation imposing a provisional anti-dumping duty. This application

---

1. See Opinion of Advocate General Jacobs in Case C-358/89 *Extrament Industrie SA v EC Council* 21 March 1991.
2. Case 323/88 *Sermes SA v Directeur des Services des Douanes de Strasbourg* [1990] ECR 3027.
3. Ibid at pp 3038-3040.
4. Case 246/87 *Continentale Produkten Gesellschaft Erhardt-Renken v Hauptzollamt München-West* [1989] ECR 1151.
5. Case 323/88 *Sermes SA v Directeur des Services des Douanes de Strasbourg* [1990] ECR 3027 at p3038.
6. Ibid at 3039.

was dismissed as Sermes did not have sufficient locus standi to challenge the regulation. However, it continued to import electric motors even after the definitive duties were imposed. Inevitably, it challenged the level of anti-dumping duties claimed by the Customs authorities and raised an action in the local courts for their recovery. In so doing, its aim was to persuade the national court to make a reference to the Court under article 177, 1st para, point (b) thereby enabling it to submit to the Court its observations challenging the validity of Regulation 864/87 in a situation where a direct action for annulment was precluded[1].

The Advocate General having noted these two features then considered from what viewpoint the Council regulation should be examined so that the Court could give a reply to the national court. He took the view and the Court concurred[2] that such a reply must include an examination of the submissions raised in the appellants observations in the main proceedings. His reason for doing so was based on the notion of judicial co-operation which characterises preliminary ruling proceedings and which he considered favoured such a solution[3].

Unlike proceedings under article 173 where a number of interested parties may have standing to challenge safeguard measures, article 177, 1st para, point (b) would in practice really only allow importers the right to raise proceedings since it is from importers that the customs authorities collect the duties. As the EC Commission noted in the *First Allied* case[4], it is impossible for exporters themselves to contest the imposition of anti-dumping duties in the national courts. At the very most, they can intervene alongside importers. It is therefore in their interests to be able to raise an action directly before the Court in order to protect their interests. As stated above, the Court rules on the validity of the Community measure, but it is outside the ambit of the Court to apply it to the facts or for that matter to make findings of fact. In practical terms, however, the Court's ruling will very often be worded in such a manner that it can be easily applied by the national courts.

4.11   Action for damages : article 215, 2nd para

In theory it is possible for an undertaking to bring an action for damages under article 215, 2nd para before the Court where it can be established that the Community authorities have acted unlawfully in adopting the measure in question.

---

1. Case 323/88 *Sermes SA v Directeur des Services des Douanes de Strasbourg* [1990] ECR 3027 at 3039.
2. Ibid, p3050 at para 13 of judgment.
3. Ibid at 3040.
4. Joined Cases 239 and 275/82 *Allied Corporation and Ors v EC Commission* [1984] ECR 1005.

It may only be in limited circumstances that an applicant would consider this course of action. In such circumstances the proper Court would be the national court[1].

The preconditions for an action for damages are difficult to establish, in that the applicant would have to show that the institutions have acted in a reckless manner in adopting the disputed measures. More importantly in practical terms, duties are refunded when the regulation imposing them has been annulled.

What is uncertain, however, is whether an applicant could successfully bring an article 215, 2nd para action to recover the interest paid on these duties. This has yet to be resolved by the Court. It would probably be the case that the Court would decline jurisdiction on the basis that the duties were collected by the customs authorities.

Claims for compensation for damages have been raised on three occasions to date in the proceedings involving safeguard measures. In *Nippon Seiko KK v EC Council and EC Commission*[2] claims were made by NSK-UK, NSK Germany and NSK-France. The claims were divided into four categories :

(a) Damages equal to the amount of the provisional duty actually paid to the customs authorities on importations effected before it was possible to arrange a bank guarantee. The amounts paid in each country were specified.

(b) Damages equal to the interest on the money which applicants had been deprived of as result of making these payments.

(c) Damages equal to the cost of the bank guarantees.

(d) Damages equal to loss of profits resulting from the applicants having to raise their prices for bearings manufactured by NSK-UK.

The Court did not address the question of damages. Advocate General Warner did[3]. He held that the claims under category (a) were inadmissible. It was well established that an action for damages did not lie against a Community institution where the claim was for the restitution of specific sums paid to national authorities. The proper court in which to raise the action was the national court[4].

---

1.   Case 26/74 *Roquette Frères v EC Commission* [1976] ECR 677.
2.   Case 119/77 *Nippon Seiko KK v EC Council and EC Commission* [1979] ECR 1303.
3.   Case 113/77 *NTN Toyo Bearing Co Ltd and Ors v EC Council* [1979] ECR 1185 at 1272.
4.   See Case 96/71 *Haegeman v EC Commission* [1972] ECR 1005.

Likewise, he held the claim under category (b) was inadmissible for the same reasons. With respect to categories (c) and (d) the Advocate General was of the opinion that these claims were properly brought before the Court. He considered, however, that the claims did not appear to rest on any general principle of a kind mentioned in article 215, 2nd para. He therefore rejected the applicants' submissions.

In the *First Allied*[1] case the applicants sought to claim damages under article 215, 2nd para. They contended that there had been a breach of a superior rule for the protection of the individual without specifying which rule. As a result they argued that a substantial loss of profits was incurred. The Court again did not address the matter. Advocate General VerLoren van Theemat held that as the measure imposing provisional duties was not unlawful, the application for damages must also be dismissed. He considered that it was impossible for a claim to succeed where loss was sustained as a result of a lawfully adopted measure[2].

In *Epichieriseon Metalleftikon Viomichanikon Kai Naftiliakon AE & Ors. v EC Council and EC Commission*[3] the Court rejected the application under article 215, 2nd para of the EEC Treaty.

It held that the decisions of the EC Council and EC Commission in connection with a proceeding relating to the possible imposition of an anti-dumping duty constituted legislative action involving choices of economic policy. In such circumstances and in accordance with the consistent case law of the Court, Community liability will only arise if there has been a sufficiently serious breach of a superior rule of law for the protection of the individual[4].

It is not clear from the judgment if all measures adopted in connection with an anti-dumping investigation will be considered as measures involving choices of economic policy. Further case law will be awaited with interest.

4.12 Conclusion

The system of judicial remedies in the European Communities, and article 173 in particular, provide the Court with the power to review the legality of acts of the institutions. The right of an individual to challenge acts of the institutions and, in

---

1. Joined Cases 239 and 275/82 *Allied Corporation v EC Commission* [1984] ECR 1005.
2. Ibid at 1048-9.
3. Case 122/86 *Epichieriseon Metalleftikon Viomichanikon Kai Naftiliakon AE and Ors v EC Council and EC Commission* [1989] ECR 3959.
4. Ibid at 3960.

particular, acts of general application depends largely on whether they have the necessary locus standi to do so.

As discussed above in the first part of the chapter, the preconditions laid down by article 173, 2nd para are very restrictive. Generally speaking, the Court has not in its jurisprudence adopted a liberal interpretation of article 173, 2nd para and in particular with respect to the concepts of "direct and individual" concern.

The Court's attitude to an individual's right to challenge safeguard measures is much more liberal. The major reason for this difference in attitude is that a restrictive interpretation would result in virtually all interested parties being unable to challenge the legality of safeguard measures imposed. Generally speaking, where appropriate, exporters, or producers, associated importers, and in limited circumstances OEMs, will have standing to challenge safeguard measures. The test to be applied by the Court is whether the economic agent in question is concerned by the findings relating to the existence of dumping complained of.

The Court has extended further the concept of locus standi in relation to safeguard measures. In a number of decisions it was prepared to confer on other interested parties, and complainants in particular, locus standi to challenge the disputed measure because they had certain procedural rights under the basic regulation in question which had been infringed or disregarded, notwithstanding the fact that those parties would not otherwise have had such locus standi.

Independent importers as a general rule will not have standing to challenge the measure in question, as they will neither be identified in the measure nor have specific findings made about them. The Court is prepared to hold that such importers would have locus standi if they could establish that they have certain attributes which are particular to them and distinguish them from all other persons. It is submitted that there is no good reason why independent importers should be treated any differently from those other undertakings referred to above. There is some justification for the view that the test to be applied, in determining an undertaking's locus standi should be based on the extent to which that undertaking was involved in the investigations. Furthermore, they will have standing to challenge quantitative restrictions where they can establish that they had entered into binding contracts prior to the imposition of the duties.

The EC Commission and EC Council have now recognised the fact that private parties should have locus standi to challenge safeguard measures. The major alternative to article 173 actions is for a natural or legal person to go to his national court in the hope that it will make a reference to the Court for a preliminary ruling on validity under article 177, 1st para, point (b). Such an action, it is submitted, does not offer the same advantages as a direct action before the Court.

CHAPTER 5 : THE AWARD OF INTERIM MEASURES IN CASES INVOLVING SAFEGUARD MEASURES

5.1   Introduction

By virtue of article 185 of the EEC Treaty, actions brought before the Court do not have suspensory effect. The Court may, if the circumstances so require, order that the application of the contested act be suspended. Under article 186 of the EEC Treaty, it may prescribe any necessary interim measures[1].

Generally speaking, the cases concerning interim measures are decided by the President of the Court. It is possible, however, for the full Court to decide the question of interim measures following an opinion of the Advocate General[2]. In the majority of cases, an order will be made within one month of the application.

By virtue of articles 36 of the Statute of the Court and 83 to 89 of the Rules of Procedure, certain conditions have to be fulfilled in an action for interim measures. First, there must be a main procedure before the Court in the context in which an application for interim measures is made[3]. Article 83(1)(2) of the Rules of Procedure further provides that an application under article 186 for the adoption of interim measures is admissible only if it is made by a party to a case before the Court and relates to that case. In *Nashua Corporation v EC Commission*[4], the applicant sought suspension of the effects of Council Regulation 535/87 imposing definitive duties. The EC Commission, the sole defendant, argued that the application for interim measures was inadmissible on the ground that the EC Council was not a party to the action. It took the view that the application could not be admissible merely because, as the applicant claimed, the Council regulation imposing definitive duties was the direct consequence of the EC Commission's decision rejecting the undertaking offered by Nashua. The Court held that :

> "In this case the decision under challenge in the main proceedings was adopted by the Commission, whereas the regulation establishing definitive anti-dumping duties, the operation of which the applicant wishes to have

---

1. See article 39 of the ECSC Treaty; articles 157 and 158 Euratom Treaty.
2. Eg Case 18/57 *Nold v High Authority* [1959] ECR 41; Case 792/79R *Camera Care Ltd v EC Commission* [1980] ECR 119.
3. Article 83(1), Rules of Procedure.
4. Case 133/87R *Nashua Corporation v EC Commission* [1987] ECR 2883 at 2886, para 6 of Order.

suspended by way of an interim measure, is the act of the Council. It follows that the Judge hearing the interlocutory proceedings is not empowered to allow such an application for an interim measure, since to do so would have the effect of suspending an act of a legislative nature, emanating from an institution which is not party to the proceedings."[1]

Second, a prima facie case on the factual and legal grounds has to be established, and further, an award of interim measures must be a matter of urgency[2]. It follows from a consistent line of decisions of the Court that the urgency required by article 83(2) of the Rules of Procedure, in regard to an application for interim measures, must be considered in relation to the need to adopt such measures in order to prevent "serious and irreparable" damage from being caused to the party requesting those measures. Third, the interim measures must be provisional[3]. Fourth, they must not prejudge the decision of the Court on the substance of the main application[4]; and finally, no appeal is possible[5].

The purpose of interim measures is to preserve the status quo pending a decision on the substance of the case. The Court has consistently held that interim measures may only be granted if they do not prejudge the decision on the substance of the case[6]. In the *Arbed* case the Court explained the objects and limits of interim measures. The Court held that if :

"their adoption is prima facie justified in fact and law, if they are urgent in the sense that it is necessary, in order to avoid serious and irreparable damage, that they should be laid down, and should take effect, before the decision of the Court on the substance of the action and if they are provisional in the sense that they do not prejudge the decision on the substance of the case, that is to say that they do not at this stage decide disputed points of law or of fact or neutralise in advance the consequences of a decision to be given subsequently on the substance of the action."[7]

There have been a number of applications for interim orders for the recovery of documents and measures of inquiry[8]. Although the Court admitted the

---

1.   Case 133/87R *Nashua Corporation v EC Commission* [1987] ECR 2883 at 2887, para 8 of the Order.
2.   Article 83(2), Rules of Procedure.
3.   Article 86(3), (4), Rules of Procedure.
4.   Article 86(4), Rules of Procedure.
5.   Article 86(1), Rules of Procedure.
6.   Cases 60 and 190/81R *IBM v EC Commission* [1981] ECR 1857 at 1862.
7.   Case 20/81R *Arbed SA and Ors v EC Commission* [1981] ECR 721 at 731, para 13 of Order.
8.   Case 121/86R *Anonymos Eteireia Epicheiriseon Metalleftikon Viomichanikon Kai Naftiliakon AE and Ors v EC Council and EC Commission* [1986] ECR 2063; Case 129/86R *Greece v EC Council and EC Commission* [1986] ECR 2071.

applications, it concluded that the applicants had not shown "serious and irreparable" damage and further it held that :

> "in the absence of exceptional circumstances which must be proved and which do not exist in this case, an application for the adoption of interim measures is not in principle an appropriate procedure for obtaining the production of documents of the kind applied for in this case. Such a measure is similar to a measure of inquiry of the kind which the Court may order under article 21 of the Statute of the Court of Justice in the context of the procedure dealing with the substance of the case."[1]

5.2   Interim measures and anti-dumping actions

Article 83(2) of the Court's Rules of Procedure provides the conditions governing the award of interim measures. First, there must be a prima facie case. Second, there must be urgency in the sense that the measures are necessary in order to avoid "serious and irreparable" harm before the decision of the Court on the main case. The concept of "serious and irreparable" damage has been further defined by the Court. In *Technointorg v EC Council*[2], it held that in establishing serious and irreparable damage, a party must at least adduce evidence showing that the damage suffered by the applicant as a result of the imposition of the anti-dumping duty is special to it[3], and that the balance of interests at stake points in its favour in the sense that the grant of the interim measures requested would not cause appreciable injury to the Community industry[4].

These criteria are normally referred to by the Court in cases which involve measures of general application. They are therefore important in any analysis of interim measures where safeguard measures are concerned.

The Court will usually first consider whether the applicant has established a prima facie case before considering the question of urgency. For example in *TEC Co Ltd v EC Council* the Court, having determined that no prima facie case existed, did not discuss whether the other conditions had been fulfilled[5]. However, in some cases the Court has declared that as the applicants had not succeeded in proving

---

1.   Case 129/86R *Greece v EC Council and EC Commission* [1986] ECR 2071 at 2076, para 17 of Order.
2.   Case 77/87R *Technointorg v EC Council* [1987] ECR 1793 at 1799, para 17 of Order.
3.   See in particular, Case 258/84R *Nippon Seiko KK v EC Council* [1984] ECR 4357.
4.   See Case 250/85R *Brother Industries Ltd v EC Council and EC Commission* [1985] ECR 3459; Case 260/85R *TEC v EC Council and EC Commission* [1985] ECR 3467; Case 273/85R *Silver Seiko Ltd v EC Council and EC Commission* [1985] ECR 3475; Joined Cases 277 and 300/85R *Canon Inc v EC Council and EC Commission* [1985] ECR 3491; Case 297/85R *Towa Sankiden Corpn v EC Council and EC Commission* [1985] ECR 3483.
5.   Case 260/85R *TEC v EC Council and EC Commission* [1985] ECR 3467.

urgency, it was not necessary to consider whether the factual and legal grounds advanced by them established a prima facie case[1].

5.2.1 Prima facie case

As stated above, the adoption of interim measures cannot be considered by the Court unless the factual and legal circumstances relied upon establish a prima facie case for granting interim measures. In some orders, this criterion is not mentioned at all, and in others in only a vague way. This seems to be the position in the cases in which interim measures have been sought where anti-dumping regulations are in issue[2]. The overriding principle for the Court seems to be that the applicant must satisfy it that there is a serious question to be tried[3].

With respect to cases involving safeguard measures, the Court is willing to accept as a minimum requirement that the applicant shows to its satisfaction that there are sufficiently serious doubts about the legality of the challenged measures. In *Raznoimport v EC Commission*[4], the Court was of the view that the applicant had established a prima facie case. It expressed serious doubts about the way in which the EC Commission adopted a constructed value as a basis of reference when prices were apparently determined by market mechanisms and secondly, in calculating the constructed value on the basis of production costs in a non-member country[5]. It also raised doubts in respect of the circumstances in which the EC Commission fixed the rate of provisional duty at 7%[6].

In the majority of cases, the applicant will use the same arguments for the application of interim measures as for the main case, in order to establish to the Court's satisfaction that the case is well founded. In *Nippon Seiko v EC Commission*, the Court noted that, as regards the factors establishing a prima facie case, the applicant expressly referred to its main application, which set out the numerous grounds of annulment[7].

The case of *TEC v EC Council*[8] is an example of a decision where the Court decided a prima facie case had not been established. In its submission, the applicant alleged that it was discriminated against, as compared with Nakajima All, which was

1.   See Case 121/86R *Anonymos Eteireia Epicheiriseon Metalleftikon Viomichanikon Kai Naaftiliakon AE and Ors v EC Council and EC Commission* [1986] ECR 2063.
2.   See for example Case 304/86R *Enital SpA v EC Council and EC Commission* [1987] ECR 267.
3.   In Case 792/79R *Camera Care Ltd v EC Commission* above, Advocate General Warner pointed to the fact that the applicant must have "at least an arguable case, in the main proceedings".
4.   Case 120/83R *Raznoimport v EC Commission* [1983] ECR 2573.
5.   Ibid at 2578-9.
6.   Ibid at 2579.
7.   Case 258/84R *Nippon Seiko KK v EC Council* [1984] ECR 4357.
8.   Case 260/85R *TEC v EC Council and EC Commission* [1985] ECR 3467.

the only Japanese producer of electronic typewriters on whom no provisional or definitive anti-dumping duty was imposed. Before the hearing, the EC Commission did in fact impose a provisional duty on the imports of electronic typewriters manufactured by Nakajima All. It was held by the Court that the imposition of this duty, although only provisional, would have substantially the same economic effect as a definitive duty. For this reason, it concluded that there was no longer any difference in treatment between TEC and Nakajima All at the date of the order. This argument had no longer any purpose and therefore the applicant had not established a prima facie case for interim measures.

5.2.2 Urgency

Once an applicant has established a prima facie case, the Court must also assess the urgency of the interim measures. In particular, the applicant must satisfy the Court that the interim measures requested are necessary for the purposes of avoiding "serious and irreparable" damage to itself[1]. This is a question of fact to be decided in every case. It must be shown to the satisfaction of the Court that the damage suffered by the applicant is special to it[2]. Furthermore, the applicant must adduce evidence that the balance of the interests at stake weighs in its favour, in the sense that the grant of the interim measures requested would not cause appreciable injury to the Community industry[3].

5.2.2.1 The damage suffered must be special to the applicant

In analysing this criterion, a distinction has to be drawn between interim measures aimed at suspending provisional anti-dumping duties; those aimed at suspending definitive anti-dumping duties; and those aimed at suspending the definitive collection of provisional anti-dumping duties.

(a)   Provisional duties

In *Raznoimport v EC Commission*[4], the applicant sought the suspension of an anti-dumping regulation imposing a provisional duty. It contended that the damage to it consisted of the risk that the patterns of trade established by it may be disrupted as a result of the obligation during the validity of the provisional duty to provide security at the time of entry of the imported nickel.

The problem facing Raznoimport was that the duty was only provisional. It did not need to be paid until it was made definitive. All that required to be done was to

---

1.   Case 69/89R *Nakajima All Precision Co v EC Council* [1989] ECR 1689.
2.   Case 258/84R *Nippon Seiko v EC Council* [1984] ECR 4357 at 4362; Case 77/87R *Technointorg v EC Council* [1987] ECR 1793; Case 358/89R *Extramet Industrie SA v EC Council* [1990] ECR 431.
3.   Eg Case 250/85R *Brother Industries v EC Council* [1985] ECR 3459.
4.   Case 120/83R *Raznoimport v EC Commission* [1983] ECR 2573.

provide security which would be reimbursed if the applicant was successful in the main application. In considering whether the damage suffered by the applicant was special to it, the Court pointed to the fact that it must have regard to the specific features of the procedure in question. It held that :

> "It must be emphasised that, under the procedure established by Regulation (EEC) No. 3017/79, the EC Council will shortly have to decide both whether to impose a definitive duty and whether to collect definitively the provisional duty. Although that does not in itself exclude the possibility of suspending the operation of the contested measures, the Court must, however, in proceedings for the adoption of interim measures, take account of the specific features of the procedure in question and of the powers which the Council will have to exercise within the prescribed period, after it has been given full information, in particular in the light of what has emerged during these proceedings for the adoption of interim measures."[1]

Because it was a provisional duty, the Court ruled that the EC Commission was under an obligation not only to continue its investigation, but to monitor from day to day any change in prices on the market of the product which was subject to the provisional duty, in order to determine whether it was necessary to maintain that duty or the rate thereof. The Court noted that :

> "in view of the characteristic features of the market of the product in question, the risk of any lasting disruption of the patterns of trade as a result of the maintenance of the provisional duty is small. It has not been established that the applicant will be unable to avoid such damage by adopting measures consistent with the obligation to co-operate which is incumbent upon it in order to mitigate the alleged damage."[2]

The Court concluded by stating that the damage facing the applicant was limited to the burden constituted by the provision of security for the payment of provisional duties. This cost was estimated at 1-2% of the amount of the provisional duty. The Court in this respect held that this :

> "disadvantage cannot constitute serious and irreparable damage such as would permit the suspension of a decision adopted in the context of a complex economic situation. Any damage which may occur can, if appropriate, be made good in the context of the action for compensation brought by the applicant."[3]

---

1.   Case 120/83R *Raznoimport v EC Commission* [1983] ECR 2573 at 2579, para 12 of Order.
2.   Ibid at 2580, para 14 of Order.
3.   Ibid, para 15 of Order.

In essence, the damage which the applicant claimed to have suffered was of a kind which may generally occur whenever a provisional duty is imposed.

The Court was again faced with an application in *Technointorg v EC Commission* for the suspension of a regulation imposing provisional anti-dumping duties[1]. It began by stating that, as the contested regulation in the main action was itself a provisional measure forming part of the procedure laid down by Regulation 2176/84, the application for interim measures must be examined in the light of the procedure laid down in that regulation[2]. The Court then proceeded to examine articles 11 and 12 of the aforesaid regulation which governed the imposition of provisional duties[3] and held that :

> "The procedure laid down by the regulation therefore implies that the Council will shortly have to decide both whether a definitive duty is to be imposed and whether the provisional duty is to be definitively collected. It must therefore be stated that to grant the applicant's request that the payment of the provisional duty should be suspended until the Court has given judgment on the main application, on condition that it provides a guarantee equivalent to the amount of the duty, would be tantamount to depriving the Council of the power conferred upon it by the aforesaid article 12 to decide whether the provisional duty should be definitively collected and to depriving that decision of any practical effect."[4]

The Court came to the view that the damage suffered by the applicant was limited to the cost of providing a guarantee for a period of four months. It held that this could not constitute serious and irreparable damage. In this respect it referred to its decision in *Raznoimport*.

In *Enital v EC Council and EC Commission* the EC Commission imposed provisional anti-dumping duties following a review by it of the price undertakings. The applicant sought to have the effect of this regulation suspended. It claimed inter alia that the Community institutions' decision to fix the date of entry for the coming into force of the contested measures at their date of publication amounted in fact to giving them retroactive effect, and that it caused them serious and irreparable damage because it had already determined its commercial policy on the basis of price undertakings already accepted[5]. The Court held that, by virtue of

1.   Case 294/86R *Technointorg v EC Commission* [1986] ECR 3979.
2.   Ibid at 3986, para 21 of Order.
3.   See Chapter 3, section 3.9.5.3 on anti-dumping duties, above.
4.   Case 294/86R *Technointorg v EC Commission* [1986] ECR 3979 at 3987, para 25 of Order.
5.   Case 304/86R *Enital SpA EC Council and EC Commission* [1987] ECR 267 at 271, para 14 of Order.

article 191, the Treaty permitted the institutions adopting the regulation to lay down therein the date on which it was to enter into force[1]. The Court further held :

> "That provisional anti-dumping duties should enter into force immediately would appear to follow from the provisional and protective nature of such duties which, in the terms of article 11 of Council Regulation 2176/84, are imposed in order to prevent injury being caused to the Community during the anti-dumping proceeding. It does not appear likely to cause serious and irreparable damage to the applicant."[2]

The applicant had therefore failed to show to the satisfaction of the Court that it would suffer serious and irreparable damage.

It is submitted that, having regard to recent case law of the Court, if the application for interim measures involves the suspension of a regulation imposing provisional duties, the Court is unlikely to grant them. This is even more so the case where the damage allegedly suffered by the applicant is limited to the cost of providing a guarantee or security for the duration of the validity of the provisional duties.

(b)   Definitive duties

In *Nippon Seiko v EC Council*[3], the applicants sought to have a regulation imposing definitive anti-dumping duties suspended until the main application was heard with the result that only a security for later payment would be required.

The applicants contended that they were suffering serious and irreparable damage on the ground that they were losing substantial sums by way of interest on the duty. This interest could not be recouped on the grounds that there was no specific Community legislation providing for the payment of interest on the repayment of anti-dumping duties[4]. The EC Council, on the other hand, argued that this damage could not be regarded as serious. The effect of a definitive anti-dumping duty was to bring about an increase in prices. This would not occur if the definitive duties were

---

1.   Case 304/86R *Enital SpA EC Council and EC Commission* [1987] ECR 267 at 272, para 16 of Order.

2.   Ibid at 272-3, para 16 of Order.

3.   Case 258/84R *Nippon Seiko KK v EC Council* [1984] ECR 4357.

4.   It has been suggested that the Court might have the power under article 176 or article 215(2) to order the payment of interest when duties under a regulation which have been annulled are refunded. If this is the case then an important argument for the suspension of duties is deprived of its basis. See Temple Lang "Judicial Review of Trade Safeguard Measures in the European Community" in (ed) B. Hawk 'Antitrust and Trade Policy in the United States and the European Community', Fordham University School of Law (1985) 643 at 669.

suspended. The Court concluded that the EC Council and the EC Commission had demonstrated that the :

"adoption of the interim measures applied for would cause substantial harm to the European Economic Community, in that merely to require the lodging of security as proposed by the applicant would have considerably less protective effect than the levying of the anti-dumping duty itself. Such a step would not take the interests of the Community's own industry sufficiently into account and would be apt to frustrate the purpose of the regulation itself. Furthermore the damage allegedly suffered by the applicant is not special to it but, on the contrary, is likely to arise in every case where anti-dumping duties are imposed. There is therefore no special feature of this case which would justify the interim measures requested."[1]

In the *Electronic Typewriter* cases[2], the Court noted that the parties had taken opposing views and submitted different figures on the level of prices and market shares of the European industry and its Japanese competitors. It held that :

"In interim proceedings it is impossible for the President of the Court, without prejudging the substance of the case, to accept figures submitted by one party in preference to those submitted by the other, unless, as is not the case here, there are other factors weighing in favour of one party's view."[3]

The Court also noted that it had a similar dilemma when determining whether the export price and normal value were compared at the same level of trade. Given that an applicant must prove that his allegations are well founded, the Court concluded that these applicants had not adduced sufficient evidence establishing that they would suffer serious and irreparable damage.

In *Technointorg v EC Council*[4], the applicant sought to have the definitive duties suspended pending the Court's judgment in the main proceedings, on condition that it continued to provide security for the performance of its obligation in the amount it was required to pay under Council Regulation 29/87.

As stated above, the applicant had already sought to have the provisional anti-dumping duties suspended on condition that it provided a security. The Court

---

1.   Case 258/84R *Nippon Seiko KK v EC Council* [1984] ECR 4357 at 4361-2, paras 19-20 of Order.
2.   See footnote 4, p213.
3.   Eg Case 273/85R *Silver Seiko Ltd v EC Council and EC Commission* [1985] ECR 3475 at para 17 of Order.
4.   Case 77/87R *Technointorg v EC Council* [1987] ECR 1793.

dismissed that application on two grounds. First, to grant the applicant's request to suspend the provisional duties until the main application had been determined would have been tantamount to depriving the EC Council of the power conferred on it by article 12 of Regulation 2176/84. Second, the President also came to the conclusion that the damage suffered by the applicant was limited to the cost of providing security for a period of four months, and that such a disadvantage could not constitute serious and irreparable damage to it[1]. In the present case the applicant, in demonstrating the urgency of the application, sought to describe the effects which were inherent in the imposition of anti-dumping duties, namely a rise in the price of its products and a diminution of its market share.

The Court concluded that the applicant had not shown that the damage suffered by it as a result of the imposition of the anti-dumping duty was special to it. It held that :

> "It is in the very nature of anti-dumping duties that they should result in an increase in the price of the product in question because their purpose is to counterbalance the dumping margin which has been established and to protect the Community industry against the injury caused by dumping."[2]

The Court concluded by stating that :

> "The damage which [the applicant] claims to suffer is of a kind which may generally occur whenever a definitive anti-dumping duty is imposed."[3]

The Court observed in *Extramet Industrie S.A. v EC Council* that an undertaking which claims that its survival is endangered following the introduction of the anti-dumping duty, which results in a loss of almost all its sales on the Community market representing approximately one-third of its production, fails to establish the imminence of that danger if it admits that its business has remained profitable and that demand for the products which it sells on the world market is increasing[4].

It is submitted that definitive anti-dumping duties are unlikely to be suspended by the Court as an interim measure, even if future payment in the shape of bank guarantees are offered, given the recent pronouncements of the Court.

---

1. Case 294/86R *Technointorg v EC Commission* [1986] ECR 3979.
2. Case 77/87R *Technointorg v EC Council* [1987] ECR 1793 at 1799 at para 16 of Order; See also Case 69/89R *Nakajima All Precision Co v EC Council* [1989] ECR 1689; Case 358/89 *Extramet Industrie SA v EC Council* [1990] ECR 431.
3. Ibid at 1800, para 19 of Order.
4. Case 358/89 *Extramet Industrie SA v EC Council* [1990] ECR 431 at 431-2.

(c) Definitive collection of provisional duties

In the very first dumping case to come before the Court, a number of Japanese manufacturers of ballbearings lodged applications to have article 3 of Council Regulation 1778/77, ordering the definitive collection of provisional duties, suspended[1].

In *NTN Toyo Bearing Co Ltd v EC Council* the applicants were prepared to maintain bank guarantees in force and for this reason did not see why it was necessary to insist on the immediate implementation of article 3 of Regulation 1778/77. They argued that the immediate payment of the sums demanded would lead to additional financing costs, with the result that they could not be sure of recovering interest on the sum paid in the event of being successful in the main action[2]. The Court held that :

> "It has not been possible to establish conclusively within the context of the present proceedings whether, in the event of NTN's being successful in the main action this expenditure would be wholly recouped.

> Having regard to the probable duration of the procedure in the main action, charges at the rate quoted by the applicant cannot be regarded as negligible."[3]

For these reasons it was prepared to order the suspension of the obligation to pay the provisional duties, on condition that the bank guarantees were maintained.

5.2.2.2 The balance of interests

The Court will balance the harm that will be caused to the applicant if the interim measures applied for are refused against that to the defendant if they are allowed.

In *Nippon Seiko v EC Council*[4], the applicant sought the suspension of definitive duties on the ground that the loss of interest on the duty would constitute irreparable damage, even though the duties would be refunded if the applicant was successful in the main application. The EC Council argued that the provision of a security would not adequately protect the interests of the Community industry. It argued that the purpose of an anti-dumping duty is to increase the price of the imported products to eliminate the effects of dumping. This purpose could not be

---

1.   Case 113/77R *NTN Toyo Bearing Co Ltd v EC Council* [1977] ECR 1721. See also Case 121/77R *Nachi Fujikoshi Corporation v EC Council* [1977] ECR 2107.
2.   Case 113/77R, above, at 1723.
3.   Ibid at 1725, para 5-6 of Order.
4.   Case 258/84R *Nippon Seiko KK v EC Council* [1984] ECR 4357.

achieved by means only of a security[1]. On the question of balancing the interests involved, the Court held that :

"The Council and Commission have been able to demonstrate that the adoption of the interim measures applied for would cause substantial harm to the European Economic Community, in that merely to require the lodging of security as proposed by the applicant would have considerably less protective effect than the levying of the anti-dumping duty itself. Such a step would not take the interests of the Community's own industry sufficiently into account and would be apt to frustrate the purpose of the regulation itself."[2]

In the *Electronic Typewriter* cases[3], the Community authorities argued that the damage suffered by Community industry as a result of undercutting by the applicants in the prices of their electronic typewriters was considerable, and that suspension of the definitive duties would undoubtedly result in the destruction of a part of the Community industry. The Court held that, in the absence of reliable and uncontested evidence to the contrary, the adoption of the interim measures applied for would cause appreciable damage to European industry[4].

Finally, in *Technointorg v EC Council*[5], the Court stressed that, in proving "serious and irreparable damage", the applicant must adduce evidence showing not only that the damage suffered is special to it but also that the balance of interests points in their favour. The applicant had adduced no such evidence. The Court stated, however, that :

"The Council and Commission, on the other hand, have shown that the adoption of the interim measure requested would cause appreciable injury to the interests of the European Economic Community. The mere requirement of a security, for which the applicant is arguing, would have considerably less protective effect than the collection of the anti-dumping duty itself, and hence such a measure would not take sufficient account of the interests of the Community industry and would be liable to nullify the effect intended by the imposition of a definitive anti-dumping duty."[6]

---

1.   Case 258/84R *Nippon Seiko KK v EC Council* [1984] ECR 4357 at 4359-60.
2.   Ibid at 4361, para 19 of Order.
3.   See footnote 4, p213.
4.   Eg Case 278/85R *Silver Seiko Ltd v EC Council and EC Commission* above at 3841, para 18 of Order.
5.   Case 77/87R *Technointorg v EC Council* [1987] ECR 1793 at para 17 of Order.
6.   Ibid at 1799/1800 para 18 of Order.

5.3   Interim measures and other safeguard measures

The principles expounded by the Court in the anti-dumping cases where there has been an application to have those duties suspended would apply equally to applications to have countervailing duties or measures under Regulations 288/82 and 2641/84 suspended. This will undoubtedly depend on whether the applicants have the requisite locus standi to challenge these duties or measures. The applicants must also adduce sufficient evidence to satisfy the Court that there is a prima facie case for the granting of interim measures, and that those measures are necessary and urgent, balancing the interests concerned in order to avoid "serious and irreparable" damage being caused to the applicant. It should be emphasised, however, that the Court may be slow to suspend the operation of quantitative restrictions, for to do so would leave Community industry unprotected and would also prejudge the ultimate result of the main application before it.

5.4   Conclusion

On the application of a natural or legal person who is seeking to have a Community measure annulled, the Court may by virtue of articles 185 and 186 prescribe any necessary interim measures it considers appropriate in the case, in order to preserve the status quo pending the decision on the substance of the case. In order to obtain an order for interim measures, it is necessary for an undertaking to show that it has fulfilled the following pre-conditions :

1.   a prima facie case; and

2.   that the measures requested are urgent in the sense that there is a "serious and irreparable" damage being caused to the applicant. "Serious and irreparable" damage has been further defined by the Court in that the applicant must show that :

   (a)   the damage suffered by it is special to it; and

   (b)   the balance of interests weigh in its favour in the sense that the granting of the interim measures requested would not cause appreciable injury to the Community industry concerned.

The case law of the Court with respect to safeguard measures has been concerned with suspension of regulations imposing anti-dumping duties. However, the principles expounded by the Court in these cases would be equally applicable to applications for interim measures involving the other safeguard measures.

To date there have been very few successful cases. The case law can be divided into three potential categories where an applicant would wish to have the effects of a regulation imposing anti-dumping duties suspended. First, it may wish to have the effects of a regulation imposing provisional anti-dumping duties suspended. The cases, however, indicate that an applicant would be unsuccessful in attempting to have the regulation suspended. Second, it may wish to have the effects of a regulation imposing definitive anti-dumping duties suspended. Again, the applicant would fair little better even if it was prepared to offer bank guarantees as security pending the outcome of the main application. Finally, an applicant may be successful if it seeks to have the effects of a regulation ordering the definitive collection of provisional anti-dumping duties suspended.

CHAPTER 6 : SUBSTANTIVE ASPECTS OF JUDICIAL REVIEW

PART 1 : THE GROUNDS OF ILLEGALITY : GENERAL

6.1   Introduction

Article 173[1] enumerates four grounds of illegality. They are :

1.   Lack of competence;

2.   Infringement of an essential procedural requirement;

3.   Infringement of the Treaty or any rule of law relating to its application; and

4.   Misuse of powers.

Under article 38 of the ECSC Treaty, acts of the EC Council and European Parliament may only be contested on two grounds, namely lack of competence and infringement of an essential procedural requirement. Some commentators[2] have grouped them into two main categories of illegality : formal illegality, which encompasses lack of competence and infringement of an essential procedural requirement; and material illegality, which encompasses infringement of the Treaty or any rule of law relating to its application and misuse of powers.

Historically, the grounds of illegality are derived from French administrative law, the equivalent French terms being *incompétence, vice de forme, violation de la loi,* and *détournement de pouvoir.* The grounds can be defined separately but invariably these definitions overlap, with the result that one set of facts may fall into more than one category. It will normally be the case that an illegality falling into either category 1, 2 or 4 will also constitute an infringement of the Treaty or any rule of law relating to its application. It does not follow, however, that the converse will be true.

---

1.   Article 146, Euratom the same four grounds are recognised.
2.   Eg Bebr "Development of Judicial Control of the European Communities" (1981) at p85.

6.2   Lack of competence

This concept covers the situation where the institution in question did not have the power to do what it purported to do. The case of *Meroni v High Authority*[1] is an example. The Court, however, treated it as an infringement of the Treaty. Under article 58 of the ECSC Treaty, delegation of powers in respect of financial arrangements had to be precisely defined. The Court found that the High Authority had delegated powers to a private body giving it a "degree of latitude which implies a wide margin of discretion"[2]. Such a delegation, the Court held, could not be regarded as being compatible with the requirements of the Treaty.

6.3   Infringement of an essential procedural requirement

Infringement of an essential procedural requirement can take many forms and will often constitute a breach of a general principle such as the right to be heard. Reference to a few decisions of the Court will give the reader some idea of the sort of illegality which is caught under this category. For example, in *Roquette Frères v EC Council*[3], a Council regulation was annulled by the Court because the European Parliament had not been consulted.

Infringement of an essential procedural requirement will often come about as a result of a failure on the part of the Community authorities to provide an adequate statement of reasons as to why a particular decision was taken. This is also an infringement of the Treaty (article 190). In *EC Commission v EC Council*[4], the EC Commission challenged two Council regulations which under the Generalised System of Preferences (GSP) granted favourable tariffs to developing countries. The EC Commission complained that the EC Council failed to specify the provisions of the Treaty on which the regulations were based as required by article 190 of the EEC Treaty. The Court held that it was essential in such a case to do so and that the resultant failure infringed the requirement in article 190 to state the reasons on which the regulations were based.

---

1.   Case 9/56 *Meroni v High Authority* [1957-58] ECR 133.
2.   Ibid at 154.
3.   Case 138/79 *Roquette Frères v EC Council* [1980] ECR 3333.
4.   Case 45/86 *EC Commission v EC Council* [1987] ECR 1493.

As stated above, breach of general principles with respect to the protection of an individual's right of defence fall into this category. For example, in *Transocean Marine Paint Association v EC Commission*[1], the Court held that :

> "a person whose interests are perceptibly affected by a decision taken by a public authority must be given the opportunity to make his point of view known."[2]

In this case, conditions were imposed on the grant of exemptions to undertakings under article 85(3) without those undertakings having been heard. The Court stated that an undertaking must be clearly informed in good time of the conditions which the EC Commission intends to be subject to the exemption and it must have the opportunity to submit its observations to the EC Commission.

6.4   Infringement of the Treaty or of rules of law relating to its application

This is by far the most important ground of illegality under article 173. It has been held to include breach of the general principles common to the laws of the Member States which have been recognised by the Court. The most important of these are considered briefly below.

6.4.1   Fundamental human rights

In the *Internationale Handelsgesellschaft* case, the Court held that "respect for fundamental rights forms an integral part of the general principles of law protected by the Court of Justice"[3]. Such rights put constraints upon the legislative and executive action of the institutions when they are applying or are obliged to apply Community rights and obligations.

6.4.2   The principle of legal certainty

This principle provides that the application of the law to a specific situation should be predictable[4]. Certain other principles will naturally follow on from this. A legal right once acquired should not be withdrawn and, more importantly, a case should be judged in the light of the law as it was at the time the event took place[5].

---

1.   Case 17/74 *Transocean Marine Paint Association v EC Commission* [1974] ECR 1063.
2.   Ibid, p1080, para 15 of judgment.
3.   Case 11/70 *Internationale Handelsgesellschaft mbH v Einfuhr- und Vorratsstelle für Getreide und Futtermittel* [1970] ECR 1125 at 1134, para 4 of judgment.
4.   Eg Case 78/74 *Deuka, Deutsche Kraftfutter GmbH, B.J. Stolp v Einfuhr- und Vorrastsstelle für Getreide un Futterwmittel* [1975] ECR 421; Cases 66, 127 and 128/79 *Amministrazione della Finanze v Srl Meridionale Industria Salumi, Fratelli Vasanelli and Fratelli Ultrocchi* [1980] ECR 1237.
5.   See Case 12/71 *Günther Henck v Hauptzollamt Emmerich* [1971] ECR 743.

The Court has also recognised the principle that a person is entitled to act and carry on his business in the reasonable expectation that the law as it exists will continue to apply[1].

6.4.3   The principle of proportionality

This principle is aimed at ensuring that the means used in a given situation are not disproportionate to the end to be achieved[2].

6.4.4   The principle of non-discrimination

In *Ruckdeschel*[3], the Court held that the prohibition of discrimination "is merely a specific enunciation of the general principle of equality which is one of the fundamental principles of Community law. This principle requires that similar situations shall not be treated differently unless differentiation is objectively justified"[4]. When the difference in treatment is objectively justified no discrimination arises[5].

6.4.5   Evaluation of economic facts and circumstances

If the question is one which concerns the validity of acts of the Community authorities in the economic sphere the Court will not as a general rule evaluate their findings or interfere with their discretion except within limited spheres. The Court has held that it will limit its review to examining whether those findings contain a manifest error or a misuse of powers or clearly exceeds the bounds of their discretion[6].

6.5   Misuse of powers

This ground of illegality relates to those situations where the Community authorities had the power to do what they did but used that power for wrongful purposes[7]. This ground of illegality is often alleged but rarely proved. An example of a case involving a misuse of powers is *Giuffrida v EC Council*[8]. This case concerned the internal competition for the post of principal administrator in the EC Council's Directorate for Regional Policy. The Court was advised that the competition had been held for the sole purpose of remedying the anomalous

---

1.   Case 112/77 *Töpfer v EC Commission* [1978] ECR 1019.
2.   Case 9/73 *Carl Schülter v Hauptzollamt Lörrach* [1973] ECR 1135.
3.   Cases 117/76 and 16/77 *Ruckdeschel & Co and Hansa-Lagerhaus Stroh & Co v Hauptzollamt Hamburg-St Annen* [1977] ECR 1753.
4.   Ibid at 1769, para 7 of judgment.
5.   Case 88/78 *Hauptzollamt Hamburg-Jonas v Hermann Kendermann* [1978] ECR 2477.
6.   Case 29/77 *Roquette Frères v Administration des Douanes* [1977] ECR 1835.
7.   See Joined Cases 3 and 4/64 *Chambre Syndicale de la Sidérurgie Française v High Authority* [1965] ECR 441 at 454/5.
8.   Case 105/75 *Giuffrida v EC Council* [1976] ECR 1395 at 1043.

administrative status of a specific official and of appointing that same official to the post declared vacant. This was contrary to recruitment procedure as well as internal competition procedure. The Court held that this constituted a misuse of powers.

PART 2 : SAFEGUARD MEASURES

6.6   Introduction

Almost all the proceedings which have come before the Court to date concerning safeguard measures involve the Community's anti-dumping laws. In these circumstances, the analysis of the Court's review of safeguard measures will concentrate on these laws, in particular on the application by the Court of the general principles referred to above and the extent to which it is prepared to review the exercise of the EC Commission's discretion where this involves highly complex economic facts and circumstances.

It will very often be the case that the Court will not consider all the submissions put forward by the applicants but instead will decide the case on one ground alone. For these reasons, the following analysis will include an examination of the Advocate General's Opinion where relevant. Generally speaking, the Advocate General will consider all the submissions of the parties in reaching his decision.

6.7   Lack of competence

In the *Japanese Ballbearing* cases, the very first set of anti-dumping cases to come before the Court[1], a number of the applicants[2] relied on inter alia this ground of illegality in their submissions.

After an investigation, the EC Commission adopted Regulation 261/77 imposing a provisional duty of 20% on ballbearings and tapered roller bearings originating in Japan. On the same date as the EC Commission accepted price undertakings from the applicants, the EC Council adopted Regulation 1778/77 imposing a suspended definitive duty of 15% as a sanction for their observance. The applicants sought to have this regulation annulled.

---

1.   Case 113/77 *NTN Toyo Bearing Co Ltd v EC Council* [1979] ECR 1185; Case 118/77 *Import Standard Office (ISO) v EC Council* [1979] ECR 1277; Case 119/77 *Nippon Seiko KK and Ors v EC Council* [1979] ECR 1303; Case 120/77 *Koyo Seiko Co Ltd and Ors v EC Council and EC Commission* [1979] ECR 1337; Case 121/77 *Nachi Fujikoshi Corp and Ors v EC Council* [1977] ECR 1363.

2.   Case 113/77 above; Case 121/77 above.

The lack of competence argument was based on the premise that the EC Commission did not have the necessary power to issue Regulation 261/77 imposing provisional duties given that the power to do so in article 15 of the basic regulation, ie Regulation 459/68 (now Regulation 2423/88), was ultra vires[1]. The applicants were in actual fact pleading the illegality of the basic regulation, namely Regulation 459/68. The EC Council disagreed with this on the basis that the economic objective to be achieved, by the adoption of provisional duties, was to allow the necessary decisions to be made within a short period of time and for this reason the EC Commission should be allowed to attain this objective. Further, the imposition of provisional measures by the EC Commission was in conformity with the separation of powers laid down in the Treaty[2]. These submissions were considered neither by the Court nor by Advocate General Warner.

Lack of competence was also relied upon by the applicants in the *Continentale Produkten Gesellschaft* case[3], which involved proceedings in respect of the refund procedure under article 15 of Regulation 2176/84. The applicants sought to show that the EC Commission had no power to decide whether they were entitled to refunds, as this was a matter for the national authorities by virtue of article 15 of Regulation 3017/79. The procedure had commenced under the old legislation, namely Regulation 3017/79, but during proceedings a new regulation - Regulation 2176/84 - had entered into force.

The EC Commission argued that the new regulation - Regulation 2176/84 - applied to proceedings already initiated but not resolved by virtue of article 19(2) of the said regulation[4]. It referred to the decision of the Court in the case of *Westzucker v Einfuhr- und Vorratsstelle für Zucker*[5] as an authority for the proposition that new legislation applied to situations which arose under earlier legislation but which as yet had not been resolved.

Advocate General Darmon in his Opinion[6] held that the EC Commission had obtained its powers from the general provisions in article 15 of Regulation 2176/84.

---

1. Case 113/77 *NTN Toyo Bearing Co Ltd v EC Council* [1979] ECR 1185 at 1196; and Case 121/77 *Nachi Fujikoshi Corp and Ors v EC Council* [1977] ECR 1363 at 1371.
2. Case 121/77 *Nachi Fujikoshi Corp and Ors v EC Council* [1977] ECR 1363 at 1372-3.
3. Case 312/84 *Continentale Produkten Gesellschaft Ehrhardt-Renken GmbH & Co v EC Commission* [1987] ECR 841.
4. Ibid at 845.
5. Case 1/73 *Westzucker v Einfuhr- und Vorratsstelle für Zucker* [1973] ECR 723 at 729.
6. Case 312/84 *Continentale Produkten Gesellschaft Ehrhardt-Renken GmbH & Co v EC Commission* [1987] ECR 841 at 856.

Further, a change in the procedural rules relating to the decision on the application was merely a matter of form. The Court agreed with the Advocate General. It held that :

> "in general provisions amending an administrative procedure and appointing the competent authorities are applicable to pending proceedings and the persons concerned may not claim to have a "vested right" to have their case dealt with by the authorities upon whom competence was conferred by the previous provisions."[1]

Given that the role and functions of the institutions are now well established under the various safeguard measures, this ground of illegality is likely only to arise when and if new legislation comes into existence, as seen by the decision of the Court in the *Continentale Produkten Gesellschaft* case above.

6.8 Infringement of essential procedural requirements

In all the cases that have come before the Court involving a review of the anti-dumping regulations, the applicants have alleged in one way or another that there has been an infringement of an essential procedural requirement. This usually takes the form of an allegation by the applicants that they have had no opportunity to see all the information relevant to the defence of their interests or that the regulation in question or part of it has not been sufficiently reasoned.

6.8.1 Defence of interests and confidentiality

6.8.1.1 Defence of interests

In the first *Japanese Ballbearing* cases[2], some of the applicants alleged that there had been an infringement of an essential procedural requirement on the basis that inter alia the EC Commission had failed to give them the opportunity to see all the information which was relevant to the defence of their interests[3]. The EC Council argued that there was no obligation on the part of the EC Commission to produce all the evidence on which it had acted or on how it had used that material. The applicants, they contended, were only entitled to be appraised of the factual material.

---

1. Case 312/84 *Continentale Produkten Gesellschaft Ehrhardt-RenkenGmbH & Co v EC Commission* [1987] ECR 841 at 865, para 4.
2. Above at footnote 1, p229.
3. See for example Case 121/77 *Nachi Fujikoshi Corpn v EC Council* [1977] ECR 1363 at 1371.

The Court, in deciding the case on other grounds, did not consider whether the institutions had indeed infringed an essential procedural requirement. Advocate General Warner, in his Opinion[1], did consider the matter in greater detail. He began by enunciating the following fundamental principle of Community law that :

> "before any individual measure or decision is taken, of such a nature as directly to affect the interests of a particular person, that person has a right to be heard by the responsible authority; and it is part and parcel of that principle that, in order to enable him effectively to exercise that right, the person concerned is entitled to be informed of the facts and considerations on the basis of which the authority is minded to act. That principle, which is enshrined in many a judgment of this Court, and which applies regardless of whether there is a specific legislative text requiring its application, was reasserted by the Court only yesterday in Case 85/76 *Hoffmann-La Roche & Co AG v EC Commission*."[2]

The Advocate General stated that the EC Commission's duty was to tell the applicants, as clearly and as fully as the circumstances permitted, what its case against them was[3]. He considered, however, that the right to be heard was subject to the general proviso that it must be compatible with the requirements of good administration. This did not mean that the EC Commission were not obliged to explain to the applicants in a satisfactory manner why so restrictive an interpretation of the exporter's rights was necessitated by practical considerations[4]. He agreed that regard should be had to the provisions relating to confidential information but did not see that this prevented each of the applicants making representations on the question of their own alleged dumping[5]. The Advocate General concluded that there had been an infringement of an essential procedural requirement within the meaning of that phrase in article 173 of the Treaty.

In *Sermes SA v Directeur des services des douanes de Strasbourg*[6], the applicants argued inter alia that by not giving them an opportunity to confront the complainants, the Community authorities had infringed article 7 of Regulation 2176/84, or alternatively the applicants' right to a fair hearing. Article 7(6) of Regulation 2176/84, in particular, provided that the EC Commission were required, on request, to give the parties directly concerned an opportunity to meet, so that opposing views could be presented and any rebuttal argument put forward.

---

1.   Case 113/77 *NTN Tokyo Bearing Co Ltd v EC Council* [1979] ECR 1185 at 1212 et seq.
2.   Ibid at 1261.
3.   Ibid at 1265.
4.   Ibid at 1262-3.
5.   Ibid at 1263.
6.   Case 323/88 *Sermes SA v Directeur des services des douanes de Strasbourg* [1990] ECR 3027.

The Court rejected Sermes' submissions. It held that :

"The expression 'parties directly concerned' must be understood in the sense given to it by the Court in regard to the admissibility of actions brought against an anti-dumping regulation. As appears from the order of the Court in Case 279/86 *Sermes v EC Commission* [1987] ECR 3109, Sermes does not belong to any of the categories of traders who the Court has held are entitled to bring proceedings directly against regulations imposing an anti-dumping duty in respect of imports of certain electric motors originating in certain State trading countries. Moreover, Sermes has produced no evidence to show that it did in fact request a meeting."[1]

The Court has recently, in a number of cases, been required to consider more fully the extent of an interested party's right to a fair hearing in an anti-dumping proceeding. In *Al Jubail Fertiliser Company and Ors v EC Council and EC Commission*[2], the applicants sought a declaration under article 173, 2nd para that article 1 of Regulation 3339/87 imposing a definitive anti-dumping duty on imports of urea originating in Libya and Saudi Arabia was void on the basis that they were inter alia denied the right to a fair hearing.

In support of their submission, the applicants argued that they had not :

— been informed in advance of the reasons why the EC Council rejected their request for an allowance to take account of the differences in the level of trade and in the quantities sold in Saudi Arabia and the Community;

— been warned in advance of the change in the type of anti-dumping duty imposed;

— received an answer to the questions which they had raised regarding the determination of injury threshold;

— received an explanation of why the EC Commission in granting an allowance for warehousing used a figure which was lower than that which they had supplied.

---

1.   Case 323/88 *Sermes SA v Directeur des services des douanes de Strasbourg* [1990] ECR 3027 at 3056, para 43 of judgment.

2.   Case C-49/88 *Al Jubail Fertiliser Co (SAMAD) and Saudi Arabian Fertiliser Co (SAFCO) v EC Council* [1991] 3 CMLR 377.

The Court accepted that the applicants had not been given a fair hearing. It referred to article 7(4)(a) and (b) of Regulation 2176/84 and held that :

> "according to the well established case law of the Court (see most recently the judgment of 18 June 1991 in Case C-260/89 *ERT* [1991] ECR), fundamental rights form an integral part of the general principles of law, whose observance is ensured by the Court. Consequently, it is necessary when interpreting article 7(4) of the basic regulation to take account in particular of the requirements stemming from the right to a fair hearing, a principle whose fundamental character has been stressed on numerous occasions in the case law of the Court (see in particular the judgment of 17 October 1989 Case 85/87, *Dow Benelux v EC Commission* [1989] ECR 3137). Those requirements must be observed not only in the course of proceedings which may result in the imposition of penalties, but also in investigative proceedings prior to the adoption of anti-dumping regulations which, despite their general scope, may directly and individually affect the undertakings concerned and entail adverse consequences for them.
>
> It should be added that, with regard to the right to a fair hearing, any action taken by the Community institutions must be all the more scrupulous in view of the fact that, as they stand at present, the rules in question do not provide all the procedural guarantees for the protection of the individual which may exist in certain national legal systems."[1]

The Court noted that the applicants were entitled to all the information relevant to the defence of their interests insofar as the disclosure of such information was compatible with the obligation not to disclose business secrets. Notwithstanding this the Court held that :

> "In any event, the undertakings concerned should have been placed in a position during the administrative procedure in which they could effectively make known their views on the correctness and relevance of the facts and circumstances alleged and on the evidence presented by the EC Commission in support of its allegations concerning the existence of dumping and the resultant injury."[2]

The Court concluded that there was nothing in the documents before the Court, namely internal memoranda and letters, to show that the Community authorities had discharged their duty in placing before the applicants all the information

---

1.   Case C-49/88 *Al Jubail Fertiliser Co (SAMAD) and Saudi Arabian Fertiliser Co (SAFCO) v EC Council* [1991] 3 CMLR 377 at 414, paras 15 and 16 of judgment.
2.   Ibid, p414 at para 17 of judgment.

which would have enabled them to effectively defend their interests. It conceded that the Community authorities may in terms of article 7(4)(c), supply the information orally. Nonetheless, they were not relieved from their obligation to ensure that they had tangible evidence enabling them, if necessary, to prove that such information was actually communicated[1].

The Court concluded that the applicants' right to a fair hearing had been infringed with the exception of the lack of information concerning the method of calculating the anti-dumping duty, as this information was not essential to the defence of the applicants' interests[2]. The Court's ruling is to be welcomed in that it advocates greater transparency in anti-dumping cases.

In *Bureau européen des unions de consommateurs (BEUC) v EC Commission*[3], the applicants argued that the EC Commission had infringed the principle of a right to a fair hearing by refusing to grant it access to the non-confidential file in connection with the anti-dumping investigation concerning imports of audio cassette and audio cassette tapes originating in Japan, the Republic of Korea and Hong Kong.

BEUC took the view that prior to the adoption of any individual measure or decision which affects the interest of that person, they should have the right to be heard by the competent authorities and told of the basis upon which they intend to act. Article 7(4)(a) of Regulation 2176/84, it argued, was not restricted to the categories of persons expressly mentioned therein since the right to a fair hearing constituted a fundamental principle of Community law which must be guaranteed in the absence of an express provision.

The Court rejected BEUC's submissions. It held that an organisation such as BEUC could not, in the absence of an express provision, rely on a fundamental principle of the right to a fair hearing in order to claim access to the non-confidential file submitted during the anti-dumping investigation[4]. It was for the Community legislature to consider whether Regulation 2423/88 should grant an association like BEUC the right to consult the non-confidential file[5]. It observed, however, that there was nothing in the wording of article 7(4)(a) to prevent the EC Commission

---

1.   Case C-49/88 *Al Jubail Fertiliser Co (SAMAD) and Saudi Arabian Fertiliser Co (SAFCO) v EC Council* [1991] 3 CMLR 377 at 415, para 20 of judgment; see also Opinion of Advocate General Darmon at p400.
2.   Ibid, p415 at para 24 of judgment.
3.   Case 170/89 *Bureau européen des unions de consommateurs (BEUC) v EC Commission* [1992] 1 CMLR 820.
4.   Ibid, pp849-850 at para 19 of judgment.
5.   Case 170/89 *Bureau européen des unions de consommateurs (BEUC) v EC Commission* [1992] 1 CMLR 820, p851 at para 30 of judgment.

from permitting persons who have a legitimate interest to inspect the non-confidential file[1].

BEUC also argued that it was illogical to refuse them access to inspect the non-confidential file given that where it is granted permission to intervene in an action for annulment at the instance of an exporter it would have the right, by virtue of article 93(4) of the Court's Rules of Procedure, to inspect all non-confidential documents produced during the Court proceedings.

The applicants' argument confused two different procedures, namely an anti-dumping investigation on the one hand and a proceeding before the Court for the annulment of a regulation adopting protective measures on the other, both of which had different purposes and different objectives. The Court noted that :

> "Anti-dumping proceedings are intended first, to ensure that imports into the Community are not the subject of dumping causing injury to Community industry and, secondly, to enable the institutions to adopt the necessary measures within a reasonable period if required by the interests of the Community. Proceedings before the Court, on the other hand, are intended, as article 164 of the EEC Treaty provides, to ensure that "the law is observed".

> The fact that a consumer organisation may, where appropriate, be granted leave by the Court to intervene in proceedings before it and obtain the right of access as an intervener to non-confidential documents produced by the parties to the proceedings does not therefore mean that such a right should also be granted in administrative anti-dumping proceedings."[2]

In the *Second Allied*[3] case, the applicants complained that they were not informed of the main facts and considerations on the basis of which it was intended to recommend to the EC Council the imposition of definitive duties and the definitive collection of the amounts secured by means of a provisional duty. They alleged that an exporter should be allowed the opportunity to question the EC Commission's interpretation of the information provided, even if that information comes mainly from the exporter in question[4]. The EC Council contended that two of the three applicants did not request information. Furthermore, Allied was informed of the essential factors taken into account and in particular the method of determining normal value, as indeed were the other applicants. The rights of defence afforded to applicants in competition matters, they argued, could not be transposed to the

1. Ibid, p851 at para 29 of judgment.
2. Ibid, pp850-851, paras 25 and 26 of judgment.
3. Case 53/83 *Allied Corporation v Council of the European Communities* [1985] ECR 1621.
4. Ibid at 1654.

anti-dumping field, since the Community authorities have no power to require the production of information[1]. Information could only be provided in reply to a request, the submission of which was subject to precise rules and time limits.

Advocate General VerLoren van Themaat held that in his opinion it was sufficient that the information was provided to the applicants in order to allow them to present argument on the decisive points at issue. The applicants right of defence had not therefore been infringed[2].

The rights of defence argument was also relied upon by the applicants in *Technointorg v EC Commission and EC Council*[3]. The EC Commission had based its findings on the information available in view of the fact that the exporters had failed to co-operate with their investigation. The applicants denied that they had refused to co-operate with the EC Commission, stating that it had failed to request information or even indicate the usefulness of providing such information, with the result that their rights of defence had been infringed by not having a fair hearing[4].

The EC Council in reply contended that the EC Commission was perfectly entitled to base their findings on the information available, especially when the exporters had failed to complete the questionnaire sent to them. They pointed to the fact that the EC Commission did not have the power to carry out compulsory inspections of the exporters' premises outside the Community. For this reason there was a need for full information and full co-operation, especially since the EC Commission had to consider whether undertakings offered were acceptable[5].

The Court concurred with Advocate General Slynn who upheld the EC Council's submission that the EC Commission were entitled to proceed on the basis of the information available.

In conclusion, it is submitted that there is a duty on the Community authorities to inform the applicants clearly and fully of the case against them and in so doing it is a fundamental principle of Community law that an applicant is entitled to a fair hearing. The applicant's right, however, to defend his interests will not have been

---

1.   Ibid.
2.   Case 53/83 *Allied Corporation v Council of the European Communities* [1985] ECR 1621 at 1637.
3.   Joined Cases 294/86 and 77/87 *Technointorg v EC Commission and EC Council* [1988] ECR 6077.
4.   Ibid at 6082.
5.   Ibid at 6083.

infringed where that applicant refuses to co-operate with the EC Commission's investigation.

6.8.1.2 Confidential information

The right to examine all information in order to defend one's interests and the right to business confidentiality require to be reconciled. These two conflicting objectives, while giving rise to an uncertain legal position, have major implications when it comes to the question of judicial review.

Interested parties have under each of the safeguard measures the right to have information treated as confidential if certain conditions are satisfied[1] and the corresponding right to information in order to defend their interests[2]. Article 8(1)(a) of Regulation 2423/88 provides that neither the EC Council, EC Commission nor the Member States shall reveal any confidential information with regard to an anti-dumping or anti-subsidy investigation without the permission from the party submitting such information.

"Confidentiality" covers only information whose "disclosure is likely to have a significantly adverse effect upon the supplier or the source of such information"[3]. To have information treated as confidential, it must be requested, justified and accompanied by a "non-confidential summary of the information or a statement of the reasons why the information is not susceptible of such summary"[4]. If the information is not justified as confidential and the supplier does not want it disclosed, it can be disregarded but cannot be disclosed[5]. Likewise, if a non-confidential summary can be made and the supplier refuses, the information can be disregarded. Regulation 2423/88 allows disclosure of the following information :

— general information

— the reasons on which decisions are based in terms of the regulation

— the evidence relied on by the Community institutions to the extent that this is required in order to explain those reasons to the Court.

---

1.   See generally, Chapter 3 section 3.9.3.
2.   Section 6.8.1.1 above.
3.   Article 8(3), Council Regulation (EEC) 2423/88.
4.   Article 8(2)(b), Council Regulation (EEC) 2423/88.
5.   Article 8(4), Council Regulation (EEC) 2423/88.

The Court first considered the question of confidentiality in *Celanese Chemical Company Inc v EC Council and EC Commission*[1]. The applicant sought to claim confidentiality in relation to five categories of information which it regarded as forming part of its business secrets and which concerned sales prices; the structure of production costs; the identity of certain customers; the quantities sold; and market shares. They referred to the fact that as the undertakings concerned were outside the jurisdiction of the Community authorities, they could only be expected to co-operate on condition that guarantees were given with respect to confidential information where their business secrets were concerned.

The Court held that :

"The request for confidential treatment put forward by the applicant is accepted. Protection of the business secrets of undertakings under investigation in anti-dumping proceedings must take account of the special nature of such investigations."[2]

The Court also stated that, in the event of the EC Council and the EC Commission refusing to apply confidential treatment to the documents to be examined, the applicant must have the chance to withdraw them[3]. Finally, it held that it reserved the right to decide the use which it makes of the confidential information where it conflicts with its duty to state reasons for its judgment or that imposed upon the Advocate General to deliver his Opinion in public. If such an event does arise, the Court can exclude from its file any such document or part thereof. In so doing, however, the Court will take into account, when deciding the case, the exclusion of such material[4].

The Court's most important pronouncement on the question of confidentiality was its decision in *Timex Corporation v EC Council and EC Commission*[5]. Timex argued that the EC Commission refused to supply it with information gathered from Hong Kong undertakings which had been selected as reference undertakings for the determination of constructing the normal value. Such information, it argued, was relevant in terms of article 7(4)(a) of Regulation 3017/79 to the defence of its interests[6]. The Community authorities in reply contended that article 7(4)(a)

---

1.   Case 236/81 *Celanese Chemical Company Inc v EC Council and EC Commission* [1982] ECR 1183.
2.   Case 236/81 *Celanese Chemical Company Inc v EC Council and EC Commission* [1982] ECR 1183 at 1186, para 9 of judgment.
3.   Ibid at 1186-7, para 11 of judgment.
4.   Ibid at 1187, para 13 of judgment.
5.   Case 264/82 *Timex Corporation v EC Council and EC Commission* [1985] ECR 849.
6.   Ibid at 855.

related only to the parties to the investigation thereby excluding the Hong Kong authorities[1].

Secondly, Timex alleged that the EC Commission had failed to supply samples of watch dials and cases. The Community authorities argued that article 7(4)(c) only required them to supply information and not samples. It further alleged that in this respect such information was not given with the result that it was impossible for it to obtain useful samples[2].

Thirdly, Timex claimed that the EC Commission merely sent it a list of the items made and assembled in Hong Kong without prices. Article 8 of Regulation 3017/79, they argued, could not be invoked on the grounds that the protection of business confidentiality should be limited to what was strictly necessary. This was not the case here since the information from the Hong Kong authorities could have been disclosed to it in other ways without disclosing confidential information[3]. In reply to this submission, the Community authorities argued that in order to secure the co-operation of undertakings in non-member countries it was necessary to respect business confidentiality or their sources of information would dry up. Whilst article 8 attempted to reconcile the requirements of information and business confidentiality, it required nevertheless strict observance of such confidentiality. They considered that the alternatives proposed by Timex were impracticable given that the prices of the reference undertakings were similar[4].

The Court concluded that the Community authorities' interpretation of article 7(4)(a) of Regulation 3017/79 was too restrictive. It held that :

> "the aim of article 7(4)(a) of Regulation 3017/79 is to ensure that the traders or manufacturers concerned may inspect the information gathered by the Commission during the investigation so that they may effectively put forward their points of view. However, the protection of rights guaranteed by that provision must where necessary be reconciled with the principle of confidentiality, which is given general recognition in article 214 of the EEC Treaty, and which, as far as the procedure under Regulation 3017/79 is concerned, specifically laid down in article 8 of that regulation."[5]

---

1.   Ibid.
2.   Ibid.
3.   Case 264/82 *Timex Corporation v EC Council and EC Commission* [1985] ECR 849 at 855-856.
4.   Ibid at 856.
5.   Ibid at 868-9, para 24 of judgment.

The Court held further that :

"The expression 'any party to an investigation' in article 7(4)(a) of Regulation 3017/79 must be interpreted as meaning not only the parties which are the subject of the investigation but also the parties whose information has been used, as in this case, to calculate the normal value of the relevant products, since such information is just as relevant to the defence of the complainants' interests as the information supplied by the undertakings carrying out the dumping."[1]

With reference to the second argument, the Court was of the view that the EC Commission had a *duty* either to make samples available to the applicant or, failing that, to provide the information requested to enable the applicant to identify the items in question[2].

Advocate General Darmon in his Opinion qualified the Community authorities' argument that respecting business confidentiality was necessary in order to secure the co-operation of undertakings in non-member countries when he held that :

"Nobody denies that the voluntary co-operation of undertakings in non-member countries is indispensable for the conduct of an investigation since their consent is needed in order to obtain the information sought. Nevertheless, in securing such co-operation, the rules governing the right to be heard according to all the parties must be respected, otherwise the regulation would not have required them to request confidential treatment beforehand."[3]

The Court concluded that there had been a breach of an essential procedural requirement rejecting the Community authorities' contention that the information concerning the prices of the items assembled in Hong Kong were confidential. It held that :

"The Community institutions are bound by article 214 of the EEC Treaty to respect the principle of confidential treatment of information about undertakings, particularly about undertakings in non-member countries which have expressed their readiness to co-operate with the Commission, even if no express request for such treatment is received under article 8 of Regulation 3017/79. That obligation, however, must be interpreted in such a

---

1.   Ibid at 869, para 25 of judgment.
2.   Case 264/82 *Timex Corporation v EC Council and EC Commission* [1985] ECR 849 at 855-856 at 869, para 27 of judgment, emphasis added.
3.   Ibid at 857.

way that the rights provided by article 7(4)(a) of that regulation are not deprived of their substance.

It follows that in the present case the Commission ought to have made every effort, as far as was compatible with the obligation not to disclose business secrets, to provide the applicant with information relevant to the defence of its interests, choosing, if necessary on its own initiative, the appropriate means of providing such information. Mere disclosure of the items referred to in the calculation of the normal value without any figures does not satisfy those imperative requirements. That conclusion is all the more warranted in view of the fact that the normal value was determined on the basis of the constructed value of the like product, within the meaning of article 2(5)(b) of Regulation 3017/79, so that Timex was entirely dependent for the defence of its interests on the factors on which the Commission based its calculation."[1]

This meant that article 1 of the regulation in question was void. The applicant sought not to have it declared void but to have a higher duty substituted. The Court allowed the provision to be maintained in terms of article 174, 2nd para, until the Community authorities adopted the necessary measure needed to comply with the judgment.

In *Al Jubail Fertiliser Company and Ors v EC Council and EC Commission*[2], the applicants had criticised the EC Commission inter alia for its failure to reply to the questions they raised concerning the determination of injury threshold and in particular, regarding the choice of the representative Community producer and the level of its production costs on the ground that such information was confidential. The amount of the anti-dumping duty was fixed in the contested regulation by reference to injury and not to the dumping margin. In these circumstances, access to such information was essential to the defence of the applicants' interests.

The Court, following its reasoning in *Timex*[3] and observing that there was an obligation on the Community authorities not to disclose business secrets, held that the failure to provide the information requested constituted a denial of the applicants' right to a fair hearing[4].

1.   Ibid at 870-1, paras 29-30 of judgment.
2.   Case 49/88 *Al Jubail Fertiliser Company and Ors v EC Council and EC Commission* [1991] 3 CMLR 377.
3.   Case 264/82 *Timex Corporation v EC Council and EC Commission* [1985] ECR 849 at 871, para 30 of judgment.
4.   Case 49/88 *Al Jubail Fertiliser Company and Ors v EC Council and EC Commission* [1991] 3 CMLR 377 at 414, paras 17 and 21 of judgment.

Article 13(3) of Regulation 2423/88 states that the amount of the duty to be imposed should not exceed the dumping margin and therefore should be less if such lesser duty would be adequate to remove injury. In the *Second Allied* case[1], the Court held that an exporter or producer knows that he can reduce the duty if he can prove to the satisfaction of the Court that the injury caused is less than the margin of dumping. It will be the case, however, that its access to such information is more often than not subject to article 8 of Regulation 2423/88 allowing confidential treatment of such information if requested.

In concluding, it is submitted that the principle of confidential treatment of information about undertakings and, in particular, undertakings in non-member countries which have co-operated with the Community authorities, must be respected. However, this principle must always be reconciled with the right of an interested party to examine all information relevant to the defence of their interests. In so doing, an interested party should be placed in a position during the anti-dumping investigation in which it can make known its views on the correctness and relevance of the facts and circumstances alleged and on the evidence presented by the EC Commission in support of its allegations concerning the existence of dumping and resultant injury[2]. As discussed above, the Court suggested in *Timex* that more information should be given, though the duty of disclosure does not reach the standard required in competition cases[3].

A system of disclosing information to lawyers under a form of confidentiality bond like that which exists in the United States would go a long way in ensuring that the defence of an applicant's interests are protected. The idea of introducing such a system in the Community was considered at great length by Advocate General Darmon in the *Al Jubail* case[4]. He observed that under the American system, the Trade Agreements Act 1979 introduced the concept of an "Administrative Protective Order" which permits an interested party's lawyer to have sight of confidential documents lodged with the relevant administrative authorities, the International Trade Administration (ITA) and the International Trade Commission (ITC), subject to the condition that he respects their confidentiality even in dealings with his client. The Court of International Trade will issue an "Administrative Protective Order" either when the competent authorities during the investigation refuse the disclosure of confidential information or when an application is made which

1.   Case 53/83 *Allied Corporation v Council of the European Communities* [1985] ECR 1621.
2.   Case 49/88 *Al Jubail Fertiliser Company and Ors v EC Council and EC Commission* [1991] 3 CMLR 377 at 414, para 17 of judgment.
3.   Case 264/82 *Timex Corporation v EC Council and EC Commission* [1985] ECR 849 at 870, para 30 of judgment.
4.   Case 49/88 *Al Jubail Fertiliser Company and Ors v EC Council and EC Commission* [1991] 3 CMLR 377, pp408-411, Opinion delivered on 7 February 1991. Advocate General Darmon was also the Advocate General in Case 264/82 *Timex Corporation v EC Council and EC Commission*, above.

challenges decisions adopted by the competent authorities. In granting or refusing the Order, the Court will take into consideration the following factors : the age and origin of such information to determine its sensitivity; the relevance of the documents with regard to the decision adopted; the reasons given in the application; the specificity of the information requested; the observance of equitable principles and the status of the applicant's lawyer.

Advocate General Darmon took the view that such a system could be transposed into Community law. He posed the question, "Are the legal difficulties insuperable?" and observed that :

> "Advocates, solicitors and barristers are required to observe the rules of professional ethics in all the Member States, no matter whether those rules are imposed by the legislature or by the profession itself. A breach of confidentiality is, in principle, punished under the domestic legal order of every Member State. Furthermore, the rules of civil liability should enable undertakings injured by an unlawful disclosure of their confidential information to take action against the counsel or lawyer who committed the breach. It is difficult to see what arguments could support the view that, even given the same guarantees, European lawyers are not in a position to perform the same function as officers of the Court as their American counterparts. Moreover, any improper conduct could be punished by denying the guilty party further access, for a period to be determined, to the confidential data on file in an anti-dumping proceeding. Such a penalty would be particularly effective since there are not many legal firms that act in dumping cases.

> It could apparently be included in the basic Council regulation if the decision were taken to introduce into Community law machinery similar to the "administrative protective order". In that event it would be appropriate to involve in the establishment of the system the professional lawyers' organisations operating at a European level - by way of a protocol if need be."[1]

6.8.2   The statement of reasons

In almost all the anti-dumping proceedings brought before the Court, the applicants have argued that the measure imposing either provisional or definitive duties had not been sufficiently reasoned in one way or another. In the *Mini Ballbearing* cases[2] the Court, in rejecting the applicants' submissions that the

---

1. Case 49/88 *Al Jubail Fertiliser Company and Ors v EC Council and EC Commission* ibid, at pp 410-411.
2. Case 240/84 *NTN Toyo Bearing Co Ltd and Ors v EC Council* [1987] ECR 1809; Case 255/84 *Nachi Fujikoshi Corp v EC Council* [1987] ECR 1861; Case 256/84 *Koyo Seiko Co Ltd v EC Council* [1987] ECR 1899; Case 258/84 *Nippon Seiko KK v EC Council* [1987] ECR 1923; Case 260/84 *Minebea Co Ltd v EC Council* [1987] ECR 1975.

measure in question was not sufficiently reasoned, reiterated a principle it had consistently followed and in particular had stated in *Nicolet Instrument v Hauptzollamt Frankfurt am Main*[1] that :

"The statement of reasons required by article 190 of the Treaty must disclose in a clear and unequivocal fashion the reasoning followed by the Community authority which adopted the measure in question in such a way as to make the persons concerned aware of the reasons for the measure and thus enable them to defend their rights and to enable the Court to exercise its supervisory function."[2]

In *Gestetner Holdings plc v EC Council and EC Commission*[3], the applicant contended that by simply referring to its traditional practice of not accepting undertakings from importers, the EC Commission had failed to comply with the requirements of article 190. The Court reiterated the above principle and held that the requirements of article 190 had been satisfied. The practice of not accepting undertakings offered by importers was based on article 10 of Regulation 2176/84 and article 7 of the GATT Anti-dumping Code. Since the photocopiers were purchased for importation, the reasons for justifying the refusal of undertakings offered by importers were applicable[4].

In determining whether there are sufficient reasons, the Court will invariably take into account the nature of the measure in question and the power exercised. In *Epicheiriseon Metalleftikon Viomichanikon Kai Naftiliakon and Ors v EC Council*[5], the applicants sought a declaration that Council Decision 86/59 terminating the anti-dumping proceeding concerning imports of dead burned natural magnesite from China and North Korea was void. They maintained inter alia that the decision was based on an inadequate statement of reasons in that it merely noted the absence of injury without taking into account the fact that dumping was taking place.

---

1.   Case 203/85 *Nicolet Instrument v Hauptzollamt Frankfurt am Main* [1986] ECR 2049.
2.   See for example Case 240/84 *NTN Toyo Bearing Co Ltd v EC Council* above at 1857, para 31 of judgment; Case 256/84 *Koyo Seiko Co Ltd v EC Council* above at 1919, para 29 of judgment and Case 258/84 *Nippon Seiko KK v EC Council* above at 1966, para 28 of judgment.
3.   Case 156/87 *Gestetner Holdings plc v EC Council and EC Commission* [1990] ECR 781. See also Case 171/87 *Canon Inc v EC Council*; Case 175/87 *Matsushita Electrical Industrial Co Ltd and Matsushita Electric Trading Co Ltd v EC Council* and Case 178/87 *Minolta Camera Care Co Ltd v EC Council* (1992) Transcripts 10 March. The Court in rejecting the applicants arguments that the contested regulation did not contain an adequate statement of reasons regarding the determination of dumping relied on the principles laid down in *Gestetner*.
4.   Case 156/87 *Gestetner Holdings plc v EC Council and EC Commission* [1990] ECR 781 at 844-845.
5.   Case 121/86 *Epicheiriseon Metalleftikon Viomichanikon Kai Naftiliakon and Ors v EC Council* [1989] ECR 3919. See also Case 129/86 *Greece v EC Commission* .

The Court began by stating that the applicants' arguments (including the above) required to be considered in the light of the observations it had made with respect to the discretion accorded to the Community authorities in the field of anti-dumping law and in particular its judgment in *Fediol*[1].

The Court rejected the applicants' argument. It observed that in determining whether the dumped imports had caused injury to Community industry, article 4(1) of Regulation 2176/84 did not preclude this assessment from being made independently from the other two pre-conditions required for the imposition on an anti-dumping duty, namely, a finding of dumping and the need to act in the interests of the Community. Furthermore, it was clear from articles 2 and 4 of Regulation 2176/84 that the findings of dumping and injury were based on different factors which could be analysed separately[2].

In these circumstances, the Court concluded that the assessment of injury carried out by the Community authorities was not arbitrary nor unreasonable[3]. The Court noted that the Community authorities had relied on several matters of fact relating essentially to the impact of the imports in question on Community industry in coming to the conclusion that there was a lack of injury capable of justifying the imposition of a definitive duty[4]. Furthermore, this assessment was in conformity with the criteria laid down in article 4(2) of Regulation 2176/84 in the context of the examination of injury[5].

The Court will also consider the attitude of the parties and the extent to which they have co-operated with the Community authorities during the investigation. In the *First Allied* case[6], the EC Commission imposed a provisional duty on imports of certain chemical fertilisers originating in the United States upon the withdrawal of price undertakings by the applicants. The duty was based on information available when the undertakings were withdrawn.

The applicants alleged that the EC Commission had infringed an essential procedural requirement in that the duty to state reasons on which the measure was based was not discharged by the fact that it was taken as a matter of urgency. It was, they argued, necessary to state the reasons on which the condition of urgency itself was based. The statement of reasons must be sufficient, consistent, relevant

---

1.   Ibid, p3950 at para 8 of judgment; Case 187/85 *Fediol v EC Commission* [1987] ECR 4155.
2.   Ibid, p3951 at para 11 of judgment.
3.   Ibid, p3951 at para 14 of judgment.
4.   Ibid, p3951 at para 12 and 13 of judgment.
5.   Ibid, p3951 at para 14 of judgment.
6.   Case 239 and 275/82 *Allied Corporation v EC Commission* [1984] ECR 1005.

and must be such as to allow the Court to exercise its power of review[1]. The EC Commission replied by stating that the measure in question was based on article 10(6) of Regulation 3017/79 and therefore it was permitted to apply the provisional measures on the basis of the information available to it. The statement of reasons, it argued, had to be consistent with the nature of the measure in question and the power exercised. In fact, argued the EC Commission, it could refer to the reasons stated in the earlier measures[2].

The Court did not expressly deal with the question of whether there had been an infringement of an essential procedural requirement, preferring to base its decision on other grounds. By holding, however, that the EC Commission was correct in proceeding on the basis of information available to it when the price undertakings were given, it is submitted that the Court agreed, albeit impliedly, with the EC Commission that its statement of reasons were sufficient[3].

In the *Second Allied* case[4], the applicants sought to have the regulations imposing definitive duties annulled on the ground that inter alia insufficient reasons were given for the method of determining normal value[5]. The EC Commission argued that the choice of method for determining normal value was chosen as a result of the applicants' failure to co-operate as a result of which they could not claim that they did not know the reasons[6]. The Advocate General in his Opinion suggested that the statement of reasons was not adequate but considered that a more adequate statement of reasons would not have led to a different result[7]. The Court held that :

"If a firm does not co-operate in an anti-dumping investigation carried out by the Commission and the information available does not enable it to establish the normal value on one of the bases mentioned in article 2 of Regulation 3017/79, the Commission is entitled to take as a basis the prices which the firm undertakes to observe, which may be considered to be closest to economic reality, unless the Commission possesses information indicating that those prices no longer correspond to economic reality."[8]

The Court has also recognised that the duty to provide sufficient reasons must be balanced with the duty not to disclose confidential information. In *Technointorg v*

---

1.   Ibid at 1017.
2.   Ibid at 1019.
3.   Ibid at 1031-3.
4.   Case 53/83 *Allied Corporation v Council of the European Communities* [1985] ECR 1621.
5.   Ibid at 1645.
6.   Ibid.
7.   Case 53/83 *Allied Corporation v Council of the European Communities* [1985] ECR 1621 at 1628.
8.   Ibid, p1658, para 13 of judgment.

EC Commission and EC Council[1], the applicants alleged that article 190 of the EEC Treaty had been infringed in that there were insufficient reasons given as to why Community interest should prevail and why a duty of 33% was required to remove injury[2]. The EC Council contended that the statement of reasons as to the rate of duty to be imposed was sufficient. They argued that a more detailed explanation would have resulted in their having to disclose confidential information regarding individual Community producers' profitability[3]. The Advocate General held and the Court concurred that the measure was sufficiently reasoned to comply with article 190. They did not therefore have to consider whether a more detailed explanation would result in disclosing confidential information.

In *Epicheiriseon Metalleftikon Viomichanikon Kai Naftiliakon and Ors v EC Council*[4], the applicants argued inter alia that the data on which the EC Council decision to terminate the anti-dumping proceeding was based was inaccurate and conflicted both with official statistics and with the EC Commission's earlier decisions, proposals and findings. They maintained that there was no data relating to the imports of the product in question originating in North Korea from 1982 and to imports of the same product originating in China from the second quarter of 1983 to the first five months of 1985. Furthermore, the EC Commission's non-confidential files did not contain questionnaires on those aspects or any non-confidential summaries as provided for by article 8(2)(b) of the basic regulation. The Community authorities contended that the questionnaires at issue were confidential. In any event, the EC Commission asserted that it had supplied the applicants with all the information. The Community authorities were unable to supply non-confidential summaries of the questionnaires.

Advocate General Tesauro in his Opinion[5] recalled that the obligation of confidentiality must be interpreted in such a way that the rights conferred by the basic regulation are not deprived of their substance. He took the view that there was an inadequate statement of reasons given the absence of information relating to the volume of imports from those countries covered by the investigation[6]. For this reason, he concluded the decision in question was void.

The Court did not agree with the Advocate General. It observed that the contested decision was based on a set of data concerning not only imports of the product in

---

1. Joined Cases 294/86 and 77/87 *Technointorg v EC Commission and EC Council* [1988] ECR 6077.
2. Ibid at 6084-6.
3. Ibid at 6086.
4. Case 121/86 *Epicheiriseon Metalleftikon Viomichanikon Kai Naftiliakon and Ors v EC Council* [1989] ECR 3919.
5. Case 121/86 *Epicheiriseon Metalleftikon Viomichanikon Kai Naftiliakon and Ors v EC Council* [1989] ECR 3919 at 3930.
6. Ibid, pp3941-3943.

question into the Community, but also the increase in Community production, the increase in the utilisation of production capacity of all Community producers, a rise in their sales on the Community market, a rise in the market share held by them, a rise in their average sale prices, improved profits and an increase in the number of persons employed[1].

Furthermore, it accepted the EC Commission's claim that the questionnaires at issue were confidential and that the applicants had been adequately informed by the EC Commission of the data use during the investigation into injury[2].

In conclusion it is submitted that the Court will be satisfied that article 190 has been complied with if the statement of reasons provided by the Community authorities discloses in a clear and unequivocal manner the reasoning followed by them so as to enable the affected parties to defend their interests and the Court to exercise its supervisory jurisdiction. In deciding whether there is sufficient reasoning the Court will take into account the nature of the measure in question, the power exercised and the extent to which the applicant has co-operated with the Community authorities. Further, the duty to provide sufficient reasons will have to be reconciled with the duty not to disclose confidential information.

6.9   Infringement of the Treaty or rules relating to its application

This is by far the most important ground relied on by interested parties challenging Community acts imposing protective measures. As stated above, the Court has included within this category breaches of general principles common to the laws of the Member States. The first part of this section will concentrate on the extent to which the Court takes into account these general principles in reviewing Community safeguard measures. An analysis of the extent to which provisions of international agreements such as the GATT can be invoked by interested parties will also be considered.

Invariably, the adoption of safeguard measures are associated with investigations of a very complex and technical nature. For this reason, the Community authorities, in exercising their powers, are endowed with a wide discretion. The second part of this section will concentrate on the extent to which the Court is prepared to review the exercise of such discretion.

---

1.   Ibid, p3956 at para 37 of judgment.
2.   Ibid, p3956 at para 36 of judgment.

6.9.1   General principles

6.9.1.1 Non-discrimination

As stated above, the principle of non-discrimination is part of an overall principle of equality, ie similar situations are not to be treated differently. The applicants have in a number of anti-dumping cases sought to rely on the principle. It normally arises as the result of the EC Commission treating one exporter differently from another either by imposing a duty or a lower duty.

In some of the *Plain Paper Photocopies* cases[1], the applicants, in challenging the Community authorities determination of Community industry, maintained inter alia that by bringing only companies established in Japan within the scope of article 13(10) of Regulation 2176/84 whilst disregarding Community producers and, in particular, Rank Xerox which carried out the same "screwdriver" activities, the Community authorities treated similar cases dissimilarly.

The Court rejected this argument. It stated that article 13(10) was introduced after the contested regulation was adopted. Furthermore, it was concerned with the imposition of anti-dumping duties on products assembled or produced in the Community from components originating in the exporting country or countries in question, not with the definition of Community industry[2].

A number of the applicants in the first *Japanese Ballbearing* cases[3] alleged that this principle had been infringed. In particular, in *Nippon Seiko KK v EC Council and EC Commission*[4], the applicants argued that a provisional duty of 20% was imposed on products manufactured by themselves and NTN Toyo Bearing Company Limited whereas only a rate of 10% was imposed on products manufactured by Koyo and Nachi.

The regulation imposing definitive duties required the definitive collection of provisional duties to the extent that they did not exceed the rate of duty fixed in the definitive regulation. As a result of the difference in the provisional duties imposed, this meant collection at a rate of 15% for NTN Toyo Bearing Company Limited and Nippon Seiko KK on the one hand, and at a rate of 10% for Koyo and

---

1. Case 179/87 *Sharp Corporation v EC Council* [1992] 2 CMLR 415; Case 176/87 *Konishiroku Photo Industry Co Ltd v EC Council*; Case 175/87 *Matsushita Electric Industrial Co Ltd and Matsushita Electric Trading Co Ltd v EC Council*; Case 174/87 *Ricoh Co Ltd v EC Council*; Case 188/87 *Sanyo Electric Co Ltd v EC Council*; all (1992) Transcripts 10 March.
2. Case 179/87 *Sharp Corporation v EC Council*, above, at 427, para 36 of judgment.
3. Above at footnote 1, p229.
4. See Case 119/77 *Nippon Seiko KK v EC Council and EC Commission* [1979] ECR 1303; see also Case 113/77 *NTN Toyo Bearing Co Ltd* [1979] ECR 1185.

Nachi on the other. The applicants contended that this was inter alia contrary to a general principle of Community law namely, the principle of non-discrimination[1]. The EC Council in reply argued that the more lenient treatment of Koyo and Nachi was as a result of their good fortune on the basis that they could not order collection of provisional duties on their products at a rate of more than 10%.

The Court did not consider these submissions, deciding the case on other grounds. Advocate General Warner was of the opinion, however, that no discrimination had taken place. He noted that the principle meant different treatment of persons in like situations. He concluded that the situation of Koyo and Nachi differed from that of Nippon Seiko KK and NTN Toyo Bearing Company Limited. It was clear, he argued, that the EC Council would have collected provisional duties at a rate of 15% on the products of Koyo and Nachi if it had been possible to do so[2].

In *Technointorg v EC Council and EC Commission*[3], the applicants alleged that the Community authorities had breached the general principle of non-discrimination by refusing to accept the undertakings offered by them while at the same time accepting those from the Yugoslav and East German exporters. The EC Council in reply contended that the undertakings were defective. They argued that the price increases were insufficient to eliminate injury. Further, full price increases were not due to take place until 1989/90 when the applicant's new factory was to go into production.

The Court held that :

> "the fact that the Commission refused to accept the undertakings offered by Technointorg although it did accept undertakings offered by the exporters from the German Democratic Republic and Yugoslavia does not constitute arbitrary discrimination. As is stated in Recital 34 of the provisional regulation, the undertakings offered by those exporters had the effect of raising prices by an amount sufficient to eliminate the injury, and it was possible to ensure that those undertakings were actually adhered to."[4]

The Court, having noted the reasons put forward by the EC Commission for refusing the undertakings, agreed with the EC Council that the undertakings were

---

1.   Case 119/77 *Nippon Seiko KK v EC Council and EC Commission*, above, at 1316.
2.   Case 113/77 *NTN Toyo Bearing Co Ltd* [1979] ECR 1185 at 1268-9.
3.   Joined Cases 294/86 and 77/87 *Technointorg v EC Commission and EC Council* [1988] ECR 6077.
4.   Joined Cases 294/86 and 77/87 *Technointorg v EC Commission and EC Council* [1988] ECR 6077 at 6118, para 49 of judgment.

inadequate and that the conditions necessary to enable the EC Commission to verify whether they were adhered to were not satisfied.

In *NMB v EC Commission*[1], the applicants argued primarily that the contested decisions, which rejected in part their requests for refunds on anti-dumping duties levied in 1985 and 1986 on imports of ball bearings originating in Singapore, were unlawful because these were based on an incorrect interpretation of the basic regulation then in force, namely Regulation 2176/84 and in particular article 2(8)(b). In short, the applicants, who were associated importers, maintained they were discriminated against as compared to independent importers in the calculation of refunds of anti-dumping duties.

The applicants were all wholly owned European subsidiaries of the Japanese parent company. The partial rejection of the applicants' requests for refunds was due to the fact that in calculating the constructed export price, the EC Commission deducted the anti-dumping duties paid by the applicants in accordance with article 2(8)(b) of Regulation 2176/84 owing to their association with the exporter.

The applicants noted that article 16 of Regulation 2176/84, in accordance with the GATT Anti-dumping Code, provided that the only precondition to a refund of anti-dumping duties was proof that the duty paid exceeded the actual dumping margin. In their view, where an associated importer had increased his resale price within the Community by an amount equal to the dumping margin previously established and where there was no change of any significance to the other factors, such an increase eliminated dumping.

In such circumstances, an associated importer should be able to obtain a refund of the duties paid. To arrive at such a conclusion, the applicants maintained that the payment of anti-dumping duties should not be regarded as a cost borne between importation and resale and therefore should not be deducted in constructing the export price.

Such an interpretation, they argued, was necessary so as to avoid unjustified discrimination between associated and independent importers. They noted that where an independent importer has paid the anti-dumping duties he may apply for a refund if the exporter has increased his price equal to or greater than the dumping margin independently of payment of anti-dumping duties. Pending refund of the

---

1.   Case C-188/88 *NMB v EC Commission* (1992) Transcript 10 March.

duties, the independent importer can either make a single increase in the price charged to his customers, thereby absorbing the duties, or make a double increase in the price charged to his customers, thereby passing on the duties. On the other hand, an associated importer, owing to the EC Commission's practice, will require to charge his customer, ie the first independent buyer in the Community, a double increase representing the anti-dumping duties together with an increase sufficient to eliminate the dumping independently of payment of the duties.

In his Opinion[1], Advocate General Tesauro accepted the applicants' interpretation following a detailed analysis of the legislation. He formed the view that in order to bring dumping to an end, all an associated importer need do is increase his resale price to an independent purchaser by an amount equal to the dumping margin found to exist and no more. He observed that if a greater increase were required, it would mean that the imported product would be unfairly placed at a disadvantage by comparison with the competing Community product. Such a situation would mean a movement away by the Community authorities from a defence of trade to protectionism. He concluded that such a system was discriminatory.

The Court, however, were not persuaded by the Advocate General's reasoning. They rejected the applicants' interpretation, holding that it was contrary to the actual wording of the provision, ie article 2(8)(b), which expressly provided that anti-dumping duties are to be deducted in constructing the export price. Furthermore, the provision made no distinction between the procedure for review and refund[2].

The Court also held that the alleged difference in treatment of independent and associated importers did not constitute discrimination. The difference in treatment was justified by the difference in their respective situations in relation to dumping. Its reasoning was as follows :

"Whereas independent importers are not involved in the dumping, importers who are associated with the exporter are thereby placed on the other side of the "dumping fence" in the sense that they participate in the practices which constitute dumping and, in any event, are in a position to have full knowledge of the circumstances underlying it.

The fact that they are in different situations affects the conduct of independent importers and associated importers with respect to the passing on of anti-dumping duties to their customers.

1.　　　Case C-188/88 *NMB v EC Commission* (1992) Transcript 10 March.
2.　　　Ibid at para 30 of judgment.

As the Commission correctly stated, independent importers may be expected to pass on the anti-dumping duties to their customers since otherwise they would incur a loss of interest on the amounts paid and suffer the effects of any currency devaluation and, since they have no knowledge of the facts on the basis of which the dumping margin was established, they would run the risk of not being granted the refund despite the increase in the export price.

That does not apply to associated importers, who may refrain from passing on the anti-dumping duties, since they are aware of the commercial practices underlying the dumping and consequently are not in any doubt and run no risks with respect to the possibility of obtaining a refund.

Consequently, if the anti-dumping duties were not deducted in constructing the export price, associated importers would be in a more favourable position than independent importers."[1]

In deciding whether the Community authorities have treated an exporter or other affected party in a discriminatory manner compared to the other parties under investigation, the Court will take into account the degree of discretion accorded to them. In *Silver Seiko v EC Council*[2], normal value for the applicants was established on the basis of domestic prices as there were sufficient sales on the domestic market. Silver Seiko argued that they had been discriminated against as compared to those undertakings which had insufficient sales on the domestic market. For those undertakings, the lowest profit margin, ie that established for Canon Inc, was used in constructing a normal value.

The Court rejected this argument and held that :

"the situation of Silver Seiko for which a real profit margin was established, cannot be regarded as identical to that of TEC and Sharp, with respect to which, in the absence of real information, a degree of discretion had necessarily to be accorded to the institutions."[3]

In two of the Electronic Typewriter cases - *TEC v EC Council*[4] and *Sharp v EC Council*[5] - the applicants alleged that the Community authorities had breached the principle of non-discrimination by failing to impose a provisional duty on

1.   Case C-188/88 *NMB v EC Commission* (1992) Transcript 10 March, at para 35-39.
2.   Joined Cases 273/85 and 107/86 *Silver Seiko v EC Council* [1988] ECR 5927.
3.   Joined Cases 273/85 and 107/86 *Silver Seiko v EC Council* [1988] ECR 5927 at 5976, para 18 of judgment.
4.   Joined Cases 260/85 and 106/86 *TEC v EC Council* [1988] ECR 5855.
5.   Case 301/85 *Sharp v EC Council* [1988] ECR 5813.

Nakajima All Precision & Co Ltd. In *TEC v EC Council*, they contended that in calculating the normal value applicable to their products, the profit margin used was discriminatory since it was much higher than that established for Nakajima whose circumstances in Tec's opinion were wholly comparable to its own[1]. The EC Council in reply argued that Nakajima was different from the other undertakings subject to the investigations. It argued that it was basically a factory operation making a limited number of products which were sold to a limited number of customers[2].

In his Opinion[3], Advocate General Slynn agreed with the EC Council in concluding that there was no discrimination between the applicants and Nakajima. He held that Nakajima was in essence a factory without a conventional sales force or sales structure. It would be unreasonable to apply the same profit margin for a company with different characteristics[4].

More importantly, in its judgment the Court held that :

> "discrimination in favour of Nakajima could not, even if it were established, lead to the annulment of the regulation imposing a definitive anti-dumping duty on TEC, which was adopted on the basis of findings correctly made in the course of the anti-dumping investigation and in accordance with the rules laid down by Regulation 2176/84."[5]

On the other hand, in *Nakajima All Precision Co Ltd v EC Council*[6], the Court was not prepared to take into account as it had in the *Electronic Typewriter* cases, cited above, Nakajima's different sales structure. Nakajima sought to have the Council regulation imposing a definitive duty on its exports of dot matrix printers to the Community annulled.

Nakajima had not sold dot matrix printers in Japan, as it produced only for export and sold only to independent importers. As a result it did not have a vertical sales structure with its own related sales companies in the domestic market and therefore did not have the same costs. In constructing normal value, the Community authorities added to Nakajima's costs of production, selling, general and

---

1.   Joined Cases 260/85 and 106/86 *TEC v EC Council* [1988] ECR 5855 at 5863.
2.   Ibid at 5865.
3.   Ibid at 5884 et seq.
4.   Ibid at 5893.
5.   Ibid at 5918, para 18 of judgment. the Court reached a similar conclusion in Case 301/85 *Sharp v EC Council* [1988] ECR 5813.
6.   Case C-69/89 *Nakajima All Precision Co Ltd v EC Council* (1991) Transcript 7 May 1991.

administrative expenses and profit incurred by Japanese producers of the product in question who had profitable sales in the domestic market.

The Court held that the fact that Nakajima had been treated in a particular way in the *Electronic Typewriter* cases did not give it the right to be treated in an identical manner in the present case. Furthermore, it would be discriminatory to treat Nakajima in a different manner from other Japanese producers that did sell in the domestic market through related sales companies merely because it had no domestic sales.

The principle cannot be invoked where the Community authorities are not responsible for the difference in treatment of persons in like situations. In *Nashua Corporation v EC Council and EC Commission*[1], the applicant claimed that the EC Council had infringed the principle prohibiting discrimination by applying anti-dumping duties at a standard rate to all imports of plain paper photocopiers. This resulted in it paying a higher duty in absolute terms than a related manufacturer of a Japanese subsidiary. The Court held that the difference resulted not from the imposition of anti-dumping duties, but from the exporter's sales policy of selling at lower prices to its subsidiaries in the Community than the price it sold to Nashua[2]. Nor can there be discrimination where the Community authorities in constructing the normal value for products sold to OEMs use a single profit margin where they lack the information necessary to evaluate each exporter's profit margin individually[3].

The principle of non-discrimination means that persons in like or identical situations should not be treated differently. This is a matter to be decided on the facts of each case. In determining whether there has been a breach of the principle, the Court will take into account the discretion accorded to the Community authorities. Most importantly, the Court has indicated that different treatment may not necessarily lead to an annulment of a regulation imposing definitive anti-dumping duties where these duties have been imposed as a result of findings correctly made.

6.9.1.2 Legal certainty
The principle of legal certainty is aimed at ensuring that the law to be applied to a given situation is predictable. There are a number of other principles which flow

---

1. Cases 133 and 150/87 *Nashua Corporation v EC Council and EC Commission* [1990] ECR 719.
2. Ibid at 47, paras 40-41 of judgment.
3. Case 172/87 *Canon Inc v EC Council*, judgment of 10 March 1992 at para 13 of judgment.

from this, in particular that a person should be able to act in the reasonable expectation that the law as it exists will continue to apply.

Article 7(9)(a) of Regulation 2423/88 provides that the conclusion of an anti-dumping proceeding "should normally take place within one year of initiation of the proceeding". In *Continentale Produkten Gesellschaft Erhardt-Renken GmbH & Co v Hauptzollamt München-West*[1] the Court observed that :

> "the period mentioned in article 7(9) of the basic regulation is a guide rather than a mandatory period. This is clear both from the wording of the provision in question, which uses the word "normally", and from the nature of the anti-dumping proceeding itself, whose progress does not depend solely on the efforts of the Community authorities. However, it follows from article 7(9) that the anti-dumping proceeding must not be extended beyond a reasonable period to be assessed according to the particular circumstances of each case."[2]

In that case the proceedings lasted 32 months. This was due to special circumstances which prevented the EC Commission from concluding the investigations within a one year period. These included inter alia political events and currency depreciation occurring in Turkey at that time; inadequate co-operation of the Turkish exporters; the need for lengthy negotiations with the Association of Turkish Textile Exporters (TTEA) and the fact that the Turkish exporters themselves requested an extension of the investigation period[3].

In the circumstances, the Court concluded that although the proceedings had been unusually long they did not exceed a reasonable period[4].

The Court came to a similar conclusion in *Epicheiriseon Metalleftikon Viomichanikon Kai Naftiliakon and Ors v EC Council*[5]. In that case, the applicants contended that by allowing the proceedings in question to be pending for four years, the EC Council had infringed not only article 7(9)(a) but also the principles of legal certainty, protection of legitimate expectations[6] and resolution of disputes. The Court rejected their argument. It referred to its decision in the

---

1. Case 246/87 *Continentale Produkten Gesellschaft Erhardt-Renken GmbH & Co v Hauptzollamt München-West* [1989] ECR 1151.
2. Ibid, p1172 at para 8 of judgment.
3. Ibid, p1172 at para 9 of judgment.
4. Ibid.
5. Case 121/86 *Epicheiriseon Metalleftikon Viomichanikon Kai Naftiliakon and Ors v EC Council* [1989] ECR 3919; see also Case 129/86 *Greece v EC Council* [1989] ECR 3963.
6. Case 129/86 *Greece v EC Council and EC Commission* ibid, this aspect was emphasised by the Greek Government.

Continentale Produkten-Gesellschaft case and accepted that the Community authorities were not in a position to terminate the proceedings within a one year period due to the complexity of the proceedings and the contradictory conclusions reached by the experts[1].

As stated above[2], normal value will normally be calculated by reference to sales on the domestic market so long as these permit a proper comparison. This requirement will be satisfied if those sales are sufficiently representative to serve as a basis for the determination of normal value, ie the sales on the domestic market reflect normal behaviour on the part of the purchaser and the selling prices are determined by demand and supply. Since its anti-dumping procedure concerning electronic typewriters originating in Japan[3], the practice of the Community authorities has been to consider this requirement as satisfied where a producer's domestic sales exceed 5% of its export sales to the Community[4]. This threshold is aimed at providing a degree of legal certainty as regards the assessment by the Community authorities as to whether or not sales on the domestic market are representative.

This practice has recently been challenged in *Goldstar Co Ltd v EC Council*[5]. Goldstar, a member of the South Korean Goldstar Group which manufactured electrical and electronic goods including compact disc players for both the Korean and world markets sought a declaration under article 173, 2nd para of the EEC Treaty that the Council regulation imposing a definitive anti-dumping duty on compact disc players exported to the Community by Goldstar was void. Its action was based on a number of grounds including inter alia that the use by the Community authorities of the prices actually paid or payable on the domestic market to establish normal value for some of its models was incorrect. It maintained that the concept "ordinary course of trade" presupposed a sufficient volume of sales in absolute terms on a representative market. This was not the case, it argued, on the Korean market. The EC Council was wrong to assess the volume of domestic sales only in relative terms by reference to the 5% threshold, and further, it failed to take into account the characteristics and size of the Korean market for compact disc players, which during the reference period amounted to only 5,000 sales.

---

1. Case 121/86 *Epicheiriseon Metalleftikon Viomichanikon Kai Naftiliakon and Ors v EC Council* ibid, at 3953, para 23 of judgment.
2. See Chapter 3, section 3.3.2.
3. Commission Regulation (EEC) 3643/84 (OJ L335/43 1984) and Council Regulation (EEC) 1698/85 (OJ L163/1 1985.)
4. The Court has also applied this threshold in deciding if the Community authorities have chosen the appropriate analogue country where state trading countries are involved. See Joined Cases 305/86 and 160/87 *Neotype Techmashexport v EC Commission and EC Council* [1990] ECR 2945; Case 16/90 *Detlef Nölle v Hauptzollamt Bremen Freihafen* (1991) Transcript 22 October.
5. Case 105/90 *Goldstar Co Ltd v EC Council* [1992] 1 CMLR 996.

The Court rejected Goldstar's arguments and held that the EC Council was entitled not to depart from its practice of applying the 5% threshold. It began by noting that article 2(3)(a) of the basic regulation presupposes that in establishing normal value, regard must be had to the prices actually paid or payable in the ordinary course of trade. This principle could only be derogated from in accordance with article 2(3)(b) of the basic regulation where there were no sales of the like product in the ordinary course of trade or when such sales did not permit a proper comparison[1]. As regards the concept of "ordinary course of trade" the Court held that :

> "The ordinary course of trade is a concept which relates to the nature of sales themselves. It is designed to exclude, for the determination of the normal value, situations in which sales on the domestic market are not made under conditions corresponding to the ordinary course of trade, in particular where a product is sold at a price below production costs or where transactions take place between parties which are associated or have a compensatory arrangement with each other."[2]

The Court held that Goldstar had never stated that its domestic sales were made under conditions which did not correspond to the ordinary course of trade. In coming to this conclusion, the Court had then to consider whether or not the sales on the domestic market permitted a proper comparison, ie were the domestic sales sufficiently representative to serve as a basis for the determination of the normal values. Such sales would be, so long as they reflected a normal behaviour on the part of the purchasers and where the selling prices were determined by supply and demand.

The Court noted that it was the normal practice of the Community authorities to consider this requirement satisfied where the domestic sales of the producer concerned exceeded 5% of its export sales to the Community. In the present case, the EC Council determined that Goldstar's sales of compact disc players on the Korean market exceeded 5% of its export sales to the Community. Therefore, in absence of any exceptional circumstances, it considered that it was entitled to establish normal value on the basis of prices actually paid or payable.

As regards this practice generally the Court held that :

> "that practice offers the traders concerned a degree of legal certainty as regards the assessment made by the Community institutions of the question whether or

---

1.   Case 105/90 *Goldstar Co Ltd v EC Council* [1992] 1 CMLR 996 at 1022, para 12 of judgment.
2.   Ibid, p1022 at para 13 of judgment.

not sales on the domestic market are representative. In the light of that guarantee the 5% criterion should be upheld, and may be departed from only in exceptional circumstances.

Such circumstances may arise when the total volume of sales on the domestic market is not sufficiently large for selling prices to be determined by supply and demand."[1]

Advocate General Van Gerven in his Opinion[2] took a similar view whilst observing that the Community authorities had curtailed their discretion under articles 2(3)(a) and 2(3)(b) of the basic regulation in the interest of ensuring legal certainty[3]. He further considered that the characteristics and, in particular, the total size of the domestic market and the extent of competition in the domestic market would constitute special circumstances which would permit the Community authorities to derogate from the 5% threshold[4].

Goldstar had maintained that the volume of its domestic sales of compact disc players during the reference period amounted to only 5,000 units. The Court noted that the Korean market during the reference period was characterised by a relatively small volume of sales and a relatively stable level of prices. It took the view that in such circumstances the EC Council was entitled to apply the 5% threshold. This was even more so the case given that the number of domestic sales corresponded to 14% of the export sales of Korean compact disc players to the Community[5].

With regard to Goldstar's argument that the 5% threshold related to the volume of domestic sales in relative and not absolute terms, the Court observed that it would be impossible, given that the volume of sales in absolute terms vary from one sector of the economy to another, to fix an absolute minimum threshold. This could only be assessed by reference to the specific features of each individual case. In this respect the Court held that :

"To accept a departure from the 5% practice on account of the specific features of each individual case would, however, have the effect of jeopardising the legal certainty which that practice is designed to bring to the assessment of the question whether or not an exporter's sales on its domestic market are

1.   Case 105/90 *Goldstar Co Ltd v EC Council* [1992] 1 CMLR 996 at 1022-1023 at para 17 and 18 of judgment.
2.   Ibid at 1003.
3.   Ibid, p1008 at para 8 of his Opinion.
4.   Ibid, pp1009-1010 at para 10-12 of his Opinion.
5.   Ibid, p1023 at para 21 of judgment.

representative. Accordingly, a small volume of sales in absolute terms does not in itself constitute a factor permitting a departure from the 5% practice."[1]

In two of the *Electronic Typewriter* cases, the applicants[2] argued that the Community authorities had breached the principle on the ground that the normal value as constructed was unpredictable and arbitrary. This, they alleged, was due to the inclusion of an excessive profit margin and the inclusion of selling expenses of sales companies on the domestic market. Both TEC and Sharp had insufficient sales on the domestic market, with the result that normal value was constructed in terms of article 2(3)(b)(ii) of Regulation 2176/84. The profit margin used was based on the lowest margin calculated for those undertakings which had sufficient domestic sales, ie Canon Inc.

TEC, in particular, argued that this was arbitrary and unpredictable. It was arbitrary because it was impossible for the applicants to gauge the profit margins of one company from those of another. It was unpredictable in that they could not ascertain the profit margins realised by another company. This meant that it was impossible to know how to set prices in order to avoid dumping[3]. The EC Council replied by stating that it was legitimate for the Community authorities to have regard to the profit margins realised by the other manufacturers. It was not contrary to the principle of legal certainty, they contended, in that the objective of this principle had to be reconciled with the requirements of the anti-dumping procedure. It was a fact of life that the exporter would not have access to all the information, in particular, to that which was confidential[4]. This was in line with the law as laid down in the GATT rules and Community legislation[5]. Further, the legislation allowed for cases in which an undertaking could not calculate the dumping margin beforehand (ie non-market economies). Lastly, the methods prescribed in article 2(3) of Regulation 2176/84 depended on circumstances which an undertaking could not have foreseen[6].

Advocate General Slynn rejected the submissions that legal certainty had been violated. The profit figures, he argued, related only to sales on the domestic market which exceeded 5% volume of exports to the Community. This threshold was introduced to safeguard legal certainty[7]. He also refuted the argument put forward by TEC based on unpredictability, in that it was always possible for an

---

1. Case 105/90 *Goldstar Co Ltd v EC Council* [1992] 1 CMLR 996 at 1023, para 23 of judgment.
2. Joined Cases 260/85 and 106/86 *TEC v EC Council* 1988] ECR 5855; Case 301/85 *Sharp v EC Council* [1988] ECR 5813.
3. Joined Cases 260/85 and 106/86 *TEC v EC Council* ibid, at 5862.
4. Ibid at 5863-5865.
5. Case 301/85 *Sharp v EC Council* [1988] ECR 5813 at 5819.
6. Ibid at 5820.
7. Eg Joined Cases 260/85 and 106/86 *TEC v EC Council* [1988] ECR 5855 at 5889.

exporter to raise his prices and request a review[1]. The principle of legal certainty, he argued, had to be balanced with the principle of equal treatment. To use a hypothetical margin for those companies who had no sales and a real margin for those that had would result in inequality. Further, there was no provision in the regulation which stated that the EC Commission must continue to use a hypothetical margin when normal profit had been established[2].

The Court, in concurring with the Advocate General, held that a certain degree of unforseeability did not constitute an infringement of the principle of legal certainty where, as in the present case, it was not possible to take real prices as a basis in calculating the normal value[3].

TEC again relied on the principle of legal certainty in arguing that it was wrong in constructing normal value to include in the cost of production selling expenses of TEC Electronics Company Limited, the sales subsidiary of TEC Limited. It contested that such practice was not consistent with the previous practice of the Community authorities. Further, it was arbitrary in that it included in the cost of production the expenses of a company which had never sold electronic typewriters[4].

The Court held that :

> "the division of production and sales activities within a group made up of legally distinct companies can in no way alter the fact that the group is a single economic entity which carries out in that way activities that, in other cases, are carried out by what is in legal terms as well a single entity.
>
> There would be discrimination if expenses necessarily included in the selling price of a product when it was sold by a sales department forming part of the manufacturer's organisation were not included when that product was sold by a company which although financially controlled by the manufacturer, was a legally distinct entity."[5]

It agreed with the Advocate General, who held that irrespective of the corporate structure of an undertaking, article 2(3)(b)(ii) of Regulation 2176/84 permitted the Community authorities to look beyond the purely formal division and assess production cost on a reasonable basis including selling expenses of the whole operation no differently from the way they would if dealing with a single

---

1.   Ibid at 5890.
2.   Ibid.
3.   Ibid at 5917, para 15 of judgment.
4.   See submissions Joined Cases 260/85 and 106/86 *TEC v EC Council* ibid at 5984-5889.
5.   Ibid at 5919, para 28-29 of judgment.

corporation[1]. Neither the Advocate General nor the Court considered it necessary to determine whether the principle of legal certainty had been breached.

In the *Mini Ballbearing* cases[2], some of the applicants[3] contested the method by which the EC Commission had calculated the dumping margin. In determining the dumping margin, normal value was established on the weighted average method and export price on the transaction-by-transaction method. This latter method was preferred where export prices varied both above and below normal value, since use of weighted averages would result in a finding that no dumping was occurring at all[4]. The applicants argued that, by using the transaction-by-transaction method to establish export price, the Community authorities had breached the principle of legitimate expectation, commercial certainty and sound administration in that they had used the weighted average method on previous occasions[5].

In answering the applicants' submission, the Court held that article 2(13)(b) of Regulation 3017/79 provided that the transaction-by-transaction method was just one of the methods which could be used by the Community authorities in calculating the dumping margin in situations where prices vary as they did in the present case[6]. It concurred with Advocate General Mancini that the charges raised by the applicants had been answered by its previous decision in the case of *Faust v EC Commission*[7]. It held that :

> "where the institutions enjoy a margin of discretion in the choice of the means needed to achieve their policies, traders cannot claim to have a legitimate expectation that the means originally chosen will be maintained, since these may be altered by the institutions in the exercise of their powers."[8]

In *Brother Industries Ltd v EC Council*[9], the applicants argued that the lack of detailed rules regarding the calculation of the dumping margin prevented traders,

---

1.   Joined Cases 260/85 and 106/86 *TEC v EC Council* 1988] ECR 5855 at 5897.
2.   Above at footnote 2, p244.
3.   Case 256/84 *Koyo Seiko Co Ltd v EC Council* [1987] ECR 1899; Case 258/84 *Nippon Seiko KK v EC Council*, above.
4.   See Chapter 3, section 3.3.6.
5.   See the applicants' submissions in Case 256/84 *Koyo Seiko Co Ltd v EC Council* [1987] ECR at 1906-1909 and Case 258/84 *Nippon Seiko KK v EC Council and EC Commission* [1979] ECR at 1935-1941.
6.   Case 256/84 *Koyo Seiko Co Ltd v EC Council* [1987] ECR ibid, at 1917, para 19 of judgment; Case 258/84 *Nippon Seiko KK v EC Council and EC Commission* [1979] ECR ibid, at 1967, para 33 of judgment.
7.   Case 52/81 *Faust v EC Commission* [1982] ECR 3745.
8.   Case 256/84 *Koyo Seiko Co Ltd v EC Council* [1987] ECR 1917, at para 20 of judgment; Case 258/84 *Nippon Seiko KK v EC Council and EC Commission* [1979] ECR at 1967, para 34 of judgment.
9.   Case 250/85 *Brother Industries Ltd v EC Council* [1988] ECR 5683 at 5698.

even diligent and prudent ones, from taking the appropriate action to avoid the imposition of an anti-dumping duty. The Court held that :

"... the rules laid down by Regulation 2176/84 leave a measure of discretion to the Community institutions, in particular the Commission in an anti-dumping investigation, as regards fixing a provisional duty and proposing a definitive duty to the Council, and the fact that the EC Commission exercises that discretion without explaining in detail and in advance the criteria which it intends to apply in every specific situation does not constitute a breach of the principle of legal certainty."[1]

The retroactive nature of a regulation imposing a definitive anti-dumping duty as permitted by article 13(4)(a) of Regulation 2423/88 does not infringe the principle of legitimate expectation. In *Continentale Produkten Gesellschaft Erhardt-Renken GmbH & Co v Hauptzollamt München West*[2], the applicants maintained that the principle was infringed given that the regulation imposing the definitive duties was retroactive as regards contracts concluded prior to its entry into force but performed thereafter. It should have made provision for the total exemption from duties of imports carried out pursuant to old contracts.

The Court rejected this argument. It held that :

"Since an anti-dumping proceeding was still in progress, a circumspect and prudent trader knew, or ought to have known, that the imposition of an anti-dumping duty was possible and could therefore have taken that possibility into account when signing contracts with his suppliers. Consequently, the legitimate expectation of traders was not infringed."[3]

Furthermore, the lack of any transitional provision in a regulation imposing a definitive anti-dumping duty cannot contravene this principle[4].

In the first *Japanese Ballbearing* cases[5], one of the applicants, Import Standards Office[6], sought to argue that the Community authorities, by definitively collecting provisional duties, had violated the principle of legal certainty of undertakings. The collection of provisional duties was only competent where definitive duties

---

1. Ibid 5725 at para 29 of judgment.
2. Case 248/87 *Continentale Produkten Gesellschaft Erhardt-Renken GmbH & Co v Hauptzollamt München West* [1987] ECR 1151.
3. Ibid, p1174 at para 17.
4. Ibid.
5. Above at footnote 1, p229.
6. Case 118/77 *Import Standard Office (ISO) v EC Council* [1979] ECR 1277.

had been imposed. If undertakings had been accepted as they were in the present case then such collection should have been abandoned. The Court, without making reference to whether the principle had been breached or not, held that there was no need to order the collection of provisional duties if the undertakings were acceptable, as they were in the present case[1].

Article 14 of Regulation 2423/88 provides that the decision to accept an undertaking may be reviewed at the request of a Member State, on the initiative of the EC Commission or at the request of an interested party who submits evidence of changed circumstances. In *Sermes S.A. v Directeur des Services des douanes de Strasbourg*[2], the applicants argued that the EC Council regulation at issue, which imposed a definitive anti-dumping duty on certain multiphase electric motors following a review of price undertakings previously given, was void. They maintained that there was insufficient evidence of changed circumstances, contrary to article 14 and the principle of legal certainty.

The Court rejected their arguments, holding that neither the documents before it nor the arguments presented to it indicated that the Community authorities had misdirected themselves in their assessment of the evidence produced by the complainants, GIMELEC (Association of Electrical Equipment and Industrial Electronics Industries) which disclosed changed circumstances[3].

Advocate General Van Gerven observed that the decision to substitute an anti-dumping duty for a price undertaking did not in itself infringe the principle of legal certainty[4]. He referred to the Court's judgment in *Nippon Seiko v EC Council* where it held that :

> "Where the institutions enjoy a margin of discretion in the choice of the means needed to achieve their policies, traders cannot claim to have a legitimate expectation that the means originally chosen will be maintained, since these may be altered by the institutions in the exercise of their powers."[5]

The Advocate General considered that this was more so the case when it appeared that the means originally chosen, namely the acceptance of price undertakings, does not bring an end to the injurious effects of the dumped imports[6].

---

1.   Ibid, pp1298-9 at paras 49-55 of judgment.
2.   Case 323/88 *Sermes SA v Directeur des Services des douanes de Strasbourg* [1990] ECR 3027.
3.   Ibid, p3051 at para 17 of judgment.
4.   Ibid at 3041.
5.   Case 258/84 *Nippon Seiko KK v EC Council* [1987] ECR 1923 at 1967, para 34 of judgment.
6.   Case 323/88 *Sermes SA v Directeur des Services des douanes de Strasbourg* [1990] ECR 3027 at 3041.

It is submitted that the Community authorities enjoy a large measure of discretion in ensuring that their policies are effective and as such traders cannot legitimately expect that the practice originally adhered to will continue. This has allowed the Community authorities to change their practice to cover situations not governed by the legislation in existence at the time. A failure by the authorities to explain in detail and in advance the criteria applied in a given situation will not constitute a breach of legal certainty.

6.9.1.3 The principle of proportionality

The principle of proportionality is aimed at ensuring that the means used must be proportionate to the end to be achieved in a given situation. Article 13(3) of Regulation 2423/88 is an example of this principle. It provides that "the amount of such duties (definitive) shall not exceed the dumping margin provisionally estimated or finally established ... it should be less if such lesser duty would be adequate to remove the injury". In other words, a lower duty should be imposed if such a duty would be sufficient to eradicate the injury to Community industry.

This provision was considered at length by Advocate General VerLoren van Themaat in the *Second Allied* case[1]. The applicants in their submissions argued that the interests of the Community could not simply be equated with the interests of certain producers and completely ignore the interests of consumers. Further, the interests of the Community did not justify the definitive duties imposed[2].

Advocate General VerLoren van Themaat pointed out that the EC Council had a wide discretion in defining what amounted to the "interests of the Community". He objected, however, to the reasoning of the Community authorities which he considered did not justify the imposition of duties equivalent to the dumping margin. The EC Council gave the following as its reasons for imposing the duty it did :

> "The results of its [the Commission] investigation [ie into the dumping margin] provided as accurate a basis for the determination of the level of dumping as possible and that lower levels would constitute a bonus for Allied Corporation's withdrawal from its undertaking and subsequent non-co-operation and the withdrawal from their undertakings by Kaiser and Transcontinental."[3]

---

1.   Case 53/88 *Allied Corporation v Council of the European Communities* [1990] ECR I 3917.
2.   Ibid at 1650-52.
3.   See para 24 of Council Regulation (EEC) 101/83, OJ L15/1 1983.

He contended that the withdrawal from an undertaking should not on its own affect the care and objectivity with which the fresh investigation should be carried out. Likewise, the refusal to co-operate could not in itself justify the above passage[1].

As far as the Advocate General was concerned, this was the only passage in the regulation which could be regarded as an explanation for the non-application of the last sentence of article 13(3) of Regulation 3017/79. It was, he noted, of decisive importance that the Community authorities did not state any reasons regarding the extent of injury found[2]. The Advocate General concluded that the anti-dumping duty imposed on the applicants should not result in a higher level of import prices than those which applied to their American competitors at the time when the regulation was adopted. A considerably lower level than the one imposed would have been sufficient to remove the injury caused by the dumping[3].

The Court, in concurring with the Advocate General's Opinion, began by reiterating the general rule that the EC Council, when adopting an anti-dumping regulation, is required to ascertain the amount of duty which is necessary in order to remove the injury. The Court noted that the EC Council in the preamble to Regulation 101/83 did not deal with this issue. It held that :

"In the preamble to Regulation 101/83, the Council deals in detail with the question whether the injury was caused by imports from the United States or by sales on the French market by producers established in other Member States. It does not however discuss the question of the amount of duties necessary in order to receive the injury; its only reference in that connection is to the Commission's view that lower levels would constitute a bonus for Allied Corporation's withdrawal from its undertaking and subsequent non-co-operation and the withdrawal from their undertakings by Kaiser and Transcontinental. That consideration is not relevant to the application of article 13(3) of the regulation. Examination of the case has not disclosed any other factors indicating that the Council took into account that article in fixing the amount of the anti-dumping duties. It must therefore be concluded that the regulation was adopted in disregard of article 13 and that it must therefore be declared void."[4]

---

1. Case 53/88 *Allied Corporation v Council of the European Communities* [1990] ECR I 3917 at 1635.
2. Ibid at 1635.
3. Ibid at 1656.
4. Case 53/88 *Allied Corporation v Council of the European Communities* [1990] ECR I 3917 at 1659, para 19 of judgment.

In *NTN Toyo Bearing Co Ltd v EC Council*, the applicant[1], like those in the *Allied* case above, argued that in fixing the rate of duty the Community authorities did not comply with article 13(3) of Regulation 2176/84. In so doing they had contravened the principle of porportionality by virtue of the fact that the duty imposed should be proportionate to the injury suffered.

Advocate General Mancini referred to the Court's judgment in the *Allied* case and noted in particular that when the EC Council adopts an anti-dumping regulation "it is required to ascertain whether the amount of the duties is necessary in order to remove the injury"[2]. He then referred to the preamble of the contested regulation, concluding that in the light of the explanations, the rates of duty fully met the objectives pursued by the legislature[3].

The Court concluded that the principle of proportionality had not been infringed. It referred, in particular, to the fact that the Community authorities had established that the overall sales of small bearings produced by the Community industry decreased by 13.3% between 1979-83 and the market share fell from 72 to 60.9%. Further, substantial damage was caused to Community industry both financially and with respect to employment[4]. In such circumstances, the imposition of anti-dumping duties could not be regarded as contrary to the principle.

In *Nachi Fujikoshi Corporation v EC Council*[5], the applicants alleged that the Community authorities, by not accepting the undertakings offered, had breached the principle of proportionality. The Court concluded, however, that the Community authorities' refusal was within their discretion and that the applicants had not established that their reasons for rejecting the undertakings exceeded this discretion.

The principle of proportionality, if breached by the Community authorities, will automatically lead to the measure or parts thereof in question to be declared void. The principle, it is submitted, unlike other general principles, is one which cannot be qualified or limited in any respect.

1.　　Case 240/84 *NTN Toyo Bearing Co Ltd v EC Council* [1987] ECR 1809.
2.　　Ibid, at 1847.
3.　　Ibid.
4.　　Ibid at 1858, paras 37-38 of judgment.
5.　　Case 255/84 *Nachi Fujikoshi Corporation v EC Council* [1987] ECR 1923 at 1893-4, paras 37-43 of judgment.

6.9.2   The effect of international agreements in Community law

The Community safeguard measures are based on provisions of the General Agreement on Tariffs and Trade ("the GATT") or on the GATT codes negotiated at the Tokyo Round of Multilateral Trade negotiations. This invariably raises the question - to what extent can an interested party challenge a Community safeguard measure on the ground that it was incompatible with the Community's Treaty obligations?

In answering this question the Court will have to consider the status and effect of International agreements in question from two basic standpoints :

1.   whether the agreement binds the Community; and

2.   whether it is capable of conferring rights on individuals which they can invoke in the national courts, ie whether such provisions can be directly effective. Clearly, if an interested party could rely on a directly effective provision in the national courts then it could rely on such a provision in proceedings brought before the Court under article 173 of EEC Treaty.

The GATT and, in particular, its anti-dumping code is the most important international agreement as far as safeguard measures are concerned. It is an example of an international agreement entered into by the Member States and third parties before the creation of the European Communities. Under international law, such agreements have to be respected. This is reflected in article 41 of the Vienna Convention on the Law of Treaties[1] and also in article 234 of the EEC Treaty. Article 234, 1st para states that the rights for third countries arising from the Member States' pre-existing international agreements and obligations for the Member States are not affected by the EEC Treaty[2].

The Court has stated that its jurisdiction extends to considering all those grounds capable of invalidating those measures. For this reason, it is obliged to examine whether their validity may be affected by reason of the fact that they are contrary to a rule of international law[3].

---

1.   8 Int. Leg Materials (1969), 679.
2.   See also Case 10/61 *EC Commission v Italian Republic* [1962] ECR 11.
3.   Case 21-24/72 *International Fruit Co* [1972] ECR 1219 at 1226; see also Case 9/73 *Schülter v Hauptzollamt Lörrach* [1973] ECR 1135 at 1157.

More particularly, in the *SPA* case[1], the Court was called upon to deal precisely with its jurisdiction in relation to the GATT. The Italian Supreme Court of Cassation, when making its reference to the Court, questioned whether the latter had the jurisdiction to interpret the GATT in cases other than those where the interpretation or the legality of the Community measure were at issue. In answer to this question the Court held that :

"it is important that the provisions of the GATT should, like the provisions of all other agreements binding the Community, receive uniform application throughout the Community. Any difference in the interpretation and application of provisions binding the Community as regards non-member countries would not only jeopardise the unity of the commercial policy, which according to article 113 of the Treaty must be based on uniform principles, but also create distortions in trade within the Community, as a result of differences in the manner in which the agreements in force between the Community and non-member countries were applied in the various Member States."[2]

In order for the validity of a Community measure to be set aside because it is contrary to Community law, the Community has to be bound by the particular rule of international law.

The Community is effectively the successor to the rights and obligations of its Member States under the GATT by virtue of the fact that it has exclusive competence in the area of external trade and commercial matters. In the *International Fruit Co* case, the Court held that :

"The Community has assumed the functions inherent in the tariff and trade policy, progressively during the transitional period and in their entirety on the expiry of that period, by virtue of articles 111 and 113 of the Treaty.

By conferring those powers on the Community, the Member States showed their wish to bind it by obligations entered into under the General Agreement.

It therefore appears that, insofar as under the EEC Treaty the Community has assumed the powers previously exercised by the Member States in the area governed by the General Agreement, the provisions of that agreement have the effect of binding the Community."[3]

---

1. Joined Cases 267-269/81 *Amministrazione dlle Finanze dello Stato v Scoieta Petrolifera Italiana Spa (SPI) and SpA Michelin Italiana (ASMI)* [1983] ECR 801.
2. Ibid at 828, para 14 of judgment.
3. Case 21-24/72 *International Fruit Co* [1972] ECR 1219 at 1227, paras 14, 15 and 18 of judgment.

It would be fair to say that in recognising that an international agreement is part of Community law, the Court is seeking to protect the uniform application of that law as much as, if not more than, it is seeking to enforce the relevant provisions of that international agreement.

Given that the Court recognises that the Community is bound by the GATT, the next question which arises is the extent to which the provisions of the GATT are "directly effective"[1]. In other words, for an individual to challenge the validity of a Community measure on the basis that it is contrary to a provision of the GATT, the latter provision must be capable of conferring rights on the individual which he can enforce in the national court. To be directly effective, a provision must be clear and precise and must be unconditional, ie it must leave no discretion on the authorities by whom they are to be applied[2].

It is not clear the extent to which the Court has transposed these criteria into its jurisprudence on the direct effect of international agreements. Generally speaking, the Court's reasoning relies heavily on the special features of the international agreement in question in establishing whether the provision is directly effective.

In the *Kupferberg*, case the Court was faced with the question of whether a provision of the Free Trade Agreement between the Community and Portugal was directly effective[3]. The Court held that the provision in question did confer rights on individuals which they could invoke in the national courts. Its reasoning was as follows :

"The governments which have submitted observations to the Court do not deny the Community nature of the provisions of agreements concluded by the Community. They contend, however, that the generally recognised criteria for determining the effects of provisions of a purely Community origin may not be applied to provisions of a free trade agreement concluded by the Community with a non-member country.

In that respect the governments base their arguments in particular on the distribution of powers in regard to the external relations of the Community, the principle of reciprocity governing the application of free trade agreements, the institutional framework established by such agreements in order to settle

---

1. See generally Bourgeois "The effect of International Agreements in EEC Law: Are the Dice Cast?" 82 Mich. L. Rev. 1250; Pescatore "The Doctrine of Direct Effect: An Infant Disease of Community Law" 1983 ELRev. 155.
2. See for example Case 26/62 *Van Gend en Loos* [1963] ECR 1.
3. Case 104/81 *Hauptzollamt Mainz v C A Kupferberg KG aA* [1982] ECR 3641.

differences between the contracting parties and safeguard clauses allowing the parties to derogate from the agreements.

It is true that the effects within the Community of provisions of an agreement concluded by the Community with a non-member country may not be determined without taking account of the international origin of the provisions in question. In conformity with the principles of public international law Community institutions which have power to negotiate and conclude an agreement with a non-member country are free to agree with that country what effect the provisions of the agreement are to have in the internal legal order of the contracting parties. Only if that question has not been settled by the agreement does it fall for decision by the courts having jurisdiction in the matter, and in particular by the Court of Justice within the framework of its jurisdiction under the Treaty, in the same manner as any question of interpretation relating to the application of the agreement in the Community.

According to the general rules of international law there must be bona fide performance of every agreement. Although each contracting party is responsible for executing fully the commitments which it has undertaken it is nevertheless free to determine the legal means appropriate for attaining that end in its legal system unless the agreement, interpreted in the light of its subject matter and purpose, itself specifies those means. Subject to that reservation the fact that the courts of one of the parties consider that certain of the stipulations in the agreement are of direct application whereas the courts of the other party do not recognise such direct application is not in itself such as to constitute a lack of reciprocity in the implementation of the agreement.

As the governments have emphasised, the free trade agreements provide for joint committees responsible for the administration of the agreements and for their proper implementation. To that end they may make recommendations and, in the cases expressly provided for by the agreement in question, take decisions.

The mere fact that the contracting parties have established a special institutional framework for consultations and negotiations inter se in relation to the implementation of the agreement is not in itself sufficient to exclude all judicial application of that agreement. The fact that a court of one of the parties applies to a specific case before it a provision of the agreement involving an unconditional and precise obligation and therefore not requiring any prior intervention on the part of the joint committee does not adversely affect the powers that the agreement confers on that committee.

As regards the safeguard clauses which enable the parties to derogate from certain provisions of the agreement it should be observed that they apply only in specific circumstances and as a general rule after consideration within the joint committee in the presence of both parties. Apart from specific situations which may involve their application, the existence of such clauses, which, moreover, do not affect the provisions prohibiting tax discrimination, is not sufficient in itself to affect the direct applicability which may attach to certain stipulations in the agreement.

It follows from all the foregoing considerations that neither the nature nor the structure of the Agreement concluded with Portugal may prevent a trader from relying on the provisions of the said Agreement before a court in the Community.

Nevertheless the question whether such a stipulation is unconditional and sufficiently precise to have direct effect must be considered in the context of the Agreement of which it forms part. In order to reply to the question on the direct effect of the first paragraph of article 21 of the Agreement between the Community and Portugal it is necessary to analyse the provision in the light of both the object and purpose of the Agreement and of its context. The purpose of the Agreement is to create a system of free trade in which rules restricting commerce are eliminated in respect of virtually all trade in products originating in the territory of the parties, in particular by abolishing customs duties and charges having equivalent effect and eliminating quantitative restrictions and measures having equivalent effect.

Seen in that context the first paragraph of article 21 of the Agreement seeks to prevent the liberalisation of the trade in goods through the abolition of customs duties and charges having equivalent effect and quantitative restrictions and measures having equivalent effect from being rendered nugatory by fiscal practices of the Contracting Parties. That would be so if the product imported of one party were taxed more heavily than the similar domestic products which it encounters on the market of the other party.

It appears from the foregoing that the first paragraph of article 21 of the Agreement imposes on the Contracting Parties an unconditional rule against discrimination in matters of taxation, which is dependent only on a finding that the products affected by a particular system of taxation are of like nature, and the limits of which are the direct consequence of the purpose of the Agreement. As such this provision may be applied by a court and thus produce direct effects throughout the Community."[1]

---

1.   Case 104/81 *Hauptzollamt Mainz v C A Kupferberg KG aA* [1982] ECR 3641 at 3663-3665, paras 15-26 of judgment.

The Court recognised that it was not sufficient to exclude the direct effect of certain provisions on the basis that there existed a special institutional framework for consultations and negotiations nor the possibility that the contracting parties could derogate from the Agreement by virtue of the safeguard clauses contained therein.

The decision in *Kupferberg* did not result in the Court having a change of attitude towards the direct effect of the GATT provisions, which will be discussed below. There are a number of reasons why this may be the case. First, the Free Trade Agreement with Portugal was a bilateral treaty whereas the GATT is a multilateral agreement, though it should be noted that the Court's decision in *Bresciani*, discussed below, concerned a multilateral agreement, namely the Yauondé Convention (now Lomé Convention). Second and most important, the aim of the Free Trade Agreement with Portugal was to create a free trade area which goes beyond the scheme and objectives of the GATT.

Apart from the decision in *Kupferberg*, the Court has in several other cases held provisions of association agreements to be directly effective[1]. Such agreements create a close relationship between the Community and the non-Member States involved.

In *Bresciani*, the Court was confronted with the question of whether article 2(1) of the Yauondé Convention (now replaced by the Lomé Conventions) conferred rights upon individuals which they could invoke in the national courts. The Court held that it was directly effective, on the basis that article 2(1) of the Convention expressly referred to article 13 of the EEC Treaty. As such, the Community had undertaken the same obligations towards the Associated States as the Member States had with respect to one another[2].

In *Pabst & Richarz*, which concerned a provision of the Association Agreement with Greece, the Court stated :

"That provision [article 53(1)], the wording of which is similar to that of article 95 of the Treaty, fulfils, within the framework of the Association between the Community and Greece, the same function as article 95 ...It accordingly follows from the wording of article 53(1) cited above, and from the objective and the nature of the Association Agreement of which it forms part that that provision precludes a national system of relief from providing more favourable tax treatment for domestic spirits than for those imported from

---

1.   Case 87/75 *Bresciani* [1976] ECR 129; Case 17/81 *Pabst and Richarz* [1982] ECR 1331.
2.   Case 87/75 *Bresciani* ibid, at 141-2, para 25 of judgment.

Greece. It contains a clear and precise obligation which is not subject, in its implementation or effects, to the adoption of any subsequent measure."[1]

The Court was first confronted with the question of whether a provision of the GATT was directly effective in the *International Fruit Company* case[2] and in particular article XI thereof. The Court held that in order to establish whether provisions of the GATT had direct effect it was necessary to consider the spirit, the general scheme and the terms of the General Agreement[3]. It concluded that article XI was not capable of conferring on the citizens of the Community rights which they could invoke before the national courts. Its reasons for reaching this conclusion were as follows :

"This Agreement [GATT] which, according to its preamble, is based on the principle of negotiations undertaken on the basis of 'reciprocal and mutually advantageous arrangements' is characterised by the great flexibility of its provisions, in particular those conferring the possibility of derogation, the measures to be taken when confronted with exceptional difficulties and the settlement of conflicts between contracting parties."[4]

Advocate General Myras in his Opinion reached the same conclusion. He held that :

"Article XI contains exceptions and derogations which in practice have been shown to leave States and, *mutatis mutandis*, the Community a discretion such as excludes individuals from the principle established by that article subjective rights capable of being profitably invoked before a Court."[5]

A year later the Court again had to determine whether another provision of the GATT - article II(1) - was directly effective[6]. It stated that this had to be answered in the light of the meaning, structure and wording of the General Agreement[7]. By applying its reasoning in the *International Fruit Company* case, the Court concluded that article II(1) did not confer rights on individuals which they could invoke in the national courts.

---

1.   Case 17/81 *Pabst and Richarz* [1982] ECR 1331 at 1350, paras 26-27 of judgment.
2.   Case 21-24/72 *International Fruit Co* [1972] ECR 1219.
3.   Ibid at 1227, paras 20 of judgment.
4.   Ibid at 1227, para 21 of judgment.
5.   Ibid at 1239.
6.   Case 9/73 *Schülter v Hauptzollamt Lörrach* [1973] ECR 1135.
7.   Ibid at 1157, para 29 of judgment.

In a number of cases referred to the Court by the Italian Supreme Court of Cassation[1], it confirmed its reasoning in the *International Fruit Company* case in holding that article V of the GATT did not confer rights on individuals which they could enforce in the national courts. It did, however, emphasise "the Community's obligation to ensure that the provisions of the GATT are observed in its relations with non-Member States which are parties to the GATT"[2]. This was reiterated by the Court in the *Second Fediol* case[3] when it concluded that the concept of a subsidy in article 3 of Regulation 2176/84 presupposed the grant of an economic advantage through a charge on the public account. It held that :

"The concept of a subsidy thus understood is not incompatible with the Community's obligations under international law, in particular under GATT and agreements concluded in the framework thereof."[4]

The Court in the *Third Fediol* case[5] has gone one step further and has held that for the purposes of the New Commercial Policy Instrument - Regulation 2641/84 - individuals can rely directly on the provisions of the GATT. It held that :

"... Since Regulation 2641/84 entitles the economic agents concerned to rely on the GATT provisions in the complaint which they lodge with the Commission in order to establish the illicit nature of the commercial practices which they consider to have harmed them, those same economic agents are entitled to request the Court to exercise its powers of review over the legality of the Commission's decision applying those provisions."[6]

In considering the merits of the case the Court went even further. It was prepared to give its own interpretation on the GATT provisions invoked by the applicant rather than restricting its review to question whether the EC Commission's interpretation of the GATT provisions was within its discretion[7]. Such a development is to be welcomed and even more so given that the Court was prepared to interpret the GATT provisions itself.

The decision re-opens the issue of whether the EC Commission's practices and interpretation of the anti-dumping regulation (Regulation 2423/88) are also in accordance with the GATT and the GATT Anti-dumping Code. It is arguable,

---

1.   Case 266/81 *SIOT*, [1983] ECR 731; Case 267-9/81 *SpA (SPI and SAMI)* [1983] ECR 801; Joined Cases 290 and 291/81 *Singer and Geigy* [1983] ECR 847.
2.   Case 266/81 *SIOT*, ibid, 780, paras 27 and 28 of judgment.
3.   Case 188/85 *Fediol (No 2) v EC Commission* [1988] ECR 4193.
4.   Ibid at 4226, para 13 of judgment.
5.   Case 70/87 *Fediol v EC Commission* [1989] ECR 1781.
6.   Ibid at 1831 para 22 of judgment.
7.   Ibid.

however, that the Court would distinguish its decision in the *Third Fediol* case if it was required to rule on the direct effect of the GATT provisions so far as the anti-dumping rules are concerned. In the *Third Fediol* case, the Court noted that the GATT rules formed part of the rules of public international law of which specific mention is made in article 2(1) of Regulation 2641/84. The regulation, however, does not set out which of the GATT rules may be relied upon by an individual who is attempting to establish that there is an illicit commercial practice. The Anti-dumping Rules, on the other hand, more or less incorporate the rules laid down in the GATT and the Anti-dumping Code[1].

The question of the effect of the GATT and, in particular, the effect of the Anti-dumping Code, has arisen in two recent cases. In *Nakajima All Precision Co Ltd v EC Council*[2], the applicants argued that the method for constructing the normal value as provided for in article 2(3)(b)(ii) of the basic regulation was contrary to articles 2(4) and 2(6) of the GATT Anti-dumping Code. The EC Council maintained that the provisions of the Code like those of the GATT itself were not directly effective.

The Court avoided the need to consider this argument by holding that the applicants were not claiming direct effect but only challenging the legality of the basic regulation on the basis that it violated the EEC Treaty. The Court concluded that the Community was bound by the Code as much as by the GATT itself and must respect its provisions. Article 2(3)(b)(ii) did not violate the Code owing to the fact that it was reasonable within the parameters of the Code provisions.

In *Goldstar Co Ltd v EC Council*[3] the applicants claimed inter alia that the EC Council had infringed article 2(3)(b)(ii) of Regulation 2423/88 in establishing the constructed value of the compact disc player, model GCD13, by reference to the profit margin realised on the sales of models sold on the domestic market since these profits did not correspond to profits normally realised on that market. They maintained that the EC Council should have referred to the profits made by all the other Korean producers on the basis of article 2(4) of the Anti-dumping Code and in particular the final sentence which provided that :

"As a general rule, the addition for profit shall not exceed the profit normally realised on sales of products of the same general category in the domestic market of the country of origin."

---

1.   See generally Rabe and Schütte "EC Anti Dumping Law: current issues in the light of the Jurisidiction of the Court" 26 CMLRev. 644.
2.   Case C-69/89 *Nakajima All Precision Co Ltd v EC Council* (1991) Transcript 7 May, at para 64 of judgment.
3.   Case 105/90 *Goldstar Co Ltd v EC Council* [1992] 1 CMLR 996.

In its view, the words "profit normally realised" must be understood as referring to the average profit realised collectively by all the producers of the country of origin on sales of the like product on the domestic market. Therefore, the first method of calculation for the profit margin provided for in article 2(3)(b)(ii) of Regulation 2423/88, which refers to the profit realised by the producer concerned, was contrary to article 2(4) of Anti-dumping Code.

Advocate General Van Gerven took the view that Goldstar's argument was based on a misinterpretation of the Anti-dumping Code. The interpretation that the addition for profit may not be higher than the profit realised by the producer concerned on the sales of like products on the domestic market, he considered, was more in keeping with the aim of establishing a constructed value. Such an interpretation was consistent with the Court's rulings[1] where it held that the purpose of constructing the normal value is to determine the selling price of a product as it would be if that product were sold in its country of origin or in the exporting country[2].

The Court considered, however, that article 2(4) of the Anti-dumping Code was couched in general terms and did not make it clear whether it related to the profits realised by the exporter concerned or the average profit realised by all the producers collectively on the domestic market[3].

It referred to its decision in *Nakajima All Precision Co Ltd v Council* and on the basis of the principles laid down in that case held that :

> "The profit margin must therefore be calculated primarily by reference to the profit realised by the producer on profitable sales of like products on the domestic market. Only if the data are unavailable, unreliable or not suitable for use is the profit margin to be calculated by reference to the profits realised by other producers on sales of the like product.
>
> In giving priority in that way to the use of data relating to the individual producer concerned, article 2(3)(b)(ii) of the basic regulation seeks to ensure that the constructed normal value corresponds as closely as possible to what the situation would have been if the producer had actually sold the product in question on the domestic market in sufficient quantities. That provision thus

---

1. See Case 250/85 *Brother v EC Council* [1988] ECR 5683, at para 18 of judgment; Joined Cases 277 and 300/85 *Canon v EC Council* [1988] ECR 5731 at para 26 of judgment; Joined Cases 273/85 and 107/86 *Silver Seiko v EC Council* [1988] ECR 5927 at para 16 of judgment; Case 69/89 *Nakajima All Precision Co Ltd v EC Council* (1991) Transcript 7 May, para 64 of judgment.
2. Case 105/90 *Goldstar Co Ltd v EC Council* [1992] 1 CMLR 996 at 1013-1014 para 20 of Opinion.
3. Ibid, p1025 at para 32 of judgment.

ensures that each undertaking is assessed by reference to its own specific characteristics."[1]

The Court observed that such characteristics must include the pricing policy pursued by the producer concerned on the domestic market. The data relating to the profits generated by the applicants cannot be disregarded simply because its profit margin is high in relation to that realised by other producers on that market[2]. In such circumstances, the EC Council was entitled to calculate the profit margin for the constructed normal value of the GCD 13 model on the basis of profits realised by Goldstar on the sales of its other models on the Korean market.

As a corollary to the above, reference is often made to the preamble of the basic anti-dumping regulation where it states that :

"the Community is required to take account of their interpretation [the rules] by the Community's major trading partners as reflected in legislation or established practice."

The Court has held, however, that the Community is not obliged to follow the practice of one of its trading partners, even a major partner (United States), in interpreting an element in the determination of anti-dumping duties[3].

The recognition by the Court that the Community is bound by Treaties like the GATT is more often aimed at protecting the uniform application of Community law than at enforcing international law. In this respect, the Court has observed that the Community is bound by the GATT and its codes. It does not follow, however, that just because an international agreement is part of Community law or that the Community is bound by it that it is therefore enforceable by individuals.

What is important, as a result of the Court's jurisprudence in the GATT and Free Trade Association cases, is that a clause in an agreement which bears a close relationship to the Community, irrespective of whether it has been applied in a reciprocal manner by the other party, is enforceable by an individual, if such a provision is precise and unconditional. The Court's decision in the *Third Fediol* case is a source of encouragement to interested parties affected by Community acts imposing safeguard measures. It is reassuring to know that the Court is prepared to

---

1. Case 105/90 *Goldstar Co Ltd v EC Council* [1992] 1 CMLR 996 at 1025, paras 36 and 37 of judgment.
2. Ibid, p1026 at para 38 of judgment.
3. Case 250/85 *Brother Industries Ltd v EC Council* [1988] ECR 5683.

recognise the direct effect of the GATT provisions, albeit only in relation to the New Commercial Policy Instrument to date.

6.10 The evaluation of economic facts and circumstances - the extent to which the Court will review the exercise of the Community authorities' discretion

The imposition of safeguard measures involves investigations of a highly technical and complex nature. Naturally, the legislation which permits the Community authorities to impose such measures confers on them a wide discretion in exercising the powers with which they are endowed.

Advocate General Roemer in *Germany v EC Commission*[1] was of the opinion that the exercise of powers which confers a wide discretion should be subject to judicial review by the Court to ensure effective control. The crucial factor is the extent to which the Court may exercise such review. As early as its decision in *Consten & Grundig*, the Court stated its position with respect to its review of the Community authorities' discretion. It held that :

"the exercise of the Commission's powers necessarily implies complex evaluation on economic matters. A judicial review of these evaluations must take account of their nature by confining itself to an examination of relevance of the facts and of the legal consequences which the Commission deduces therefrom."[2]

The Court's objective is to examine only the relevance and accuracy of the facts and the legal consequences which, according to the EC Commission, flow from them. However, in situations where the facts are complex, it is much more difficult to avoid an evaluation of the findings of the Community authorities.

In such situations, the Court will not seek to substitute its own evaluation of the facts for that of the competent institution. Rather, it will attempt to examine whether the evaluation of the findings of that institution contains a patent error or constitutes a misuse of powers. Inevitably, the Court is placed in the dilemma of respecting the legitimate limits of the institution's discretion which is indispensible to the operation of the Community on the one hand, while on the other, protecting the interests of the applicant and respecting the rule of law.

---

1.   Case 34/62 *Germany v EC Commission* [1963] ECR 149 at 152.
2.   Case 56 and 58/64 *Etablissements Consten SARL and Grundig Verkaufs-GmbH v EC Commission* [1966] ECR 299 at 347.

The Court has on numerous occasions in its jurisprudence regarding anti-dumping laws made reference to the extent to which it is prepared to review the exercise of the discretion given to the Community authorities under these laws. In *Fediol*, the Court stated the following general rule when it held that :

"complainants may not be refused the right to put before the Court any matters which would facilitate a review as to whether the Commission has observed the procedural guarantees to complainants by Regulation 3017/79 and whether or not it has committed manifest errors in its assessment of the facts, has omitted to take into consideration any essential matters of such a nature as to give rise to a belief in the existence of subsidisation or has based the reasons for its decision on considerations amounting to a misuse of powers. In that respect, the Court is required to exercise its normal powers of review over a discretion granted to a public authority, even though it has no jurisdiction to intervene in the exercise of the discretion reserved to the Community authorities by the aforementioned regulation."[1]

The Court reiterated this principle in the *Mini Ballbearing* cases referring to its judgment in the *Remia* case[2]. It noted that the choice between the different methods of calculating the dumping margin in article 2(13)(b) of Regulation 3017/79 required an appraisal of complex economic situations. In so doing it held that it must :

"limit its review of such an appraisal to verifying whether the relevant procedural rules have been complied with, whether the statement of reasons for the decision is adequate, whether the facts on which the choice is based have been accurately stated and whether there has been a manifest error of appraisal or a misuse of powers."[3]

An analysis of the Court's pronouncements regarding the exercise of discretion by the Community authorities can best be understood by considering the areas in which this discretion arises. They are as follows :

    6.10.1   The calculation of dumping
    6.10.2   The determination of injury
    6.10.3   The determination of Community interests
    6.10.4   The calculation of duties and the refusal to accept undertakings
    6.10.5   Evaluation.

---

1.   Case 191/82 *Fediol v EC Commission* [1983] ECR 2913 at 2935-6, para 30 of judgment.
2.   Case 42/84 *Remia BV v EC Commission* [1985] ECR 2545.
3.   See for example Case 240/84 *NTN Toyo Bearing Co Ltd and Ors v EC Council* [1987] ECR 1809 at 1854, para 19 of judgment.

6.10.1   The calculation of dumping

In the *Continentale Produkten* case[1], the applicants had brought an action before the Court to annul a decision by the EC Commission refusing refund duties under article 16 of Regulation 2176/84, on the basis that they had not adduced sufficient evidence for their claims. The applicants in their submissions contended that the actual normal values for their Turkish suppliers were lower than those originally established by Regulation 789/82 on the basis of which definitive duties were imposed. Normal value was constructed as there were insufficient sales on the domestic market. The EC Commission contended that the refundable amount was merely the difference between the duty collected and the "normal values" as determined definitively in Regulation 789/82. The applicants maintained, however, that the sums to be reimbursed should be calculated on the basis of their suppliers' actual individual "normal values".

Advocate General Darmon concluded, and the Court concurred, that article 16 could not permit the method of calculating the normal value to be changed by substituting real prices for constructed value[2]. This also applied to the export price. Article 16, he argued, enabled an applicant to have the normal value etc recalculated if and only if special factors applied.

More importantly, the Advocate General recognised that the Community authorities had in this area a wide discretion. He noted that the control exercised by the Court was limited to manifest error of assessment and misuse of powers. In this respect he referred to the *Fediol* decision. He concluded that no misuse of powers had been alleged. As regards manifest error which the applicant had to prove, no such error had been established[3].

When the imported product originates from a state trading country (ie a non-market economy), the Community authorities are not able to establish normal value on the basis of the prices of the product on the domestic market because those prices do not reflect market forces. For that reason, article 2(5) of Regulation 2423/88 provides that in such a case normal value is to be determined "in an appropriate and not unreasonable manner" by reference either to the price at which the like product of a market economy third country is actually sold for consumption on the domestic market of that country or to other countries, or the constructed value of the like product in a market economy third country, or when neither of the above provides a sufficient basis, the price actually paid or payable in the Community for the like product.

---

1.   Case 312/84 *Continentale Produkten Gesellschaft Ehrhardt-Renken GmbH & Co v EC Commission* [1987] ECR 841.
2.   Ibid at 860-1.
3.   Ibid at 861.

The Community authorities have a discretion in determining how normal value is to be established in terms of article 2(5)[1].

In *Technointorg v EC Council and EC Commission*, article 2(5) was used to calculate normal value as the USSR was a non-market economy. The EC Commission chose Yugoslavia as the analogue country and established normal value on the basis of domestic prices on the Yugoslav market. The applicants were unhappy with Yugoslavia being chosen owing to the differences in income levels and manufacturing processes in the two countries. Normal value, therefore, should have been constructed. The EC Council was of the view that normal value in Yugoslavia should only have been constructed if there were circumstances which made it unreasonable to use domestic prices, otherwise they were entitled to use these latter prices.

The Court held that :

"it is unnecessary to have recourse to the constructed value unless it would be unreasonable in the circumstances to use the domestic price. That value must be calculated in such a way that the results obtained are as close as possible to the normal value based on the domestic price. In that regard the institutions have a discretion and Technointorg has not established that, by choosing to base the normal value in this case on the prices on the Yugoslav market, they have used it erroneously."[2]

In *Neotype Techmashexport v EC Commission and EC Council*[3], the applicants argued that the Yugoslav prices did not afford an appropriate and reasonable basis of comparison owing to the fact that the size of the Yugoslav market was sufficient and that there were practically no imports into Yugoslavia capable of providing any competition.

The Court observed that article 2(5) conferred on the Community authorities a discretion in the choice of the market economy as a reference country for the purpose of establishing normal value. It concurred with Advocate General Van Gerven[4] in holding that the Community authorities had not exceeded the limits of their

---

1.   Joined Cases 294/86 and 77/87 *Technointorg v EC Council and EC Commission* [1988] ECR 6077. See also Case 16/90 *Detlef Nölle v Hauptzollamt Bremen Freihafen* (1991) Transcript 22 October, at paras 12-13 of judgment.

2.   Ibid at 6113, para 30 of judgment.

3.   Joined Cases 305/86 and 160/87 *Neotype Techmashexport v EC Commission and EC Council* [1990] ECR 2945.

4.   Joined Cases 305/86 and 160/87 *Neotype Techmashexport v EC Commission and EC Council* [1990] ECR 2945 at 2977.

discretion by choosing the Yugoslav prices as a basis of comparison[1]. With respect to Neotype's arguments, it noted that the size of the domestic market was not in principle a factor capable of being taken into consideration in the choice of a reference country as determined by article 2(5), insofar as during the period of investigation there was a sufficient number of transactions to ensure the representative nature of the market in relation to the exports in question. In this context, the Court referred to the Community authorities' practice of fixing the minimum level of representativity of the domestic market for the purposes of calculating the normal value in accordance with article 2(3) of basic regulation at 5% of exports which it approved in *Brother v EC Commission*[2]. No evidence was placed before it establishing that the Yugoslav market was not representative in this sense[3].

Furthermore, the alleged absence of imports was not of itself sufficient to render the Yugoslav market as inappropriate given that there were three producers of electric motors who were in competition with one another thereby ensuring that the prices were representative[4].

The selection of the analogue country arose again in *Detlef Nölle v Hauptzollamt Bremen Freihafen*[5] in the context of an article 177 reference on the validity of a Council regulation imposing a definitive duty on the imports of paint brushes from China. The EC Commission, in determining normal value, used the domestic sales of producers of the like product on the Sri Lankan market. Nölle had suggested Taiwan, maintaining that Sri Lanka did not afford an appropriate and reasonable basis of comparison for the determination of normal value.

They argued inter alia that the volume of sales in Sri Lanka was lower than the volume of Chinese exports to the Community, especially when one observed that there were only two producers in Sri Lanka as compared with one hundred and fifty medium sized companies manufacturing the product in China. Secondly, the Sri Lankan producers had to import the necessary raw materials whereas the Chinese producers had access to these locally.

The Court in its judgment carefully and fully examined the decisions taken by the Community authorities. It observed that it was necessary for it in the exercise of its

1. Ibid, p3002 at para 34 of judgment.
2. Case 250/85 *Brother Industries Ltd v EC Council* [1988] ECR 5683.
3. Joined Cases 305/86 and 160/87 *Neotype Techmashexport v EC Commission and EC Council* [1990] ECR 2945 at 3001, para 31 of judgment.
4. Ibid, pp3001-3002 at para 32 of judgment.
5. Case 16/90 *Detlef Nölle v Hauptzollamt Bremen Freihafen* (1991) Transcript 22 October.

review to ensure that the Community authorities had taken account of all relevant considerations in choosing a suitable Third Country and that the matter had been examined with the care required to establish that normal value had been fixed in "an appropriate and reasonable manner"[1].

The Court concluded that the EC Commission had not taken fully account of the information known to it, given doubts that existed as to the appropriateness of Sri Lanka, nor had it properly considered Nölle's proposal, Taiwan. In particular, the Court applied the 5% threshold criterion in determining if domestic sales on the Sri Lankan market were representative for establishing normal value. It noted that China exported about 60 million brushes to the Community whereas Sri Lanka's total production amounted to 750,000 brushes, thereby representing 1.25% of Chinese exports to the Community. This, however, did not necessarily imply that the choice of Sri Lanka was inappropriate and unreasonable. On the other hand, such a small figure was an indication of the low representativity of the market[2]. Furthermore, the Court considered it important that the Sri Lankan producers had to import their raw materials whereas the Chinese producers could obtain these domestically. This factor was relevant and required to be taken into account when determining the selection of analogue country[3].

Some commentators[4] have suggested that all interested parties should be given the opportunity to make known their views on the selection of an analogue country. Furthermore, where an alternative analogue country is proposed and this proposal is accompanied by sufficient evidence, the EC Commission should give it serious consideration. Time limits could be built in to the existing procedure so as to avoid any delays caused by such a system. Such a proposal, it is submitted, would have the effect of ensuring that the Community authorities give serious consideration to their choice of analogue country while at the same time taking account of the interested parties' views.

In constructing normal value, article 2(3)(b)(ii) of Regulation 2423/88 permits the Community authorities to include an amount for a reasonable profit margin. What is reasonable is not defined in the regulation thereby endowing the EC Commission with a discretion as to what this amount should be.

1.	Case 16/90 *Detlef Nölle v Hauptzollamt Bremen Freihafen* (1991) Transcript 22 October, a t para 13 of judgment.
2.	Ibid at paras 20-22 of judgment.
3.	Ibid at para 26 of judgment.
4.	See Vermulst and Hooijer [1992] CMLRev. 380-404.

In *TEC v EC Council*[1], the EC Commission, in an attempt to arrive at a constructed normal value as close as possible to that which would have been established if there had been domestic sales, took into account profit margins actually realised for sales of electronic typewriters on the domestic market. This amounted to 47.92%. The applicants contended that this was contrary to existing practice, which had never before resulted in a profit margin exceeding 10% and was also incompatible with the rule in article 2(3)(b)(ii) of Regulation 2176/84 that the profit should not exceed that realised on sales of products in the same general category.

In his Opinion, Advocate General Slynn relied on the Court's judgment in *Nippon Seiko*[2] where the Court had held that where the Community authorities were required to appraise complex economic situations the Court was limited in its review of such appraisal to verifying whether the relevant procedural rules had been complied with, whether the facts had been accurately stated and whether there had been a manifest error of appraisal or misuse of powers. He noted that the purpose of the constructed normal value was to act as a substitute for the domestic selling price where there were no domestic sales or where these did not permit a proper comparison. He concluded that article 2(3)(b)(ii) did not require that the profit had to be realised by the same company but only that it should be realised by sales of goods of the same general category, ie electronic typewriters. This was, therefore, within the EC Commission's power of appraisal[3]. The Court duly concurred with the Advocate General's Opinion. It held that :

> "there is nothing in article 2(3)(b)(ii) of Regulation 2176/84 to preclude the view that the profit margin adopted by the institutions could, in the context of their power of appraisal, be regarded as a reasonable margin."[4]

In all the *Electronic Typewriter* cases, where there were sufficient domestic sales, the products were sold through a sales subsidiary. The Community authorities held that these were not independent from the parent company but that they formed one economic entity. As the Court held in *Brother v EC Council*[5], the division of production and sales activities within a group made up of legally distinct companies can in no way alter the fact that the group is a single economic entity which organises in that way activities that, in other cases, are carried out by what is in legal terms as well a single entity. In calculating normal value, they therefore disregarded the sales price from the parent company to the sales company as these did not represent arm's length prices[6].

1.　　Joined Cases 260/85 and 106/86 *TEC v EC Council* [1988] ECR 5855.
2.　　Case 258/84 *Nippon Seiko KK v EC Council* [1987] ECR 1899 at 1964, para 21 of judgment.
3.　　Joined Cases 260/85 and 106/86 *TEC v EC Council* [1988] ECR 5855 at 5889.
4.　　Ibid at 5916-7, para 13 of judgment.
5.　　Case 250/85 *Brother Industries Ltd v EC Commission* [1988] ECR 5683 at para 16 of judgment.
6.　　See also judgments of 10 March 1992, not yet reported : Case 179/87 *Sharp Corporation v EC Council* [1992] 2 CMLR 415; Case 176/87 *Konishiroku Photo Industry Co Ltd v EC Council*; Case

In *Canon Inc v EC Council*[1], the applicants argued that these transfer prices, ie those from the parent to the sales company, were fair and reliable and therefore could have been used as the basis for calculating normal value. Failing that, normal value should have been constructed on the basis of prices to third countries.

Advocate General Slynn held that the Community authorities had a discretion which they could exercise and did so by disregarding the transfer prices from Canon Inc to its subsidiary Canon Sales Ltd for the purposes of constructing normal value, on the basis that they were associated. In this respect, Canon had failed to show that the discretion was exceeded or improperly used. Article 2(3)(a) of Regulation 2176/84, he argued, included in its scope the price charged by its sales company to its customers. The prices charged by Canon Sales Ltd to its customers were plainly "in the ordinary course of trade" within the meaning of article 2(3)(a), and the Community authorities were entitled to use them for the purpose of establishing normal value as they did[2].

As to those models which were not sold on the domestic market or which were sold in insufficient quantities, the Community authorities had a discretion on the reading of article 2(3)(b) to choose between either constructing the normal value or using third country export prices. The applicant had not shown that this discretion was wrongly applied[3] whereas the EC Council had explained the reasons for the Community authorities' choice in the definitive duty regulation. The Court concurred with the Advocate General. It held that :

> "Article 2(3)(b) does not indicate that use of the price for exportation to a third country is to take precedence over construction of the normal value. The institutions therefore enjoy a margin of discretion in that respect and Canon has not shown that that discretion has been abused."[4]

Where a producer has no domestic sales of the like product, the Community authorities will normally construct normal value by adding to that producer's cost of production an amount for selling, general and administrative expenses and profit based on the findings for those producers which have profitable sales on the domestic market. Following the decision of the Court in *Nakajima All*

175/87 *Matsushita Electric Industrial Co Ltd* and *Matsushita Electric Trading Co Ltd v EC Council*; Case 174/87 *Ricoh Co Ltd v EC Council*; Case 177/87 *Sanyo Electric Co Ltd v EC Council*; Case 178/87 *Minolta Camera Care Co Ltd v EC Council*; Case 171/87 *Canon v EC Council*. All the applicants made a joint submission on similar grounds. The Court as in the *Electronic typewriter* cases rejected their submissions.

1.   Joined Cases 277 and 300/85 *Canon Inc v EC Council* [1988] ECR 5731.
2.   Ibid at 5774.
3.   Ibid at 5775.
4.   Ibid at 5800, para 17 of judgment.

Precision Co Ltd v EC Council[1], this practice will also apply not only to foreign producers who do not have any domestic sales but who have different sales structures. Nakajima did not sell dot matrix printers in Japan but produced for export and sold only to independent importers. More importantly, it did not have a vertical structure with its own domestic sales related companies. Consequently, it did not incur the same costs. The Court held that the EC Commission, by adding an amount for selling general and administrative costs and profit based on the findings of producers who did sell profitably on the domestic market, to Nakajima's costs of production in constructing normal value, had acted in conformity with the basic regulation.

This decision is unfortunate in that it penalises a foreign producer like Nakajima for being more competitive. The Court was in effect making an assumption. It assumed that if Nakajima did sell on the domestic market it would sell through related sales companies rather than to independent distributors. Consequently, the Court is placing the burden of proving that would not do so on the foreign producer in question. Arguably, it should be for the Community authorities, who are required to establish dumping and injury, to provide such proof.

Once the normal value and the export price have been established, the Community authorities will then calculate the dumping margin. Prior to Regulation 2423/88, where prices varied, article 2(13)(b) and (c) allowed the Community authorities to assess the export price by either establishing it on the basis of the transaction-by-transaction method or by reference to weighted average prices.

In the *Mini Ballbearing* cases[2], the charge was concerned with whether, in determining the dumping margin, the normal value and export price must be assessed by the use of the same method or by different methods when domestic prices and export prices fluctuated appreciably. The normal value was assessed by reference to the weighted average price for all transactions on the domestic market and reduced to a single figure. The export price, on the other hand, was assessed by reference to the transaction-by-transaction method. This method sought to exclude exports whose prices were in excess of the normal value, otherwise prices in excess of normal value and prices below normal value could be offset against one another, thereby mathematically cancelling out any dumping margin, whilst leaving intact the effects of injury to Community industry.

---

1.   Case 69/89 *Nakajima All Precision Co Ltd v EC Council* (1991) Transcript 7 May.
2.   See footnote 2, p244 above; see also Case 178/87 *Minolta Camera Care Co Ltd v EC Council* (1992) Transcript 10 March 1992.

The applicants contended that the method of calculation involved a manifest error of fact and law. They argued that article 2(13) of Regulation 2176/84 allowed for a choice to be made between the different methods but did not allow them to be combined. Its effect was to leave out of account the large number of export sales made at non-dumping prices and to establish the existence of dumping even where export prices did not differ on average from internal consumption on the Japanese market.

Advocate General Mancini concluded that this was an area in which the Community authorities had been entrusted with the task of appraising complex economic matters involving choices of a technical nature, and as such the Court's powers of review would be limited to determining whether that power of appraisal had been subject to manifest error or misuse of powers[1]. He noted that there was no obligation on the Community authorities to use only one of the criteria in article 2(13)(b), which he concluded was designed to prevent economic injury resulting from selective dumping practices being concealed by carefully orchestrated manipulation of higher and lower prices[2].

The Court agreed with the Advocate General. It held that :

> "The fact that the methods of calculation [for normal value and export price] which may be used are independent is confirmed by provisions of article 2(13)(b) and (c) of Regulation 3017/79, which merely state the various possibilities for calculating the dumping margin without imposing any requirement that the methods chosen for calculating the normal value and that export price should be similar or identical."[3]

The Court also concurred with the Advocate General in concluding that the choice between the different methods of calculation specified in article 2(13) required an appraisal of complex economic issues and, as such, its review was limited to ensuring that the procedural rules had been complied with, the facts accurately stated and whether there had been a manifest error of appraisal or misuse of powers. The Court was of the opinion that the applicants' argument was almost tantamount to alleging that the Community authorities had made a manifestly incorrect appraisal of the facts in adopting a method of assessing the dumping margin which took into account only a proportion of the transactions on the export market[4].

---

1.   See Case 240/84 *NTN Toyo Bearing Co Ltd v EC Council* [1987] ECR 1809 at 1844.
2.   Ibid.
3.   See Case 240/84 *NTN Toyo Bearing Co Ltd v EC Council* [1987] ECR at 1853, para 14 of judgment.
4.   See Case 255/84 *Nachi Fujikoshi v EC Council* [1987] ECR 1861 at 1890, para 22 of judgment.

It was of the view that such a line of argument could not be accepted. It held that :

> "the transaction-by-transaction method used by the Commission, like the weighted average method, takes account of all sales and quantities sold for export and involves establishment or weighted average of export prices. This method differs from weighted average method inasmuch as prices above the normal value are artificially reduced to the level of normal value and then included in the calculation of the weighted average of all the prices charged on the export market."[1]

The Court concluded that the EC Commission did not commit any manifest error in its appraisal of the facts by applying the transaction-by-transaction method to calculate the dumping margin. It agreed with the Advocate General that this was the only method applicable of dealing with certain manoeuvres in which dumping was disguised by charging different prices. It noted that the application of the weighted average method in such a situation would not meet the purpose of the anti-dumping proceedings, since that method would mask sales at dumping prices by those at what were known as "negative" dumping prices and would thus in no way eliminate the injury suffered by the Community industry concerned[2].

6.10.2   The determination of injury

The Court has held that article 4 of the basic regulation confers a wide discretionary power on the EC Commission as regards the period to be taken into consideration for the purpose of determining injury[3]. Generally speaking, the information regarding injury caused to Community industry will be provided by the complainant industry. As a result, this information will for the most part be subject to the rules relating to confidential information in terms of article 8 of Regulation 2423/88[4]. This was noted by Advocate General Warner in the first *Japanese Ballbearing* cases. He stated that the findings of injury and of its cause were necessarily based in large part on the confidential information supplied by the European industry which the EC Commission was precluded from disclosing. The findings of injury like the determination of dumping was, according to the Advocate General, based on the assessment by the institutions of complex economic

---

1.   Case 255/84 *Nachi Fujikoshi v EC Council* [1987] ECR 1861 at para 23 of judgment.
2.   Case 240/84 *NTN Toyo Bearing Co Ltd v EC Council* [1987] ECR 1809 at 1855, paras 23/24 of judgment.
3.   See Case 121/86 *Epicheiriseon Metalleftikon Viomichanikon Kai Naftiliakon and Ors v EC Council* [1989] ECR 3919 at 3952, para 20 of judgment. The Court noted that the Commission had taken into consideration a period of approximately four years, in conformity with Community practice in this area. See also Case 129/86 *Greece v EC Council* [1987] ECR 1189. See also Case 69/89 *Nakajima All Precision Co Ltd v EC Council* (1991) Transcript 7 May. The Court rejected Nakajima's argument that the Commission was wrong to include 1983 in its examination of injury given that the investigation into dumping covered the period from March 1986 to April 1987.
4.   See for example Case 69/89 *Nakajima All Precision Co Ltd v EC Council*, (1991) Transcript 7 May.

facts not readily open to judicial review. He implied that judicial review would be limited to determining whether that assessment was actuated by improper motives or on the basis of manifest error[1].

In such circumstances, the Community authorities will have a wide discretion in determining whether injury has been caused to Community industry as a result of dumping. This was borne out by the decision in the *First Allied* case[2]. The applicants challenged a Commission regulation imposing a provisional duty after undertakings had been withdrawn. They contended that this had been adopted on the basis of incorrect information. In particular, the EC Commission had failed to take into account three new facts namely, a decision of the French government on production and marketing of fertiliser, the rise in the value of the dollar and the decline in imports of nitrogen fertiliser into the Community, which would have had a bearing on the assessment of injury to Community industry.

The Court concluded that the arguments put forward by the applicants were not of such a nature as to constitute proof that the EC Commission committed a number of manifest errors in its assessment of whether injury was caused to the European fertiliser industry as a result of dumping. In particular, with reference to those arguments regarding the rise in the value of the dollar and decline in imports, the Court held that :

> "although it is true that the volume of imports of nitrogen solution fertiliser originating in the United States into the Community fell in 1981-82, imports of that product increased substantially in the first quarter of 1982, in spite of the increase in the value of the dollar. It follows that this factor has not had the effect of compensating for injury caused to European producers."[3]

In *Neotype Techmashexport v EC Commission and EC Council*[4], the applicants disputed the manner in which the EC Council determined injury including inter alia that there could be no injury owing to the fact that the number of electric motors produced in the Community increased as compared with the market share of the state trading countries which decreased.

1.   See footnote 2, p244.
2.   Joined Cases 239 and 275/82 *Allied Corporation v EC Commission* [1984] ECR 1005.
3.   Ibid at 1035, para 29 of judgment.
4.   Joined Cases 305/86 and 160/87 *Neotype Techmashexport v EC Commission and EC Council* [1990] ECR I 2945. See also Joined Cases 304/86 and 185/87 *ENITAL v EC Commission* [1990] ECR 2939; Joined Cases 320/86 and 186/87 *Stanko France v EC Commission and EC Council* [1990] ECR 3013, Case 157/87 *Electroimpex v EC Council* [1990] ECR 3021.

As regards reduction in market share for imported electric motors, the Court observed :

"in accordance with article 4(2) of Regulation 2176/84, the examination of injury must take account of a whole series of factors and no single factor can in itself be decisive."[1]

In this respect, it noted that whilst the market share of the imports decreased, the EC Council made a determination of injury in accordance with several factors set out in article 4(2) of Regulation 2176/84. In particular, the resale prices of imported electric motors significantly undercut the cost and selling prices of the Community producers; Community producers had sustained operating losses of between 2 and 25% of the cost price; and employment directly related to the production of electric motors continued to decline[2].

Having regard to these factors, the Court held that the EC Council, in the absence of a challenge to the accuracy of the determination of injury, could not be said to have exceeded the limits of its discretionary power by concluding that Community producers had suffered significant injuries caused by the dumped imports in question, in spite of a reduction in the exporters' market share[3].

In a number of *Plain Paper Photocopier* cases[4], the applicants challenged the Community authorities' analysis of the factors used in determining injury and maintained that the Community producers did not suffer injury. In their view, the injury, as determined by the Community authorities, did not come about as a result of the imports in question, but from the policy followed by the Community producers and the inferiority of their machines as compared with the Japanese products.

The Court referred to articles 4(1) and 4(2) of Regulation 2176/84 and in concurring with Advocate General Mischo held that :

"It is therefore in the exercise of their discretion that the institutions are called upon to analyse the said factors and to use such of the assessment factors

---

1.   Joined Cases 305/86 and 160/87 *Neotype Techmashexport v EC Commission and EC Council* [1990] ECR I 2945 at 3005, para 50 of judgment.
2.   Ibid, p3005 at para 51 of judgment.
3.   Ibid, p3006 at para 52 of judgment.
4.   Case 179/87 *Sharp Corporation v EC Council* [1992] 2 CMLR 415; Case 176/87 *Konishiroku Photo Industry Co Ltd v EC Council*; Case 175/87 *Matsushita Electric Industrial Co Ltd and Matsushita Electric Trading Co Ltd v EC Council*; Case 174/87 *Ricoh Co Ltd v EC Council*; Case 177/87 *Sanyo Electric Co Ltd v EC Council*, (1992) Transcripts 10 March. All the applicants made joint submissions regarding "injury".

listed for that purpose in article 4(2) as they deem to be relevant in each particular case. In the present case the institutions carried out a detailed examination of the factors mentioned in article 4(2)."[1]

It referred, in particular, to the volume of Japanese exports and the undercutting of the Community producers' prices. It observed that the Community authorities were entitled to consider that the Japanese imports prevented a more favourable development of plain paper photocopier sales and rentals by the Community producers. Furthermore, the prices of the imported products were the same as or even lower than the prices of the Community producers[2].

As far as the impact of the dumped imports on the Community industry in question was concerned, the Court noted that not only had there been a fall in the Community producers market share, but their profitability also fell[3].

Article 4(1) of Regulation 2423/88 provides that injury caused by factors other than the effects of dumping must not be attributed to the dumped imports. As a result of the Court's decision in *Extramet Industrie S.A. v EC Council*[4], the Community authorities are obliged to consider, in appropriate cases, the competitive situation on the Community market in order to discount the possibility of self inflicted injury on the part of Community industry.

Extramet maintained that the injury suffered by Péchiney, the sole producer of calcium metal in the Community, was self inflicted. In particular, its refusal to supply them meant that Extramet had to import the products from China and the USSR. The EC Council, on the other hand, argued that the alleged abuse of a dominant position on the part of Péchiney could not be considered in an anti-dumping proceeding.

The Court did not comment on the relationship between an anti-dumping proceeding on the one hand and competition policy on the other. It simply held that the Community authorities had not effectively examined the question of whether Péchiney had contributed to its injury by refusing to supply Extramet[5].

---

1.   Case 179/87 *Sharp Corporation v EC Council* [1992] 2 CMLR 415, p429 at para 46 of judgment.
2.   Ibid, p429 at paras 47 and 48 of judgment.
3.   Ibid, p429 at paras 49 of judgment.
4.   Case C-358/89 *Extramet Industrie SA v EC Council* (1992) Transcript 11 June 1992.
5.   Ibid at para 20 of judgment.

Advocate General Jacobs recognised the difficulty of reconciling recourse to anti-dumping measures with considerations of competition or anti-trust policy but accepted that cases may arise where failure to take account of competition policy considerations might lead to the adoption of anti-dumping measures which produce effects which are inconsistent with that policy[1]. He therefore considered it essential that proper account be taken of competition policy considerations when the imposition of anti-dumping duties was being considered[2].

By virtue of article 4(5) of Regulation 2423/88, the Community authorities, in considering whether injury has been caused to Community industry, may exclude those producers who are related to the exporter or importer or who are themselves importers of the allegedly dumped or subsidised product. The Court has recently held that it is for the Community authorities in the exercise of this discretion to determine by reference to all the relevant facts whether such producers should be excluded[3]. It further held that they will not exceed this discretion where they include producers that have imported certain models of the allegedly dumped product in order to present a full range of models to their customers, which was rendered impossible by the depressed prices imposed by the Japanese imports[4]. The Community authorities will also not have exceeded their discretion if they decide not to exclude a producer which had imported the dumped product if the volume of those imports was minimal in relation to the producer's entire range of products, and even if they had caused injury to the other Community producers[5].

6.10.3   The determination of Community interests

Community legislation, unlike the GATT rules or the anti-dumping laws of the Community's trading partners, permits the Community authorities when imposing anti-dumping duties to take into account Community interests. The term "interests of the Community" has not been defined and it is therefore inevitable that the Community authorities enjoy in this respect a very wide discretion. Naturally, they have, when the matter has been queried by exporters, claimed that this is an area not subject to review by the Court.

---

1. Paras 30-33 of his Opinion delivered on 8 April 1992.
2. Ibid at para 33.
3. Case 156/87 *Gestetner Holdings plc v EC Commission and EC Council* [1990] ECR 781. See also Case 179/87 *Sharp Corporation v EC Council* [1992] 2 CMLR 415; Case 176/87 *Konishiroku Photo Industry Co Ltd v EC Council*; Case 175/87 *Matsushita Electric Industrial Co Ltd and Matsushita Electric Trading Co Ltd v EC Council*; Case 174/87 *Ricoh Co Ltd v EC Council*; Case 177/87 *Sanyo Electric Co Ltd v EC Council*; (1992) Transcripts 10 March. The Court rejected the applicants argument that Rank Xerox, Océ and Olivetti should have been excluded form Community industry owing to the fact that those Community producers had links with Japanese exporters and themselves effected imports from Japan.
4. Case 156/87 *Gestetner Holdings plc v EC Commission and EC Council* ibid, at 847/8, paras 47-49 of judgment. See also, eg, Case 179/87 *Sharp Corporation v EC Council* p427 at para 34 of judgment; Case 69/89 *Nakajima All Precision Co Ltd v EC Council*, (1991) Transcript 7 May.
5. Case 156/87 *Gestetner Holdings plc v EC Commission and EC Council* ibid, at 849-850, paras 56-61 of judgment. See also, eg, Case 179/87 *Sharp Corporation v EC Council* ibid, p428 at para 38 of judgment.

In *Fediol*[1], the applicant sought to have annulled the refusal of the EC Commission to initiate anti-subsidy proceedings in respect of soya imports from Brazil. The case was concerned generally with the question of "Community interests" in relation to the initiation of proceedings.

The EC Commission did not deny that the failure to institute an anti-subsidy proceeding may affect the applicant's interests. However, the interests must be significant in that there must be a "distinct" change in the applicant's legal position. It argued that there could be no such effect in this case because protective measures were, according to their nature in law, "measures belonging exclusively in the area of commercial policy ... adopted essentially in the general economic interest". For this reason, an anti-subsidy proceeding was not intended principally to protect individuals. Furthermore, in view of the discretion vested in the EC Commission, the applicant could not be acknowledged to have a right to require the initiation of an investigation[2].

The applicant was of the view that the EC Commission's arguments were aimed at obtaining judicial recognition of a discretionary power free from control by the Court, in relation to the initiation of a compensatory proceeding. It considered that the existence of a discretionary power free from review by the Court in this respect could not be deduced from the concept of Community interest[3].

The Advocate General agreed with the applicant that it was entitled to a proper exercise of discretion free from misuse of power or a patent disregard of Community law[4]. She was of the opinion that even if the EC Commission had a discretion with regard to the initiation of proceedings, this was not free from review. In the present case, the refusal to initiate proceedings, she noted, did not relate to the interests of the Community, but rather was concerned with whether there was sufficient evidence[5].

The Court held that :

> "whilst it is true that the EC Commission, when exercising the powers assigned to it in Regulation 3017/79, is under a duty to establish objectively the facts concerning the existence of subsidisation practices and of injury caused thereby to Community undertakings, it is no less true that it has a wide discretion to

---

1.   Case 191/82 *Fediol v EC Commission* [1983] ECR 2913.
2.   Ibid at 2946-7.
3.   Ibid at 2947.
4.   Ibid at 2947.
5.   Ibid at 2948-9.

decide, in terms of the interests of the Community, any measures needed to deal with the situation which it has established."[1]

In the light of these considerations, the Court had to determine whether the applicant had the right to bring an action. It detailed at length the complainant's procedural rights under the regulation and held that :

"the complainants may not be refused the right to put before the Court any matters which would facilitate a review as to whether the EC Commission has observed the procedural guarantees granted to the complainants by Regulation 3017/79 and whether or not it has committed manifest errors in its assessments of the facts, has omitted to take into consideration any essential matters of such a nature as to give rise to a belief in the existence of subsidisation or has based the reasons for its decision on considerations amounting to misuse of powers. In that respect the Court is required to exercise its normal powers of review over a discretion granted to a public authority, even though it has no jurisdiction to intervene in the exercise of the discretion reserved to the Community authorities by the aforementioned regulation."[2]

This corresponds with the Court's understanding of its limits in the review of the Community authorities' discretion when matters of a complex and economic nature are at issue. Ultimately, the Court's review will extend to ensuring that the Community authorities have not committed a manifest error of appraisal or a misuse of powers.

In the *Second Allied* case[3], the Court had to consider those entities in the Community whose interests would be affected by the imposition of duties. The applicants contended that the interests of the Community should be interpreted as those of the Community as a whole, and not as the particular interest of certain Community producers. In particular, it argued that the interests of consumers were not examined[4]. In reply, the EC Council noted that an analysis of the interests of the Community involved a wide discretion in assessing political and economic circumstances, and the weighing up of various factors internal and external to the Community. The interests of consumers and, in particular, their long-term interests, were taken into account. Given such a discretion, the Court must limit its review to determining whether a manifest error or a misuse of power had been committed[5].

---

1.   Case 191/82 *Fediol v EC Commission* [1983] ECR 2913 at 2934-5, para 26 of judgment.
2.   Ibid at 2935, para 30 of judgment. See also Case 156/87 *Gestetner Holdings plc v EC Council* [1990] ECR 781 at para 63 of judgment.
3.   Case 53/83 *Allied Corporation v EC Council* [1985] ECR 1621.
4.   Ibid at 1651.
5.   Case 53/83 *Allied Corporation v EC Council* [1985] ECR 1621 at 1652.

The Court decided in favour of the applicants on the basis that article 13(3) of Regulation 3017/79 had been breached[1]. It did not, however, make reference to the extent to which the Court would review the exercise of discretion on the part of the Community authorities with respect to the interests of those entities which would be affected by the imposition of duties. It stated that it did not relieve the Community authorities of their obligation to state the reasons why, in their view, intervention was necessary[2].

In a number of the recent *Plain Paper Photocopier* cases[3], the Court was asked to consider whether the Community authorities had committed a manifest error in their appraisal of Community interests.

In *Sharp v EC Council*[4], the applicants maintained that the evaluation of Community interests by the Community authorities was distorted by the fact that they regarded a number of the Community producers which were dependent upon and benefited from the dumped imports as belonging to the producers making up Community industry. Secondly, they did not take into account the limited nature of Community production in the small photocopier sector. Furthermore, the Community authorities attached more importance to the interests of the Community producers than those of the OEM importers, such as Gestetner and Agfa-Gevaert, and in protecting those producers it paid no regard to the prices to be paid by consumers.

The Court, relying on its decision in *Gestetner*[5], held that the Community authorities had not committed any error of appraisal in their determination of the Community interests. More particularly, the Court observed that according to the Community authorities :

"In the absence of anti-dumping duties it would be doubtful whether an independent Community PPC industry could survive although it is necessary in order to maintain and develop the technique required in manufacturing reprographic equipment and in order to preserve a large number of jobs. That concern arose in particular from the take-over, in the course of the investigation, of the business of one of the Community producers by a Japanese manufacturer. The institutions therefore took the view that the need to protect Community industry was more important than the need to protect the

---

1.   Ibid at p1659, para 19 of judgment.
2.   Ibid at 1634.
3.   Case 179/87 *Sharp Corporation v EC Council* [1992] 2 CMLR 415; Case 176/87 *Konishiroku Photo Industry Co Ltd v EC Council*; Case 175/87 *Matsushita Electric Industrial Co Ltd and Matsushita Electric Trading Co Ltd v EC Council*; Case 174/87 *Ricoh Co Ltd v EC Council*; Case 177/87 *Sanyo Electric Co Ltd v EC Council*, (1992) Transcripts 10 March. All the applicants made joint submission regarding "the Community interest."
4.   Case 179/87 *Sharp Corporation v EC Council* [1992] 2 CMLR 415.
5.   Case 156/87 *Gestetner Holdings Plc v EC Council* [1990] ECR 781 at 843, para 63 of judgment.

immediate interests of consumers, as is explained in paragraph 99 of the preamble to the contested regulation, and the need to protect importers."[1]

The *First Allied* case[2], was concerned more particularly with the question of discretion in relation to the "interests of the Community" in imposing provisional duties where an undertaking had been removed. The EC Commission argued that the term "interests of the Community" was imprecise and therefore was not amenable to judicial review. The Advocate General agreed that the EC Commission enjoyed a wide discretion in deciding whether to impose provisional duties under article 10 of Regulation 3017/79. This discretion, the Advocate General noted, became even wider where an undertaking had been removed under article 10(6). He concluded and the Court concurred by holding that the authorities were under no obligation to attach any decisive significance to the new facts submitted by the applicants[3].

The discretion afforded to the Community authorities by the term "interests of the Community" is sufficiently wide to permit them to depart from previous practice. In *Canon v EC Council*[4], the applicants argued that in assessing injury to Community industry, the authorities took no account of whether the European producers were efficient. In previous cases it had calculated the level of duty needed to remedy injury by reference not to *all* producers, but in relation to the most efficient. However, in the present case, it had departed from this practice by basing its injury finding on the average between the efficient and the inefficient producers.

Advocate General Slynn rejected this argument. He argued that, where there was injury caused by dumping, the regulation stated that duties could be imposed if it was in the interests of the Community. He noted that the concept was not defined with the result that this gave the Community authorities a wide discretion. Given this, the authorities were not bound to follow previous practice[5]. The Court made no reference to the extent of the authorities' discretion but held nevertheless that :

> "the fact that a Community producer is facing difficulties attributable in part to causes other than the dumping is not a reason for depriving that producer of all protection against the injury caused by the dumping."[6]

---

1. Case 179/87 *Sharp Corporation v EC Council* [1992] 2 CMLR 415 at 431, para 59 of judgment.
2. Case 239 and 275/82 *Allied Corporation v EC Commission* [1984] ECR 1005.
3. Ibid at 1048.
4. Joined Cases 277 and 300/85 *Canon Inc v EC Council* [1988] ECR 5731.
5. Joined Cases 277 and 300/85 *Canon Inc v EC Council* [1988] ECR 5731 at 5790-5791.
6. Ibid at 5809, para 63 of judgment.

6.10.4 The determination of an anti-dumping duty and refusal to accept undertakings

6.10.4.1 The determination of an anti-dumping duty

The method of fixing anti-dumping duties is laid down in article 13 of Regulation 2423/88. It provides that such duties are to be imposed by regulation and that "such regulation shall indicate in particular the amount and the type of duty imposed". The Court has held that those provisions leave the Community authorities with a wide discretionary power to determine, in each case, the "type of duty" which is such as to afford the most effective defence against dumped imports[1].

The matter has again been considered by the Court in *Neotype Technomeshexport v EC Commission and EC Council*[2]. The applicants argued that the basic regulation then in force, namely Regulation 2176/84, did not give the EC Council power to impose an anti-dumping duty which varied according to the price at which the imported product was resold for the first time to an independent buyer.

The EC Council had considered it appropriate to fix the amount of the anti-dumping duty as the difference between the minimum price and the customs value of the imported product as determined by article 6 of Regulation 1224/80.

The EC Council maintained that they were at liberty to impose anti-dumping measures in the form which appeared to them most appropriate in order to eliminate injury caused by dumping. In so doing, they frequently made use of a variable duty calculated according to the difference between a minimum price and the export price (or price paid by the first independent purchaser).

Advocate General Van Gerven[3] noted that neither Regulation 2176/84 nor the GATT dumping provisions stipulated the form to be taken by anti-dumping measures. The Court also observed that :

"Under article 13(2) of Regulation 2176/84 regulations imposing an anti-dumping duty are to indicate in particular the amount and type of duty imposed, together with certain other matters. Accordingly, the institutions are

---

1. Case 189/88 *Cartorobica SpA v Ministero delle Finanze dello State* [1990] ECR 1269 at 1298 paras 24 and 25 of judgment.
2. Joined Cases 305/86 and 160/87 *Neotype Technomeshexport v EC Commission and EC Council* [1990] I ECR 2945.
3. Joined Cases 305/86 and 160/87 *Neotype Technomeshexport v EC Commission and EC Council* [1990] I ECR 2945 at p2988.

free to choose, within the limits of their margin of discretion, between the different types of duty."[1]

The Court held that the EC Council had not exceeded the limits of its discretionary power. In particular, it noted that a variable duty was generally more favourable to the traders in question given that it makes it possible to avoid anti-dumping duties, provided that the imports are effected at prices above the minimum price fixed[2].

In *Nashua Corporation v EC Council and EC Commission*, the applicant was of the view that the same method used for calculating the dumping margin should be used to calculate the anti-dumping duty to be imposed. The Court held that :

"For the calculation of the anti-dumping duty, article 13(3) of Regulation 2176/84 merely requires the institutions not to exceed either the dumping margin established or the extent of the injury, if a lower duty than the dumping margin would be adequate to remove the injury. The institutions thus enjoy a wide discretion in choosing the method for calculating the duty and are not obliged to adopt for that purpose the same method as that used for determining the dumping margin."[3]

In a number of the other *Plain Paper Photocopier* cases[4], the applicants argued that the Community authorities were in breach of article 13(3) of Regulation 2176/84 in fixing the level of the definitive duties.

In *Sharp v EC Council*[5], the applicant argued inter alia that the EC Commission was wrong to consider that a profit margin of 12% was necessary to ensure for the Community producers a reasonable profit or return on the sale of photocopiers. They maintained that this margin was excessive given that the profits on small photocopiers was lower than the profits on plain paper photocopiers as a whole.

---

1.   Ibid, p3007 at para 58 of judgment.
2.   Ibid, p3007 at para 60 of judgment.
3.   Cases 133 and 150/87 *Nashua Corpn v EC Commission* [1990] ECR 719 at 777, para 36 of judgment.
4.   Case 179/87 *Sharp Corporation v EC Council* [1992] 2 CMLR 415; Case 176/87 *Konishiroku Photo Industry Co Ltd v EC Council*; Case 175/89 *Matsushita Electric Industrial Co Ltd and Matsushita Electric Trading Co Ltd v EC Council*; Case 174/87 *Ricoh Co Ltd v EC Council*; Case 177/87 *Sanyo Electric Co Ltd v EC Council*, (1992) Transcripts 10 March. All the applicants made joint submissions regarding the calculation of the anti-dumping duty.
5.   Case 179/87 *Sharp Corporation v EC Council* [1992] 2 CMLR 415.

The Court rejected this argument as it appeared neither from the documents before the Court nor from the argument at the hearing that the Community authorities had exercised their discretion incorrectly[1]. More particularly, it observed that the Community authorities had chosen this margin so as to allow the Community producers as a whole a reasonable return commensurate with the risk represented by investing in the development of new products. In these circumstances, they considered that it was inappropriate to take into account the profits made on supplies or other operations related to photocopiers[2].

6.10.4.2 Refusal to accept undertakings

The Community authorities when terminating proceedings, may accept price undertakings rather than impose duties. The reasons for adopting such a course of action are self-explanatory. They allow a controversial situation to be settled amicably, they save time and, above all, are flexible. The acceptance of price undertakings are, however, completely at the discretion of the EC Commission. Of all the categories discussed to date, this undoubtedly is the one category where the Court will be slow to review the exercise of that discretion.

In the *Mini Ballbearing* cases, some of the applicants[3] complained that the Community authorities failed to take into account the undertakings offered. Advocate General Mancini noted that the EC Commission was required, in the exercise of the powers conferred upon it by Regulation 3017/79, to establish in an objective manner whether there was evidence of dumping practised by undertakings from outside the Community. The Court, however, had held in *Fediol* that it was no less true that the EC Commission had a very wide discretion to select in terms of the interests of the Community the most appropriate measures for dealing with the situation which it had established[4]. In these circumstances, he concluded that it was for the EC Commission alone to consider whether a price undertaking would have been sufficient to safeguard the Community's economic interests. The Court noted that there was no provision in Regulation 3017/79 which compelled the Community authorities to accept price undertakings offered[5]. It was clear from article 10 of Regulation 3017/79 that it was for the Community authorities in the exercise of their discretionary power to determine whether such undertakings were acceptable[6].

---

1.   Ibid, p432 at para 64 of judgment.
2.   Ibid, p431-432 at para 63 of judgment.
3.   Case 240/84 *NTN Toyo Bearing Co Ltd v EC Council*, [1987] ECR 1809; Case 256/84 *Koyo Seiko Co Ltd v EC Council* [1985] ECR 1351; Case 258/84 *Nippon Seiko KK v EC Council* [1987] ECR 1923; and Case 260/84 *Minebea Co Ltd v EC Council* [1987] ECR 1975.
4.   Ibid at 1846-7.
5.   See Case 258/84 *Nippon Seiko KK v EC Council* [1987] ECR 1923 at 1971, para 51 of judgment; Case 260/84 *Minebea Co Ltd v EC Council* [1987] ECR 1975 at 2011, para 48 of judgment.
6.   Case 260/84 *Minebea Co Ltd v EC Council*, above.

In *Technointorg v EC Commission and EC Council*[1], the applicants had also offered price undertakings which the EC Commission refused on the basis that these were unacceptable. The Court followed its decision in the *Mini Ballbearing* cases by holding that no provision of Regulation 2176/84 compelled the Community authorities to accept price undertakings. On the contrary, it followed on from article 10 of Regulation 2176/84 that it was for the Community authorities to assess whether undertakings offered were acceptable[2]. The Court concluded that, by refusing to accept the undertakings offered by Technointorg, the EC Commission had not exceeded the limits of its discretion[3].

The above decisions related to undertakings offered by exporters. In *Nashua Corporation v EC Commission and EC Council*[4] the Court had to consider the refusal by the EC Commission to accept an undertaking from the applicant, an original equipment manufacturer (OEM). Because the products under consideration were purchased for importation into the Community, Nashua was regarded as an importer. The Court noted that the practice of the Community authorities in not accepting undertakings from importers was based not only on article 10 of Regulation 2176/84 but also on article 7 of the GATT Anti-dumping Code.

The Court held that the Community authorities had not exceeded their discretion in refusing to accept the undertakings offered. This was justified on two grounds :

> "First, acceptance of the undertaking offered by an importer would have the effect of encouraging him to continue to obtain supplies from outside the Community at dumped prices. Secondly, other importers would have to receive the same treatment and this, on account of the large number of companies involved, would make it extremely difficult to monitor compliance with the undertakings."[5]

6.10.5   Evaluation
Inevitably, as more and more undertakings from third countries which manufacture "high-tech" consumer goods are investigated for dumping, the Court is drawn into the dilemma of determining the extent of its review on the exercise of the powers which confer a margin of discretion on the Community authorities.

---

1.   Joined Cases 294/86 and 77/87 *Technointorg v EC Commission and EC Council* [1988] ECR 6077.
2.   Ibid at 6117, para 45 of judgment.
3.   Ibid, para 48 of judgment.
4.   Joined Cases 133 and 150/87 *Nashua Corpn v EC Commission* [1990] ECR 719.
5.   Ibid, para 46 of judgment.

The Court has, from the inception of the European Economic Community, held that the exercise of powers by the Community authorities which confer on them a wide discretion should be subject to its review. As the findings of the Community authorities are of a highly complex and technical nature in anti-dumping cases, the Court has adopted the general principle that its review is limited to verifying whether the relevant procedural rules have been complied with, whether the reasons for the decision are adequate, whether the facts on which the choice is made are accurate, and most importantly, whether there has been a manifest error of appraisal or a misuse of powers. The onus of proving the latter lies fairly and squarely on the shoulders of the applicant. To date, this has proved to be an insurmountable hurdle to discharge.

The Court has held that the Community authorities have not exceeded the margin of discretion by attempting to construct a normal value which is as close as possible to that which would have been established if there had been sufficient sales in the ordinary course of trade on the domestic market. Likewise, it has approved the inclusion of a profit margin in the constructed normal value which reflected profits realised by the sales of the products in the same general category. Where a sales company operates as a sales department of a parent company, the Court has condoned the practice of the Community authorities of including their selling expenses when constructing normal value. Where state trading countries are concerned, the Court will, in the exercise of its review, ensure that the Community authorities have taken account of all relevant considerations in selecting an analogue country which allows normal value to be established in "an appropriate and reasonable manner".

When domestic and export prices vary appreciably, the Court has approved the practice of the Community authorities to assess export prices on a transaction-by-transaction basis in order to avoid negative dumping. It has held that the choice of method used to establish the dumping margin does not have to be the same in assessing normal value and export price.

Owing to the fact that the majority of information on which the Community authorities base their findings of injury is confidential, the Court is reluctant to review these findings. It appears to be the case that the Court considers that the protection of Community industry is paramount. It has held that the Community authorities had not exceeded their discretion by not excluding Community producers when considering the effects of the dumped products on Community industry, where those producers had imported the dumped product. This will be the case where the Community authorities show that this was done in order to enable a producer to complete its range of models, or where the imports were minimal even though this caused injury to the other Community producers. On the other hand, the Community authorities are obliged to take into account the competitive situation on the Community market so as to ensure that the injury caused to Community industry is not self inflicted.

It has also held that the term "interests of the Community" confers on the Community authorities a sufficiently wide discretion to enable them to decide what are the appropriate measures required to deal with a given situation. This discretion will be even wider when an applicant has violated a price undertaking. However, the Court will exercise its review in the exercise of that discretion where the procedural rights of an interested party are at issue.

The Court has held that the choice of duty to be imposed is at the discretion of the Community authorities. With respect to the acceptance or refusal of an undertaking, the Court has noted that, generally speaking, these are subject to more practical considerations and for this reason, it is submitted that the Court will be less likely, if at all, to review the exercise of the EC Commission powers in this respect.

6.11   Misuse of powers

This ground of illegality, because of the difficulties in proving it, has rarely been relied upon by an applicant in the cases that have come before the Court.

In *Brother Industries Ltd v EC Council*[1], the applicants argued that the margin of profit (71.18%) included in the normal value of the three Brother models for which normal value was constructed was excessively high and was wrongly determined. They contended that this constituted inter alia a misuse of powers[2]. Advocate General Slynn, whilst agreeing that the selling, general and administrative expenses were miscalculated, held the applicant had adduced no proof of any misuse of powers and he accordingly rejected the allegation[3].

Likewise in *Sermes v Directeur des Services des douanes de Strasbourg*[4], the Court rejected the applicants' argument that the Council regulation imposing a definitive duty on multiphase electric motors was vitiated by a misuse of powers inasmuch as

1.   Case 250/85 *Brother Industries Ltd v EC Council* [1988] ECR 5683.
2.   Ibid at 5693.
3.   Case 250/85 *Brother Industries Ltd v EC Council* [1988] ECR 5683 at 5674-5.
4.   Case 323/88 *Sermes SA v Directeur des Services des douanes de Strasbourg* [1990] I ECR 3027.

the EC Council allowed itself to be guided by interests of a Community industry and not by the Community interest. The Court noted that :

> "A decision is vitiated by a misuse of powers only if it appears, on the basis of objective, relevant and consistent indications, to have been adopted in order to achieve purposes other than those for which it was intended (Judgment in Case C-198/87 *Kerzmann v Court of Auditors* [1989] ECR 2083 - see summary of Judgment, paragraph 2)."[1]

It observed that the EC Council had set out its reasons in the contested regulation which led it to take the view that the interests of the Community required the adoption of protective measures. At the same time, the applicants, in challenging the existence of a Community interest, merely made assertions without substantiating them[2].

In *Nippon Seiko KK v EC Council*[3], the applicants alleged that the EC Council, by imposing definitive duties as a sanction to compel compliance with the price undertakings given, had misused their powers[4]. Without making an express reference as to whether the EC Council had misused its power, the Court held that by virtue of the anti-dumping regulation it was unlawful for one and the same anti-dumping procedure to be terminated on the one hand by the EC Commission's acceptance of a price undertaking and on the other by imposition by the EC Council of a definitive anti-dumping duty[5].

In *Import Standard Office v EC Council*[6], the applicants argued that the order to definitively collect the provisional duties constituted a misuse of powers because its real purpose was to pave the way for the adoption by the EC Council of definitive duties[7]. Advocate General Warner was of the opinion that this argument was misconceived, first because there was no evidence that this was the EC Council's real purpose, and second because the point was founded on an erroneous premise. He noted that there was nothing in the basic regulation which precluded the EC Council from ordering the definitive collection of the provisional duties. He concluded that it was open for the EC Council, while assenting to the acceptance of the undertaking, to decide the fate of the provisional duty[8].

---

1.   Ibid, p3054 at para 33 of judgment.
2.   Ibid, p3054 paras 34 and 35 of judgment.
3.   Case 119/77 *Nippon Seiko KK and Ors v EC Council* [1979] ECR 1303.
4.   Ibid at 1317.
5.   Ibid at 1329.
6.   Case 118/77 *Import Standard Office (ISO) v EC Council* [1979] ECR 1277.
7.   Case 118/77 *Import Standard Office (ISO) v EC Council* [1979] ECR 1277 at 1289.
8.   Ibid at 1250.

CONCLUSION

The system of judicial remedies in the European Community and article 173 in particular, provide the Court with the power to review the legality of acts of the Community authorities. It is undoubtedly the case that the Community authorities enjoy a large measure of discretion in the exercise of their powers under the legislation governing anti-dumping and other safeguard measures. In this respect it is important that the Community authorities which apply the law are also bound by it. For this very reason, the Court has stated that it has the power to review the exercise of the powers which confer a margin of discretion on the Community authorities, albeit in a limited manner. By so doing the Court is able to exercise an element of control over them and so ensure that the rule of law is observed.

The right of a natural or legal person to challenge an act of the institutions and, in particular, acts of general application depends on whether they have the necessary locus standi to do so. The Court has adopted a distinct and separate approach to the admissibility of actions involving anti-dumping and other safeguard measures. Its reason for doing so was to allow interested parties, who would otherwise not have had the opportunity, to challenge the legality of Community acts imposing anti-dumping and other safeguard measures.

The test applied by the Court to determine whether an applicant has sufficient locus standi to challenge measures imposing anti-dumping duties is whether the economic agent in question was concerned by the findings relating to the existence of dumping complained of. Generally speaking, exporters or producers, associated importers and, in limited circumstances, original equipment manufacturers (OEMs) will have the requisite locus standi. Exporters or producers can normally establish that they were identified in the measure adopted or that they were concerned by the preliminary investigations. Associated importers and OEMs will have locus standi where they can establish that their sales prices have been used in the determination of dumping. The Court has, however, extended the scope of locus standi where anti-dumping and other safeguard measures are involved. In a number of decisions, it was prepared to confer locus standi on other interested parties, notably complainants, because they had certain procedural rights which were guaranteed by the legislation in question. This was all the more important where those parties would otherwise not have had locus standi.

Independent importers as a general rule will not have locus standi as they will neither be identified in the measure nor have specific findings made about them. In special circumstances, the Court is prepared to hold that independent importers have locus standi providing that they can establish that they are affected by particular attributes which differentiate them from all other persons. Otherwise, they will be required to challenge the collection of anti-dumping duties in the national courts. It is submitted that there is no good reason why independent importers should be differentiated from those other undertakings cited above. Arguably, a more appropriate and fairer test would be one based on the extent to which such importers were involved in the investigation.

The EC Commission and the EC Council have recognised the fact that private parties should have locus standi, and rightly so, given that the Community authorities should be the proper defendants in any action challenging Community acts imposing anti-dumping and other safeguard measures. The alternative is an action by the importers who bear the duties in the Member States and ultimately a ruling by the Court in terms of article 177, 1st para, point (b) of the EEC Treaty.

Prior to the final judgment of the Court, parties often attempt to obtain an award of interim measures. Certain conditions have to be fulfilled before the Court will make such an award. An applicant will have to establish a prima facie case and must show to the satisfaction of the Court that the measures are urgent. They will be urgent if "serious and irreparable" damage is being caused to the applicant and if the balance of interests point in their favour in the sense that the grant of interim measures would not cause appreciable injury to Community industry.

To date there have been few successful cases. What is not in doubt is that an applicant would not be successful in having the effects of a regulation imposing either provisional or definitive anti-dumping duties suspended, even if bank guarantees were offered pending the outcome of the main application. It is submitted that these general propositions would be equally applicable to an application for interim measures involving other safeguard measures.

The grounds of illegality in article 173 upon which the Court will review the merits of a case involving anti-dumping and other safeguard measures, are lack of competence, misuse of powers, infringement of an essential procedural requirement and an infringement of the Treaty or a rule relating to its application. An applicant will not usually allege lack of competence or misuse of powers as it would be required to discharge a heavy onus of proof in respect of each of these grounds of illegality. It is more often the case that an applicant will rely on allegations relating to a breach of an essential procedural requirement or an infringement of the Treaty or a rule relating to its application.

A breach of an essential procedural requirement as a ground of illegality is aimed at ensuring that an applicant's rights of defence are protected and that it is made fully aware of the reasons why the particular decision was taken. The Court has stated that it will ensure that an applicant's right to a defence of his interests is protected and, in particular, it is a fundamental principle that an applicant is entitled to a fair hearing. This duty will be discharged according to the Court where the Community authorities provide the applicant with sufficient information to allow it to present a case. At the same time, the right to examine all the information has to be balanced with the duty not to disclose confidential information, otherwise undertakings fearing that their business secrets may be disclosed will not co-operate. It is difficult to envisage under the present rules how further information could be disclosed other than by some form of confidentiality bond between lawyers like the system that exists in the United States.

The Community authorities are also under an obligation to provide a statement of reasons for their decisions so as to enable the applicant to defend its rights and allow the Court to exercise its supervisory jurisdiction. This obligation, like the obligation to provide information, has to be reconciled with the duty not to disclose confidential information. The Court will take into account the nature of the measure in question, the power exercised and the extent to which the applicant has co-operated with the authorities in deciding whether the statement of reasons are sufficient. It is fair to say that the EC Commission and the EC Council regulations are now more detailed, and for the most part sufficiently reasoned, as a result of the Court's case law and new legislation. This is to be welcomed and encouraged. The more transparent the Community acts imposing anti-dumping duties and other safeguard measures are, the less likely it is that affected parties will object on the grounds of insufficient reasoning.

By far the most important ground of illegality is that relating to an infringement of the Treaty or a rule relating to its application. In exercising its power of review based on this ground, the Court has had to consider the application of the general principles common to the laws of the Member States, which are now an important part of its jurisprudence.

The applicants have on a number of occasions invoked the principle of non-discrimination. This principle is aimed at ensuring that persons in like or identical situations are treated equally and is a question of fact to be decided in each case. It is submitted, however, that even if an applicant can show that there has been discrimination where the duties have been imposed as a result of findings correctly made, the Court will not necessarily annul the measure in question.

Where the Community authorities have departed from previous practice and, in particular, in the calculation of dumping, the Court has held that traders cannot claim to have a legitimate expectation that the means originally chosen will be maintained, since these may be altered by the Community authorities in the exercise of their powers. Furthermore, the Court has held that the failure by the Community authorities to explain or provide in advance the criteria which they intend to apply in a given case when imposing a provisional or definitive duty does not constitute a breach of the principle of legal certainty.

Where the Community authorities have breached the principle of proportionality, ie that the means used in a given situation must be proportionate to the end to be achieved, the Court will annul the measure in question or the offending part of it. In particular, when a provision in the legislation allows for a lesser duty to be applied and if such a lesser duty is sufficient in the circumstances to remove the injury, failure to do so will mean that the measure in question or parts thereof will be annulled. Such a principle is important given that the aim of the anti-dumping duties or other safeguard measure is to remove the injury to Community industry but not such that the exporter in question is discriminated against vis-à-vis other exporters.

Occasionally, an applicant may allege that the powers exercised by the Community authorities were not in conformity with the GATT rules. This invariably raises the question of whether provisions of international agreements, and in particular the GATT, are directly effective. The Court has held that the Community is bound by the GATT and has emphasised that there is an obligation on the Community to ensure that its provisions are observed in relations with non-Member States which are parties to the GATT. Until recently, the Court has not been prepared to hold that the provisions of the GATT are directly effective. In the third *Fediol* case it was held that the GATT provisions are directly effective in relation to the New Commercial Policy Instrument. This decision is to be welcomed.

Because investigations associated with anti-dumping measures are of a highly complex and technical nature, the Community authorities are endowed with a wide margin of discretion in the exercise of their powers. The Court has from the inception of the European Economic Community held that the exercise of powers by the Community authorities which confer on them a wide discretion should be subject to its review. It has, in relation to anti-dumping and other safeguard measures, adopted the general principle that its review is limited to verifying whether the relevant procedural rules have been complied with, whether the reasons for the decision are adequate, whether the facts on which the choice is made are accurate and, most importantly, whether there has been a manifest error of appraisal or misuse of powers.

The Court has held that the Community authorities did not exceed their powers when they constructed a normal value which was as close as possible to that which would have been established if there had been sufficient sales on the domestic market. Likewise it has approved the inclusion of a profit margin in the constructed normal value which reflected the profit realised by the sales of the product in the same general category on the domestic market. Where a sales company operates as a sales department of a parent company, the Court has condoned the practice of the Community authorities to include the sales company's selling expenses when constructing normal value.

In constructing the dumping margin, the Court has approved the practice of assessing the export price when these vary by the transaction-by-transaction method in order to avoid negative dumping. The authorities, in determining the dumping margin, do not have to use the same method in assessing normal value and export price. The choice of method is within the authorities' discretion and, by choosing a method corresponding to a particular situation, this discretion had not been exceeded.

The Court considers the protection of Community industry as paramount. Where a complainant industry has imported the dumped product, the Community authorities may exclude such producers. In a recent number of cases, the Community authorities did not exclude such Community producers because either the producer imported the dumped product in order to complete its range of models or these imports were minimal even though they caused injury to the other Community producers.

It has also held that the term "interests of the Community" confers on the Community authorities a sufficiently wide discretion to enable them to decide what measures are appropriate to deal with a given situation. This discretion will be even wider when an applicant has violated a price undertaking. The Court will, however, exercise its review in the exercise of that discretion where the procedural rights of an interested party are in issue. The decision to accept or refuse an undertaking is one subject to practical considerations. For this reason, the Court will be less likely, if at all, to review the exercise of the EC Commission's powers in this respect.

Owing to economic and political pressures and, more importantly, to the size of the task and the length of time involved, the Court is unwilling to evaluate the factual assessment upon which the Community authorities have imposed anti-dumping or other safeguard measures.

The Court has proposed that the jurisdiction of the Court of First Instance be extended to all direct actions brought by individuals. For the most part the EC Commission is in favour, given that such a transfer of jurisdiction would allow the Court to concentrate on its primary role of interpreting Community law for the national courts. It is not in favour of extending the jurisdiction of the Court of First Instance where the review of anti-dumping measures is involved, given that a second tier to the judicial system would render the decision-making process even more cumbersome.

In this respect, the EC Commission has proposed a reform to the administrative procedure by reducing it to one stage, ie it would have the power to impose both provisional and definitive duties. Such a move, it contends, would alleviate its fears regarding the transfer of jurisdiction. The EC Commission has also suggested that the imposition of duties would be subject to prior consultation with the Member States in the form of the Anti-dumping Committee. Such a proposal would, it is submitted, allay any political obstacles to such a change. Arguably, given the technical and complex nature of anti-dumping investigations, the room for political intervention is very limited.

Such a change is to be welcomed. At the same time the jurisdiction of the Court of First Instance should be extended to cover the review of anti-dumping and other safeguard measures. This would mean, it is submitted, that a review of the Community authorities' decisions would be given greater consideration and scrutiny.

APPENDICES

APPENDIX 1

EXCERPTS FROM THE GENERAL AGREEMENT ON TARIFFS AND TRADE

Article VI

Anti-dumping and Countervailing Duties

1.   The contracting parties recognise that dumping, by which products of one country are introduced into the commerce of another country at less than the normal value of the products, is to be condemned if it causes or threatens material injury to an established industry in the territory of a contracting party or materially retards the establishment of a domestic industry. For the purposes of this Article, a product is to be considered as being introduced into the commerce of an importing country at less than its normal value, if the price of the product exported from one country to another

- (a)   is less than the comparable price, in the ordinary course of trade, for the like product when destined for consumption in the exporting country, or,

- (b)   in the absence of such domestic price, is less than either
    - (i)   the highest comparable price for the like product for export to any third country in the ordinary course of trade or
    - (ii) the cost of production of the product in the country of origin plus a reasonable addition for selling cost and profit.

Due allowance shall be made in each case for differences in conditions and terms of sale, for differences in taxation, and for other differences affecting price comparability.

2.   In order to offset or prevent dumping, a contracting party may levy on any dumped product an anti-dumping duty not greater in amount than the margin of dumping in respect of such product. For the purposes of this Article, the margin of dumping is the price difference determined in accordance with the provisions of paragraph 1.

3.   No countervailing duty shall be levied on any product of the territory of any contracting party imported into the territory of another contracting party in excess of an amount equal to the estimated bounty or subsidy determined to have been granted, directly or indirectly, on the manufacture, production or export of such product in the country of origin or exportation, including any special subsidy to the transportation of a particular product. The term "countervailing duty" shall be understood to mean a special duty levied for the purpose of offsetting any bounty or

subsidy bestowed, directly or indirectly, upon the manufacture, production or export of any merchandise.

4 . No product of the territory of any contracting party imported into the territory of any other contracting party shall be subject to anti-dumping or counter-vailing duty by reason of the exemption of such product from duties or taxes borne by the like product when destined for consumption in the country of origin or exportation, or by reason of the refund of such duties or taxes.

5. No product of the territory of any contracting party imported into the territory of any other contracting party shall be subject to both anti-dumping and countervailing duties to compensate for the same situation of dumping or export subsidisation.

6.(a) No contracting party shall levy any anti-dumping or countervailing duty on the importation of any product of the territory of another contracting party unless it determines that the effect of the dumping or subsidisation, as the case may be, is such as to cause or threaten material injury to an established domestic industry, or is such as to retard materially the establishment of a domestic industry.

(b) The CONTRACTING PARTIES may waive the requirement of sub-paragraph (a) of this paragraph so as to permit a contracting party to levy an anti-dumping or countervailing duty on the importation of any product for the purpose of offsetting dumping or subsidisation which causes or threatens material injury to an industry in the territory of another contracting party exporting the product concerned to the territory of the importing contracting party. The CONTRACTING PARTIES shall waive the requirements of sub-paragraph (a) of this paragraph, so as to permit the levying of a countervailing duty, in cases in which they find that a subsidy is causing or threatening material injury to an industry in the territory of another contracting party exporting the product concerned to the territory of the importing contracting party.

(c) In exceptional circumstances, however, where delay might cause damage which would be difficult to repair, a contracting party may levy a countervailing duty for the purpose referred to in sub-paragraph (b) of this paragraph without the prior approval of the CONTRACTING PARTIES; Provided that such action shall be reported immediately to the CONTRACTING PARTIES and that the countervailing duty shall be withdrawn promptly if the CONTRACTING PARTIES disapprove.

7. A system for the stabilisation of the domestic price or of the return to domestic producers of a primary commodity, independently of the movements of export prices, which results at times in the sale of the commodity for export at a price lower than the comparable price charged for the like commodity to buyers in

the domestic market, shall be presumed not to result in material injury within the meaning of paragraph 6 if it is determined by consultation among the contracting parties substantially interested in the commodity concerned that :

(a) the system has also resulted in the sale of the commodity for export at a price higher than the comparable price charged for the like commodity to buyers in the domestic market, and

(b) the system is so operated, either because of the effective regulation of production, or otherwise, as not to stimulate exports unduly or otherwise seriously prejudice the interests of other contracting parties.

Ad Article VI

Paragraph 1

1. Hidden dumping by associated houses (that is, the sale by an importer at a price below that corresponding to the price invoiced by an exporter with whom the importer is associated, and also below the price in the exporting country) constitutes a form of price dumping with respect to which the margin of dumping may be calculated on the basis of the price at which the goods are resold by the importer.

2. It is recognised that, in the case of imports from a country which has a complete or substantially complete monopoly of its trade and where all domestic prices are fixed by the State special difficulties may exist in determining price comparability for the purposes of paragraph 1, and in such cases importing contracting parties may find it necessary to take into account the possibility that a strict comparison with domestic prices in such a country may not always be appropriate.

Paragraphs 2 and 3

Note 1 As in many other cases in customs administration, a contracting party may require reasonable security (bond or cash deposit) for the payment of anti-dumping or countervailing duty pending final determination of the facts in any case of suspected dumping or subsidisation.

Note 2 Multiple currency practices can in certain circumstances constitute a subsidy to exports which may be met by countervailing duties under paragraph 3 or can constitute a form of dumping by means of a partial depreciation of a country's currency which may be met by action under paragraph 2. By "multiple currency practices" is meant practices by governments or sanctioned by governments.

Paragraph 6(b)

Waivers under the provisions of this sub-paragraph shall be granted only on application by the contracting party proposing to levy an anti-dumping or countervailing duty, as the case may be.

Article XVI

Subsidies

Section A - Subsidies in General

1.   If any contracting party grants or maintains any subsidy, including any form of income or price support, which operates directly or indirectly to increase exports of any product from, or to reduce imports of any product into, its territory, it shall notify the CONTRACTING PARTIES in writing of the extent and nature of the subsidisation, of the estimated effect of the subsidisation on the quantity of the affected product or products imported into or exported from its territory and of the circumstances making the subsidisation necessary. In any case in which it is determined that serious prejudice to the interest of any other contracting party is caused or threatened by any such subsidisation, the contracting party granting the subsidy shall, upon request, discuss with the other contracting party or parties concerned or with the CONTRACTING PARTIES, the possibility of limiting the subsidisation.

Section B - Additional Provisions on Export Subsidies

2.   The contracting parties recognise that the granting by a contracting party of a subsidy on the export of any product may have harmful effects for other contracting parties, both importing and exporting, may cause undue disturbance to their normal commercial interests, and may hinder the achievement of the objectives of this Agreement.

3.   Accordingly, contracting parties should seek to avoid the use of subsidies on the export of primary products. If, however, a contracting party grants directly or indirectly any form of subsidy which operates to increase the export of any primary product from its territory, such subsidy shall not be applied in a manner which results in that contracting party having more than an equitable share of world export trade in that product, account being taken of the shares of the contracting parties in such trade in the product during a previous representative period, and any special factors which may have affected or may be affecting such trade in the product .

4.   Further, as from 1 January 1958 or the earliest practicable date thereafter, contracting parties shall cease to grant either directly or indirectly any form of subsidy on the export of any product other than a primary product which subsidy results in the sale of such product for export at a price lower than the comparable price charged for the like product to buyers in the domestic market. Until 31 December 1957 no contracting party shall extend the scope of any such subsidisation beyond that existing on 1 January 1955 by the introduction of new, or the extension of existing, subsidies.

5.   The CONTRACTING PARTIES shall review the operation of the provisions of this Article from time to time with a view to examining its effectiveness, in the light of actual experience, in promoting the objectives of this Agreement and avoiding subsidisation seriously prejudicial to the trade or interests of contracting parties.

Ad Article XVI

The exemption of an exported product from duties or taxes borne by the like product when destined for domestic consumption, or the remission of such duties or taxes in amounts not in excess of those which have accrued, shall not be deemed to be a subsidy.

Section B

1.   Nothing in Section B shall preclude the use by a contracting party of multiple rates of exchange in accordance with the Articles of Agreement of the International Monetary Fund.

2.   For the purposes of Section B, a "primary product" is understood to be any product of farm, forest or fishery, or any mineral, in its natural form or which has undergone such processing as is customarily required to prepare it for marketing in substantial volume in international trade.

Paragraph 3

1.   The fact that a contracting party has not exported the product in question during the previous representative period would not in itself preclude that contracting party from establishing its right to obtain a share of the trade in the product concerned.

2.   A system for the stabilisation of the domestic price or of the return to domestic producers of a primary product independently of the movements of export prices, which results at times in the sale of the product for export at a price lower

than the comparable price charged for the like product to buyers in the domestic market, shall be considered not to involve a subsidy on exports within the meaning of paragraph 3 if the CONTRACTING PARTIES determine that :

(a) the system has also resulted, or is so designed as to result, in the sale of the product for export at a price higher than the comparable price charged for the like product to buyers in the domestic market; and

(b) the system is so operated, or is designed so to operate, either because of the effective regulation of production or otherwise, as not to stimulate exports unduly or otherwise seriously to prejudice the interests of other contracting parties.

Notwithstanding such determination by the CONTRACTING PARTIES, operations under such a system shall be subject to the provisions of paragraph 3 where they are wholly or partly financed out of government funds in addition to the funds collected from producers in respect of the product concerned.

Paragraph 4

The intention of paragraph 4 is that the contracting parties should seek before the end of 1957 to reach agreement to abolish all remaining subsidies as from 1 January 1958; or, failing this, to reach agreement to extend the application of the standstill until the earliest date thereafter by which they can expect to reach such agreement.

Article XIX

Emergency Action on Imports of Particular Products

1. (a) If, as a result of unforeseen developments and of the effect of the obligations incurred by a contracting party under this Agreement, including tariff concessions, any product is being imported into the territory of that contracting party in such increased quantities and under such conditions as to cause or threaten serious injury to domestic producers in that territory of like or directly competitive products, the contracting party shall be free, in respect of such product, and to the extent and for such time as may be necessary to prevent or remedy such injury, to suspend the obligation in whole or in part or to withdraw or modify the concession.

(b) If any product, which is the subject of a concession with respect to a preference, is being imported into the territory of a contracting party in the circumstances set forth in subparagraph (a) of this paragraph, so as to cause or threaten serious injury to domestic producers of like or directly competitive products in the territory of a contracting party which receives or received such preference, the importing contracting party shall be free, if that other contracting party so requests, to suspend the relevant obligation in whole or in part or to withdraw or modify the concession in respect of the product, to the extent and for such time as may be necessary to prevent or remedy such injury.

2.   Before any contracting party shall take action pursuant to the provisions of paragraph 1 of this Article, it shall give notice in writing to the CONTRACTING PARTIES as far in advance as may be practicable and shall afford the CONTRACTING PARTIES and those contracting parties having a substantial interest as exporters of the product concerned an opportunity to consult with it in respect of the proposed action. When such notice is given in relation to a concession with respect to a preference, the notice shall name the contracting party which has requested the action. In critical circumstances, where delay would cause damage which it would be difficult to repair, action under paragraph 1 of this Article may be taken provisionally without prior consultation, on the condition that consultation shall be effected immediately after taking such action.

3.(a)   If agreement among the interested contracting parties with respect to the action is not reached, the contracting party which proposes to take or continue the action shall, nevertheless, be free to do so, and if such action is taken or continued, the affected contracting parties shall then be free, not later than ninety days after such action is taken, to suspend, upon the expiration of thirty days from the day on which written notice of such suspension is received by the CONTRACTING PARTIES, the application to the trade of the contracting party taking such action, or, in the case envisaged in paragraph l(b) of this Article, to the trade of the contracting party requesting such action, of such substantially equivalent concessions or other obligations under this Agreement the suspension of which the CONTRACTING PARTIES do not disapprove.

(b)   Notwithstanding the provisions of sub-paragraph (a) of this paragraph, where action is taken under paragraph 2 of this Article without prior consultation and causes or threatens serious injury in the territory of a contracting party to the domestic producers of products affected by the action, that contracting party shall, where delay would cause damage difficult to repair, be free to suspend, upon the taking of the action and throughout the period of consultation, such concessions or other obligations as may be necessary to prevent or remedy the injury.

Article XXIII

Nullification or Impairment

1.   If any contracting party should consider that any benefit accruing to it directly or indirectly under this Agreement is being nullified or impaired or that the attainment of any objective of the Agreement is being impeded as the result of

    (a)   the failure of another contracting party to carry out its obligations under this Agreement, or

    (b)   the application by another contracting party of any measure, whether or not it conflicts with the provisions of this Agreement, or

    (c)   the existence of any other situation,

the contracting party may, with a view to the satisfactory adjustment of the matter, make written representations or proposals to the other contracting party or parties which it considers to be concerned. Any contracting party thus approached shall give sympathetic consideration to the representations or proposals made to it.

2.   If no satisfactory adjustment is effected between the contracting parties concerned within a reasonable time, or if the difficulty is of the type described in paragraph l(c) of this Article, the matter may be referred to the CONTRACTING PARTIES. The CONTRACTING PARTIES shall promptly investigate any matter so referred to them and shall make appropriate recommendations to the contracting parties which they consider to be concerned, or give a ruling on the matter, as appropriate. The CONTRACTING PARTIES may consult with contracting parties, with the Economic and Social Council of the United Nations and with any appropriate inter-governmental organisation in cases where they consider such consultation necessary.

If the CONTRACTING PARTIES consider that the circumstances are serious enough to justify such action, they may authorise a contracting party or parties to suspend the application to any other contracting party or parties of such concessions or other obligations under this Agreement as they determine to be appropriate in the circumstances. If the application to any contracting party of any concession or other obligation is in fact suspended, that contracting party shall then be free, not later than sixty days after such action is taken, to give written notice to the Executive Secretary to the CONTRACTING PARTIES of its intention to withdraw from this Agreement and such withdrawal shall take effect upon the sixtieth day following the day on which such notice is received by him.

APPENDIX 2

AGREEMENT ON IMPLEMENTATION OF ARTICLE VI OF THE GENERAL AGREEMENT ON TARIFFS AND TRADE

The Parties to this Agreement (hereinafter referred to as "Parties"),

Recognising that anti-dumping practices should not constitute an unjustifiable impediment to international trade and that anti-dumping duties may be applied against dumping only if such dumping causes or threatens material injury to an established industry or materially retards the establishment of an industry;

Considering that it is desirable to provide for equitable and open procedures as the basis for a full examination of dumping cases;

Taking into account the particular trade, development and financial needs of developing countries;

Desiring to interpret the provisions of Article VI of the General Agreement on Tariffs and Trade (hereinafter referred to as "General Agreement" or "GATT") and to elaborate rules for their application in order to provide greater uniformity and certainty in their implementation; and

Desiring to provide for the speedy, effective and equitable settlement of disputes arising under this Agreement;

Hereby agree as follows :

PART I - ANTI-DUMPING CODE

Article 1

Principles

The imposition of an anti-dumping duty is a measure to be taken only under the circumstances provided for in Article VI of the General Agreement and pursuant to investigations initiated[1] and conducted in accordance with the provisions of this Code. The following provisions govern the application of Article VI of the General Agreement in so far as action is taken under anti-dumping legislation or regulations.

---

1.   The term "initiated" as used hereinafter means the procedural action by which a Party formally commences an investigation as provided in paragraph 6 of Article 6.

Article 2

Determination of Dumping

1. For the purpose of this Code a product is to be considered as being dumped, ie introduced into the commerce of another country at less than its normal value, if the export price of the product exported from one country to another, is less than the comparable price, in the ordinary course of trade, for the like product when destined for consumption in the exporting country.

2. Throughout this Code the term "like product" ("produit similaire") shall be interpreted to mean a product which is identical, ie alike in all respects to the product under consideration, or in the absence of such a product, another product which, although not alike in all respects, has characteristics closely resembling those of the product under consideration.

3. In the case where products are not imported directly from the country of origin but are exported to the country of importation from an intermediate country, the price at which the products are sold from the country of export to the country of importation shall normally be compared with the comparable price in the country of export. However, comparison may be made with the price in the country of origin, if, for example, the products are merely transhipped through the country of export, or such products are not produced in the country of export, or there is no comparable price for them in the country of export.

4. When there are no sales of the like product in the ordinary course of trade in the domestic market of the exporting country or when, because of the particular market situation, such sales do not permit a proper comparison, the margin of dumping shall be determined by comparison with a comparable price of the like product when exported to any third country which may be the highest such export price but should be a representative price, or with the cost of production in the country of origin plus a reasonable amount for administrative, selling and any other costs and for profits. As a general rule, the addition for profit shall not exceed the profit normally realised on sales of products of the same general category in the domestic market of the country of origin.

5. In cases where there is no export price or where it appears to the authorities[1] concerned that the export price is unreliable because of association or a compensatory arrangement between the exporter and the importer or a third party, the export price may be constructed on the basis of the price at which the imported products are first resold to an independent buyer, or if the products are not resold to

---

1. When in this Code the term "authorities" is used, it shall be interpreted as meaning authorities at an appropriate, senior level.

an independent buyer, or not resold in the condition as imported, on such reasonable basis as the authorities may determine.

6.   In order to effect a fair comparison between the export price and the domestic price in the exporting country (or the country of origin) or, if applicable, the price established pursuant to the provisions of Article VI:l(b) of the General Agreement, the two prices shall be compared at the same level of trade, normally at the ex-factory level, and in respect of sales made at as nearly as possible the same time. Due allowance shall be made in each case, on its merits, for the differences in conditions and terms of sale, for the differences in taxation, and for the other differences affecting price comparability. In the cases referred to in paragraph 5 of Article 2 allowance for costs, including duties and taxes, incurred between importation and resale, and for profits accruing, should also be made .

7.   This Article is without prejudice to the second Supplementary Provision to paragraph 1 of Article VI in Annex I of the General Agreement.

Article 3

Determination of Injury[1]

1.   A determination of injury for purposes of Article VI of the General Agreement shall be based on positive evidence and involve an objective examination of both (a) the volume of the dumped imports and their effect on prices in the domestic market for like products, and (b) the consequent impact of these imports on domestic producers of such products.

2.   With regard to volume of the dumped imports the investigating authorities shall consider whether there has been a significant increase in dumped imports, either in absolute terms or relative to production or consumption in the importing country. With regard to the effect of the dumped imports on prices, the investigating authorities shall consider whether there has been a significant price undercutting by the dumped imports as compared with the price of a like product of the importing country, or whether the effect of such imports is otherwise to depress prices to a significant degree or prevent price increases, which otherwise would have occurred, to a significant degree. No one or several of these factors can necessarily give decisive guidance.

3.   The examination of the impact on the industry concerned shall include an evaluation of all relevant economic factors and indices having a bearing on the

---

1.   Under this Code the term "injury" shall, unless otherwise specified, be taken to mean material injury to a domestic industry, threat of material injury to a domestic industry or material retardation of the establishment of such an industry and shall be interpreted in accordance with the provisions of this Article.

state of the industry such as actual and potential decline in output, sales, market share, profits, productivity, return on investments, or utilisation of capacity; factors affecting domestic prices; actual and potential negative effects on cash flow, inventories, employment, wages, growth, ability to raise capital or investments. This list is not exhaustive, nor can one or several of these factors necessarily give decisive guidance.

4.   It must be demonstrated that the dumped imports are, through the effects[1] of dumping, causing injury within the meaning of this Code. There may be other factors[2] which at the same time are injuring the industry, and the injuries caused by other factors must not be attributed to the dumped imports.

5.   The effect of the dumped imports shall be assessed in relation to the domestic production of the like product when available data permit the separate identification of production in terms of such criteria as : the production process, the producers' realisations, profits. When the domestic production of the like product has no separate identity in these terms the effects of the dumped imports shall be assessed by the examination of the production of the narrowest group or range of products, which includes the like product, for which the necessary information can be provided.

6.   A determination of threat of injury shall be based on facts and not merely on allegation, conjecture or remote possibility. The change in circumstances which would create a situation in which the dumping would cause injury must be clearly foreseen and imminent[3].

7.   With respect to cases where injury is threatened by dumped imports, the application of anti-dumping measures shall be studied and decided with special care.

Article 4

Definition of Industry

1.   In determining injury the term "domestic industry" shall be interpreted as referring to the domestic producers as a whole of the like products or to those of

---

1.   As set forth in paragraphs 2 and 3 of this Article.
2.   Such factors include, inter alia, the volume and prices of imports not sold at dumping prices, contraction in demand or changes in the patterns of consumption, trade restrictive practices of and competition between the foreign and domestic producers, developments in technology and the export performance and productivity of the domestic industry.
3.   One example, though not an exclusive one, is that there is convincing reason to believe that there will be, in the immediate future, substantially increased importation's of product at dumped prices.

them whose collective output of the products constitutes a major proportion of the total domestic production of those products, except that

(i) when producers are related[1] to the exporters or importers or are themselves importers of the allegedly dumped product, the industry may be interpreted as referring to the rest of the producers;

(ii) in exceptional circumstances the territory of a Party may, for the production in question, be divided into two or more competitive markets and the producers within each market may be regarded as a separate industry if (a) the producers within such market sell all or almost all of their production of the product in question in that market, and (b) the demand in that market is not to any substantial degree supplied by producers of the product in question located elsewhere in the territory. In such circumstances, injury may be found to exist even where a major portion of the total domestic industry is not injured provided there is a concentration of dumped imports into such an isolated market and provided further that the dumped imports are causing injury to the producers of all or almost all of the production within such market.

2. When the industry has been interpreted as referring to the producers in a certain area, ie a market as defined in paragraph l(ii), anti-dumping duties shall be levied[2] only on the products in question consigned for final consumption to that area. When the constitutional law of the importing country does not permit the levying of anti-dumping duties on such a basis, the importing Party may levy the anti-dumping duties without limitation only if (l) the exporters shall have been given an opportunity to cease exporting at dumped prices to the area concerned or otherwise give assurances pursuant to Article 7 of this Code, and adequate assurances in this regard have not been promptly given, and (2) such duties cannot be levied on specific producers which supply the area in question.

3. Where two or more countries have reached under the provisions of Article XXIV:8(a) of the General Agreement such a level of integration that they have the characteristics of a single, unified market, the industry in the entire area of integration shall be taken to be the industry referred to in paragraph 1 above.

4. The provisions of paragraph 5 of Article 3 shall be applicable to this Article.

---

1. An understanding among Parties should be developed defining the word "related" as used in this Code.
2. As used in this Code "levy" shall mean the definitive or final legal assessment or collection of a duty or tax.

Article 5

Initiation and Subsequent Investigation

1.   An investigation to determine the existence, degree and effect of any alleged dumping shall normally be initiated upon a written request by or on behalf of the industry[1] affected. The request shall include sufficient evidence of (a) dumping; (b) injury within the meaning of Article VI of the General Agreement as interpreted by this Code and (c) a causal link between the dumped imports and the alleged injury. If in special circumstances the authorities concerned decide to initiate an investigation without having received such a request, they shall proceed only if they have sufficient evidence on all points under (a) to (c) above.

2.   Upon initiation of an investigation and thereafter, the evidence of both dumping and injury caused thereby should be considered simultaneously. In any event the evidence of both dumping and injury shall be considered simultaneously (a) in the decision whether or not to initiate an investigation, and (b) thereafter, during the course of the investigation, starting on a date not later than the earliest date on which in accordance with the provisions of this Code provisional measures may be applied, except in the cases provided for in paragraph 3 of Article 10 in which the authorities accept the request of the exporters.

4.   An application shall be rejected and an investigation shall be terminated promptly as soon as the authorities concerned are satisfied that there is not sufficient evidence of either dumping or of injury to justify proceeding with the case. There should be immediate termination in cases where the margin of dumping or the volume of dumped imports, actual or potential, or the injury is negligible.

4.   An anti-dumping proceeding shall not hinder the procedures of customs clearance.

5.   Investigations shall, except in special circumstances, be concluded within one year after their initiation.

---

1.   As defined in Article 4.

Article 6

Evidence

1.   The foreign suppliers and all other interested parties shall be given ample opportunity to present in writing all evidence that they consider useful in respect to the anti-dumping investigation in question. They shall also have the right, on justification, to present evidence orally.

2.   The authorities concerned shall provide opportunities for the complainant and the importers and exporters known to be concerned and the governments of the exporting countries, to see all information that is relevant to the presentation of their cases, that is not confidential as defined in paragraph 3 below, and that is used by the authorities in an anti-dumping investigation, and to prepare presentations on the basis of this information.

3.   Any information which is by nature confidential (for example, because its disclosure would be of significant competitive advantage to a competitor or because its disclosure would have a significantly adverse effect upon a person supplying the information or upon a person from whom he acquired the information) or which is provided on a confidential basis by parties to an anti-dumping investigation shall, upon cause shown, be treated as such by the investigating authorities. Such information shall not be disclosed without specific permission of the party submitting it[1]. Parties providing confidential information may be requested to furnish non confidential summaries thereof. In the event that such parties indicate that such information is not susceptible of summary, a statement of the reasons why summarisation is not possible must be provided.

4.   However, if the authorities concerned find that a request for confidentiality is not warranted and if the supplier is either unwilling to make the information public or to authorise its disclosure in generalised or summary form, the authorities would be free to disregard such information unless it can be demonstrated to their satisfaction from appropriate sources that the information is correct[2].

5.   In order to verify information provided or to obtain further details the authorities may carry out investigations in other countries as required, provided they obtain the agreement of the firms concerned and provided they notify the representatives of the government of the country in question and unless the latter object to the investigation.

---

1.   Parties are aware that in the territory of certain Parties disclosure pursuant to a narrowly drawn protective order may be required.
2.   Parties agree that requests for confidentiality should not be arbitrarily rejected.

6.   When the competent authorities are satisfied that there is sufficient evidence to justify initiating an anti-dumping investigation pursuant to Article 5, the Party or Parties the products of which are subject to such investigation and the exporters and importers known to the investigating authorities to have an interest therein and the complainants shall be notified and a public notice shall be given.

7.   Throughout the anti-dumping investigation all parties shall have a full opportunity for the defence of their interests. To this end, the authorities concerned shall, on request, provide opportunities for all directly interested parties to meet those parties with adverse interests, so that opposing views may be presented and rebuttal arguments offered. Provision of such opportunities must take account of the need to preserve confidentiality and of the convenience to the parties. There shall be no obligation on any party to attend a meeting and failure to do so shall not be prejudicial to that party's case.

8.   In cases in which any interested party refuses access to, or otherwise does not provide, necessary information within a reasonable period or significantly impedes the investigation, preliminary and final findings[1,] affirmative or negative, may be made on the basis of the facts available.

9.   The provisions of this Article are not intended to prevent the authorities of a Party from proceeding expeditiously with regard to initiating an investigation, reaching preliminary or final findings, whether affirmative or negative, or from applying provisional or final measures, in accordance with the relevant provisions of this Code.

Article 7

Price Undertakings

1.   Proceedings may[2] be suspended or terminated without the imposition of provisional measures or anti-dumping duties upon receipt of satisfactory voluntary undertakings from any exporter to revise its prices or to cease exports to the area in question at dumped prices so that the authorities are satisfied that the injurious effect of the dumping is eliminated. Price increases under such undertakings shall not be higher than necessary to eliminate the margin of dumping.

2.   Price undertakings shall not be sought or accepted from exporters unless the authorities of the importing country have initiated an investigation in accordance with the provisions of Article 5 of this Code. Undertakings offered need not be

---

1.   Because of different terms used under different systems in various countries the term "finding" is hereinafter used to mean a formal decision or determination.
2.   The word "may" shall not be interpreted to allow the simultaneous continuation of proceedings with the implementation of price undertakings except as provided in paragraph 3.

accepted if the authorities consider their acceptance impractical, for example, if the number of actual or potential exporters is too great, or for other reasons.

3.   If the undertakings are accepted, the investigation of injury shall nevertheless be completed if the exporter so desires or the authorities so decide. In such a case, if a determination of no injury or threat thereof is made, the undertaking shall automatically lapse except in cases where a determination of no threat of injury is due in large part to the existence of a price undertaking. In such cases the authorities concerned may require that an undertaking be maintained for a reasonable period consistent with the provisions of this Code.

4.   Price undertakings may be suggested by the authorities of the importing country, but no exporter shall be forced to enter into such an undertaking. The fact that exporters do not offer such undertakings, or do not accept an invitation to do so, shall in no way prejudice the consideration of the case. However, the authorities are free to determine that a threat of injury is more likely to be realised if the dumped imports continue.

5.   Authorities of an importing country may require any exporter from whom undertakings have been accepted to provide periodically information relevant to the fulfilment of such undertakings, and to permit verification of pertinent data. In case of violation of undertakings, the authorities of the importing country may take, under this Code in conformity with its provisions, expeditious actions which may constitute immediate application of provisional measures using the best information available. In such cases definitive duties may be levied in accordance with this Code on goods entered for consumption not more than ninety days before the application of such provisional measures, except that any such retroactive assessment shall not apply to imports entered before the violation of the undertaking.

6.   Undertakings shall not remain in force any longer than anti-dumping duties could remain in force under this Code. The authorities of an importing country shall review the need for the continuation of any price undertaking, where warranted, on their own initiative or if interested exporters or importers of the product in question so request and submit positive information substantiating the need for such review.

7.   Whenever an anti-dumping investigation is suspended or terminated pursuant to the provisions of paragraph 1 above and whenever an undertaking is terminated, this fact shall be officially notified and must be published. Such notices shall set forth at least the basic conclusions and a summary of the reasons therefor.

Article 8

Imposition and Collection of Anti-dumping Duties

1.   The decision whether or not to impose an anti-dumping duty in cases where all requirements for the imposition have been fulfilled and the decision whether the amount of the anti-dumping duty to be imposed shall be the full margin of dumping or less, are decisions to be made by the authorities of the importing country or customs territory. It is desirable that the imposition be permissive in all countries or customs territories Parties to this Agreement and that the duty be less than the margin, if such lesser duty would be adequate to remove the injury to the domestic industry.

2.   When an anti-dumping duty is imposed in respect of any product, such anti-dumping duty shall be collected in the appropriate amounts in each case, on a non-discriminatory basis on imports of such product from all sources found to be dumped and causing injury, except as to imports from those sources, from which price undertakings under the terms of this Code have been accepted. The authorities shall name the supplier or suppliers of the product concerned. If, however, several suppliers from the same country are involved. and it is impracticable to name all these suppliers, the authorities may name the supplying country concerned. If several suppliers from more than one country are involved, the authorities may name either all the suppliers involved, or, if this is impracticable, all the supplying countries involved.

3.   The amount of the anti-dumping duty must not exceed the margin of dumping as established under Article 2. Therefore, if subsequent to the application of the anti-dumping duty it is found that the duty so collected exceeds the actual dumping margin, the amount in excess of the margin shall be reimbursed as quickly as possible.

4.   Within a basic price system the following rules shall apply, provided that their application is consistent with the other provisions of this Code :

> If several suppliers from one or more countries are involved, anti-dumping duties may be imposed on imports of the product in question found to have been dumped and to be causing injury from the country or countries concerned, the duty being equivalent to the amount by which the export price is less than the basic price established for this purpose, not exceeding the lowest normal price in the supplying country or countries where normal conditions of competition are prevailing. It is understood that for products which are sold below this already established basic price, a new anti-dumping investigation shall be carried out in each particular case, when so demanded by the interested parties and the demand is supported by relevant evidence In cases where no dumping is found,

anti-dumping duties collected shall be reimbursed as quickly as possible. Furthermore, if it can be found that the duty so collected exceeds the actual dumping margin, the amount in excess of the margin shall be reimbursed as quickly as possible.

5.   Public notice shall be given of any preliminary or final finding whether affirmative or negative and of the revocation of a finding. In the case of affirmative finding each such notice shall set forth the findings and conclusions reached on all issues of fact and considered material by the investigating authorities, and the reasons and basis therefor. In the case of a negative finding, each notice shall set forth at least the basic conclusions and a summary of the reasons therefor. All notices of findings shall be forwarded to the Party or Parties the products of which are subject to such finding and to the exporters known to have an interest therein.

Article 9

Duration of Anti-dumping Duties

1.   An anti-dumping duty shall remain in force only as long as, and to the extent necessary to counteract dumping which is causing injury.

2.   The investigating authorities shall review the need for the continued imposition of the duty, where warranted, on their own initiative or if any interested party so requests and submits positive information substantiating the need for review.

Article 10

Provisional Measures

1.   Provisional measures may be taken only after a preliminary affirmative finding has been made that there is dumping and that there is sufficient evidence of injury, as provided for in (a) to (c) of paragraph 1 of Article 5. Provisional measures shall not be applied unless the authorities concerned judge that they are necessary to prevent injury being caused during the period of investigation.

2.   Provisional measures may take the form of a provisional duty or, preferably, a security - by cash deposit or bond - equal to the amount of the anti-dumping duty provisionally estimated, being not greater than the provisionally estimated margin of dumping. Withholding of appeasement is an appropriate provisional measure, provided that the normal duty and the estimated amount of

the anti-dumping duty be indicated and as long as the withholding of appeasement is subject to the same conditions as other provisional measures.

3.   The imposition of provisional measures shall be limited to as short a period as possible, not exceeding four months or, on decision of the authorities concerned, upon request by exporters representing a significant percentage of the trade involved to a period not exceeding six months.

4.   The relevant provisions of Article 8 shall be followed in the application of provisional measures.

Article 11

Retroactivity

1.   Anti-dumping duties and provisional measures shall only be applied to products which enter for consumption after the time when the decision taken under paragraph 1 of Article and paragraph 1 of Article 10, respectively, enters into force, except that in cases :

(i)   Where a final finding of injury (but not of a threat thereof or of a material retardation of the establishment of an industry) is made or, in the case of a final finding of threat of injury, where the effect of the dumped imports would, in the absence of the provision measures, have led to a finding of injury, anti-dumping duties may be levied retroactively for the period for which provisional measures, if any, have been applied.

If the anti-dumping duty fixed in the final decision is higher than the provisionally paid duty, the difference shall not be collected. If the duty fixed in the final decision is lower than the provisionally paid duty or the amount estimated for the purpose of the security, the difference shall be reimbursed or the duty recalculated, as the case may be.

(ii)   Where for the dumped product in question the authorities determine
   (a)   either that there is a history of dumping which caused injury or that the importer was, or should have been, aware that the exporter practices dumping and that such dumping would cause injury, and

(b)   that the injury is caused by sporadic dumping (massive dumped imports of a product in a relatively short period) to such an extent that in order to preclude it recurring, it appears necessary to levy an anti-dumping duty retroactively on those imports.

the duty may be levied on products which were entered for consumption not more than 90 days prior to the date of application of provisional measures.

2.   Except as provided in paragraph 1 above where a finding of threat of injury or material retardation is made (but no injury has yet occurred) a definitive anti-dumping duty may be imposed only from the date of the finding of threat of injury or material retardation and any cash deposit made during the period of the application of provisional measures shall be refunded and any bonds released in an expeditious manner.

3.   Where a final finding is negative any cash deposit made during the period of the application of provisional measures shall be refunded and any bonds released in an expeditious manner.

Article 12

Anti-dumping Action on behalf of a Third Country

1.   An application for anti-dumping action on behalf of a third country shall be made by the authorities of the third country requesting action.

2.   Such an application shall be supported by price information to show that the imports are being dumped and by detailed information to show that the alleged dumping is causing injury to the domestic industry concerned in the third country. The government of the third country shall afford all assistance to the authorities of the importing country to obtain any further information which the latter may require.

3.   The authorities of the importing country in considering such an application shall consider the effects of the alleged dumping on the industry concerned as a whole in the third country that is to say the injury shall not be assessed in relation only to the effect of the alleged dumping on the industry's exports to the importing country or even on the industry's total exports.

4.   The decision whether or not to proceed with a case shall rest with the importing country. If the importing country decides that it is prepared to take

action, the initiation of the approach to the CONTRACTING PARTIES seeking their approval for such action shall rest with the importing country.

Article 13

Developing Countries

It is recognised that special regard must be given by developed countries to the special situation of developing countries when considering the application of anti-dumping measures under this Code. Possibilities of constructive remedies provided for by this Code shall be explored before applying anti-dumping duties where they would affect the essential interests of developing countries.

PART II

Article 14

Committee on Anti-dumping Practices

1.   There shall he established under this Agreement a Committee on Anti-dumping Practices (hereinafter referred to as the Committee) composed of representatives from each of the Parties. The Committee shall elect its own Chairman and shall meet not less than twice a year and otherwise as envisaged by relevant provisions of this Agreement at the request of any Party. The Committee shall carry out responsibilities as assigned to it under this Agreement or by the Parties and it shall afford Parties the opportunity of consulting on any matters relating to the operation of the Agreement or the furtherance of its objectives. The GATT secretariat shall act as the secretariat to the Committee.

2.   The Committee may set up subsidiary bodies as appropriate.

3.   In carrying out their functions, the Committee and any subsidiary bodies may consult with and seek information from any source they deem appropriate. However, before the Committee or a subsidiary body seeks such information from a source within the jurisdiction of a Party, it shall inform the Party involved. It shall obtain the consent of the Party and any firm to be consulted.

4.   Parties shall report without delay to the Committee all preliminary or final anti-dumping actions taken. Such reports will be available in the GATT secretariat for inspection by government representatives. The Parties shall also submit, on a semi-annual basis, reports of any anti-dumping actions taken within the preceding six months.

Article 15

Consultation, Conciliation and Dispute Settlement[1]

1.   Each Party shall afford sympathetic consideration to, and shall afford adequate opportunity for consultation regarding, representations made by another Party with respect to any matter affecting the operation of this Agreement.

2.   If any Party considers that any benefit accruing to it, directly or indirectly, under this Agreement is being nullified or impaired, or that the achievement of any objective of the Agreement is being impeded, by another Party or Parties, it may, with a view to reaching a mutually satisfactory resolution of the matter, request in writing consultations with the Party or Parties in question. Each Party shall afford sympathetic consideration to any request from another Party for consultation. The Parties concerned shall initiate consultation promptly.

3.   If any Party considers that the consultation pursuant to paragraph 2 has failed to achieve a mutually agreed solution and final action has been taken by the administering authorities of the importing country to levy definitive anti-dumping duties or to accept price undertakings, it may refer the matter to the Committee for conciliation. When a provisional measure has a significant impact and the Party considers the measure was taken contrary to the provisions of paragraph 1 of Article 10 of this Agreement, a Party may also refer such matter to the Committee for conciliation. In cases where matters are referred to the Committee for conciliation, the Committee shall meet within thirty days to review the matter, and, through its good offices, shall encourage the Parties involved to develop a mutually acceptable solution [2].

4.   Parties shall make their best efforts to reach a mutually satisfactory solution throughout the period of conciliation.

5.   If no mutually agreed solution has been reached after detailed examination by the Committee under paragraph 3 within three months, the Committee shall, at the request of any party to the dispute, establish a panel to examine the matter, based upon :

    (a)   a written statement of the Party making the request indicating how a benefit accruing to it, directly or indirectly, under this Agreement has been nullified or impaired, or that the achieving of the objectives of the Agreement is being impeded, and

---

1.   If disputes arise between Parties relating to rights and obligations under this Agreement, Parties should complete the dispute settlement procedures under this Agreement before availing themselves of any rights which they have under the GATT.

2.   In this connection the Committee may draw Parties' attention to those cases in which, in its view, there are no reasonable bases supporting the allegations made.

(b)   the facts made available in conformity with appropriate domestic procedures to the authorities of the importing country.

6.   Confidential information provided to the panel shall not be revealed without formal authorisation from the person or authority providing the information. Where such information is requested from the panel but release of such information by the panel is not authorised, a non-confidential summary of the information, authorised by the authority or person providing the information, will be provided.

7.   Further to paragraphs 1-6 the settlement of disputes shall mutatis mutandis be governed by the provisions of the understanding regarding Notification, Consultation, Dispute Settlement and Surveillance. Panel members shall have relevant experience and be selected from Parties not parties to the dispute.

PART III

Article 16

Final Provisions

1.   No specific action against dumping of exports from another Party can be taken except in accordance with the provisions of the General Agreement, as interpreted by this Agreement[1].

Acceptance and accession
2. (a) This Agreement shall be open for acceptance by signature or otherwise by governments contracting parties to the GATT and by the European Economic Community.

(b) This Agreement shall be open for acceptance by signature or otherwise by governments having provisionally acceded to the GATT, on terms related to the effective application of rights and obligations under this Agreement, which take into account rights and obligations in the instruments providing for their provisional accession.

(c) This Agreement shall be open to accession by any other government on terms, related to the effective application of rights and obligations under this Agreement, to be agreed between that government and the Parties, by the deposit with the

---

1.   This is not intended to preclude action under other relevant provisions of the General Agreement, as appropriate.

Director General to the CONTRACTING PARTIES to the GATT of an instrument of accession which states the terms so agreed.

(d) In regard to acceptance, the provisions of Article XXVI:5(a) and (b) of the General Agreement would be applicable.

Reservations

3.   Reservations may not be entered in respect of any of the provisions of this Agreement without the consent of the other Parties.

Entry into force

4.   This Agreement shall enter into force on 1 January 1980 for the governments[1] which have accepted or acceded to it by that date. For each other government it shall enter into force on the thirtieth day following the date of its acceptance or accession to this Agreement.

Denunciation of the 1967 Agreement

5.   Acceptance of this Agreement shall carry denunciation of the Agreement on Implementation of Article VI of the General Agreement on Tariffs and Trade, done at Geneva on 30 June 1967, which entered into force on 1 July 1968, for Parties to the 1967 Agreement. Such denunciation shall take effect for each Party to this Agreement on the date of entry into force of this Agreement for each such Party.

National legislation

6 (a) Each government accepting or acceding to this Agreement shall take all necessary steps, of a general or particular character, to ensure, not later than the date of entry into force of this Agreement for it, the conformity of its laws, regulations and administrative procedures with the provisions of this Agreement as they may apply for the Party in question.

(b) Each Party shall inform the Committee of any changes in its laws and regulations relevant to this Agreement and in the administration of such laws and regulations.

Review

7.   The Committee shall review annually the implementation and operation of this Agreement taking into account the objectives thereof. The Committee shall annually inform the CONTRACTING PARTIES to the GATT of developments during the period covered by such reviews.

---

1.   The term "government" is deemed to include the competent authorities of the European Economic Community.

Amendments

8.　　The Parties may amend this Agreement having regard, inter alia, to the experience gained in its implementation. Such an amendment, once the Parties have concurred in accordance with procedures established by the Committee, shall not come into force for any Party until it has been accepted by such Party.

Withdrawal

9.　　Any Party may withdraw from this Agreement. The withdrawal shall take effect upon the expiration of sixty days from the day on which written notice of withdrawal is received by the Director-General to the CONTRACTING PARTIES to the GATT. Any Party may upon such notification request an immediate meeting of the Committee.

Non-application of this Agreement between particular Parties

10.　　This Agreement shall not apply as between any two Parties if either of the Parties, at the time either accepts or accedes to this Agreement, does not consent to such application.

Secretariat

11.　　This Agreement shall be serviced by the GATT secretariat.

Deposit

12.　　This Agreement shall be deposited with the Director-General to the CONTRACTING PARTIES to the GATT, who shall promptly furnish to each Party and each contracting party to the GATT a certified copy thereof and of each amendment thereto pursuant to paragraph 8, and a notification of each acceptance thereof or accession thereto pursuant to paragraph 2, and of each withdrawal therefrom pursuant to paragraph 9 of this Article.

Registration

13.　　This Agreement shall be registered in accordance with the provisions of Article 102 of the Charter of the United Nations.

Done at Geneva this twelfth day of April nineteen hundred and seventy-nine in a single copy in the English, French and Spanish languages, each text being authentic.

ANNEX

The following statement was circulated on 11 April 1979 at the request of the delegations of Austria, Canada, European Communities, Japan, Sweden, Switzerland and the United States.

"With regard to the Agreement on Implementation of Article VI of the General Agreement on Tariffs and Trade (MT/NTM/W/232 and Add. 1 and Corr. l) it is understood that paragraph 6[1] of Article 15 of the Agreement concerning the settlement of disputes arising under the Agreement is to be interpreted to mean that the measures which may be authorised by the Committee on Anti-dumping Practices for the purpose of the Agreement may include all such measures as can be authorised under Articles XXII and XXIII of the General Agreement."

* * *

The following statement was circulated on 19 October 1979 at the request of the delegations of Austria, Brazil, Canada, Colombia, European Communities, Egypt, Finland, Japan, Norway, Romania, Sweden, Switzerland and United States.

"With regard to the Agreement on Implementation of Article VI of the General Agreement on Tariffs and Trade (MTN/NTM/W/232/Rev. 1), the above-noted delegations, cognisant of the commitment in Article 13 of the Agreement that special regard must be given by developed countries to the special situation of developing countries when considering the application of anti-dumping measures under this Code, agree that :

1. In developing countries, governments play a large role in promoting economic growth and development in accordance with their national priorities, and their economic regimes for the export sector can be different from those relating to their domestic sectors resulting inter alia in different cost structures. This Agreement is not intended to prevent developing countries from adopting measures in this context, including measures in the export sector, as long as they are used in a manner which is consistent with the provisions of the General Agreement on Tariffs and Trade, as applicable to these countries.

2. In the case of imports from a developing country, the fact that the export price may be lower than the comparable price for the like product when destined for domestic consumption in the exporting country does not *per se* justify

---

1.   In the final version of the Agreement as reproduced herein, paragraph 6 has become paragraph 7.

an investigation or the determination of dumping unless the other factors mentioned in Article 5 :1 are also present. Due consideration should be given to all cases where, because special economic conditions affect prices in the home market, these prices do not provide a commercially realistic basis for dumping calculations. In such cases the normal value for the purposes of ascertaining whether the goods are being dumped shall be determined by methods such as a comparison of the export price with the comparable price of the like product when exported to any third country or with the cost of production of the exported goods in the country of origin plus a reasonable amount for administrative, selling and any other costs and for profits."

* * *

The following statement was circulated on 19 October 1979 at the request of the delegations of Austria, Brazil, Canada, Colombia, European Communities, Egypt, Finland, Japan, Norway, Romania, Sweden, Switzerland and United States.

"It is recognised that developing countries may face special problems initially in adapting their legislation to the requirements of the Code, including administrative and infrastructural problems, in carrying out anti-dumping investigations initiated by them. Accordingly, the Committee on Anti-dumping Practices may grant, upon specific request and on conditions to be negotiated on a case-by-case basis, time-limited exceptions in whole or in part from obligations which relate to investigations undertaken by a developing country under this Agreement.

Developed countries Parties to this Agreement shall endeavour to furnish, upon request and on terms to be agreed, technical assistance to developing countries Parties to this Agreement, with regard to the implementation of this Agreement, including training of personnel, and the supplying of information on methods, techniques and other aspects of conducting investigations on dumping practices."

APPENDIX 3

AGREEMENT ON INTERPRETATION AND APPLICATION OF ARTICLES VI, XVI AND XXIII OF THE GENERAL AGREEMENT ON TARIFFS AND TRADE

The signatories[1] to this Agreement,

Noting that Ministers on 12-14 September 1973 agreed that the Multilateral Trade Negotiations should, inter alia, reduce or eliminate the trade restricting or distorting effects of non-tariff measures, and bring such measures under more effective international discipline,

Recognising that subsidies are used by governments to promote important objectives of national policy,

Recognising also that subsidies may have harmful effects on trade and production,

Recognising that the emphasis of this Agreement should be on the effects of subsidies and that these effects are to be assessed in giving due account to the internal economic situation of the signatories concerned as well as to the state of international economic and monetary relations,

Desiring to ensure that the use of subsidies does not adversely affect or prejudice the interests of any signatory to this Agreement, and that countervailing measures do not unjustifiably impede international trade, and that relief is made available to producers adversely affected by the use of subsidies within an agreed international framework of rights and obligations,

Taking into account the particular trade, development and financial needs of developing countries,

Desiring to apply fully and to interpret the provisions of Articles VI, XVI and XXIII of the General Agreement on Tariffs and Trade[2] (hereinafter referred to as "General Agreement" or "GATT") only with respect to subsidies and countervailing measures and to elaborate rules for their application in order to provide greater uniformity and certainty in their implementation,

---

1.   The term "signatories" is hereinafter used to mean Parties to this Agreement.
2.   Wherever in this Agreement there is reference to "the terms of this Agreement" or the "articles" or "provisions or this Agreement" it shall be taken to mean, as the context requires, the provisions of the General Agreement as interpreted and applied by this Agreement.

Desiring to provide for the speedy, effective and equitable resolution of disputes arising under this Agreement,

Have agreed as follows :

PART I

Article 1

Application of Article VI of the General Agreement[1]

Signatories shall take all necessary steps to ensure that the imposition of a countervailing duty[2] on any product of the territory of any signatory imported into the territory of another signatory is in accordance with the provisions of Article VI of the General Agreement and the terms of this Agreement.

Article 2

Domestic procedures and related matters

1.   Countervailing duties may only be imposed pursuant to investigations initiated[3] and conducted in accordance with the provisions of this Article. An investigation to determine the existence, degree and effect of any alleged subsidy shall normally be initiated upon a written request by or on behalf of the industry affected. The request shall include sufficient evidence of the existence of (a) a subsidy and, if possible, its amount, (b) injury within the meaning of Article VI of the General Agreement as interpreted by this Agreement[4] and (c) a causal link between the subsidised imports and the alleged injury. If in special circumstances the authorities concerned decide to initiate an investigation without having received such a request, they shall proceed only if they have sufficient evidence on all points under (a) to (c) above.

---

1.   The provisions of both Part I and Part II of this Agreement may by invoked in parallel: however, with regard to the effects of a particular subsidy in the domestic market of the importing country, only one form of relief (either a countervailing duty or an authorised countermeasure) shall be available.

2.   The term "countervailing duty" shall be understood to mean a special duty levied for the purpose of off-setting any bounty or subsidy bestowed directly or indirectly upon the manufacture, production or export of any merchandise, as provided for in Article VI:3 of the General Agreement.

3.   The term "initiated" as used hereinafter means procedural action by which a signatory formally commences an investigation as provided in paragraph 3 of this Article.

4.   Under this Agreement the term "injury" shall, unless otherwise specified, be taken to mean material injury to a domestic industry, threat of material injury to a domestic industry or material retardation of the establishment of such an industry and shall be interpreted in accordance with the provisions of Article 6.

2.   Each signatory shall notify the Committee on Subsidies and Countervailing Measures[1] (a) which of its authorities are competent to initiate and conduct investigations referred to in this Article and (b) its domestic procedures governing the initiation and conduct of such investigations.

3.   When the investigating authorities are satisfied that there is sufficient evidence to justify initiating an investigation, the signatory or signatories, the products of which are subject to such investigation and the exporters and importers known to the investigating authorities to have an interest therein and the complainants shall be notified and a public notice shall be given. In determining whether to initiate an investigation, the investigating authorities should take into account the position adopted by the affiliates of a complainant party[2] which are resident in the territory of another signatory.

4.   Upon initiation of an investigation and thereafter, the evidence of both a subsidy and injury caused thereby should be considered simultaneously. In any event the evidence of both the existence of subsidy and injury shall be considered simultaneously (a) in the decision whether or not to initiate an investigation and (b) thereafter during the course of the investigation, starting on a date not later than the earliest date on which in accordance with the provisions of this Agreement provisional measures may be applied.

5.   The public notice referred to in paragraph 3 above shall describe the subsidy practice or practices to be investigated. Each signatory shall ensure that the investigating authorities afford all interested signatories and all interested parties[3] a reasonable opportunity, upon request, to see all relevant information that is not confidential (as indicated in paragraphs 6 and 7 below) and that is used by the investigating authorities in the investigation, and to present in writing, and upon justification orally, their views to the investigating authorities.

6.   Any information which is by nature confidential or which is provided on a confidential basis by parties to an investigation shall, upon cause shown, be treated as such by the investigating authorities. Such information shall not be disclosed without specific permission of the party submitting it[4]. Parties providing confidential information may be requested to furnish non-confidential summaries thereof. In the event such parties indicate that such information is not susceptible of summary, a statement of reasons why summarisation is not possible must be provided.

---

1.   As established in Part V of this Agreement and hereinafter referred to as "the Committee".
2.   For the purpose of this Agreement "party" means any natural or juridical person resident in the territory of any signatory.
3.   Any "interested signatory" or "interested party" shall refer to a signatory or a party economically affected by the subsidy in question.
4.   Signatories are aware that in the territory of certain signatories disclosure pursuant to a narrowly drawn protective order may be required.

7.　　However, if the investigating authorities find that a request for confidentiality is not warranted and if the party requesting confidentiality is unwilling to disclose the information, such authorities may disregard such information unless it can otherwise be demonstrated to their satisfaction that the information is correct[1].

8.　　The investigating authorities may carry out investigations in the territory of other signatories as required, provided they have notified in good time the signatory in question and unless the latter objects to the investigation. Further, the investigating authorities may carry out investigations on the premises of a firm and may examine the records of a firm if (a) the firm so agrees and (b) the signatory in question is notified and does not object.

9.　　In cases in which any interested party or signatory refuses access to, or otherwise does not provide, necessary information within a reasonable period or significantly impedes the investigation, preliminary and final findings[2], affirmative or negative, may be made on the basis of the facts available.

10.　　The procedures set out above are not intended to prevent the authorities of a signatory from proceeding expeditiously with regard to initiating an investigation, reaching preliminary or final findings, whether affirmative or negative, or from applying provisional or final measures, in accordance with relevant provisions of this Agreement.

11.　　In cases where products are not imported directly from the country of origin but are exported to the country of importation from an intermediate country, the provisions of this Agreement shall be fully applicable and the transaction or transactions shall, for the purposes of this Agreement, be regarded as having taken place between the country of origin and the country of importation.

12.　　An investigation shall be terminated when the investigating authorities are satisfied either that no subsidy exists or that the effect of the alleged subsidy on the industry is not such as to cause injury.

13.　　An investigation shall not hinder the procedures of customs clearance.

14.　　Investigations shall, except in special circumstances, be concluded within one year after their initiation.

15.　　Public notice shall be given of any preliminary or final finding whether affirmative or negative and of the revocation of a finding. In the case of an

---

1.　　Signatories agree that requests for confidentiality should not be arbitrarily rejected.
2.　　Because of different terms used under different systems in various countries the term "finding" is hereinafter used to mean a formal decision or determination.

affirmative finding each such notice shall set forth the findings and conclusions reached on all issues of fact and law considered material by the investigating authorities, and the reasons and basis therefor. In the case of a negative finding each notice shall set forth at least the basic conclusions and a summary of the reasons therefor. All notices of finding shall be forwarded to the signatory or signatories the products of which are subject to such finding and to the exporters known to have an interest therein.

16.   Signatories shall report without delay to the Committee all preliminary or final actions taken with respect to countervailing duties. Such reports will be available in the GATT secretariat for inspection by government representatives. The signatories shall also submit, on a semi-annual basis, reports on any countervailing duty actions taken within the preceding six months.

Article 3

Consultations

1.   As soon as possible after a request for initiation of an investigation is accepted, and in an event before the initiation of any investigation, signatories the products of which may be subject to such investigation shall be afforded a reasonable opportunity for consultations with the aim of clarifying the situation as to the matters referred to in Article 2, paragraph 1 above, and arriving at a mutually agreed solution.

2.   Furthermore, throughout the period of investigation, signatories the products of which are the subject of the investigation shall be afforded a reasonable opportunity to continue consultations, with a view to clarifying the factual situation and to arriving at a mutually agreed solution[1].

3.   Without prejudice to the obligation to afford reasonable opportunity for consultation, these provisions regarding consultations are not intended to prevent the authorities of a signatory from proceeding expeditiously with regard to initiating the investigation, reaching preliminary or final findings, whether affirmative or negative, or from applying provisional or final measures, in accordance with the provisions of this Agreement.

4.   The signatory which intends to initiate any investigation or is conducting such an investigation shall permit, upon request, the signatory or signatories the products of which are subject to such investigation access to non-confidential

---

1.   It is particularly important, in accordance with the provisions of this paragraph, that no affirmative finding whether preliminary or final be made without reasonable opportunity for consultations having, been given. Such consultations may establish the basis for proceeding under the provisions of Part VI of this Agreement.

evidence including the non-confidential summary of confidential data being used for initiating or conducting the investigation.

Article 4

Imposition of countervailing duties

1.   The decision whether or not to impose a countervailing duty in cases where all requirements for the imposition have been fulfilled and the decision whether the amount of the countervailing duty to be imposed shall be the full amount of the subsidy or less are decisions to be made by the authorities of the importing signatory. It is desirable that the imposition be permissive in the territory of all signatories and that the duty be less than the total amount of the subsidy if such lesser duty would be adequate to remove the injury to the domestic industry.

2.   No countervailing duty shall be levied[1] on any imported product in excess of the amount of the subsidy found to exist, calculated in terms of subsidisation per unit of the subsidised and exported products[2].

3.   When a countervailing duty is imposed in respect of any product, such countervailing duty shall be levied, in the appropriate amounts, on a non-discriminatory basis on imports of such product from all sources found to be subsidised and to be causing injury, except as to imports from those sources which have renounced any subsidies in question or from which undertakings under the terms of this Agreement have been accepted.

4 .   If, after reasonable efforts have been made to complete consultations, a signatory makes a final determination of the existence and amount of the subsidy and that, through the effects of the subsidy, the subsidised imports are causing injury, it may impose a countervailing duty in accordance with the provisions of this section unless the subsidy is withdrawn.

---

1.   As used in this Agreement "levy" shall mean the definitive or final legal assessment or collection of a duty or tax.
2.   An understanding among the signatories should be developed setting out the criteria for the calculation of the amount of the subsidy.

5. (a) Proceedings may[1] be suspended or terminated without the imposition of provisional measures or countervailing duties, if undertakings are accepted under which :

    (i)   the government of the exporting country agrees to eliminate or limit the subsidy or take other measures concerning its effects; or

    (ii)   the exporter agrees to revise its prices so that the investigating authorities are satisfied that the injurious effect of the subsidy is eliminated. Price increases under undertakings shall not be higher than necessary to eliminate the amount of the subsidy. Price undertakings shall not be sought or accepted from exporters unless the importing signatory has first (l) initiated an investigation in accordance with the provisions of Article 2 of this Agreement and (2) obtained the consent of the exporting signatory. Undertakings offered need not be accepted if the authorities of the importing signatory consider their acceptance impractical, for example if the number of actual or potential exporters is too great, or for other reasons.

(b) If the undertakings are accepted, the investigation of injury shall nevertheless be completed if the exporting signatory so desires or the importing signatory so decides. In such a case, if a determination of no injury or threat thereof is made, the undertaking shall automatically lapse, except in cases where a determination of no threat of injury is due in large part to the existence of an undertaking; in such cases the authorities concerned may require that an undertaking be maintained for a reasonable period consistent with the provisions of this Agreement.

(c) Price undertakings may be suggested by the authorities of the importing signatory, but no exporter shall be forced to enter into such an undertaking. The fact that governments or exporters do not offer such undertakings or do not accept an invitation to do so, shall in no way prejudice the consideration of the case. However, the authorities are free to determine that a threat of injury is more likely to be realised if the subsidised imports continue.

6.   Authorities of an importing signatory may require any government or exporter from whom undertakings have been accepted to provide periodically information relevant to the fulfilment of such undertakings, and to permit verification of pertinent data. In case of violation of undertakings, the authorities of the importing signatory may take expeditious actions under this Agreement in conformity with its provisions which may constitute immediate application of provisional measures using the best information available. In such cases definitive

---

1.   The word "may" shall not be interpreted to allow the simultaneous continuation of proceedings with the implementation of price undertakings, except as provided in paragraph 5(b)of this Article.

duties may be levied in accordance with this Agreement on goods entered for consumption not more than ninety days before the application of such provisional measures, except that any such retroactive assessment shall not apply to imports entered before the violation of the undertaking.

7.   Undertakings shall not remain in force any longer than countervailing duties could remain in force under this Agreement. The authorities of an importing signatory shall review the need for the continuation of any undertaking, where warranted, on their own initiative, or if interested exporters or importers of the product in question so request and submit positive information substantiating the need for such review.

8.   Whenever a countervailing duty investigation is suspended or terminated pursuant to the provisions of paragraph 5 above and whenever an undertaking is terminated, this fact shall be officially notified and must be published. Such notices shall set forth at least the basic conclusions and a summary of the reasons therefor.

9.   A countervailing duty shall remain in force only as long as, and to the extent necessary to counteract the subsidisation which is causing injury. The investigating authorities shall review the need for continued imposition of the duty where warranted on their own initiative or if an interested party so requests and submits positive information substantiating the need for review.

Article 5

Provisional measures and retroactivity

1.   Provisional measures may be taken only after a preliminary affirmative finding has been made that a subsidy exists and that there is sufficient evidence of injury as provided for in Article 2, paragraph 1(a) to (c). Provisional measures shall not be applied unless the authorities concerned judge that they are necessary to prevent injury being caused during the period of investigation.

2.   Provisional measures may take the form of provisional countervailing duties guaranteed by cash deposits or bonds equal to the amount of the provisionally calculated amount of subsidisation .

3.   The imposition of provisional measures shall be limited to as short a period as possible, not exceeding four months.

4.   The relevant provisions of Article 4 shall be followed in the imposition of provisional measures.

5.   Where a final finding of injury (but not of a threat thereof or of a material retardation of the establishment of an industry) is made or in the case of a final finding of threat of injury where the effect of the subsidised imports would, in the absence of the provisional measures, have led to a finding of injury, countervailing duties may be levied retroactively for the period for which provisional measures, if any, have been applied.

6.   If the definitive countervailing duty is higher than the amount guaranteed by the cash deposit or bond, the difference shall not be collected. If the definitive duty is less than the amount guaranteed by the cash deposit or bond, the excess amount shall be reimbursed or the bond released in an expeditious manner.

7.   Except as provided in paragraph 5 above, where a finding of threat of injury or material retardation is made (but no injury has yet occurred) a definitive countervailing duty may be imposed only from the date of the finding of threat of injury or material retardation and any cash deposit made during the period of the application of provisional measures shall be refunded and any bonds released in an expeditious manner.

8.   Where a final finding is negative any cash deposit made during the period of the application of provisional measures shall be refunded and any bonds released in an expeditious manner.

9.   In critical circumstances where for the subsidised product in question the authorities find that injury which is difficult to repair is caused by massive imports in a relatively short period of a product benefiting from export subsidies paid or bestowed inconsistently with the provisions of the General Agreement and of this Agreement and where it is deemed necessary, in order to preclude the recurrence of such injury, to assess countervailing duties retroactively on those imports, the definitive countervailing duties may be assessed on imports which were entered for consumption not more than ninety days prior to the date of application of provisional measures.

Article 6

Determination of injury

1.   A determination of injury[1] for purposes of Article VI of the General Agreement shall involve an objective examination of both (a) the volume of subsidised imports and their effect on prices in the domestic market for like

---

1.   Determinations of injury under the criteria set forth in this Article shall be based on positive evidence. In determining threat of injury the investigating authorities, in examining the factors listed in this Article, may take into account the evidence on the nature of the subsidy in question and the trade effects likely to arise therefrom.

products[1] and (b) the consequent impact of these imports on domestic producers of such products.

2.   With regard to volume of subsidised imports the investigating authorities shall consider whether there has been a significant increase in subsidised imports, either in absolute terms or relative to production or consumption in the importing signatory. With regard to the effect of the subsidised imports on prices, the investigating authorities shall consider whether there has been a significant price undercutting by the subsidised imports as compared with the price of a like product of the importing signatory, or whether the effect of such imports is otherwise to depress prices to a significant degree or prevent price increases, which otherwise would have occurred, to a significant degree. No one or several of these factors can necessarily give decisive guidance.

3.   The examination of the impact on the domestic industry concerned shall include an evaluation of all relevant economic factors and indices having a bearing on the state of the industry such as actual and potential decline in output, sales, market share, profits, productivity, return on investments, or utilisation of capacity; factors affecting domestic prices; actual and potential negative effects on cash flow, inventories, employment, wages, growth, ability to raise capital or investment and, in the case of agriculture, whether there has been an increased burden on Government support programmes. This list is not exhaustive, nor can one or several of these factors necessarily give decisive guidance.

4.   It must be demonstrated that the subsidised imports are, through the effects[2] of the subsidy, causing injury within the meaning of this Agreement. There may be other factors[3] which at the same time are injuring the domestic industry, and the injuries caused by other factors must not be attributed to the subsidised imports.

5.   In determining injury, the term "domestic industry" shall, except as provided in paragraph 7 below, be interpreted as referring to the domestic producers as a whole of the like products or to those of them whose collective output of the products constitutes a major proportion of the total domestic production of those products, except that when producers are related[4] to the

---

1.   Throughout this Agreement the term "like product" (*"produit similaire"*) shall be interpreted to mean a product which is identical, ie alike in all respects to the product under consideration or in the absence of such a product, another product which although not alike in all respects, has characteristics closely resembling those of the product under consideration.

2.   As set forth in paragraphs 2 and 3 of this Article.

3.   Such factors can include *inter alia*, the volume and prices of non-subsidised imports of the product in question contraction in demand or changes in the pattern of consumption, trade restrictive practices of and competition between the foreign and domestic producers, developments in technology and the export performance and productivity of the domestic industry.

4.   The Committee should develop a definition of the word "related" as used in this paragraph.

exporters or importers or are themselves importers of the allegedly subsidised product the industry may be interpreted as referring to the rest of the producers.

6.   The effect of the subsidised imports shall be assessed in relation to the domestic production of the like product when available data permit the separate identification of production in terms of such criteria as : the production process, the producers' realisation, profits. When the domestic production of the like product has no separate identity in these terms the effects of subsidised imports shall be assessed by the examination of the production of the narrowest group or range of products, which includes the like product, for which the necessary information can be provided.

7.   In exceptional circumstances the territory of a signatory may, for the production in question, be divided into two or more competitive markets and the producers within each market may be regarded as a separate industry if (a) the producers within such market sell all or almost all of their production of the product in question in that market, and (b) the demand in that market is not to any substantial degree supplied by producers of the product in question located elsewhere in the territory. In such circumstances injury may be found to exist even where a major portion of the total domestic industry is not injured provided there is concentration of subsidised imports into such an isolated market and provided further that subsidised imports are causing injury to the producers of all or almost all of the production within such market.

8.   When the industry has been interpreted as referring to the producers in a certain area as defined in paragraph 7 above, countervailing duties shall be levied only on the products in question consigned for final consumption to that area. When the constitutional law of importing signatory does not permit the levying of countervailing duties on such a basis, the importing signatory may levy the countervailing duties without limitation, only if (a) the exporters shall have been given an opportunity to cease exporting at subsidised prices to the area concerned or otherwise give assurances pursuant to Article 4, paragraph 5, of this Agreement, and adequate assurances in this regard have not been promptly given, and (b) such duties cannot be levied only on products of specific producers which supply the area in question.

9.   Where two or more countries have reached under the provisions of Article XXIV:8(a) of the General Agreement such a level of integration that they have the characteristics of a single, unified market the industry in the entire area of integration shall be taken to be the industry referred to in paragraphs 5 to 7 above.

PART II

Article 7

Notification of subsidies[1]

1.   Having regard to the provisions of Article XVI:1 of the General Agreement, any signatory may make a written request for information on the nature and extent of any subsidy granted or maintained by another signatory (including any form of income or price support) which operates directly or indirectly to increase exports of any product from or reduce imports of any product into its territory.

2.   Signatories so requested shall provide such information as quickly as possible and in a comprehensive manner, and shall be ready, upon request, to provide additional information to the requesting signatory. Any signatory which considers that such information has not been provided may bring the matter to the attention of the Committee.

3.   Any interested signatory which considers that any practice of another signatory having the effects of a subsidy has not been notified in accordance with the provisions of Article XVI:1 of the General Agreement may bring the matter to the attention of such other signatory. If the subsidy practice is not thereafter notified promptly, such signatory may itself bring the subsidy practice in question to the notice of the Committee.

Article 8

Subsidies - General Provisions

1.   Signatories recognise that subsidies are used by governments to promote important objectives of social and economic policy. Signatories also recognise that subsidies may cause adverse effects to the interests of other signatories.

2.   Signatories agree not to use export subsidies in a manner inconsistent with the provisions of this Agreement.

---

1.   In this Agreement, the term "subsidies" shall be deemed to include subsidies granted by any government or any public body within the territory of a signatory. However, it is recognised that for such signatories with different federal systems of government, there are different divisions of powers. Such signatories accept nonetheless the international consequences that may arise under this Agreement as a result of the granting of subsidies within their territories.

3.   Signatories further agree that they shall seek to avoid causing, through the use of any subsidy

(a)   injury to the domestic industry of another signatory[1],

(b)   nullification or impairment of the benefits accruing directly or indirectly to another signatory under the General Agreement[2], or

(c)   serious prejudice to the interests of another signatory[3].

4.   The adverse effects to the interests of another signatory required to demonstrate nullification or impairment[4] or serious prejudice may arise through

(a)   the effects of the subsidised imports in the domestic market of the importing signatory,

(b)   the effects of the subsidy in displacing or impeding the imports of like products into the market of the subsidising country, or

(c)   the effects of the subsidised exports in displacing[5] the exports of like products of another signatory from a third country market[6].

Article 9

Export subsidies on products other than certain primary products[7]

1.   Signatories shall not grant export subsidies on products other than certain primary products.

---

1.   Injury to the domestic industry is used here in the same sense as it is used in Part I of this Agreement.
2.   Benefits accruing directly or indirectly under the General Agreement include the benefits of tariff concessions bound under Article II of the General Agreement.
3.   Serious prejudice to the interests of another signatory is used in this Agreement in the same sense as it is used in Article XVI:1 of the General Agreement and includes threat of serious prejudice.
4.   Signatories recognise that nullification or impairment of benefits may also arise through the failure of a signatory to carry out its obligations under the General Agreement or this Agreement. Where such failure concerning export subsidies is determined by the Committee to exist, adverse effects may, without prejudice to paragraph 9 of Article 18 below, be presumed to exist. The other signatory will be accorded a reasonable opportunity to rebut this presumption.
5.   The term "displacing" shall be interpreted in a manner which takes into account the trade and development needs of developing countries and in this connection is not intended to fix traditional market shares.
6.   The problem of third country markets so far as certain primary products are concerned is dealt with exclusively under Article 10 below.
7.   For purposes of this Agreement "certain primary products" means the products referred to in Note Ad Article XVI of the General Agreement, Section B, paragraph 2, with the deletion of the words "or any mineral".

2.   The practices listed in points (a) to (l) in the Annex are illustrative of export subsidies.

Article 10

Export subsidies on certain primary products

1.   In accordance with the provisions of Article XVI:3 of the General Agreement, signatories agree not to grant directly or indirectly any export subsidy on certain primary products in a manner which results in the signatory granting such subsidy having more than an equitable share of world export trade in such product, account being taken of the shares of the signatories in trade in the product concerned during a previous representative period, and any special factors which may have affected or may be affecting trade in such product.

2.   For purposes of Article XVI:3 of the General Agreement and paragraph 1 above :

   (a)   "more than an equitable share of world export trade" shall include any case in which the effect of an export subsidy granted by a signatory is to displace the exports of another signatory bearing in mind the developments on world markets;

   (b)   with regard to new markets traditional patterns of supply of the product concerned to the world market, region or country, in which the new market is situated shall be taken into account in determining "equitable share of world export trade";

   (c)   "a previous representative period" shall normally be the three most recent calendar years in which normal market conditions existed.

3.   Signatories further agree not to grant export subsidies on exports of certain primary products to a particular market in a manner which results in prices materially below those of other suppliers to the same market.

Article 11

Subsidies other than export subsidies

1.   Signatories recognise that subsidies other than export subsidies are widely used as important instruments for the promotion of social and economic policy objectives and do not intend to restrict the right of signatories to use such subsidies

to achieve these and other important policy objectives which they consider desirable. Signatories note that among such objectives are :

(a) the elimination of industrial, economic and social disadvantages of specific regions,

(b) to facilitate the restructuring, under socially acceptable conditions, of certain sectors, especially where this has become necessary by reason of changes in trade and economic policies, including international agreements resulting in lower barriers to trade,

(c) generally to sustain employment and to encourage re-training and change in employment,

(d) to encourage research and development programmes, especially in the field of high technology industries,

(e) the implementation of economic programmes and policies to promote the economic and social development of developing countries,

(f) redeployment of industry in order to avoid congestion and environmental problems.

2.   Signatories recognise, however, that subsidies other than export subsidies, certain objectives and possible form of which are described, respectively, in paragraphs 1 and 3 of this Article, may cause or threaten to cause injury to a domestic industry of another signatory or serious prejudice to the interests of another signatory or may nullify or impair benefits accruing to another signatory under the General Agreement, in particular where such subsidies would adversely affect the conditions of normal competition. Signatories shall therefore seek to avoid causing such effects through the use of subsidies. In particular, signatories, when drawing up their policies and practices in this field, in addition to evaluating the essential internal objectives to be achieved, shall also weigh, as far as practicable, taking account of the nature of the particular case, possible adverse effects on trade. They shall also consider the conditions of world trade, production (eg price, capacity utilisation etc) and supply in the product concerned.

3.   Signatories recognise that the objectives mentioned in paragraph 1 above may be achieved, inter alia, by means of subsidies granted with the aim of giving an advantage to certain enterprises. Examples of possible forms of such subsidies are : government financing of commercial enterprises, including grants, loans or guarantees; government provision or government financed provision of utility, supply distribution and other operational or support services or facilities;

government financing of research and development programmes; fiscal incentives; and government subscription to, or provision of, equity capital.

Signatories note that the above form of subsidies are normally granted either regionally or by sector. The enumeration of forms of subsidies set out above is illustrative and non-exhaustive, and reflects these currently granted by a number of signatories to this Agreement.

Signatories recognise, nevertheless, that the enumeration of forms of subsidies set out above should be reviewed periodically and that this should be done, through consultations, in conformity with the spirit of Article XVI:5 of the General Agreement.

4.   Signatories recognise further that, without prejudice to their rights under this Agreement, nothing in paragraphs 1-3 above and in particular the enumeration of forms of subsidies creates, in itself, any basis for action under the General Agreement, as interpreted by this Agreement.

Article 12

Consultations

1.   Whenever a signatory has reason to believe that an export subsidy is being granted or maintained by another signatory in a manner inconsistent with the provisions of this Agreement, such signatory may request consultations with such other signatory.

2.   A request for consultations under paragraph 1 above shall include a statement of available evidence with regard to the existence and nature of the subsidy in question.

3.   Whenever a signatory has reason to believe that any subsidy is being granted or maintained by another signatory and that such subsidy either causes injury to its domestic industry, nullification or impairment of benefits accruing to it under the General Agreement, or serious prejudice to its interests, such signatory may request consultations with such other signatory.

4.   A request for consultations under paragraph 3 above shall include a statement of available evidence with regard to (a) the existence and nature of the subsidy in question and (b) the injury caused to the domestic industry or, in the case of nullification or impairment, or serious prejudice, the adverse effects caused to the interests of the signatory requesting consultations.

5.   Upon request for consultations under paragraph 1 or paragraph 3 above, the signatory believed to be granting or maintaining the subsidy practice in question shall enter into such consultations as quickly as possible. The purpose of the consultations shall be to clarify the facts of the situation and to arrive at a mutually acceptable solution.

Article 13

Conciliation, dispute settlement and authorised countermeasures

1.   If, in the case of consultations under paragraph 1 of Article 12, a mutually acceptable solution has not been reached within thirty days[1] of the request for consultations, any signatory party to such consultations may refer the matter to the Committee for conciliation in accordance with the provisions of Part VI.

2.   If, in the case of consultations under paragraph 3 of Article 12, a mutually accepted solution has not been reached within sixty days of the request for consultations, any signatory party to such consultations may refer the matter to the Committee for conciliation in accordance with the provisions of Part VI.

3.   If any dispute arising under this Agreement is not resolved as a result of consultations or conciliation's, the Committee shall, upon request, review the matter in accordance with the dispute settlement procedures of Part VI.

4.   If, as a result of its review, the Committee concludes that an export subsidy is being granted in a manner inconsistent with the provisions of this Agreement or that a subsidy is being granted or maintained in such a manner as to cause injury, nullification or impairment, or serious prejudice, it shall make such recommendations[2] to the parties as may be appropriate to resolve the issue and, in the event the recommendations are not followed, it may authorise such countermeasures as may be appropriate, taking into account the degree and nature of the adverse effects found to exist, in accordance with the relevant provisions of Part VI.

---

1.   Any time periods mentioned in this Article and in Article 18 may be extended by mutual agreement.
2.   In making such recommendations, the Committee shall take into account the trade, development and financial needs of developing country signatories.

PART III

Article 14

Developing countries

1. Signatories recognise that subsidies are an integral part of economic development programmes of developing countries.

2. Accordingly, this Agreement shall not prevent developing country signatories from adopting measures and policies to assist their industries, including those in the export sector. In particular the commitment of Article 9 shall not apply to developing country signatories, subject to the provisions of paragraphs 5 through 8 below.

3. Developing country signatories agree that export subsidies on their industrial products shall not be used in a manner which causes serious prejudice to the trade or production of another signatory.

4 . There shall be no presumption that export subsidies granted by developing country signatories result in adverse effects, as defined in this Agreement, to the trade or production of another signatory. Such adverse effects shall be demonstrated by positive evidence, through an economic examination of the impact on trade or production of another signatory.

5. A developing country signatory should endeavour to enter into a commitment[1] to reduce or eliminate export subsidies when the use of such export subsidies is inconsistent with its competitive and development needs.

6. When a developing country has entered into a commitment to reduce or eliminate export subsidies, as provided in paragraph 5 above, counter-measures pursuant to the provisions of Parts II and VI of this Agreement against any export subsidies of such developing country shall not be authorised for other signatories of this Agreement, provided that the export subsidies in question are in accordance with the terms of the commitment referred to in paragraph 5 above.

7. With respect to any subsidy, other than an export subsidy, granted by a developing country signatory, action may not be authorised or taken under Parts II and VI of this Agreement, unless nullification or impairment of tariff concessions or other obligations under the General Agreement is found to exist as a result of such subsidy, in such a way as to displace or impede imports of like products into the market of the subsidising country, or unless injury to domestic industry in the

---

1.   It is understood that after this Agreement has entered into force, any such proposed commitment shall be notified to the Committee in good time.

importing market of a signatory occurs in terms of Article VI of the General Agreement, as interpreted and applied by this Agreement. Signatories recognise that in developing countries, governments may play a large role in promoting economic growth and development. Intervention by such governments in their economy, for example through the practices enumerated in paragraph 3 of Article 11, shall not, per se, be considered subsidies.

8.   The Committee shall, upon request by an interested signatory, undertake a review of a specific export subsidy practice of a developing country signatory to examine the extent to which the practice is in conformity with the objectives of this Agreement. If a developing country has entered into a commitment pursuant to paragraph 5 of this Article, it shall not be subject to such review for the period of that commitment.

9.   The Committee shall, upon request by an interested signatory, also undertake similar reviews of measures maintained or taken by developed country signatories under the provisions of this Agreement which affect interests of a developing country signatory.

10.   Signatories recognise that the obligations of this Agreement with respect to export subsidies for certain primary products apply to all signatories.

PART IV

Article 15

Special situations

1.   In cases of alleged injury caused by imports from a country described in NOTES AND SUPPLEMENTARY PROVISIONS to the General Agreement (Annex I, Article VI, paragraph 1, point 2) the importing signatory may base its procedures and measures either

(a)   on this Agreement, or, alternatively

(b)   on the Agreement on Implementation of Article VI of the General Agreement on Tariffs and Trade.

2.   It is understood that in both cases (a) and (b) above the calculation of the margin of dumping or of the amount of the estimated subsidy can be made by comparison of the export price with

(a)   the price at which a like product of a country other than the importing signatory or those mentioned above is sold, or

(b)   the constructed value[1] of a like product in a country other than the importing signatory or those mentioned above.

3.   If neither prices nor constructed value as established under (a) or (b) of paragraph 2 above provide an adequate basis for determination of dumping or subsidisation then the price in the importing signatory, if necessary duly adjusted to reflect reasonable profits, may be used.

4.   All calculations under the provisions of paragraph 2 and 3 above shall be based on prices or costs ruling at the same level of trade, normally at the ex factory level, and in respect of operations made as nearly as possible at the same time. Due allowance shall be made in each case, on its merits, for the difference in conditions and terms of sale or in taxation and for the other differences affecting price comparability, so that the method of comparison applied is appropriate and not unreasonable.

PART V

Article 16

Committee on Subsidies and Countervailing Measures

1.   There shall be established under this Agreement a Committee on Subsidies and Countervailing Measures composed of representatives from each of the signatories to this Agreement. The Committee shall elect its own Chairman and shall meet not less than twice a year and otherwise as envisaged by relevant provisions of this Agreement at the request of any signatory. The Committee shall carry out responsibilities as assigned to it under this Agreement or by the signatories and it shall afford signatories the opportunity of consulting on any matters relating to the operation of the Agreement or the furtherance of its objectives. The GATT secretariat shall act as the secretariat to the Committee.

2.   The Committee may set up subsidiary bodies as appropriate.

---

1.   Constructed value means cost of production plus a reasonable amount for administration, selling and any other costs and for profits.

3.   In carrying out their functions, the Committee and any subsidiary bodies may consult with and seek information from any source they deem appropriate. However, before the Committee or a subsidiary body seeks such information from a source within the jurisdiction of a signatory, it shall inform the signatory involved.

PART VI

Article 17

Conciliation

1.   In cases where matters are referred to the Committee for conciliation failing a mutually agreed solution in consultations under any provision of this Agreement, the Committee shall immediately review the facts involved and, through its good offices, shall encourage the signatories involved to develop a mutually acceptable solution.[1]

2.   Signatories shall make their best efforts to reach a mutually satisfactory solution throughout the period of conciliation.

3.   Should the matter remain unresolved, notwithstanding efforts at conciliation made under paragraph 2 above, any signatory involved may, thirty days after the request for conciliation, request that a panel be established by the Committee in accordance with the provisions of Article 18 below.

Article 18

Dispute settlement

1.   The Committee shall establish a panel upon request pursuant to paragraph 3 of Article 17[2]. A panel so established shall review the facts of the matter and, in light of such facts, shall present to the Committee its findings concerning the rights and obligations of the signatories party to the dispute under the relevant provisions of the General Agreement as interpreted and applied by this Agreement.

2.   A panel should be established within thirty days of a request therefor[3] and a panel so established should deliver its findings to the Committee within sixty days after its establishment.

---

1.   In this connection, the Committee may draw signatories' attention to those cases in which, in its view, there is no reasonable basis supporting the allegations made.

2.   This does not preclude, however, the more rapid establishment of a panel when the Committee so decides, taking into account the urgency of the situation.

3.   The parties to the dispute would respond within a short period of time, ie seven working days, to nominations of panel members by the Chairman of the Committee and would not oppose nominations except for compelling reasons.

3.   When a panel is to be established, the Chairman of the Committee, after securing the agreement of the signatories concerned, should propose the composition of the panel. Panels shall be composed of three or five members, preferably governmental, and the composition of panels should not give rise to delays in their establishment. It is understood that citizens of countries whose governments[1] are parties to the dispute would not be members of the panel concerned with that dispute.

4.   In order to facilitate the constitution of panels, the Chairman of the Committee should maintain an informal indicative list of governmental and non-governmental persons qualified in the fields of trade relations, economic development, and other matters covered by the General Agreement and this Agreement, who could be available for serving on panels. For this purpose, each signatory would be invited to indicate at the beginning of every year to the Chairman of the Committee the name of one or two persons who would be available for such work .

5.   Panel members would serve in their individual capacities and not as government representatives, nor as representatives of any organisation. Governments would therefore not give them instructions with regard to matters before a panel. Panel members should be selected with a view to ensuring the independence of the members, a sufficiently diverse background and a wide spectrum of experience.

6.   To encourage development of mutually satisfactory solutions between the parties to a dispute and with a view to obtaining their comments, each panel should first submit the descriptive part of its report to the parties concerned, and should subsequently submit to the parties to the dispute its conclusions, or an outline thereof, a reasonable period of time before they are circulated to the Committee.

7.   If a mutually satisfactory solution is developed by the parties to a dispute before a panel, any signatory with an interest in the matter has a right to enquire about and be given appropriate information about that solution and a notice outlining the solution that has been reached shall be presented by the panel to the Committee.

8.   In cases where the parties to a dispute have failed to come to a satisfactory solution, the panels shall submit a written report to the Committee which should set forth the findings of the panel as to the questions of fact and the application of the relevant provisions of the General Agreement as interpreted and applied by this Agreement and the reasons and bases therefor.

---

1.   The term "governments" is understood to mean governments of all member countries in cases of customs unions.

9.   The Committee shall consider the panel report as soon as possible and, taking into account the findings contained therein, may make recommendations to the parties with a view to resolving the dispute. If the Committee's recommendations are not followed within a reasonable period, the Committee may authorise appropriate countermeasures (including withdrawal of GATT concessions or obligations) taking into account the nature and degree of the adverse effect found to exist. Committee recommendations should be presented to the parties within thirty days of the receipt of the panel report.

PART VII

Article 19

Final provisions

1.   No specific action against a subsidy of another signatory can be taken except in accordance with the provisions of the General Agreement, as interpreted by this Agreement[1].

Acceptance and accession

2. (a)   This Agreement shall be open for acceptance by signature or otherwise, by governments contracting parties to the GATT and by the European Economic Community.

    (b)   This Agreement shall be open for acceptance by signature or otherwise by governments having provisionally acceded to the GATT, on terms related to the effective application of rights and obligations under this Agreement, which take into account rights and obligations in the instruments providing for their provisional accession.

    (c)   This Agreement shall be open to accession by any other government on terms, related to the effective application of rights and obligations under this Agreement, to be agreed between that government and the signatories, by the deposit with the Director-General to the CONTRACTING PARTIES to the GATT of an instrument of accession which states the terms so agreed.

    (d)   In regard to acceptance, the provisions of Article XXVI:5(a) and (b) of the General Agreement would be applicable.

---

1.   This paragraph is not intended to preclude action under other relevant provisions of the General Agreement, where appropriate.

Reservations

3.   Reservations may not be entered in respect of any of the provisions of this Agreement without the consent of the other signatories.

Entry into force

4.   This Agreement shall enter into force on 1 January 1980 for the governments[1] which have accepted or acceded to it by that date. For each other government it shall enter into force on the thirtieth day following the date of its acceptance or accession to this Agreement.

National legislation

5.   (a)   Each government accepting or acceding to this Agreement shall take all necessary steps, of a general or particular character, to ensure, not later than the date of entry into force of this Agreement for it, the conformity of its laws, regulations and administrative procedures with the provisions of this Agreement as they may apply to the signatory in question.

     (b)   Each signatory shall inform the Committee of any changes in its laws and regulations relevant to this Agreement and in the administration of such laws and regulations.

Review

6.   The Committee shall review annually the implementation and operation of this Agreement taking into account the objectives thereof. The Committee shall annually inform the CONTRACTING PARTIES to the GATT of developments during the period covered by such reviews[2].

Amendments

7.   The signatories may amend this Agreement having regard, inter alia, to the experience gained in its implementation. Such an amendment, once the signatories have concurred in accordance with procedures established by the Committee, shall not come into force for any signatory until it has been accepted by such signatory.

Withdrawal

8.   Any signatory may withdraw from this Agreement. The withdrawal shall take effect upon the expiration of sixty days from the day on which written notice of withdrawal is received by the Director-General to the CONTRACTING

---

1.   The term "governments" is deemed to include the competent authorities of the European Economic Community.

2.   At the first such review, the Committee shall, in addition to its general review of the operation of the Agreement, offer all interested signatories an opportunity to raise questions and discuss issues concerning specific subsidy practices and the impact on trade, if any, of certain direct tax practices.

PARTIES to the GATT. Any signatory may upon such notification request an immediate meeting of the Committee.

Non-application of this Agreement between particular signatories
9.   This Agreement shall not apply as between any two signatories if either of the signatories, at the time either accepts or accedes to this Agreement, does not consent to such application.

Annex
10.   The annex to this Agreement constitutes an integral part thereof.

Secretariat
11.   This Agreement shall be serviced by the GATT secretariat.

Deposit
12.   This Agreement shall be deposited with the Director-General to the CONTRACTING PARTIES to the GATT, who shall promptly furnish to each signatory and each contracting party to the GATT a certified copy thereof and of each amendment thereto pursuant to paragraph 7, and a notification of each acceptance thereof or accession thereto pursuant to paragraph 2, and of each withdrawal therefrom pursuant to paragraph 8 of this Article.

Registration
13.   This Agreement shall be registered in accordance with the provisions of Article 102 of the Charter of the United Nations.

Done at Geneva this twelfth day of April nineteen hundred and seventy-nine in a single copy, in the English, French and Spanish languages, each text being authentic.

ANNEX

Illustrative List of Export Subsidies

(a) The provision by governments of direct subsidies to a firm or an industry contingent upon export performance.

(b) Currency retention schemes or any similar practices which involve a bonus on exports.

(c) Internal transport and freight charges on export shipments, provided or mandated by governments, on terms more favourable than for domestic shipments.

(d) The delivery by governments or their agencies of imported or domestic products or services for use in the production of exported goods, on terms or conditions more favourable than for delivery of like or directly competitive products or services for use in the production of goods for domestic consumption, if (in the case of products) such terms or conditions are more favourable than those commercially available on world markets to their exporters.

(e) The full or partial exemption, remission, or deferral specifically related to exports, of direct taxes[1] or social welfare charges paid or payable by industrial or commercial enterprises[2].

(f) The allowance of special deductions directly related to exports or export performance, over and above those granted in respect to production for domestic consumption, in the calculation of the base on which direct taxes are charged.

(g) The exemption or remission in respect of the production and distribution of exported products, of indirect taxes[1] in excess of those levied in respect of the production and distribution of like products when sold for domestic consumption.

(h) The exemption, remission or deferral of prior stage cumulative indirect taxes[1] on goods or services used in the production of exported products in excess of the exemption, remission or deferral of like prior stage cumulative indirect taxes on goods or services used in the production of like products when sold for domestic consumption; provided, however, that prior stage cumulative indirect taxes may be exempted, remitted or deferred on exported products even when not exempted, remitted or deferred on like products when sold for domestic consumption, if the prior stage cumulative indirect taxes are levied on goods that are physically incorporated (making normal allowance for waste) in the exported product[3].

(i)   The remission or drawback of import charges[1] in excess of those levied on imported goods that are physically incorporated (making normal allowance for waste) in the exported product; provided, however, that in particular cases a firm may use a quantity of home market goods equal to, and having the same quality and characteristics as, the imported goods as a substitute for them in order to benefit from this provision if the import and the corresponding export operations both occur within a reasonable time period, normally not to exceed two years.

(j)   The provision by governments (or special institutions controlled by governments) of export credit guarantee or insurance programmes, of insurance or guarantee programmes against increases in the costs of exported products[4] or of exchange risk programmes, at premium rates, which are manifestly inadequate to cover the long-term operating costs and losses of the programmes[5].

(k)   The grant by governments (or special institutions controlled by and/or acting under the authority of governments) of export credits at rates below those which they actually have to pay for the funds so employed (or would have to pay if they borrowed on international capital markets in order to obtain funds of the same maturity and denominated in the same currency as the export credit), or the payment by them of all credits, or part of the costs incurred by exporters or financial institutions in obtaining credits, in so far as they are used to secure a material advantage in the field of export credit terms.

Provided, however, that if a signatory is a party to an international undertaking on official export credits to which at least twelve original signatories[6] to this Agreement are parties as of 1 January 1979 (or a successor undertaking which has been adopted by those original signatories), or if in practice a signatory applies the interest rates provisions of the relevant undertaking, an export credit practice which is in conformity with those provisions shall not be considered an export subsidy prohibited by this Agreement.

(l)   Any other charge on the public account constituting an export subsidy in the sense of Article XVI of the General Agreement.

NOTES

1. For the purpose of this Agreement :

The term "direct taxes" shall mean taxes on wages, profits, interest, rents, royalties, and all other forms of income, and taxes on the ownership of real property;

The term "import charges" shall mean tariffs, duties, and other fiscal charges not elsewhere enumerated in this note that are levied on imports;

The term "indirect taxes" shall mean sales, excise, turnover, value added, franchise, stamp, transfer, inventory and equipment taxes, border taxes and all taxes other than direct taxes and import charges;

"Prior stage" indirect taxes are those levied on goods or services used directly or indirectly in making the product;

"Cumulative" indirect taxes are multi-staged taxes levied where there is no mechanism for subsequent crediting of the tax if the goods or services subject to tax at one stage of production are used in a succeeding stage of production;

"Remission" of taxes includes the refund or rebate of taxes.

2. The signatories recognise that deferral need not amount to an export subsidy where, for example, appropriate interest charges are collected. The signatories further recognise that nothing in this text prejudges the disposition by the CONTRACTING PARTIES of the specific issues raised in GATT document L/4422.

The signatories reaffirm the principle that prices for goods in transactions between exporting enterprises and foreign buyers under their or under the same control should for tax purposes be the prices which would be charged between independent enterprises acting at arm's length. Any signatory may draw the attention of another signatory to administrative or other practices which may contravene this principle and which result in a significant saving of direct taxes in export transactions. In such circumstances the signatories shall normally attempt to resolve their differences using the facilities of existing bilateral tax treaties or other specific international mechanisms, without prejudice to the rights and obligations of signatories under the General Agreement, including the right of consultation created in the preceding sentence.

Paragraph (e) is not intended to limit a signatory from taking measures to avoid the double taxation of foreign source income earned by its enterprises or the enterprises of another signatory.

Where measures incompatible with the provisions of paragraph (e) exist, and where major practical difficulties stand in the way of the signatory concerned bringing such measures promptly into conformity with the Agreement, the signatory concerned shall, without prejudice to the rights of other signatories under the General Agreement or this Agreement, examine methods of bringing these measures into conformity within a reasonable period of time.

In this connection the European Economic Community has declared that Ireland intends to withdraw by 1 January 1981 its system of preferential tax measures related to exports, provided for under the Corporation Tax Act of 1976, whilst continuing nevertheless to honour legally binding commitments entered into during the lifetime of this system.

3. Paragraph (h) does not apply to value-added tax systems and border-tax adjustment in lieu thereof; the problem of the excessive remission of value-added taxes is exclusively covered by paragraph (g).

4. The signatories agree that nothing in this paragraph shall prejudice or influence the deliberations of the panel established by the GATT Council on 6 June 1978 (C/M/126).

5. In evaluating the long-term adequacy of premium rates, costs and losses of insurance programmes, in principle only such contracts shall be taken into account that were concluded after the date of entry into force of this Agreement.

6. An original signatory to this agreement shall mean any signatory which adheres *ad referendum* to the Agreement on or before 30 June 1979.

APPENDIX 4

COUNCIL REGULATION (EEC) 2423/88
of 11 July 1988

on protection against dumped or subsidised imports from countries not members of the European Economic Community[1]

THE COUNCIL OF THE EUROPEAN COMMUNITIES,

Having regard to the Treaty establishing the European Economic Community, and in particular Article 113 thereof,

Having regard to the Regulations establishing the common organisation of agricultural markets and the Regulations adopted under Article 235 of the Treaty applicable to goods manufactured from agricultural products, and in particular the provisions of those Regulations which allow for derogation from the general principle that protective measures at frontiers may be replaced solely by the measures provided for in those Regulations,

Having regard to the proposal from the Commission,

Whereas by Regulation (EEC) 2176/84[2], as amended by Regulation (EEC) 1761/87[3], the Council adopted common rules for protection against dumped or subsidised imports from countries which are not members of the European Economic Community;

Whereas these rules were adopted in accordance with existing international obligations, in particular those arising from Article VI of the General Agreement on tariffs and trade (hereinafter referred to as "GATT"), from the Agreement on Implementation of Article VI of the GATT (1979 Anti-dumping Code) and from the Agreement on Interpretation and Application of Articles VI, XVI and XXIII of the GATT (Code on Subsidies and Countervailing Duties);

Whereas in applying these rules it is essential, in order to maintain the balance of rights and obligations which these Agreements sought to establish, that the Community take account of their interpretation by the Community's major trading partners, as reflected in legislation or established practice;

---

1.   OJ L209 11.7.88 p1.
2.   OJ L201 30.7.84 p1.
3.   OJ L167 26.6.87 p9.

Whereas it is desirable that the rules for determining normal value should be presented clearly and in sufficient detail; whereas it should be specifically provided that where sales on the domestic market of the country of export or origin do not for any reason form a proper basis for determining the existence of dumping, recourse may be had to a constructed normal value; whereas it is appropriate to give examples of situations which may be considered as not representing the ordinary course of trade, in particular where a product is sold at prices which are less than the costs of production, or where transactions take place between parties which are associated or which have a compensatory arrangement; where it is appropriate to list the possible methods of determining normal value in such circumstances;

Whereas it is expedient to define the export price and to enumerate the necessary adjustments to be made in those cases where reconstruction of this price from the first open-market price is deemed appropriate;

Whereas, for the purpose of ensuring a fair comparison between export price and normal value, it is advisable to establish guidelines for determining the adjustments to be made in respect of differences in physical characteristics, in quantities, in conditions and terms of sale and to draw attention to the fact that the burden of proof falls on any person claiming such adjustments;

Whereas the term "dumping margin" should be clearly defined and the Community's established practice for methods of calculation where prices or margins vary codified;

Whereas it seems advisable to lay down in adequate detail the manner in which the amount of any subsidy is to be determined;

Whereas it seems appropriate to set out certain factors which may be relevant for the determination of injury;

Whereas it is necessary to lay down the procedures for anyone acting on behalf of a Community industry which considers itself injured or threatened by dumped or subsidised imports to lodge a complaint; whereas it seems appropriate to make it clear that in the case of withdrawal of a complaint, proceedings may, but need not necessarily, be terminated;

Whereas there should be co-operation between the Member States and the Commission both as regards information about the existence of dumping or subsidisation and injury resulting therefrom, and as regards the subsequent examination of the matter at Community level; whereas, to this end, consultations should take place within an advisory committee;

Whereas it is appropriate to lay down clearly the rules of procedure to be followed during the investigation, in particular the rights and obligations of the Community authorities and the parties involved, and the conditions under which interested parties may have access to information and may ask to be informed of the essential facts and considerations on the basis of which it is intended to recommend definitive measures;

Whereas it is desirable to state explicitly that the investigation of dumping or subsidisation should normally cover a period of not less than six months immediately prior to the initiation of the proceeding and that final determinations must be based on the facts established in respect of the investigation period;

Whereas to avoid confusion, the use of the terms 'investigation' and 'proceeding' in this Regulation should be clarified;

Whereas it is necessary to require that when information is to be considered as being confidential, a request to this effect must be made by the supplier, and to make clear that confidential information which could be summarised but of which no non-confidential summary has been submitted may be disregarded;

Whereas, in order to avoid undue delays and for administrative convenience, it is advisable to introduce time limits within which undertakings may be offered;

Whereas, it is necessary to lay down more explicit rules concerning the procedure to be followed after withdrawal or violation of undertakings;

Whereas it is necessary that the Community's decision-making process permit rapid and efficient action, in particular through measures taken by the Commission, as for instance the imposition of provisional duties;

Whereas, in order to discourage dumping, it is appropriate to provide, in cases where the facts as finally established show that there is dumping and injury, for the possibility of definitive collection of provisional duties even if the imposition of a definitive anti-dumping duty is not decided on, on particular grounds;

Whereas it is essential, in order to ensure that anti-dumping and countervailing duties are levied in a correct and uniform manner, that common rules for the application of such duties be laid down; whereas, by reason of the nature of the said duties, such rules may differ from the rules for the levying of normal import duties;

Whereas experience gained from the implementation of Regulation (EEC) 2176/84 has shown that assembly in the Community of products whose importation in a finished state is subject to anti-dumping duty may give rise to certain difficulties;

Whereas in particular :

— where assembly or production is carried out by a party which is related or associated to any of the manufacturers whose exports of the like product are subject to an anti-dumping duty, and

— where the value of the parts or materials used in the assembly or production operation and originating in the country of origin of the product subject to an anti-dumping duty exceeds the value of all other parts or materials used,

such assembly or production is considered likely to lead to circumvention of the anti-dumping duty;

Whereas, in order to prevent circumvention, it is necessary to provide for the collection of an anti-dumping duty on products thus assembled or produced;

Whereas it is necessary to lay down the procedures and conditions for the collection of duty in such circumstances;

Whereas the amount of anti-dumping duty collected should be limited to that necessary to prevent circumvention;

Whereas provision should be made for the review of Regulations and decisions to be carried out, where appropriate, in part only;

Whereas, in order to avoid abuse of Community procedures and resources, it is appropriate to lay down a minimum period which must elapse after the conclusion of a proceeding before such a review may be conducted, and to ensure that there is evidence of a change in circumstances sufficient to justify a review;

Whereas it is necessary to provide that, after a certain period of time, anti-dumping and countervailing measures will lapse unless the need for their continued existence can be shown;

Whereas appropriate procedures should be established for examining applications for refunds of anti-dumping duties; whereas there is a need to ensure that refund procedures apply only in respect of definitive duties or amounts of any provisional duty which have been definitively collected, and to streamline the existing procedures for refunds;

Whereas this Regulation should not prevent the adoption of special measures where this does not run counter to the Community's obligations under the GATT;

Whereas agricultural products and products derived therefrom might also be dumped or subsidised; whereas it is, therefore, necessary to supplement the import rules generally applicable to these products by making provision for protective measures against such practices;

Whereas, in addition to the above considerations, which, in essence, led to the adoption of Regulation (EEC) 2176/84, experience has shown that it is necessary to define more precisely certain of the rules to be applied and the procedures to be followed in the context of anti-dumping proceedings.

Whereas, for the determination of normal value, it is appropriate to ensure that when this is based on domestic prices, the price should be that actually paid or payable in the ordinary course of trade in the exporting country or country of origin and, therefore, the treatment of discounts and rebates should be clarified, in particular, with regard to deferred discounts which may be recognised if evidence is produced that they were not introduced to distort the normal value. It is also desirable to state more explicitly how normal value is established on the basis of constructed value, in particular, that the selling, general and administrative expenses and profit should be calculated, depending on the circumstances, by reference to the expenses incurred and the profit realised on profitable sales made by the exporter concerned or by other producers or exporters or on any reasonable basis. In addition, it is appropriate to state that, where the exporter neither produces nor sells the like product in the country of origin, the normal value shall normally be established by reference to the prices or costs of the exporter's supplier. Finally, it is considered necessary to define more precisely the conditions under which sales at a loss may be considered as not having been made in the ordinary course of trade;

Whereas, for the determination of export prices, it is advisable to ensure that this is based on the price actually paid or payable and, therefore, the treatment of discounts and rebates should be clarified. In cases where the export price has to be reconstructed, it is necessary to state that the costs to be used in this reconstruction include those normally borne by an importer but paid by any party which appears to be associated with the importer or exporter;

Whereas, for the comparison of normal value and export prices, it is necessary to ensure that this is not distorted by claims for adjustments relating to factors which are not directly related to the sales under consideration or by claims for factors already taken into account. It is therefore appropriate to define precisely the differences which affect price comparability and to lay down more explicit rules on how any adjustment should be made, in particular, for differences in physical characteristics, transport, packing, credit, warranties and other selling expenses. With regard to such selling expenses, it is appropriate, for reasons of clarity, to specify that no allowance should be made for general selling expenses since such expenses are not directly related to the sales under consideration with the exception of salesmen's salaries which should not be treated differently to commissions paid. For reasons of administrative convenience, it is also appropriate to specify that claims for individual adjustments which are insignificant should be disregarded;

Whereas, it is expedient to clarify Commuity practice with regard to the use of averaging and sampling techniques;

Whereas, in order to avoid undue disruption to proceedings, it is advisable to clarify that the supply of false or misleading information may lead to such information being disregarded and any claims to which it refers being disallowed;

Whereas, experience has shown that, it is necessary to prevent the effectiveness of anti-dumping duties being eroded by the duty being borne by exporters. It is appropriate to confirm that, in such circumstances, additional anti-dumping duties may be imposed, where necessary retroactively;

Whereas, experience has also shown that the rules relating to the expiry of anti-dumping and countervailing measurs should be clarified. For this purpose and in order to facilitate the administration of these rules, provision should be made for the publication of a notice of intention to carry out a review;

Whereas, it is appropriate to state more explicitly the methods to be used in the calculation of the amount to any refund, thus confirming the consistent practice of the Commission, as regards refunds and the relevant principles contained in the notice which the Commission has published concerning the reimbursement of anti-dumping duties[1];

Whereas it is appropriate to take advantage of this opportunity to proceed to a consolidation of the rules in question,

HAS ADOPTED THIS REGULATION :

---

1.   OJ C266 22.10.86 p2.

Article 1

Applicability

This Regulation lays down provisions for protection against dumped or subsidised imports from countries not members of the European Economic Community.

Article 2

Dumping

A. PRINCIPLE

1. An anti-dumping duty may be applied to any dumped product whose release for free circulation in the Community causes injury.

2. A product shall be considered to have been dumped if its export price to the Community is less than the normal value of the like product.

B. NORMAL VALUE

3. For the purposes of this Regulation, the normal value shall be :

    (a)   the comparable price actually paid or payable in the ordinary course of trade for the like product intended for consumption in the exporting country or country of origin. This price shall be net of all discounts and rebates directly linked to the sales under consideration provided that the exporter claims and supplies sufficient evidence that any such reduction from the gross price has actually been granted. Deferred discounts may be recognised if they are directly linked to the sales under consideration and if evidence is produced to show that these discounts were based on consistent practice in prior periods or on an undertaking to comply with the conditions required to qualify for the deferred discount.

    (b)   when there are no sales of the like product in the ordinary course of trade on the domestic market of the exporting country or country of origin, or when such sales do not permit a proper comparison :

        (i)   the comparable price of the like product when exported to any third country, which may be the highest such export price but should be a representative price; or

  (ii) the constructed value, determined by adding cost of production and a reasonable margin of profit. The cost of production shall be computed on the basis of all costs, in the ordinary course of trade, both fixed and variable, in the country of origin, of materials and manufacture, plus a reasonable amount for selling, administrative and other general expenses. The amount for selling, general and administrative expenses and profit shall be calculated by reference to the expenses incurred and the profit realised by the producer or exporter on the profitable sales of like products on the domestic market. If such data is unavailable or unreliable or is not suitable for use they shall be calculated by reference to the expenses incurred and profit realised by other producers or exporters in the country of origin or export on profitable sales of the like product. If neither of these two methods can be applied the expenses incurred and the profit realised shall be calculated by reference to the sales made by the exporter or other producers or exporters in the same business sector in the country of origin or export or on any other reasonable basis.

 (c) where the exporter in the country of origin neither produces nor sells the like product in the country of origin, the normal value shall be established on the basis of prices or costs of other sellers or producers in the country of origin in the same manner as mentioned in subparagraphs (a) and (b). Normally the prices or costs of the exporter's supplier shall be used for this purpose.

4. Whenever there are reasonable grounds for believing or suspecting that the price at which a product is actually sold for consumption in the country of origin is less than the cost of production as defined in paragraph 3(b)(ii), sales at such prices may be considered as not having been made in the ordinary course of trade if they :

 (a) have been made in substantial quantities during the investigation period as defined in Article 7(1)(c); and

 (b) are not at prices which permit recovery, in the normal course of trade and within the period referred to in paragraph (a) of all costs reasonably allocated.

In such circumstances, the normal value may be determined on the basis of the remaining sales on the domestic market made at a price which is not less than the cost of production or on the basis of export sales to third countries or on the basis of the constructed value or by adjusting the sub-production-cost price referred to above in order to eliminate loss and provide for a reasonable profit. Such normal value calculations shall be based on available information.

5. In the case of imports from non-market economy countries and, in particular, those to which Regulations (EEC) 1765/82[1] and (EEC) 1766/82[2] apply, normal value shall be determined in an appropriate and not unreasonable manner on the basis of one of the following criteria :

(a) the price at which the like product of a market economy third country is actually sold :

(i) for consumption on the domestic market of that country; or

(ii) to other countries, including the Community; or

(b) the constructed value of the like product in a market economy third country;

(c) if neither price nor constructed value as established under (a) or (b) provides an adequate basis, the price actually paid or payable in the Community for the like product, duly adjusted, if necessary, to include a reasonable profit margin.

6. Where a product is not imported directly from the country of origin but is exported to the Community from an intermediate country, the normal value shall be the comparable price actually paid or payable for the like product on the domestic market of either the country of export or the country of origin. The latter basis might be appropriate inter alia, where the product is merely trans-shipped through the country of export, where such products are not produced in the country of export or where no comparable price for it exists in the country of export.

7. For the purpose of determining normal value, transactions between parties which appear to be associated or to have a compensatory arrangement with each other may be considered as not being in the ordinary course of trade unless the Community authorities are satisfied that the prices and costs involved are comparable to those involved in transactions between parties which have no such link.

C. EXPORT PRICE

8. (a) The export price shall be the price actually paid or payable for the product sold for export to the Community net of all taxes, discounts and rebates actually granted and directly related to the sales under consideration. Deferred discounts shall also be taken into consideration if they are actually granted and directly related to the sales under consideration.

---

1.   OJ L195 5.7.82 p1.
2.   OJ L195 5.7.82 p21.

(b)   In cases where there is no export price or where it appears that there is an association or a compensatory arrangement between the exporter and the importer or a third party, or that for other reasons the price actually paid or payable for the product sold for export to the Community is unreliable, the export price may be constructed on the basis of the price at which the imported product is first resold to an independent buyer, or if the product is not resold to an independent buyer, or not resold in the condition imported, on any reasonable basis. In such cases, allowance shall be made for all costs incurred between importation and resale, including all duties and taxes, and for a reasonable profit margin. These costs shall include those normally borne by an importer but paid by any party either in or outside the Community which appears to be associated or to have a compensatory arrangement with the importer or exporter.

Such allowances shall include, in particular, the following :

(i)   usual transport, insurance, handling, loading and ancillary costs;

(ii)   customs duties, any anti-dumping duties and other taxes payable in the importing country by reason of the importation or sale of the goods;

(iii)   a reasonable margin for overheads and profit and/or any commission usually paid or agreed

D. COMPARISON

9. (a)   The normal value, as established under paragraphs 3 to 7, and the export price, as established under paragraph 8, shall be compared as nearly as possible at the same time. For the purpose of ensuring a fair comparison, due allowance in the form of adjustments shall be made in each case, on its merits, for the differences affecting price comparability, ie for differences in :

(i)   physical characteristics;

(ii)   import charges and indirect taxes;

(iii)   selling expenses resulting from sales made :
        —   at different levels of trade, or
        —   in different quantities, or
        —   under different conditions and terms of sale.

(b)   Where an interested party claims an adjustment it must prove that its claim is justified.

10. Any adjustments to take account of the differences affecting price comparability listed in paragraph 9(a) shall, where warranted, be made pursuant to the rules specified below.

(a)   Physical characteristics :

The normal value as established under paragraphs 3 to 7 shall be adjusted by an amount corresponding to a reasonable estimate of the value of the difference in the physical characteristics of the product concerned.

(b)   Import charges and indirect taxes :

Normal value shall be reduced by an amount corresponding to any import charges or indirect taxes, as defined in the notes to the Annex, borne by the like product and by materials physically incorporated therein, when destined for consumption in the country of origin or export and not collected or refunded in respect of the product exported to the Community.

(c)   Selling expenses (ie) :

(i)   Transport, insurance, handling, loading and ancillary costs :

Normal value shall be reduced by the directly related costs incurred for conveying the product concerned from the premises of the exporter to the first independent buyer. The export price shall be reduced by any directly related costs incurred by the exporter for conveying the product concerned from its premises in the exporting country to its destination in the Community. In both cases these costs comprise transport, insurance, handling, loading and ancillary costs.

(ii)   Packing :

Normal value and export price shall be reduced by the respective, directly related costs of the packing for the product concerned.

(iii)   Credit :

Normal value and export price shall be reduced by the cost of any credit granted for the sales under consideration.

The amount of the reduction shall be calculated by reference to the normal commercial credit rate applicable in the country of origin or export in respect of the currency expressed on the invoice.

(iv) Warranties, guarantees, technical assistance and other after-sales services :

Normal value and export price shall be reduced by an amount corresponding to the direct costs of providing warranties, guarantees, technical assistance and services.

(v) Other selling expenses :

Normal value and export price shall be reduced by an amount corresponding to the commissions paid in respect of the sales under consideration. The salaries paid to salesmen, ie personnel wholly engaged in direct selling activities, shall also be deducted.

(d) Amount of the adjustment :

The amount of any adjustment shall be calculated on the basis of relevant data for the investigaiton period or the data for the last available financial year.

(e) Insignificant adjustments :

Claims for adjustments which are insignificant in relation to the price or value of the affected transactions shall be disregarded. Ordinarily, individual adjustments having an *ad valorem* effect of less than 0.5% of that price or value shall be considered insignificant.

E. ALLOCATION OF COSTS

11. In general, all cost calculations shall be based on available accounting data, normally allocated, where necessary, in proportion to the turnover for each product and market under consideration.

F. LIKE PRODUCT

12. For the purposes of this Regulation, 'like product' means a product which is identical, ie, alike in all respects, to the product under consideration, or, in the absence of such a product, another product which has characteristics closely resembling those of the product under consideration.

G. AVERAGING AND SAMPLING TECHNIQUES

13. Where prices vary :

— normal value shall normally be established on a weighted average basis,

— export prices shall normally be compared with the normal value on a transaction-by-transaction basis except where the use of weighted averages would not materially affect the results of the investigation,

— sampling techniques, eg the use of the most frequently occurring or representative prices may be applied to establish normal value and export prices in cases in which a significant volume of transactions is involved.

H. DUMPING MARGIN

14. (a) "Dumping margin" means the amount by which the normal value exceeds the export price.

(b) Where dumping margins vary, weighted averages may be established.

Article 3

Subsidies

1. A countervailing duty may be imposed for the purpose of offsetting any subsidy bestowed, directly or indirectly, in the country of origin or export, upon the manufacture, production, export or transport of any product whose release for free circulation in the Community causes injury.

2. Subsidies bestowed on exports include, but are not limited to, the practices listed in the Annex.

3. The exemption of a product from import charges or indirect taxes, as defined in the Notes to the Annex, effectively borne by the like product and by materials physically incorporated therein, when destined for consumption in the country of origin or export, or the refund of such charges or taxes, shall not be considered as a subsidy for the purposes of this Regulation.

4. (a) The amount of the subsidy shall be determined per unit of the subsidised product exported to the Community.

(b)   In establishing the amount of any subsidy the following elements shall be deducted from the total subsidy :

        (i)   any application fee, or other costs necessarily incurred in order to qualify for, or receive benefit of, the subsidy;

        (ii)   export taxes, duties or other charges levied on the export of the product to the Community specifically intended to offset the subsidy.

        Where an interested party claims a deduction, it must prove that the claim is justified.

(c)   Where the subsidy is not granted by reference to the quantities manufactured, produced, exported or transported, the amount shall be determined by allocating the value of the subsidy as appropriate over the level of production or exports of the product concerned during a suitable period. Normally this period shall be the accounting year of the beneficiary.

        Where the subsidy is based upon the acquisition or future acquisition of fixed assets, the value of the subsidy shall be calculated by spreading the subsidy across a period which reflects the normal depreciation of such assets in the industry concerned. Where the assets are non-depreciating, the subsidy shall be valued as an interest-free loan.

(d)   In the case of imports from non-market economy countries and in particular those to which Regulations (EEC) 1765/82 and (EEC) 1766/82 apply, the amount of any subsidy may be determined in an appropriate and not unreasonable manner, by comparing the export price as calculated in accordance with Article 2(8) with the normal value as determined in accordance with Article 2(5). Article 2(10) shall apply to such a comparison.

(e)   Where the amount of subsidisation varies, weighted averages may be established.

Article 4

Injury

1. A determination of injury shall be made only if the dumped or subsidised imports are, through the effects of dumping or subsidisation, causing injury ie, causing or

threatening to cause material injury to an established Community industry or materially retarding the establishment of such an industry. Injuries caused by other factors, such as volume and prices of imports which are not dumped or subsidised, or contraction in demand, which, individually or in combination, also adversely affect the Community industry must not be attributed to the dumped or subsidised imports.

2. An examination of injury shall involve the following factors, no one or several of which can necessarily give decisive guidance :

   (a)   volume of dumped or subsidised imports, in particular whether there has been a significant increase, either in absolute terms or relative to production or consumption in the Community;

   (b)   the prices of dumped or subsidised imports, in particular whether there has been a significant price undercutting as compared with the price of a like product in the Community;

   (c)   the consequent impact on the industry concerned as indicated by actual or potential trends in the relevant economic factors such as :

        — production,
        — utilisation of capacity,
        — stocks,
        — sales,
        — market share,
        — prices (ie, depression of prices or prevention of price increases which otherwise would have occurred),
        — profits,
        — return on investment,
        — cash flow,
        — employment.

3. A determination of threat of injury may only be made where a particular situation is likely to develop into actual injury. In this regard account may be taken of factors such as :

   (a)   rate of increase of the dumped or subsidised exports to the Community;

   (b)   export capacity in the country of origin or export, already in existence or which will be operational in the foreseeable future, and the likelihood that the resulting exports will be to the Community;

   (c)   the nature of any subsidy and the trade effects likely to arise therefrom.

4. The effect of the dumped or subsidised imports shall be assessed in relation to the Community production of the like product when available data permit its separate identification. When the Community production of the like product has no separate identity, the effect of the dumped or subsidised imports shall be assessed in relation to the production of the narrowest group or range of production which includes the like product for which the necessary information can be found.

5. The term "Community industry" shall be interpreted as referring to the Community producers as a whole of the like product or to those of them whose collective output of the products constitutes a major proportion of the total Community production of those products except that :

— when producers are related to the exporters or importers or are themselves importers of the allegedly dumped or subsidised product the term "Community industry" may be interpreted as referring to the rest of the producers;

— in exceptional circumstances the Community may, for the production in question, be divided into two or more competitive markets and the producers within each market regarded as a Community industry if,

(a) the producers within such market sell all or almost all their production of the product in question in that market, and

(b) the demand in that market is not to any substantial degree supplied by producers of the product in question located elsewhere in the Community.

In such circumstances injury may be found to exist even where a major proportion of the total Community industry is not injured, provided there is a concentration of dumped or subsidised imports into such an isolated market and provided further that the dumped or subsidised imports are causing injury to the producers of all or almost all of the production within such market.

Article 5

Complaint

1. Any natural or legal person, or any association not having legal personality, acting on behalf of a Community industry which considers itself injured or threatened by dumped or subsidised imports may lodge a written complaint.

2. The complaint shall contain sufficient evidence of the existence of dumping or subsidisation and the injury resulting therefrom.

3. The complaint may be submitted to the Commission, or a Member State, which shall forward it to the Commission. The Commission shall send Member States a copy of any complaint it receives.

4. The complaint may be withdrawn, in which case proceedings may be terminated unless such termination would not be in the interest of the Community.

5. Where it becomes apparent after consultation that the complaint does not provide sufficient evidence to justify initiating an investigation, then the complainant shall be so informed.

6. Where, in the absence of any complaint, a Member State is in possession of sufficient evidence both of dumping or subsidisation and of injury resulting therefrom for a Community industry, it shall immediately communicate such evidence to the Commission.

Article 6

Consultations

1. Any consultations provided for in this Regulation shall take place within an Advisory Committee, which shall consist of representatives of each Member State, with a representative of the Commission as chairman. Consultations shall be held immediately on request by a Member State or on the initiative of the Commission.

2. The Committee shall meet when convened by its chairman. He shall provide the Member States, as promptly as possible, with all relevant information.

3. Where necessary, consultation may be in writing only; in such case the Commission shall notify the Member States and shall specify a period within which they shall be entitled to express their opinions or to request an oral consultation.

4. Consultation shall in particular cover :

    (a)   the existence of dumping or of a subsidy and the methods of establishing the dumping margin or the amount of the subsidy;

    (b)   the existence and extent of injury;

(c)   the causal link between the dumped or subsidised imports and injury;

(d)   the measures which, in the circumstances, are appropriate to prevent or remedy the injury caused by dumping or the subsidy and the ways and means for putting such measures into effect.

Article 7

Initiation and subsequent investigation

1. Where, after consultation it is apparent that there is sufficient evidence to justify initiating a proceeding the Commission shall immediately :

(a)   announce the initiation of a proceeding in the *Official Journal of the European Communities*; such announcements shall indicate the product and countries concerned, give a summary of the information received, and provide that all relevant information is to be communicated to the Commission; it shall state the period within which interested parties may make known their views in writing and may apply to be heard orally by the Commission in accordance with paragraph 5;

(b)   so advise the exporters and importers known to the Commission to be concerned as well as representatives of the exporting country and the complainants;

(c)   commence the investigation at Community level, acting in co-operation with the Member States; such investigation shall cover both dumping or subsidisation and injury resulting therefrom and shall be carried out in accordance with paragraphs 2 to 8; the investigation of dumping or subsidisation shall normally cover a period of not less than six months immediately prior to the initiation of the proceeding.

2. (a)   The Commission shall seek all information it deems to be necessary and, where it considers it appropriate, examine and verify the records of importers, exporters, traders, agents, producers, trade associations and organisations.

(b)   Where necessary the Commission shall carry out investigations in third countries, provided that the firms concerned give their consent and the government of the country in question has been officially notified and raises no objection. The Commission shall be assisted by officials of those Member States who so request.

3. (a) The Commission may request Member States :

    — to supply information,

    — to carry out all necessary checks and inspections, particuarly amongst importers, traders and Community producers,

    — to carry out investigations in third countries, provided the firms concerned give their consent and the government of the country in question has been officially notified and raises no objection.

    (b) Member States shall take whatever steps are necessary in order to give effect to requests from the Commission. They shall send to the Commission the information requested together with the results of all inspections, checks or investigations carried out.

    (c) Where this information is of general interest or where its transmission has been requested by a Member State, the Commission shall forward it to the Member States, provided it is not confidential, in which case a non-confidential summary shall be forwarded.

    (d) Officials of the Commission shall be authorised, if the Commission or a Member State so requests, to assist the officials of Member States in carrying out their duties.

4. (a) The complainant and the importers and exporters known to be concerned, as well as the representatives of the exporting country, may inspect all information made available to the Commission by any party to an investigation as distinct from internal documents prepared by the authorities of the Community or its Member States, provided that it is relevant to the defence of their interests and not confidential within the meaning of Article 8 and that it is used by the Commission in the investigation. To this end, they shall address a written request to the Commission indicating the information required.

    (b) Exporters and importers of the product subject to investigation and, in the case of subsidisation, the representatives of the country of origin, may request to be informed of the essential facts and considerations on the basis of which it is intended to recommend the imposition of definitive duties or the definitive collection of amounts secured by way of a provisional duty.

(c) (i) requests for information pursuant to (b) shall :

    (aa) be addressed to the Commission in writing,

    (bb) specify the particular issues on which information is sought,

    (cc) be received, in cases where a provisional duty has been applied, not later than one month after publication of the imposition of that duty;

(ii) the information may be given either orally or in writing as considered appropriate by the Commission. It shall not prejudice any subsequent decision which may be taken by the Commission or the Council. Confidential information shall be treated in accordance with Article 8;

(iii) information shall normally be given no later than 15 days prior to the submission by the Commission of any proposal for final action pursuant to Article 12. Representations made after the information is given shall be taken into consideration only if received within a period to be set by the Commission in each case, which shall be at least 10 days, due consideration being given to the urgency of the matter.

5. The Commission may hear the interested parties. It shall so hear them if they have, within the period prescribed in the notice published in the *Official Journal of the European Communities*, made a written request for a hearing showing that they are an interested party likely to be affected by the result of the proceeding and that there are particular reasons why they should be heard orally.

6. Furthermore the Commission shall, on request, give the parties directly concerned an opportunity to meet, so that opposing views may be presented and any rebuttal argument put forward. In providing this opportunity the Commission shall take account of the need to preserve confidentiality and of the convenience of the parties. There shall be no obligation on any party to attend a meeting and failure to do so shall not be prejudicial to that party's case.

7. (a) This Article shall not preclude the Community authorities from reaching preliminary determinations or from applying provisional measures expeditiously.

    (b) In cases in which any interested party or third country refuses access to, or otherwise does not provide, necessary information within a reasonable period, or significantly impedes the investigation, preliminary or final findings, affirmative or negative, may be made on the basis of the facts available. Where the Commission finds that any interested party or third country has supplied it with false or misleading information, it may disregard any such information and disallow any claim to which this refers.

8. Anti-dumping or countervailing proceedings shall not constitute a bar to customs clearance of the product concerned.

9. (a) An investigation shall be concluded either by its termination or by definitive action. Conclusion should normally take place within one year of the initiation of the proceeding.

   (b) A proceeding shall be concluded either by the termination of the investigation without the imposition of duties and without the acceptance of undertakings or by the expiry or repeal of such duties or by the termination of undertakings in accordance with Articles 14 or 15.

Article 8

Confidentiality

1. Information received in pursuance of this Regulation shall be used only for the purpose for which it was requested.

2. (a) Neither the Council, nor the Commission, nor Member States, nor the officials of any of these, shall reveal any information received in pursuance of this Regulation for which confidential treatment has been requested by its supplier, without specific permission from the supplier.

   (b) Each request for confidential treatment shall indicate why the information is confidential and shall be accompanied by a non-confidential summary of the information, or a statement of the reasons why the information is not susceptible of such summary.

3. Information will ordinarily be considered to be confidential if its disclosure is likely to have a significantly adverse effect upon the supplier or the source of such information.

4. However, if it appears that a request for confidentiality is not warranted and if the supplier is either unwilling to make the information public or to authorise its disclosure in generalised or summary form, the information in question may be disregarded.

The information may also be disregarded where such request is warranted and where the supplier is unwilling to submit a non-confidential summary, provided that the information is susceptible of such summary.

5. This Article shall not preclude the disclosure of general information by the Community authorities and in particular of the reasons on which decisions taken in pursuance of this Regulation are based, or disclosure of the evidence relied on by the Community authorities in so far as necessary to explain those reasons in court proceedings. Such disclosure must take into account the legitimate interest of the parties concerned that their business secrets should not be divulged.

Article 9

Termination of proceedings where protective measures are unnecessary

1. If it becomes apparent after consultation that protective measures are unnecessary, then, where no objection is raised within the Advisory Committee referred to in Article 6(1), the proceeding shall be terminated. In all other cases the Commission shall submit to the Council forthwith a report on the results of the consultation, together with a proposal that the proceeding be terminated. The proceeding shall stand terminated if, within one month, the Council, acting by a qualified majority, has not decided otherwise.

2. The Commission shall inform any representatives of the country of origin or export and the parties known to be concerned and shall announce the termination in the *Official Journal of the European Communities* setting forth its basic conclusions and a summary of the reasons therefor.

Article 10

Undertakings

1. Where, during the course of an investigation, undertakings are offered which the Commission, after consultation, considers acceptable, the investigation may be terminated without the imposition of provisional or definitive duties.

Save in exceptional circumstances, undertakings may not be offered later than the end of the period during which representations may be made under Article 7(4)(c)(iii). The termination shall be decided in conformity with the procedure laid down in Article 9(1) and information shall be given and notice published in accordance with Article 9(2). Such termination does not preclude the definitive collection of amounts secured by way of provisional duties pursuant to Article 12(2).

2. The undertakings referred to under paragraph 1 are those under which :

(a)   the subsidy is eliminated or limited, or other measures concerning its injurious effects taken, by the government of the country of origin or export; or

(b)   prices are revised or exports cease to the extent that the Commission is satisfied that either the dumping margin or the amount of the subsidy, or the injurious effects thereof, are eliminated. In case of subsidisation the consent of the country of origin or export shall be obtained.

3. Undertakings may be suggested by the Commission, but the fact that such undertakings are not offered or an invitation to do so is not accepted, shall not prejudice consideration of the case. However, the continuation of dumped or subsidised imports may be taken as evidence that a threat of injury is more likely to be realised.

4. If the undertakings are accepted, the investigation of injury shall nevertheless be completed if the Commission, after consultation, so decides or if request is made, in the case of dumping, by exporters representing a significant percentage of the trade involved or, in the case of subsidisation, by the country of origin or export. In such a case, if the Commission, after consultation, makes a determination of no injury, the undertaking shall automatically lapse. However, where a determination of no threat of injury is due mainly to the existence of an undertaking, the Commission may require that the undertaking be maintained.

5. The Commission may require any party from whom an undertaking has been accepted to provide periodically information relevant to the fulfilment of such undertakings, and to permit verification of pertinent data. Non-compliance with such requirements shall be construed as a violation of the undertaking.

6. Where an undertaking has been withdrawn or where the Commission has reason to believe that it has been violated and where Community interests call for such intervention, it may, after consultations and after having offered the exporter concerned an opportunity to comment, apply provisional anti-dumping or countervailing duties forthwith on the basis of the facts established before the acceptance of the undertaking.

Article 11

Provisional duties

1. Where preliminary examination shows that dumping or a subsidy exists and that there is sufficient evidence of injury caused thereby and the interests of the Community call for intervention to prevent injury being caused during the proceeding, the Commission, acting at the request of a Member State or on its own initiative, shall impose a provisional anti-dumping or countervailing duty. In such cases, release of the products concerned for free circulation in the Community shall be conditional upon the provision of security for the amount of the provisional duty, definitive collection of which shall be determined by the subsequent decision of the Council under Article 12(2).

2. The Commission shall take such provisional action after consultation or, in cases of extreme urgency, after informing the Member States. In this latter case, consultations shall take place 10 days at the latest after notification to the Member States of the action taken by the Commission.

3. Where a Member State requests immediate intervention by the Commission, the Commission shall within a maximum of five working days of receipt of the request, decide whether a provisional anti-dumping or countervailing duty should be imposed.

4. The Commission shall forthwith inform the Council and the Member States of any decision taken under this Article. The Council, acting by a qualified majority, may decide differently. A decision by the Commission not to impose a provisional duty shall not preclude the imposition of such duty at a later date, either at the request of a Member State, if new factors arise, or on the initiative of the Commission.

5. Provisional duties shall have a maximum period of validity of four months. However, where exporters representing a significant percentage of the trade involved so request or, pursuant to a notice of intention from the Commission, do not object, provisional anti-dumping duties may be extended for a further period of two months.

6. Any proposal for definitive action, or for extension of provisional measures, shall be submitted to the Council by the Commission not later than one month before expiry of the period of validity or provisional duties. The Council shall act by a qualified majority.

7. After expiration of the period of validity of provisional duties, the security shall be released as promptly as possible to the extent that the Council has not decided to collect it definitively.

Article 12

Definitive action

1. Where the facts as finally established show that there is dumping or subsidisation during the period under investigation and injury caused thereby, and the interests of the Community call for Community intervention, a definitive and anti-dumping or countervailing duty shall be imposed by the Council, acting by qualified majority on a proposal submitted by the Commission after consultation.

2. (a) Where a provisional duty has been applied, the Council shall decide, irrespective of whether a definitive anti-dumping or countervailing duty is to be imposed, what proportion of the provisional duty is to be definitively collected. The Council shall act by a qualified majority on a proposal from the Commission.

   (b) The definitive collection of such amount shall not be decided upon unless the facts as finally established show that there has been dumping or subsidisation, and injury. For this purpose, "injury" shall not include material retardation of the establishment of a Community industry, nor threat of material injury, except where it is found that this would, in the absence of provisional measures, have developed into material injury.

Article 13

General provisions on duties

1. Anti-dumping or countervailing duties, whether provisional or definitive, shall be imposed by Regulation.

2. Such Regulation shall indicate in particular the amount and type of duty imposed, the product covered, the country of origin or export, the name of the supplier, if practicable, and the reasons on which the Regulation is based.

3. The amount of such duties shall not exceed the dumping margin provisionally estimated or finally established or the amount of the subsidy provisionally estimated or finally established; it should be less if such lesser duty would be adequate to remove the injury.

4. (a)   Anti-dumping and countervailing duties shall be neither imposed nor increased with retroactive effect. The obligation to pay the amount of these duties is incurred in accordance with Directive 79/623/EEC[1].

   (b)   However, where the Council determines :

   (i)   for dumped products :

   —   that there is a history of dumping which caused injury or that the importer was, or should have been, aware that the exporter practices dumping and that such dumping would cause injury, and

   —   that the injury is caused by sporadic dumping, ie massive dumped imports of a product in a relatively short period, to such an extent that, in order to preclude it recurring, it appears necessary to impose an anti-dumping duty retroactively on those imports; or

   (ii)   for subsidised products :

   —   in critical circumstances that injury which is difficult to repair is caused by massive imports in a relatively short period of a product benefiting from export subsidies paid or bestowed inconsistently with the provisions of the GATT and of the Agreement on Interpretation and Application of Articles VI, XVI and XXIII of the GATT, and

   —   that it is necessary, in order to preclude the recurrence of such injury, to assess countervailing duties retroactively on these imports; or

   (iii) for dumped or subsidised products :

   —   that an undertaking has been violated,

   the definitive anti-dumping or countervailing duties may be imposed on products in relation to which the obligation to pay import duties under Directive 79/623/EEC has been or would have been incurred not more than 90 days prior to the date of application of provisional duties, except that in the case of violation of an undertaking such retroactive assessment

---

1.   OJ L179 17.7.79 p31.

shall not apply to imports which were released for free circulation in the Community before the violation.

5. Where a product is imported into the Community from more than one country, duty shall be levied at an appropriate amount on a non-discriminatory basis on all imports of such product found to be dumped or subsidised and causing injury, other than imports from those sources in respect of which undertakings have been accepted.

6. Where the Community industry has been interpreted as referring to the producers in a certain region, the Commission shall give exporters an opportunity to offer undertakings pursuant to Article 10 in respect of the region concerned. If an adequate undertaking is not given promptly or is not fulfilled, a provisional or definitive duty may be imposed in respect of the Community as a whole.

7. In the absence of any special provisions to the contrary adopted when a definitive or provisional anti-dumping or countervailing duty was imposed, the rules on the common definition of the concept of origin and the relevant common implementing provisions shall apply.

8. Anti-dumping or countervailing duties shall be collected by Member States in the form, at the rate and according to the other criteria laid down when the duties were imposed, and independently of the customs duties, taxes and other charges normally imposed on imports.

9. No product shall be subject to both anti-dumping and countervailing duties for the purpose of dealing with one and the same situation arising from dumping or from the granting of any subsidy.

10. (a) Definitive and anti-dumping duties may be imposed, by way of derogation from the second sentence of paragraph 4(a), on products that are introduced into the commerce of the Community after having been assembled or produced in the Community, provided that :

— assembly or production is carried out by a party which is related or associated to any of the manufacturers whose exports of the like product are subject to a definitive anti-dumping duty,

— the assembly or production operation was started or substantially increased after the opening of the anti-dumping investigation,

— the value of parts or materials used in the assembly or production operation and originating in the country of exportation of the product subject to the anti-dumping duty exceeds the value of all other parts or materials used by at least 50%.

In applying this provision, account shall be taken of the circumstances of each case, and, inter alia, of the variable costs incurred in the assembly or production operation and of the research and development carried out and the technology applied within the Community.

In that event the Council shall, at the same time, decide that parts or materials suitable for use in the assembly or production of such products and originating in the country of exportation of the product subject to the anti-dumping duty can only be considered to be in free circulation in so far as they will not be used in an assembly or production operation as specified in the first subparagraph.

(b) Products thus assembled or produced shall be declared to the competent authorities before leaving the assembly or production plant for their introduction into the commerce of the Community. For the purposes of levying an anti-dumping duty, this declaration shall be considered to be equivalent to the declaration referred to in Article 2 of Directive 79/695/EEC[1].

(c) The rate of the anti-dumping duty shall be that applicable to the manufacturer in the country of origin of the like product subject to an anti-dumping duty to which the party in the Community carrying out the assembly or production is related or associated. The amount of duty collected shall be proportional to that resulting from the application of the rate of the anti-dumping duty applicable to the exporter of the complete product on the cif value of the parts or materials imported; it shall not exceed that required to prevent circumvention of the anti-dumping duty.

(d) The provisions of this Regulation concerning investigation, procedure, and undertakings apply to all questions arising under this paragraph.

11. (a) Where the exporter bears the anti-dumping duty, an additional anti-dumping duty may be imposed to compensate for the amount borne by the exporter.

(b) When any party directly concerned submits sufficient evidence showing that the duty has been borne by the exporter, eg that the resale price to the first independent buyer of the product subject to the anti-dumping

---

1.   OJ L205 13.8.79 p19.

duty is not increased by an amount corresponding to the anti-dumping duty, the matter shall be investigated and the exporters and importers concerned shall be given an opportunity to comment.

When it is found that the anti-dumping duty has been borne by the exporter, in whole or in part, either directly or indirectly and where Community interests call for intervention, an additional anti-dumping duty shall, after consultation, be imposed in accordance with the procedures laid down in Articles 11 and 12.

This duty may be applied retroactively. It may be imposed on products in relation to which the obligation to pay import duties under Directive 79/623/EEC has been incurred after the imposition of the definitive anti-dumping duty, except that such assessment shall not apply to imports which were released for free circulation in the Community before the exporter bore the anti-dumping duty.

(c)   Insofar as the results of the investigation show that the absence of a price increase by an amount corresponding to the anti-dumping duty is not due to a reduction in the costs and/or profits of the importer for the product concerned then the absence of such price increase shall be considered as an indicator that the anti-dumping duty has been borne by the exporter.

(d)   Article 7(7)(b) applies within the context of investigations under this paragraph.

Article 14

Review

1. Regulations imposing anti-dumping or countervailing duties and decisions to accept undertakings shall be subject to review, in whole or in part, where warranted.

Such review may be held either at the request of a Member State or on the initiative of the Commission. A review shall also be held where an interested party so requests and submits evidence of changed circumstances sufficient to justify the need for such review, provided that at least one year has elapsed since the conclusion of the investigation. Such requests shall be addressed to the Commission which shall inform the Member States.

2. Where, after consultation, it becomes apparent that review is warranted, the investigation shall be re-opened in accordance with Article 7, where the

circumstances so require. Such re-opening shall not *per se* affect the measures in operation.

3. Where warranted by the review, carried out either with or without re-opening of the investigation, the measures shall be amended, repealed or annulled by the Community institution competent for their introduction. However, where measures have been taken under the transitional provisions of an Act of Accession the Commission shall itself amend, repeal or annul them and shall report this to the Council; the latter may, acting by a qualified majority, decide that different action be taken.

Article 15

1. Subject to the provisions of paragraph 3, 4 and 5, anti-dumping or countervailing duties and undertakings shall lapse after five years from the date on which they entered into force or were last modified or confirmed.

2. The Commission shall normally, after consultation and within six months prior to the end of the five year period, publish in the *Official Journal of the European Communities* a notice of the impending expiry of the measure in question and inform the Community industry known to be concerned. This notice shall state the period within which interested parties may make known their views in writing and may apply to be heard orally by the Commission in accordance with Article 7(5).

3. Where an interested party shows that the expiry of the measure would lead again to injury or threat of injury, the Commission shall, after consultation, publish in the *Official Journal of the European Communities* a notice of its intention to carry out a review of the measure. Such notice shall be published prior to the end of the relevant five year period. The measure shall remain in force pending the outcome of this review.

However, where the initiation of the review has not been published within six months after the end of the relevant five year period the measure shall lapse at the end of that six month period.

4. Where a review of a measure under Article 14 is in progress at the end of the relevant five year period, the measure shall remain in force pending the outcome of such review. A notice to this effect shall be published in the *Official Journal of the European Communities* before the end of the relevant five year period.

5. Where anti-dumping or countervailing duties and undertakings lapse under this Article the Commission shall publish a notice to that effect in the *Official Journal*

of the European Communities. Such notice shall state the date of expiry of the measure.

Article 16

Refund

1. Where an importer can show that the duty collected exceeds the actual dumping margin or the amount of the subsidy, consideration being given to any application of weighted averages, the excess amount shall be reimbursed. This amount shall be calculated in relation to the changes which have occurred in the dumping margin or the amount of the subsidy which were established in the original investigation for the shipments to the Community of the importer's supplier. All refund calculations shall be made in accordance with the provisions of Articles 2 or 3 and shall be based, as far as possible, on the same method applied in the original investigation, in particular, with regard to any application of averaging or sampling techniques.

2. In order to request the reimbursement referred to in paragraph 1, the importer shall submit an application to the Commission. The application shall be submitted via the Member State in the territory of which the products were released for free circulation and within three months of the date on which the amount of the definitive duties to be levied was duly determined by the competent authorities or of the date on which a decision was made definitively to collect the amounts secured by way of provisional duty.

The Member State shall forward the application to the Commission as soon as possible, either with or without an opinion as to its merits.

The Commission shall inform the other Member States forthwith and give its opinion on the matter. If the Member States agree with the opinion given by the Commission or do not object to it within one month of being informed, the Commission may decide in accordance with the said opinion. In all other cases, the Commission shall, after consultation, decide whether and to what extent the application should be granted.

Article 17

Final provisions

This Regulation shall not preclude the application of :

1.   any special rules laid down in agreements concluded between the Community and third countries;

2.   the Community Regulations in the agricultural sector and of Regulations (EEC) 1059/69[1], (EEC) 2730/75[2], and (EEC) 2783/75[3]; this Regulation shall operate by way of complement to those Regulations and in derogation from any provisions thereof which preclude the application of anti-dumping or countervailing duties;

3.   special measures, provided that such action does not run counter to obligations under the GATT.

Article 18

Repeal of existing legislation

Regulation (EEC) 2176/84 is hereby repealed.

References to the repealed Regulation shall be construed as references to this Regulation.

---

1.   OJ L141 12.6.69 p1.
2.   OJ L281 1.11.75 p20.
3.   OJ L282 1.11.75 p104.

Article 19

Entry into force

This Regulation shall enter into force on the third day following its publication in the *Official Journal of the European Communities.*

It shall apply to proceedings already initiated.

This Regulation shall be binding in its entirety and directly applicable in all Member States.

Done at Brussels, 11 July 1988.

For the Council
The President
P. ROUMELIOTIS

ANNEX

ILLUSTRATIVE LIST OF EXPORT SUBSIDIES

(a)   The provision by governments of direct subsidies to a firm or an industry contingent upon export performance.

(b)   Currency retention schemes or any similar practices which involve a bonus on exports.

(c)   Internal transport and freight charges on export shipments, provided or mandated by governments, on terms more favourable than for domestic shipments.

(d)   The delivery by governments or their agencies of imported or domestic products or services for use in the production of exported goods, on terms or conditions more favourable than for delivery of like or directly competitive products or services for use in the production of goods for domestic consumption, if (in the case of products) such terms or conditions are more favourable than those commercially available on world markets to their exporters.

(e)   The full or partial exemption, remission, or deferral specifically related to exports, of direct taxes or social welfare charges paid or payable by industrial or commercial enterprises. Notwithstanding the foregoing, deferral of taxes and charges referred to above need not amount to an export subsidy where, for example, appropriate interest charges are collected.

(f)   The allowance of special deductions directly related to exports or export performance, over and above those granted in respect to production for domestic consumption, in the calculation of the base on which direct taxes are charged.

(g)   The exemption or remission in respect of the production and distribution of exported products, or indirect taxes in excess of those levied in respect of the production and distribution of like products when sold for domestic consumption. The problem of the excessive remission of value added tax is exclusively covered by this paragraph.

(h)   The exemption, remission or deferral of prior stage cumulative indirect taxes on goods or services used in the production of exported products in excess of the exemption, remission or deferral of like prior stage cumulative indirect taxes on goods or services used in the production of like products when sold for domestic consumption; provided, however, that prior stage cumulative

406

indirect taxes may be exempted, remitted or deferred on exported products even when not exempted, remitted or deferred on like products when sold for domestic consumption, if the prior stage cumulative indirect taxes are levied on goods that are physically incorporated (making normal allowance for waste) in the exported product. This paragraph does not apply to the value added tax systems and border tax adjustments related thereto.

(i) The remission or drawback of import charges in excess of those levied on imported goods that are physically incorporated (making normal allowance for waste) in the exported product; provided, however, that in particular cases a firm may use a quantity of home market goods equal to, and having the same quality and characteristics as, the imported goods as a substitute for them in order to benefit from this provision if the import and the corresponding export operations both occur within a reasonable time period, normally not to exceed two years. This paragraph does not apply to value added tax systems and border tax adjustments related thereto.

(j) The provision by governments (or special institutions controlled by governments) of export credit guarantee or insurance programmes, of insurance or guarantee programmes against increases in the costs of exported products or of exchange risk programmes, at premium rates, which are manifestly inadequate to cover the long-term operating costs and losses of the programmes.

(k) The grant by governments (or special institutions controlled by and/or acting under the authority of governments) of export credits at rates below those which they actually have to pay for the funds so employed (or would have to pay if they borrowed on international capital markets in order to obtain funds of the same maturity and denominated at the same currency as the export credit), or the payment by them of all or part of the costs incurred by exporters or financial institutions in obtaining credits, in so far as they are used to secure a material advantage in the field of export credit terms. Provided, however, that if the country of origin or export is a party to an international undertaking on official export credits to which at least 12 original signatories to the Agreement on Interpretation and Application of Articles VI, XVI and XXIII of the GATT are parties as of 1 January 1979 (or a successor undertaking which has been adopted by those original signatories), or if in practice the country of origin or export applies the interest rate provisions of the relevant undertaking, an export credit practice which is in conformity with those provisions shall not be considered an export subsidy.

(l) Any other charge on the public account constituting an export subsidy in the sense of Article XVI of the GATT.

Notes :

For the purposes of this Annex the following definitions apply :

1   The term "direct taxes" shall mean taxes on wages, profits, interest, rents, royalties, and all other forms of income, and taxes on the ownership of real property.

2   The term "import charges" shall mean tariffs, duties, and other fiscal charges not elsewhere enumerated in these Notes that are levied on imports.

3   The term "indirect taxes" shall mean sales, excise, turnover, value added, franchise, stamp, transfer, inventory and equipment taxes, border taxes and all taxes other than direct taxes and import charges.

4   "Prior stage" indirect taxes are those levied on goods or services used directly or indirectly in making the product.

5   "Cumulative" indirect taxes are multi-staged taxes levied where there is no mechanism for subsequent crediting of the tax if the goods or services subject to tax at one stage of production are used in a succeeding stage of production.

6   "Remission" of taxes includes the refund or rebate of taxes.

APPENDIX 5

COUNCIL REGULATION (EEC) 288/82
of 5 February 1982

on common rules for imports[1]

THE COUNCIL OF THE EUROPEAN COMMUNITIES,

Having regard to the Treaty establishing the European Economic Community, and in particular Article 113 thereof,

Having regard to the instruments establishing common organisation of agricultural markets and to the instruments concerning processed agricultural products adopted in pursuance of Article 235 of the Treaty, in particular the provisions of those instruments which allow for derogation from the general principle that all quantitative restrictions or measures having equivalent effect may be replaced solely by the measures provided for in those same instruments,

Having regard to the proposal from the Commission,

Whereas the common commercial policy must be based on uniform principles; whereas the import rules established by Regulation (EEC) 926/79[2] are an important aspect of that policy;

Whereas the liberalisation of imports, that is to say the absence of any quantitative restrictions subject to exceptions and derogations provided for in Community rules, is the starting point for common rules in this field;

Whereas the Commission must be informed by the Member States of any danger created by trends in imports which might call for protective measures;

Whereas, in such a case, the Commission must examine import terms and conditions, import trends, the various aspects of the economic and commercial situation, and the measures, if any, to be taken;

Whereas it may become apparent that there should be either Community surveillance or surveillance at national level over certain of these imports;

---

1. OJ L35 9.2.82 p1. This regulation incoporates amendments made by Regulations (EEC) 1243/86, 2727/90, 3859/91 and 848/92. The Annexes to the regulation have not been reproduced here.
2. OJ L131 29.5.79 p15.

Whereas in this case the putting into free circulation of the products concerned should be made subject to production of an import document satisfying uniform criteria; whereas that document must, on declarations or on simple application by the importer, be issued or endorsed by the authorities of the Member States within a certain period but without the importer thereby acquiring any right to import; whereas the document must therefore be valid only during such period as the import rules remain unchanged;

Whereas it is in the interest of the Community that the Member States and the Commission should make as full an exchange as possible of information resulting from either Community surveillance or surveillance at national level;

Whereas it is for the Commission and the Council to adopt the protective measures called for by the interests of the Community with due regard for existing international obligations; whereas, therefore, protective measures against a country which is a contracting party to GATT may be considered only if the product in question is imported into the Community in such greatly increased quantities and on such terms or conditions as to cause, or threaten to cause, substantial injury to Community producers of like or directly competing products, unless international obligations permit derogation from this rule;

Whereas Member States should be empowered, in certain circumstances and provided that their actions are on an interim basis only, to take protective measures individually;

Whereas Articles 14(6) and 16(1) of Regulation (EEC) 926/79 provide that the Council shall decide on the adjustments to be made to that Regulation;

Whereas a review of the Regulation, in the light of experience gained in applying it, has shown that it is necessary to adopt more precise criteria for assessing possible injury and to introduce an investigation procedure while still allowing the Commission and the Member States to introduce appropriate measures in urgent cases;

Whereas to this end more detailed provisions should be introduced on the opening of investigations, on the checks and inspections required, on the hearing of those concerned, the treatment of information obtained and the criteria for assessing injury;

Whereas the provisions on the investigations introduced by this Regulation do not prejudice Community or national rules concerning professional secrecy;

Whereas, furthermore, in a desire for simplicity and greater transparency of import arrangements, it seemed preferable to draw up a list of quantitative restrictions still applicable at national level rather than a common liberalisation list;

Whereas a procedure should be available for application where import restrictions maintained by certain Member States are amended; whereas in order to prevent these autonomous amendments from constituting obstacles to the implementation of the common commercial policy and from injuring the interests of the Community or one of its Member States, these amendments should be subject to prior consultation and, where necessary, to an authorisation procedure;

Whereas, in addition, the provisions of the Agreement on import licencing procedures signed within the framework of GATT should be transposed into Community law, in particular so as to ensure a greater transparency of the systems of restrictions applied by the Member States;

Whereas the Regulation this amended should be published in its entirety,

HAS ADOPTED THIS REGULATION :

TITLE I

General Principles

Article 1

1. This Regulation shall apply to imports of products covered by the Treaty originating in third countries, except for

— textile products subject to specific common import rules for the duration of those rules, subject to measures which may be taken regarding these products in accordance with Title IV,

— the products originating in State-trading countries listed in Regulation (EEC) 925/79[1];

— the products originating in the People's Republic of China listed in Regulation (EEC) 2532/78[2],

— products originating in Cuba.

1. OJ L131 29.5.79 p1.
2. OJ L306 31.10.78 p1.

2. Importation into the Community of the products referred to in paragraph 1 shall be free, and therefore not subject to any quantitative restriction, without prejudice to

— measures which may be taken under Title V,

— measures maintained under Title VI,

— quantitative restrictions for the products listed in Annex I and maintained in the Member States indicated opposite these products in that Annex. [However, the application of quantitative restrictions to the placing in free circulation of products originating in the [Yugoslav Republics of Bosnia-Herzegovina, Macedonia and Montenegro and the Republics of Croatia and Slovenia][1] and listed in the said Annex I shall be suspended until [31 December 1992][2], except in the case of imports into Spain and Portugal of products falling within the CN codes listed in Annex Ia without prejudice to the measures which may be taken under Titles V and VI.][3]

Article 2

The Council may, acting by a qualified majority on a proposal from the Commission, decide to delete certain products from Annex I, if it considers that such action is not liable to create a situation where the reintroduction of protective measures would be justified.

TITLE II

Community information and consultation procedure

Article 3

The Commission shall be informed by the Member States should trends in imports appear to call for surveillance or protective measures. This information shall contain the available evidence on the basis of the criteria laid down in Article 9. The Commission shall pass on this information to all the Member States forthwith.

---

1.   Text replaced by Council Regulation (EEC) 848/92 (OJ L89 4.4.92).
2.   Text replaced by Council Regulation (EEC) 3859/91 (OJ L362 31.12.91 p83).
3.   Text added by Council Regulation (EEC) 2727/90 (OJ L262 26.9.90 p11).

Article 4

Consultations may be held, either at the request of a Member State or on the initiative of the Commission. They shall take place within eight working days following receipt by the Commission of the information provided for in Article 3 and, in any event, before the introduction of any measure of surveillance or protective measure by the Community.

Article 5

1. Consultation shall take place within an advisory committee (hereinafter called "the Committee") which shall consist of representatives of each Member State with a representative of the Commission as chairman.

2. The Committee shall meet when convened by its chairman. He shall provide the Member States, as promptly as possible, with all relevant information.

3. Consultation shall cover in particular :

   (a)   terms and conditions of importation, import trends, and the various aspects of the economic and commercial situation as regards the produce in question;

   (b)   the measures, if any, to be taken.

4. Consultations may be in writing if necessary. The Commission shall in this event inform the Member States, which may express their opinion or request oral consultations within a period of five to eight working days to be decided by the Commission.

TITLE III

Community investigation procedure

Article 6

1. Where, after consultation it is apparent to the Commission that there is sufficient evidence to justify an investigation, the Commission shall :

   (a)   announce the opening of an investigation in the *Official Journal of the European Communities*; such announcements shall give a summary of the information received, and stipulate that all relevant information is to be

413

communicated to the Commission; it shall state the period within which interested parties may make known their views in writing;

(b)   commence the investigation, acting in co-operation with the Member States.

2. The Commission shall seek all information it deems to be necessary and, where it considers it appropriate, after consulting the Committee, endeavour to check this information with importers, traders, agents, producers, trade associations and organisations.

The Commission shall be assisted in this task by staff of the Member State on whose territory these checks are being carried out, provided this Member State so wishes.

3. The Member States shall supply the Commission, at its request and following procedures laid down by it, with all information at their disposal on developments in the market of the product being investigated.

4. The Commission may hear the interested natural and legal persons. Such parties must be heard where they have applied in writing within the period laid down in the notice published in the *Official Journal of the European Communities*, showing that they are actually likely to be affected by the outcome of the investigations and that there are special reasons for them to be heard orally.

5. Where the information requested by the Commission is not supplied within a reasonable period, or the investigation is significantly impeded, findings may be made on the basis of the facts available.

Article 7

1. At the end of the investigation, the Commission shall submit a report on the results to the Committee.

2. If the Commission considers that no Community surveillance or protective measures are necessary, it shall publish in the *Official Journal of the European Communities*, after consulting the Committee, a notice that the investigations are closed, stating the main conclusions of the investigations.

3. If the Commission considers that Community surveillance or protective measures are necessary, it shall take the necessary decisions in accordance with Title IV and V.

4. The provisions of this Title shall not preclude the taking, at any time, of surveillance measures in accordance with Articles 10 to 14 or, in an emergency, protective measures in accordance with Articles 15 to 17.

In the latter case, the Commission shall immediately take the investigation measures it considers to be still necessary. The results of the investigation shall be used to re-examine the measures taken.

Article 8

1. Information received in pursuance of this Regulation shall be used only for the purpose for which it was requested.

2. (a) Neither the Council, nor the Commission, nor Member States, nor the officials of any of these, shall reveal any information of a confidential nature received in pursuance of this Regulation, or any information provided on a confidential basis, without specific permission from the supplier of such information.

   (b) Each request for confidentiality shall state the reasons why the information is confidential.

      However, if it appears that a request for confidentiality is unjustified and if the supplier of the information wishes neither to make it public nor to authorise its disclosure in general terms or in the form of a summary, the information concerned may be disregarded.

3. Information will in any case be considered to be confidential if its disclosure is likely to have a significantly adverse effect upon the supplier or the source of such information.

4. The above paragraphs shall not preclude reference by the Community authorities to general information and in particular to reasons on which decisions taken in pursuance of this Regulation are based. These authorities must, however, take into account the legitimate interest of the legal and natural persons concerned that their business secrets should not be divulged.

Article 9

1. The examination of the trend of imports, of the conditions in which they take place and of the substantial injury or threat of substantial injury to Community

producers resulting from such imports, shall cover in particular the following factors :

(a)　the volume of imports, in particular where there has been a significant increase, either in absolute terms or relative to production or consumption in the Community;

(b)　the prices of the imports, in particular where there has been a significant price undercutting as compared with the price of a like product in the Community;

(c)　the consequent impact on the Community producers of similar or directly competitive products as indicated by trends in certain economic factors such as :

— 　production,
— 　utlisation of capacity,
— 　stocks,
— 　sales,
— 　market share,
— 　prices (ie depression of prices or prevention of price increases which would normally have occurred),
— 　profits,
— 　return on capital employed,
— 　cash flow,
— 　employment.

2. Where a threat of serious injury is alleged the Commission shall also examine whether it is clearly foreseeable that a particular situation is likely to develop into actual injury. In this regard account may be taken of factors such as :

(a)　rate of increase of the exports to the Community;

(b)　export capacity in the country of origin or export, already in existence or which will be operational in the foreseeable future, and the likelihood that the resulting exports will be to the Community.

TITLE IV

Surveillance

Article 10

1. Where developments on the market in respect of a product originating in a third country covered by this Regulation threaten to cause injury to Community producers of like or directly competing products and where the interests of the Community so require, importation of that product may be made subject, as the case may be, to :

(a)   retrospective Community surveillance carried out according to the procedures laid down in the Decision referred to in paragraph 2, or

(b)   prior Community surveillance carried out according to the procedures laid down in Article 11.

In these cases the product together with the indication "EUR" shall be entered in Annex II.

2. Where the decision to impose surveillance is taken simultaneously with the liberalisation of importation of the product in question, that decision shall be taken by the Council, acting by a qualified majority on a proposal from the Commission. In all other cases it shall be taken by the Commission and Article 15(5) shall apply.

3. The surveillance measures shall be of limited duration. Unless otherwise provided, they shall cease to be valid at the end of the second half calendar year following that in which they were introduced.

Article 11

1. Products under prior Community surveillance may be put into free circulation only on production of an import document. Such document shall be issued or endorsed by Member States, free of charge, for any quantity requested and within a maximum of five working days following submission, in accordance with the national laws in force, either of a declaration or simply of an application by any Community importer, regardless of his place of business in the Community, without prejudice to the observance of the other conditions required by the regulations in force.

2. Subject to any provision to the contrary made when surveillance was imposed and under the procedure there followed, the declaration or application by the importer must give :

    (a)   the name and address of the importer;

    (b)   a description of the product with the following particulars :

        — commercial description,

        — tariff heading, or reference number, of the product in the goods nomenclature used for foreign trade purposes by the country concerned,

        — country of origin,

        — exporting country;

    (c)   the cif price free-at-frontier and the quantity of the product in units customarily used in the trade in question;

    (d)   the proposed date or dates as well as the place or places of importation.

Member States may request further particulars.

3. Paragraph 2 shall not preclude the putting into free circulation of the product in question if the unit price at which the transaction is effected exceeds that indicated in the import document, or if the total value or quantity of the products to be imported exceeds the value or quantity given in the import document by less than 5%. The Commission, having heard the opinions expressed in the Committee and taking account of the nature of the products and other special features of the transactions concerned, may fix a different percentage, which, however, should not normally exceed 10%.

4. Import documents may be used only for such time as arrangements for the liberalisation of imports remain in force in respect of the transactions concerned and in any event not beyond the expiry of a period laid down, with regard to the nature of the products and other special features of the transactions, at the same time and by means of the same procedure as the imposition of surveillance.

5. Where the decision taken under Article 10 so requires, the origin of products under Community surveillance must be proved by a certificate of origin. This paragraph shall not prejudice other provisions concerning the production of any such certificate.

6. Where the product under prior Community surveillance is not liberalised in a Member State, the import authorisation granted by that Member State may replace the import document.

Article 12

1. Where importation of a product has not been made subject to prior Community surveillance within a period of eight working days following the end of consultations, the Member State, having informed the Commission under Article 3 may carry out surveillance over such importation at national level.

2. In cases of extreme urgency the Member State may carry out surveillance at national level after informing the Commission in accordance with Article 3. The latter shall inform the other Member States.

3. The Commission shall be informed, upon the entry into force of the surveillance, of the detailed rules for its application and shall amend Annex II by means of a notice published in the *Official Journal of the European Communities*, by entering the name of the Member State applying the surveillance opposite the product in question.

Article 13

Products under national surveillance may be put into free circulation only on production of an import document. Such document shall be issued or endorsed by the Member State, free of charge, for any quantity requested and within a maximum of five working days following submission of a declaration or simply of an application by any Community importer, regardless of his place of business in the Community, without prejudice to the observance of the other conditions required by the regulations in force. Import documents may be used only for such time as arrangements for the liberalisation of imports remain in force in respect of the transactions concerned.

Article 14

1. Member States shall communicate to the Commisison within the first 10 days of each month in the case of Community surveillance and within the first 20 days of each quarter in the case of national surveillance :

(a)   in the case of prior surveillance, details of the sums of money (calculated on the basis of cif prices) and quantities of goods in respect of which import documents were issued or endorsed during the preceding period;

(b)   in every case, details of imports during the period preceding the period referred to in subparagraph (a).

The information supplied by Member States shall be broken down by product and by countries.

Different provisions may be laid down at the same time and by the same procedure as the surveillance arrangements.

2. Where the nature of the products or special circumstances so require, the Commission may, at the request of a Member State or on its own initiative, amend the timetables for submitting this information.

3. The Commisison shall inform the Member State.

TITLE V

Protective measures

Article 15

1. Where a product is imported into the Community in such greatly increased quantities and/or on such terms or conditions as to cause, or threaten to cause, substantial injury to Community producers of like or directly competing products, and where a critical situation, in which any delay would cause injury which it would be difficult to remedy, calls for immediate intervention in order to safeguard the interests of the Community, the Commission may, acting at the request of a Member State or on its own initiative :

(a)   limit the period of validity of import documents within the meaning of Article 11 to be issued or endorsed after the entry into force of this measure;

(b) alter the import rules for the product in question by providing that it may be put into free circulation only on production of an import authorisation, the granting of which shall be governed by such provisions and subject to such limits as the Commission shall lay down pending action, if any, by the Council under Article 16.

The measures referred to in (a) and (b) shall take effect immediately.

2. Where the establishment of a quota constitutes a withdrawal of liberalisation, account shall be taken in particular of :

— the desirability of maintaining, as far as possible, traditional trade flows,

— the volume of goods exported under contracts concluded on normal terms and conditions before the entry into force of a protective measure within the meaning of this Title, where such contracts have been notified to the Commission by the Member State concerned,

— the need to avoid jeopardising achievement of the aim pursued in establishing the quota.

3. (a) The measures referred to in this Article shall apply to every product which is put into free circulation after their entry into force. They may be limited to imports intended for certain regions of the Community.

(b) However, such measures shall not prevent the putting into free circulation of products already on their way to the Community provided that the destination of such products cannot be changed and that those products which, under Articles 10 and 11 may be put into free circulation only on production of an import document are in fact accompanied by such a document.

4. Where intervention by the Commission has been requested by a Member State, the Commission shall take a decision within a maximum of five working days of receipt of such request.

5. Any decision taken by the Commission under this Article shall be communicated to the Council and to the Member States. Any Member State may, within one month following the day of communication, refer such decision to the Council.

6. If a Member State refers the decision taken by the Commission to the Council, the Council shall, by a qualified majority, confirm, amend or revoke the decision of the Commission.

If within three months of the referral of the matter to the Council, the latter has not given a decision, the measure taken by the Commission shall be deemed revoked.

Article 16

1. Where the interests of the Community so require, the Council may, acting by a qualified majority on a proposal from the Commission, adopt appropriate measures :

  (a)   to prevent a product being imported into the Community in such greatly increased quantities and/or on such terms or conditions as to cause, or threaten to cause, substantial injury to Community producers of like or directly competing products;

  (b)   to allow the rights and obligations of the Community or of all its Member States to be exercised and fulfilled at international level, in particular those relating to trade in primary products.

2. Article 15(2) and (3) shall apply.

Article 17

1. In the following cases a Member State may, as an interim protective measure, alter the import rules for a particular product by providing that it may be put into free circulation only on production of an import authorisation, the granting of which shall be governed by such provisions and subject to such limits as that Member State shall lay down :

  (a)   where there exists in its territory a situation such as that defined as regards the Community in Article 15(1);

  (b)   where such measure is justified by a protective clause contained in a bilateral agreement between the Member State and a third country.

2. (a)   The Member State shall inform the Commission and the other Member States by telex of the reasons for and the details of the proposed measures. The Commission and the other Member States shall treat this information in strictest confidence. The Commission shall forthwith convene the Committee. The Member State may take these measures after having heard the opinions expressed by the Committee.

(b) Where a Member State claims that the matter is especially urgent, consultations shall take place within a period of five working days following information transmitted to the Commission; at the end of this period, the Member State may take these measures. During this period the Member State may make imports of the product in question subject to production of an import authorisation to be granted under the procedure and within the limits to be laid down at the end of the said period.

3. The Commission shall be notified by telex of the measures immediately following their adoption.

4. The notification shall be equivalent to a request within the meaning of Article 15(4). The measures shall operate only until the coming into operation of the decision taken by the Commission. However, where the Commission decides not to introduce any measure or adopts measures pursuant to Article 15, different from those taken by the Member State, its decision shall apply as from the sixth day following its entry into force, unless the Member State which has taken the measures refers the decision to the Council; in that case, the national measures shall continue to operate until the entry into force of the decision taken by the Council and for the maximum of one month following referral of the matter to the latter. The Council shall take a decision before the expiry of that period. The Council may under the same conditions decide in certain cases to extend this period, which may, in no fashion, exceed a total of three months.

The preceding subparagraph does not affect the Member States' right of recourse under Article 15(5) and (6).

5. This Article shall apply until 31 December 1984. Before 31 December 1983, the Commission shall propose to the Council amendments to be made to it. The Council shall act, before 31 December 1984 by a qualified majority, upon the Commission proposal. However, the provisions relating to protective measures :

— justified by a safeguard clause contained in a bilateral agreement shall not be effected by that time limit,

— concerning imports of products which have been liberalised in certain Member States but subject to quota in other shall apply until 31 December 1987.

Article 18

1. While any measure of surveillance or protective measure applied in accordance with Titles IV and V is in operation, consultations within the Committee shall be held, either at the request of a Member State or on the initiative of the Commission. The purpose of such consultations shall be :

(a)   to examine the effects of the measure;

(b)   to ascertain whether its application is still necessary.

2. Where, as a result of the consultations referred to in paragraph 1, the Commission considers that any measure referred to in Articles 10, 12, 15 or 16 should be revoked or amended it shall proceed as follows;

(a)   where the Council has acted on a measure, the Commission shall propose that it be revoked or amended; the Council shall act by a qualified majority;

(b)   in all other cases, the Commission shall amend or revoke Community protective measures and measures of surveillance. Where this decision concerns national measures of surveillance, it shall apply as from the sixth day following its publication in the *Official Journal of the European Communities*, unless the Member State which has taken the measure refers it to the Council; in that case the national measure shall continue to operate until the entry into force of the decision taken by the Council, but in no event after the expiry of a period of three months following referral of the matter to the latter. The Council shall act before the expiry of that period.

TITLE VI

Transitional and final provisions

[*Article 19*

1. By 31 December 1988 at the latest, the Council shall decide on the adjustments to be made to this Regulation for the purpose of greater uniformity of rules for imports. The Council shall act by a qualified majority on a proposal from the Commission and with due regard to the progress of the common commercial policy.

2. Pending such adjustments :

(a) as regards the products to which Regulation (EEC) 3420/83[1] applies, Member States may make imports subject to the requirement that not only the origin of the products concerned, but also the country of purchase or the country of provenance shall be among the countries to which this Regulation applies;

(b) import documents required for Community surveillance under Article 11 shall be valid only in the Member States which have issued or endorsed them;

(c) the Benelux countries and the Italian Republic may retain the automatic licence or import-declaration formalities currently applied by them to imports originating in Japan and Hong Kong;

(d) until 30 June 1987, the Benelux countries and Ireland may retain, for textile products not covered by any specific common import rules, national surveillance over the imports of such products, including imports under automatic licences. The same applies to Ireland in respect of footwear imports under headings 64.01-11 to 19, 64.02-21 to 99, 64.03-00 and 64.04-10, 90 of the NIMEXE code;

(e) this Regulation shall not preclude the continuance until 30 June 1988 of measures taken by the Italian Republic - pursuant to the Ministerial Decree of 6 May 1976, including the list annexed thereto and the subsequent amendments to it - making subject to special authorisation the importation of articles, machinery and equipment, whether used or new but in poorly maintained condition, falling within Chapters 84, 85, headings Nos. 86.01 to 86.04 and Chapters 87 and 93 of the Common Customs Tariff.

3. Member States shall notify the Commission, at its request, of any rules and other particulars concerning the procedures for the submission of requests for licences, including the conditions relating to admissibility of persons, enterprises or institutions who submit such requests. Any intended changes to these rules shall also be notified to the Commission.

---

1 OJ L346, 8.12.1983 p6.

Article 20

1.Where a Member State which applies an import restriction referred to in the last indent of Article 1(2) intends to change it, it shall inform the Commission and the other Member States thereof.

2. (a)   At the request of the Commission or a Member State, the measures referred to in paragraph 1 shall be the subject of prior consultation within the Committee.

    (b)   If the Commission does not request, on its own initiative, consultations within five working days of receiving the information referred to in paragraph 1, nor at the request of a Member State received sufficiently early before the end of the said period, the Member State concerned may put the proposed measure into effect.

    (c)   In other cases, the consultation procedure shall commence within five working days of expiry of the period provided for in (b).

3. (a)   If, after consultation, no objection has been raised by the other Member States or by the Commission, the Commission shall forthwith inform the Member State concerned, which may put the proposed measure into effect immediately.

    (b)   In other cases, the Member State concerned may not put the proposed measure into effect until two weeks after the opening of the consultation.

    (c)   If, within this period, the Commission submits to the Council, under Article 113 of the Treaty, a proposal meeting the objections raised, the proposed measure may not be put into effect until the Council has acted.

4. In cases of extreme urgency and until 30 June 1988, the following provisions shall apply :

    (a)   when a quota has been exhausted and the economic requirements of a Member State call for additional imports from the non-member country or countries benefiting from the quota, the Member State concerned may, without prior notification, open additional import facilities up to a maximum of 20% of the quantity or value of the exhausted quota; it shall forthwith inform the Commission and the other Member States thereof. The emergency procedure laid down in this paragraph shall not apply once the opening of negotiations with the non-member country concerned has been authorised;

426

(b) at the request of any Member State or of the Commission, subsequent consultation under the terms of paragraph 3 shall be held on measures taken by the Member State under this paragraph.

5. Where a Member State intends to make a unilateral change to its import arrangements for a petroleum product which is entered in Annex I and referred to in Article 3 of Council Regulation (EEC) No 802/68 of 27 June 1968 on the common definition of the concept of the origin of goods[1], it shall, inform the Commission and the other Member States thereof. The procedure laid down in paragraphs 2, 3 and 4 shall be applicable in this case; the other provisions of this Regulation shall not apply.

Article 21

1. This Regulation shall not preclude the fulfilment of obligations based on special provisions of agreements between the Community and non-member countries.

2. (a) Without prejudice to other Community provisions, this Regulation shall not preclude the adoption or application by Member States :

   (i) of prohibitions, quantitative restrictions measures of surveillance on grounds public morality, public policy or public security, the protection of health and life of humans, animals or plants, the protection of national treasures possessing artistic historic or archaeological value, or the protection of industrial and commercial property;

   (ii) of special formalities concerning foreign exchange :

   (iii) of formalities introduced pursuant to international agreements in accordance with the Treaty;

   (b) Member States shall inform the Commission the measures or formalities to be introduced amended pursuant to this paragraph. In cases extreme urgency, the national measures or formalities in question shall be communicated to the Commission as soon as they are adopted.][2]

---

1.   OJ L148, 28.6.1968 p1.
2.   Articles 19, 20 and 21 replaced by Council Regulation (EEC) 1243/86 (OJ L113 30.4.86 p1).

Article 22

1. This Regulation shall be without prejudice to the operation of the instruments establishing the common organisation of agricultural markets or of Community or national administrative provisions derived therefrom or of the specific instruments adopted under Article 235 of the Treaty applicable to goods resulting from the processing of agricultural products; it shall operate by way of complement to those instruments.

2. However, in the case of products covered by the instruments referred to in paragraph 1, Articles 10 to 14 and 18 shall not apply to those in respect of which the Community rules on trade with third countries require the production of a licence or other import document.

Articles 15, 17 and 18 shall not apply to those products in respect of which such rules make provision for the application of quantitative import restrictions.

Article 23

The Commission shall publish at regular intervals an updated text of Annexes I and II which will take account of Acts adopted in accordance with this Regulation both by the Community and by Member States. The Commission shall be informed of the introduction, amendment or repeal of all national measures.

Article 24

Regulation (EEC) 926/79 is hereby repealed.

References to the repealed Regulation shall be understood as referring to this Regulation.

Article 25

This Regulation shall enter into force on the day of its publication in the *Official Journal of the European Communities.*

This Regulation shall be binding in its entirety and directly applicable in all Member States.

Done at Brussels, 5 February 1982.

For the Council
The President
L. TINDEMANS

APPENDIX 6

COUNCIL REGULATION (EEC) 2641/84
of 17 September 1984

on the strengthening of the common commercial policy with regard in particular to protection against illicit commercial practices[1]

THE COUNCIL OF THE EUROPEAN COMMUNITIES,

Having regard to the Treaty establishing the European Economic Community, and in particular Article 113 thereof,

Having regard to the rules establishing the common organisation of agricultural markets and the rules adopted under Article 235 of the Treaty, applicable to goods processed from agricultural products, and in particular those provisions thereof which allow for derogation from the general principle that any quantitative restriction or measure having equivalent effect may be replaced solely by the measures provided for in those instruments,

Having regard to the proposal from the Commission,

Having regard to the opinion of the European Parliament[2],

Having regard to the opinion of the Economic and Social Committee[3],

Whereas the common commercial policy must be based on uniform principles, notably with regard to commercial protection; whereas Council Regulation (EEC) 2176/84 of 23 July 1984 on protection against dumped or subsidised imports from countries not members of the European Economic Community[4] and the rules for imports laid down pursuant to Regulation (EEC) 288/82[5], as amended by Regulations (EEC) 899/83[6], (EEC) 1765/82[7] and (EEC) 1766/82[8], as amended by Regulations (EEC) 35/83[9] and (EEC) 101/84[10], constitute important components of that policy;

1.	OJ L252 20.9.84 p1.
2.	OJ C205 1.8.83 p2.
3.	OJ C211 8.8.83 p24.
4.	OJ L201 30.7.84 p24.
5.	OJ L35 9.2.82 p1.
6.	OJ L103 21.4.83 p1.
7.	OJ L195 5.7.82 p1.
8.	OJ L195 5.7.82 p21.
9.	OJ L5 7.1.83 p12.
10.	OJ L14 17.1.84 p7.

Whereas in the light of experience and of the conclusions of the European Council of June 1982, which considered that it was of the highest importance to defend vigorously the legitimate interests of the Community in the appropriate bodies, in particular GATT, and to make sure the Community, in managing trade policy, acts with as much speed and efficiency as its trading partners, it has become apparent that the common commercial policy needs to be strengthened, notably in the fields not covered by the rules already adopted;

Whereas to this end it is advisable to provide the Community with procedures enabling it :

— to respond to any illicit commercial practice with a view to removing the injury resulting therefrom,

— to ensure full exercise of the Community's rights with regard to the commercial practices of third countries;

Whereas, in particular, the Community should be enabled to remove the injury resulting from third countries' practices whose illicit nature is evident from their incompatibility regarding international trade practices either with international law or with the generally accepted rules;

Whereas the measures taken under the procedures in question should, however, be without prejudice to other measures in cases not covered by this Regulation which might be adopted directly pursuant to Article 113 of the Treaty;

Whereas the Community must act in compliance with its international obligations and, where such obligations result from agreements, maintain the balance of rights and obligations which it is the purpose of those agreements to establish;

Whereas it is necessary to confirm, by establishing a formal complaints procedure, the right of Community industry to submit to the Commission any complaint regarding illicit commercial practices by third countries;

Whereas for the purposes of implementation of this Regulation there should be co-operation between the Member States and the Commission and, to this end, arrangements should be made for consultations within an advisory committee;

Whereas it is appropriate to lay down clearly the rules of procedure to be followed during the examination, in particular the rights and obligations of the Community authorities and the parties involved, and the conditions under which interested parties may have access to information and may ask to be informed of the essential facts and considerations resulting from the examination procedure;

Whereas, in conducting the defence of its commercial interests, the Community needs to have at its disposal a decision-making process which permits rapid and effective action,

HAS ADOPTED THIS REGULATION :

Article 1

Aims

This Regulation establishes procedures in the matter of commercial policy which, subject to compliance with existing international obligations and procedures, are aimed at :

(a) responding to any illicit commercial practice with a view to removing the injury resulting therefrom;

(b) ensuring full exercise of the Community's rights with regard to the commercial practices of third countries.

Article 2

Definitions

1. For the purposes of this Regulation, illicit commercial practices shall be any international trade practices attributable to third countries which are incompatible with international law or with the generally accepted rules.

2. For the purposes of this Regulation, the Community's rights shall be those international trade rights of which it may avail itself either under international law or under generally accepted rules.

3. For the purposes of this Regulation, injury shall be any material injury caused or threatened to Community industry.

4. The term "Community industry" shall be taken to mean all Community producers :

— of products identical or similar to the product which is the subject of illicit practices or of products competing directly with that product, or

— who are consumers or processors of the product which is the subject of illicit practices, or all those producers whose combined output constitutes a major proportion of total Community production of the products in question; however :

(a) when producers are related to the exporters or importers or are themselves importers of the product alleged to be the subject of illicit practices, the term "Community industry" may be interpreted as referring to the rest of the producers;

(b) in particular circumstances, the producers within a region of the Community may be regarded as the Community industry if their collective output constitutes the major proportion of the output of the product in question in the Member State or Member States within which the region is located provided that :

(i) where the illicit practice concerns imports into the Community, their effect is concentrated in that Member State or those Member States,

(ii) where the illicit practice concerns Community exports to a third country, a significant proportion of the output of those producers is exported to the third country concerned.

Article 3

Complaint on behalf of Community producers

1. Any natural or legal person, or any association not having legal personality, acting on behalf of a Community industry which considers that it has suffered injury as a result of illicit commercial practices may lodge a written complaint.

2. The complaint must contain sufficient evidence of the existence of illicit commercial practices and the injury resulting therefrom. Proof of injury must be given on the basis of the factors indicated in Article 8.

3. The complaint shall be submitted, to the Commission, which shall send a copy thereof to the Member States.

4. The complaint may be withdrawn, in which case the procedure may be terminated unless such termination would not be in the interests of the Community.

5. Where it becomes apparent after consultation that the complaint does not provide sufficient evidence to justify initiating an investigation, then the complainant shall be so informed.

Article 4

Referral by a Member State

1. Any Member State may ask the Commission to initiate the procedures referred to in Article 1.

2. It shall supply the Commission with the necessary evidence to support its request. Where illicit commercial practices are alleged, proof thereof and of the injury resulting therefrom must be given on the basis of the factors indicated in Article 8.

3. The Commission shall notify the other Member States of the requests without delay.

4. Where it becomes apparent after consultation that the request does not provide sufficient evidence to justify initiating an investigation, then the Member State shall be so informed.

Article 5

Consultation procedure

1. For the purpose of consultations pursuant to this Regulation, an advisory committee, hereinafter referred to as 'the Committee', is hereby set up and shall consist of representatives of each Member State, with a representative of the Commission as chairman.

2. Consultations shall be initiated at the request of a Member State or on the initiative of the Commission. The chairman of the Committee shall provide the Member States, as promptly as possible, with all relevant information in his possession.

3. The Committee shall meet when convened by its chairman.

4. Where necessary, consultations may be in writing. In such case the Commission shall notify in writing the Member States who, within a period of eight working days from such notification shall be entitled to express their opinions in writing or to request oral consultations.

Article 6

Community examination procedure

1. Where, after consultation, it is apparent to the Commission that there is sufficient evidence to justify initiating an examination procedure and that it is necessary in the interest of the Community, the Commission shall act as follows :

(a) it shall announce the initiation of an examination procedure in the *Official Journal of the European Communities*; such announcement shall indicate the product and countries concerned, give a summary of the information received, and provide that all relevant information is to be communicated to the Commission; it shall state the period within which interested parties may make known their views in writing and may apply to be heard orally by the Commission in accordance with paragraph 5;

(b) it shall so officially notify the representatives of the country or countries which are the subject of the procedure, with whom, where appropriate, consultations may be held;

(c) it shall conduct the examination at Community level, acting in co-operation with the Member States.

2. (a) If necessary, and notably in cases of allegations of illicit commercial practices, the Commission shall seek all the information it deems necessary and attempt to check this information with the importers, traders, agents, producers, trade associations and organisations, provided that the undertakings or organisations concerned give their consent.

(b) Where necessary, the Commission shall carry out investigations in the territory of third countries, provided that the governments of the countries concerned have been officially notified and raise no objection within a reasonable period.

(c) The Commission shall be assisted in its investigation by officials of the Member State in whose territory the checks are carried out, provided that the Member State in question so requests.

3. Member States shall supply the Commission, upon request, with all information necessary for the examination, in accordance with the detailed arrangements laid down by the Commission.

4. (a)   The complainants and the exporters and importers concerned, as well as the representatives of the principal exporting or importing country or countries concerned, may inspect all information made available to the Commission except for internal documents for the use of the Commission and the administrations, provided that such information is relevant to the protection of their interests and not confidential within the meaning of Article 7 and that it is used by the Commission in its examination procedure. The persons concerned shall address a reasoned request in writing to the Commission, indicating the information required.

    (b)   The complainants and the exporters and importers concerned and the representatives of the principal exporting or importing country or countries concerned may ask to be informed of the principal facts and considerations resulting from the examination procedure.

5. The Commission may hear the parties concerned. It shall hear them if they have, within the period prescribed in the notice published in the *Official Journal of the European Communities*, made a written request for a hearing showing that they are a party primarily concerned by the result of the procedure.

6. Furthermore, the Commission shall, on request, give the parties primarily concerned an opportunity to meet, so that opposing views may be presented and any rebuttal argument put forward. In providing this opportunity the Commission shall take account of the wishes of the parties and of the need to preserve confidentiality. There shall be no obligation on any party to attend a meeting and failure to do so shall not be prejudicial to that party's case.

7. When the information requested by the Commission is not supplied within a reasonable time or where the investigation is significantly impeded, findings may be made on the basis of the facts available.

8. The Commission shall take a decision as soon as possible on the opening of a Community examination procedure following any complaint or request made in accordance with Articles 3 and 4; the decision shall normally be taken within 45 days of referral; this period may be extended to 60 days in special circumstances.

9. When it has concluded its examination the Commission shall report to the Committee. The report should normally be presented within five months of the announcement of initiation of the procedure, unless the complexity of the examination is such that the Commission extends the period to seven months.

Article 7

Confidentiality

1. Information received pursuant to this Regulation shall be used only for the purpose for which it was requested.

2. (a) Neither the Council, nor the Commission, nor Member States, nor the officials of any of these, shall reveal any information of a confidential nature received pursuant to this Regulation, or any information provided on a confidential basis by a party to an examination procedure, without specific permission from the party submitting such information.

   (b) Each request for confidential treatment shall indicate why the information is confidential and shall be accompanied by a non-confidential summary of the information or a statement of the reasons why the information is not susceptible of such summary.

3. Information will normally be considered to be confidential if its disclosure is likely to have a significantly adverse effect upon the supplier or the source of such information.

4. However, if it appears that a request for confidentiality is not warranted and if the supplier is either unwilling to make the information public or to authorise its disclosure in generalised or summary form, the information in question may be disregarded.

5. This Article shall not preclude the disclosure of general information by the Community authorities and in particular of the reasons on which decisions taken pursuant to this Regulation are based. Such disclosure must take into account the legitimate interest of the parties concerned that their business secrets should not be divulged.

Article 8

Examination of injury

1. An examination of injury shall involve in particular the following factors :

   (a) the volume of Community imports or exports concerned, notably where there has been a significant increase or decrease, either in absolute terms or relative to production or consumption on the market in question;

(b) the prices of the Community producers' competitors, in particular in order to determine whether there has been, either in the Community or on third country markets, significant undercutting of the prices of Community producers;

(c) the consequent impact on Community industry as defined in Article 2(4) and as indicated by trends in certain economic factors such as :

— production,
— utilisation of capacity,
— stocks,
— sales,
— market share,
— prices (that is, depression of prices or prevention of price increases which would normally have occurred),
— profits,
— return on capital,
— investment,
— employment.

2. Where a threat of injury is alleged, the Commission shall also examine whether it is clearly foreseeable that a particular situation is likely to develop into actual injury. In this regard, account may also be taken of factors such as;

(a) the rate of increase of exports to the market where the competition with Community products is taking place;

(b) export capacity in the country of origin or export, which is already in existence or will be operational in the foreseeable future, and the likelihood that the exports resulting from that capacity will be to the market referred to in point (a).

3. Injury caused by other factors which, either individually or in combination, are also adversely affecting Community industry must not be attributed to the practices under consideration.

Article 9

Termination of the procedure

1. When it is found as a result of the examination procedure that the interests of the Community do not require any action to be taken, the procedure shall be terminated in accordance with Article 12.

2. (a) When, after an examination procedure, the third country or country concerned take(s) measures which are considered satisfactory the procedure may also be terminated in accordance with the provisions of Article 11.

   (b) The Commission shall supervise the application of these measures, where appropriate on the basis of information supplied at intervals, which it may request from the third countries concerned and check as necessary.

   (c) Where the measures taken by the third country or countries concerned have been rescinded, suspended or improperly implemented or where the Commission has grounds for believing this to be the case or, finally, where a request for information made by the Commission as provided for by point (b) has not been granted, the Commission shall inform the Member States, and where necessary and justified by the results of the investigation and the new facts available any measures shall be taken in accordance with Article 11.

Article 10

Adoption of commercial policy measures

1. Where it is found as a result of the examination procedure that action is necessary in the interests of the Community in order to :

   (a) respond to any illicit commercial practice with the aim of removing the injury resulting therefrom; or

   (b) ensure full exercise of the Community's rights with regard to the commercial practices of third countries

the appropriate measures shall be determined in accordance with the procedure set out in Article 11.

2. Where the Community's international obligations require the prior discharge of an international procedure for consultation or for the settlement of disputes, the measures referred to in paragraph 3 shall only be decided on after that procedure has been terminated, and taking account of the results of the procedure.

3. Any commercial policy measures may be taken which are compatible with existing international obligations and procedures, notably :

(a) suspension or withdrawal of any concession resulting from commercial policy negotiations;

(b) the raising of existing customs duties or the introduction of any other charge on imports;

(c) the introduction of quantitative restrictions or any other measures modifying import or export conditions or otherwise affecting trade with the third country concerned.

4. The corresponding decisions shall state the reasons on which they are based and shall be published in the *Official Journal of the European Communities*. Publications shall also be deemed to constitute notification to the countries and parties primarily concerned.

Article 11

Decision-making machinery

1. The decisions referred to in Articles 9 and 10 shall be adopted in accordance with the following provisions.

2. Where a response to an illicit commercial practice within the meaning of Article 1(a) is to be made :

(a) where the Community follows formal international consultations or dispute settlement procedures, decisions relating to the initiation, conduct, or termination of such procedures shall be taken in accordance with Article 12;

(b) where the Community, after the conclusion of such an international procedure, has to take a decision on the measures of commercial policy to be adopted, the Council shall act, on the proposal from the Commission, in accordance with Article 113 of the Treaty, by a qualified majority, not later than 30 days after receiving the proposal.

3. Where the full exercise of the Community's rights within the meaning of Article 1(b) is to be ensured, the Council shall act, on the proposal from the Commission, in accordance with Article 113 of the Treaty, by a qualified majority, not later than 30 days after receiving the proposal.

Article 12

Should reference be made to the procedure provided for in this Article, the matter shall be brought before the Committee by its chairman.

The Commission representative shall submit to the Committee a draft of the decision to be taken. The Committee shall discuss the matter within a period to be fixed by the chairman, depending on the urgency of the matter.

The Commission shall adopt a decision which it shall communicate to the Member States and which shall apply after a period of 10 days if during this period no Member State has referred the matter to the Council.

The Council may, at the request of a Member State and acting by a qualified majority revise the Commission's decision.

The Commission's decision shall apply after a period of 30 days if the Council has not given a ruling within this period, calculated from the day on which the matter was referred to the Council.

Article 13

This Regulation shall not apply in cases covered by other existing rules in the common commercial policy field. It shall operate by way of complement to the :

— rules establishing the common organisation of agricultural markets and their implementing provisions;

— specific rules adopted under Article 235 of the Treaty, applicable to goods processed from agricultural products.

It shall be without prejudice to other measures which may be taken pursuant to Article 113 of the Treaty.

Article 14

This Regulation shall enter into force on the third day following its publication in the *Official Journal of the European Communities*.

This Regulation shall be binding in its entirety and directly applicable in all Member States.

Done at Brussels, 17 September 1984.

For the Council
The President
P. BARRY

APPENDIX 7

BIBLIOGRAPHY

Agreement on Implementation of Article VI of the General Agreement on Tariffs and Trade, reprinted in *Basic Instruments and Selected Documents*, 26th Supplement (1980) (Geneva : GATT)

Alexander & Grabandt, *National Courts entitled to ask Preliminary Rulings under Article 177 of the EEC Treaty: The Case Law of the Court of Justice*, 19 CMLRev 413-420

Arnull, *Judicial review of anti-dumping measures - further developments*, (1983) ELRev 403-5

Atwood, J., *EEC's new measures against unfair practices in international trade*, 19 International Lawyer 361 (1985)

Balassa, *Tokyo Round and developing countries*, 14 JWTL 93

    The new protectionism and international economy, 12 JWTL 409

    Studies in Trade Liberalisation : Problems and Prospects for Industrial Countries (1967)

Barcelo, *The anti-dumping law : repeal/revise it*, Mich. Y.B. International Legal Studies, Vol 1, 53-93 (1979)

    Antidumping laws as barriers to trade, 57 Cornell Law Rev (1972), p491

    Subsidies, countervailing duties and anti-dumping after the Tokyo Round, 13 Cornell International L.J. (1980), pp257-88

Barav, *The judicial power of the European Economic Community*, 53 Southern California L.R. (1980), 461

    Direct and individual concern : an almost insurmountable barrier to the admissibility of individual appeal to the European Court, 11 CMLRev 191

Brand, *Private Parties and GATT Dispute Resolution : Implications of Panel Report on Section 337 of US Tariff Act of 1930*, 24 JWTL (Vol 3) 5

Bebr, *Agreements concluded by the EEC and their possible direct effects : From International Fruit Co. (No. 3)* to *Kupferberg,* 20 CMLRev 35

Rule of law within the European Communities, Institut d'Etude Européennes Université Libre de Bruxelles 1965

Development of judicial control of European Communities (1981)

Bellis, J. F., *Judicial review of EEC anti-dumping and anti-subsidy determinations after Fediol : the emergence of a new admissibility test,* 21 CMLRev 539

La règlementation anti-dumping de la Communauté économique européenne, 15 Cahiers de Droit Européen (1979), pp495-539

Judicial review of EEC anti-dumping and anti-subsidy determinations after Fediol : the emergence of a new admissibility test, 21 CMLRev 539-551

Beseler, J. F., *EEC protection against dumping and subsidies from Third Countries,* 6 CMLRev 327-352

Beseler, J. F. and Williams, A. N., *Anti-dumping and anti-subsidy law; The European Communities,* (1986)

Bourgeois, *Tokyo Round Agreements on Technical Barriers to Trade and Government Procurement in International and EEC Perspective,* 19 CMLRev 5

Effects of International Agreements in EEC Law : Are the Dice Cast?, 82 Mich. L.Rev 1250

EC anti-dumping enforcement - selected second generation issues in (ed.) B. Hawk, *Anti Trust and Trade Policy in the United States and the European Community* (1985) pp563-602

EC Rules against "Illicit Trade Practices" - Policy Cosmetics or International Law Enforcement? in (ed.) B. Hawk *North American and Common Market Anti Trust and Trade Laws,* (1988) Chapter 6

The Common Commercial Policy - Scope and Nature of the Powers in (ed.) Volker *Protectionism in the EEC* p4

Bourgeois & Laurent, *Le "nouvel instrument de politique commerciale" : un pas en avant vers l'élimination des obstacles aux échanges internationaux,* 21 Revue Trimestrielle de Droit Européen (1985) at 41

Briet, *Antidumping in de EEG - DE Kinderschoenen ontgroeid?* SEW (1982) 145

Bronckers, *Private response to foreign unfair trade practices US & EEC Complaint Procedures*, 6 Northwestern J. International Law and Bus. (1985) 201

   A legal analysis of protectionist measures affecting Japanese imports into the EC in (ed.) Volker *Protectionism and the European Community*, (1983) pp 53-98

   Selective Safeguard Measures in Multilateral Trade Relations (1985)

Brown, L. N. & Jacobs, F. A., *The Court of the European Communities* 2nd ed. (1983)

Brownlie, *Principles of Public International Law* (1979) (3rd edn)

Bryan, *Taxing unfair international trade practices. A study of US antidumping and countervailing duty laws*, 1980

Burnside, A., *Enforcement of EEC Competition Law by Interim Measures*, 19 JWTL 34

Canal-Forgues & Ostrihansky, *New Developments in the GATT Dispute Settlement Procedure*, 24 JWTL (vol. 2) 67

Cuanne & Stanbrook, *Dumping and subsidies. The law and procedures governing the imposition of anti-dumping and countervailing duties in the European Community* (1983)

Curzon, V., *Industrial Policy in the European Community*, Trade Policy Research Centre (1981)

Curzon & Curzon, *The Management of Trade Relations in the GATT* in (ed.) Shonfield *International Economic Relations of Western World* [1959-71] (1976), Vol 1, pp143-286

Curzon & Curzon, *Hidden barriers to international trade* and *Global assault on non-tariff barriers*, Thames Essay No. 3 (1972)

Curzon-Price, *Industrial Policies in EEC* (1981)

Daillier, P., *La pratique communautaire de lutte contre le dumping*, Revue du Marché (1979) 557-568

Dale, *Antidumping in a liberal trade order* (1980)

Dam, *GATT as an international organisation*, 3 JWTL 375

   The GATT (1970)

Dashwood, *Annotation on Case 113/77 and other anti-dumping cases*, 17 CMLRev (1980) 119

Davey, W. J., *An analysis of European Communities legislation and practice relating to anti dumping and countervailing duties* in (ed.) B. Hawk *Anti-Trust and Trade Policy in International Trade* (1983), pp39-128

 Anti-dumping laws : a time for restriction in (ed.) B. Hawk *North American and Common Market Anti-Trust and Trade Laws* (1988), Chapter 8

De Bandt, *EEC Anti Dumping Rules : A practical approach*, 12 International Law 523

De Bus, M. D., *La CEE et le code sur les subventions et les droits compensateurs*, 17 RTDE (1981) 33

De Jong, H. W., *The significance of dumping in international trade*, 2 JWTL 162-188

De Smedt, *EEC Anti-dumping Policy. New Developments*, 14 International Law 223

Denton, *The NCPI and Akzo v Dupont* (1988) ELRev 28

Denton et al, *Subsidy issues in international commerce* (1972)

Didier, P., *EEC Anti-dumping Rules and Practices*, 17 CMLRev 349-369

 Deux années d'application du nouveau règlement anti-dumping de la C.E.E., 18 Cahiers de Droit Européen (1982), 21-54

Diebold, *Industrial Policy as an International Issue* (1980)

Dinnage, J., *Locus Standi and Article 173* [1979] ELRev 15

Donner, *The Role of the Lawyer in European Community* (1968)

Edward, D. A. O. and Lane, R. C., *Introduction to European Community Law*, reprinted from Stair Encyclopaedia Vol 3 (1986)

Ehlermann, *Scope and extent of the capacity of the Community to act on the international plane*, House of Lords Select Committee on European Affairs, Report 1985.

Ehrenhaft, P. D., *An administrator's look at anti-dumping duty laws in US trade policy*, Mich. Y.B. International Leg. Studies, (1979) Vol 1, 97-114 .

 Protection against international price discrimination : United States countervailing and antidumping duties, 58 Columbia Law Review 44

Epstein, *The illusory conflict between anti-dumping and anti-trust law*, XVIII Anti Trust Bulletin 1-22 (1973)

European Research Associates, *EEC Protectionism* (Vols. 1 and 2)

Evans, *The Kennedy Round in American Trade Policy*

> *Subsidies and countervailing duties in GATT : present law and future prospects*, 3 Int. T. de L.J. 211 (1979)

Ewing, *Non-tariff barriers and non-adjustment or international trade*, 18 JWTL 63

First Annual Report of Commission of European Communities on the Community's anti-dumping and anti-subsidy activities (1983), EC Commission, DOCUMENTS, COM(83) 519/final/2 (Microfiche No. EN-83-175)

Fisher, *The Anti-Dumping Law of the US : A Legal and Economic Analysis*, 5 Law & Policy in International Bus. (1973) 85

The General Agreement on Tariffs and Trade, reprinted in *Basic Instruments and Selected Documents*, Vol 1 (1952) (Geneva : GATT)

Gilistra, *Anti-dumping policy in the EEC in practice* in (ed.) Volker *Protectionism and the European Community* (1983) pp147-180

Greenway, *Multilateral trade policy in the 1980's* Lloyds Bank Review, Jan. 1984, No. 151

Harding, *The private interest in challenging Community action*, (1980) ELRev 354

Hartley, *The Japanese Ballbearing Judgments*, (1979) ELRev 265/7

> *The foundations of European Community law : an introduction to the constitutional and administrative law of the European Community* (1981)

Hartley, *International Agreements and the EEC Legal System : Some Recent Developments* (1983) ELRev 383

Hiscocks, R. I., *International Price discrimination. The Discovery of the Predatory Dumping Act of 1916*, International Lawyer (1977)

Hudec, *GATT or GABB*, 80 Yale L.J. 1299

Hofbauer & Schott, *Trading for growth : The Next Round of Trade Negotiations* 11 Inst. Int'l. Econ. (1985) 79

Hunnings, *Enforceability of EEC-EFTA Free Trade Agreements*, (1977) ELRev 163

Ianni, *International Treatment of State Trading*, 16 JWTL , 480-496

International Trade, *Dumping*, 20 Harvard International L.J., pp193-201

International Trade, *GATT Legislation - the TAA of 1979*, Harvard International L.J. (1979), pp687-695

Jackson, J. H., *World Trade and the Law of GATT* (1969)

> *Responses to Foreign "Unfair" Actions* in (ed.) Jackson *Legal Problems of International Economic Relations*, 1977

Jackson et al, *Implementing the Tokyo Round : Legal Aspects of Changing International Rules*, 81 Mich. L.Rev 267

> *The Jurisprudence of International Trade : the DISC Case in GATT* 72 AJIL (1978) 747

Jacobs (ed.), *European Law and the Individual* (1976)

Kelly, *Non-Tariff Barriers* in (ed.) *Balassa Studies in Trade Liberalisation : Problems and Prospects for Industrial Countries* (1967)

Klabbers & Vrengdenhil, *Dispute settlement in GATT : Disc and its successor*, (1986) LIEI 115

Kock, K., *International Trade Policy and the GATT 1947-67* (1968)

Kojima, *Hidden barriers to trade in Japan*, 7 JWTL 137

Kuypers, *Some reflections on the legal position of private complainants in various procedures relating to commercial policy*, (1983) LIEI 115

Lesguillons, H, *Le régime anti dumping de la Communauté européenne*, Droit et Pratique du Commerce International (1978) 459-505 (vol. 4)

Levitt, *International trade import restrictions*, Harvard Int'l L.J. 21, pp561-/7 (1980)

Lowe, *Extraterritorial Jurisdiction* An Annotated Collection of Legal Materials (1983)

Mackenzie Stuart, *The non-contractual liability of EEC*, Maccabaean Lecture in Jurisprudence (1975)

McGovern, *International Trade Regulation* (1982)

Mann, *The function of judicial decision in European economic integration*

Meesen, *Application of rules of public international law within Community law*, 13 CMLRev 485

Meier, *Problems of Trade Policy* (1973)

Merciai, *Safeguard measures in GATT*, 15 JWTL 125

Mestmäcker, *Providing fair conditions of competition under the Free Trade Agreements of the EEC*, 3 Northwestern J. International Law & Bus. (1981) 296-319

Metzger, *Injury and Market Disruption from Imports* in *Williams Commission Papers 1* (1971) at p167

Middleton, *Negotiating on non-tariff distortions of trade*

   GATT Standards Code, 14 JWTL 201

Norall, *Judicial review of anti dumping measures : further developments* (1984) ELRev 46.

Norall, *The New Amendments to the EC's Basic Anti-Dumping Regulation*, 26 CMLRev 83-101

Note : *A legal guide to Tokyo Round*, 13 JWTL 436

Oldekop D. & Van Bael I., *European Antidumping Law and Procedure*, Antidumping Law : Policy and Implementation, Mich. Yearbook of International Legal Studies (Vol 1) (1979), pp230-244

O'Keefe, *Appeals against an Order to refer under Article 177 of the EEC Treaty* [1983] ELRev 87-104

Olechowski & Sampson, *Trade Restrictions in the EEC, the US and Japan*, 14 JWTL, pp220/23

Paisley, S. E., *A Guide to EEC Law in Northern Ireland* (1986)

Parry, A. & Hardy, S., *EEC Law* (1972)

Pestieau, *Revising GATT Approach to Subsidies : A Canadian View* in (ed.) Warnecke *International Trade and Industrial Policies* (1978) at p95

Pescatore, *The doctrine of "direct effect" : an infant disease of Community law*, (1983) ELRev 155

Petersmann, *Application of GATT by the ECJ*, 20 CMLRev 397

Participation of the EEC in GATT : International law and EEC law aspects in (ed.) O'Keefe & Schermers *Mixed Agreements* (1983) pp167-198

Pevtchin, G., *Allied II : Limits on the extent of injury under the EEC anti-dumping rules* in (ed.) B. Hawk *Anti Trust and Trade Policy in the United States and the European Community* (1985) pp605-622

Phegan, C, *GATT Article XVI.3 : Export subsidies and equitable shares*, 16 JWTL 251

Rabe, H.-J. & Schötte, M., *EC Anti dumping law : current issues in the light of the jurisdiction of the Court*, 26 CMLRev 643-674

Rasmussen, *Why is Article 173 EEC interpreted against private plaintiffs*, (1980) ELRev 112

Report on the Community's anti-dumping activities (1981) Working Documents 1-422/81, European Parliament

Riesenfield, *The treatment of confidential information in antidumping cases : a comment on the Celanese case*, 21 CMLRev 533

Rodgers, R. P., *The illusory conflict between antidumping and antitrust : a comment*, Antitrust Bulletin (1974)

Schermers, *Judicial Protection in the European Communities*, 3rd edn (1983)

Community Law and International Law, 12 CMLRev 77

The direct application of Treaties with Third States : Polydor and Pabst cases, 19 CMLRev 564

Internal effect of EEC Treaty making in (ed.) O'Keefe & Schermers *Essays in European Law and Integration* (1982)

Shonfield, A., *International Economic Relations of the Western World*, Vol 1 Politics and Trade (1976)

Smit & Herzog, *The Law of the European Economic Community : A Commentary on the EEC Treaty* (1976)

Sohn, *Generally accepted international rules*, 61 Washington L. Rev (1986) 1073

Stanbrook, *The impact of Community interest and injury determination on anti-dumping measures in the EEC* in (ed.) B. Hawk *Anti Trust and Trade Policy in the United States and the European Community*, (1985) pp623-642

Steenbergen, *The New Commercial Policy Instrument*, 22 CMLRev 421

   Trade regulation after the Tokyo Round in (ed.) Volker *Protectionism and the European Community* (1983) pp181-199

Stegeman, *Anti-dumping Policy and the Consumer*, 19 JWTL 466

Stein & Vining, *Citizen Access to Judicial Review of Administrative Action in Transitional and Federal Context* in (ed.) Jacobs *European Law and the Individual* 116

Temple Lang, *EEC Competition Actions in Member States' Courts - claim for damages declarations and injunctions for breach of Community anti-trust law* in (ed.) B. Hawk *Anti Trust and Trade Policy in the United States and the European Community* (1983) pp219-304

Temple Lang, *Judicial Review of Trade Safeguard Measures in the European Community* in (ed.) B. Hawk *Antitrust and Trade Policy in the United States and the European Community* (1985) pp643-694

Thirty Years of Community Law, EC Commission

Thomas, *New US anti-dumping law : some advice to exporters*, 15 JWTL 323-330

Toth, *Legal Protection of Individuals in the European Communities* (1978)

Ugonis, M. & Puifferat, J., *La nouvelle législation anti dumping de la Communauté*, Revue du Marché Commun No. 255, Mars (1982), pp117-119

Usher, *European Court Practice* (1983)

Van Bael, *Ten years of EEC anti-dumping enforcement*, 13 JWTL 395-408

   The EEC Anti Dumping Rules - A Practical Approach, International Lawyer (1978) 523-545

   EEC anti-dumping law and procedure revisited, 24 JWTL (Vol 2) 5

Van Bael & Bellis, *International Trade Law and Practice of the European Community - EEC Anti Dumping and other Trade Protection Laws* (1985)

Vance, A. P., *Judicial Review of Anti Dumping Orders in US and EEC*, N.Y. Law School L. Rev, pp577-607

Van Dijk, *Judicial review of governmental action and the requirement of an interest to sue* (1980)

Vaughan, *The Law of the European Communities* (Vols. 1 & 2) (1986)

Vermulst, E., *Dumping in the US and the European Community : a comparative analysis,* (1984) LIEI 103-47

Vermulst, E., *Anti Dumping Law and Practice in the United States and the European Community* (1987)

Verstrynge, *Current anti trust policy issues in EEC : some reflections on the second generation of EEC Competition Policy* in (ed.) B. Hawk *Anti Trust and Trade Policy in International Trade* (1984) pp673-698

Viner, J., *Dumping : A problem in international trade,* Chicago, University of Chicago Press, 1923, reprinted in Kelley (1966)

Volker, *The Direct Effect of International Agreements in the EEC's Legal Order,* (1983) LIEI 131

Protectionism in the EEC

Wall. E. H., *The Court of Justice of the European Communities* (1966)

Warnecke, *International Trade and Industrial Policies* (1978)

White, *Effects of International Treaties within the Community Order,* (1975-6) ELRev 402

Whitt, R. S., *The Politics of Procedure : An examination of the GATT dispute settlement panel and Article XXI, Defense in the context of the US embargo of Nicaragua* (1987) Law Policy & Int'l Bus. 603

Wyatt, D. and Dashwood, A., *The Substantive Law of the EEC,* 2nd ed. (1987)

Zoller, *Remedies for Unfair Trade : European and US Views,* (1985) 18 Cornell International Law Journal, 227-245

APPENDIX 8 : ANTI-DUMPING PROCEEDINGS INITIATED SINCE 1 JANUARY 1980

PRODUCT	COUNTRY	INITIATION	PROVISIONAL DUTY	DEFINITIVE DUTY	UNDERTAKING	OTHER	COURT
Chemical fertiliser	USA	OJ C47 26.2.80 p2; Corrigendum OJ C112 7.5.80 p18; Review OJ C219 30.8.86 p2	OJ L212 15.5.80 p43; OJ L330 6.12.80 p1; OJ L214 22.7.82 p7; OJ L246 21.8.82 p5; OJ L322 18.11.82 p4	OJ L39 12.2.81 p4; OJ C179 16.7.82 p4; OJ L15 17.1.83 p1			Joined Cases 239 and 275/82 Allied Corporation, Demufert SA, Transcontinental Fertiliser Co and Kaiser Aluminium and Chemical Corporation v EC Commission [1984] ECR 1005; Case 53/83 Allied Corporation, Demufert SA, Transcontinental Fertiliser Co and Kaiser Aluminium and Chemical Corporation v EC Council [1985] ECR 1621
Louvre doors	Taiwan	OJ C77 27.3.80 p5; OJ C187 13.7.83 p3				OJ L158 16.6.81 p5 (no duty)	
Polyester yarn	USA	OJ C129 30.5.80 p2; Corrigendum OJ C149 18.6.80 p19; Review OJ C48 23.2.82 p2; Review OJ C257 25.9.84 p3; Notice of impending expiry OJ C72 27.3.90 p4	OJ L235 2.9.80 p1; OJ L279 23.10.80 p18; OJ L294 4.11.80 p5	OJ L358 31.12.80 p91; OJ L322 11.11.81 p2; OJ L89 3.4.82 p1; OJ L50 25.2.83 p1; OJ L246 13.9.85 p57 (amendment)			
Pressure sensitive paper masking tape	USA	OJ C130 31.5.80 p3				OJ L344 19.12.80 p57 (no duty)	
Vinyl acetate monomer	USA	OJ C169 9.7.80 p2; OJ C164 2.7.86 p2 (reopened)	OJ L311 21.11.80 p13; OJ L73 19.3.81 p3	OJ L129 15.5.81 p1; OJ L213 14.8.87 p32 (amendment)	OJ L311 21.11.80 p13; Lapsed 21.11.85 OJ C300 23.11.85 p4		Case 236/81 Celanese Co Inc v EC Council and EC Commission [1982] ECR 1183. Removed OJ C83 21.3.83 p5
Mechanical wrist watches	USSR	OJ C181 19.7.80 p3; Corrigendum OJ C202 7.8.80 p7; Review OJ C284 7.11.85 p3; Review OJ C24 1.2.90 p6	OJ L11 16.1.82 p14; OJ L125 7.5.82 p1	OJ L207 15.7.82 p1; OJ L213 4.8.87 p5; OJ L50 24.2.88 p5 (amended); OJ L331 16.11.88 p44 (amended)		OJ L256 20.9.90 p10 (definitive duties repealed)	Case 264/82 Timex Corporation v EC Commission and EC Council [1985] ECR 861

PRODUCT	COUNTRY	INITIATION	PROVISIONAL DUTY	DEFINITIVE DUTY	UNDERTAKING	OTHER	COURT
Lithium hydroxide	USA USSR	OJ C181 19.7.80 p4		OJ L228 30.8.80 p59			
Styrene monomer	USA	OJ C189 26.7.80 p4; OJ C231 12.9.86 p5 (reopened)	OJ L42 14.2.81 p14; OJ L132 19.5.81 p17	OJ L154 13.6.81 p10		OJ L258 8.9.87 p20 (no injury)	
Edible and pharmaceutical gelatine	Sweden	OJ C219 27.8.80 p2				OJ L320 27.11.80 p41 (no duty)	
Furfural	Dominican Republic Spain China	OJ C219 27.8.80 p3				OJ L189 11.7.81 p57 (no injury)	
Potato granules	Canada	OJ C221 29.8.80 p2	OJ L116 28.4.81 p11	OJ L243 26.8.81 p1	OJ L243 26.8.81 p16	OJ C231 12.9.86 p6 (duty lapsed)	
Tube and pipe fittings of malleable cast iron	Brazil	OJ C249 26.9.80 p2			OJ L145 3.6.81 p29		
Paraxylene	Puerto Rico USA Virgin Islands	OJ C286 5.11.80 p2	OJ L158 16.6.81 p7	OJ L296 15.10.81 p1; OJ L364 19.12.81 p3; OJ C124 15.5.82 p2; OJ L101 20.4.83 p1	OJ L158 16.5.81 p7; OJ L101 20.4.83 p1		
Orthoxylene	Puerto Rico USA	OJ C286 5.11.80 p3	OJ L141 27.5.81 p29	OJ L270 25.9.81 p1; OJ L353 9.12.81 p1; OJ C124 15.5.82 p2; OJ L101 20.4.83 p4			Case 307/81 Alusuisse Italia SpA v EC Commission and EC Council [1982] ECR 3463
Louvre doors	Malaysia Singapore	OJ C286 5.11.80 p4			OJ L135 22.5.81 p33	OJ L135 22.5.81 p33 (no duty)	

PRODUCT	COUNTRY	INITIATION	PROVISIONAL DUTY	DEFINITIVE DUTY	UNDERTAKING	OTHER	COURT
Hermetic compressors for refrigerating equipment	Brazil Spain Hungary Japan Singapore	OJ C296 14.11.80 p2; Corrigendum OJ C317 4.12.80 p15				OJ L113 25.4.81 p53 (no duty)	
Certain textured polyester fabrics	USA	OJ C337 24.12.80 p7	OJ L133 20.5.81 p17	OJ L262 16.9.81 p1; Corrigendum OJ L120 4.5.85 p18			
Monochrome portable television sets	South Korea	OJ C25 5.2.81 p3				OJ L364 19.12.81 p49 (no injury)	
Fluid cracking catalysts	USA	OJ C29 10.2.81 p2; OJ C136 5.6.81 p2			OJ L11 16.2.82 p25		
Upright pianos	GDR Poland Czechoslovakia USSR	OJ C35 18.2.81 p2; OJ C181 23.7.81 p3; Notice of expiry OJ C326 30.12.89 p5	OJ L101 16.4.82 p30; Corrigendum OJ L115 29.4.82 p22	OJ L238 13.8.82 p1; Corrigendum OJ L271 21.9.82 p20	OJ L101 16.4.82 p45; OJ L332 20.12.84 p79; OJ L26 31.1.85 p5		
Phenol and its salts	USA	OJ C51 10.3.81 p4	OJ L195 18.7.81 p22; OJ L322 11.11.81 p1	OJ L12 18.1.82 p1; OJ L89 3.4.82 p2			
Codeine and its salts	Poland Hungary Czechoslovakia Yugoslavia	OJ C72 1.4.81 p2				OJ L16 20.1.83 p30 (no entry)	
Plywood and similar laminated wood products	Canada USA	OJ C117 20.5.81 p2				OJ L338 25.1.81 p42 (no duty)	
Polypropylene film	Japan	OJ C155 24.6.81 p2			OJ L172 18.6.82 p44; undertaking lapsed OJ C335 30.12.86 p11		
Polyester cotton yarn	USA	OJ C157 26.6.81 p2				OJ L48 20.2.82 p30 (no duty)	

PRODUCT	COUNTRY	INITIATION	PROVISIONAL DUTY	DEFINITIVE DUTY	UNDERTAKING	OTHER	COURT
Certain refrigerators	Czechoslovakia GDR Hungary Poland Romania USSR Yugoslavia	OJ C162 2.7.81 p3			OJ L184 29.6.82 p23; undertaking lapsed OJ C335 30.12.86 p11		
Fibre building board	Bulgaria Hungary	OJ C164 4.7.81 p2			OJ L181 25.6.82 p18; undertaking lapsed OJ C335 30.12.86 p11		
Fibre building board	Czechoslovakia Finland Norway Poland Romania Spain USSR Sweden	Review OJ C164 4.7.81 p3; OJ C6 9.1.85 p5; (reopened) Review OJ C165 24.6.88 p88; Notice of impending expiry OJ C172 1.7.88 p3; Review OJ C150 17.6.89 p3; Notice of impending expiry OJ C176 23.6.89 p51; OJ C243 23.9.89 p3 (expiry)	OJ L181 25.6.82 p19; OJ L295 21.10.82 p1; OJ L241 31.8.83 p9; OJ L61 2.3.84 p22	OJ L361 24.12.83 p6; OJ L170 29.6.84 p68	OJ L181 25.6.82 p19; OJ L49 22.2.83 p6; OJ L361 24.12.83 p47; OJ L46 25.2.86 p23; undertaking lapsed OJ C178 7.7.87 p8		

PRODUCT	COUNTRY	INITIATION	PROVISIONAL DUTY	DEFINITIVE DUTY	UNDERTAKING	OTHER	COURT
Standard multiphase electric motors with a power rating exceeding 0.75kw but not more than 0.75kw (inclusive)	Bulgaria GDR Czechoslovakia Hungary Poland Romania USSR Yugoslavia	Review OJ C197 5.8.81 p2; OJ C305 26.11.85 p2; OJ C282 8.11.86 p2 (reopened and extension); Notice of impending expiry OJ C256 2.10.91 p6; OJ C37 15.2.92 p21; Notice of expiry OJ C80 31.3.92 p7	OJ L85 31.3.82 p9; OJ L280 1.10.86 p68; OJ L26 29.1.87 p1 (extension); Corrigendum OJ L42 12.2.87 p54; OJ L102 14.4.87 p5	OJ L220 29.7.82 p36; OJ L83 27.3.87 p1; Corrigendum OJ L102 14.4.87 p35; OJ L218 7.8.87 p2	OJ L85 31.3.82 p9; OJ L220 29.7.82 p36; OJ L95 5.4.84 p28; OJ L123 9.5.84 p22; OJ L280 1.10.86 p66 (repealed); OJ L83 27.3.87 p53		Case 279/86 Sermes SA v EC Commission [1987] ECR 3109; Case 301/86 R Frimodt Pedersen SA/s v EC Commission [1987] ECR 3123; Case 304/86R Enital SpA v EC Council and EC Commission [1987] ECR 267; Case 205/87 Nuova Ceam Srl v EC Commission [1987] ECR 4428; Joined Cases 305/86 and 160/87 Neotype Techmashexport v EC Council [1990] ECR 2945; Joined Cases 320/86 and 188/87 Stanko France v EC Council [1990] ECR 3013; Case 157/87 Electroimpex & Others v EC Council [1990] ECR 3021; Joined Cases 304/86 and 185/87 Enital v EC Council and EC Commission [1990] ECR 2939; Case 323/88 Sermes SA v Directeur des services des douanes de Strasbourg [1990] ECR 3027
Herbicide	Romania	Review OJ C208 18.8.81 p3; OJ C142 29.5.87 p4 (reopened); Notice of impending expiry OJ C193 31.7.92 p2		OJ L128 11.5.82 p17	OJ L26 30.1.88 p107	OJ C335 30.12.86 p11 (duty lapsed)	
Oxalic acid	China GDR Czechoslovakia Hungary	OJ C241 19.9.81 p11; Review OJ C137 22.5.87 p4; Notice of impending expiry OJ C335 30.12.86 p11; Review OJ C216 31.8.90 p2	OJ L19 27.1.82 p26; Corrigendum OJ L34 9.2.82 p11; OJ L148 27.5.82 p37; OJ L138 1.6.91 p62; OJ L272 20.9.91 p2 (extension)	OJ L148 27.5.82 p37; OJ L326 28.11.91 p16	OJ L148 27.5.82 p51; undertaking lapsed OJ C335 30.12.86 p11; OJ L343 13.12.88 p34		
Cylinder vacuum cleaners	Czechoslovakia GDR Poland	OJ C245 25.9.81 p2			OJ L172 18.6.82 p47; undertaking lapsed OJ C335 30.12.86 p11		
Photographic enlargers for amateur use	Poland USSR Czechoslovakia	OJ C271 23.10.81 p4	OJ L212 21.7.82 p32; OJ L322 18.11.82 p3		OJ L212 21.7.82 p32; OJ L9 7.1.83 p5		

PRODUCT	COUNTRY	INITIATION	PROVISIONAL DUTY	DEFINITIVE DUTY	UNDERTAKING	OTHER	COURT
Trichloroethylene	Czechoslovakia GDR Poland Romania Spain USA	OJ C271 23.10.81 p5	OJ L223 31.7.81 p76; OJ L308 4.11.82 p5; OJ L326 23.11.82 p28		OJ L223 31.7.82 p76; OJ L308 4.11.82 p5	OJ L223 31.7.82 p76 (no duty)	
Certain welded tubes of iron or steel	Romania	OJ C299 18.11.81 p2	OJ L25 3.2.82 p5; OJ L150 29.5.82 p1		OJ L150 29.5.82 p79		
Polyvinyl-chloride resins and compounds	Czechoslovakia GDR Hungary	OJ C332 19.12.81 p2	OJ L274 24.9.82 p15; OJ L18 22.1.83 p24		OJ L274 24.9.82 p15; OJ L18 22.1.83 p26		
Paracetamol crystals or powder	China	OJ C337 24.12.81 p6; Review OJ C236 2.9.87 p2	OJ L155 22.6.88 p29; OJ L282 15.10.88 p29 (extension)	OJ L348 17.12.88 p1	OJ L236 11.8.82 p23; undertaking lapsed OJ C193 22.7.87 p2		
Decabromodiphe nylether	USA	OJ C337 24.12.81 p6; OJ C229 2.9.82 p3			OJ L319 16.11.82 p16		
Aluminium foil for household and catering use	GDR Austria Hungary Israel	OJ C8 14.1.82 p5				OJ L339 1.12.82 p58 (no injury)	
Certain pears in syrup	Australia China South Africa	OJ C33 10.2.82 p2; OJ C276 19.10.82 p7				OJ L196 18.7.83 p22 (no duty)	
Nuts of iron or steel	Taiwan	OJ C67 16.3.82 p7; Review OJ C53 28.2.92 p4				OJ L254 31.8.82 p15 (no injury)	
Sheets and plates of iron or steel	Brazil	OJ C70 19.3.82 p3; OJ C197 31.7.82 p3	OJ L128 11.5.82 p9; OJ L221 30.7.82 p17	OJ L312 9.11.82 p10; OJ L45 14.2.83 p11; OJ L131 20.5.83 p13		OJ L184 17.7.85 p7 (duty suspended)	

PRODUCT	COUNTRY	INITIATION	PROVISIONAL DUTY	DEFINITIVE DUTY	UNDERTAKING	OTHER	COURT
Methylamine, dimethylamine and trimethylamine	GDR Romania	OJ C79 31.3.82 p2	OJ L238 13.8.82 p35	OJ L348 8.12.82 p1	OJ L238 13.8.82 p35		
Acrylonitrile	USA	OJ C84 3.4.82 p2				OJ L101 20.4.83 p33 (no injury)	
Bisphenol	USA	OJ C93 14.4.82 p4	OJ L23 26.1.83 p9; OJ L136 25.5.83 p12; OJ L199 22.7.83 p4				
Light sodium carbonate	Bulgaria GDR Poland USSR Romania	OJ C93 14.4.82 p5 (reopened); Review OJ C162 21.6.88 p9	OJ L283 6.10.82 p9	OJ L32 3.2.83 p1; amendment OJ L169 26.6.86 p1; OJ L131 13.5.89 p4	OJ L337 24.11.81 p5	OJ L60 9.3.90 p14 (refund)	
Fibre building board	Brazil	OJ C113 5.5.82 p3; Review OJ C165 24.6.88 p88			OJ L47 19.2.83 p30		
Thiophen	USA	OJ C122 13.5.82 p5			OJ L295 21.10.82 p35		
Perchlorethylene	Czechoslovakia Romania Spain USA	OJ C133 25.5.82 p10			OJ L371 30.12.82 p47		
Acrylic fibres	USA	Review OJ C140 3.6.82 p8; Notice of expiry OJ C243 23.9.89 p3			OJ L55 2.3.83 p1; OJ L209 4.8.84 p1	OJ L125 11.5.85 p32 (refund)	
Ferro silicon	Venezuela Norway Iceland Sweden Yugoslavia	OJ C144 8.6.82 p2; OJ C250 24.9.82 p2; Review OJ C145 2.6.88 p4; OJ C115 6.5.92 p2		OJ L38 10.2.90 p1	OJ L57 4.3.83 p20; OJ L38 10.2.90 p1		

PRODUCT	COUNTRY	INITIATION	PROVISIONAL DUTY	DEFINITIVE DUTY	UNDERTAKING	OTHER	COURT
Heavy sodium carbonate	USA	OJ C147 11.6.82 p4; OJ C101 13.4.84 p10 (reopened); Review OJ C64 14.3.89 p6; Notice of impending expiry OJ C183 20.7.89 p10; Notice of expiry OJ C282 10.11.90 p5	OJ L317 13.11.82 p5; OJ L206 2.8.84 p15	OJ L64 10.3.83 p23; OJ L311 29.11.84 p26	OJ L317 13.11.82 p5; OJ L206 2.8.84 p15	OJ L283 16.10.90 p38 (termination); OJ L47 20.2.91 p8 (refund)	
Copper sulphate	Yugoslavia Czechoslovakia USSR	OJ C161 26.2.82 p2; OJ C331 17.12.82 p2; OJ C301 8.11.83 p2; OJ C55 28.2.84 p2 (reopened); OJ C284 7.11.85 p3 (reopened); Notice of impending expiry OJ C282 10.11.90 p4	OJ L308 4.11.82 p7; OJ L296 8.11.85 p26; OJ L62 5.3.86 p1 (extension)	OJ L274 7.10.83 p1; OJ L55 2.3.83 p4; OJ L274 7.10.83 p1: Repealed OJ L215 11.8.84 p1; OJ L113 30.4.86 p4	OJ L281 13.10.83 p22; OJ L215 11.8.84 p16; OJ L225 22.8.84 p22		Case 87/83 Zorka-Sabac OJ C163 22.6.83 p3 withdrawn OJ C334 14.12.84 p3
Natural magnesium carbonate	China	OJ C162 29.6.82 p2	OJ L371 30.12.82 p21; OJ L110 27.4.83 (extension)		OJ L66 8.3.84 p32		
Natural magnesium carbonate	China Republic of Korea	OJ C162 29.6.82 p3; OJ C149 19.6.85 p2 (continuation)	OJ L371 30.12.82 p23; OJ L110 27.4.83 p28 (extension)			OJ L70 13.3.86 p41 (no injury)	Joined Cases 121, 122/86R Anonimos Eteria Epichiriseon Metalleftikon, Viomichanikon kai Naftiliakon AE and Others v EC Council and EC Commission [1986] ECR 2063; Case 129/86R Greece v EC Council and EC Commission [1986] ECR 2071; Case 121/86 and 122/86 Anonymos Etaireia Epicheiriseon Metalleftikon Viomichanikon kai Naftiliakon AE and Others v EC Commission and EC Council [1989] ECR 3919 and 3959; Case 129/86 Greece v EC Council [1989] ECR 3963

PRODUCT	COUNTRY	INITIATION	PROVISIONAL DUTY	DEFINITIVE DUTY	UNDERTAKING	OTHER	COURT
Urea ammonium nitrate fertilisers	USA	OJ C179 16.7.82 p4; OJ C219 30.8.86 p2	OJ L33 4.2.83 p9		OJ L211 3.8.83 p1	OJ L208 30.7.87 p1 (no injury)	
Sheets and plates of iron or steel	Brazil	OJ C197 31.7.82 p3	OJ L45 17.2.83 p14				
Broad flanged beams	Spain	OJ C207 10.8.82 p4	OJ L238 13.8.82 p2; OJ L317 13.11.82 p16	OJ L30 1.2.83 p61; Corrigendum OJ L36 8.2.83 p10		OJ L116 30.4.83 p91 (suspension); OJ L165 25.6.85 p11 (definitive duties repealed)	
Barium chloride	China GDR	OJ C207 10.8.82 p5	OJ L110 27.4.83 p11	OJ L228 20.8.83 p28			
Hexamethylene-tetramine	GDR USSR Czechoslovakia Romania	OJ C211 13.8.82 p2; Corrigendum OJ C215 19.8.82 p8	OJ L40 12.2.83 p24	OJ L151 9.6.83 p9	OJ L40 10.2.83 p24		
Outboard motors	Japan	OJ C215 19.8.82 p3; OJ C305 26.11.85 p3 (reopened); Notice of impending expiry OJ C256 2.10.91 p5; OJ C304 23.11.91 p12; Review OJ C53 28.2.91 p3	OJ L152 10.6.83 p18	OJ L275 8.10.83 p1; OJ L124 13.5.87 p1	OJ L247 7.9.83 p18; OJ L82 26.3.87 p36		
Kraftliner paper and board	USA Austria Canada Finland Portugal USSR Sweden Brazil South Africa	OJ C217 21.8.82 p2 (review); OJ C109 7.5.86 p2 (review)		OJ L64 10.3.83 p25	OJ C217 21.8.82 p2; OJ L64 8.3.83 p25		Case C-189/88 Cartorobica SpA v Ministero delle Finanze dello stato [1990] ECR 1269

PRODUCT	COUNTRY	INITIATION	PROVISIONAL DUTY	DEFINITIVE DUTY	UNDERTAKING	OTHER	COURT
Polyethylene	Czechoslovakia GDR Poland USSR	OJ C230 3.9.82 p2; OJ C325 11.12.82 p3			OJ L138 27.5.83 p65		
Xanthan gum	USA	OJ C253 28.9.82 p2				OJ L268 30.9.83 p60 (no injury)	
Cellulose ester resins	USA	OJ C299 16.11.82 p3			OJ L106 23.4.83 p24		
Iron or steel coils for re-rolling	Argentina Brazil Venezuela Canada	OJ C303 20.11.82 p4; Review OJ C158 17.6.88 p3; Terminated OJ L112 25.4.89 p5	OJ L82 29.3.83 p9	OJ L210 2.8.83 p5; Suspension OJ L143 3.6.87 p16	OJ L82 29.3.83 p9; OJ L160 18.6.83 p32; Corrigendum OJ L222 13.8.83 p46; Suspended OJ L184 17.7.85 p6		
Glass textile fibre (rovings)	Czechoslovakia GDR Japan	OJ C310 27.11.82 p2; Notice of impending expiry OJ C172 1.7.88 p3; Review OJ C294 18.11.88 p4; OJ C87 8.4.89 p3	OJ L160 18.6.83 p18; OJ L283 15.10.83 p1	OJ L354 16.12.83 p15	OJ L352 15.12.83 p47; Undertaking lapsed OJ C97 18.4.89 p9		
TV image and sound recorders or reproducers	Japan	OJ C338 24.12.82 p27				OJ L86 31.3.83 p23 (termination)	
Unwrought nickel	USSR	OJ C31 5.2.83 p3	OJ L43 15.2.83 p19; OJ L159 17.6.83 p43			OJ L286 19.10.83 p29 (no injury)	
Non alloyed unwrought aluminium	Egypt USSR Norway Yugoslavia Surinam	OJ C31 5.2.83 p4; OJ C206 2.8.83 p6				OJ L161 15.6.83 p15; OJ L57 28.2.84 p119 (termination)	
U and I sections of iron or steel	South Africa	OJ C37 10.2.83 p5				OJ L181 6.7.83 p26 (no duty)	

PRODUCT	COUNTRY	INITIATION	PROVISIONAL DUTY	DEFINITIVE DUTY	UNDERTAKING	OTHER	COURT
Dicumyl peroxide	Japan	OJ C46 17.2.83 p21; Review OJ C244 18.11.88 p4; Notice of impending expiry OJ C143 1.6.88 p3	OJ L203 27.7.83 p13		OJ L329 25.11.83 p19		
Sanitary fixtures of porcelain or china	Czechoslovakia Hungary	OJ C87 29.3.83 p4			OJ L325 22.11.83 p18		
Caravans	Yugoslavia	OJ C89 31.3.83 p3			OJ L240 30.8.83 p12		
Lithium hydroxide	USSR USA China	OJ C98 12.4.83 p2		OJ L294 26.10.83 p3	OJ L294 26.10.83 p29		
Synthetic fibre hand knitting yarn	Turkey	OJ C102 15.4.83 p2; Notice of impending expiry OJ C249 23.9.88 p2; OJ C42 21.2.89 p2 (reopened); Notice OJ C53 2.3.89 p8			OJ L67 9.3.84 p60	OJ L309 31.10.89 p42 (termination)	Case 312/84 Continentale Producten Gesellschaft Ehrhardt-Reuken v EC Commission [1987] ECR 841; Case 246/87 Continentale Producten Gesellschaft Ehrhardt-Reuken v Hauptzollamt München West [1989] ECR 1151
Certain angles shapes and sections of iron or steel	Romania	OJ C109 23.4.83 p2			OJ L83 27.3.84 p9		
Choline chloride	GDR Romaina	OJ C109 23.4.83 p3	OJ L356 20.12.83 p12		OJ L117 3.5.84 p44		
Saccharin and its salts	China Korea USA	OJ C119 4.5.83 (review)				OJ L352 15.12.83 p49 (no injury)	
Exterior panel doors	Taiwan	OJ C152 10.6.83 p7				OJ L16 19.1.84 p42 (no duty)	

PRODUCT	COUNTRY	INITIATION	PROVISIONAL DUTY	DEFINITIVE DUTY	UNDERTAKING	OTHER	COURT
Vinyl acetate monomer	Canada USA	OJ C180 7.7.83 p3; Review OJ C105 25.4.89 p3	OJ 58 29.2.84 p17	OJ L170 29.6.84 p70; OJ L275 29.9.87 p1; (amended) OJ L53 1.3.90 p1		OJ L240 3.9.90 pp19, 20, 23; OJ L80 27.3.91 pp49, 51, 53 (refund)	
Ball bearings	Japan Singapore Thailand	OJ C188 14.7.83 p8; OJ C310 15.11.83 p3; OJ C101 13.4.84 p11 (reopened); OJ C179 7.7.84 p2 (extension); Review OJ C111 25.4.87 p3; OJ C159 18.6.88 p2; Notice of impending expiry OJ C74 22.3.89 p10; Review OJ C133 30.5.89 p3; OJ C126 23.5.89 p2; OJ C175 11.7.89 p3; OJ C204 20.9.89 p4; Notice OJ C100 22.4.92 p5	OJ L79 23.3.84 p8; OJ L340 28.12.84 p37; OJ L112 25.4.85 p1 (extension); OJ L129 15.5.85 p1 (amended)	OJ L193 21.7.84 p1; OJ L307 24.11.84 p15 (amended); OJ L167 27.6.85 p3; OJ L336 26.11.87 p1 (amended); OJ C132 31.5.90 p5 (continued)		OJ L59 27.2.85 p30 (no duty); OJ L113 30.4.86 p61 (no duty); OJ L148 15.6.88 pp26-28, 30 (refund); OJ L185 4.7.92 pp35, 38, 41, 44 (refund)	Case 240/84 NTN Toyo Bearing Co v EC Council [1987] ECR 1809; Case 255/84 Nachi Fujikoshi Corporation v EC Council [1987] ECR 1861; Case 256/84 R Koyo Seiko Co Ltd v EC Council and EC Commission [1985] ECR 1351; Case 256/84 Koyo Seiko Co Ltd v EC Council and EC Commission [1987] ECR 1899; Case 258/84 R Nippon Seiko KK v EC Council [1984] ECR 4357; Case 258/84 Nippon Seiko KK v EC Council [1987] ECR 1923; Case 260/84 Minebea Co Ltd v EC Council [1987] ECR 1975; Case 188/88 NMB (Deutschland) GmbH & Others v EC Commission, Judgment of 10.3.92
Horticultural glass and drawn glass	Czechoslovakia GDR Poland Romaina USSR Hungary	OJ C194 21.7.83 p4; OJ C13 19.1.84 p3 (extension); Notice OJ C183 20.7.89 p10; Notice of expiry OJ C23 31.1.90 p4			OJ L224 21.8.84 p26		

PRODUCT	COUNTRY	INITIATION	PROVISIONAL DUTY	DEFINITIVE DUTY	UNDERTAKING	OTHER	COURT
Electronic weighing scales	Japan	OJ C236 3.9.83 p5; OJ C196 25.7.84 p3 (continued); Notice of impending expiry OJ C106 28.4.90 p5; Review OJ C240 26.9.90 p3; OJ C50 26.2.91 p3	OJ L80 24.3.84 p9; OJ L275 16.10.85 p5; OJ L32 7.2.86 p4 (extended)	OJ L97 12.4.86 p1; OJ C81 26.3.91 p5 (continued)	OJ L275 16.10.85 p5		Case 191/86 Tokyo Electric Co Ltd v EC Council OJ C215 26.8.86 p4
Pentaery-thritol	Spain Sweden Canada	OJ C244 13.9.83 p2; OJ C72 13.3.84 p2 (extension); Notice of impending expiry OJ C122 14.5.92 p11	OJ L254 22.9.84 p5	OJ L13 16.1.85 p1; Corrigendum OJ L20 24.1.85 p1	OJ L88 31.3.84 p74; OJ L254 22.9.84 p5		
Artificial corundum	China Spain Czechoslovakia Yugoslavia Hungary USSR Poland	OJ C261 30.9.83 p2; OJ C201 31.7.84 p4 (extended); Review OJ C67 17.3.90 p7	OJ L255 25.9.84 p9		OJ L340 28.12.84 p82; OJ L271 23.9.86 p26; OJ L275 2.10.91 p27		
P Ropan-l-ol	USA	OJ C275 14.10.83 p3			OJ L106 19.4.84 p55		
Certain ceramic tiles	Spain	OJ C282 19.10.83 p4			OJ L168 28.6.84 p35 (no duty)		
Certain sensitised paper for colour photographs	Japan	OJ C292 28.10.83 p2			OJ L124 11.5.84 p45		
Concrete re-inforced bars	Spain	OJ C299 5.11.83 p4	OJ L303 5.11.83 p13	OJ L33 4.2.84 p15; Corrigendum OJ L65 7.3.84 p15; OJ L150 6.6.84 p15 (suspension)		OJ L165 25.6.85 p12 (duty repealed)	

PRODUCT	COUNTRY	INITIATION	PROVISIONAL DUTY	DEFINITIVE DUTY	UNDERTAKING	OTHER	COURT
Certain shovels	Brazil	OJ C348 23.12.83 p15; Notice of expiry OJ C326 30.12.89 p5	OJ L231 29.8.84 p29		OJ L330 18.12.84 p28		
Certain angles shapes and sections of iron and steel	GDR	OJ C13 19.1.84 p4; Notice of expiry OJ C243 23.9.90 p3	OJ L109 26.4.84 p11	OJ L227 24.8.84 p31	OJ L227 24.8.84 p33		
Kraftliner paper and board	Spain	OJ C21 28.1.84 p2; Notice of expiry OJ C326 30.12.89 p5			OJ L224 21.8.84 p30		
Certain skates	Czechoslovakia Hungary Romania Yugoslavia	OJ C55 28.2.84 p3; OJ C204 3.8.84 p4 (extended)				OJ L52 22.2.85 p48 (no injury)	
Asbestos-cement corrugated sheets	GDR Czechoslovakia	OJ C55 28.2.84 p4; Review OJ C246 27.9.89 p2; Notice of impending expiry OJ C52 3.3.90 p15			OJ L259 28.9.84 p48		
Oxalic acid	Brazil GDR Spain	OJ C67 8.3.84 p7; Review OJ C301 30.11.89 p3; OJ C318 20.12.89 p2; Notice of impending expiry OJ C243 23.9.89 p3; OJ C239 25.9.90 p14 (expiry)	OJ L239 7.9.84 p8	OJ L26 31.1.86 p5	OJ L239 7.9.84 p8; OJ L340 28.12.84 p50; OJ L184 17.7.90 p16; Notice OJ L190 21.7.90 p50; Corrigendum OJ L219 14.8.90 p1	OJ L239 7.9.84 p8 (no duty)	

PRODUCT	COUNTRY	INITIATION	PROVISIONAL DUTY	DEFINITIVE DUTY	UNDERTAKING	OTHER	COURT
Electronic typewriters	Japan Taiwan	OJ C83 24.3.84 p4; OJ C149 19.6.85 p3 (reopened); Review OJ C338 31.12.85 p6; OJ C338 31.12.85 p7 (extended); Notice of impending expiry OJ C5 10.1.90 p4; OJ C67 17.3.90 p9 (modified); Review OJ C141 9.6.90 p14; OJ C315 14.12.90 p6; Notice of impending expiry OJ C96 12.4.91 p5; OJ C255 1.10.91 p2 (expiry); Notice OJ C283 30.10.91 p13	OJ L335 22.12.84 p43; OJ L108 19.4.85 p18 (extended); OJ L266 9.10.85 p5	OJ L163 22.6.85 p1; OJ L288 30.10.85 p5 (amended); OJ L17 23.1.86 p2; OJ L187 9.7.86 p3; OJ L56 26.2.87 p1; OJ L18 21.1.88 p4 (amended); OJ L183 14.7.88 p1 (amended); OJ L203 28.7.88 p1 (amended)	OJ L283 4.10.86 p25	OJ L335 22.12.84 p43 (no duty); OJ L40 15.2.86 p29; (no duty); OJ L140 27.5.86 p52 (no duty)	Case 56/85 Brother Industries Ltd v EC Commission [1988] ECR 5655; Case 250/85R Brother Industries Ltd v EC Council and EC Commission [1985] ECR 3459; Case 250/85 Brother Industries Ltd v EC Council and EC Commission [1988] ECR 5683; Case 260/85R Tokyo Electric Co Ltd v EC Council [1985] ECR 3467; Case 273/85R Silver Seiko and Others v EC Council [1985] ECR 3475; Joined Cases 277 and 300/85R Canon Inc v EC Council [1985] ECR 3491; Case 297/85R Towa Sandiken Corpn v EC Council and EC Commission [1985] ECR 3483; Case 229/86 Brother Industries Ltd v EC Commission [1987] ECR 3757; Case 299/85 Tokyo Juki Industrial v EC Council and EC Commission [1987] ECR 2965; Joined Cases 260/85 and 106/86 Tokyo Electric Co Ltd v EC Council [1988] ECR 5855; Joined Cases 273/85 and 107/86 Silver Seiko v EC Council [1988] ECR 5927; Case 301/85 Sharp v EC Council [1988] ECR 5813; Case 277 and 300/85 Canon Inc v EC Council [1988] ECR 5731
Copper sulphate	Bulgaria Hungary Poland Spain	OJ C90 31.3.84 p2; Review OJ C200 30.7.88 p9	OJ L275 18.10.84 p12; OJ L205 30.7.88 p68; OJ L326 30.11.88 p1 (extended)	OJ L41 12.2.85 p11	OJ L275 18.10.84 p12; OJ L41 12.2.85 p13	OJ L275 18.10.84 p12 (no duty)	
Paraformalde-hyde	Spain	OJ C145 1.6.84 p7; Notice of impending expiry OJ C326 30.12.89 p5			OJ L282 26.10.84 p58		
Certain glass mirrors	South Africa	OJ C167 27.6.84 p2; Notice of impending expiry OJ C5 10.1.90 p4; OJ C141 9.6.90 p15 (expiry)	OJ L36 8.2.85 p10	OJ L148 7.6.85 p1			

PRODUCT	COUNTRY	INITIATION	PROVISIONAL DUTY	DEFINITIVE DUTY	UNDERTAKING	OTHER	COURT
Certain hydraulic excavators	Japan	OJ C201 31.7.84 p3; Notice of impending expiry OJ C16 23.1.90 p3; Review OJ C132 31.5.90 p4; OJ C206 18.8.90 p5; OJ C51 27.2.91 p4 (expiry)	OJ L68 8.3.85 p13	OJ L176 6.7.85 p1		OJ L108 19.4.89 p1 (refund); OJ L36 8.2.91 p25 (termination)	
Silicon carbide	China Spain Czechoslovakia Norway Poland USSR Yugoslavia	OJ C202 1.8.84 p5; Notice of impending expiry OJ C100 17.4.91 p17; Review OJ C211 13.8.91 p4; OJ C279 26.10.91 p11			OJ L287 10.10.86 p25		
Polystyrene sheets	Spain	OJ C205 4.8.84 p10; OJ C238 20.9.86 p3 (reopened)	OJ L97 4.4.85 p30	OJ L198 30.7.85 p1		OJ L95 10.4.87 p13 (duty repealed)	
Roller chains for cycles	USSR China	OJ C235 5.9.84 p9; OJ C2 6.1.88 p2 (reopened); Notice of impending expiry OJ C161 30.6.90 p7; OJ C323 22.12.90 p15 (expiry)	OJ L217 14.8.85 p7; OJ L335 13.12.85 p61 (extended); OJ L3 6.1.88 p5	OJ L40 15.2.86 p25; OJ L115 3.5.88 p1	OJ L335 13.12.85 p63; OJ L40 15.2. 86 p27		
Certain titanium 'Mill products'	Japan USA	OJ C237 7.9.84 p2				OJ L113 23.4.85 p30 (no injury)	
Glycine	Japan	OJ C265 4.10.84 p5; Notice of impending expiry OJ C50 1.3.90 p5; OJ C206 18.8.90 p5 (expiry)	OJ L107 18.4.85 p8	OJ L218 15.8.85 p1			

PRODUCT	COUNTRY	INITIATION	PROVISIONAL DUTY	DEFINITIVE DUTY	UNDERTAKING	OTHER	COURT
Plasterboard	Spain	OJ C276 16.10.84 p4; OJ C82 31.3.90 p9 (expiry)			OJ L89 29.3.85 p65		
Basic chromium sulphate	Yugoslavia	OJ C276 16.10.84 p5; Notice of impending expiry; OJ C141 9.6.90 p13; OJ C304 4.12.90 p11 (expiry)	OJ L205 3.8.85 p12	OJ L321 30.11.85 p81			
Standard wood particle board	Bulgaria USSR Czechoslavakia Poland Romania Spain Yugoslavia	OJ C305 16.11.84 p6				OJ L268 10.10.85 p22 (no injury)	
Clogs	Sweden	OJ C47 19.2.85 p2	OJ L268 10.10.85 p11; OJ L333 11.12.85 p18 (amended)	OJ L32 7.2.86 p1	OJ L32 7.2.86 p28		
Hardboard	Argentina Portugal Switzerland Yugoslavia	OJ C47 10.2.85 p3			OJ L157 12.6.86 p61	OJ L81 26.3.86 p30 (termination)	
Wire rod	Brazil Portugal Trinidad and Tobago Venezuela	OJ C48 20.2.85 p2				OJ L299 13.11.85 p18 (no duty)	
Container corner fittings of worked cast steel	Austria	OJ C56 2.3.85 p2; Notice of impending expiry OJ C82 31.8.90 p11; Review OJ C310 11.12.90 p7			OJ L256 27.9.85 p44; OJ L165 19.6.90 p37		

PRODUCT	COUNTRY	INITIATION	PROVISIONAL DUTY	DEFINITIVE DUTY	UNDERTAKING	OTHER	COURT
Certain catagories of glass	Turkey Romania Yugoslavia Bulgaria Hungary Czechoslovakia	OJ C66 14.3.85 p13; OJ C200 8.8.85 p3 (extension); Notice of impending expiry OJ C215 30.8.90 p3; OJ C55 2.3.91 p3 (expiry)			OJ L51 28.2.86 p73		
Certain tube and pipe fittings	Brazil Taiwan Yugoslavia Japan	OJ C77 23.3.85 p3				OJ L313 8.11.86 p20 (no injury)	
Ball bearings and tapered roller bearings	Poland USSR Romania Thailand	OJ C77 23.3.85 p4; OJ C153 23.7.85 p9 (withdrawn); OJ C95 16.4.85 p2; OJ C238 19.9.85 p4 (reopened)				OJ L102 18.4.86 p31 (no injury); Corrigendum OJ L108 25.4.86 p60	
Portland cement	GDR Poland Yugoslavia Spain	OJ C84 2.4.85 p5				OJ L202 25.7.86 p43 (no injury); OJ L282 3.10.86 p36 (no injury); OJ L16 22.1.91 p34 (termination)	
Hammers	China	OJ C96 17.4.85 p3				OJ L29 4.2.86 p36 (no injury)	
Stainless steel household cooking ware	South Korea	OJ C126 23.5.85 p23				OJ L74 19.3.86 p33 (no injury)	
Housed bearing units	Japan	OJ C132 30.5.85 p2 (reopened); Notice of impending expiry OJ C208 9.8.91 p4; Notice of expiry OJ C33 11.2.92 p5	OJ L221 7.8.86 p16; OJ L339 2.12.86 p4 (extension)	OJ L35 6.2.87 p32			

PRODUCT	COUNTRY	INITIATION	PROVISIONAL DUTY	DEFINITIVE DUTY	UNDERTAKING	OTHER	COURT
Certain acrylic fibres	Israel Mexico Romania Turkey	OJ C159 29.6.85 p2; OJ C117 4.5.88 p3 (reopened and review); Notice of impending expiry OJ C84 28.3.91 p6; Notice of expiry OJ C251 26.9.91 p4			OJ L272 24.9.86 p29; OJ L301 19.10.89 p1		
Photocopiers	Japan	OJ C194 2.8.85 p5; Notice of impending expiry OJ C222 27.8.91 p2; Review OJ C33 11.2.92 p4	OJ L239 26.8.86 p5; OJ L359 19.12.86 p9 (extension)	OJ L54 24.2.87 p12	OJ L54 24.2.87 p36		Case 133/87R Nashua Corporation v EC Commission [1987] ECR 2883; Case 150/87 Nashua Corporation v EC Council and EC Commission [1987] ECR 4421; Case 150/87 Nashua Corporation v EC Council and EC Commission [1990] ECR 719; Case 155/87 Gestetner Holdings plc v EC Council and EC Commission [1980] ECR 781; Case 172/87 Mital v EC Council [1992] 2 CMLR 614; Case 174/87 Ricoh v EC Council; Case 175/87 Matsushita Electric Trading Co v EC Council; Case 176/87 Konish Iroku Photo Ind v EC Council; Case 177/87 Sanyo Electric Co v EC Council; Case 178/87 Minolta v EC Council; Case 179/87 Sharp v EC Council, Judgment of 10.3.92, OJ C90 10.4.92
Binder and baler twine	Brazil Mexico	OJ C315 6.12.85 p2 (reopened); Notice of impending expiry OJ C206 7.8.91 p2; Review OJ C336 31.12.91 p5; OJ C111 30.4.92 p11			OJ L34 5.2.87 p55		
Certain freezers	GDR Yugoslavia USSR	OJ C319 11.12.85 p3; Notice of impending expiry OJ C68 16.3.91 p4; OJ C153 11.6.91 p9; Notice of expiry OJ C251 26.9.91 p4; OJ C7 11.1.92 p7	OJ L259 11.9.86 p14	OJ L6 8.1.87 p1	OJ L259 11.9.86 p14		Case 294/86R Technointorg v EC Commission [1986] ECR 3979; Case 77/87R Technointorg v EC Council [1987] ECR 1793; Case 295/86 Garelly v EC Commission [1987] ECR 3117; Joined Cases 294/86 and 77/87 Technointorg v EC Commission and EC Council [1988] ECR 6077

PRODUCT	COUNTRY	INITIATION	PROVISIONAL DUTY	DEFINITIVE DUTY	UNDERTAKING	OTHER	COURT
Certain sheets and plates of iron and steel	Yugoslavia	OJ C38 19.2.86 p3; OJ C22 28.1.88 p10 (reopened)	OJ L254 6.9.86 p18; OJ L23 28.1.88 p13; OJ L98 15.4.88 p33 (modified); OJ L123 17.5.88 p20 (extension)	OJ L188 19.7.88 p14	OJ L371 31.12.86 p84		
Potassium permanganate	Czechoslovakia GDR China	OJ C63 18.3.86 p5; OJ C37 9.2.88 p3 (reopened); OJ C216 22.8.89 p7 (reopened)	OJ L217 5.8.86 p12; OJ L35 9.2.88 p13; OJ L245 22.8.89 p5; OJ L374 22.12.89 p1 (extension)	OJ L339 2.12.86 p1; OJ L138 3.6.88 p4; OJ L42 16.2.90 p1; OJ L276 6.10.90 p1 (extension)	OJ L339 2.12.86 p32	OJ L14 19.1.91 p56 (termination)	
Paint distemper varnish and similar brushes	China	OJ C103 30.4.86 p2; OJ C257 4.10.88 p5 (reopened); Notice OJ C332 21.12.91 p5; OJ C24 31.1.92 p3	OJ L272 4.10.88 p16; OJ L303 8.11.88 p11 (amended); OJ L23 27.1.89 p5 (extension)	OJ L79 22.3.87 p24	OJ L46 14.2.87 p45; OJ L312 18.11.88 p33		Case C-16/90 D Nölle t/a "Eugen Nölle" v Hauptzollamt Bremen-Freinhafen, Judgment of 22.10.91
Synthetic textile fibres of polyesters	GDR Romania Turkey Yugoslavia	OJ C125 24.5.86 p2				OJ L103 15.4.87 p38 (no injury)	
Inner tubes and new tyre cases	Korea Taiwan	OJ C132 30.5.86 p5 (reopened)			OJ L134 31.5.88 p61		
Copper sulphate	Czechoslovakia Hungary Poland USSR	Review OJ C200 9.8.86 p4; Notice of impending expiry OJ C50 25.2.92 p2	OJ L205 30.7.88 p68	OJ L235 20.8.87 p18; OJ L259 9.9.87 p7 (amended); OJ L23 27.1.89 p1	OJ L235 20.8.87 p22		

PRODUCT	COUNTRY	INITIATION	PROVISIONAL DUTY	DEFINITIVE DUTY	UNDERTAKING	OTHER	COURT
Ferro-silicon	Brazil USSR	OJ C231 12.9.86 p4; OJ C77 24.3.87 p2 (extension); Review OJ C109 3.5.90 p5; Notice of impending expiry OJ C37 15.2.90 p22; Review OJ C115 6.5.92 p2; Notice of impending expiry OJ C122 14.5.92 p11	OJ L219 8.8.87 p24	OJ L343 5.12.87 p1; OJ L111 3.5.91 p1	OJ L219 8.8.87 p24; OJ L111 3.5.91 p47		Case C-216/91 Rima Electometalurgia SA v EC Council OJ C243 18.9.91 p7
Refrigerating units	France (to Spain)	OJ C241 25.9.86 p6 (Pursuance)				OJ L79 24.3.88 p35 (no injury/no duty)	
Ferro silicon calcium	Brazil	OJ C244 30.9.86 p13	OJ L129 19.5.87 p5; OJ L268 19.9.87 p63 (extension)	OJ L332 12.11.87 p1			
Urea	Czechoslovakia GDR Kuwait Libya Saudi Arabia USSR Trinidad and Tobago Yugoslavia Austria Hungary Malaysia USA Romania Venezeula	OJ C254 11.10.86 p3; Notice OJ C34 12.2.87 p3; OJ C271 9.10.87 p4 (extension); Notice of impending expiry OJ C121 13.5.92 p6; Review OJ C55 2.3.91 p4	OJ L121 9.5.87 p11; OJ L254 5.9.87 p20 (extension); OJ L235 25.8.88 p5; OJ L355 23.12.88 p3 (extension)	OJ L137 7.11.87 p1; OJ L52 24.2.89 p1; OJ L272 28.9.91 p10 (amended); Corrigendum OJ L290 22.10.91 p44; OJ L334 5.12.91 p1 (amended)	OJ L137 7.11.87 p1; OJ L52 24.2.89 p37	OJ L272 28.9.91 p10 (terminated)	Case 49/88 Al Jubail Fertiliser Co & Another v EC Council [1991] 3 CMLR 377
Certain sheets and plates of iron/steel	Mexico	OJ C308 2.12.86 p2; Review OJ C118 12.5.90 p3	OJ L207 29.7.87 p21	OJ L330 21.11.87 p42		OJ L35 12.2.92 p9 (definitive duties repealed)	

PRODUCT	COUNTRY	INITIATION	PROVISIONAL DUTY	DEFINITIVE DUTY	UNDERTAKING	OTHER	COURT
Microwave ovens	Japan Singapore South Korea	OJ C325 18.12.86 p5				OJ L343 13.12.88 p33 (terminated)	
Mercury	USSR	OJ C53 28.2.87 p5; Notice of impending expiry OJ C148 12.6.92 p6	OJ L227 14.8.87 p8	OJ L346 10.12.87 p27			
Certain types of electronic semi-conductors known as EPROMS	Japan	OJ C101 14.4.87 p10; Review OJ C181 17.7.92 p7		OJ L65 12.3.91 p1	OJ L65 12.3.91 p1		
Dot matrix printers	Japan	OJ C111 25.4.87 p2; OJ C327 20.12.88 p8	OJ L130 26.5.88 p12; OJ L264 24.9.88 p56 (extension)	OJ L317 24.11.88 p33; OJ L291 10.10.89 p52 (extension)			Case 69/89R Nakajima Co Ltd v EC Council [1989] ECR 1689; Case 69/89 Nakajima Co Ltd v EC Council, Judgment of 7.5.91
Kraft liner board and paper	Brazil South Africa	OJ C113 28.4.87 p2				OJ L62 8.3.88 p40 (no injury)	
Daisy wheel printers	Japan	OJ C121 7.5.87 p4	OJ L177 8.7.88 p1; OJ L302 5.11.88 p30 (extension)	OJ L5 5.1.89 p23			
Certain iron or steel coils	Algeria Mexico Yugoslavia	OJ C126 12.5.87 p2; Review OJ C118 12.5.90 p5	OJ L18 21.1.88 p1; OJ L98 13.4.88 p32 (modified); OJ L123 17.5.88 pp20, 21 (extension)	OJ L188 19.7.88 p18		(refund) OJ L60 9.3.90 p17; OJ L350 19.12.91 p11 (duties repealed)	
Oxalic acid	China Czechoslovakia	OJ C137 22.5.87 p4; Review OJ C216 31.8.90 p2	OJ L138 1.6.91 p62	OJ L326 28.11.91 p6	OJ L343 13.12.88 p34	OJ L138 1.6.91 p62 (termination)	Case 61/92 Sinochem Heilongjiang v EC Council OJ C103 23.4.92. p6
Oxalic acid	South Korea Taiwan	OJ C137 22.5.87 p5	OJ L72 18.3.88 p15	OJ L184 15.7.88 p1	OJ L160 28.6.88 p63		
Synthetic textile fibres of polyesters	Mexico Taiwan Turkey USA Romania Yugoslavia	OJ C173 1.7.87 p10; Review OJ C230 15.9.90 p3	OJ L151 17.6.88 p47; OJ L282 15.10.88 p27 (extension)	OJ L348 17.12.88 p49; Notice OJ C119 13.5.89 p15			

PRODUCT	COUNTRY	INITIATION	PROVISIONAL DUTY	DEFINITIVE DUTY	UNDERTAKING	OTHER	COURT
Polyester yarn	Mexico Taiwan South Korea Turkey	OJ C173 1.7.87 p11; Review OJ C289 17.11.90 p7	OJ L151 17.6.88 p39; OJ L257 17.9.88 p24; OJ L282 15.10.88 p28 (extension)	OJ L347 16.12.88 p10; OJ L275 2.10.91 p21 (amended)		OJ L295 2.10.91 p21 (duties repealed)	
Compact disc players	South Korea Japan	OJ C178 7.7.87 p7; Notice OJ C334 29.12.88 p6; Review OJ C173 4.7.91 p3; Notice OJ C334 28.12.91 p8	OJ L205 18.7.89 p5, Corrigendum OJ L257 2.9.89 p27; OJ L331 16.11.88 p45 (extension); OJ L87 2.4.92 p1 (amended)	OJ L13 17.1.90 p21		OJ L104 24.4.91 p44; OJ L143 7.6.91 p51, 54; OJ L151 15.6.91 p86 (refunds)	Case 105/90 Goldstar Co Ltd v EC Council [1992] 1 CMLR 996
Certain types of electronic micro-circuits known as DRAMS	Japan	OJ C181 9.7.87 p3; Review OJ C50 25.2.92 p3	OJ L20 25.1.90 p5; Corrigendum OJ L22 27.1.90 p79; Corrigendum OJ L38 10.2.90 p44; OJ L131 23.5.90 p6 (extension); OJ L292 24.10.90 p16 (amended)	OJ L193 25.7.90 p1	OJ L20 25.1.90 p5		
Certain cellular mobile radio telephones	Canada Japan Hong Kong	OJ C185 15.7.87 p2; OJ C71 17.3.88 p12 (extension)				OJ L362 30.12.88 p59 (terminated)	
Certain iron or steel sections	Yugoslavia Turkey	OJ C216 14.8.87 p2	OJ L190 21.7.88 p5	OJ L313 19.11.88 p18			
Electronic typewriters (components)	Japan	OJ C235 1.9.87 p2		OJ L101 20.4.88 p1; OJ C123 17.5.88 p88 (amended); OJ L183 14.7.88 p1 (amended); OJ L203 28.7.88 p1 (amended); OJ L101 20.4.88 p1	OJ L128 21.5.88 p39; OJ L183 14.7.88 p39; OJ L203 28.7.88 p25	OJ L101 20.4.88 p26 (no duty); OJ L101 20.4.88 p27 (no duty)	

PRODUCT	COUNTRY	INITIATION	PROVISIONAL DUTY	DEFINITIVE DUTY	UNDERTAKING	OTHER	COURT
Certain electronic scales (components)	Japan	OJ C235 1.9.87 p3		OJ L101 20.4.88 p1	OJ L189 20.7.88 p27	OJ L101 20.4.88 p28 (terminated) OJ L244 2.9.88 p1 (duties repealed) OJ L58 1.3.89 p1 (amended)	
Choline chloride	Belgium (to Spain)	OJ C255 25.9.87 p2; OJ C279 17.10.87 p8 (amended)			OJ L63 7.3.89 p32		
Video cassette recorders	Korea Japan	OJ C256 26.9.87 p19	OJ L240 31.8.88 p5; OJ L254 14.9.88 p14; OJ L355 23.12.88 p4	OJ L57 28.2.89 p55	OJ L57 28.2.89 p61		
Certain hydraulic excavators	Japan	OJ C285 23.10.87 p4				OJ L101 20.4.88 p24 (no duty)	
Certain imports of video cassette tapes	Korea Hong Kong	OJ C340 18.12.87 p6; Notice OJ C212 12.8.88 p11; Review OJ C20 21.7.90 p7; OJ C7 11.1.91 p2; OJ C266 12.10.91 p7; OJ C87 8.4.92 p9	OJ L356 24.12.88 p47; OJ L107 19.4.89 p1 (extension)	OJ L174 22.6.89 p1; OJ L343 7.12.90 p1 (amended); OJ L139 22.5.92 p1 (amended); OJ L182 2.7.92 p6 (amended)	OJ L174 22.6.89 p30		
Polyester film	Korea	OJ C7 12.1.88 p9				OJ L305 21.10.89 p31	
Calcium metal	China USSR	OJ C20 26.1.88 p3	OJ L78 21.3.89 p10; OJ L271 20.9.89 p1				Case 358/89R Extrament Industrie SA v EC Council [1990] ECR 431, Judgment of 16.5.91; Opinion of AG Jacobs 8.3.92; Judgment of Court 7.6.92
Stainless steel tubes	Austria	OJ C24 20.1.88 p3				OJ L25 28.1.89 p87 (no injury)	

PRODUCT	COUNTRY	INITIATION	PROVISIONAL DUTY	DEFINITIVE DUTY	UNDERTAKING	OTHER	COURT
Small screen TV receivers	Korea Hong Kong China	OJ C44 17.2.88 p3; OJ C288 12.11.88 p13 (extension); Notice OJ C334 29.12.88 p6; Review OJ C18 26.1.91 p3	OJ L314 28.10.89 p1; Corrigendum OJ L329 15.10.89 p43; OJ L41 15.2.90 p1 (extension); OJ L14 19.1.91 p31; OJ L122 17.5.91 p1 (extension)	OJ L107 27.4.90 p56; Corrigendum OJ L133 24.5.90 p92; OJ L275 2.10.91 p24 (amended); OJ L195 18.7.91 p1			
Plain paper photocopiers	Japan	OJ C44 17.2.88 p3 (Art 13 (10)); Notice OJ C306 1.12.88 p8 (Art 13 (10)); Notice OJ C113 4.5.89 p6		OJ L284 19.10.88 p36; OJ L355 23.12.88 p1 (amended)	OJ L284 19.10.88 p60; OJ L355 23.12.88 p66; OJ L43 15.2.89 p54; OJ L126 9.5.89 p38	OJ L34 6.2.90 p28 (termination)	
Carbon ferro chromium	South Africa Turkey Zimbabwe	Review OJ C57 1.3.88 p3				OJ L39 11.2.89 p33 (terminated)	
Hydraulic excavators	Japan	OJ C146 3.6.88 p3				OJ L249 25.5.89 p71 (no injury)	
Wheeled loaders	Japan	OJ C146 3.6.88 p4				OJ L39 11.2.89 p35 (no injury)	
Ball bearings (components)	Japan	OJ C150 8.6.88 p4				OJ L25 28.1.89 p90 (terminated)	
Glutamic acid and its salts	Korea Taiwan Indonesia Thailand	OJ C147 4.6.88 p3; Review OJ C287 5.11.91 p5	OJ L56 3.3.90 p23	OJ L167 30.6.90 p1	OJ L56 3.3.90 p23		
Ball bearings	Thailand	OJ C147 4.6.88 p6	OJ L152 16.6.90 p24	OJ L281 12.10.90 p1			
Certain sheets of iron or non alloy steel	Yugoslavia	OJ C184 14.7.88 p4	OJ L78 21.3.89 p14; OJ L133 17.5.89 p5	OJ L193 8.7.89 p11; OJ L38 10.2.90 p9 (extension)			

PRODUCT	COUNTRY	INITIATION	PROVISIONAL DUTY	DEFINITIVE DUTY	UNDERTAKING	OTHER	COURT
Certain welded tubes of iron or non alloy steel	Romania Yugoslavia	OJ C241 16.9.88 p3	OJ L294 13.10.89 p10	OJ L91 6.4.90 p8	OJ L91 6.4.90 p8		
Diesel engines	Finland Sweden	OJ C251 27.9.88 p3			OJ L76 22.3.90 p28		
Ferroboron	Japan	OJ C306 1.12.88 p7	OJ L73 20.3.90 p6	OJ L187 19.7.90 p1			
Barium chloride	China GDR	OJ C308 3.12.88 p7	OJ L227 4.8.89 p24; OJ L349 30.11.89 p1 (extension)	OJ L60 7.3.91 p1			
Amonium-paratungstate	China Korea	OJ C322 15.12.88 p4				OJ L83 30.3.90 p117 (terminated)	
Tungstic acid and tungstic oxide	China	OJ C322 15.12.88 p5	OJ L83 30.3.90 p29; OJ L195 26.7.90 p1 (extension)	OJ L264 27.9.90 p4	OJ L264 27.9.90 p57		
Tungsten metal powder	China Korea	OJ C322 15.12.88 p7				OJ L83 30.3.90 p124 (terminated)	
Tungsten carbide and fused tungsten carbide	China Korea	OJ C322 15.12.88 p7	OJ L83 30.3.90 p36; OJ L195 26.7.90 p2 (extension)	OJ L264 27.9.90 p7	OJ L264 27.9.90 p59	OJ L83 30.3.90 p86 (terminated)	
Methenamine (hexamethylenetr amine)	Bulgaria Hungary Poland Romania Czechoslovakia	OJ C322 15.12.88 p8			OJ L104 24.4.90 p14		
Photo album	Hong Kong Korea	OJ C322 15.12.88 p9			OJ L138 31.5.90 p48		
Mica	Japan	OJ C323 16.12.88 p3				OJ L284 3.10.89 p45 (termination)	

PRODUCT	COUNTRY	INITIATION	PROVISIONAL DUTY	DEFINITIVE DUTY	UNDERTAKING	OTHER	COURT
Dot matrix printers	Japan	OJ C327 20.12.88 p8 (Art 13(10))			OJ L291 10.10.89 p57; OJ L340 23.11.89 p25		
Tungsten ores and concentrates	China Hong Kong	OJ C2 4.1.89 p5	OJ L83 30.3.90 p23; OJ L195 26.7.90 p3 (extension)	OJ L264 27.9.90 p1	OJ L264 27.9.90 p55		
Audio cassettes and audio cassette tapes	Japan Korea Hong Kong	OJ C11 14.1.89 p9	OJ L313 13.11.90 p5; Corrigendum OJ L9 12.1.91 p36	OJ L119 14.5.91 p3		OJ L28 4.2.92 p25 (termination)	Case 170/89 Bureau Européen des Unions de Consommateurs v EC Commission [1992] 1 CMLR 820
Polyolefin woven bags	China	OJ C21 27.1.89 p2	OJ L187 19.7.90 p36	OJ L318 17.11.90 p2			
Silicon metal	China Hong Kong	OJ C26 1.2.89 p8	OJ L80 27.3.90 p9	OJ L198 28.7.90 p57; OJ L170 25.6.90 p1 (amended)			
Dicumyl peroxide	Japan Taiwan	OJ C39 16.2.89 p4			OJ L317 31.10.89 p49	OJ L317 31.10.89 p49 (terminated)	
NPK-fertilisers	Hungary Poland Romania Yugoslavia	OJ C55 4.3.89 p3				OJ L188 20.7.90 p63 (no injury)	
Denim	Turkey Indonesia Hong Kong Macao	OJ C73 21.3.89 p3				OJ L222 17.8.90 p50 (terminated)	
Propan-1-ol (propyl alcohol)	USA	Review OJ C140 6.6.89 p7				OJ L306 6.11.90 p23 (terminated)	
Portland cement	Yugoslavia	OJ C149 16.6.89 p4					
Video cassette recorders (components)	Japan	OJ C172 7.7.89 p7					

PRODUCT	COUNTRY	INITIATION	PROVISIONAL DUTY	DEFINITIVE DUTY	UNDERTAKING	OTHER	COURT
Lincar tungsten halogen lamp	Japan	OJ C183 20.7.89 p9	OJ L188 20.7.90 p10; OJ L318 17.11.90 p1 (extension); Corrigendum OJ L321 21.11.90 p19	OJ L14 19.1.91 p1			Case 124/91 Phoenix Electric Co Ltd v EC Council, OJ C145 4.6.91 p12; Removed OJ C274 19.10.91 p13
Potassium permanganate	USSR	OJ C192 29.7.88 p8	OJ L145 8.6.90 p9				
Welded tubes of iron or non alloy steel	Turkey Venezuela	OJ C226 2.9.89 p18	OJ L351 15.12.90 p17	OJ L91 12.4.91 p1	OJ L351 15.12.90 p17		
Single two phase electric motors	Bulgaria Romania Czechoslovakia	OJ C286 14.11.89 p11				OJ L202 31.7.90 p47 (no injury)	Case 315/90 Groupement des Industries d'equipment electrique et de l'electronique industrielle associée v EC Commission Judgment of 27.11.91 OJ C331 20.12.91 p5
Pure silk typewriter ribbon fabrics	China	OJ C300 29.11.89 p3; Review OJ C12 18.1.92 p5	OJ L174 7.7.90 p27	OJ L306 6.11.90 p21	OJ L174 7.7.90 p27		
Espadrilles	China	OJ C314 14.12.89 p15	OJ L365 28.12.90 p25; OJ L107 27.4.91 p1 (extension)	OJ L166 28.6.91 p1			
Thin polyester film	Republic of Korea	OJ C24 1.2.90 p7					
Salmon	Norway	OJ C25 2.2.90 p6				OJ L69 16.3.91 p32 (terminated)	
Certain cotton terry towelling articles	Turkey	OJ C32 10.2.90 p8				OJ L17 23.1.91 p22 (terminated)	
Aspartame	USA Japan	OJ C52 3.3.90 p12	OJ L330 29.11.90 p16; OJ L82 28.3.91 p1 (extension)	OJ L134 29.5.91 p1			Case C-233/91 Ajinomoto v EC Council OJ C291 8.11.91 p8; Case 224/91 The Nutrasweet Co v EC Council OJ C291 8.11.91 p9
Asbesto cement pipes	Turkey	OJ C63 13.3.90 p4			OJ L209 31.7.91 p37		

PRODUCT	COUNTRY	INITIATION	PROVISIONAL DUTY	DEFINITIVE DUTY	UNDERTAKING	OTHER	COURT
Imports of cotton yarn not put up for retail sale	Turkey Brazil Egypt India Thailand	OJ C72 22.3.90 p3	OJ L271 27.9.91 p17; OJ L18 25.1.92 p33 (extension)	OJ L82 27.3.92 p1		OJ L271 27.9.91 p17 (no injury); OJ L82 27.3.92 p70 (no dumping)	
Certain polyester yarns (man made staple fibres)	Republic of Korea Taiwan Indonesia India China Turkey	OJ C80 30.3.90 p6	OJ L271 3.10.91 p7; OJ L2 30.1.92 p31 (extension)	OJ L88 3.4.92 p1; Corrigendum OJ L153 5.6.92 p16; Corrigendum OJ L213 29.7.92 p36		OJ L276 3.10.91 p7 (terminated)	
Pocket lighters gas fuelled non refillable	China Republic of Korea Thailand Japan	OJ C89 7.4.90 p3; OJ C206 18.8.90 p7 (extension); Review OJ C62 11.3.92 p2	OJ L133 28.5.91 p20; OJ L272 28.9.91 p1 (extension)	OJ L326 28.11.91 p1	OJ L326 28.11.91 p31		Case 75/92 Gao Yao (Hong Kong) Hua Fa Industrial Co Ltd v EC Council OJ C113 1.5.92 p4
Video cassettee tapes	China	OJ C92 11.4.90 p6	OJ L106 26.4.91 p15; OJ L236 24.8.91 p1 (extension)	OJ L293 24.10.91 p2			
Radio broadcast receivers of a kind used in motor vehicles	South Korea	OJ C114 8.5.90 p4	OJ L34 11.2.92 p8; OJ L156 10.6.92 p1 (extension)				
Certain merchant bars and rods of alloy steel	Turkey	OJ C144 14.6.90 p4					
Semi-finished products of alloy steel	Turkey Brazil	OJ C144 14.6.90 p5	OJ L95 9.4.92 p26	OJ L182 2.7.92 p23	OJ L182 2.7.92 p23	OJ L35 12.2.92 p12 (terminated)	
Artificial corundum	Brazil Yugoslavia	OJ C159 26.6.90 p5			OJ L275 2.10.91 p27		
Dihydrostreptomycin (DHS)	China Japan	OJ C186 27.7.90 p33	OJ L187 13.7.91 p23; OJ L293 24.10.91 p1 (extension)	OJ L362 31.12.91 p1		OJ L28 4.2.92 p23 (terminated)	

PRODUCT	COUNTRY	INITIATION	PROVISIONAL DUTY	DEFINITIVE DUTY	UNDERTAKING	OTHER	COURT
Welded wire mesh	Yugoslavia	OJ C188 28.7.90 p7			OJ L123 18.5.91 p54		
Oxalic acid	India	OJ C216 31.8.90 p2	OJ L138 1.6.91 p62	OJ L326 28.11.91 p6			
High carbon ferro chromium	Albania USSR	OJ C252 6.10.90 p11				OJ L90 11.4.91 p38 (terminated)	
Potassium chloride (potash)	Belarus Russia Ukraine	OJ C274 31.10.90 p18	OJ L110 28.4.92 p5				
Synthetic fibres of polyester	India Republic of Korea	OJ C291 21.11.90 p20	OJ L197 16.7.92 p25				
Silicon metal	Brazil	OJ C296 27.11.90 p3	OJ L96 10.4.92 p7				
Wire rod	Argentina Egypt Turkey Trinidad and Tobago Yugoslavia	OJ C310 11.12.90 p9					
Outer rings of taperes roller bearings	Japan	OJ C2 4.1.91 p8	OJ L199 18.7.92 p8				
Thermal paper	Japan	OJ C16 24.1.91 p3; Notice OJ C334 28.12.91 p7	OJ L270 26.9.91 p15; OJ L11 17.1.92 p33 (extension)	OJ L81 26.3.92 p1; Corrigendum OJ L138 24.5.92 p40	OJ L81 26.3.92 p22		
Electronic micro circuits known as DRAM's	Republic of Korea	OJ C57 6.3.91 p9					
Large alluminium electrolytic capacitors	Japan	OJ C93 11.4.91 p5	OJ L152 4.6.92 p22; Corrigendum OJ L163 17.6.92 p27				

PRODUCT	COUNTRY	INITIATION	PROVISIONAL DUTY	DEFINITIVE DUTY	UNDERTAKING	OTHER	COURT
Ferro silicon	Egypt Poland	OJ C122 8.5.91 p4	OJ L183 3.7.92 p8		OJ L183 3.7.92 p40		
Woven polyolefin bags	China	OJ C157 15.6.91 p5 (investigation under Art 13 (11))					
Compact disc players	Japan Republic of Korea	OJ C174 5.7.91 p15 (investigation under Art 13 (11)); Review OJ C334 28.12.91 p8					
Magnetic disks (3.5" micro disks)	Japan Taiwan China	OJ C174 5.7.91 p16					
Imports of parts of gas fuelled, non refillable pocket lighters	Japan	OJ C202 1.8.91 p4					
Pig iron	Turkey USSR	OJ C246 21.9.91 p9					
Bicycles	Taiwan China	OJ C266 12.10.91 p6					
Silicon metal	China	OJ C273 18.10.91 p20 (investigation under Art 13 (11))		OJ L170 25.6.92 p1			
Dead burned (sintered) magnesia	China	OJ C276 23.10.91 p3					
Magnesium oxide	China	OJ C279 26.10.91 p10					
Electronic weighing scales	Singapore Republic of Korea	OJ C6 10.1.92 p2; OJ C84 4.4.92 p14 (extension)					

PRODUCT	COUNTRY	INITIATION	PROVISIONAL DUTY	DEFINITIVE DUTY	UNDERTAKING	OTHER	COURT
Unwrought manganese containing more than 96% by weight of manganese	China	OJ C15 21.1.92 p12					
Antimony trioxide	China	OJ C72 21.3.92 p6					
Imports into Spain of Portland cement	Turkey Romania Tunisia	OJ C100 22.4.92 p4					
Fluorspar	China	OJ C105 25.4.92 p23					
Photo albums	China	OJ C120 12.5.92 p10					
Compact disc players	Taiwan Singapore Malaysia	OJ C148 12.6.92 p7					
Ferro silicon	China South Africa	OJ C173 9.7.92 p8					
Manganese steel wearparts	South Africa	OJ C188 25.7.92 p3					
Gum rosin	China	OJ C195 1.8.92 p5					
Low carbon ferro-chrome (LCFECR)	Kazakhstan Russia Ukraine	OJ C195 1.8.92 p6					

ANTI-SUBSIDY PROCEEDINGS INITIATED

PRODUCT	COUNTRY	INITIATION	PROVISIONAL DUTY	DEFINITIVE DUTY	UNDERTAKING	NO INJURY	COURT
Seamless tubes of non alloy steel	Spain	OJ C264 19.10.79 p2; OJ C196 30.7.92 p3 (reopened)	OJ L196 30.7.80 p34	OJ L322 28.1.80 p30; OJ L116 30.4.83 p7 (amended)		OJ L165 23.6.81 p27 (terminated)	
Stainless steel bars	Brazil	OJ C317 18.12.79 p3				OJ L139 5.6.80 p30 (terminated)	
Womens shoes	Brazil	OJ C241 19.9.81 p10			OJ L327 14.11.81 p39		
Sheets and plates of iron or steel (ECSC)	Brazil	OJ C146 10.6.82 p4		OJ L45 17.2.83 p11		OJ L45 17.2.83 p11 (duties suspended)	
Sheets and plates of iron or steel (ECSC)	Brazil	OJ C197 30.7.82 p3		OJ L205 29.7.83 p29		OJ L205 29.7.83 p29 (duties suspended)	
Broad flanged beams (ECSC)	Spain	OJ C207 10.8.82 p4	OJ L238 13.8.82 p32; OJ L317 13.11.82 p16 (amended)	OJ L30 1.2.83 p61		OJ L116 30.4.83 p91 (duties suspended and terminated)	
Tube and pipe fittings of malleable cast iron	Spain	OJ C142 31.5.83 p3	OJ L322 19.11.83 p13	OJ L74 17.3.84 p47; OJ L297 19.10.85 p1 (amended)		OJ L103 19.4.86 p4 (duties repealed)	
Soya bean oil	Argentina Brazil	OJ C283 22.10.83 p5; OJ C76 17.3.84 p13 (extension)				OJ L106 18.4.85 p19; OJ L108 20.4.85 p28 (terminated)	
Ball bearings	Thailand	OJ C147 4.6.88 p4			OJ L152 16.6.90 p59		
Polyester fibres and polyester yarns	Turkey	OJ C33 9.2.89 p7	OJ L137 31.5.91 p8; OJ L272 28.9.91 p3		OJ L272 28.9.91 p92		

PROCEEDINGS INITITATED UNDER REGULATION 288/82

PRODUCT	COUNTRY	INITIATION	PROTECTIVE MEASURES	UNDERTAKING	OTHER	COURT
Stoneware	South Korea Taiwan	OJ C144 8.6.82 p3	OJ L369 29.12.87 p27	OJ L96 15.4.83 p8	OJ L200 23.7.83 p43 (system of automatic authorisation)	
Quartz watches	Hong Kong Japan Macao South Korea Taiwan	OJ C285 22.10.83 p5	OJ L106 19.4.84 p31		OJ L172 30.6.84 p1 (confirmation of protective measures)	
Beach slippers	China	OJ C210 10.8.84 p5			OJ L340 28.12.84 p30 (system of automatic authorisation)	
Tubes and pipes of malleable steel	Austria Brazil Portugal Spain Yugoslavia	OJ C6 9.1.85 p3				
Glass	Spain Turkey Yugoslavia	OJ C66 14.3.85 p12			OJ C128 27.5.86 p7 (termination)	
Urea	Spain	OJ C154 20.6.86 p2	OJ L303 29.10.86 p29; OJ L339 2.12.86 p21 (extension); OJ L370 30.12.86 p30			
Zip fastners	Taiwan	OJ C123 9.5.87 p3			OJ L353 16.12.87 p11 (system of automatic authorisation)	
Footwear	South Korea Taiwan China	OJ C217 15.8.87 p7; OJ C274 13.10.87 p3			OJ L155 22.6.88 p1; OJ L166 1.7.88 p6 (system of authomatic authorisation)	

PROCEEDINGS INITIATED UNDER REGULATION 2641/84

ILLICIT COMMERCIAL PRACTICE	COUNTRY	INITIATION	PROTECTIVE MEASURES	UNDERTAKING	OTHER	COURT
Exclusion of unlicensed importation of aramid fibres	USA	OJ C25 5.2.86 p2			OJ L117 5.5.87 p18 (international consultation and dispute settlement procedures)	
Unauthorised sound recordings	Indonesia	OJ C136 21.5.87 p3		OJ L123 27.5.88 p51		
Differential export taxes for soya meal	Argentina				Unpublished decision dated 22.12.86 (rejecting complaint)	
Intellectual property laws	Jordan				OJ L30 1.2.89 p67 (rejecting the complaint)	
Port charge or fee used for creation of a Harbour Management Fund	Japan	OJ C40 16.2.91 p18			OJ L74 20.3.92 p47 (suspension of examination)	
Piracy of sound recordings	Thailand	OJ C189 20.7.91 p26				